IFIP Advances in Information and Communication Technology 440

IFIP – The International Federation for Information Processing

IFIP was founded in 1960 under the auspices of UNESCO, following the First World Computer Congress held in Paris the previous year. An umbrella organization for societies working in information processing, IFIP's aim is two-fold: to support information processing within its member countries and to encourage technology transfer to developing nations. As its mission statement clearly states,

> *IFIP's mission is to be the leading, truly international, apolitical organization which encourages and assists in the development, exploitation and application of information technology for the bene t of all people.*

IFIP is a non-profitmaking organization, run almost solely by 2500 volunteers. It operates through a number of technical committees, which organize events and publications. IFIP's events range from an international congress to local seminars, but the most important are:

- The IFIP World Computer Congress, held every second year;
- Open conferences;
- Working conferences.

The flagship event is the IFIP World Computer Congress, at which both invited and contributed papers are presented. Contributed papers are rigorously refereed and the rejection rate is high.

As with the Congress, participation in the open conferences is open to all and papers may be invited or submitted. Again, submitted papers are stringently refereed.

The working conferences are structured differently. They are usually run by a working group and attendance is small and by invitation only. Their purpose is to create an atmosphere conducive to innovation and development. Refereeing is also rigorous and papers are subjected to extensive group discussion.

Publications arising from IFIP events vary. The papers presented at the IFIP World Computer Congress and at open conferences are published as conference proceedings, while the results of the working conferences are often published as collections of selected and edited papers.

Any national society whose primary activity is about information processing may apply to become a full member of IFIP, although full membership is restricted to one society per country. Full members are entitled to vote at the annual General Assembly, National societies preferring a less committed involvement may apply for associate or corresponding membership. Associate members enjoy the same benefits as full members, but without voting rights. Corresponding members are not represented in IFIP bodies. Affiliated membership is open to non-national societies, and individual and honorary membership schemes are also offered.

Bernard Grabot   Bruno Vallespir   Samuel Gomes
Abdelaziz Bouras   Dimitris Kiritsis (Eds.)

Advances in Production Management Systems

Innovative and
Knowledge-Based Production Management
in a Global-Local World

IFIP WG 5.7 International Conference, APMS 2014
Ajaccio, France, September 20-24, 2014
Proceedings, Part III

 Springer

Volume Editors

Bernard Grabot
LGP ENIT, Tarbes, France
E-mail: bernard.grabot@enit.fr

Bruno Vallespir
Université de Bordeaux, IMS, Talence, France
E-mail: bruno.vallespir@ims-bordeaux.fr

Samuel Gomes
Université de Technologie de Belfort-Montbéliard, M3M, Belfort, France
E-mail: samuel.gomes@utbm.fr

Abdelaziz Bouras
Qatar University, College of Engineering, ictQatar, Doha, Qatar
E-mail: abdelaziz.bouras@qu.edu.qa

Dimitris Kiritsis
EPFL/STI-IGM-LICP, Lausanne, Switzerland
E-mail: dimitris.kiritsis@epfl.ch

ISSN 1868-4238   e-ISSN 1868-422X
ISBN 978-3-662-52603-3   e-ISBN 978-3-662-44733-8 (e-Book)
DOI 10.1007/978-3-662-44733-8
Springer Heidelberg New York Dordrecht London

Typesetting: Camera-ready by author, data conversion by Scientific Publishing Services, Chennai, India

Printed on acid-free paper

Springer is part of Springer Science+Business Media (www.springer.com)

Preface

For the last decades, APMS has been a major event and the official conference of the IFIP Working Group 5.7 on Advances in Production Management Systems, bringing together leading experts from academia, research, and industry. Starting with the first conference in Helsinki in 1990, the conference has become a successful annual event that has been hosted in various parts of the world including Washington (USA, 2005), Wroclaw (Poland, 2006), Linköping (Sweden, 2007), Espoo (Finland, 2008), Bordeaux (France, 2009), Cernobbio (Italy, 2010), Stavanger (Norway, 2011), Rhodos (Greece, 2012), and State College (PA, USA, 2013).

By returning to Europe, APMS 2014 took place in Ajaccio (Corsica, France). This issue was organized in a collaborative way, as its organization was supported by four French universities and engineers schools: ENIT-INPT / University of Toulouse, the University of Bordeaux, the University of Lyon and the University of Technology of Belfort-Montbéliard.

The topics of APMS are similar to those of the IFIP WG 5.7. They concern all the facets of the systems of production of goods and services. For its 2014 issue, APMS selects the "Innovative and knowledge-based production management in a global-local world" theme, focusing on innovation, knowledge, and the apparent opposition between globalization of the economy and local production. 233 papers were accepted, based on blind peer-review. They were written and proposed by more than 600 authors and co-authors coming from 28 countries. The main review criteria were the paper quality and contributions to science and industrial practice. Accepted papers of registered participants are included in this volume. According to the new standard of APMS conference, full papers have been submitted and reviewed from the outset, allowing for the final proceedings to be available at the time of the conference.

Through an open call for special sessions and papers, APMS 2014 sought contributions in cutting-edge research, as well as insightful advances in industrial practice. The intent of the special sessions is to raise visibility on topics of focused interest in a particular scientific or applications area. This year, 21 special sessions were planned. They were consistent with the theme of the conference and focused on key areas of simulation, design, service, process improvement, sustainability, human & organizational aspects, agility and flexibility, maintenance, future and smart manufacturing, ontology, co-evolution of production and society, lean production, factories lifecycle, experience, knowledge & competence, and optimization.

Following the tradition of past APMS conferences, the 7th APMS Doctoral Workshop offered Ph.D. students the opportunity to present, discuss, receive feedback, and exchange comments and views on their doctoral research in an inspiring academic community of fellow Ph.D. students, experienced researchers, and professors from the IFIP WG 5.7 community.

Three awards were distributed during APMS 2014:

- Burbidge Award for best paper,
- Burbidge Award for best presentation,
- Doctoral Workshop Award.

The Scientific Committee, consisting of 78 researchers, most of them being active members of the IFIP WG 5.7, played a key role in reviewing the papers in a timely manner and providing constructive feedback to authors, allowing them to revise their manuscripts for the final draft.

Papers in these three volumes are grouped thematically as follows:

Volume 1:

- **Part I: Knowledge Discovery and Sharing**: Knowledge management, creative enterprise, quality management, design tools, system engineering, PLM, ontology, decision support system, collaboration maturity, Business Intelligence, enterprise 2.0, etc.
- **Part II: Knowledge-Based Planning and Scheduling**: Scheduling, optimization, production planning and control, assembly line balancing, decoupling points, inventory management, supply chain management, multi-echelon supply chain, analytic hierarchy process, enterprise resource planning, decision support systems, problem solving, vehicle routing, physical internet, etc.

Volume 2:

- **Part III: Knowledge-Based Sustainability**: Cleaner production, green IT, energy, energy-efficiency, risk management, disturbance management, resilience, end of life, reverse logistics, creative industry, eco-factory, environmental innovation, solidarity economy, social responsibility, glocalization, etc.
- **Part IV: Knowledge-Based Services**: Service production, service engineering, service governance, healthcare, public transportation, customer satisfaction, after sales, smart manufacturing, etc.

Volume 3:

- **Part V: Knowledge-Based Performance Improvement**: Performance measurement system, evaluation, quality, in-service inspection, inspection programs, lean, visual management, standardization, simulation, analysis techniques, value stream mapping, maturity models, benchmarking, change management, human behavior modeling, community of practice, etc.

- **Part VI: Case Studies**: sectors (petroleum industry, aeronautic industry, agribusiness, automobile, semiconductors), tools (ERP, TQM, six sigma, enterprise modeling, simulation), concepts (supply chain, globalization), etc.

We hope that these volumes will be of interest to a wide range of researchers and practitioners.

August 2014

Bernard Grabot
Bruno Vallespir
Samuel Gomes
Abdelaziz Bouras
Dimitris Kiritsis

Part VI: Case Studies section ...

...

Organization

General Chair

Bernard Grabot   ENIT-INPT/University of Toulouse, France

Doctoral Workshop Committee

Chair

Abdelaziz Bouras   University of Lyon, France & Qatar University,
                                   Qatar

Organizing Committee

Chair

Samuel Gomes   University of Technology of
                                   Belfort - Montbéliard, France

Members

Cédrick Béler   University of Toulouse, France
Abdelaziz Bouras   Qatar University, Qatar; Université Lumiere
                                   Lyon 2, France
Laurent Geneste   University of Toulouse, France
Raymond Houé   University of Toulouse, France
Daniel Noyes   University of Toulouse, France
Bruno Vallespir   University of Bordeaux, France

Organization

R-Events

Conference Secretariat

Catherine Eberstein   University of Technology of
                                   Belfort-Montbéliard, France
Cécile De Barros   Marie Robert, ENIT-LGP, INP, University of
                                   Toulouse, France

Sponsors

IFIP WG 5.7 Advances in Production Management Systems
IODE: Research Federation on Distributed Organizations Engineering
GdR MACS: CNRS Research Group on Modelling and Analysis of Complex Systems
IRTES: Research Institute on Transports, Energy and Society
Mairie d'Ajaccio

Special Sessions

Discrete event simulation for distributed production systems
    Paul-Antoine Bisgambiglia   University of Corsica, France

The practitioner's view on "Innovative and Knowledge-Based Production Management in a Global-Local World"
    Gregor von Cieminski   ZF Friedrichshafen AG, Germany

Integrated design in collaborative engineering
    Claude Baron   LAAS CNRS, France

Service manufacturing systems
    Toshiya Kaihara   Kobe University, Japan

Process improvement programmes for sustainability
    Jose Arturo Garza-Reyes   University of Derby, UK

Sustainable initiatives in developing countries
    Irenilza de Alencar Nääs   Paulista University, Brazil

Human and organizational aspects of planning and scheduling
    Ralph Riedel   TU Chemnitz, Germany

Agility and flexibility in manufacturing operations
    D. Jentsch   TU Chemnitz, Germany

Asset and maintenance management for competitive and sustainable manufacturing
    Marco Garetti   Politecnico di Milano, Italy

Manufacturing of the future
    R.S.Wadhwa   Høgskole i Gjøvik, Norway

Smart manufacturing system architecture
    Hyunbo Cho   Postech University, Republic of Korea

Production capacity pooling vs. traditional inventory pooling in an additive
manufacturing scenario
    Jan Holmström   Aalto University, Finland

Ontology based engineering
    Soumaya El Kadiri   EPFL, Switzerland

Co-evolving production and society in a global-local world
    Paola Fantini   Politecnico di Milano, Italy

Lean in high variety, low volume production
    Erlend Alfnes   Norwegian University of Science and
                                          Technology, Norway
Lean system development
    Elise Vareilles   École des Mines d'Albi, France

Managing factories lifecyle in a global-local world
    Claudio Palasciano   Politecnico di Milano, Italy

Experience, knowledge and competence management for production systems
    Laurent Geneste   INP-ENIT, France

IFIP WG5-7 research workshop
    Hermann Lödding   Hamburg University of Technology,
                                          Germany

Optimization models for global supply chain management
    Ramzi Hammami   ESC Rennes School of Business, France

Product Service System information system
    Thècle Alix   University of Bordeaux, France

International Scientific Committee

Bruno Vallespir (Chair)	University of Bordeaux, France
Erlend Alfnes	NTNU Valgrinda, Norway
Eiji Arai	Osaka University, Japan
Frédérique Biennier	INSA de Lyon, France
Umit S. Bititci	University of Stratchlyde, UK
Abdelaziz Bouras	Qatar University, Qatar; Université Lumière Lyon 2, France
Luis Manuel Camarinha-Matos	Universidade Nova de Lisboa, Portugal
Sergio Cavalieri	University of Bergamo, Italy
Stephen Childe	University of Exeter, UK

Table of Contents – Part III

Knowledge-Based Performance Improvement

Knowledge-Based Performance Improvement

Community of Practice Theory and Process Modelling: Two Tools for Better Collaboration in Research Projects

Virginie Goepp, Charlotte Munzer, and Françoise Feugeas

ICube, INSA de Strasbourg 24, bld de la Victoire 67084 – Strasbourg Cedex France
{virginie.goepp,charlotte.munzer,
francoise.feugeas}@insa-strasbourg.fr

Abstract. Today, research projects are often multi-disciplinary involving several research teams. For such projects to be a success implies, for these teams, to work together in an efficient manner. To improve collaboration we propose to work on two complementary aspects. The first aspect exploits the community of practice theory in order to define the knowledge to share and the way to share it. The second aspect applies process modelling in order to model research processes at different level of granularity (project, task, protocol). In this way, process uncertainty is reduced and a shared vision of the process is worked out. We illustrate our proposition on the SEPOLBE project that involves four research teams and a company to develop bio admixtures for concrete.

Keywords: community of practice, process modelling, BPMN, experimental protocol.

1 Introduction

In today context of fierce competition, research projects are more and more multi-disciplinary. This requires the collaboration between several research teams who have different backgrounds and are disseminated in different locations.

The collaboration enables, among other, to share expensive experimental means. However, setting up the collaboration in such a context requires overcoming the barriers linked to location and discipline. For the collaboration to be efficient the project members have to explicitly define the way they have to work together and to share knowledge. In this boarder, the Community of Practice theory and process modelling can be useful tools. The first enables the definition of the kind of knowledge shared and the way to share it. The second enables the formalization of experimental protocols in order to reduce their uncertainty and to provide a shared and unified view of them.

The remainder of the paper is structured as follows. Section 2 deals with Community of Practice theory that we apply to research projects. Section 3 deals with process modelling and BPMN (Business Process Model Notation). Section 4 applies Community of Practice Theory and process modelling to the SEPOLBE research project dedicated to develop bioadmixtures for concrete.

B. Grabot et al. (Eds.): APMS 2014, Part III, IFIP AICT 440, pp. 3–10, 2014.
© IFIP International Federation for Information Processing 2014

2   Community of Practice Theory

2.1   Definition

The notion of Community of Practice (CoP) has largely been discussed in the literature. For example, Cox in [1] makes a comparative review of four seminal works on CoPs. He shows that the ambiguities of the terms "communities" and "practice" allow the concept to be re-appropriated for different purposes.

In [2] CoPs are treated as the informal relations and understandings developed in mutual engagement on an appropriated joint enterprise. In other words, a community of practice is defined as a group that coheres through "mutual engagement" on an "appropriated enterprise", and creates a common "repertoire". It goes beyond the simple notion of team that not necessarily creates a common "repertoire". In our view, the collaboration between research teams becomes efficient when this team becomes a community of practice and shares knowledge.

In [3] the concept is redefined towards a more managerial stance, making the concept more popular and simple. Here CoPs are "groups of people who share a concern, a set of problems, or a passion about a topic, and who deepen their knowledge and expertise in this area by interacting on an ongoing basis." According to [1], this definition is much vaguer than the previous one. The definition is of a group that is somehow interested in the same thing, not closely tied together in accomplishing a common enterprise. The purpose is specifically to learn and share knowledge, not to get the job done. From this point of view a CoP has three structural features:

1. Domain: it *"... creates common ground and a sense of common identity. A well-defined domain legitimises the community by affirming its purpose and value to members and other stakeholders. The domain inspires members to contribute and participate, guides their learning, and gives meaning to their actions"* [3].
2. Community: it *"...creates the social fabric of learning. A strong community fosters interactions and relationships based on mutual respect and trust. It encourages a willingness to share ideas, expose one's ignorance, ask difficult questions, and listen carefully. Community is an important element because learning is a matter of belonging as well as an intellectual process.* [3].
3. Practice: it *"...is the specific knowledge the community develops, shares and maintains"* [3].

The definition of a CoP is interesting as it enables to consider research projects from a different point of view. In this view, the research project becomes a place in which knowledge is shared and exchanged between the different members involved.

2.2   Community of Practice Typologies

The structural features of a CoP can be refined through corresponding typologies.

Thus, for the domain, McDermott [4] indicates four types of community: (i) communities which are linked to a strategic objective; (ii) communities which focus on tactical processes, process optimisation and sharing of best practices;

(iii) project-based communities and (iv) communities developing a particular body of knowledge. A research project is generally a project based community. It is the project in itself that forms the domain of the CoP.

Concerning the community, the CoP theory provides a set of typical roles. Wenger, McDermott and Snyder [3] describe the specific role of "coordinator" as the one who organises events, connects communities and generally keeps the community alive. They identify three levels of participation in a CoP:

- *The core group*: a small group of people (10 to 15 percent of the CoP) that carries out most of the work in the community. It actively participates in discussions and identifies the topics to be addressed within the community. As the CoP matures, this group becomes the coordinator's auxiliary.
- *The active group*, 15 to 20 percent of the CoP, attends meetings regularly but not with the regularity or intensity of the core group.
- *The peripheral* group represents a large portion of the community members. They rarely participate actively but are often not as passive as they seem. They gain their own insights from observing the discussions of the other members of the community.

In a research project the coordinator is the project leader that is in charge of organizing meetings with the people involved in the project. He also writes regularly the meeting report about the project progress.

Last but not least, the practice dimension is related to what each community does. It is specific to each CoP and is related to the common repository built progressively to support the CoP functioning. The activity typology of the CoP is described in [5] as: (i) collaboration to solve everyday problems; (ii) dissemination and development of best practices, guidelines and procedures; (iii) building, organisation and management of a body of knowledge; (iv) innovation and creation of breakthrough ideas.

Generally a research project creates new knowledge and is therefore concerned with innovation and creation of breakthrough ideas.

3   Process Modelling

3.1   Definition of Process Modelling

According to [6], a business process can be defined as: *"a partially ordered set of enterprise activities that can be executed to achieve some desired end-result in pursuit of a given objective of an enterprise or a part of an enterprise"*. From this definition we can deduce the definition of a process as a partially ordered set of activities that can be executed to achieve some desired end-result in pursuit of a given objective.

Process modelling describes the task of designing semi-formal, graphical descriptions of processes [7]. Process models are designed using so-called process modelling grammars, i.e., sets of graphical constructs and rules, which define how to combine these constructs [8]. Most available grammars such as UML (Unified Modelling

Language) activity diagram or BPMN (Business Process Model Notation) are essentially graph-based flowcharting notations that exploit basic shapes such as rectangles or circles and arcs.

The act of building a process model is commonly named the *process of process modelling* [9, 10]. According to [11], this process consists in three stages: *elicitation, modelling and validation.*

During elicitation, a natural language (e.g. textual or verbal) description of the problem domain is developed by collecting relevant information objects (e.g., documents, data or informal explanations from process stakeholders), which are then verbalized using a common language. During modelling, these information objects are transformed into a formal specification (i.e. a process model) by mapping the components of the informal specification onto modelling grammar and tool. Last during validation, the model is paraphrased again in natural language in order to be able to validate the resulting text against the natural language description created during the elicitation stage [12].

In other words, process modelling enables to fix the features of a given process enabling to reduce its uncertainty. According to [13] a classical classification of uncertainty is its separation of uncertainty into: aleatory and epistemic. Aleatory uncertainty describes the intrinsic variability associated with a physical system or environment. Epistemic uncertainty, on the other hand, is due to an incomplete knowledge about a physical system or environment. Process modelling deals with Epistemic uncertainty as it enables to pinpoint the lacking knowledge about the process modelled.

3.2   BPMN

BPMN (Business Process Model Notation) is a graphical process modelling notation provided by the OMG. According to [14], its objective is to provide businesses with the capability of understanding their internal business procedures in a graphical notation and to give organizations the ability to communicate these procedures in a standard manner. Furthermore, the graphical notation has to facilitate the understanding of the performance collaborations and business transactions between the organizations.

The grammar of BPMN is rich and dedicated to describe in detail business processes. For example, it distinguishes eight different tasks: abstract task, service task, send task, receive task, user task, manual task, business rule task and script task. From this point of view BPMN is a powerful tool to model business processes.

In our view, even if it is dedicated to business processes, it can be applied to any process. We apply it to the modelling of experimental protocols in collaborative research projects. Such a modelling enables the different stakeholders involved to formalize the different steps of the experiments in order to fix it precisely. Such formalization is essential to avoid misunderstanding between the research teams. It also enables to define which experiments each team has to set up and is responsible for. In this way, it avoids the teams the checking of the experimental results of another team. This is essential to save time and money during the project.

4   Case Study: The SEPOLBE Project

4.1   Context of the Project

The SEPOLBE project is dedicated to develop bioadmixtures for concrete. These substances are conscientious of the environment and should limit the bio contamination of the concrete surface and improve the resistance to corrosion of its metallic reinforcement. This project implies four research teams and a company. The research teams have different complementary areas of competency: concrete surface analysis, physical chemistry analysis of films on steel and concrete, electro chemistry for steel corrosion inhibition, petro physics for concrete physical chemistry characterization. Competences in micro biology, chemistry and microscopy are also required to develop the substances and to analyse the surface bio contamination. The industrial partner is specialised in concrete admixtures. Its product mix already includes protection products but none of them is dedicated to biological contamination. The duration of this project is about four years. It uses extra cellular substances and has been divided into eight tasks that are scheduled on a GANTT plan providing a shared vision of the project:

— Task 1: project coordination
— Task 2: this task deals with the elaboration and characterization of the products based on the extra cellular products considered. It implies the company and the B2HM team specialized in micro biology. The target is to define the concentration of each extra cellular product in the solution and to optimize its physical chemistry. This task also includes activities linked to the eco profile and security data writing of the different formulas.
— Task 3: this task consists in elaborating test samples of "admixtured" concrete with the products from task two. These samples are then mechanically tested in order to validate the pair (product ingredients, concentration). The admixtures can modify both compressive and bending strength of the mortar samples, but values remain higher than the minimum required by the standard.
— Task 4: this task consists in validating the products' concentration and its influence on the mortar samples properties like setting time. The underlying objective is to check that the adjuvants have no negative impacts on the mortar base properties. This task implies the company and the ICube team having mechanical competencies.
— Task 5: this task consists in validating the inhibiting actions of the selected products. The objective is to choose the products having the best action against bio contamination and corrosion. Here, electro chemistry experiments are worked out by the ICube and LISE teams. The LISE team is specialized in electro chemistry.
— Task 6: this task deals with the understanding of the inhibition corrosion mechanisms exploiting the operative modes defined during the tasks 3, 4 and 5. The LISE and ICube teams are responsible for this task.
— Task 7: this task consists in the characterization of modifications of the concrete surface and the steel/mortar base interfaces. The objective is to determine how the admixtures modify the concrete porous network. Three partners are in charge of

this task: the ICube team, the company and the LPCS team, specialized in surface physical chemistry.

— Task 8: this task deals with the cleaning ability of the mortar base surfaces. The objective is to evaluate the ability of the bioadmixtures to limit the development of biofilms on the concrete surface and its impact on the cleaning concrete surface (biofilm dropping out). The ICube and B2HM teams are in charge of this task. The ICube team has to provide to the B2HM team "adequate" concrete samples. The B2HM is in charge of the contamination and cleaning tests.

4.2   The Community of Practice

The SEPOLBE project can be analysed in the light of the CoP theory. This analysis enables the improving of the project functioning towards better collaboration.

The SEPOLBE project is a project based CoP. Indeed, the four research teams and the company work together during 48 months in order to develop bioadmixtures for concrete. After project completion the CoP will be dissolved. This enables the definition of the *domain* of the CoP.

Concerning the *community* dimension, for the SEPOLBE project, we can identify a core group and an active group. The core group is represented by the project coordinator and one responsible in each research team involved. The project coordinator which is part of the ICube team checks that the tasks of the project work properly and follow the foreseen schedule. To succeed in project meetings take place twice a year. At least one representative person of each team attends to the meeting.

Concerning the *practice* dimension the SEPOLBE project mainly share innovative ideas. Indeed, the boadmixtures that have to be developed during the project are new. Therefore, during the project specific communication strategies are set up. Moreover the different stakeholders signed a contract specifying the role of each partner during the project. In this contract the problem of patent rights and scientific publications were stated. Indeed, the industrial partner wants to keep the industrial property on the bioadmixtures that have to be formulated during the project and the scientific partners in the project would like to publish the project results.

4.3   Process Modelling

We illustrate the usefulness of process modelling on task 8 and the collaboration between the ICube and B2HM teams. The ICube team has to manufacture cement base samples for the B2HM team that proceeds to bio-receptivity tests. The underlying objective is to provide samples whose bio-receptivity remains steady between the manufacturing date and the bio-receptivity tests. The B2HM team requires an average time of two or three weeks to make these tests.

The process parameters that the ICube team checks is the surface roughness, surface pH value and energy surface and their evolution over time. Indeed, according to these physical chemistry parameters are representative of the bio-receptivity. These preliminary tests aim at validating the manufacturing process and preservation conditions of the samples.

The modelling of the manufacturing process and preliminary test enable the formalization and sharing of the experimental protocols. In this way, the process is codified and each partner can rely on this description for its own work. Moreover, the model can be annotated enabling to refine the activity described.

The process model of the tablet manufacturing is given in **Fig. 1**. First of all the cement base is elaborated according to the standard. This is day zero of the samples. After turning out of the samples, they are stored in distilled water (standard curing conditions). The water/sample relation is steady over time. In this way, the humidity rate is constant (about 100%) and has therefore not to be taken into account. Then, there is a waiting time from at least two days of cement base hardening (before it is too crumbly to be polished). The polishing enables to have smooth and parallel sides. In this way, the topographical differences linked with casting can be removed. The polish activity uses three different sand papers. Then the samples are ultrasonicated in order to remove the polishing fragments. Both teams discuss on the process model about the preservation conditions and surface condition of the samples. In this way the proc ess epistemic uncertainty is fixed.

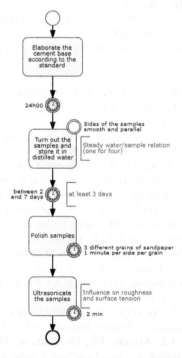

Fig. 1. Cement base sample manufacturing process of the SEPOLBE project

5   Conclusion

Research projects are more and more collaborative and multi-disciplinary with teams geographically dispersed. In this boarder, efficient collaborative work has to be ensured. To succeed in we propose to apply two tools: (i) CoP theory and (ii) process modelling. The first one enables the setting up of an appropriate collaboration context by defining the domain, community and practice features. The second one is useful to describe experimental protocols on which different teams have to work. BPMN through its rich semantics is particularly adapted, even if it is not dedicated to such a context. The SEPOLBE project shows the applicability of these tools to this particular context. In future it will be interesting to add to the BPMN semantics elements specific to experimental protocol modelling.

References

1. Cox, A.: What are communities of practice? A comparative review of four seminal works. Journal of Information Science 31(6), 527–540 (2005)
2. Wenger, E.: Communities of Practice: Learning. Meaning and Identity. Cambridge University Press, Cambridge (1998)
3. Wenger, E., McDermott, R., Snyder, W.M.: Cultivating communities of practice. Harvard Business School Press, Boston (2002)
4. McDermott, R.: Critical success factors in building communities of practice. Knowledge Management Review 3 (May-June 2000)
5. APQC, Building and Sustaining Communities of Practice: Continuing Success in Knowledge, American Productivity and Quality Centre (APQC), Texas, United States of America (2001)
6. ISO 19439, Enterprise integration - Framework for enterprise modelling (2006)
7. Ingvaldsen, J.E., Gulla, J.A.: Model-based business process mining. Information Systems Management 23, 19–31 (2006)
8. Wand, Y., Weber, R.: Research commentary: information systems and conceptual modeling – a research agenda. Information Systems Research 13, 363–376 (2002)
9. Claes, J., Vanderfeesten, I., Reijers, H.A., Pinggera, J., Weidlich, M., Zugal, S., Fahland, D., Weber, B., Mendling, J., Poels, G.: Tying process model quality to the modeling process: the impact of structuring, movement, and speed. In: Barros, A., Gal, A., Kindler, E. (eds.) BPM 2012. LNCS, vol. 7481, pp. 33–48. Springer, Heidelberg (2012)
10. Indulska, M., Recker, J., Rosemann, M., Green, P.: Business process modeling: Current issues and future challenges. In: van Eck, P., Gordijn, J., Wieringa, R. (eds.) CAiSE 2009. LNCS, vol. 5565, pp. 501–514. Springer, Heidelberg (2009)
11. Recker, J., Mendling, J., Hahn, C.: How collaborative technology supports cognitive processes in collaborative process modeling: A capabilities-gains-outcome model. Information Systems 38(8), 1031–1045 (2013)
12. Flynn, D.J., Warhurst, R.: An empirical study of the validation process within requirements determination. Information Systems Journal 4, 185–212 (1994)
13. Dantan, J.Y., Qureshi, A.J., Antoine, J.F., Eisenbart, B., Blessing, L.: Management of product characteristics uncertainty based on formal logic and characteristics properties model. CIRP Ann Manuf Technol. 62(1), 147–150 (2013)
14. OMG (2014), http://www.bpmn.org/ (last access March 27, 2014)

Quality Improvement of NLFM Manufacturing Process: Estimating Optimal Combination of Influencing Factor Levels

R.M. Chandima Ratnayake[1,*] and M. Amarathunga[2]

[1] Department of Mechanical and Structural Engineering and Materials Science,
University of Stavanger, Stavanger, Norway
chandima.ratnayake@uis.no
[2] Richard Pieris Natural Foams Ltd., Biyagama, Sri Lanka

Abstract. Natural latex foam mattresses (NLFMs) are manufactured using the latex extracted in its purest form of milky white liquid, which is tapped from the trunks of mature rubber trees. The natural latex foam mattress manufacturing (NLFMM) process undergoes several processing stages before the natural latex is converted into an ultra cushioning material with a wide range of firmness and comfort. Among the other processing steps, the gelling process has been found to play a significant role in controlling the quality of the final product, provided that quality raw materials have been supplied to the manufacturing plant. This manuscript suggests a methodology for estimating optimal levels of parameters that affect the gelling process, focusing on minimizing the influence on mattresses' surface quality deterioration. A case study has been performed in collaboration with one of the natural latex foam manufacturing plants to recognize main quality deterioration mechanisms and corresponding process parameters using the engineering robust design approach to establish the optimal combination of influencing factor levels.

Keywords: Natural latex foam manufacturing, defects minimization, engineering robust design, quality deterioration factors.

1 Introduction

Natural latex foam mattress manufacturing (NLFMM) starts with the latex, which is extracted in its purest form when tapped from the trunks of mature rubber trees [1]. The extracted natural latex is then converted into an ultra cushioning material with a wide range of firmness and comfort, through heat, vacuum, and freezing. In general, the NLFMM processes follow one of the following approaches [2]: 1. *Standard process*: this is also referred to as the Dunlop process (Note: It is a less expensive process for NLFMM whilst producing a finished product that has a steadier feel); 2. *Talalay process*: this is the most advanced NLFMM process which manufactures latex mattress cores (Note: Latex cores manufactured using the *Talalay* process have

---

* Corresponding author.

B. Grabot et al. (Eds.): APMS 2014, Part III, IFIP AICT 440, pp. 11–18, 2014.
© IFIP International Federation for Information Processing 2014

been proven to be superior in comfort and durability with a greater range of firmness, i.e. from very soft to super firm).

Currently different kinds of categorizations are used to describe NLFMs [3]. For instance, there are three main kinds of categorizations in latex mattresses: 1. Pure latex (i.e. at least 20% natural and a blend of 80% synthetic); 2. Natural latex (at least 80% natural and a blend of 20% synthetic); and 3. 100% natural latex (i.e. 2% forming additives, 2% soaping agents and 96% latex from rubber trees) [3]. The 100% NLFMM process has been selected for the current study. Generally, natural rubber is very soft and elastic, whilst synthetic rubber provides good hardness to the foam.

The natural rubber is very dilute when it is tapped from a tree, having a rubber content of about only 30%. Hence, it is concentrated before use to above 61.5% solids which has been referred to as total solid content (TSC). Usually,   60.0% of TSC is rubber and the remaining 1.5% are compounds that are unique to natural latex (proteins, phospholipids, carbohydrates, amino acids) [4]. The aforementioned unique ingredients play a significant role in explaining the behavior of natural latex [4].

The initial preservation of the raw natural rubber latex and later for NLFM requires sending latex through several processing stages. In this context, controlling the quality of the final product is of significant importance and challenging. In particular, minimizing surface defects requires the identification of optimum settings of influencing factors. This manuscript first illustrates the results of a preliminary study, which have been utilized for the identification of influencing factors in relation to major surface defects. Then the manuscript suggests an engineering robust design based approach and framework to carry out experiments. Finally, it presents the results of the experiment (i.e. optimal combination of influencing factors).

2   Industrial Challenge and Preliminary Study

2.1   Industrial Challenge

The surface quality of mattresses is assessed based on the size and number of defects that are allowed to appear on the surface (top, bottom and sides) of the mattresses that are graded for the export market. Ideally a product is said to be of exportable grade when the product has a very uniform surface all around with no surface depressions or holes appearing. Fig. 1 illustrates the basic process of the natural latex foam manufacturing.

However, it is difficult to achieve the desired surface finish, especially due to the fact that there are inherent limitations present in the NLFMM process and technology as well as in the process of extraction of the main raw material (i.e. being a "natural or living" product). In the context of NLFMM process product quality, apart from the latex compounding step (i.e. related to the quality of the raw materials), the gelation is the next significant step that has a greater effect on controlling surface finish. Hence, the gelling process has been a subject for study. The main focus has been on developing a methodology for estimating the variables' set points (or levels) to improve surface finish.

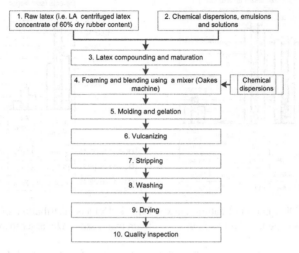

Fig. 1. The process of the natural latex foam manufacturing

2.2   Preliminary Study

A preliminary study has been carried out to investigate the different kinds of defects present in a natural foam latex mattress and their relationships to various influencing factors. Information has been gathered to obtain an overview about maturation time and different kinds of defects. Fig. 2 illustrates compounded latex maturation data.

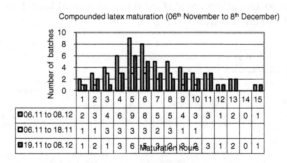

Fig. 2. Compounded latex maturation data

Fig. 3 illustrates results of preliminary defect analysis for defects size less than 5x5 cm². Fig. 4 illustrates results of preliminary defect analysis for defects size greater than 5x5 cm².

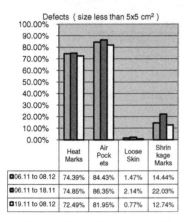

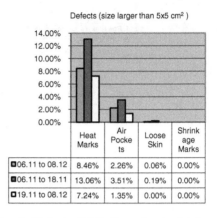

Defects (size less than 5x5 cm²)

	Heat Marks	Air Pock ets	Loose Skin	Shrin kage Marks
◙06.11 to 08.12	74.39%	84.43%	1.47%	14.44%
◙06.11 to 18.11	74.85%	86.35%	2.14%	22.03%
◻19.11 to 08.12	72.49%	81.95%	0.77%	12.74%

Defects (size larger than 5x5 cm²)

	Heat Marks	Air Pocke ts	Loose Skin	Shrink age Marks
◙06.11 to 08.12	8.46%	2.26%	0.06%	0.00%
◙06.11 to 18.11	13.06%	3.51%	0.19%	0.00%
◻19.11 to 08.12	7.24%	1.35%	0.00%	0.00%

Fig. 3. Defects distribution of natural latex foam mattresses (size less than 5×5 cm²)

Fig. 4. Defects distribution of natural latex foam mattresses (size larger than 5×5 cm²)

Table 1 illustrates the main surface defects *vs.* related codes which have been identified in a preliminary prioritization study of the surface finish.

Table 1. Main surface defects vs. related codes

Surface defect	Code
Heat marks	2
Loose skin	13
Shrinkage marks/lake marks	15

A fish bone diagram has been developed to understand the influence of different factors' interaction with the surface finish [5]. Using a fish bone diagram, the major influencing factors that affect the surface finish of natural latex foam mattresses have been identified and are illustrated in Fig. 5.

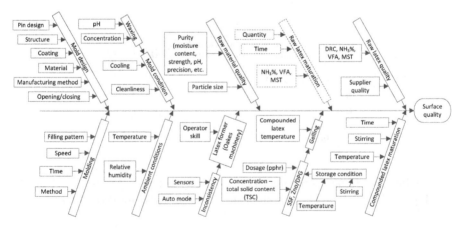

Fig. 5. Factors affecting the surface quality of natural latex foam mattresses (fish bone diagram) [Note: mechanical stability time (MST)]

Table 2 illustrates the parameters influencing quality deterioration that have been identified from the preliminary investigation.

Table 2. Parameters influencing quality deterioration

Symbol	Quality deterioration influencing factor	Units	Levels		
			1	2	3
A	Raw latex maturation	days	30	37	44
B	Compounded latex maturation	hours	2	8	14
C	SSF dosage	pphr	0.9	1.5	2.2
D	ZnO/DPG dosage	pphr	2	4	6
E	Mold Temperature	^{0}C	30	40	50
F	NH_3 content of latex	W/W %	0.18	0.22	0.28
G	pH of PEG (mold releasing agent)	pH	7	10.5	12

Parts of additive per hundred parts of rubber (pphr); Diphenyl Guanidine (DPG); PolyEthylene Glycol (PEG)

Hence, it is vital to develop a methodology to estimate the optimal combination of quality deterioration influencing factors in order to make the necessary improvements to surface quality in terms of reducing the number and size of the surface defects that appear on manufactured latex foam mattresses.

3   Methodology

3.1   Matrix Experiments Using Orthogonal Arrays

An efficient way to study the effect of several control factors simultaneously is to plan matrix experiments using orthogonal arrays which have been introduced in the engineering robust design approach (ERDA) [6,7]. A matrix experiment consists of a set of experiments which provides the possibility to change the settings of the various product or process parameters, which it is necessary to study, from one experiment to another [8,9]. For processes that involve many factors, experiments are conducted using special matrices called *Orthogonal Arrays* [10]. After conducting a matrix experiment, the data from all experiments are taken together and analyzed to determine the effects of the various parameters [7], [6].

3.2   Analysis Approach

The following steps are adapted from the literature applying the ERDA in designing the experiments and finding the optimal internal vibration settings which give the best surface finish [6].

* *Identify the challenge:* In this study, the challenge is to investigate the optimal combination of influencing factor settings which minimizes the surface defects.

- *Determination of the performance characteristic(s) and the measuring system:* The surface finish is evaluated by visual inspection and the use of appropriate measuring devices. According to the classification, the smaller the number of defects, the better the surface finishes.
- *Determination of the variables (parameters) affecting the performance characteristic(s):* There are various factors affecting the NLFM surface finish (see Fig. 5). Considering the case study on "surface quality improvements for latex foam mattresses", the significant process parameters have been identified as: Polyethylene Glycol (A), raw latex maturation (B), compounded latex maturation (C), SSF (D), ZnO/DPG (E), mold temperature (F), ammonia content of latex (G) (see Table 2).
- *Determination of the number of levels and values of the controllable variables (parameters):* In this case, only the controllable parameters are discussed. For example, Table 4 gives three levels for the variable raw latex maturation time (i.e. 30, 37 and 44 days). Only 18 experiments are needed to study the entire experimental parameters using the *L18* orthogonal array.
- *Determination of loss function and the performance statistics:* The "smaller-is-better" (SMB) loss function is selected for calculating signal to noise ratios (S/N ratios) for surface defects [11] [see Equation (1)].

$$S/N \ ratio \ (\eta_i) = -10 \ log_{10} \left\{ \left(\frac{1}{n} \right) \sum_{i=1}^{n} \frac{1}{y_{ij}^2} \right\} \tag{1}$$

where

n = number of replications

y_{ij} = performance indicator value ($i = 1,2 \ldots n$ and $j=1,2,3 \ldots n$).

- *Conducting experiments and recording of results.*
- *Analyzing data and selection of the optimum value of the controllable variables.*
- *Verifying the results.*
- *Re-establishing and documenting the NLFMM process parameters.*

Under the optimum set-points, the corresponding η_{opt} is calculated using the additive model for factor effects (see (2) suggested by [6].

$$S/N \ ratio \ (\eta) = \alpha + \alpha_i^A + \alpha_j^B + \alpha_k^C + \alpha_l^D + \alpha_m^E + \alpha_n^F + \varepsilon_{ijklmn} \tag{2}$$

where

α = overall mean S/N ratio for surface defects count over all the possible combinations

$i,j,k,l,m.n$ = particular levels of each of the parameters which were selected (so in this model i,j,k,l,m,n must all take on one of the values 1, 2 or 3)

α_i^A = deviation from α caused by setting parameter "A" at level i (similarly, other terms in Equation (2) are defined)

ε_{ijklmn} = error term.

The calculated η_{opt} represents the theoretical level of defect value at optimum settings found by experimentation. However, a verification experiment shall be performed to investigate the accuracy of the optimum settings. Fig. 6 provides a framework to illustrate the calculation and experimentation approach.

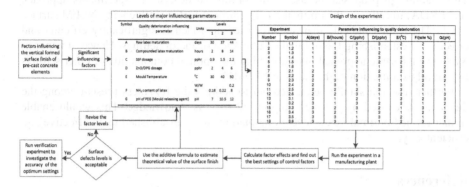

Fig. 6. Framework for experimentation, estimation of best settings and verification

4   Results and Discussion

The levels of the factors to minimize the affect to surface finish of NLFM have been established based on the final analysis of the matrix experiment results and further discussions with a team of expert personnel. For the raw latex maturation time, level 3 (i.e. 44 days) has been shown to be the best level. However, due to the practical limitations of having such a long maturation in the latex storage tanks, the team has decided to purchase latex with 21 days' minimum maturation and issuing it for the manufacturing process after it reaches 30 days minimum.

For the compounded latex maturation time, levels 1 and 2 have indicated more or less the same effect on the defect code numbers 2, 13 and 15. Therefore, the team decided to adopt six hours minimum (within levels 1 and 2), while the raw latex maturation is 30 days minimum. For instance, if the raw latex maturation is closer to 44 days, then the compounded latex maturation has to be closer to level 1 (i.e. two hours).

For the SSF dosage, level 1 (0.9 pphr) has been shown to be the optimum level to reduce defect code number 2; however, its performance in reducing defect code number 13 is poor. Hence, the team decided to reduce the SSF dosage by 0.1 pphr from the present operating level.

For ZnO/DPG dosage, level 3 (i.e. 6 pphr) has indicated a greater effect in reducing defect code number 13; however, on average level 2 has a similar effect in reducing other defects, as well as having a good control over maintaining other parameters. Hence, the team has decided to increase the ZnO/DPG dosage by 0.1 pphr as it reduces defect code number 13.

For mold temperature, level 1 (i.e. 30 ^{0}C) has the greatest effect in reducing defect code number 2. For defect code number 13, level 3 (i.e. 50 ^{0}C) is indicated to be the best. Therefore, the team decided to adopt level 1 as the optimum level in order to reduce defect code number 2 to a greater extent.

For NH_3 content, the present operating level seems to be the best at controlling defects as well as other tested parameters. Also, for the factor pH of PEG, level 2 (10.5 pH) has been proven to be the best level for most of the tested parameters.

5   Conclusion

This manuscript proposes the use of the optimized design of experiments approach (i.e. ERDA) to estimate the optimal combination of factors influencing NLFM surface finish. The results indicate that the suggested approach is significantly efficient and effective in establishing the optimal combination of factor settings. Hence, it is possible to use the same approach in establishing the optimal combination of other settings by careful examination of the existing NLFMM.

Further research should be carried out to address the fuzziness present among the factor levels caused by the incorporation of experts' knowledge. This would enable further refined optimal factor level combinations to be established in an effective and efficient way.

References

1. Nawamawat, K., Sakdapipanich, J.T., Ho, C.C., Ma, Y., Song, J., Vancso, J.G.: Surface Nanostructure of Hevea Brasiliensis Natural Rubber Latex Particles, Colloid. Surface. A: Physicochemical and Engineering Aspects 390(1-3), 157–166 (2011)
2. Jones, K.P.: CHAPTER 1 – Historical Development of the World Rubber Industry. Dev. Crop Sci. 23, 1–25 (1992)
3. Ryan, J.: Latex as a Comfort Layer (2014),
   http://www.factory-beds-direct.co.uk/
   latex-as-a-comfort-layer (accessed on April 21, 2014)
4. Sansatsadeekul, J., Sakdapipanich, J., Rojruthai, P.: Characterization of Associated Proteins and Phospholipids in Natural Rubber Latex. J. Biosci. Bioeng. 111(6), 628–634 (2011)
5. Ratnayake, R.M.C.: Framework for Computing Machining Parameter Settings in CNC Machines: An Industrial Case Study. Int. J. Comput. Sys. Eng. (2014),
   http://www.inderscience.com/info/ingeneral/
   forthcoming.php?jcode=ijcsyse
6. Phadke, M.S.: Quality Engineering using Robust Design. PTR Prentice-Hall Inc., Englewood Cliffs (1989)
7. Ratnayake, R.M.C.: Small and Medium Enterprises Project Finance: Identifying Optimum Settings of Controllable Factors. Int. J. Appl. Decision Sci. 7(2), 136–150 (2014)
8. Ratnayake, R.M.C., Valbo, I.: Use of Robust Design Technique in Job Shop Manufacturing: A Case Study of Die-Sinking Electro Discharge Machining. Int. J. Perform. Eng. 10(2), 153–160 (2014)
9. Taguchi, G., Phadke, M.S.: Quality Engineering through Design Optimization. In: Conf. Record GLOBECOM 84 Meeting. IEEE Communications Society, Atlanta (1984)
10. McEwan, W., Belavendram, N., Abou-Ali, M.: Taguchi Methods and Expert Systems in Fabrication Design. Int. J. Pres. Ves. Pip. 53(1), 47–61 (1992)
11. Kamaruddin, S., Zahid Khan, A., Foong, S.H.: Application of Taguchi Method in the Optimization of Injection Moulding Parameters for Manufacturing Products from Plastic Blend. IACSIT Int. J. Eng. Tech. 2(6) (December 2010) ISSN: 1793–8236

Lean Production and Just in Time:
A Case Study of the e-procurement Application[*]

Demésio Carvalho de Sousa, Rodrigo Franco Gonçalves,
Marinalva Rodrigues Barboza, Rose Reis de Souza, and Oduvaldo Vendrametto

Paulista University-UNIP, Graduate Program in Production Engineering,
Dr. Bacelar St. 1212, São Paulo, Brazil
sousamtm@gmail.com

Abstract. Guided for an increasingly competitive market, companies
have sought to attend consumer expectations by offering the best
product, quality, flexibility, agility and cost effectively. Studies have
been shown that the Just in Time (JIT) has proven to meet these requirements. Allied to information technology through e-procurement,
using the JIT has boosted results. Practical results of this combination
are presented in this paper, through a case study in a large multinational
company in the food sector. The purpose of this article is to identify and
present the benefits of using the JIT philosophy in the implementation
of e-procurement in the purchasing and routing company.

Keywords: ERP, B2B, Supply Chain.

1 Introduction

Just in time (JIT) is an important philosophy in logistical activities, especially when it
refers to lean production, initially of used by Toyota Motor Company in 70's. Mainly
since 80's so far, the JIT philosophy which is one of the pillars of lean production has
been used in several of companies segments with success such as: cost, time, reliability, quality and flexibility [1;4;10].

The variables that form the primary activities and the value chain has suffered
alteration with the information technology introduction, it evolves machines, equipment, raw materials, supplies and other consumable items which are already commonly associated with primary activities [2; 9; 11].

The objective of this paper is to present the results gotten by an American multinational company (called XPTO Brazil, on this study), active in Brazilian market and it
is a producer of food and beverages that through JIT philosophy, associated to an
e-procurement tool, provided improvement in the purchasing process and company
routing.

---

[*] The authors wish to thank the CAPES.

B. Grabot et al. (Eds.): APMS 2014, Part III, IFIP AICT 440, pp. 19–26, 2014.
© IFIP International Federation for Information Processing 2014

2   Backgrounds

2.1   Lean Production

Through a reverse logistical Lean Manufacturing and JIT study has realized other discoveries about philosophy contributions in areas related to logistics. The lack of integration between the key areas studied by authors that are Collecting, Inventory, Remanufacturing and Distribution. Through a long bibliographic review, the authors could get the JIT performance results in five sectors, such as: cost, speed, flexibility, quality and reliability. It's believed that JIT contribute for the process of remanufacturing as optimization of line production, involving the acquisition of resources and diagnosis of any activity in advance [3; 6; 13].

2.2   E-procurement

E-procurement is a buying   application based on   the Internet/Intranet or a place service that boosts the trade purchasing partners, maximize the commerce efficiency along the chain supplies and provides e-commerce strategy skills on the Internet.

The solution of e-procurement facilitates the cooperative purchases through the Internet. According to the author, the tool has the power of turning into the purchasing process because it spreads in all steps identified by supply manager. E-procurement is the most revolutionary aspect of B2B and it will change completely and definitely the way of companies do business, replacing the physical process that involve trade. [2; 5; 8; 10]. The (table 1) presents some e-procurement types, its main models and features [6].

Table 1. Models of e-procurement

Ecommerce templates	Main features
Networks EDI Electronic Data Interchange.	Range of commercial and customer opinions. Simple transactional capabilities. Processing in series. Shift to value-added networks and reactive expensive way.
Applications requisition Business-to-Employee (B2E).	Quick Shopping for corporate employees. Automation of approval and standardization of the requisition process. Provides the buyer management tool suppliers.
Corporate procurement portals.	Better control over the procurement process and allows business rules of most companies are consistently implemented. Customize with prices negotiated in a multi-vendor catalog. Management cost analysis.
Trade first generation.	Industrial content, jobs and news. New sales channel for distributors and manufacturers. Service bundling and catalogues.
Trade second generation.	Automating the process of requesting and-order transactions. Discovery of suppliers, prices and products/services. Catalogues management and credit.
Trade third generation.	Synchronized operations and satisfaction in real time. Transparency in the process leading to restriction of demand and supply chain. Alternative information for inventory.
Industrial consortiums.	Next step in the evolution of corporate procurement portals.

Source: Adaptation by Kalakota and Robinson [7].

2.3   Just in Time

Experiencing a post - WWII environment, Japan saw an opportunity to gain competitive advantage to optimize their processes through the use of quality tools and standardization, based on items of verification and control at all stages of the production process, generating customer value [1; 10]. JIT is used in a pull production system which produces only on demand, after the completion of an application in the amount and at the desired time, since it does not allow anticipation of purchases, production or transportation [4; 9; 11].

The stock is part of the assets of a company and thus directly influences the working capital. In this context, the JIT philosophy aims to meet demand instantaneously with perfect quality and no waste. Note in this context that the primary activities are essential to the achievement of logistics objectives are also those that contribute the largest share of logistics costs [1; 5; 12].

3   Methodology

3.1   Case Study

The methodology used has been the application of a case study supported by a review of JIT philosophy and the application of an e-procurement platform in a specific view. The identification of weaknesses and strengths of XPTO Company was accomplished through the interviews with Supplies and Information Technology Directors, being guided by theme and goals as follow:

Needing evaluation in order to determine the Planning, Warehousing, Handling and Storage Control, aiming at the service optimization and costs reduction through the concept of Lean Production, Just in Time and the application of an e-Procurement Platform. The specific objectives of the case study are:

a) Evaluate the application of Just in Time and Lean Production concepts in XPTO Company Brazil identifying possible opportunities of improvement.
b) Understanding the main techniques for storage sizing in order to attend business needs of a company, its warehousing and handling, focusing on Lean Production.
c) Evaluate the results gotten through the application of e-procurement platform and its improvements in productive process and Just in Time.

It has showed by the directors, reports, prints, graphs, sheets, floor plans and these documents have been used for the identification of weaknesses and opportunities of improvement and these ones served as a reference for the elaboration of proposals following the theme and goals pre-established and can be viewed in SWOT matrix and for being strategy information they will not be presented in their totality in this article.

On the documental analysis was possible to identify that: "XPTO Brazil firmly believes that the international trade strengths the stability and peace when it promotes the economic growing, the opportunities and the mutual understanding".

3.2   SWOT Analysis

The identification of strengths, weaknesses, threads and opportunities was the critical factor of success for the suitability of theme and proposed goals in this study, guided the incorporation of the best market practices and available technology following concepts and specific scientific methodology.

a) Evaluate the application of Just in Time and Lean Production concepts at XPTO Brazil identifying possible improvements opportunities.
- Strength: overview of all storages in movement in the company.
- Weakness: Absence of improvement actions and data analysis comparing them with scientific literature.
- Opportunity: Integrating SAP-ERP system with e-procurement.

b) Understanding the main techniques for a storage sizing in order to attend the business necessities of a company, its warehousing and movement, focusing on Lean Production.
- Strength: ERP (Enterprise Resource Planning) System of routes managing and supplies.
- Weakness: analysis and improvements lack using the data and information from ERP-SAP linked to scientific methodology.

c) Evaluate the results have gotten through the e-procurement Platform Application and its improvement in productive process and in Just in time.
- Strength: Emphasized only the improvement opportunity.
- Weakness: Lack of ERP (Enterprise Resource Planning) - SAP integration with a supplies module, being this also not contemplated in the organization core-business
- Opportunity: implementation of an e-procurement Platform linking the ERP-SAP with supplies area.

3.3   The Nature of Strategy of the Company Business Unit

Each business unit of XPTO Brazil follows the net and search international corporate strategy in order to provide the best conditions of understanding the benefits Logistics foundations, being that the business unit chosen was a distribution center of the company and the pilot project was also the unit studied for the e-procurement implementation, automatize the purchasing system from all over the group XPTO Brazil through an e-procurement Platform linking the ERP (Enterprise Resource Planning) - SAP with the supplies area, aiming at the lead time optimization, gains of competitiveness and cost reduction, being the strategy adopted to Brazil branch.

4   Results and Discussion

Through the analysis of the case study was possible to realize that the project of a warehouse should evaluate many factors in its interrelation with the performance and the company costs, in order to find the system that optimize the operations. The company studied (XPTO Brazil) showed layout organization failures, caused by the lack of planning from the top management, mainly related to the fleet control, management of distribution centers and optimization of purchasing process through the utilization of Information Technology.

The solution of Purchasing Service (Outsourcing) to the XPTO Brazil searched attending initially the purchasing necessities of: MRO (maintenance, repair and operations) for some of its plants. In the case of a success from pilot project will be expanded to other 9 existent plants. The activity objectives to reduce the charge of XPTO Brazil buyers and in the same time to provide a service with focused professionals in cost reduction and operational optimization regulated by a Service Level Agreement Index.

The (figure1) presents the first initial result got and shows the utilization of ERP in search of the excellence of the delivery level, excelling by the punctuality and the major customer satisfaction, the outcome presents an efficiency of 67% initially in a score from 0 to 100%. The result is provided by a system and it is based on references pre-established related to the planning and logistical control section focusing on JIT, where were noted several dispersed and geographically overlapping points.

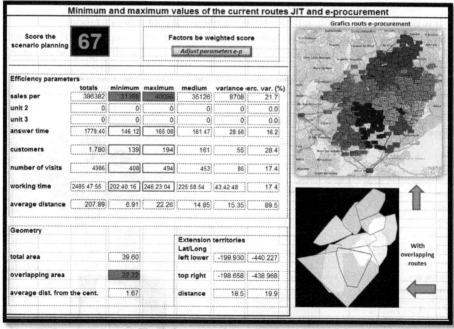

Fig. 1. Scenario of the areas and routes

Next, it has been resized the routes, according to (figure 2), that optimized the routes in order to reduce the delivery distances purposed to respective sale outlets. The results departed from 1.032,77 meters to 588,31 meters, getting a reduction of 444,46 meters in a distance to be covered a month.

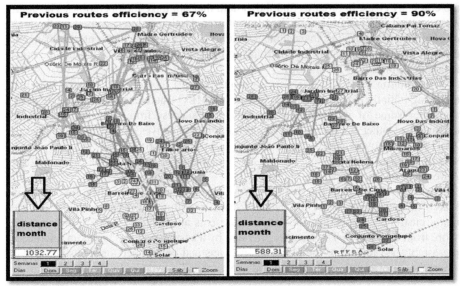

Fig. 2. Scenario routes restructured

It is noted as results gotten through the warehouse layout reorganization:

At the beginning, the total available area for warehousing occupied 1.104 m^2 being 594 m^2 occupied by end products warehouse area and after the bibliographic research

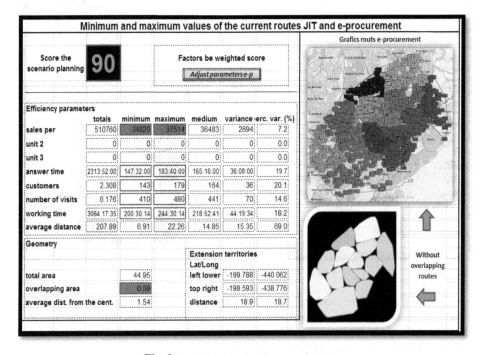

Fig. 3. Scenario restructured areas and routes

was implemented an improvement with the collaboration of a new layout in which the total warehouse area pass through disposing of 1.284 m^2, being 714 m^2 intended to warehouse area according to the purchasing planning planned by e-procurement.

This way, the gain of physical space is of 180 m^2 and 120 m^2 through the Warehousing Physical Planning that provided a distribution more balanced of areas and installations allowing a possible cost reduction, as well as it avoided a regression on the flow of processing materials.

The (figure 3) presents the improvements after the suitability of control references, the improvement of efficiency reached to 90% validating one of the JIT objectives, after the utilization of ERP and the e-procurement platform in the search of delivery level, excelling for punctuality and the major customer satisfaction.

The results are in accordance with the 3 objectives outlined in this case study because it resulted in a gain in efficiency of 13 % for the company searched. Note that the integration of SAP and e-procurement resulted in creating value for customers and stakeholders.

5   Conclusions

Lean Production and Just in Time philosophy associated to an e-procurement application has provided to the multinational company a remarkable improvement in its lead time, optimizing the return of purchasing process and the planned routing company.

This structural change was supported by the adoption of the best practices in the supplies area, in other words, automatize the purchasing system of all the group of American multinational.

With the implementation of the e-procurement Platform linking ERP (Enterprise Resource Planning) SAP with the supplies area, aiming at the lead time optimization as possible to observe competitiveness gains in supplies area and the company passed through evaluating in a systemic way its business, adapting to the present view of Corporate Logistics and aligning its core business.

References

1. Ballou, R.H.: The evolution and future of logistics and supply chain management. European Business Review 19(4), 332–348 (2007)
2. Brunnelli, M.A.: Purchasing. Consultants see big future on e-commerce. Conference Board, 2001. Research report 1294-01-RR, Conference. E-business strategies in the global marketplace: e-procurement and other challenges.Twente University, Netherlands (1999)
3. Chang, H., Tsai, Y.-C., Hsu, C.-H.: E-procurement and supply chain performance. Supply Chain Management: An International Journal 18(1), 34–51 (2013)
4. Hing, K.C., Shizhao, Y., Chanb, F.T.S.: Implementing just in time philosophy to reverse logistics systems: a review. International Journal of Production Research 48(21), 1, 6293–6313 (2010)
5. ITRG (info-tech research group), (2002) A success guide for e-procurement, London, Canada, International - Organizacion of Supreme Audit Institutions (2005) e-procurement
6. Kalakota, R., Robinson, M.: E-business 2.0: Roadmap for Success. Addison-Wesley Professional (2001)

7. Liu, S., Mcmahon, C.A., Culley, S.J.: A review of structured document retrieval (SDR) technology to improve information access performance in engineering document management. Computers in Industry 59(1), 3–16 (2008)
8. NEEF, Dale. E-procurement: From strategy to implementation. FT Press (2001)
9. Porter, M.E., Millar, V.E.: How information gives you competitive advantage (1985)
10. Presutti, J.R., William, D.: Supply management and e-procurement: creating value added in the supply chain. Industrial Marketing Management 32(3), 219–226 (2003)
11. Schönsleben, P.: Integral logistics management: Operations and Supply Chain Management Within and Across Companies, 4th edn. Auerbach Publications (2012)
12. Slack, N.: The flexibility of manufacturing systems. International Journal of Operations & Production Management 25(12), 1190–1200 (2005)
13. Yang, M.G.M., Hong, P., Modi, S.B.: Impact of lean manufacturing and environmental management on business performance: an empirical study of manufacturing firms. International Journal of Production Economics 129(2), 251–261 (2011)

Multidisciplinary Management: Model of Excellence in the Management Applied to Products and Services

Evandro Prestes Guerreiro, Pedro Luiz de Oliveira Costa Neto,
and Ulysses Martins Moreira Filho

Paulista University-UNIP
Dr. Bacelar St. 1212, 04026-002, São Paulo – SP, Brazil
egprestes@yahoo.com, {politeleia,moreiraf}@uol.com.br

Abstract. The Multidisciplinary Management is the guiding vision of modern organizations and the systems thinking which requires new approaches to organizational excellence and quality management process. The objective of this article is to present a model for multidisciplinary management of quality applied to products and services based on American, Japanese, and Brazilian National Quality Awards. The methodology used to build this model of Management Excellence starts from an analysis of the specific features of each Quality Award and the principle of a multidisciplinary administration, serving as support for the management of process excellence and results. The proposed model enables to manage organizational outcomes with sustainability, and to identify and place the task priorities in order of importance and urgency in the corporate environment. This strategy shall bring feedback for organizational results excellence.

Keywords: Administration, Multidisciplinary Management, Model of Excellence, Quality Award.

1 Introduction

The management thought grounded in the cartesian model and in mathematical logic or evolutionary thesis is not enough to fill a space of contradictions that is beyond its philosophical approaches. This is a truth, even valuing the competent systematization of Scientific Theory made by engineer Frederick Winslow Taylor (1856-1915), and adapted in Henri Ford's (1863-1947) factories focusing on operational efficiency in the industrial process, and Jules Henri Fayol (1841-1925) who founded the Classical Theory of Administration, to understand the administration process beyond than thought Taylor or Ford, seen with the strategic and tactical look of a director or manager [1].

Fayol's contribution was decisive in shaping the thinking and the study of modern organizations, especially when he structured the four functions of management: Planning, Organizing, Directing and Controlling. Undeniably, the formal logic of cartesian thinking enabled the student, simplifying the complexity of the organizational structure at levels of management processes, making it easier to

B. Grabot et al. (Eds.): APMS 2014, Part III, IFIP AICT 440, pp. 27–34, 2014.

modern teaching of managers about their practices, with what is known as a General Theory of Administration. On the other hand, what to do when the Administrative Thought can not diagnose the evolution of modern enterprise systems?

The answer may lie in the own management model. The word model, derived from the latin "modulus", leading to mold, shape, and although used in different contexts and different meanings, implies somehow the idea of the organizing and ordering of parts that make up a set. Corroborating this idea, a model is, by definition, an abstraction of reality, which may replace complexity for simplicity [2]. In other words, a model is and remains a tool that, when combined with the knowledge and experience and used properly, can help the organization to find solutions to old and new problems [3].

Another vital feature of a management model is that it fosters innovation, in order to create competitive advantages in relation to its competitors, and this requires an organizational culture focused on learning and innovation, thereby reinforcing the valuable asset that an organization has, which is its human capital, as a result creating a healthy environment for knowledge creation [4].

The management model is the body of knowledge in an organization that enables the self-sustainability of the business, being essential to stimulate organizational learning, coupled with the development of specific competences able to operate a system that wins customers' preference, but also ensures excellence of the process as a whole and in a multidisciplinary way.

2   Objective

Presenting a quality management multidisciplinary model applied to products and services with the Management multidisciplinary model – MGM, based on the National Awards of the American, Japanese and Brazilian Quality.

3   Contextualization and Methodology

In this study, we selected three management models that are substantiated on the fundamentals and indicators of quality, that after each management cycle are subjected to the diagnosis of their processes and outcomes: Malcolm Baldrige National Quality Award (USA), National Quality Award (Brazil) and Japanese Quality Award (Japan), by presenting a deep learning in the way of "manage". It is important to say that all of the Quality Awards had its origins in 1951 with the establishment of the Deming Prize by the Japanese, honoring William Edwards Deming, dedicated to quality control focusing on the guaranteed 14 Deming points of quality, in the development of new products and the application that master's business philosophy.

The United States established the Malcolm Baldrige National Quality Award in 1987 with the Public Law 100-07. The American model of quality in the 90s also served as the basis for the proliferation of management models in all Southeast Asia. In Japan this award was called Japanese Quality Award.

The Brazilian Program of Quality and Productivity was formalized in 1986 with the aim of preparing Brazilian companies to a new reality: globalization. As a result of this movement the National Quality Foundation, was created and launched the Brazilian National Quality Award in 1991.

Table 1 shows the main characteristics of the three models that supported the proposed management model.

Table 1. Models of the Quality Awards. (Source: author, 2014)

Quality award	Brief historic settings	Core values and concepts	Criteria	Purpose
Malcolm Baldrige National Quality Award (USA) [5]	Created in 1987 by Public Law 100-07 based on the Deming Prize, under the supervision of Deming, Juran and Feigenbaum. It is administered by by NIST - National Institute of Standards and Technology	Systems perspective; Visionary leadership; Focus on the future; Managing for innovation; Agility; Organizational and personal learning; Valuing workforce members and partners; Customer- driven excellence; Social responsibility; Management by facts; Focus on results and creating value.	1- Leadership; 2- Strategic planning; 3- Customer focus; 4- Measurement, analysis, and knowledge management; 5- Workforce focus; 6- Process management; 7- Results.	Promotes the strengthening of management best practices, facilitates internal communication and serves to better understand the system of management, planning, training and judgment to customers, as well as their strategies and action plans focused on the market.
National Quality Award (Brasil) [6]	Created in 1991 based on the Malcolm Baldrige Award. it is administered by FNQ-National Quality Foundation.	Systemic thinking; Network actuation; Agility; Fundamental decisions; Organizational learning; Innovation; Visionary leardership; Vision of the future; Customers and market knowledge; Social responsibility; Valuing people and the culture; Process oriented; Value generation.	1- Leadership; 2- Strategic planning; 3- Customer focus; 4- Information and knowledge; 5- Workforce focus 6- Process management 7- Results.	The Management Excellence Model proposed by the National Quality Foundation, uses PDCL cycle (Plan, Do, Check, Learn), to meet the needs and expectations of its customers, which must be identified, understood and used, so that products can be developed, creating the need to conquer and retain them, acting to contribute to the Socio Environmental development.
Japan Quality Award (Japan) [7]	Created in 1995 based on the Malcolm Baldrige Award, incorporating Japanese practices. It is administered by JPC – SED – Japanese Productivity Center for Socio-Economic Development.	Customer - driven quality; Leadership; Process-oriented; Creating "Knowledge"; Agility; Partnership and fairness.	1- Leadership of senior leaders; 2- Social responsibility of management; 3- Understanding and responding to customer and Market needs; 4- Strategic planning and deployment; 5- Improving employer and organizational capacities; 6- Customer value creating process; 7- Information management 8- Activity results.	It is a tool for changing the way of managing creating a culture for managing competitivity. Looks for companies that continue to create value through continuous process of self-innovation, to transform their global management systems in customer-oriented structures.

The methodology used to build up the Model of Excellence in Management applied to products and services, was developed in three steps:

Step1 –Bibliography Research: Analyze the specific characteristics of each Quality Award and the principle of a Multidisciplinary Management, working as a support for the management of excellence in the processes and results.

Step 2- Multidisciplinary Process: Integrating each component of the system considered as quality indicators, starting of the Action Method, that substantiate the strategic thought, based on the specific technology of each product and / or service, which drives to excellence of the result.

Step 3 - Person as manager: Enabling and maximizing the technical and management skills that enable systemic understanding of the Management Multidisciplinary Model, applied to the development of the objective conditions of quality control in the results in high performance corporate environments.

4   Theoretical Background

Frederick W. Taylor (1856-1915), in his work "Principles of Scientific Management" [8], published in 1911 observed that the production of each worker could be maximized by at least two thirds of his capacity, however was not reached due to a kind of systematic vagrancy. To resolve this issue, he thought that workers should be seen as instruments of production and, as such, should be monitored and controlled to achieve effectiveness and the operational efficiency of the organization. Taylor signaled that "the basic unit of scientific management was the function and construction of a formal structure required first establishing objectives and then dividing the work into smaller units (simple tasks), which would be placed as a coordinated system (the workers tasks rationalization)" [9]. The production process must be integrated and collaborative among the stakeholders that, directly or indirectly, make up the corporate system. Therefore, suggests that teamwork with the leader and other workers is responsible for organizational success.

Henri Fayol (1841-1925), in turn, complements the observations of Taylor when developing a study on the organizational structure, seeking to understand how the relationship between the corporate sectors can interfere with productivity. As show "Fayol believed in general and unique principles of sound administration and the role that scientific prediction and the proper methods of administration would play in improving business results" [10]. The same authors continue their analysis with presentation of the six interrelated operational groups proposed by Fayol: technical operations, sales, financial, safety, accounting and administration operations.

Management is one of the functions of the company, but differs from the others by its specificity and macro importance. "None of the other functions is responsible for formulate the overall program of action of the company, build its social body, coordinate efforts, harmonize the actions " [11]. The purpose of Fayol was to structure the organization as a whole, stating that the functions of management are: predicting, organizing, commanding, coordinating and controlling.

Unlike Taylor and Fayol, who presented a prescriptive theoretical orientation, Max Weber [12] formulated his theoretical approach as an ideal model from a descriptive approach to organizational structure, assuming that organizations function as a closed system, and the bureaucracy is their ideal and most efficient form of organization which, even being impossible to be found in practice, seeks to address the corporate whole and focuses on the internal environment of the organization, in detriment of its external environment.

5   Multidisciplinary Management and Its Management Model

A multidisciplinary approach is grounded in disciplinarity, which organizes scientific knowledge, establishing the division and specialization of labour [13], as proposed by Taylor, Fayol and Weber in their studies, aiming to respond to the complexity of the diversity of the investigated object, but preserving their autonomy and border compared to other areas of knowledge, using specific theories, language and techniques.

The Multidisciplinary Management considers that the focus on the task allowed Taylor managerial mechanisms to be revolutionary at his time, increasing productivity, reducing fatigue of the workers and optimizing the economic viability of the process, reaching more profitable results in the production line, therefore, an unique contribution to organizations. On the other hand, the task is part of a much larger purpose, since it is the middle of the process, the start and end of the activity needing to be properly controlled and supervised, what requires the contributions of Fayol and Weber to organize and structure the stages that precede and exceed the task itself.

This model understand that the present corporate environment information enables the production of knowledge, needed to establish a quality management and organizational learning. Moreover, like any model, the development of the method of intervention requires the kind of technology and strategy to be employed for reaching the benefit of the best result and the people involved in the process.

To manage in a multidisciplinary way, according to the MMM model, means to be enough technically competent to manage people to become autonomous, have efficient processes, efficient procedures, visionary plans, political diversity of interests and new administrative paradigms, able to guide the creation of new models of technical competence and excellence in organizational management. Each dimension, which integrates multidisciplinary management, challenges the ability of the organizational manager, not only as a strategist, but mainly as an entrepreneurial leader in administrative and technical tools of corporate management, implemented though what we call 6P system:

1. **Persons:** form the intellectual capital of the whole entire organizational system, prepared to address specific and general problems in the field of knowledge management and corporate learning;
2. **Process:** stages of development of productive organization, composed of input and consumption, from tangible and intangible resources needed to produce the intended result;
3. **Procedures:** techniques and methods applied in the production process, with the objectives of the tasks interpretation, understanding the goals of results and optimizing resources to achieve operational efficiency of production;
4. **Plans:** strategic systematization of corporate sustainability, from the drafting stages of increasingly customized output in terms of economic efficiency, productivity and profitability, assessing the trends in the consumer market and innovating solutions to practical problems of the clients;

5. **Policies:** ability to understand and manage the diversity of interests involved in the organizational process, creating real conditions for disseminating the shared investments, objectives, resources, capabilities, partnerships, strategic alliances and intellectual capital;

6. **Paradigms:** transformation of the disciplinary mental model in a multidisciplinary model that joins the process of technological innovation, optimizes resources sustainably, promotes intellectual capital as a source of learning and knowledge production in the context of corporate governance, decision making and organizational culture.

The Multidisciplinary Management Model – MMM is shown in Figure 1

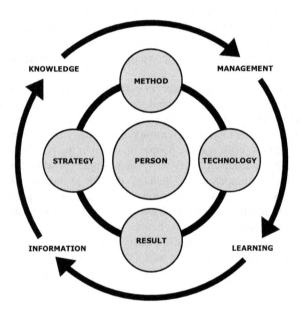

Fig. 1. Multidisciplinary Management Model – MMM. (Source: authors, 2014)

6   Discussion

Multidisciplinary Management helps to better understand the process of applying Multidisciplinary Management Model – MMM, guiding decision making about the use of the most appropriate administrative tools to a particular management problem, such us to develop a product or service, or to adopt a strategic choice to better position the organization in the market.

The main contribution of the Malcolm Baldrige National Quality Award was challenging U.S. companies in the "Quest for Excellence" and "Excellence in Performance" to compete with Japanese products.

The National Quality Award in Brazil led to the beginning of a change in Brazilian entrepreneurial mindset, influenced the curricula of the Administration courses in the country since 1995 and brought a new managerial vision to Brazilian managers and enterprises owners.

The Japanese Quality Award contributes to strengthen broader approaches to the management improvement activities within the industrial community in Japan. It also provided the impetus for the creation of local awards systems and is currently being pursued in ten regions, including Fukui, Nigata, Chiba, Mie and Tochigi.

The proposed model is aligned with the core values and concepts recommended by the Malcolm Baldrige National Quality Award (USA), National Quality Award (Brazil) and Japanese Quality Award (Japan).

7   Conclusions

Linear administration proposed by disciplinarity gradually turns to the search for a Multidisciplinary Management, able to update and innovate models and management practices, responding to the demands of the complexity of the Information Age.

The study about the National Quality Awards of U.S., Japanese, and Brazilian served to identify common points of each award, which strengthen each other, but also possible to observe weaknesses of cultural context, requiring the difference of the management style, according to nationality or the origin of each person. This observation was consolidated at the MMM model proposed in this research, placing the center of the system, the person as manager.

The proposed Multidisciplinary Management Model enables managing organizational outcomes and sustainability, identifies and places the task priorities in order of importance and urgency in the corporate environment. This strategy brings a feedback of excellence to organizational results.

References

1. Morin, E., Carvalho, M.D.C., Assis, E. (org.): The interaction between knowledge and education – Complexity: the seven knowledge and other essays. Cortez, São Paulo (2002)
2. Have, S.T., et al.: Management Models. Prentice Hall, New York (2005)
3. Ferreira, V.C.P., et al.: Management Models. FGV Management, Rio de Janeiro (2008)
4. Krogh, G.V., Ichiro, K., Nonaka, I.: Facilitating the creation of knowledge: Reinventing Business with the Power of Continuous Innovation. Campus, Rio de Janeiro (2001)
5. MALCOLM BALDRIGE NACIONAL AWARD. Criteria for Performance Excellence. Gaithersburg, USA (2013-2014)
6. FNQ – NATIONAL QUALITY FOUNDATION, Criteria for Excellence. National Quality Foundationm, Sao Paulo (2013)
7. ASO – JAPAN QUALITY AWARD, Asian Productivity Organization (2005), http://www.apo-tokyo.org/productivity/014_prod.htm (accessed on February, 26, 2013)
8. Taylor, F.W.: The Principles of Scientific Management (1911), http://www.ibiblio.org/eldritch/fwt/t1.html (accessed on: January 7, 2014)

9. Silva, R.O.: Theories of Administration. Prentice Hall, New York (2008)
10. Sobral, F.: Administration – Theory and Practice in the Brazilian context. Pearson Prentice Hall, Sao Paulo (2008)
11. Fayol, H.: Industrial and General Administration. Atlas, Sao Paulo (1995)
12. Weber, M.: Economy and Society: Fundamentals of comprehensive Sociology. UNB, Brasilia (1998)
13. Nicolescu, B., et al. (orgs.): Education and Transdisciplinarity. UNESCO, Brasilia (2000)

Evaluating Human Work in the Digital Factory
- A New German Guideline -

Gert Zülch

Karlsruhe Institute of Technology, ifab-Institute of Human and Industrial Engineering,
Kaiserstrasse 12, D-76131 Karlsruhe, Germany
gert.zuelch@gefora-beratung.de

Abstract. Over a period of several years a Guideline Committee of the Association of German Engineers (VDI) engaged in the development of a part of a guideline for computer-aided modelling and ergonomic evaluation of working people in digital factory tools. The subject of this part is to document the state of the art in analysis, evaluation and assessment of stresses and strains through work tasks. Broken down according to the separate aspects of engineering mechanics, it looks at existing anthropometric and physiological functionalities of evaluating human labour, with a distinction made between those that are already required as standard and those that are still considered to be optional and are only applied in a few procedures. It appears that the evaluation methods used often lead to different assessments, and that some necessary functions are not yet realized. Further progress is therefore required from an ergonomic perspective.

Keywords: Human models, ergonomics, workplace design, physical stress, evaluation.

1 VDI Guidelines for Representing Humans in the Digital Factory

The digital factory already has a proven way of securing the planning of parts manufacturing and assembly systems. In 2008, the Technical Committee "Digital Factory" within the Association of German Engineers (VDI) started with the publication of a series of guidelines for digital factory planning. The first part of this guideline series, VDI Guideline 4499 Part 1 [1], looks at the basics of digital factory planning. The other parts of this guideline series, each of which is developed by a separate Guideline Committee, involved special tools, such as the digital factory operation.

Currently a VDI Guideline Committee is dealing with the ergonomic analysis, evaluation and assessment of stresses and strains of working people through work tasks with tools of the digital factory. Digital human models were first developed in the mid-1980s as progress was made with the processing of graphical data. Today, digital human models are one of the fundamental tools used in connection with the digital factory. But the graphical representations and the available ergonomic evaluations differ substantially from each other in some cases. After more than 25 years of

B. Grabot et al. (Eds.): APMS 2014, Part III, IFIP AICT 440, pp. 35–42, 2014.

developing digital human models, the question we now face is which human models come into consideration for certain ergonomic aspects, and what limitations the procedures still have.

Figure 1 shows an exemplary virtual representation of a manual assembly system. The new guideline part focuses on the methods available in Germany. Stresses and strains caused by the working environment will be the subject of a future part of the guideline. The current Guideline Committee is composed of representatives from science and software companies as well as industrial users. The draft VDI Guideline 4499 Part 4 [3] was published in 2012. After processing of objections, the final version will appear along with an English translation in mid-2014.

Fig. 1. Visualization of an assembly system [Software: 2]

The new guideline part is different to VDI Guideline 3633 Part 6 [4], already published in 2001, in that it deals with the "Representation of human resources in simulation models". This guideline part is based on a longer-term perspective of human resources from one shift up to many months. In contrast, the focus of the new VDI Guideline 4499 Part 4 is on the dynamic analysis of operations in the second and minute range, and on the evaluation of static working situations.

2   Functionalities of Ergonomic Human Models

The structure of the Guideline 4499 Part 4 is based on the different aspects of engineering mechanics, namely geometry, kinematics, statics and dynamics. While from an ergonomic perspective the first two aspects are part of anthropometric design, the latter two constitute physiological work design. For each of these aspects, underlying functionalities are listed that an ergonomic human model should include as well as those that are optional but are present in at least one of the tools available in Germany. The following gives an overview of the characteristic options for modelling and ergonomic evaluation and assessment.

2.1   Geometric Analysis

The geometry of the work system first and foremost concerns the spatial layout of the workplace with furnishings, as well as the geometry of work objects, workpiece carriers and equipment. Here it is apparent that much of the data used in CAD models has no relevance for ergonomic issues, for example tolerances and contact areas between the internal parts of a pre-assembled workpiece.

The second aspect concerns the dimensions of the human body. The statistical percentage values from existing standards and data collections suffice for this purpose, although these usually relate to an unclothed human body. There is much less standardized data on the appropriate clothing, particularly in the case of protective clothing, which represents a problem when examining a person's freedom of movement.

Another problem is the variability of the human body depending on posture. There are only standards relating to the hip or seat width of the human body. It is highly likely that the recently concluded series of studies conducted as part of the SizeGermany project [5] will provide a new set of underlying data. Although these studies are aimed at the clothing industry, they will certainly influence the standardization of body dimensions in other fields.

2.2   Kinematic Analysis

Kinematic analysis and evaluation relates on the one hand to the zones of movement of human limbs and also to the time required to carry out these movements. The joints of the human body and the way the limbs move present a particular problem. This is because of the range of relative movements between the surfaces of the limbs and sliding elements, as well as the relationships between the limbs involved in a movement. One example of this is the way in which the shoulder follows when working with your hands above your head. Assuming inflexible limbs and hinge or point-shaped joints, these movements can be approximated using engineering kinematics. These technical conveniences result in a certain degree of inaccuracy in the movement paths and reaching distances when compared with real body movements.

Movement paths can be calculated using forward or inverse kinematics. There are a number of ways to calculate a movement path from a starting point to a destination, for example by applying the principle of minimizing joint excursion based on having the joints at a comfortable angle. But in many cases it is not yet clear which way is the most appropriate one.

Another problem is the speed at which the body motions are carried out. The current state of the art is that the necessary time evaluation is carried out on the basis of predetermined time systems or standard times. Figure 2 visualizes a manual operation together with the Gantt chart representation of the operation sequence and a time evaluation by means of MTM-UAS.

However, the time evaluation by means of a system of predetermined times can only serve as an approximation, for example if movement paths encounter obstacles and loads have to be transported. It is known that the load on the muscles (and therefore also the time required to complete the movement) depends not only on the horizontal reaching distance but also on the angle as well as the starting distance and destination distance from the body. Adding the vertical excursion of the hand/arm system as a third dimension further modifies the amount of time required as we would expect.

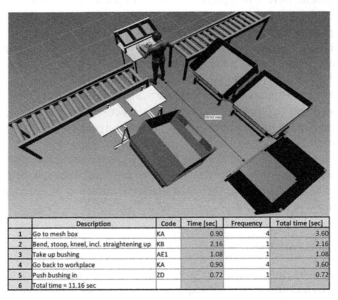

	Description	Code	Time [sec]	Frequency	Total time [sec]
1	Go to mesh box	KA	0.90	4	3.60
2	Bend, stoop, kneel, incl. straightening up	KB	2.16	1	2.16
3	Take up bushing	AE1	1.08	1	1.08
4	Go back to workplace	KA	0.90	4	3.60
5	Push bushing in	ZD	0.72	1	0.72
6	Total time = 11.16 sec				

Fig. 2. Workplace layout and time evaluation with MTM-UAS [3, p. 18, transl; Software: 2]

The paths followed by the various parts of the human body and the time required to perform these movements are usually measured by means of motographic recording using real test subjects. However, applying this to human modelling processes requires synthesizing algorithms that allow the parameterized calculation of movement paths and their time requirements. Biomechanical approaches from some research laboratories aimed at developing humanoid robots and in the field of sports science show how this can be done.

2.3   Static Analysis

From a static perspective, the movements of the human body are subject to internal and external forces and torques. Therefore, a distinction is made between posture when working (static work posture) and isometric holding work, i.e. of a weight. It may be necessary to further specify the static work down to hand, finger, leg and foot forces and the corresponding torques.

One particular problem is presented by postures that are imposed by the physical dimensions of the work situation. This is especially the case if parts of the body are resting on parts of the work system. Although it is possible in principle to calculate the state of equilibrium for the imposed posture, but this is not done in existing procedures. Instead, posture is represented as a drawing taking into account the geometric properties of the human body. Furthermore, this does not take into account the deformation of the body's surface.

There are a number of methods for analysing, evaluating and assessing human static posture and holding work based on kinematic assumptions or even practical approaches. They include the OWAS method (Figure 3) developed in Finland as well as the Guidance Characteristic Method that is widely used in Germany. Interactive calculation forms for the latter method are available on the internet. It also takes into account the time required for a particular static posture or holding task in the form of frequencies per shift.

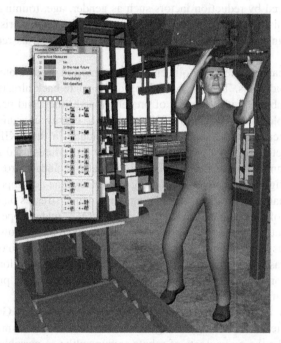

Fig. 3. Evaluation of overhead work using the OWAS method [3, p. 20; Software: 6]

Both methods provide an assessment of static work and indications of the need for redesign measures, albeit in different levels of detail. However, a dynamic assessment is not carried out as static work is only analysed at a specific point in time that is known to the user to be critical.

The static methods include the NIOSH load capacity method from the US and the RULA method from the UK. Based on the evaluation results, an assessment of the predicted stress on individual limbs is made using a traffic light assessment. The methods mentioned also take external forces into account, allowing both static posture and holding work to be evaluated.

It is apparent that Anglo-American evaluation methods dominate international human modelling procedures, while tools developed in Germany are typically not integrated into standard digital factory planning procedures. For example, the VDI method of determining load limits, which has been known in Germany for years, is available as a stand-alone computing procedure but not as a tool for the digital factory. It should be noted that the various methods for evaluation of static working in extreme cases can lead to different assessments of operations [7, pp. 114].

2.4   Dynamic Analysis

In the course of digital factory planning, dynamic aspects of human modelling are generally represented by taking into account the frequency or duration of movements under the influence of external forces and torques. The maximum possible forces and torques are reduced by reduction factors such as gender, age, training and frequency of movement. This principle is followed by the Guidance Characteristic Method, for example, for lifting and carrying, pushing and pulling, as well as repetitive manual work operations.

In other applications, the metabolic energy consumption is calculated based on systems of predefined loads. These kinds of approaches date back already to the 1920s. They can be combined with a system of predetermined times, and presented in table form. For example, the calculation of the metabolic energy consumption in accordance with Spitzer, Hettinger and Kaminski is included in the EKIDES procedure. However, this method is not a part of digital factory procedures used in Germany. At least the American human models JACK and JILL also include a prospective evaluation of human fatigue and recovery according to the formulae developed by Rohmert.

On the other hand, methods for calculating the dynamic stresses on human subjects to the influence of forces and accelerations are a largely undeveloped field with regard to digital factory planning. Military applications have been known already since the mid-1980s, especially with regard to aircraft piloting, which have been further developed for crash investigations in the field of automotive development. Another field of application can be found in sports science, for example the procedures being developed in Germany by Chemnitz University of Technology.

Other aspects of human modelling have been developed in Germany by the Karlsruhe Institute of Technology alongside the development of humanoid robots: If one hopes to make the movements of robots as humanlike as possible it is necessary to analyse human motions. Not only does this involve analysing the geometric properties and paths of motion of humans, but also the mass of their limbs and their inertia properties. The aim is then to synthesize motion paths, i.e. generating movements in accordance with the principles of forward dynamics or also inverse dynamics (analogous to forward kinematics and inverse kinematics). However, the principles according to which the motion paths should be generated, such as the principle of minimum torque, are yet largely unclear. These approaches therefore still require validation in comparison to real motion paths.

However, dynamic applications from the field of factory planning are not currently known. For example, while it is conceivable that the stress on the spine when walking on a floor with suspension properties could be evaluated, this has not yet been tested, and certainly not integrated into the digital factory procedures. Comparable applications are well known from the design of automobile seats and merely require transferring in order to be able to evaluate work stresses or even work aids provided by the suspension properties of a work platform.

Anatomical human models that take muscles, sinews and tendons into account in addition to limbs and joints show the way in this regard. The work of MIRALab at the University of Geneva in Switzerland deserves a particular mention in this regard. Figure 4 shows an example of the Danish human model AnyBody when getting in and getting out of a passenger car. The aggregated muscle activity is shown as a function of the handle height.

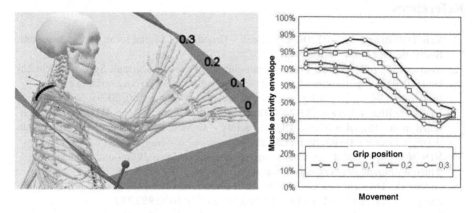

Fig. 4. Aggregated muscle activity during entry and exit from a car [3, p. 22; Software: 8]

3   Need for Further Development

The discussion of digital human models by the current VDI Guideline Committee based on the various aspects of engineering mechanics not only revealed the extent to which ergonomic aspects are already incorporated into various tools of the digital factory, but also their limitations. While anthropometric design can be seen as covered as a matter of standard in a wide area, there are still a number of questions with regard to physiological work design. It is apparent that evaluation options from the German-speaking world are rare in commercial tools. It is also proving particularly disadvantageous in operating practice that evaluation methods developed for the same ergonomic aspects sometimes produce different assessments. There continue to be deficits regarding the analysis of collisions between model elements, both for rigid bodies and particularly for flexible objects and their deformation as a result of collisions.

The examples given here show that the modelling of humans in digital factory tools is still far from adequate for the purpose of conducting ergonomic evaluations and assessments at a comprehensive level of work systems that only exist in a virtual form. The risk-assessment of future work systems in the interest of prospective occupational health and safety also poses a number of methodical questions. These mainly pertain to the evaluation and assessment of successive load cycles for a single type of stress and for several types of stress working simultaneously, both issues requiring further fundamental ergonomic research.

Acknowledgement. In his role as coordinator of the work presented here in summary, the author would like to thank all the members of the VDI Guideline Committee and everybody, especially from software companies, who have contributed their support.

References

1. VDI 4499 Blatt 1:2008-02: Digitale Fabrik – Grundlagen; Digital factory – Fundamentals. Beuth, Berlin (2008)
2. Systemes, D. (ed.): Virtual Ergonomics Solutions. Fellbach: Dassault Systemes Deutschland (2009), http://www.3ds.com/de/products/delmia/solutions/human-modeling/overview/#vid1 (accessed December 30, 2009)
3. VDI 4499 Blatt 4, Entwurf:2012-04: Digitale Fabrik – Ergonomische Abbildung des Menschen in der Digitalen Fabrik; Digital Factory – Ergonomic representation of humans in the digital factory. Beuth, Berlin (2012)
4. VDI 3633 Blatt 6:2001-10: Simulation von Logistik-, Materialfluss- und Produktionssystemen Abbildung des Personals in Simulationsmodellen. Beuth, Berlin (2001)
5. Gröber, A.: Deutsche wachsen weiter – aber eher in die Breite. Die Welt (April 21, 2009), http://www.welt.de/wissenschaft/article3595128/Deutsche-wachsen-weiter-aber-eher-in-die-Breite.html (accessed April 13, 2014)
6. Siemens PLM Software (ed.): Jack and Process Simulate Human, http://www.plm.automation.siemens.com/en_us/products/tecnomatix/assembly_planning/jack/index.shtml (accessed May 25, 2009)
7. Zülch, G.: Perspektiven der Menschmodellierung als Werkzeug der digitalen Fabrikplanung. In: Schenk, M. (ed.) Digital Engineering – Herausforderung für die Arbeits- und Betriebsorganisation, pp. 105–124. GITO, Berlin (2009)
8. AnyBody Technology (ed.): Occupational Health. Anybody Technology A/S, Aalborg (2011), http://www.anybodytech.com/index.php?id=166 (accessed April 13, 2014)

Differentiation and Customer Decoupling Points: Key Value Enablers for Mass Customization

Joanna Daaboul[1] and Catherine Marie Da Cunha[2]

[1] Laboratoire Roberval UMR CNRS 7337, Department of Mechanical Systems Engineering,
UTC – Université de Technologie de Compiègne, Compiègne, France
[2] Lunam Universite, Ecole Centrale De Nantes - IRCCyN UMR CNRS 6597 - 1 Rue de la Noë,
Nantes, France

Abstract. Mass customization draws a twofold benefit: cost reduction, inherited from mass production techniques, and good response to customers' requirements, inherited from customization. Two main decisions, relevant to design and manufacturing, are required for proper implementation of mass customization. Firstly, product features should be split between standard and customizable ones. This will position the differentiation points. Secondly, processes should be split between Make-to-Stock and Make-to-order. This will position the customer-order decoupling point. The impact of these 2 criteria on enterprise and customer value will be evaluated through the creation of a generic causal diagram. Following, a real case study on ALPINA industries is simulated and analyzed. The computational results highlight the joint impact of the two decisions on the overall performance. Hence, the results advocate that these two levers should then be considered, simultaneously, when implementing mass customization.

Keywords: Mass customization, value, decoupling point, differentiation points.

1 Introduction

Many companies in different fields (Adidas, Nike, DELL, Woonio for customized furniture, Spreadshirt for customized shirts, Louis Vuitton, Motorola, BMW etc.) implemented Mass Customization (MC). It enables to benefit both from costs reduction (mass production) and good response to customers' requirements (customization). Even though MC was the center of many research projects (trying to better identify this strategy, understand its enablers and how it can be implemented successfully), many questions remained unanswered. There are two main decisions when implementing MC:

1. What customization to offer to the customer: which components of the product will be standard and which will be customized, thus where to position the product differentiation points (PDP).
2. How to produce a mass customized product: which processes will be Make-to-Stock (MTS) and which will be Make-to-order (MTO), thus where to position the customer-order-decoupling-point (CODP).

B. Grabot et al. (Eds.): APMS 2014, Part III, IFIP AICT 440, pp. 43–50, 2014.
© IFIP International Federation for Information Processing 2014

Until now those two questions were often answered separately. This paper advocates that PDP and CODP should be considered simultaneously when defining the best MC customization strategy for a company. The paper is organized as follows: section 2 presents a definition and a literature review for the three main concepts: value, PDP, and CODP. Section three describes the methodology used. Section 4 presents a case study and finally a conclusion in section 5 on the opportunities for MC.

2   Literature Review

2.1   Value

Based on a literature review combined with an empirical study, Daaboul et al. (2012b) concluded that value can be identified as "the amount of satisfaction created, by fulfilling a certain physical, biological, or psychological need of a beneficiary party". Many criteria (such as cost, delay, perceived quality, and perceived price) influence it. It can be objective or subjective. It depends on circumstances and is related to the specific goals of the beneficiary party. Different performance indicators are used as its measurement. Value has different beneficiary parties. Those can be the customer, suppliers, enterprise, stakeholders, etc. All those form a value network which is a group of partners collaborating together in order to generate value. A value network, unlike a value chain, is not a linear sequential order of activities transforming materials into products. It allows the consideration of the interactions between the different activities, and relies on the definition of value being multicriteria, subjective and with different beneficiary parties (Daaboul et al., 2014). For the enterprise, the financial value (its objective value) is measured by its profit. Its subjective value is measured by its image, customer loyalty, ranking among completion, etc. For the customer, value is purely subjective. It is measured by dividing the perceived quality (of the product and related services) to the perceived price.

2.2   Product Differentiation Point (PDP)

The product differentiation point denominates an operation that transforms a product common to all the products of the same family to a customized or personalized product (finished or not). This transformation can be done by the adjunction of specialized components and/or by the action of a special process. PDP can be multiple, as many attributes can differentiate products among a family. Figure 1 schematizes the multiple product differentiation points that enable obtaining a final product from common inventories. PDPs are not limited to technological products. For instance in the agro-food industry, the large variety of formats and/or packaging, which creates customization, compensates the relative simplicity of the product (van Donk 2001).

The choice of PDP encompasses the 2 dimensions of MC optimization: product and process. Product differentiation is either studied on the product portfolio angle (how many different options should be offered) or on the position in the chain angle (should the PDP be moved to the customer: postponement). The differentiation may occur in any attribute of the product including price and localization. A good localization of PDP is closely linked not only to the process used, but also to the information describing the demand (Zhang et al. 2013).

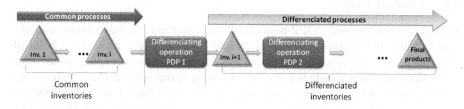

Fig. 1. Multiple PDPs

2.3   CODP

Ji et al. (2007) defined the CODP as "the breaking point between productions for stock based on forecast and customization that responds to customer demand. It is also the breaking point between MTS and MTO, namely, activities before CODP are driven by forecast while activities after CODP are driven by real customer order demand". The CODP position is a main factor in classifying MC systems (Daaboul et al. 2012a). It does not determine what the customization offer is, but influences it, and determines how this offer is being satisfied. According to the literature, the location of the CODP can be at one of the 5 following points: design, production, assembly, "distribution, and consumer (Martinez-Olvera and Shunk 2006).

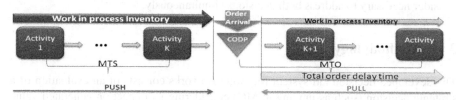

Fig. 2. CODP position

When determining the CODP position (Figure 2), the main factors to consider are: production process, setup time, production technology cost, customer service level, production utilization rate, and the requirements of work in process for storage conditions and time (Ji et al. 2007). Many authors have presented an optimization problem to define the optimal position of the CODP such as Olhager (2003), Ji et al. (2007), Shao and Jia (2008) and Abbey et al. (2013). The CODP position should be determined based on the overall value generated by the system for each beneficiary party (e.g. customers, shareholders, company). In fact, the CODP position influences the performance of the network via its impact on costs (cost of resources, cost of materials, inventory cost, production cost, transportation cost), delays (setup time, processing time, delivery delays, order delay time, etc.), and quality (conforming commands, customer perceived quality of the product and the service, etc.). Its position should be optimized by taking into consideration not only capacity constraints, cost and time, but also the product differentiation points and the customization possibilities offered to the customer.

2.4   Coupled Analysis

The question of PDP and CODP positioning were often considered as exclusive alternatives. Zinn and Bowersox (1988) addressed both questions; naming the point of differentiation "form postponement" and the customer-order-decoupling-point "time postponement". They concluded that product price is the variable that justifies form postponement while uncertainty is determinant for time postponement. Nevertheless in their model form postponement can only occur after the customer order is received. Su et al (2005) considered form and time postponement as exclusive alternatives. They have concluded that once the number of products increases above some threshold, the time postponement structure is preferred under both performance metrics (cost and waiting time). According to them, form postponement structure is more favorable in the case of higher arrival time and process time variations. Time postponement is more favorable in the case of higher interest rates. Hegde et al (2005) developed a framework to address what degrees of customization to offer. Their results showed that product conformance gradually decreased when the degree of customization exceeded the manufacturing threshold. This paper advocates that the decision on the customization offer should be made simultaneously with the decision on the manufacturing system configuration, and in particular with the CODP determination. Fujita et al. (2012) propose a mathematical model for strategy-level simultaneous design of module commonalization and supply chain configuration. They consider necessary to address both decisions simultaneously.

3   Methodology

The developed decision aid system for value networks consists of an evaluation of a strategic decision (such as moving to MC) considering its impact on generated value for all partners. It is based on a what-if analysis and comparison of different possible scenarios. In step 3 of the methodology shown in Figure 3, possible TO-BE scenarios are defined. In our case, a TO-BE scenario consists of a combination of CODP position and PDPs position. This is realized by identifying possible PDP positions, possible CODP positions and then by identifying all possible combination of these positions. Step 4 analyses the results.

A specific library was developed by Daaboul et al. (2013) for discrete event simulation software: Arena (Rockwell Automation). It is intended to model and simulate easily and in short time, large and complex value networks. It concentrates on value evaluation. It also permits easy modeling and simulation of different PDPs and

CODPs. It is formed of seven modules: order generator, decision activity, trigger, execution activity, partner, variant, and physical flow. The library permits evaluating customer perceived value and value for enterprise.

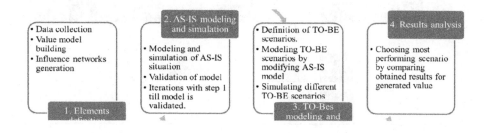

Fig. 3. Methodology for evaluation of value network evolution

4 Case Study: Alpina (Footwear Industry)

4.1 Alpina

To challenge the hypothesis that CODP and PDP are linked, a real case was studied. It concerns a shoemaking industry in Slovenia, named Alpina which was founded in 1947. Nowadays, Alpina is a worldwide company with 1800 employees and with production and sales companies in 11 different countries. In 2011 Alpina sold more than 500000 pairs, what means world n°1 in production of cross ski country boots with more than 30% part of the world market.

4.2 Shoe Parts and Shoe Process

A shoe is formed essentially of an upper, outsole, insole, midsole, eyelets, buckle, laces, and accessories. After analysis and discussions with Alpina, two possible PDPs were identified. The first PDP is at the laced shoe stage, meaning that the customer can only customize the color of the laces. The second PDP is at the upper stage, meaning that the customer may customize the color of its shoe, the type and color of the outsole, and the laces.

The shoe production process essentially consists of seven main processes: outsole production, insole and midsole production, cutting upper parts, stitching upper parts, lasting upper and assembling it to the soles, cleaning the shoes, and adding laces. This process leads to five possible CODPs (CODP 1 before outsole production, CODP2 before cutting upper parts, CODP3 before stitching upper parts, CODP4 before lasting upper, and CODP5 before adding laces. Figure 4 shows both the process and the shoe parts.

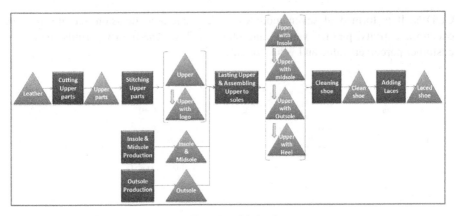

Fig. 4. Simplified shoe fabrication process

4.3   Simulation of Value Network of Alpina

Needed data (concerning products, processes, supply chain, distributor, suppliers, etc.) were collected from the enterprise using different templates and many interviews with different departments of Alpina. An empirical study realized by Alpina permitted obtaining the perceived quality attributes (fitting, aesthetics, material, thermal comfort, flexibility, weight, stability, breathability, durability and waterproofing, brand name, ecological level, shop assistance, customization time and number of proposed product variants). Thus all needed data for building the value model was provided by the real world. The performance indicators measuring customer value were chosen in coherence with the firm's strategy. Concerning the service related attributes, they are chosen according to (Daaboul et al., 2011).

The value network with PDP 1 and CODP 1 stands for the AS-IS situation. After collecting all needed data, this scenario was simulated and validated by Alpina. After validating the AS-IS scenario (scenario 1), 8 other scenarios were identified. The scenario formed of PDP 2 and CODP 5 is not feasible since it is not possible to have such customization of the shoe and have the customer order decoupling point positioned at the last stage.

4.4   Results

The obtained results were validated by Alpina. The results were coherent with other analysis and studies realized at Alpina. As shown in Figure 5, the value for Alpina is higher in the case of PDP at position 1. This is due to the fact that Alpina was not ready to make the necessary changes and investments such as changing its agreements with its suppliers in order to offer MC shoes. Whereas the customer perceived value has a less predictable behavior. It is impacted by many indicators such as product perceived quality, offered customization, and order delay. The results (Figure 5) show that the value for Alpina is higher for PDP1 than PDP2 no matter the position of CODP. The value for Alpina is highest when the CODP is further in the chain

(CODP5). In addition it reduces dramatically for CODP 1, 2, 3 & 4 compared to CODP5. This is due to:

- An increase in cost of raw material caused by the increase in the required stock for each material.
- Reduced economies of scale as the size of the production batch in the case of MC is equal to 1.
- An increase in the cost of usage of resources, since the execution time of an activity increased with increasing set-up time.
- A slight increase in transportation costs caused by increased late orders that require faster delivery therefore more expensive.
- A slight increase in turnover. As part of the MC, Alpina estimated a 5% increase in sales. However, this increase in sales (an increase of 37,559 Euros) was not sufficient to cover the additional costs.

The Pareto Front for Alpina's results was built. It shows the dominating combinations of CODP and PDP.

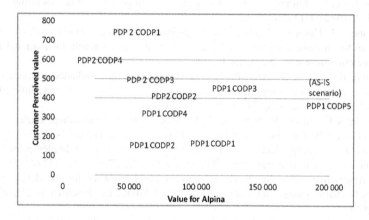

Fig. 5. Scenarios' performance and Pareto front

5   Discussion and Conclusion

The case study validates the adopted framework. The results obtained validate the hypothesis of considering both CODP and PDP positions in defining the best MC strategy for a company. PDP and CODP are the two main acting variables defining the customization strategy. They do not only define the type of MC but influence greatly both customer perceived value and enterprise value. Thus deciding on a MC strategy should be made in light of the influence of those two variables on the value for the different partners. Offering high customization might not always better satisfy the customer.

(Mason-Jones and Towill, 1999) stressed that to maximize competitive opportunity CODP position should be considered jointly with information decoupling point (when information from forecast and market meet). The early usage of distorted information could improve capacity management. Hence, future work is needed in order to investigate the joint impact of CODP, PDP and the information decoupling point (IDP).

References

1. Abbey, J.D., Guide, V.D.R., Souza, G.C.: Delayed Differentiation for Multiple Lifecycle Products. Production and Operations Management 22(3), 588–602 (2013)
2. Daaboul, J., Da Cunha, C., Bernard, A., Laroche, F.: Design for Mass Customization: Product variety vs. Process variety. Process variety. CIRP Annals 23(6), 169–174 (2011)
3. Daaboul, J., Bernard, A., Laroche, F.: Extended value network modelling and simulation for mass customization implementation. Journal of Intelligent Manufacturing 23(6), 2427–2439 (2012a)
4. Daaboul, J., Da Cunha, C., Bernard, A., Laroche, F.: Value of personalized products: modelling the customer perception. In: Chesbrough, H., Piller, F. (eds.) Proceedings of The 2011 World Conference on Mass Customization, Personalization, and Co-Creation (MCPC 2011), Raleigh, NC, vol. 1, pp. 978–971 (2012b), http://Lulu.com ISBN: 978-1-4716-3023-1
5. Daaboul, J., Le Duigou, J., Da Cunha, C., Bernard, A.: Value networks: pulling the triggers. A combined approach of modelling and simulation for performance evaluation. International Journal of Computer Integrated Manufacturing (2013), doi:10.1080/0951192X.2013.834478
6. Daaboul, J., Castagna, P., Da Cunha, C., Bernard, A.: Value network modelling and simulation for strategic analysis: A discrete event simulation approach. International Journal of Production Research (2014), doi:10.1080/00207543.2014.886787
7. Fujita, K., Amaya, H., Akai, R.: Mathematical model for simultaneous design of module commonalization and supply chain configuration toward global product family. Journal of Intelligent Manufacturing 24(5), 991–1004 (2012)
8. Hegde, V.G., Kekre, S., Rajiv, S., Tadikamalla, P.R.: Customization: Impact on Product and Process Performance. Production and Operations Management 14(4), 388–399 (2005)
9. Ji, J., Qi, L., Gu, Q.: Study on CODP Position of Process Industry Implemented Mass Customization. Systems Engineering - Theory and Practice 27(12), 152–157 (2007)
10. Martínez-Olvera, C., Shunk, D.: Comprehensive framework for the development of a supply chain strategy. International Journal of Production Research 44(21), 4511–4528 (2006)
11. Mason-Jones, R., Towill, D.: Using the information decoupling point to improve supply chain performance. International Journal of Logistics Management 10(2), 13–26 (1999)
12. Olhager, J.: Strategic positioning of the order penetration point. International Journal of Production Economics 85(3), 319–329 (2003)
13. Shao, X.-F., Jia, J.-H.: Evaluation of postponement strategies in mass customization with service guarantees. International Journal of Production Research 46(1), 153–171 (2008)
14. Su, J., Chang, Y., Ferguson, M.: Evaluation of postponement structures to accommodate mass customization. Journal of Operations Management 23(3-4), 305–318 (2005)
15. Van Donk, D.P.: Make to stock or make to order: The decoupling point in the food processing industries. International Journal of Production Economics 69(3), 297–306 (2001)
16. Zhang, J., Shou, B., Chen, J.: Postponed product differentiation with demand information update. International Journal of Production Economics 141(2), 529–540 (2013)
17. Zinn, W., Bowersox, D.J.: Planning physical distribution with the principle of postponement. Journal of Business Logistics 9(2), 117–136 (1988)

Alignment of the Purchasing Strategy to the Business Strategy: An Empirical Study on a Harbour Cranes Company

Sandra Martínez[1], Miguel Mediavilla[1], Jenny Bäckstrand[2], and Carolina Bernardos[3]

[1] GLOBOPE Research and Consulting, San Sebastián, Spain,
{sandra.martinez,miguel.mediavilla}@globope.es
[2] School of Engineering, Jönköping University, Jönköping, Sweden
Jenny.Backstrand@jth.hj.se
[3] Department of Economic Analyis, University of Zaragoza
472387@unizar.es

Abstract. The purchasing function is assuming an increasingly relevant role within companies in the last decades. This is due to a fact that purchasing strategy can contribute to develop competitive advantages. Therefore, it is important to align the purchasing strategy with the company business strategy. On the other hand, category management can be used as the basic unit of strategic purchasing analysis, which measures the competitive improvement in purchasing management. It its known that a differentiated purchasing strategy involves managing suppliers within the different categories, so that, it is considered that there should be a leadership to level category by purchasing managers to improve the company competitiveness. Hence, this paper contributes by presenting how aligned business and purchasing strategies and product categorization leads to increased competitiveness –by presenting an empirical study on a harbor cranes company.

Keywords: Purchasing function, purchasing strategy, category management, business strategy.

1 Introduction

In the past few decades the purchasing function has changed from a passive administrative role into a strategic function [1, 2, 3, 4] having direct responsibility for the costs of goods purchased (e.g. materials, products or services), as well as supplier management. This change has increased the impact and influence of the purchasing function to achieve competitive advantages for the business, as other business functions do. Moreover, this development is logical, as the sourced components represent a large and growing percentage of the total cost of a product, as well as these components have a crucial importance depending on its quality and performance [5].

The purchasing strategy is the process of planning, implementing, evaluating and controlling the strategic and operative purchasing decisions. These decisions lead all

B. Grabot et al. (Eds.): APMS 2014, Part III, IFIP AICT 440, pp. 51–58, 2014.
© IFIP International Federation for Information Processing 2014

activities of the purchasing function toward opportunities that are consistent with the capabilities of the company in order to achieve the long-term objectives [6]. Hence, in order to get competitive advantages, the purchasing strategy must be aligned with the overall strategy of the company. Furthermore, different purchasing strategies are needed for different types of purchased items [7, 8].

The literature shows that in this era of purchasing it is necessary to provide solutions to different challenges, risks and characteristics. Neverthelessone of the most important challenges is to align the purchasing strategy with the business strategy, .In order to achieve a better alignment, one key step is to define the appropriate purchasing strategy for each purchasing category in order to achieve the goal defined within the business strategy [6], [9, 10, 11, 12].

Therefore, the research question would be: How can the alignment of purchasing strategy with business strategy and product categorization improve the competitiveness of a company?

In order to give an answer this question, this paper will illustrate through an empirical study how aligned strategies lead to increased competitiveness. First, the paper presents a brief literature review; then the adopted research methodological approach is presented. Then, a case study carried out on a harbor cranes company is explained. Finally, the paper concludes by highlighting the contribution of the research.

2   Literature Review

Strategic Alignment

The purchasing function is assuming an increasingly relevant role within companies. This is due to a fact that purchasing strategy can contribute to get competitive advantages. Therefore, it is important to align the purchasing strategy with the business strategy of the company.

Generally, business strategy is concerned with developing distinct competences and competitive advantages [13]. One approach to business-level strategy is the competitive strategies, introduced by Porter [14], that drive an actor to compete as cost leader, differentiator, or a focused provider.

For manufacturing actors, the competitive business strategy is translated into competitive priorities and operationalized through functional strategies [15, 16, 17]. According to previous research, purchasing strategy also requires the identification of competitive priorities [16], [18] in order to support business strategy. However, different purchasing strategies are needed for different types of purchased items. Additionally alternative ways of categorizing or classifying items and/or suppliers is necessary.

Necessities for a competitive purchasing strategy configuration are external resources, location, suppliers network design, purchasing organization (from process and functional perspectives) and standardization and improvement of the purchasing and procurement processes. Additionally the globalization necessarily affect the purchasing function, forcing it to be global too [19]. Van Weele [2] defined global purchasing as "the activity for searching and obtaining goods, services and other resources on a possible worldwide scale, to comply with the needs of the company and with a view to continuing and enhancing the current competitive position of the company". It includes all phases of the purchasing process, starting even before the definition of the specification list, through supplier selection and buying, up to the follow-up and evaluation phase. Moreover, global purchasing management is one of the first steps to define and design a global supply chain [20].

Category Management

To define a category strategy it is advisable to have systematic classifications [21] to help defining and visualizing the different categories. One of the most commonly used tools for categorization was developed by Kraljic [7], who proposed a matrix that classifies items into categories according to their profit impact and supply risk. This matrix has become the standard in models of purchasing categories [4], [22].

In the early 90s in the UK new principles of management throughout the supply chain was developed, the so called "Efficient Consumer Response" (ECR). Its best known process, Category Management (CM) [23, 24], is defined as 'a process that involves managing product categories as business units and customizing them on a store-by-store basis to satisfy customer needs' [8] and shifted the focus from brand management approach to a category management approach [25]. Later, CM was also adapted to categorize purchased items [26].

According to Mediavilla et al. [27] and Errasti [5], proper category management requires to:

1. Categorize items.
2. Set achievable goals within the business strategy.
3. Prioritize the purchasing categories.
4. Define strategic objectives of purchasing and consequently establish improvement projects and their deployment. These targets should be aligned with the business strategy.
5. Set management indicators for each project phases.
6. Ensure lasting results.

Therefore this CM can be used as the basic unit of strategic analysis, which measures the competitive improvement on purchasing management [4], [23, 24].

A differentiated purchasing strategy then involves managing the suppliers within the different categories. According to some authors [2], [4] it is considered that there should be a leadership by purchasing managers per category to improve the competitiveness of the company.

3   Research Methodology

The research is based on a literature review and a case study following the constructive research methodology. Constructive research is an approach that aims to produce solutions to explicit problems and is closely related to the concept of innovative constructivism [28]. This approach develops an innovative solution, which is theoretically grounded, to a relevant practical problem. An essential component of constructive research is the generation of new learning and knowledge in the process of constructing the solution [29]. The case study as such is exploratory in nature. Two of the researchers have been actively involved in the project transition of the case company. Thus, facets of action research have also been deployed. In action research both researchers and clients are actively engaged in solving a client-initiated project dealing with a certain business problem [30, 31, 32]. The company selected for the case faced the challenge of aligning its purchasing strategy to a recently changed business strategy, providing an interesting case for academics.

The main data collection and observation period lasted for 5 months during 2013 and consisted of meetings, interviews and company internal documentation. The researchers attended meetings once a week with the Purchasing Manager, CEO, Chief Engineer, Supply Chain Manager, Quality Manager and Sales Manager. The first phase of the case research included meetings and interviews that focused on understanding the harbor cranes industry and the company specific portfolio of products. During the second phase, researchers, together with Purchasing and Quality Manager, mapped the main processes within procurement function. . Finally, the third phase focused on developing and deploying new strategy of purchasing management based on Mediavilla et al. [8] and Errasti [5].

4   Case Research

The case company is a Spanish provider of integral solutions for container terminals, i.e that the company designs, manufactures, transports and erects container-handling cranes. Moreover, the case company has also its own software and hardware to optimize terminal management (terminal automation). The case company is the regional supplier for Europe, Mediterranean, North and South Atlantic side of the Americas and this company is part of an international corporation.

In order to develop and deploy a new purchasing strategy, to the first step was to push a   proper category management by:

1. Splitting the products on purchasing categories.
2. Defining the main contribution of each given purchasing category to the business strategy (E.g. competitive advantage on costs or lead-time). This is the so-called purchasing strategy per category. [5][8]
3. Prioritization of levers per category, seeking levers which could reinforce the given competitive advantage
4. Deployment of purchasing strategies per category by applying the selected levers. The prioritization could be based on the potential competitive improvements (E.g. saving or qualitative impact) and implementation effort.
5. Establishment management indicators: potential cost savings per crane.
6. Control system to review achieved results and strategy coherence along the time.

The following is an example of how the category management was carried out for a specific purchasing category in the case company.

1. The analyzed product was divided on in 42 purchasing categories. However, in this case research the focus will be on one category, called 'mechanical elements' which is composed by products such as sheaves. This category could be manufactured by a large number of suppliers, which decreases the possible supply risk but will not optimize the cost if the company is not able to create the appropriate competition. Moreover, this category has a medium profit impact. Therefore, according Kraljic's matrix [7] this category is a leverage item (see Figure 1).

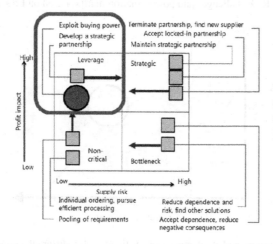

Fig. 1. Purchasing strategies for all portfolio quadrants, based on Kraljic's matrix [7], [33]

2. The main contribution to the business strategy that the category "mechanical elements" has is to improve the purchasing cost (i.e. the purchasing strategy is to reduce costs on this category). Therefore, the selected levers (i.e. how to achieve the purchasing strategy) were to introduce new suppliers and to standardize the components. Taking into account the risk/challenges and purchasing power matrix (figure 2) [5, 33], The recommended purchasing policy is to exploit purchasing power by increasing the competition between different suppliers, pushing the purchasing strategy of reducing costs. Likewise, it is also suggested to establish supplier relation case by case in order to exploit the purchasing power [5] (see Figure 2).

3. The analyzed category, according to the prioritization, belongs to the first wave of implementation according to Errasti [5], meaning that the ease of implementation is medium or high and the potential savings are medium or high too (see Figure 3).

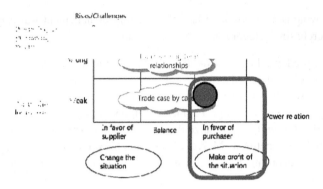

Fig. 2. Risk/challenges and power relation matrix, based on Errasti [5]

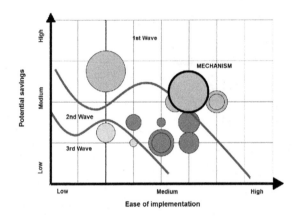

Fig. 3. Potential savings and implementation difficulties for different purchasing categories, based on Errasti [5]

4. The target was to have three new suppliers and to eliminate the current supplier due to quality problems and non-compliance with delivery dates. The company executed supplier scouting actively.

5. As a result of the strategy implementation, the supplier basis was changed and a cost reduction of approx. 50% was achieved. That situation is totally aligned to the purchasing strategy as well as to the contribution that the category made to the business strategy.

6. Currently, the company continues working to strengthen relations and establish long-term agreements with the new suppliers.

Result

Two of the three suppliers were located in a low cost country and the third one was located in Spain. The Spanish supplier was a supplier totally oriented to short delivery times and for unexpected situations.

5   Contribution

The case research shows that the use of the category management (i.e. to categorize items in purchasing categories, set purchasing strategic objectives, prioritize the purchasing categories according to the potential savings and implementation difficulties, define and deploy improvement projects, set management indicators and ensure lasting results) and the alignment of the purchasing strategy with business strategy allow to improve company competitiveness.

References

1. Ellram, L.M., Carr, A.: Strategic purchasing: a history and review of the literature. Journal of Supply Chain Management 30(1), 9–19 (1994)
2. Van Weele, A.J.: Purchasing and supply chain management: Analysis, strategy, planning and practice. Cengage Learning EMEA (2005)
3. Alinaghian, L.S., Aghadasi, M.: Proposing a model for purchasing system transformation, Glasgow, Scotland. Paper presented at the EurOMA 16th Conference (2006)
4. Monczka, R., Handfield, R., Giunipero, L., Patterson, J.: Purchasing and supply chain management, 4th edn. Cengage Learning, USA (2009)
5. Errasti, A.: Gestión de compras en la empresa. Ediciones Pirámide (Grupo Anaya), Madrid, España (2012)
6. Carr, A.S., Smeltzer, L.R.: An empirically based operational definition of strategic purchasing. European Journal of Purchasing and Supply Management 3(4), 199–207 (1997)
7. Kraljic, P.: Purchasing must become supply management. Harvard Business Review 61(5), 109–117 (1983)
8. Nielsen Marketing Research.: Category management - Positioning your organization to win. American Marketing Association, NTC Business books (1992)
9. Lindblom, A., Olkkonen, R., Ollila, P., Hyvönen, S.: Suppliers' roles in category management: a study of supplier-retailer relationships in Finland and Sweden. Industrial Marketing Management 38(8), 1006–1013 (2009)
10. Slack, N., Lewis, M.: Operations strategy. Financial Times/Prentice Hall (2002)
11. Carter, J.R., Narasimhan, R.: Is purchasing really strategic? International Journal of Purchasing and Materials Management 32(1), 20–28 (1996)
12. Bäckstrand, J.: A Method for Customer-driven Purchasing - Aligning Supplier Interaction and Customer-driven Manufacturing [Doctoral dissertation]. Jönköping University, Jönköping (2012)
13. Andrews, K.R.: The Concept of Strategy. Irwing Publishing, Homewood (1984)
14. Porter, M.E.: Competitive Strategy: Techniques for Analyzing Industries and Competitors. Free Press, New York (1980)
15. Ward, P.T., McCreery, J.K., Ritzman, L.P., Sharma, D.: Competitive Priorities in Operations Management. Decision Sciences 29(4), 1035–1046 (1998)
16. Krause, D.R., Pagell, M., Curkovic, S.: Toward a measure of competitive priorities for purchasing. Journal of Operations Management 19(4), 497–512 (2001)
17. Kroes, J.R., Ghosh, S.: Outsourcing congruence with competitive priorities: Impact on supply chain and firm performance. Journal of Operations Management 28(2), 124–143 (2010)

18. Watts, C.A., Kim, K.Y., Hahn, C.K.: Linking purchasing to corporate competitive strategy. International Journal of Purchasing and Materials Management 28(4), 2–8 (1992)
19. Martínez, S.: Framework for configuring production and logistics networks of SMEs and SBUs within an internationalization process, Dissertation, Tecnun, University of Navarra, San Sebastián, Spain (2013)
20. Leenders, M., Fearon, H.E., Flynn, A.E., Johnson, P.F.: Purchasing and Supply Management. McGraw Hill/Irwin, New York (2002)
21. Lilliecreutz, J., Ydreskog, L.: Supplier classification as an enabler for a differentiated purchasing strategy. Best Practice Procurement: Public and Private Sector Perspective 8, 73–81 (2001)
22. Gelderman, C.J., Van Weele, A.J.: Purchasing portfolio models: a critique and update. Journal of Supply Chain Management 41(3), 19–28 (2005)
23. Gruen, T.W., Shah, R.H.: Determinants and outcomes of plan objectivity and implementation in category management relationships. Journal of Retailing 76(4), 483–510 (2000)
24. Dewsnap, B., Hart, C.: Category management: a new approach for fashion marketing? European Journal of Marketing 38(7), 809–834 (2004)
25. Dussart, C.: Category management: Strengths, limits and developments. European Management Journal 16(1), 50–62 (1998)
26. O'Brien, J.: Category Management in Purchasing: A strategic approach to maximize business profitability. Kogan, London (2009)
27. Mediavilla, M., Zubizarreta, X., Errasti, A., Chackelson, C.: Logística Sanitaria: Retos y Nuevas Tendencias, World-Class Hospital Logistics. Ulma Handling Systems and GLOBOPE Research & Consulting, Spain (2014)
28. Meredith, J.: Theory building through conceptual methods. International Journal of Operations and Production Management 13(5), 3–11 (1993)
29. Mendibil, K., Macbryde, J.C.: Designing effective team-based performance measurement systems: an integrated approach. Production Planning and Control 16(2), 208–225 (2005)
30. Westbrook, R.: Action Research: A new paradigm for research in production and operations management. International Journal of Operations and Production Management 15(12), 6–20 (1995)
31. Rowley, J.: Using Case Studies in Research. Management Research News 25(1) (2002)
32. Voss, C., Tsikriktsis, N., Frohlich, M.: Case Research in operations management. International Journal of Operations and Production Management 22(2), 195–219 (2002)
33. Gelderman, C.J., Van Weele, A.J.: Handling measurement issues and strategic directions in Kraljic's purchasing portfolio model. Journal of Purchasing and Supply Management 9(5-6), 207–216 (2003)

Application of Quality Tools for Process Improvement to Reduce Scrap in an Aluminum Smelter

Marcos de Oliveira Morais, Antônio Sérgio Brejão,
and Pedro Luiz de Oliveira Costa Neto

Paulista University, UNIP, Postgraduate Studies Program in Production Engineering,
Dr. Bacelar St. 1212, São Paulo, Brazil
marcostecnologia@ig.com.br

Abstract. This paper presents a use of quality tools for the improvement of an aluminum smelting process under pressure by reducing the waste. This type of analysis has been useful in a developing country like Brazil, with the present example shown in such promising reality. The main tool used was the cause and effect diagram, enabling the discovery of the main causes of the problem, the removal of which led to a reduction in scrap that is of extreme relevance to the organization, as statistically proven.

Keywords: Quality tools, Cause and Effect Diagram, Scrap reduction, Productivity, Process improvement.

1   Introduction

Upon market opening and globalization, companies needed to upgrade and become more competitive, being forced to eliminate wastes in the entire production process, so the processes have become more streamlined, accurate and efficient.

Such reality was experienced in Brazil as a developing country and became stronger with the phenomenon of globalization and, in the specific case of this nation, with the market opening policy adopted in 1990, during the term of President Fernando Collor de Mello.

With the increasing requirements for high quality, an issue raised involving the entire organization and work project, defined as the function of specifying the activities for an individual or group in the organizational environment [1].

Scrap, represented by parts rejected by quality control which are impossible to be reworked, is considered one of the biggest problems in the industry, as it demonstrates the inefficiency of the process. Also, we cannot disregard it or manipulate the numbers so they can be satisfactory; if such problem exists, it should be treated and minimized to the maximum extend possible

This article presents a case of process improvement in an aluminum smelter using appropriate techniques, in particular the cause and effect diagram, whose methodology is attributed to Kaoru Ishikawa.

Grabot et al. (Eds.): APMS 2014, Part III, IFIP AICT 440, pp. 59–67, 2014.

2   Theoretical Background

The advancement in failure minimization for optimization can generate great rewards. For many companies, something that begins as an attempt to minimize a problem gradually evolves and becomes a coordinated effort to develop creative valuable solutions [2].

Obviously all production processes deal with wastes, but they must be measured within standard limits for the production of a particular material. In the event of a product failure, a new set of customer needs arises: how to get service restored and how to be compensated for associated unwanted losses [3].

Deming emphasized the importance of product cost, which often does not consider such loss, thus directly affecting the company, burdening the product and passing the value to the customer [4].

All people involved in the organization must be aware of the problems and how they impact the company. The overall quality and operational performance planning, as well as its implementation, focuses completely on the needs and development of the entire labor force [5].

Factors such as manpower, raw materials, customer service, energy, etc. should be considered and evaluated, taking into account the delivery of the final product to the client, having the continuous improvement as an integral part of the quality management system [6]. Regarding labor force, behavioral issues need to be closely linked to production processes for the development of a work design that is associated with the concept of empowerment involving work organization based on team. It occurs when employees that usually have juxtaposed skills collectively perform a specific task and possess high degree of description of how to actually perform the task [7].

Reducing the cost of production, material and shoddy products increases the contribution margin, taking into account higher profits. The development of a customer-oriented operational strategy begins with a corporate strategy that aligns the overall goals of the company with its essential processes.

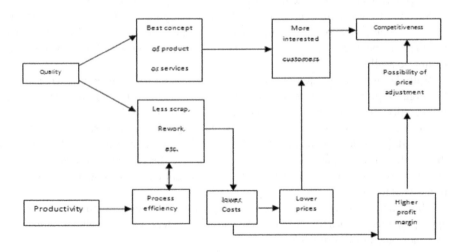

Fig. 1. Quality, productivity and competitiveness. Adapted from [8].

Observing Figure 1, it is possible to understand the flow of competitive priorities: link between corporate strategy and operational strategy.

3   Methodology

This article used the action-research methodology, which is a type of empirically-based social research, designed and carried out in close association with an action or with the solution of a collective problem in which researchers and representative participants in the situation or problem are involved in a cooperative or participatory way [9]. This type of approach may be used in an organization (company or school, for example), in which hierarchy or groups with problematic relationships are present, in order to contribute to the best possible form of problem solving, including the arising of solutions and proposals for actions corresponding to solutions, since they represent the perfect strategy when issues such as how and why are raised, when the researcher has little control over events and when the focus is on contemporary phenomena inserted in some real-life context [10].

This work refers to the description and deepening of knowledge in an industry of aluminum casting under pressure, referring to a particular item labeled as substrate.

After identifying the most relevant nonconformity of the process, the possible causes of non-compliance were mapped using brainstorming tools and Cause and Effect Diagram.

4   Results and Discussion

An analysis conducted in company between February and August 2013 showed a high rate of housing product scrap, directly affecting the client and therefore the organization.

The referred values shown in Figure 2 are related to the production, scrap and scrap percentage.

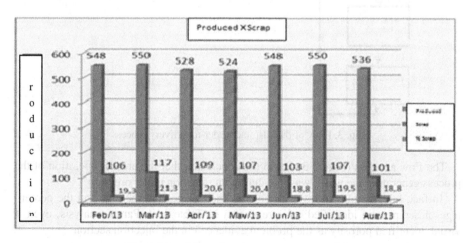

Fig. 2. Material produced versus scrap material

For the purposes of analysis and to perfectly know the process, a flow chart was made and is shown in Figure 3.

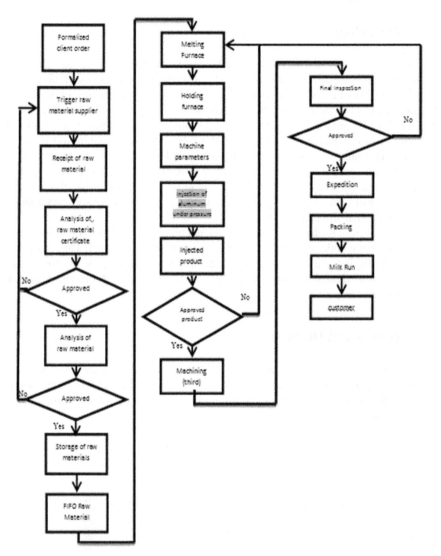

Fig. 3. Flow of the customer order-to-delivery process

The flow analysis (Figure 3) led to the conclusion that the critical operation of the process generating the waste was the aluminum injection under pressure.

In fact, the five most relevant problems, their respective sections and the percentage of scrap were identified and are shown in Table 1. A Pareto analysis, even if visual, identified porosity as the problem evidenced in the injection section.

Table 1. Stratification of problems

Problem	Section	Percentage
Porosity	Injection	71%
Cold joint	Injection	12%
Crack	Injection	11%
Breaking	Transportation	4%
Dimensional	Machining	2%

The rate established by and acceptable to the company for the section of injection is 5% of scrap, the same value reported in product cost spreadsheet shown in Figure 2. In the period considered, such average percentage was 19.81%.

The authors developed a scrap control, shown in Figure 4, to check and indicate the regions with the highest porosity in the part. The verification worksheet details the part per quadrant and region, facilitating the visualization of the most critical point, thus making the scrap reducing action more effective. In the sheet it is possible to

	CONTROL OF SCRAP (HOUSING).					
DATE:	**22/12/2013**					
AREA	**CAV. 01**	**CAV. 02**	**CAV. 03**	**CAV. 04**	**TOTAL**	**AREA OF PART**
A	27	16	24	22	89	
B	25	23	19	23	90	
C	18	24	22	21	85	
D	31	32	33	32	128	
E	32	33	35	31	131	
F	33	31	35	32	131	
G	34	29	27	31	121	
H	34	30	34	33	131	
Defects	234	218	229	225	906	
PRODUCED TOTAL		**550**			Parts	

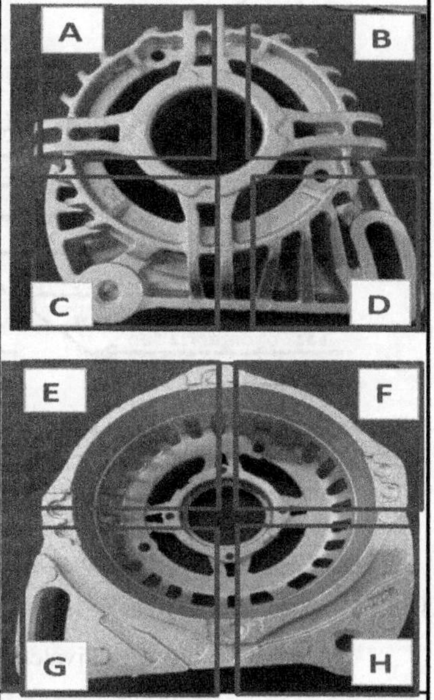

Fig. 4. Scrap control spreadsheet

identify the area of the part, its cavity, and the total and produced amounts, as well as the percentage of scrap.

The scrap control spreadsheet identifies the number of cavities and the quadrant of the part, facilitating the indication and subsequent analysis of the most critical points of the product. The action focus was porosity, since it corresponds to the highest percentage of rejection. After the completion of data collection, a multidisciplinary team was composed of all the people in charge of all sections involved, in order to work on the existing problems, having porosity as the main focus, since it represents 71% of the problems found in the analyzed parts.

Developing people is not just giving them information so that they improve their knowledge, skills and abilities and become more efficient in what they do; it is above all things giving them basic training so they can develop new attitudes, solutions, ideas, concepts, modify their habits and behaviors and become more effective in what they do. [11]

The team used the Ishikawa diagram, shown in Figure 5, to help in the identification of possible causes and their potential effects on porosity, so that direct action on the issue could be taken.

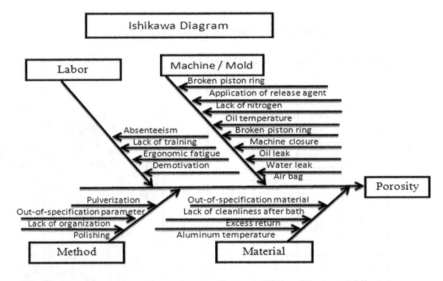

Fig. 5. Analysis of the problem using the Cause and Effect Diagram (Ishikawa)

Table 2 of equivalence was used to identify the criticality of the problem, adapted from FMEA 4th edition [12].

Table 2. Equivalence of degree of relationship with problem

Equivalence	
10 and 9	Extremely serious failure, improper temperature.
8 and 7	Very serious failure, may compromise raw material quality.
6 and 5	Serious failure, verify process sheet.
4 and 3	Medium failure, improper handling.
2 and 1	Minor failure, probably will not affect customer's product.

In the following analysis, the seriousness problem indicators have been associated with the causes identified in Ishikawa diagram, as shown in Table 3.

Table 3. Degree of relationship with problem

CAUSE	EFFECT	RELATIONS HIP WITH PROBLEM
Out-of-spec. parameter	Incorrect adjustment	8
Pulverization	Affects the filling of cavities	3
Lack of nitrogen	Poor compaction of material	5
Machine closure	Leak of material during injection	8
Oil leak	Low pressure during injection	6
Water leak	Lack of compression and cold joint	5
Concentration of release agent	Lack of compression	6
Lack of air bag	Accumulation of gases inside the cavity	6
Aluminum temperature	Above specification: generates porosity	10
	Below specification: generates cold joint	6
Excess return	Excess sludge, generating gases in raw material	9
Lack of cleanliness in the bath	Gas accumulated in the bottom of the crucible	8

Table 4 summarizes critically the main steps of aluminum injection that should be checked and the direct actions to be taken to improve the score.

Table 4. Ranking of the most critical issues in degree of relationship with the problem

Cause	Effect	Relationship
Aluminum temperature	Above specification: generates porosity	10
Excess return	Excess sludge, generating gases in the raw material	9
Lack of cleanliness in the bath	Gas accumulated in the bottom of the crucible	8
Out-of-spec. parameter	Incorrect adjustment	8
Machine closure	Leak of material during the injection, lack of compression	8

During September 2013 and January 2014 the improvement actions, which are not detailed in this article, and follow-up for analysis and verification were performed. After the improvements made in the process, were obtained the results shown in Figure 6.

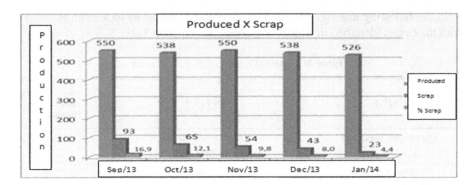

Fig. 6. Result after analyzing and taking action

An Aspin-Welch test, as described in [13], applied not strictly regarding the absolute statistical accuracy, has proven, based on the valūes $x_1 = 19.8\overline{1}$, $x_2 = 10.24$, $s^2_1 = 0.931$, $s^2_2 = 21.783$, $n_1 = 7$, $n_2 = 5$, the significant reduction of the percentage of scrap to the level of significance of 1%, with clearance ($t_4 = 4.516 > t_{4,1\%} = 3.747$). It is worthwhile to mention that the percentage of rejects after improvement actions are clearly decreasing, certainly due to the monitoring and identification of such improvements, reaching the acceptable level in January 2014.

5   Conclusions

This paper tells as an aimed improvement in process was achieved in an actual industry condition, by using quality tools. To allow such goal, there were some changes in the process under study in relation to labor, process and concepts.

Increased contribution margin can be achieved with the optimization of production processes and a balanced cost reduction strategy that will provide the organization with a better management, thus making it more competitive in the market in which it operates. Furthermore, involving people is crucial for the effective success of the whole process.

There was an effective reduction in scrap, favoring a possible reduction in the price of the item, if necessary, or even a larger effective gain for the company. One should, however, proceed with the analysis so that further improvements are effectively proven.

References

1. Richard, D.I.: Production and operations management – A life cycle approach, 3rd edn. Homewood - Illinois (1981)
2. Savitz, A.W.: A empresa sustentável: o verdadeiro sucesso é lucro com responsabilidade social e ambiental. Elsevier, Rio de Janeiro (2007)
3. Juran, J.M.: A qualidade desde o projeto: novos passos para o planejamento da qualidade em produtos e serviços. Cengage Learning, São Paulo (2011)

4. Deming, W.E.: Qualidade: a revolução na administração. Marques - Saraiva, Rio de Janeiro (1990)
5. Paladini, E.P.: Avaliação estratégica da qualidade. Atlas, São Paulo (2002)
6. Joseph, B.S.: Administração da qualidade total: o aperfeiçoamento contínuo; teoria e prática. Ibrasa, São Paulo (1997)
7. Slack, N.: Administração da produção, 2nd edn. Atlas, São Paulo (2002)
8. Costa Neto, P.L.O., Canuto, S.: A Administração com Qualidade: conhecimentos necessários para a gestão moderna. 1º reimpressão. Blucher, São Paulo (2012)
9. Turrioni, J.B.M., Carlos, H.P.: Pesquisa-ação na Engenharia de Produção. In: Miguel, P.A.C. (ed.) Metodologia de Pesquisa em Engenharia de Produção e Gestão de Operações, 2nd edn., Elsevier ABEPRO, Rio de Janeiro (2012)
10. Thiollent, M.: Metodologia da Pesquisação, 18th edn. Cortez, São Paulo (2011)
11. Chiavenato, I.: Teoria da Administração Geral, 8th edn. Editora Campus
12. AIAG, FMEA Manual, 4th edn (2010)
13. Costa Neto, P.L.O.: Estatística, 2nd edn. Blucher, São Paulo (2002)

Fuzzy Symbolic Handling of Industrial Instantaneous and Trend Performance Expressions

Vincent Clivillé, Lamia Berrah, and Laurent Foulloy

Laboratoire d'Informatique, Systèmes, Traitement de l'Information et de la Connaissance,
Annecy le Vieux, France
{vincent.cliville,lamia.berrah,laurent.foulloy}@univ-savoie.fr

Abstract. This study subscribes to the performance expression and the control of the achievement of an industrial objective. Temporal trajectory is considered for describing such an achievement, which links the initial instant of the corresponding action plan to the final one. At each milestone, instantaneous and trend performances are expressed. The purpose is thus to simultaneously handle the previous kinds of expression in order to define a meaningful piece of information that takes into account the obtained results along the considered temporal horizon. A rule-based aggregation is retained in this sense. Moreover, according to the visual management principles, symbolic fuzzification and deffuzification are used, and colored emoticons are proposed in this sense.

Keywords: Industrial objectives, Instantaneous performance expressions, Trend performance expressions, Visual management, Fuzzy logic.

1 Introduction

This study deals with the simultaneous handling of "instantaneous" performance expressions and "trend" ones, with regards to the achievement of tactical industrial objectives. This achievement can be described by a temporal trajectory. Such a trajectory is defined in coherence with the duration of the execution of the associated action plan. At the initial instant, the objective achievement is planned as being null, while at the final one, it is supposed to be totally achieved, in accordance with the expected value.

In order to control the objective temporal trajectory, milestones are introduced. These milestones generally correspond to the end of sets of actions of the considered action plan, being thus a kind of check point for the decision-maker for reacting with regards to the expressed performances. Rightly, performance expressions are provided by Performance Indicators – PI's – and Performance Measurement Systems – PMS's – [6], [7]. These expressions are the result of comparison mechanisms of the expected objectives with the acquired measures [2], [1], [5]. They are conventionally computed under numeric formats, at each milestone. That is what we can call "instantaneous" expressions. In this work, we look for the definition of a kind of enriched performance expression that not only handles the instantaneous result but also the trend one,

B. Grabot et al. (Eds.): APMS 2014, Part III, IFIP AICT 440, pp. 68–75, 2014.
© IFIP International Federation for Information Processing 2014

according to the obtained performances until the considered milestone. According to us, such an expression allows the decision-maker to have a more meaningful piece of information about the given objective achievement.

Subscribing to some principles of the visual management [4], [9], [11], we choose to describe this enriched performance expression under a symbolic form, namely coloured emoticons. Fuzzy inference mechanisms are used in this sense. Indeed, for the sake of simplicity, graphical representation has been progressively introduced in manufacturing companies during the two last decades. Providing visual pieces of information has been highlighted with the Toyota Production System, namely the Kanban flow control or the 5S management [8], [4]. For instance, the last version of the ISO 9000 standard explains how to formalise PI's through ten parameters, and gather them into visual scorecards. The visual representation is based on values, colours, curves, graphics or icons, by also considering trend data (see Fig. 1).

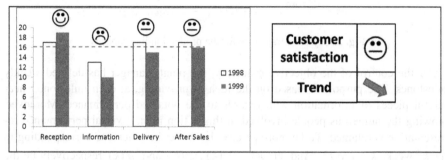

Fig. 1. Example of PI visual representation inspired by the French version of ISO 9000

Besides, the industrial practice shows that many visual formats are used for expressing performances, such as the emoticons, the traffic lights or the weather symbols. Nevertheless, the association between performance expressions and symbols generally remains implicit, while a systematic formal processing would ensure a commensurate handling. Dealing with this drawback, this article is organised as follows. In Section 2, we present the proposed fuzzy formalism. The developed ideas are illustrated by examples extracted from the case study, which is submitted by a bearings manufacturing company, around the "manufacturing Capacity" action plan. Finally, we conclude by some remarks and prospective investigations.

2   Fuzzy Processing

2.1   Case Study and Background

The bearings manufacturing company being considered works for automotive and aeronautics companies, spatial and several other high-tech activities. One of the most important Original Equipment Manufacturers in Europe, its market shares have continuously grown over the last ten years. The different bearing families are produced in specific plants and the production of a given type of bearing is made in a dedicated line which ensures the whole customer demand. Due to the success of innovative products, the submitted problem has concerned the increase of the capacity of one production line, leading thus the plant manager, who is the tactical decision-maker, to the declaration of an objective of a *capacity of 30 000 pieces par week at the end of 2013's last trimester*; knowing that the capacity at the beginning of the trimester was 27 000 pieces. Fig. 2 gives the objective trajectory planned in this sense.

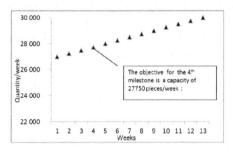

Fig. 2. Objective trajectory for the production line capacity

For the control of the objective trajectory, the plant manager has defined weekly milestones. The purpose is based on the idea of providing, at each milestone, meaningful pieces of information with regards to the obtained performance. Moreover, knowing the numerous people involved in this action plan, a visual performance representation is retained. To be more precise, let k be the milestone corresponding to the kth week, $k = 1$ to 13. And let $o(k)$, $m(k)$, $p(k)$ and $p'(k)$ respectively be the objective, the measure, the instantaneous and the trend performance expressions, with regards to the production capacity. The idea developed here is to take advantage of the instantaneous performance behaviour to introduce some kind of weighting by the performance trend. The following processing is proposed.

1 $p(k)$ and $p'(k)$ are fuzzified, into linguistic fuzzy subsets.

2 $p(k)$ and $p'(k)$ are aggregated in $C(k)$ by means of a fuzzy rule base.

3 $C(k)$ is defuzzified into a coloured emoticon $e(k)$.

2.2   Instantaneous and Trend Performance Expression Fuzzification

We choose to express the instantaneous performance expression $p(k)$ by the ratio $p(k) = \dfrac{m(k)}{o(k)}$. The performance expression trend is obtained from the backward approximation of the first derivate with a first order accuracy and a period of 4 weeks is used: $\forall k > 0$, $p'(k) = \dfrac{p(k) - p(k - \min(k,4))}{\min(k,4)}$.   (1)

The symbolic fuzzification goes the same way for the two expressions. The symbolic fuzzification of $p(k)$ denoted φ, relies on the fuzzy meaning of the linguistic terms, *i.e.* the membership function associated with each term [12]. Let $p(k)$ be characterised by the set of linguistic terms $L_1 == \{$Very Good, Good, Medium, Bad$\}$, for short $L_1 == \{$VG, G, M, B$\}$. Let the membership functions of these terms, *i.e.* their fuzzy meaning, be represented in Fig. 3. Using Zadeh's writing for discrete fuzzy subsets [13], and considering $k = 2$ as an example, the symbolic fuzzification of $p(2) = 97.85\%$ is $\varphi(p(2)) = A = 0.85/VG + 0.15/G + 0/M + 0/B$. It means that $p(2)$ is described by the term *Very Good* with a degree of 0.85 and by the term *Good* with a degree of 0.15. The symbolic fuzzification of the trend is a linguistic fuzzy subset of $L_2 = \{$*Decreasing, Stable, Increasing*$\}$, for short $L_2 = \{D, S, I\}$. The membership functions associated with these linguistic terms are given in Fig. 3. For example, the performance trend is $p'(2) = 1.41$, and its symbolic fuzzification is $\varphi(p'(2)) = B = 0.27/I + 0.73/S + 0/D$, *i.e.* the trend is stable with a small increase.

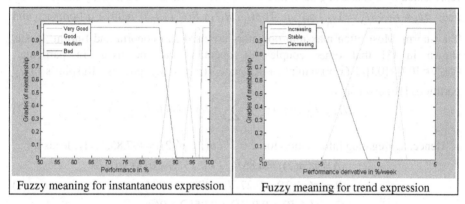

| Fuzzy meaning for instantaneous expression | Fuzzy meaning for trend expression |

Fig. 3. Fuzzy meanings of the linguistic terms describing the performance expressions

2.3   Aggregation of the Instantaneous and Trend Performance Expressions

In order to aggregate the two linguistic fuzzy subsets representing respectively the instantaneous and trend performances, we choose to use a rule based aggregation. Such a mechanism captures, more easily, various cases. The rule base used in the case study presented here is given in Table 1. The typical cases are expressed as couples of linguistic values, for example (VG, D), where the instantaneous performance is *Very Good* but its trend is *Decreasing*. Each typical case is associated with a fuzzy evaluation defined on a set of emoticons $L_3 = \{\text{☺}, \text{☻}, \text{☹}\}$. Using a fuzzy set of emoticons instead of a unique crisp emoticon provides a more precise way to code the aggregation. For example, assume that for (VG, D), we consider that aggregated evaluation can be characterised as a happy one, *i.e.* ☺, but may be also a neutral one, *i.e.* ☻, and certainly more happy than a neutral. This type of smooth natural language description can be captured by expressing that the fuzzy subset 0.7/☺ + 0.3/☻ is associated with (VG, D), according to Zadeh's conventional description one for discrete fuzzy subsets.

Table 1. Fuzzy rule base for the typical cases related to the Capacity action plan

	D	**S**	**I**
VG	0.7/☺ + 0.3/☻	1/☺	1/☺
G	0.4/☺ + 0.5/☻ + 0.1/☹	0.6/☺ + 0.4/☻	0.8/☺ + 0.2/☻
M	0.5/☻ + 0.5/☹	1/☻	0.5/☺ + 0.5/☻
B	1/☹	0.3/☻ + 0.7/☹	0.1/☺ + 0.3/☻ + 0.6/☹

This table is the graph of a fuzzy relation R defined on the Cartesian product $L_1 \times L_2 \times L_3$. Let X be a fuzzy subset of L and $l \in L$. $X(l)$ denotes the grade of membership of l in X. Let A be a fuzzy subset of L_1 and B be a fuzzy subset of L_2. Thanks to Zadeh's compositional rule of inference [13], the aggregation process is represented by a function g such that $C = g(A,B)$ with C being a fuzzy subset of L_3 and: $\forall l_3 \in L_3, C(l_3) = \perp_{(l_1,l_2) \in L_1 \times L_2} T(A(l_1), B(l_2), R(l_1, l_2, l_3))$ with $\perp$ a t-conorm and T a t-norm. Most often max-min operators are used as t-conorm and t-norm. It was shown in [3] that other couples of operators can be used. In particular, $\forall x, y \in [0,1] \times [0,1], \perp(x,y) = \min(x+y, 1)$ and $T(x,y) = x.y$ preserve Ruspini's fuzzy partitions [10] and lead to:

$$\forall l_3 \in L_3, C(l_3) = \sum_{(l_1,l_2) \in L_1 \times L_2} A(l_1) B(l_2) . R(l_1, l_2, l_3). \tag{2}$$

Hence, aggregating information for $k = 2$, $(p(2), p'(2)) = (97.85, 1.41)$, leads to:

$$A = \varphi(p(2)) = 0.85/VG + 0.15/G + 0/M + 0/B$$
$$B = \varphi(p'(2)) = 0.27/I + 0.73/S + 0/D \tag{3}$$
$$C = g(A, B) = 0.95/☺ + 0.05/☻ + 0/☹$$

Even if at this step, the plant manager can characterise every week his performances by an expression on the basis of $\varphi(p)$ and $\varphi(p')$, a final processing is necessary to propose a visual handling of this expression.

2.4   The Emoticon-Based Scorecard

The idea is now to defuzzify the fuzzy subset defined on the set of emoticons into a unique colored emoticon whose smile, makes it easily understandable. Indeed, conventionally, two parameters characterise such an emoticon: its smile, on the one hand, and its colour one the other hand, knowing that there is a kind of equivalence between them. Let C be a fuzzy subset of L_3, α_i the grade of membership and $y_i \in Y$ a value, respectively associated with each emoticon. The symbolic defuzzification δ is

defined by: $y = \delta(C) = \dfrac{\sum\limits_i \alpha_i . y_i}{\sum\limits_i \alpha_i}.$ (4)

Two symbolic defuzzifications are used at the same time. The first one refers to the intensity of the smile and the second one with the colour of the emoticon. The smile is drawn as part of an ellipsis which is associated with a parameter $s \in [-1, 1]$. When $s = 1$, the emoticon means full happiness. It means that the value 1 is associated with ☺. In the same way, -1 and 0 are respectively associated with ☹ and ☺. Moreover, a "happy" emoticon means a satisfactory situation and the green colour is the conventional one for this type of case. If the colour is defined in the RGB space and each color component is defined in [0, 1], then the vector $c = [0\,1\,0]$, representing the green colour, is associated with ☺. In the same way, red and yellow colours, *i.e.* vectors [1 0 0] and [1 1 0] are respectively associated with ☹ and ☺. For example, given $C = 0.95/☺ + 0.05/☺ + 0/☹$, we have $s = 0.95$ and $c = [0.05\,1\,0]$ which lead to the left hand side emoticon in Fig. 4. In the same way $C = 0/☺ + 0.8/☺ + 0.2/☹$ produces the right hand side one.

Fig. 4. Examples of generated emoticons

It is interesting to note that the fuzzy approach makes it quite simple to capture human expertise for the aggregation of the performance and it trend. Nevertheless, the generated information is not trivial and would have been quite complex had it been represented by mathematical equations. Fig. 5 shows this point. It represents the surface of the emoticon parameter s, *i.e.* the smile intensity, in function with the performance and its trend. The colours of the surface are the emoticon colours.

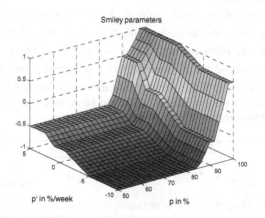

Fig. 5. The smiley parameter surface

2.5   Illustrations

Figure 6 summarises the instantaneous and trend performance expressions that correspond to the six first weeks of the Capacity action plan. Note that the same scorecard could be refreshed every week until the 13th week of the year 2013. Then expressions are thus fuzzified thanks to the previous φ functions. Results for $\varphi(p')$ are given in Table 2. For instance $\varphi(p'(6)) = 0/I + 0.41/S + 0.59/D$.

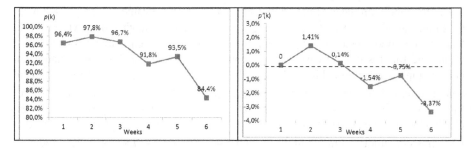

Fig. 6. Instantaneous and trend performance expression for the first six weeks

Table 2. fuzzification of the trend performance expression

	1	2	3	4	5	6
p'(k)		1,41%	0,14%	-1,54%	-0,75%	-3,37%
I (Increasing)	-	0,27	-	-	-	-
S (Stable)	1,00	- 0,73	1,00	0,87	1,00	0,41
D (Decreasing)	-	-	-	0,13	-	0,59

The next step consists in aggregating the fuzzification of $p(6)$, which is $\varphi(p(6)) = 0/VG + 0/G + 0/M + 1/B$, with the fuzzification of $p'(6)$. Using Table 1, we obtain $C(6) = 0/☺ + 0.12/☻ + 0.83/☹$. C is now defuzzified to give a coloured emoticon. For instance, the smile parameter for the 6th week is $s(6) = -0.88$, which characterises an unsmiling mouth, while the RGB vector is $c(6) = [1\,0.12\,0]$, which is an orange colour very close to the red one. It produces the following unhappy emoticon, . Thus the plant manager builds a scorecard (Fig. 7) which respectively gathers, for a considered week, the objective and measure $(o(k), m(k))$. On the left hand side of the scorecard, the performance and emoticon trajectories are displayed from the beginning of the action plan. As it can be seen, a strong and quick corrective action must be undertaken to improve the performance.

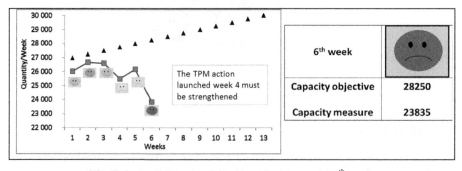

Fig. 7. Scorecard for the Capacity action plan at the 6th week

3   Conclusion

Taking trend performance expression into account can be seen as an enrichment of the traditional way of instantaneously expressing performances. Moreover, visual management is useful, in industrial improvement processes, to facilitate the decision. In this sense an information processing has been proposed which aggregates the instantaneous and the trend expressions based on fuzzification mechanisms and inference rules. This aggregated piece of information is displayed in the form of emoticons which ensure an easy and common understanding for most people involved in the improvement action plans. The case study is in progress and should give feedback about the interest and the practical difficulties to deploy this visual management in industrial company. Further development of this work concerns the generalisation of this type of visual temporal approach particularly when many objectives have to be simultaneously reached. An extension of this model is also envisaged for the performance analysis of the temporal trajectories being considered as a whole.

References

[1] Berrah, L., Mauris, G., Haurat, A., Foulloy, L.: Global vision and performance indicators for an industrial improvement approach. Computers in Industry 43(3), 211–225 (2000)

[2] Fortuin, L.: Performance indicators, why, where and how? European Journal of Operational Research 34, 1–9 (1988)

[3] Foulloy, L., Benoit, E.: Building a class of fuzzy equivalence relations. Fuzzy Sets and Systems 157(11), 1417–1437 (2006)

[4] Greif, M.: The visual factory, building participation through shared information. Productivity Press, Portland (1991)

[5] Kaplan, R., Norton, D.: The Balanced Scorecard: Measures that drive performances. Harvard Business Review (1992)

[6] Neely, A., Gregory, M., Platts, K.: Performance measurement system design: a literature review and research agenda. International Journal of Operations and Production Management 48(4), 80–116 (1995)

[7] Nudurupati, S.S., Bititci, U.S., Kumar, V., Chan, F.T.S.: State of the art literature review on performance measurement. Computers & Industrial Engineering 60(2), 279–290 (2011)

[8] Ohno, T.: Toyota Production System: Beyond Large-scale Production. Production Press (1988)

[9] Platts, K., Tan, K.H.: Strategy visualisation: knowing, understanding, and formulating. Management Decision 42(5), 667–676 (2004)

[10] Ruspini, E.: A new approach to clustering. Information and Control 15(1), 22–32 (1969)

[11] Tergan, S.O., Keller, T.: Knowledge and Information Visualization: Searching for Synergies. Lecture Notes in Computer Science / Information Systems and Applications, incl. Internet/Web, and HCI. Springer (2005)

[12] Zadeh, L.: Quantitative fuzzy semantics. Information Sciences 3, 159–176 (1971)

[13] Zadeh, L.: Outline of a new approach to the analysis of complex systems and decision processes. IEEE Transactions on Systems, Man, and Cybernetics, SMC-3, 28–44 (1973)

A Framework for Production System Design: Insights from Industrial Experience

Nico J. Vandaele[1,2] and Catherine J. Decouttere[1]

[1] Katholieke Universiteit Leuven, Faculty of Business and Economics,
Naamsestraat 69, 3000 Leuven
[2] KULAK, E. Sabbelaan 53, 8500 Kortrijk
{Nico.Vandaele,Catherine.Decouttere}@kuleuven.be

Abstract. In this paper we want to share our findings from our industrial experience in the field of system design, more precisely in production system design. We start by the observation that many rigorous designs of production systems are not facing the implementation success they suggest. We indicate three basic reasons for this: limited stakeholder involvement, lack of out-of-the-box thinking and the dominance of financial and technical evaluation criteria. Based on these findings, we suggest a five step approach: the stakeholder analysis, the definition of key performance indicators, the scenario generation, the scenario ranking and the scenario implementation.

Keywords: Scenario generation, production system design, multi-criteria evaluation, stakeholder analysis.

1 Introduction

If it comes to radical changes of production systems in the light of global-local considerations, the design of new production systems has to be much more far reaching than currently practiced. This is because the production systems of the future have to respond to the needs of many different stakeholders, which are often conflictive in their performance evaluation of the new production system [7,10]. The literature is teeming of rigorous papers, which model and optimize production systems [11]. However, much too often these extremely promising designs are not implemented as they are reported and many of these designs are abandoned before they are able to prove their full potential. The question raises: "What is the reason for this?" Since decades we make use of the best modelling approaches, optimizing methodologies and computer power [16]. Based on our experience from different modelling and implementation projects [15], we believe that there are several reasons for this, ranging from a limited stakeholders' involvement, over a lack of out-of-the-box thinking towards a missing link between quantitative and qualitative approaches towards production system design. In order to counteract these observations, contemporary production system design should build upon knowledge generated both inside as well as outside the current as-is production system.

B. Grabot et al. (Eds.): APMS 2014, Part III, IFIP AICT 440, pp. 76–82, 2014.

The contribution of this paper is three-fold: (1) we embrace the modelling of production systems with a stakeholder perspective; (2) we extend the construction, evaluation and ranking of the different production system design scenarios to include value based performance measures and (3) we use the outcomes of analytical models of production systems in a multi-criteria ranking methodology.

Section 2 explores the reasons of weak implementation of developed production system models. Section 3 proposes a five step framework to counteract these findings. We conclude, including examples, in section 4.

2 Reasons for Implementation Difficulties and a Glance at Their Countermeasures

Limited Stakeholders' Involvement. All too often new systems are designed upon the request of a single or a limited set of stakeholders [4]. At first sight, this makes the production system design process efficient as the concerns of only a few stakeholders are not that difficult to grasp and are most likely not conflicting due to their one-sided origin. The required performance measures are defined in a short notice and the number of elective scenario's fulfilling these performance measures is usually rather small. Therefore, often financial or technological performance measures suffice as the stakeholders' origin is internal to the organization whereto the production system belongs. In the same atmosphere, the goal of the new production system often boils down to a single performance measure, mostly a financial one under which technological issues are covered. As a consequence, optimization can be used effectively to further specify the optimal parameter settings of the design scenario [8]. This optimal design scenario is ready for implementation. However, as soon as this scenario is facing practical circumstances and considerations put forward by stakeholders belonging to the environment into which the production system is implemented, the scenario will suffer and will most likely be prohibited to deliver its expected performance. Even if the optimal design scenario is not left aside, it will definitely be amended to accommodate the environmental criticism [15]. These undesirable effects and amendment efforts could have been avoided if a critical number of stakeholders would have been incorporated earlier in the design process [9]. Later in this paper we will preserve the involvement of all important stakeholders via a stakeholders' analysis in order to list up all relevant key performance indicators (KPI's).

Lack of Out-of-the-Box Design Options. The composition of new radical design scenarios is a function of the different ways of thinking that are involved in the scenario building process. If only a small number of stakeholders is considered, there is a great chance that the new designs are close to the as-is system, leading to incremental scenario's with either marginal improvements or with significant, but one-dimensional improvements. Building upon our experience for instance in health care system design [15], it became clear that taking into account a variety of relevant stakeholders increases both the number as well as the diversity of the design scenarios. This offers a big chance to open up new ways of operation and performance possibilities. New building blocks for the production system are brought to the design table in order to serve the outlined set of KPI's. As a consequence, these different stakeholders with their diverse performance criteria turn the single optimization problem outlined above into a multi-objective evaluation, as can be seen in Table 1.

Table 1. A balanced evaluation of a production system: technology, economies and values

Multi – KPI Evaluation		
Technology	Economies	Human Values
Flow	Profit	Safety
Skills	Investments	Fairness
Process complexity	Operating cost	Ecological footprint
Product Quality	Time to market	Motivation

This is an adapted version of a figure reported earlier in literature [13]. The key issue is that all important KPI's are listed and that a praticular balance is preserved between technological, economical and value based KPI's in order to keep all stakeholders engaged. This is crucial for the succes of the implementation process.

The Dominance of Quantitative Financial and Technological KPI's. If different scenario's are to be assessed with respect to a complex set of KPI's a lot of qualitative aspects come into the picture. It is very tempting to either neglect the qualitative aspects like value based performance indicators in favour of more quantitative metrics of a technological or economic nature [14]. This poses a problem as some of the less tangible KPI's are nevertheless linked to important stakeholders. For instance, customer perceived value serves as a commonly used KPI for the stakeholders from the external demand side of a production system [15]. At this point, we strongly support the inclusion of KPI's which try to measure qualitative aspects of the KPI set if no straight quantitative metrics are available. As a consequence, we end up with a multi-criteria evaluation of the production system scenarios which makes the use of a ranking method mandatory. Although different ranking methods are presented in literature [13], we really do want to avoid the use of weighting scoring models. The advantage seems to be that this brings us back to a single objective function (like utility functions), which is beneficial for optimization purposes. However, it shifts the discussion away from the relevance of the criteria itself towards a discussion related to the weights of the different criteria. This is no step forward. Instead, we opt for a non-parametric ranking method, as we will explain later in the sequel of this paper.

3   A Framework

In this section we propose a framework which boils down to a five step approach. This framework has been initially developed through our research in R&D portfolio management where a model based decision support approach has been proposed and applied for assessing, ranking and selection within an R&D portfolio context [14]. The basic reason within R&D portfolio management is that when it comes to the ranking of R&D projects, the value based dimensions are often very hard to incorporate next to the typical financial or cost based objective functions and their corresponding technological constraints. We proposed a non-parametric approach, where value based measures can be included in the overall assessment, ranking and selection of projects in the portfolio [13]. This framework is currently being elaborated and refined in order to be useful for supply chain design contexts. This paper deals with the application into a production system context.

3.1 Stakeholder Analysis and Production System Definition

The stakeholders involved in a production system design effort can be categorized using a two-fold dichotomy: one dichotomy relates to the focus of the stakeholders and deals with the fact that the stakeholder is part of the supply or demand side of the production system. The other dichotomy describes the origin of the stakeholder: either internal or external to the production system. Together with some examples, this can be seen in Table 2.

Table 2. The two-fold stakeholders' dichotomy

		Focus	
		Supply	Demand
Origin	Internal	Shareholder Employee Manager	User Customer Intermediary
	External	Regulatory body Supply Chain Partners Institutional body	Government Public opinion Society at large

From the supply and demand point of view, the production system is defined as a collection of resources organized together in order to serve a particular set of flows as visualized in Fig 1. This is the traditional viewpoint from an analytical modelling perspective: resources are part of the supply side of the production system and flows originate outside the production system in the environment, are processed through the resources of the production system in a number of steps and at the end leave the system again to re-join the environment. We define the set of resources and their relationships as the supply side of the production system. Examples of important stakeholders are definitely the shareholders, employees and managers in general. In most analytic models, the demand side is assumed to be exogenous: the origin and the characterization of flows lies outside the production system. However, this supply side contains considerable opportunities in terms of stakeholder analysis as there are: the customers, users, intermediaries, …[5]. Opportunities can be found for instance in different flows serving different market segments, various evolutions through time (both in mix changes and product/service flow portfolio changes), geographical evolutions, etc. All of these demand side opportunities may eventually turn into different scenarios as will be discussed in section 3.3 of this paper. This concludes the internal supply and demand view of the production system.

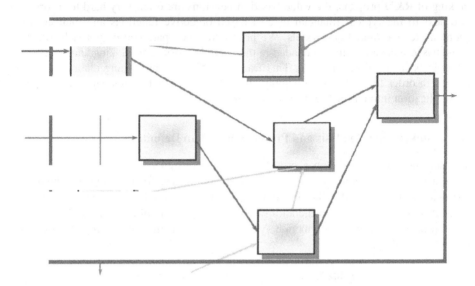

Fig. 1. The production system as a flow system

If it comes to an in-depth stakeholder analysis [6], other important external stake-holders can be located in the system's environment. On the supply side various supply chain partners, regulatory bodies, institutional bodies and the like are further shaping the stakeholders' group. On the demand side, more remote stakeholders are located in the public opinion, in the social media or the community at large, for instance the incorporation of sustainability in production systems. Also ethical and social aspects like working conditions, general welfare of human beings and the environmental concerns are examples of external stakeholders' perspectives on the demand side.

3.2   Production System KPI's and Requirements

If these stakeholders' viewpoints are relevant they must be reflected in the KPI set to evaluate the production system design scenarios. Revealing these KPI's is not always trivial and enough effort has to be devoted to gathering the stakeholders' views and the detection of the KPI's they are standing for [1]. Mostly, stakeholders also bear thresholds in their minds, against which the production system design scenario will be put. This can later on be used in the next step as a criterion to allow a scenario to be part of the long list of feasible and acceptable scenarios. This typical iterative process ends with a KPI set which is a specific instance of the general statement in Fig 1. Without going into detail, we want to stress the importance of finding appropriate metrics for these KPI's. These metrics should be robust, clearly defined and numerical. The latter includes scaled metrics which are typically used for measuring the more intangible KPI's.

3.3   Scenario Generation and Validation

From the stakeholders' opinions and their derived KPI's, building blocks for the production system will emerge. Both existing and new building blocks will be combined into different scenarios. At this point the traditional analytical modelling comes into the picture and contributes its inherent value: every scenario needs to be modelled as rigorously as possible in order to get the best parameter setting for a given scenario [2,3]. If particular aspects can be optimized, this should be done [12]. Subsequently, every scenario modelled will be assessed against the complete set of KPI's outlined in the previous step, which is a broader set than the KPI's delivered by the analytical model only. As this KPI set eventually contains thresholds induced by particular stakeholders, a scenario not passing the thresholds can be left aside in this phase. So the output of this phase is a long list of feasible scenarios endorsed by the stakeholders through their KPI's and potential thresholds.

3.4   Ranking of Production System Scenarios

This phase relies on a decision support model for scenario ranking. The long list of feasible scenarios is ranked according to the multi-criteria performance defined by the set of KPI's. Many methodologies can be put forward. We rely on Data Envelopment Analysis (DEA), which is a non-parametric ranking procedure. At this point, we can build upon our experience in the R&D portfolio management area where DEA has been applied successfully to rank the various design alternatives in the development of new products and services [14]. The major difference with production systems is that in an R&D context, the help of analytic flow models like we used in the previous step for the design of production systems is not available. In the production system design context, the existence of an analytical model should be exploited.

3.5   Production System Scenario Selection and Implementation

One of the consequences of using a non-parametric method for multi-criteria scenario ranking is the occurrence of multiple 'best' scenarios, called peers. From a practical point of view this is quite natural and for the decision support the segregation between the peers and the other scenario's is important and very useful. The final decision board will be exposed to this set of peers. Very often, if one scenario is finally chosen for implementation, the set of peers contains useful scenarios to construct fall back plans if the dynamics of the environment change the setting for the scenario chosen and implemented.

4   Conclusions and Further Research

\In this paper we reflected on production system design based on our experience in industry. It turned out that rigorous modelling is not always sufficient to reach successful implementations. In an attempt to counteract these effects, we suggest a five step approach, including stakeholder analysis and definition of a set of key performance indicators, scenario generation and scenario ranking leading to the implementation a stakeholder bought-in production system design.

Future research challenges include the quest for more refined KPI metrics and the development of an adequate visualization for better insight and decision making in the various steps.

Acknowledgments. This research has been supported by the GSK Research Chair.

References

1. Beyan, O.D., Baykal, N.: A knowledge based search tool for performance measures in health care systems. Journal of Medical Systems 36(1), 201–221 (2012)
2. Brailsford, S.C.: System dynamics: What's in it for healthcare simulation modelers? In: Simulation Conference, WSC 2008, pp. 1478–1483. IEEE (Winter 2008)
3. Brailsford, S.C., Lattimer, V., Tarnaras, P., Turnbull, J.: Emergency and on-demand health care: modelling a large complex system. Journal of the Operational Research Society 55(1), 34–42 (2004)
4. Clarkson, P.J., Buckle, P., Coleman, R., Stubbs, D., Ward, J., Jarrett, J., Lane, R., Bound, J.: Design for patient safety: a review of the effectiveness of design in the UK health service. Journal of Engineering Design 15(2), 123–140 (2004)
5. Decouttere, C., Vandaele, N.: A broader view on health care system design and modelling, 2013, KBI Research Report 1323, KU Leuven 37 pp. (submitted for publication)
6. Donaldson, K., Ishii, K., Sheppard, S.: Customer value chain analysis. Research in Engineering Design 16(4), 174–183 (2006)
7. Elias, A.A., Cavana, R.Y., Jackson, L.S.: Stakeholder analysis for R&D project management. R&D Management 32(4), 301–310 (2002)
8. Freeman, R.E.: Strategic management: A stakeholder approach. Cambridge University Press (2010)
9. Lambrecht, M. R. and Vandaele, N. J. (1996). A general approximation for the single product lot sizing model with queueing delays. *European Journal of Operational Research*, 95(1):73 – 88.
10. Mitchell, R.K., Agle, B.R., Wood, D.J.: Toward a theory of stakeholder identification and salience: Defining the principle of who and what really counts. The Academy of Management Review 22(4), 853–886 (1997)
11. Solaimani, S., Guldemond, N., Bouwman, H.: Dynamic stakeholder interaction analysis: Innovative smart living design cases. Electronic Markets, 1–12 (2013)
12. Suri, R., Sanders, J., Kamath, M.: Performance evaluation of production networks. In: Logistics of Production and Inventory, Elsevier Science Publishers (1993)
13. Vandaele, N., Nieuwenhuyse, I.V., Cupers, S.: Optimal grouping for a nuclear magnetic resonance scanner by means of an open queueing model. European Journal of Operational Research 151(1), 181–192 (2003)
14. Vandaele, N., Landrieux, B., Decouttere, C.: The Sustainable Reconciliation between Technological, Financial and People Aspects in R&D Portfolio Management. In: Proceedings of the 6th IEEE International Conference on Management of Innovation and Technology, pp. 57–61 (2012)
15. Vandaele, N.J., Decouttere, C.J.: Sustainable R&D portfolio assessment. Decision Support Systems 54(4), 1521–1532 (2013)
16. Whitt, W.: The queueing network analyzer. The Bell System Technical Journal 62(9), 2779–2815 (1983)

Improvement of Human-Plant Interactivity via Industrial Cloud-Based Supervisory Control and Data Acquisition System

Tomáš Lojka and Iveta Zolotová

Department of Cybernetics and Artificial intelligence, Košice, Slovakia
{tomas.lojka,iveta.zolotova}@tuke.sk

Abstract. Industrial companies look for the best way to be perfectly optimized, failure resistant, how to handle increasing amounts of information, and have more open and reliable union with their customers and suppliers. This paper focuses on the improvement of industry performance through the integration of SCADA/HMI (Supervisory Control and Data Acquisition/Human Machine Interface), SOA (Serviced Oriented Architecture) and cloud computing. This paper's contribution is in a failover and high availability solution for small and medium industry companies. The contribution is based on the integration of the cloud and SCADA/HMI, and contains a developed SOA load balancer for better accessibility to the cloud. This whole solution improves performance, reliability and availability. It is cost-effective and includes a mobile device implementation for controlling and monitoring systems.

Keywords: Cloud manufacturing, database systems, data storage systems, network-attached storage, SCADA/HMI systems, SOA.

1 Introduction

Industrial companies intend to reduce their operating costs and expenses. Therefore, they need solutions that will help them have full, real-time control over an entire plant [1]. The needed features of such solutions are stability, flexibility, fault-tolerance, high accessible storage of information and good connectivity. This will make every internal and external process more effective, highly available, and cost-effective. The communication interactivity and complexity will be enlarged.

One of the recent technological waves, cloud computing, fulfils industrial companies' needs [2]. Cloud computing brings the option of integration a SCADA/HMI and the cloud [3]. The integration can reduce industrial companies' costs, increase reliability, security and system stability with fail tolerance to industrial companies' systems errors [1]. This leads to "smart" industrial companies like homes in IBM vision [4]. In SDACA/HMI and cloud implantation, local parts of an industrial company's ICS (Information and Control System) are moved out to the cloud. The SCADA/HMI and cloud integration also brings a solution to the increasing demands for the amount of quick, easy and secured access to the information inside industrial companies,

B. Grabot et al. (Eds.): APMS 2014, Part III, IFIP AICT 440, pp. 83–90, 2014.

where information is important not only for critical control. The amount of information in an ICS increases every year and with new parts in the ICS. Industrial companies struggle with processing and saving large amounts of data and ensuring the security of manufacture information. Industrial companies easily overcome demands of increasing amount of information with hosting a SCADA/HMI (2) in the cloud with using cloud benefits (2) and risks (2.1).

We defined our SCADA/HMI cloud-based solution (3) with a failover SOA (Service Oriented Architecture) and a failover MySQL cluster (4) to reach improvements in performance, reliability and availability, and to find a cost-effective solution with the involved mobile device implementation for controlling and monitoring systems. The solution is aimed at small industrial companies which want to manage their own cloud. This solution was created to fulfil small industrial companies' requirements in a cost-efficient way. Moreover, this solution is open enough to supporters and customers, but not publicly open to the internet. In this solution, we chose a SOA and cloud (private, realized with VMware). Service-oriented architecture is also used for communication with mobile clients, and separated load balancer service.

2   Hosting a SCADA/HMI in the Cloud

There are many options how to implement a SCADA/HMI system in the cloud to get all benefits from a cloud-based SCADA/HMI system.

A cloud-based SCADA/HMI system provides robust remote access and independency of the client platform. We identified three option how to host a SCADA/HMI in the cloud to reach best contribution for our implementation:

- **Outside cloud-based SCADA/HMI** is situated outside of the cloud, SCADA/HMI is connected to the cloud. Data is transmitted to the cloud and classified. [3] Main purpose is data analysis and easy access to data. Data is mainly stored in the cloud to be always available and secure. Additional reporting and analysis services are implemented in the cloud to increase the efficiency of data acquisition and historization. Clients retrieve data from the cloud. [3]
- **Inside cloud-based SCADA/HMI** is running in the cloud and it is connected to the technological layer [2]. In this solution, cloud applications are remotely connected to the technological layer. Commands are sent to the technological layer and then processed. Data is polled from the technological layer and remotely sent to the cloud.
- **Inside/Outside cloud-based SCADA/HMI** is primarily running outside of the cloud, while some SCADA/HMI application runs in the cloud as well.

In our implementation, we focused on the inside cloud-based SCADA/HMI, which is depicted in Fig. 1.

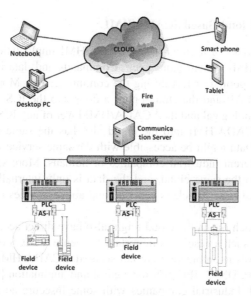

Fig. 1. Inside cloud-based SCADA/HMI system with the technological layer, communication server and firewall to protect the access to the technological layer. The SCADA/HMI application runs in the cloud and the cloud clients are connected to the application.

Our purpose was to integrate the benefits of the cloud, such as high availability, virtualization, load balancing, uptime etc. Integration provides multi-use remote access where the SCADA/HMI system is guest in the cloud environment. Hosting a SCADA/HMI in the cloud allows a user to track data with various hardware platforms (smartphones, tablets, notebook and so on).

Big benefit of a cloud-based SCADA/HMI solution is data accessibility. This accessibility ensures stable access to data. Data informational content in ICS is important for decreasing the risks of bad decisions due to no or insufficiently information.

The cloud supports sharing information and increases the speed of accessing manufacture data, also for customers. For example, if a customer (another industrial company) urgently needs to change their production and needs raw materials with other quality, then the industrial company can easily change the requirements of product quality in the supplier's industrial company.

An ICS has internal or external suppliers which maintain, explore and upgrade the ICS. In such situations, it is beneficial for suppliers to have a distributed ICS solution in the cloud due the increased complexity between the supplier and customer.

Another example, the supplier of conveyers can easily reach data about conveyers, analyse them, predict and prevent failures and decrease the downtime in production.

Implementing a SCADA/HMI in the cloud means reaching benefits such as optimization, flexibility, scalability, availability and better cost-efficiency [2].

On the other hand, connection of the cloud and a SCADA/HMI has negatives as well. These are described in sub-section 2.1.

2.1   Risks of a Cloud-Based SCADA/HMI

We identified the risks of a cloud base SCADA/HMI implantation. First, the cloud makes a SCADA/HMI system more open. Commands and data in the cloud can be sniffed, modified, spoofed or lost during the communication. Moreover, the connection of a SCADA/HMI and the cloud opens a door into the ICS. The attackers then can access the technological and the SCADA/HMI layer of any ICS.

Integrating a SCADA/HMI into the cloud also has the same risks like a typical cloud realization. Data might be accessible with the same service with different security access for different industrial companies or humans. More specifically, another client has access to the same cloud, and the data is only internally separated. There might be a potential risk. Attackers can find and abuse services or applications running in the cloud.

Applications which run in the cloud might also have direct access to the ICS technological layer. In such a case, it is important to secure the ICS communication, because some protocols in automation are not secured. SCADA/HMI systems regularly use MODBUS/TCP, DNP3, IEC-140 for control and automation [1]. Some protocols lack protection [6]. Industrial companies with some insecure communication protocols are more prone to attacks (man-in-the-middle (MiTM) attacks) [7].

The cloud offers big benefits for a SCADA/HMI or other layers of the ICS, but its security might not be reliable. The data is not the only thing that is supposed to be encrypted and secured inside the cloud. The connection to the technological layer and other parts of any ICS, which are not usually part of the cloud, require security measures as well. A simple solution for security is separating the data. Data which is important to suppliers or customers might be secured and placed in the cloud. Direct connection to the technological layer is risky. An alternative is creating a hybrid cloud. Another solution might be a gateway to field devices with a special protocol. This gateway creates two separated layers. The first one is for an internal SCADA/HMI part and the other layer is used for the cloud SCADA/HMI part [1].

3   Analysis of the Cloud-Based SCADA/HMI Solution and Connectivity in Laboratory Conditions

We implemented an inside cloud-based SCADA/HMI solution using a private cloud and the ICS with the SCADA/HMI system from Wonderware and Rockwell Automation [8]. We extended the ICS with cloud benefits, to share information from the SCADA/HMI and MES (Manufacturing Execution Systems) layer and used it in education exercises. Clients can then work with data anywhere and extend their own SCADA/HMI solution with cloud stored data from real technology process. Technological process is without risks and the connection to the field devices is limited.

Also, we consider the option if someone unauthorized gets access to the cloud stored data or some students try to do something unauthorized.

To design a cost-effective solution for a small company, and a solution with closed technological, layers we chose to use a private cloud. Another reason was the situation when providers do some changes in their security or service functionality.

The SCADA/HMI and another layer of the ICS might be sensitive to such changes, which might endanger processes in the industrial company (for example slowing down query execution). We used our own private cloud solution and with OpenVPN (Open Virtual Private Net) access (for external customers and suppliers) to have better security, be more flexible in customization and see all needed sources for realization.

In our solution for the SCADA/HMI and the cloud implementation, we firstly created a storage place. We implemented a NAS (Network Attached Storage) with a CIFS (Common Internet File System) [9]. A NAS is a storage device for VMware virtual machines. This implementation enables HA (High Availability) and gives independence to the SCADA/HMI application from the hardware implementation on the server side. If the physical server fails, another server will be used to continue processing data. Data is not bound to the server but to the data storage. In our solution, we implemented an outside SCADA/HMI cloud solution. This solution can be set in a small industrial company which needs to share large amount of data to their customers, suppliers or internal workers. The solution will be used to share data from the SCADA/HMI layer.

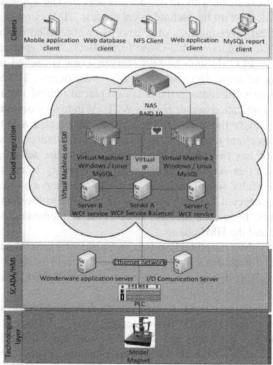

Fig. 2. Improvement of Human-plant Interactivity with better cloud accessibility

Data storage systems should meet selected requirements (high availability, reliability and others) [2]. These requirements might be in conflict. For example, availability, scalability and data consistency might be in conflict [1, 2]. In our solution, we used MySQL Cluster [11], where we gave more importance to data availability [10].

Not only storing data is important, but also the infrastructure for accessing it. Because we chose the implementation of a private cloud in our experiment, we implemented a service oriented architecture (SOA) in our architecture with a service that retrieves data from the communication server. The communication server communicates with the technological layer of our ICS. The service is also used to saving data to the cloud storage and its retrieval. The service communicates with HMI clients.

4   Realised Solution in Laboratory

We created and tested solution, in which data is accessible to every client. We chose the database to store data from technological process, but we also chose NFS due to its advantage of quick saving of reports in the cloud. For users are the documents accessible from NAS with the utilities which NAS has. Data is available through MySQL servers, which were realized on virtual machines on an ESXI server from VMware.

Our solution is extended with an application server. The application server is intended to communicate with the technological process, HMI clients and data storage.

The technological layer consists of a laboratory controlled model. The model is controlled by a PLC (Programmable Logic Controller). The application server communicates with the PLC through an OPC server. Data is cached in the application server. If the value of same data changes, a new event occurs. The application server writes (updates/inserts) the data to the database placed behind the application server in the event. The application server hosts a WCF (Windows Communication Foundation) service. To satisfy the failover requirement, we created a SOA load balancer. This balancer sends client requests to the service. If the balancer fails to communicate with the service or has insufficient low response from the service, it transmits the client request to another service. The balancer has memory where it saves a request after it was successfully sent. In our solution, we used service-oriented architecture (SOA) which is connected to the technological layer and to the data storage and also to the HMI clients. Inside the service, there is an implemented connection to the MySQL database and the HMI clients.

The MySQL database is placed on two independent virtual machines, which are clustered with the storage NAS. It is configured to use raid 10. Both virtual machines have their own MySQL instance and are connected together with a heartbeat connection [11].

These servers have one virtual IP address, which is used by the application server and MySQL clients (for example, MySQL report client). Virtual machines run Windows Server 2008 R2, but Linux can be used as well. Data is secured with MySQL security. MySQL data is accessible from every place inside the private network. The MySQL database stores data from the technological layer and critical controls commands from the HMI layer. This data is accessible for every SCADA/HMI application on a device or a PC.

MySQL client is not supported by many SCADA/HMI systems. However, there are libraries which can be implemented to allow the use of MySQL. The access to data ensures tolerance to faults, which is guaranteed with ours created cluster and the heartbeat connection of MySQL [11].

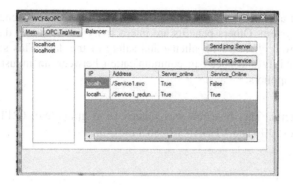

Fig. 3. Graphical interpretation of the SOA load balancer

The HMI clients can connect to the service through an installed application or through a website. These clients are used like mobile HMI applications for manufacture operators.

Clients can connect to the NAS (for example, with a web browser) and access files. Clients can use FTP, NFS and SMD protocols. These clients are mainly oriented for downloading created reports, saving and sharing business documents.

The last client type is a client application for a direct connection to the MySQL service.

Fig. 4. Mobile web application client for model Magnet

5   Conclusions

The main purpose of every industrial company is to build an effective system and reduce its costs. This paper described solutions, benefits and risks of integrating a SCADA/HMI and cloud computing. Our selected solution was introduced as a solution for small industrial companies to store their production data through the SOA service, which is implemented over a realized SCADA/HMI from Wonderware System Platform. The benefit and contribution of this solution is in parallel data processing with a SCADA/HMI and the cloud, which doesn't influence the realized SCADA/HMI system, Others benefits are interactivity of the stored data with report analysis tools, web clients, NFS clients and safety of the data. This solution should increase the stability and speed in communication between an industrial company, customers and suppliers.

Acknowledgments. This research was funded by a grant (No. 021TUKE-4/2012) from the KEGA (50%) and VEGA - 1/0286/11 (50%).

References

1. Alcaraz, C., Agudo, I., Nunez, D., Lopez, J.: Managing Incidents in Smart Grids à la Cloud. In: 2011 IEEE Third International Conference on Cloud Computing Technology and Science (CloudCom), pp. 527–531 (2011)
2. DeCandia, G., Hastorun, D., Jampani, M., Kakulapati, G., Lakshman, A., Pilchin, A., Sivasubramanian, S., Vosshall, P., Vogels, W.: Dynamo: amazon's highly available key-value store. In: SOSP 2007, pp. 205–220. ACM, New York (2007)
3. Youseff, L., Butrico, M., Da Silva, D.: Toward a Unified Ontology of Cloud Computing. In: Grid Computing Environments Workshop, GCE 2008, pp. 1–10 (2008)
4. Drungilas, D., Bielskis, A.A.: Cloud Interconnected Affect Reward based Automation Ambient Comfort Controller. Electronics and Electrical Engineering 18(10), 49–52 (2012)
5. Finn, A., Vredevoort, H., Lownds, P., Flynn, D.: Microsoft Private Cloud Computing Copyright © 2012 by John Wiley & Sons, Inc., Indianapolis, Indiana Published simultaneously in Canada (2012)
6. Alcaraz, C., Fernandez, G., Roman, R., Balastegui, A., Lopez, J.: Secure Management of SCADA Networks. New Trends in Network Management, CEPIS by Novática (ATI, Spain) 9(6), 22–28 (2008)
7. Yang, Y., McLaughlin, K., Littler, T., Sezer, S., Im, E.G., Yao, Z.Q., Pranggono, B., Wang, H.F.: Man-in-the-middle attack test-bed investigating cyber-security vulnerabilities in Smart Grid SCADA systems. In: International Conference on Sustainable Power Generation and Supply (SUPERGEN 2012), pp. 1–8 (2012)
8. Liguš, J., Zolotová, I., Karch, P., Ligušová, J.: Information and control system of traverse and its integration into cybernetic centre. Electronics and Electrical Engineering (6), 147–152 (2010)
9. Pavlík, M., Mihaľ, R., Laciňák, L., Zolotová, I.: Supervisory control and data acquisition systems in virtual architecture built via VMware vSphere platform. In: Recent Researches in Circuits and Systems: Proceedings of the 16th WSEAS International Conference on Circuits (part of CSCC 2012), Kos Island, Greece, pp. 389–393 (2012)
10. Petersen, K., Spreitzer, M., Terry, D., Theimer, B.M.: Replicated database services for world-wide applications. In: EW 7: Proceedings ofthe 7th Workshop on ACMSIGOPS European Workshop, pp. 275–280. ACM, New York (1996)
11. Davies, A.: High Availability MySQL Cookbook. Packt Publishing Ltd. (2010)

Key Performance Indicators Used as Measurement Parameter for Plant-Wide Feedback Loops

(Work in Progress)

Charlotta Johnsson

Department of Automatic Control
Lund University, Lund, Sweden
charlotta.johnsson@control.lth.se

Abstract. Feedback is a fundamental concept in automatic control. Feedback loops are used extensively in industrial applications today and there are work-procedures for designing traditional single parameter control loops. In the work procedure it is important to select control-parameters, manipulated parameters and control-strategies. A similar work-procedure could also be used for designing plant-wide control feedback loops. Key performance Indicators is thus an important concept since they can be used as control-parameters. In this paper an analogy between the single-loop and plant-wide approach is discussed, and key performance indicators from the new international standard ISO 22400 are presented.

Keywords: key performance indicators, plant-wide control, feedback loops.

1 Introduction

Feedback is a fundamental concept in automatic control. Feedback loops are used extensively in industrial applications today. The feedback loops are used to assure that the output signal is controlled so that its value approaches the value of the reference signal. In a traditional production plant within the process industry, there can be as many as 1000 feedback loops, each one controlling a single parameter such as a level, a concentration or a temperature. The most frequently used controller is the PID controller. There are methods describing the procedure to create feedback loops. The first step in this method is to select the control parameters (i.e. to think what parameter that should be controlled) and how this value should be measured (i.e. what should be used as measurement signal).

This paper examines how the concept of feedback loops could be used for plant wide control and how key performance indicators could be used as the equivalent to the measurement signal. The paper further gives examples of commonly used key performance indicators and it describes the work that is done within the international standard ISO 22400 [1] [2], currently under development. Further, the requirements for plant wide control are compared with the traditional concepts of automatic control and feedback loops. The first section of the paper describes traditional concepts of

B. Grabot et al. (Eds.): APMS 2014, Part III, IFIP AICT 440, pp. 91–99, 2014.
© IFIP International Federation for Information Processing 2014

automatic control and single parameter feedback loops, the second section discussed plant wide control. Thereafter a presentation of commonly used key performance indicators is given, and a discussion about the similarities of plant-wide control and traditional feedback loops is given. The final section contains the conclusions.

2   Single Parameter Feedback Loops

At production plants in the process industries there are many variables that need to be monitored and controlled. Feedback loops can be used to control these variables. Often, one feedback loops is used to control one variable, e.g. level, temperature or concentration. A feedback loops is shown in Figure 1.

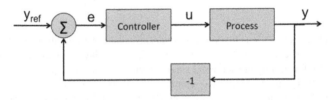

Fig. 1. Feedback loop

Important blocks in the feedback loops are:
- Process: The system that should be controlled, i.e. the system for which you would like to assure that the output is made equal to the reference signal.
- Controller: The task of the controller is to calculate a control signal $u(t)$ based on the control error $e(t)$ so that the output signal $y(t)$ approaches and eventually equals the reference signal $y_{sp}(t)$.

Important variables in the feedback loops are:
- Reference signal $y_{sp}(t)$: the reference signal is the desired value of the output signal $y(t)$.
- Control error $e(t)$:   the input to the controller is the control error $e(t)$, i.e. the difference between the reference signal $y_{sp}(t)$ and the output signal $y(t)$.
- Control signal $u(t)$: the output of the controller is the control signal $u(t)$, also refered to as the manipulated variable.
- Output signal $y(t)$: the output signal is the measured value of the output from the process.

The PID controller is by far the most commonly used controller in industry today. There are billions of control loops [3] and the PID controller is used for more than 95% of all control loops [4]. The PID controller concept is also taught in most intro-ductory automatic control courses, i.e. most control engineers are well aware of the basic principles of feedback. A common work-procedure used when designing traditional single parameter control loops is given in Table 1.

Table 1. Work procedure used when designing single-parameter control loops

Step	Activity
Step-1	select the control-parameter and the corresponding sensors i.e., select the variable that should be controlled (compare output signal) and select how it should be measured.
Step-2	select the manipulated-variable and the corresponding actuator, i.e. select the variable that should be used as control signal and select how it could be manipulated.
Step-3	construct the control loop, i.e. pair the manipulated-variable with the control-parameter.
Step-4	select the type of controller, tune the controller parameters and search for an optimal set-point.

At production plants in the process industries it is not uncommon to have as many as 1000-10000 variables and about 100-1000 feedback loop at each site. All variables are saved in an historical database. Each feedback loop is of importance for the performance of the plant, however, it is also of importance to get indications of the plant's overall performance. A dilemma is that the single control loops do not have their focus on the overall plant performance but rather on a local part of the plant.

3   Plant Wide Control

An enterprise, having one or more production sites could be structured in a hierarchical fashion. A hierarchy used for this purpose is presented in the international standard IEC 62264 [5] also known as [6], see Figure 2. The term production plant is not explicitly used in this hierarchy and is understood as either a production site or a production area.

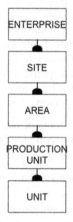

Fig. 2. The role based equipment hierarchy of IEC 62264 [5]

According to the role-based equipment hierarchy defined in IEC 62264 [5], an enterprise contains one or more sites, which in turn contains one or more production areas. Each production area has one or more production units and each production unit has one or more units, see Figure 2.

The enterprise determines which products to produce and at which site they should be produced. Sites are usually geographically grouped, and are used for rough-cut planning and scheduling. Areas are usually grouped by their geographic location and by their products. Each area produces one or more products, either end products for external sale or intermediates for further use by other areas at the site. Production units generally include all equipment required for a segment of continuous production. A production unit in the process industry could be e.g. a reactor or a distillation column. Units are composed of lower level elements, such as equipment modules, sensors and actuators [7]. At the unit level there might be several single parameter control loops, each one dedicated to control the performance of a single parameter, compare Figure 2. The single parameter control loops do not have their focus on the overall plant performance but rather on a local part of the plant.

Step 1 in the work-procedure for single parameter control loops (compare Table 1), is to select the control-parameter and its sensor. In many cases the control-parameter could be measured directly simply by placing a sensor at the correct place. When controlling a production-plant, the selection of a control-parameter might not be as trivial and it might not be possible to direclty, using a single sensor, measure the control-parameter. In many cases, the control-parameter corresponds to an indicator, i.e. a value that itself is calculated from one or many measures in the plant. These indicators are sometimes refered to as key performance indicators (KPIs).

Step 2 in the work-procedure for single parameter control loops (compare Table 1), is to select the manipulated-variable. In many cases the manipulated-variable could be modified simply by introducing an actuator at the correct place. When controlling a production-plant, the selection of a manipulated-variable might not be as trivial and it might not be possible to direclty, using a single actuator, modify the manipulated-variable.

Step 3 in the work-procedure for single parameter control loops (compare Table 1), is to construct the control loop, i.e. pair the manipulated-variable with the control-parameter. This concept seems reasonable to use also when dealing with plant wide control. Step 4 is to select the type of controller, tune the controller parameters and search for an optimal set-point (compare Table 1). This could be a hard task, however there are known structures for controllers (e.g. PID controller) and known tuning methods (e.g. Ziegler-Nichols or Step responses). When it comes to plant-wide control, this is not as obvious. Today, the correspondance of a plant-wide controller would be the human plant manager or a similar person.

The concept of plant-wide control, could be translated to the concept of classical feedback loops by making the following comparison, the concept is illustrated in Figure 3:

- Controller = plant manager or a similar person
- Process = the complete plant
- Reference signal = the business objective
- Control error = the difference between the business objective and the Key Perofrmance Indicator

- Control-signal = the action taken by the plant manager to assure that the performance of the plant (compare output signal) is approaching and eventually becomes equal to the business objective (compare reference signal).
- Output signal = the key performance indicator.

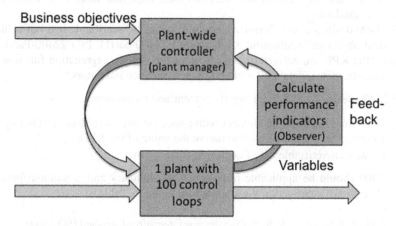

Fig. 3. Concept of plant-wide control

A possible work-procedure for plant-wide control is shown in Table 2.

Table 2. Work procedure used when designing plant-wide control loops

Step	Activity
Step-1	select the key performance indicator its corresponding definition i.e., select the indicator that should be controlled (compare output signal) and find out how it should be calculated.
Step-2	Select "manipulated-indicator" , i.e. understands what variables that should be manipulated in order to make a change in a key performance indicator in a desired direction.
Step-3	construct the control loop, i.e. pair the manipulated-indicator with the key-performance indicator.
Step-4	select the "plant-wide controller". This often corresponds to a human person. It is important to have decision support systems for this person, so that he or she can take good decisions. The decisions taken corresponds to the control-signal.

The development of the international standard ISO 22400 [1] [2] could be seen as an attempt to help defining good key performance indicators (compare good mearurement-variables).

4   Step1: Key Performance Indicators

ISO 22400 is an international standard currently under development. The title is "Key Performance indicators (KPIs) for Manufacturing Operations Management". This work was started in 2009 and the intent is to develop an international standard in 4 parts. ISO22400-Part1 and ISO22400-Part2 are in its final stage and about to be released as International standards.

ISO 22400 defines a Key Performance Indicator as "Quantifiable level of achieving a critical objective" (definition 3.1.4. in ISO 22400-part1). ISO 22400-Part1 [1] also states "the KPIs are derived directly from or through an aggregation function of, physical measurements, data and/or other key performance indicators."

ISO 22400 defines a KPI by giving its content and its context.

- Content: a quantifiable element with a specific unit of measure (including the formula that should be used to derive the value of the KPI).
- Context: a verifiable list of conditions that are met.

ISO 22400 should be applicable in both discrete industry and continuous/process industry. The 34 KPIs defined in the standard are listed in Table 3.

Table 3. A list of the 34 KPIs from the new international standard ISO 22400

Worker Efficiency	Production process ratio	Finished goods ratio
Allocation Ratio	Actual to planned scrap ratio	Integrated goods ratio
Throughput rate	First pass yield	Production loss ratio
Allocation efficiency	Scrap ratio	Storage and transportation loss ratio
Utilization efficiency	Rework ratio	Other loss ratio
Overall equipment effectiveness index	Fall off ratio	Equipment load ratio
Net equipment effectiveness index	Machine capability index	Mean operating time between failures
Availability	Critical machine capability index	Mean time to failure
Effectiveness	Process capability index	Mean time to restoration
Quality Ratio	Critical process capability index	Corrective maintenance ratio
Setup Rate	Comprehensive energy consumption	
Technical efficiency	Inventory turns	

The KPIs defined in ISO22400 are intended to be examples of the most frequently used KPIs in industry today, i.e. a palette of KPIs from which companies can select the one that best corresponds to their business objective. It is recognized that some of the KPIs are better suited for discrete industry and others are better suited for continuous/process industry.

Example: Availability and Utilization efficiency

Two of the 24 KPIs that are defined in ISO 22400-Part2 are Availability and Utilization Efficiency [2].

Availability is defined as the Actual-Production-Time (APT) divided by the Planned-Busy-Time (PBT).

- APT: Actual Production Time shall be the time during which a work unit is producing, It includes only the value adding functions.
- PBT: Planned Busy Time shall be the operating time minus the planned downtime.

Utilization Efficiency is defined as Actual-Production-Time (APT) divided by Actual-Unit-Busy-Time (AUBT).

- APT: Actual Production Time shall be the time during which a work unit is producing, It includes only the value adding functions.
- AUBT: Actual Unit Busy Time shall be the actual time that a work unit is used for the execution of a production order.

Availability is thus an indicator of how much of a plant's time that is used for production whereas Utilization efficiency is an indicator of how much of a plant's capacity is utilized. The two concepts are therefore not providing an indication of the same thing.

In discrete industry a machine and/or a plant is often used to its full capacity when it is used, however, it is not unusual that a machine and/or plant is simple waiting for a new job to be assigned. The concept of Availability is therefore frequently used in discrete industries. In continuous/process industry, a unit and/or a plant is often continuously, however it is sometimes used with reduced capacity. The concept of Utilization efficiency is therefore used in continuous industries.

In order to help making the calculations of Availability and Utilization Efficiency, as well as other KPIs, in a consistent way ISO 22400 also contains time models explaining how the measures used in the formulas should be achieved.

End-Example

The definition of KPIs will help finding good control-parameters in the work-procedure for plant-wide control (Compare step 1 in table 1 and table 2). There is currently nothing in ISO 22400 that has a clear linking to the succeeding steps in the work-procedure for plant-wide control. The work of defining key performance indicators will also be an answer to the industry-wide problem of having "poor visibility into plant operations" and to start utilizing "the hidden resource that data is known to be".

5   Industry Relevance

MESA has identified a company as a Business- Mover if the company has improved [8]:

- More than 10% on one or many of the financial metrics, or
- More than 1% on over half of the financial metrics.

MESA has further identified that the companies identified as Business-Movers:

- Have well identified Key Performance Indicators (KPIs),
- Have informed employees, and
- Use IT-systems to get measurements, calculate KPIs and display the results.

This stresses the fact that it is important for a company, interested in controlling and improving the performance of a plant, to understand what control-parameters they have access to (compare Step 1 in Table 1 and Table 2). Future research should also help identifying manipulated-indicators (compare Step-2 in table 1 and Table 2) and suitable control-actions.

6   Conclusion

Feedback is a fundamental concept in automatic control. Feedback loops are used extensively in industrial applications today and there are work-procedures for designing traditional single parameter control loops. In the work procedure it is important to select control-parameters, manipulated parameters and control-strategies. A similar work-procedure could also be used for designing plant-wide control feedback loops. The international standard ISO 22400 [1] [2] is helping defining commonly used Key Performance Indicators, these can be used as control-parameters. Future research also needs to focus on how the manipulated-parameters can be selected and how decision support systems can be used for selecting suitable plant wide control strategies.

Acknowledgment. The author C. Johnsson would like to thank the Vinnova-funded research environment LCCC in which environment the author participates, and the PIC-project founded by SSF, Sweden.

References

1. ISO/DIS-22400-1 (2013): "Key performance indicators for Manufacturing operations management - Part 1: Overview, Concepts and " International Standardization Organisation (ISO) (draft) (2013)
2. ISO/DIS-22400-2 (2013): Key performance indicators for Manufacturing operations management - Part 2: Definitions and descriptions. International Standardization Organisation (ISO) (draft) (2013)

3. Soltesz, K.: On automation of the PID tuning procedure. Licentiate Thesis ISRN LUTFD2/TFRT–3254–SE, Department of Automatic Control, Lund University, Sweden (2012)
4. Åström, K., Murray, R.: Feedback Systems: An Introduction for Scientists and Engineers. Princeton University Press, Princeton and Oxford (2012), http://www.cds.caltech.edu/~murray/amwiki
5. IEC 62264: Enterprise-Control System Integration, Part 1 Models and terminology. International Elechtrotechnical Commission (IEC) (2003)
6. ISA-95.00.01 (2009): Enterprise-Control System Integration, Part 1: Models and Terminology. International Society of Automation (ISA) (2009)
7. Lindholm, A., Johnsson, C.: A tool for utility disturbance management. presented at INCOM 2012 (2012)
8. MESA (2006): "Metrics that Matters", Manufacturing Enterprise Solutions Association (MESA), report of (2006)

Focusing Early Phases in Production System Design

Carin Rösiö and Jessica Bruch

Mälardalen University, School of Innovation, Design and Engineering, Eskilstuna, Sweden
{Carin.rosio,Jessica.bruch}@mdh.se

Abstract. It is a well-known fact that it is in the early phases of production system design where the most important decisions are made. If the production system is not designed in a proper way, this will eventually end up with disturbances and problems during serial production and it is in the early phases the potential to influence is greatest. The purpose with this paper is therefore to describe how to work and what activities to focus on in early phases of production system design by proposing a structured production system design model focusing on the early phases which can be applied by practitioners and academics. Six production system design projects were studied in three real-time case studies and three retrospective case studies. Combined with literature studies a production system design model is developed describing the initial phases of initiation, project definition and concept including activities and decision points.

Keywords: Production system design, manufacturing industry, early phases

1 Introduction

There is an increasing need for efficient production system design due to the fact that manufacturing companies must be able to handle issues such as increasing individualization of customer demands, fluctuating consumption and permanent pressure on product cost and quality [1]. European manufacturing companies have a high standard and a strong position in industrial engineering with innovative and customized product solutions, however, they lose market shares in mass production [2]. Attractive product solutions are not enough, a successful production activity is also required in order to be competitive. The potential of an effective production system design process is often not prioritized enough in manufacturing companies even though it is shown that a number of competitive advantages can be achieved such as fast ramp up, shorter time to market, robust production systems, increased market shares, higher customer acceptance, improved levels of output and increased efficiency [3]. Although manufacturing companies have started to focus on production system design, many find it difficult to coordinate the production system design process and work in a structured and systematic way [4, 5]. There are numerous explanations for the difficulties in production system design. It has been argued for example that the nature of the production system design process is not well defined, i.e. there are many different definitions and interpretations of the process and work activities involved [6]. Part of the reason is that companies have focused on the product development because they

B. Grabot et al. (Eds.): APMS 2014, Part III, IFIP AICT 440, pp. 100–107, 2014.
© IFIP International Federation for Information Processing 2014

saw it as a way to achieve competitive advantages, while the production system development process is seldom seen as a means to achieve the best possible production system [7]. Thus, although the term development process is well known in manufacturing companies, it is usually applied in the product development and not in the production system required to produce the products. It is, however, important to note that the design of production systems is both a technically challenging and organisationally complex activity on its own right, and the context where it operates is more multifaceted than is commonly described in the simultaneous-engineering literature [8]. As a result, the design of production systems needs to trigger separate control and coordination of the specific set of activities required to move the project through the development process from idea to detailed design.

Overall, it can be concluded that the design of production systems is challenging but previous research provides only limited insights and guidance for managers into how those challenges can be handled. Recent studies in the area of production system design confirm that production system development generally takes place rather ad hoc and without having a long term plan [9, 10]. The potential of gaining a competitive edge by improving the way the production system is designed is hence ignored. It is a clearly shown that it is in the early phases of production system design where the most important decisions are made. If the production system is not designed in a proper way, this will eventually end up with disturbances and problems during serial production. The result is evidently low capacity utilization, high production cost and hence low profitability. The more resources that are established early in the process, the more opportunities there are to influence the production system design [11]. The purpose with this paper is therefore to describe how to work and what activities to focus on in early phases of production system design by proposing a structured production system design model focusing on the early phases which can be applied by practitioners and academics. The results presented in this paper is a step towards a formalized production system design model offering improved understanding of how the design of production systems can be improved.

2   Frame of Reference

To succeed in production system design, dedication is required as well as a shift in attention from the operations phase to the under-utilized potential of the design of production systems. Although earlier research has contributed to improved knowledge about production system design and development [e.g. 11, 12, 13-16] there is still no agreement on the approaches to use in industry. When summarizing the approaches described in literature a number of stages and activities could be distinguished, Figure 1 where the design process should be considered as an iterative, cyclic process affected in its execution by each project context [13]. In a production system design process the problem is normally defined in an initial stage, where the project is initiated and defined in terms of e.g. project leader, budget, and time plan. Thereafter, an analysis of the background including present as well as future production systems and products including market research and environmental requirements is made. Based on this, objectives for the production system are formulated. The detailed design subsequently includes first designing conceptual production system alternatives. These early phases are focused on in this paper. The alternatives are thereafter evaluated in order to choose one final solution. The chosen production system is finally designed in detail.

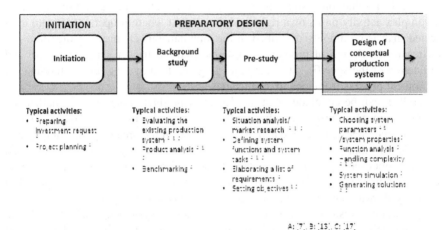

Fig. 1. Typical activities carried out in early phases of production system design

The production system design process can be considered as a part of the new product development process. Prior research on product development best practices highlights that successful projects follow a formalized and structured cross-functional stage-gate model for the product development process [17]. A structured and systematic production system design process should tell what should be done and when, what techniques and tools will be needed at each stage, what information needs to be collected, and what the output or result of each stage would be [18]. A framework should include both prescriptive and explanatory elements. While the prescriptive elements assist practitioners to carry out activities in a certain way, the explanatory elements refer to how things are perceived [19]. A framework useful for practitioners should consist of a number of logically sequential steps that support a structured work approach to the decision making process [19]. A useful framework need also to be simple to be widely used by engineers, efficient with minimum trial-and-error actions and versatile to be applicable in different situations [20]. Based on the summarized phases and activities in Figure 1. these requirements are inadequately met. A study evaluating the usability of the structured production system design process proposed by Bellgran and Säfsten [7] showed that the usage leads to increased learnability, efficiency, effectiveness, and satisfaction [21] and the contribution was largest in the early phases of the production system design process by putting emphasis on the planning and providing a structure to follow. Thus, focus on early phases is consequently crucial and worth to be highlighted.

3   Research Methodology

Data was collected by the case study methodology [22] where each case represented a production system design project. The cases had an embedded design where the project was studied and the embedded unit of analysis was the production system design process including both the actual process and the documented models that were used. All cases were selected based on theoretical sampling with the goal of extending the emergent theory [23]. Six production system design projects were studied in three real-time case studies and three retrospective case studies at four different large global manufacturing companies. All interviews were recorded and transcribed. To enhance validity, real-time studies were combined with retrospective studies [24]. Through real-time studies post-rationalization was avoided, thus increasing internal validity. Data was gathered by semi-structured interviews, observations and document studies [22], Table 1.

Table 1. Information of case studies

Case study	Type and Duration	Data Collection Techniques	No interviews (single/group) Duration [min]
Case A	Real time	Observations, Documentations Interviews	Face to face, 10 (10/0), 40-90
Case B	Retrospective	Documentation, Interviews	Face to face, 2 (1/1) 65-76
Case C	Retrospective	Interviews	Face to face, 3 (3/0) 63-72
Case D	Retrospective	Observations, Documentations Interviews	Face to face, 6 (6/0) 46-85
Case E	Real time	Observations, Documentations Interviews	Face to face, 8 (8/0) 30-80
Case F	Real time	Observations, Documentations Interviews	Face to face, 7 (7/0) 45-107, Telephone, 1 (0/1), 72

Before the study started the research design was carefully described and discussed with the representatives of the company. The role of the researcher varied due to the combination of real-time and retrospective studies. In case study A, E, and F one of the researchers was present at the site during one-three months to follow the production system design project. Observations were made at production system design meetings and daily contact was maintained with the production system design team. Before and after the visit at the site, contact was kept with key persons in the production system design team. As an initial activity in all the case studies, semi-structured interviews were carried out based on an interview guide which was sent to the respondents beforehand. Respondents involved in the production system design projects were identified at different levels in the organization, such as vice president R&D, strategic operations managers, operations managers, project managers, industrial engineers, and production engineers. Before an interview started, the terminology used was presented to the respondents in order to avoid misunderstandings. All initial interviews were recorded and transcribed. After the interviews were conducted relevant documentation was collected, such as project management models, production system design support, support for requirement specifications, and checklists and support used by individuals, all of which were made fully available. In all cases an on-going dialogue was held with involved key persons until rich descriptions of the single cases were achieved [22]. Observations were carried out including attendance on project meetings and development activities in the project as well as at one meeting with the system supplier. Field notes were carefully written through the whole case study [22], by which all activities were documented concerning what activity was done, how it was done, when it was done, and what people were involved.

4   Empirical Findings

The case studies showed that the production systems were designed according to structured stage-gate models including seven stages or phases including (1) initiation, (2) project definition/pre-study, (3) concept study, (4) detailed design and final development, (5) implementation/industrialization and commercialization, (6) follow-up/launch, and (7) disposal. The models used were mainly focused on product design but did also include a few activities related to the design of production systems. However, the process gave limited support to production system design. None of the stage-gate models in the cases included all activities that needed to be carried out when designing the production system. In addition to the stage-gate models additional support was used. This support was either individual or used by whole organizations. Individual support included e.g. individual checklists that consisted of important issues to remember throughout the production system design process and were used by the production engineers. Support more widely used often included models for requirement specifications. Several of the design activities were undertaken based on the production engineers' skills. In all cases except Case A the projects were carried out by a project leader derived from product design. In Case A the project had two equal project leaders, one responsible for product design and the other one responsible for the industrialization including all activities related to production system design. In the cases were the project leader derived from product design there was a strong focus on product design related issues. In all projects a knowledge existed that production system design should be integrated with product design and the production engineers were part of the project team from the early start to have the possibility to affect the product design. However, product design engineers were not required to give feedback to the production system concept. In reality production engineering was not represented in the initial two phases, i.e. initiation and project definition for the overall new product development project.

Several of the projects that were studied had a lack of in-house competence in design of production systems, i.e. there were few production engineers or industrial engineers. Further, the production system engineer's often prioritized problems occurred in the running production. The production engineer normally had the main part of the responsibility and did not work in a group of diverse competences as in the product development teams. This resulted in less priory on production system design activities that were not absolutely necessary to do in that point of time. To strengthen production system design competence, external equipment suppliers were often used for production system design. The external equipment suppliers were involved in the concept study or the detailed design. This often resulted in a lack of long term view, a system not clearly founded in the manufacturing strategy and a lack of knowledge among the production personnel after system implementation.

5   Production System Design Model

As described in literature a design process should tell what should be done and when, what techniques and tools will be needed at each stage, what information needs to be collected, and what the output or result of each stage would be [18]. Based on empirical and theoretical data a production system design model is proposed. An overview of the proposed model is described in Figure 2.

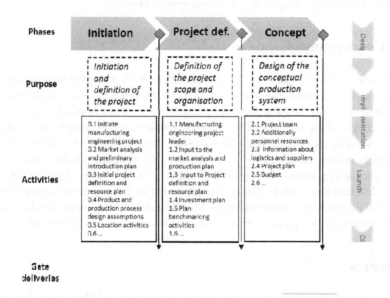

Fig. 2. Production system design model describing the earlier phases

In the initiation phase the project should is initiated and clearly defined by either the manufacturing engineering department (rationalization, replacement, quality, safety, environment etc.), the product development projects (new or changed products), or by the strategy board (Capacity, insourcing etc.). After the project is initiated the project scope and the organization should be defined. Projects conducted by project leaders derived from product design where production system design was not equal [9, 10] was a tendency showed in the case studies. The fact that there often was a lack of production engineers and the running production was prioritized instead of production system development [9, 10] was also obvious. To compete with production and in order to successfully design production systems it is crucial to create a project organization with all necessary competences early in the project. It was found successful to have a project leader responsible for production system design who is equal to the project leader responsible for product design to create a balance between product development and production system development. Time and resources are needed in order to focus on production system design and work in a cross functional team. In this phase commission directive should also be formulated and signed by steering committee which include scope, demand and goals of the manufacturing engineering project.

The conceptual design is a crucial project phase for the production system since in the early phases the decision space is often large while the cost for changes is low [11]. To put effort on the conceptual design and the requirement specification will keep the overall costs down in the long run. Based on commission directive the preliminary concept is formulated in details including e.g. time plan, layout, budget, and capacity and machine utilization. This ends up in a concept study report including all information needed to design the production system in detail.

6   Conclusions

The purpose with this paper was to describe how to work and what activities to focus in early phases of production system design by proposing a structured production system design model focusing the early phases which can be applied by practitioners and academics. There is a lack of focus on production system design and projects are mainly owned by as well as focused on product design. Based on a detailed production system design model activities were specified resulting in the concept study report. The design model should be used as a complement to already established product development models. The results presented in this paper was a step toward a formalized production system design model offering improved understanding of production systems design process including how it is carried out, who is involved, etc.

References

1. Wiendahl, H.-P., Heger, C.L.: Justifying Changeability: A Methodical Approach to Achieving Cost Effectiveness. International Journal for Manufacturing Science and Production 6(1-2), 33–39 (2004)
2. Westkämper, E.: New Trends in Production. In: Dashchenko, A.I. (ed.) Reconfigurable Manufacturing Systems and Transformable Factories, pp. 15–26. Springer, Heidelberg (2006)
3. Hayes, R., et al.: Operations, Strategy, and Technology: Pursuing the Competitive Edge. Strategic Direction. John Wiley & Sons, Hoboken (2005)
4. Bruch, J., Bellgran, M.: Characteristics affecting management of design information in the production system design process. International Journal of Production Research 51(11), 3241–3251 (2013)

5. Rösiö, C., Säfsten, K.: Reconfigurable Production System Design - theoretical and practical challenges. Journal of Manufacturing Technology Management 24(7) (2013)
6. Cochran, D.S., et al.: A decomposition approach for manufacturing system design. Journal of Manufacturing Systems 20(6), 371–389 (2001-2002)
7. Bellgran, M., Säfsten, K.: Production Development: Design and Operation of Production Systems. Springer, London (2010)
8. Pisano, G.P.: The Development Factory: Unlocking the Potential of Process Innovation. Harvard Business Review Press, Boston (1997)
9. Bruch, J.: Management of Design Information in the Production System Design Process. In: School of Innovation Design and Engineering, Mälardalens University (2012)
10. Rösiö, C.: Supporting the Design of Reconfigurable Production Systems. In: School of Innovation Design and Engineering, Mälardalen University (2012)
11. Blanchard, B.S., Fabrycky, W.J.: Systems Engineering and Analysis, 3rd edn. Prentice-Hall, Inc., Upper Saddle River (1998)
12. Bennett, D.J., Forrester, P.L.: Market-Focused Production Systems: Design and Implementation. Prentice Hall International, Hemel Hempstead (1993)
13. Wu, B.: Manufacturing Systems Design and Analysis: Context and techniques, 2nd edn. Chapman & Hall, London (1994)
14. Bellgran, M.: Systematic Design of Assembly Systems: Preconditions and Design Process Planning. In: Department of Mechanical Engineering. Linköping University, Linköping (1998)
15. Kulak, O., Durmusoglu, M.B., Tufekci, S.: A complete cellular manufacturing system design methodology based on axiomatic design principles. Computers and Industrial Engineering 48(4), 765–787 (2005)
16. Rampersad, H.K.: Integrated and Simultaneous Design for Robotic Assembly. Wiley Series in Product Development: Planning, Designing, Engineering. In: Cross, N., Roozenburg, N. (eds.). John Wiley & Sons, Nwe York (1994)
17. Griffin, A.: PDMA Research on New Product Development Practices: Updating Trends and Benchmarking Best Practices. Journal of Product Innovation Management 14(6), 429–458 (1997)
18. Love, D.: The design of manufacturing systems. In: Warner, M. (ed.) International Encyclopedia of Business and Management, pp. 3154–3174. International Thomson Business Press, London (1996)
19. McIvor, R.: A practical framework for understanding the outsourcing process. Supply Chain Management: An International Journal 5(1), 22–36 (2000)
20. Houshmand, M., Jamshidnezhad, B.: An extended model of design process of lean production systems by means of process variables. Robotics and Computer-Integrated Manufacturing 22(1), 1–16 (2006)
21. Arnesson, F., Bengtsson, J.: Usability Evaluation of a Production System Development Framework. In: School of Engineering 2012. Jönköping University, Jönköping (2012)
22. Yin, R.K.: Case Study Research: Design and Methods, 4th edn. SAGE, Thousands Oaks (2009)
23. Eisenhardt, K.M.: Building Theories from Case Study Research. Academy of Management Review 14(4), 532–550 (1989)
24. Leonard-Barton, D.: A Dual Methodology for Case Studies: Synergistic Use of a Longitudinal Single Site with Replicated Multiple Sites. Organization Science 1(3), 248–266 (1990)

Global and Regional Production Networks:
A Theoretical and Practical Synthesis

Farhad Norouzilame[1,*], Robert Moch[2], Ralph Riedel[2], and Jessica Bruch[1]

[1] Mälardalen University, Department of Product Realization, Eskilstuna, Sweden
{farhad.norouzilame,jessica.bruch}@mdh.se
[2] Chemnitz University of Technology, Department of Factory Planning and Factory
Management, Chemnitz, Germany
{robert.moch,ralph.riedel}@mb.tu-chemnitz.de

Abstract. The growth of research interest in networked production has brought up numerous important concepts aimed at production networks. Still the actual research object seems to be ambiguous, making the exact application of findings insufficient. It appears that there are two main notions of the term Production Network. The first meaning is derived by a single versus a multi-organizational perspective while the second meaning comes from a regional versus global view. Obviously indistinctness exists in this field of research and clarification of terms and concept is required. The objective of this paper is to give an overview of the existing theories in accordance with the industrial practice providing a model to bridge the academic theories to industrial practice.

Keywords: production network, literature review, case study.

1   Introduction

The affects of globalization on manufacturing is indisputable. The fragmentation of production processes and the international dispersion of tasks and activities within them have led to the emergence of borderless production systems in shape of sequential chains or complex networks commonly referred to as global value chains [1]. Most middle sized and large companies are now creating an international market and have to build and/or manage an international network of operations either due to their organic growth or via M&A activities [2]. The rationale behind such action lies principally within three main categories; (1) access to low-cost production, (2) access to skills and knowledge, and (3) proximity to market [3]. Multinational companies strive to acquire, create, and use technological assets across national borders [4].

The mentioned factors and the growth of developing economies in the world have accelerated the trend of moving from stand-alone factories toward more globalized production. The management of international networks remains an under researched area [2], and networked production of multiple organizations is also moving into focus of research [5]. To improve the competiveness of firms, not only the global

---

* Corresponding author.

B. Grabot et al. (Eds.): APMS 2014, Part III, IFIP AICT 440, pp. 108–115, 2014.

production network of one enterprise but also the interplay of locally linked production of buyers and suppliers gains importance. These inter-organizational relations are not only spotted by the discipline of Supply Chain Management which discusses global versus domestic concepts without specifying their view on very production-intrinsic challenges [6].

This paper provides an overall understanding of the *production network* concept by presenting a brief summary of the related literature along with two cases as real-life implications. The paper opens up with the introduction to the topic followed by the research methodology. Later on, some concepts are elaborated in details under reference framework section. Finally, the findings and conclusions are presented.

2   Research Method

The methodology used in this study is a combination of literature review and a multiple case study. The literature review is based on searching the keywords *production, manufacturing, network, global, international and* the German equivalent words along with combination of those terms on the databases *Science Direct, Scopus, Elsevier, and SpringerLink* via different search engines. Totally about 200 articles have been analyzed in the first phase further reduced to 18 directly related to the topic of *production networks* which are referred to in Table-1. The case study approach is chosen since it allowed an in-depth study of the phenomenon in its real-world context plus conformity to answer the *how* and *why* questions [7]. Case-A is a global manufacturing company headquartered in Sweden with total number employees of approximately 1250 with eleven production sites in six different countries, four of them located in BRIC countries. The core business of the company is the production of mechanical and electromechanical solutions for commercial vehicles, construction and mining industries, and general industry. Case-B is a network of seven companies including eight plants in total located in Germany. Six of the companies are SMEs; the other is a large company. The network's focus is to produce gearboxes for energy industry. 14 semi-structured interviews have been performed in total which of 10 were conducted at Case-A and four at Case-B.

2.1   Global Production Network and Regional Production Network

Global Production Networks (GPNs) and Global Value Chains (GVCs) are two schools of Globalization studies, with their roots on Global Commodity Chains (GCCs) having some common works, as well as some differences on concepts and focus [8]. A global production network is a manufacturing network i.e. a network consisting of wholly owned factories, i.e. belonging to the same company [9] on a global scale.

A regional Production Network (RPN) is a cooperation of geographically close companies to produce a certain product. The RPN can be developed by an addressable strategic network or is formed through latent informal network structures of manufacturing enterprises [10, 11]. As long as the production cooperation is carried out, this temporary network exists. Depending on its product portfolio, an enterprise can be part of more than one RPN.

2.2   Supply Chain Management and Networked Production

Within business studies, networked value-adding processes are focused by the field of SCM which aims to establish standard measurements, functions and reference models to analyse, describe and manage networked processes. This approach is not restricted to production and manufacturing, it is also involving e.g. marketing, resellers and distributors [6]. Besides *Business Studies* discipline, there are also approaches within the *Mechanical Engineering* and *Production Management* field. One general approach describes the formation of *Production Networks* as "cross-company cooperation" and clearly differentiates between Production Networks and Supply Chains [12]. Another concept within the discipline of mechanical engineering to describe, explain and manage networked production of different enterprises is the *competence-cell-based network* approach. Among others [11] and [13] contribute to this concept mainly aiming SME networks. Furthermore an inter-organizational process model for networked production is the *Extended Aachener PPS-Model* – production planning and control model of the RWTH Aachen University [14]. Completing these ideas of inter-organizational production networks, the concept of *Strategic Production Network* is also defined as cooperation of different enterprises [15, 16].

3   Findings

3.1   Literature Findings

To identify certain concepts and clarify their attributes, two main characteristics were ascertained based on literature study. The first characteristic is *ownership* of a network i.e. having one or multiple owners. The second characteristic is called *geographical reach*, which describes the range of the concept from regional to global scale. The summary of the findings are shown in table 1.

Table 1. Classification *of the literature review summary*

Literature	Ownership	Geographical reach
[11], [13], [16], [17], [18], [19]	multiple-owner	regional/local
[12], [14], [15]	multiple-owner	regional/global
[3], [20], [21], [22], [23], [24]	single owner	global
[25]	N/A	regional/national/global
[26], [27]	N/A	global

Based on the literature study, two major streams and interpretations of the term *production network* appear. One stream leans toward to the concept of GPN owned by one organisation and being led globally. The other stream refers to the RPN concept consisting of different companies with different ownership managed in a mutual manner on the basis of certain regional closeness and production dependency.

3.2   Reflections from the Case Studies

Networks on a Global Level

Global production networks are supposed as fully owned factories branding the mother company which are able to supply the customers with locally-produced products but to a global standard of quality. They provide some advantages beside the challenges mainly due to the global environment summarized in table 2. One example of such networks is demonstrated in figure-1 along with one global customer in order to depict the structure of such networks.

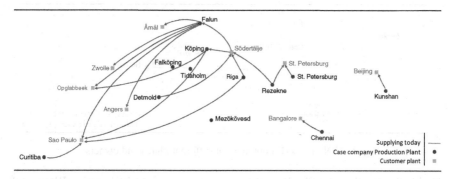

Fig. 1. GPN of the case-A along with a major global customer's plants

Foreign-exchange rate variations affect the development of costs and consequently the global production network. From the global profitability prospective, companies have to make sure that over time, the investments pay off otherwise they might be urged to move the business to other locations.

Local cost of capital interest rates in one hand is the value of the local currency; on the other hand is the inflation and interest rate cost. This must be considered as it could affect the production costs in the respective country.

Understanding the global customers' strategy: by knowing about the end-customers' demands, production companies (especially contract manufacturers) could see the trend and the increase/decrease in the volume.

Culture: despite having a global standard to run production, the local culture will be a part of the "total". So, it must be initially defined how much of the core values of the mother company could be implemented locally. Apparently, there would always be a sort of local variants due to the local culture. Thus, it would be useful to have resources, people in specific, to carry the core values of the mother company.

Local legislations and regulations such as import/export regulations or the salary system in certain countries have great impacts on GPNs.

Custom duties This is also affecting as the duties could affect the network especially when it comes to importing equipments and machinery to the host country.

Global managers who travel around the system are required to make sure that the plants continue over time to maintain the core values of the mother company and not inventing their customized system.

Networks on Regional Level

RPNs which are comprised of SMEs, continuously struggle with their production costs due to not having the potential to decrease it through mass production. Furthermore, relevant production steps on the network are distributed among diverse partners, thus, planning, controlling and coordinating the processes becomes intricate. Beside, SMEs involved in RPNs strongly depend on network partners' quality and delivery performance. They also face too much logistic processes and the challenge of integrating IT solutions to all network partners for managing the information flow.

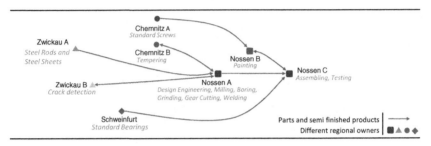

Fig. 2. RPN of case-B contained of different plants and owners

Beside the mentioned difficulties, there are advantages of SMEs within RPNs such as the capability to co-develop with the customers in a one-to-one manner because of the regional closeness and manageable number. This leads to sophisticated products, with exact fulfillment of functions and quality. Furthermore, an individual project management from the design stage to service can be realized. Additionally the production processes become flexible by adjusting the production system by means of changing the cooperating partners (Figure-2). The challenges and opportunities of the two types of production networks are summarized in table-2 resulted from the interviews performed in both case companies.

Table 2. The challenges and opportunities concerning RPN and GPN

	Challenges	Opportunities
Global Production Network (Single-owner)	Foreign-exchange rates (Currencies)	Using the global redundancy for achieving volume flexibility
	Local cost of capital interest rates	
	Understanding the global customers' strategy	Competence transfer reduces R&D costs on development and minimize risk
	Culture	Global sourcing perspective achieved by global footprint
	Local legislations and regulations	
	Custom duties (toll)	Economy of scale due to the glocal presence
	Global managers (people)	One production system within the whole network
		Local presence gives easier logistics for local market

Table 2. (*Continued.*)

Regional Production Network (Multiple-owner)	Higher production costs Intricate coordination of required production steps within supply chain / production network Dependency on network partners quality and delivery reliability High amount of logistic processes Difficult to apply inter-organizational IT standards for cooperation partners	Sophisticated product development with possibility to generate individual product functions and variations due to closeness to customers Exact quality accordance to customers' requirements and individual project management due to a lower amount of customers compared to larger companies Flexible adjustment of production to market needs due to changeability of cooperation partners

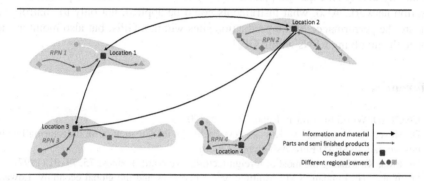

Fig. 3. Proposed model synthesizing GPN and RPN concepts

4   Conclusion

The article presents two main streams of interpretation out of the term Production Network which are found in literature and also represented by two cases. Figure 3 sums up both concepts in one theoretical model linking global and regional production networks with our given definitions.

Regarding this model a scenario could be supposed; an enterprise in one location and an existing regional network decides to start a new production site in another country. Starting the business in a new location triggers the formation of a new regional production network to produce the desired product. Therefore, concerning the terms regional and global, two questions arise; (1) how large a "region" could be? And (2) how small "global" could be?

There should be no difference in the concept of RPN even if some suppliers are not located within a certain geographical region. Also if new locations of one company spread only over one continent, the concept of GPN would still apply. Therefore, the naming of those two concepts can be misleading and can cause confusion as well. However, the naming of those concepts which points out their actual structure will facilitate further research within this discipline. For future work the dependence of those concepts on geographical location should be reconsidered.

Defining the boundaries for the usage of the term "region" and "global" can affect the definition of those concepts. Thus, we suggest keeping the boundaries of the region and global open and not limited it to the geographical borders whether a country or a continent, but still having a directing definition:

RPNs are comprised of multiple production plants in a specific geographical area with certain closeness shaped by different owners with a common product. GPNs are entirely owned production plants spread over a certain reach of distance to capture foreign markets.

Enterprises should be aware of the usage of those concepts to apply research findings concerning their own interests and objectives. Besides, there are a lot of potentials in linking the concepts of RPN and GPN. This can support enterprises with their important decision making processes, for instance when starting a new production facility during an expansion phase to be able to start an effective production cooperation network. Also, what instruments could be applied, not only to control and compare the performance of the production sites within a GPN, but also monitor and manage the involving RPNs within GPN.

References

1. UNCTAD, World Investment Report, Geneva (2013)
2. De Meyer, A., Vereecke, A.: Key Success Factors in the Creation of Manufacturing Facilities Abroad. INSEAD Euro-Asia Centre (2000)
3. Ferdows, K.: Making the most of foreign factories. Harvard Business 75, 73–91 (1997)
4. Dunning, J.H., Lundan, S.M.: Multinational enterprises and the global economy. Edward Elgar Publishing (2008)
5. Hayes, R.H.: Pom Forum: Operations Management's Next Source of Galvanizing Energy? Production and Operations Management 17(6), 567–572 (2008)
6. Harrison, T.P.: Principles for the Strategic Design of Supply Chains. In: The Practice of Supply Chain Management: Where Theory and Application Converge, pp. 3–12. Springer US (2004)
7. Yin, R.K.: Case study research: Design and methods, vol. 5. Sage (2009)
8. Sakuda, L.O.F.: Afonso Global value chains, global production networks: towards global netChains synthesis? In: Capturing Value in International Manufacturing and Supply Networks. Institute for Manufacturing, Cambridge (2012)
9. Feldmann, A.: A strategic perspective on plants in manufacturing networks. In: Production Economics. Linköping Universitet, Sweden (2011)
10. Moch, R., Riedel, R., Müller, E.: Key Success Factors for Production Network Coordination. In: Zaeh, M.F. (ed.) Enabling Manufacturing Competitiveness and Economic Sustainability, pp. 327–332. Springer International Publishing (2014)
11. Müller, E.: Production planning and operation in competence-cell-based networks. Production Planning & Control 17(2), 99–112 (2006)
12. Wiendahl, H.-P., Lutz, S.: Management of variable production networks. In: Strategic Production Networks, pp. 368–388. Springer (2002)
13. Zimmermann, M., et al.: An approach for the quantitative consideration of soft-facts for planning and controlling networked production structures. Production Planning & Control 17(2), 189–201 (2006)

14. Schuh, G., Stich, V.: Gestaltung der überbetrieblichen Produktionsplanung und -steuerung. In: Schuh, G., Stich, V. (eds.) Produktionsplanung und -steuerung 2, pp. 9–148. Springer, Heidelberg (2012)
15. Possel-Doelken, F., Zheng, L., Tang, D.: Cooperation Between Production Companies. In: Strategic Production Networks, Springer, Heidelberg (2002)
16. Wirth, S., Baumann, A.: Innovative Unternehmens-und Produktionsnetze. Wissenschaftliche Schriftenreihe H (August 1998)
17. Baum, H., Schütze, J.: A Model of Collaborative Enterprise Networks. Procedia CIRP 3, 549–554 (2012)
18. Baumann, A.: Kompetenzzellenbasierte regionale Produktionsnetze. Diplomarbeiten Agentur (2003)
19. Monauni, M., Foschiani, S.: Agility Enablers in Manufacturing Systems - Contributions of the Production Network Perspective. In: Zaeh, M.F. (ed.) Enabling Manufacturing Competitiveness and Economic Sustainability, pp. 333–337. Springer International Publishing (2014)
20. Shi, Y., Gregory, M.: International manufacturing networks—to develop global competitive capabilities. Journal of Operations Management 16(2), 195–214 (1998)
21. Bartlett, C.A., Ghoshal, S.: Managing across borders: The transnational solution, vol. 2. Taylor & Francis (1999)
22. Vereecke, A., Van Dierdonck, R.: The strategic role of the plant: testing Ferdows's model. International Journal of Operations & Production Management 22(5), 492–514 (2002)
23. Ernst, D.: Global production networks and the changing geography of innovation systems. Implications for developing countries. Economics of Innovation and New Technology 11(6), 497–523 (2002)
24. Maritan, C.A., Brush, T.H., Karnani, A.G.: Plant roles and decision autonomy in multinational plant networks. Journal of Operations Management 22(5), 489–503 (2004)
25. Henderson, J., et al.: Global production networks and the analysis of economic development. Review of International Political Economy 9(3), 436–464 (2002)
26. Vereecke, A., Van Dierdonck, R., De Meyer, A.: A typology of plants in global manufacturing networks. Management Science 52(11), 1737–1750 (2006)
27. Levy, D.L.: Political contestation in global production networks. Academy of Management Review 33(4), 943–963 (2008)

An Engineer-To-Order Mass Customization Development Framework

Jacob Bossen, Michael Natapon Hansson, Ole Madsen,
Kjeld Nielsen, and Thomas Ditlev Brunø

Department of Mechanical and Manufacturing Engineering, Aalborg University, Denmark
jacobbossen@gmail.com

Abstract. Developers of automated manufacturing systems are often catego-
rised as Engineer-To-Order companies, relying on the ability to offer solutions
that are tailored to the individual consumer. Managing product variety and enabling reusability between solutions becomes key concepts towards increasing
competitiveness and revenue, in which Engineer-To-Order companies may
benefit from adopting Mass Customization concepts. As automated manufacturing systems tends to be software intensive, it become equally important to enable reusability for physical components and for software related artefacts. In
parallel to Mass Customization, Software Product Line Engineering has
emerged as a way for software developers to manage variability and reusability.
This paper seeks to combine the concepts of Mass Customization and Software
Product Line Engineering, by introducing a development framework applicable
for Engineer-To-Order companies offering automated manufacturing systems.

Keywords: Mass Customization, Software Product Line Engineering,
Engineer-To-Order, Software Intensive Manufacturing Systems.

1   Introduction

According to the manifesto presented at the latest MCPC conference in Aalborg, Denmark: ``the era of Mass Production is over" [13]. This is a widely supported statement,
and Kumar [10] even emphasises it further by stating that companies will be struggling
for survival, if they do not adapt their strategy to the structural changes in markets. The
major structural changes is – in this context – the demand for shorter time-to-market,
increased product variety and reduced cost. With regards to manufacturing, the increasing demand for product variety will force a definitive shift in the manufacturing paradigm from Mass Production (economy of scale) towards Mass Customization (economy of scope) and Mass Personalisation (value differentiation) [6].

Products from traditional Engineer-To-Order businesses (ETOs) are similar to products from the pre-Mass Production paradigm, where each product was tailored to the
individual customer. The production methods have been developed since, but in principle, they still suffer under the labour intensive work compared to other product types.
For high wage countries, the ETO products are hence cost expensive to produce, since
a lot of resources must be allocated to the engineering related aspects of production,
and keeps the ETO businesses under a rising pressure in a global competitive market.

B. Grabot et al. (Eds.): APMS 2014, Part III, IFIP AICT 440, pp. 116–123, 2014.
© IFIP International Federation for Information Processing 2014

This has triggered some of the ETOs to standardise their engineering work, and either offer less variety, or instead offer variety in a Mass Customization approach. By offering less product variety, the ETO is though compromising with their business foundation.

This paper is based on a case of a Danish manufacturing systems developer, who offer fully automated robotic solutions for surface treatment. To cope with their customers' high demand for product variety, the company offers completely tailored and high technology solutions that are cost expensive with regards to development time. The company has until now been first movers with regards to technology, but the cost expensive development creates a rising competitive environment, as competitors catch up with the technology. The issue of obtaining a more cost effective development process – while still being able to offer similar product variety as they do currently – is in many ways similar to, what moves companies in other domain towards Mass Customization and Mass Personalisation research. The research question of this paper is hence summarised to: "How can Mass Customization capabilities be utilised with regards to creating an efficient development process for ETOs with software intensive products?" The question is answered through a literature study on Mass Customization and ETO products together with a proposal of a development framework that links concepts found in the literature.

2   Related Work

Traditional ETO products are similar to personalised products in the sense that the scope is to develop customer specific solutions. Talking about Mass Customization and Mass Personalisation, the scope is however also to do it at costs similar to Mass Production [6], which bring us to the scope of the next generation ETO products. To distinguished Mass Customization and Mass Personalisation, work by Bossen and Hansson [2] proposed to see a mass personalised product as a product, where the user can design the product in collaboration with the manufacturer (co-created product) given continuous freedom within predefined boundaries (personalised modules), combined with freedom of choice (customised modules) and company decided fixed choices (common modules). In other words, Mass Personalisation is a variant of Mass Customization, and hence it is reasonable to say, that the majority of Mass Customization research is relevant for mass personalised products and modern cost efficient ETO products.

Mass Customization has over the years been defined in different ways but work from Salvador et al. [15] summarise it to *"Providing customers what they want when they want"*. The same authors emphasise that in practice, the implementation of a Mass Customization strategy must not be seen as the destination for the company, but rather a process that will never end. In the same work, the authors defines Mass Customization as having three common capabilities, which every mass customiser to some extent must posses. These three capabilities are defined as: "(1) the ability to identify the product attributes along which customer needs diverge, (2) the ability to reuse or recombine existing organisational and value-chain resources and (3) the ability to help customers identify or build solutions to their own needs." The capabilities are called Solution Space Development, Robust Process Design and Choice Navigation respectively. Each one of them has been proven to be essential to be a mass customiser but few companies can claim to posses them all to perfection.

The transition from mass producer to a mass customiser is discussed exhaustively in literature, but the relevancy of moving an ETO business to a Mass Customization business is somehow less debated. However, work done by Haug et al. [4] focus on this issue, and the conclusion is, that even though not all definitions of Mass Customization includes an ETO business – and that an ETO business will never produce end-products near Mass Customization cost – it is still reasonable to label some of them as mass customisers. The authors claim that an ETO business must divide the development process into work packages which in some cases can be fully or partly automated (separation of concerns). This creates a need for standardising the engineering work to a partly predefined solution space, and a consistent specification process that supports customer co-creation in the development process.

As the company – which this paper is based on – develops automated manufacturing systems that are highly software intensive, another important aspect is to understand how Mass Customization is applicable to software development.

Much like the producers of physical goods, software producers have been looking towards means to avoid developing software systems from scratch, and instead, developing software product lines with reusable parts that can be shared across a product line. One of the paradigms is referred to as Software Product Line Engineering (SPLE), and is based on the principles of Mass Customization [14]. An important aspect to SPLE is the separation in development process between the establishing of the platform and reusable parts, and the derivation of the individual products with the product specific parts [3]. Pohl et al. [14] and Apel et al. [1] separates the development process even further into aspects concerning requirement establishment and realisation, and suggest a framework for implementation. The general separation of concerns principle links quite well to work on Mass Customization and ETO products by Haug et al. [4].

One of the key challenges with the SPLE approach and ETO products is to cope with the transition from ETO to Mass Customization. According to   Krueger [9] there are three adoption approaches to initiate the transition; a proactive approach, an extractive approach, and a reactive approach. The proactive approach can be described as a big-bang design strategy [5], where product lines are developed from scratch and follows a step-by-step waterfall approach to design and implement a product line [9]. The extractive approach is a refactoring strategy [17], where the goal is to structure the existing legacy solutions in a companies product portfolio in a more systematic way [9]. The reactive approach is an evolution design strategy, where an initial version of product line is designed   and implemented, and gradually extending and redesigning the product line to cover more products [1].

All of the approaches have advantages and disadvantages, but for small software ETOs the extractive approach seems beneficial because the incremental adoption also yields a lower upfront investment compared to the proactive approach. This is in general because the extraction process may only concern focusing on specific parts of the product and incrementally including more parts [17]. The downside of the extractive approach is, that implementation of the product line is potentially limited by the structure and code practises of the legacy products, since these not necessarily was implemented in structured way. This limitation means, that the refactoring process do not result in an easy maintainable structuring of the product line [1].

2.1 Research Gap

Based on the related work identified in section 2, it can be concluded that SPLE can be used for ETO companies developing software intensive manufacturing systems. Furthermore, since SPLE originally builds on Mass Customization and basically treat the same purpose, this paper assumes that the three fundamental capabilities of Mass Customization can be linked to SPLE, and thereby enable use of research from SPLE and vice versa. One example is the performance assessment research that is essential for continues improvement of the capabilities.

We conclude that a need for an ETO Mass Customization developing framework – that links the Mass Customization capabilities and SPLE – exist.

3   MC Development Framework for ETO Businesses

With basis in the essential capabilities of Mass Customization and development concepts from SPLE, we propose a product development framework for ETO product developers (see figure 2). The framework is divided according to activities related to each of the Mass Customization capabilities, and the distinctive engineering aspects. This differentiation separates the concerns of developing end-products, developing the product line, and the extraction of the potential reusable legacy artefacts. These aspects are referred to as Application Engineering, Domain Engineering and Reverse Engineering respectively. The aspect of Domain and Application Engineering are basic aspects of SPLE, whereas the aspect of Reverse Engineering is included, in order to emphasise the continues evolution of the product line through legacy reuse. Hence this framework has a focus on transforming personalised/product specific parts into reusable artefacts. In order to support continuous improvement of capabilities, we have – with inspiration from Kristal et al. [8] and Nielsen [11] – included Performance Assessment in the framework as a supporting capability. By including it as a capability of the framework, we underline the need for research addressing how to conduct Performance Assessment in this context.

Furthermore we emphasise, that the proposed framework is seen from a development viewpoint, which has similarities to the non-traditional Mass Customization process view from Haug et al. [4]. In general we believe that Mass Customization must be seen from one or more product views and several process views. Examples of process views is for instance sales, development and commissioning, where this paper focus on the development viewpoint.

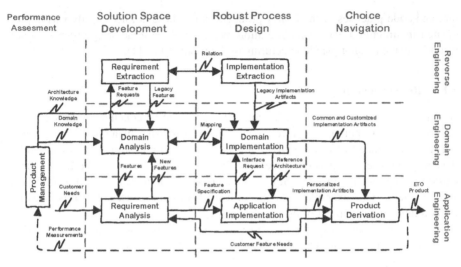

Fig. 1. Mass Customization development framework for ETO businesses

3.1   Solution Space Development

Solution Space Development is about understanding and managing the behavioural requirements for the product that are derived from customer needs. The actual process of identifying the customer needs are though not a part of Solution Space Development in the framework, since we believe this activity is allocated to a sales viewpoint. The focus of Solution Space Development is therefore to align customer needs to solution space and vice versa. This correlates with the original intention of Solution Space Development from section 2, besides the development of customer needs. Solution Space Development is conducted by expressing and managing communality and variability in terms which are understandable for developers but not necessarily for customers. This correlates with Kang and Lee [7]. A popular SPLE approach in this context is to express needs according to features, which may be defined as a behavioural product functionality that originates from a specific customer need [1].

As in traditional SPLE, the framework includes the aspect of Application Engineering and Domain Engineering. Together these continuously cover the processes of analysing if 1) a feature already exist as a reusable artefact, 2) a new feature should be developed as a reusable artefact, or 3) a new feature should be developed as a product specific artefact [14]. For ETO companies, the entire business strategy relies on tailoring end-products with customer specific features, which in most cases will involve constantly extending the end-products with features that are not already developed. A vital aspect for ETO companies in Solution Space Development is hence, the ability to recover any product specific features from legacy products, that may resemble the possible new features derived from the Requirement Analysis in the Application

Engineering aspect. This requires, that the company is able to acquire knowledge, regarding whether or not a customer specific feature already exist in the solution space. This is related to the aspect of Reverse Engineering, and the supporting capability Performance Assessment.

3.2   Robust Process Design

From a development viewpoint, Robust Process Design concerns the actual realisation of the features identified in the solution space. Robust Process Design is focussing on continuously improving the product related artefacts, in order to identify, if they may be reused or recombined into a stream of different end-products. This involves consideration towards how communality and variability is implemented, but also when variability is implemented.

Both in traditional Mass Customization and SPLE, architecture- and platform development are vital processes to secure reusability and managing variability which are related to the Domain Engineering aspect [3]. Since the demand for product specific parts are higher for ETO companies, it is important to allow the architecture to be extended with the product specific parts developed during Application Engineering. This may be handled by a static- or dynamic approach. The static approach involves clearly specifying where variation points exits in the architecture in order to interface product specific parts. The dynamic approach may be viewed as a contentiously evolution of the architecture to address the integration of product specific parts. Whether the static or dynamic approach is used, it always involves implementing variation points in the platform or in the customisable parts of the architecture. These implementations must however be monitored to justify the relevancy of the variation point in the future, and is related to Performance Assessment.

As product specific parts continuously grow in numbers – in form of legacy products – an important ability for software ETOs, is to reuse existing implementation solution if possible. This is related to the Reverse Engineering aspect. However, the intention is not to force developers to extract, and refactor product specific parts from legacy products, if the integration process is difficult. Therefore, an equally important ability in robust process design, is to access whether or not refactoring legacy products is worthwhile in the current situation, or if it will be more beneficial to develop from scratch.

3.3   Choice Navigation

In the product development viewpoint, choice navigation concerns the process of assisting the developer in configuring the end-product that satisfies the requirements of the customer. This may involve assisting tools such as a configurators or procedural specifications, to navigate the developer towards deriving an end-product. Depending on the production tools, the process of creating an end-product may either be conducted manually, automatically, or in a combination of both.

4   Discussion

By introducing the Performance Assessment supporting capability, a development team has the possibility to monitor how e.g. a Mass Customization transition process is advancing. This activity is called Product Management in the framework, and is responsible for collecting, measuring and calculating Performance Assessment data. The Mass Customization performance assessment research from Nielsen et al. [12] is useful here, but also the linking of Mass Customization and quality management from Kristal et al. [8] and Storbjerg et al. [16] is highly relevant. Possible implications by using Performance Assessment is for instance – but not limited to – the ability to measure profitability. Profitability may in this context be linked to the decision of when to include a new feature to the product line, based on the frequency of a specific personalised feature use.

By introducing viewpoints, it is envisioned that the Mass Customization capabilities are utilised in multiple stages of the production process besides the development viewpoint. For developers of automated manufacturing systems, a vital process is the actual integration of the solution in the production environment, which requires an effective commissioning process. How the Mass Customization capabilities are utilised in the different viewpoints, and how many process viewpoints that exist, must therefore be further investigated.

5   Conclusion

The literature study shows that SPLE research achievements are highly relevant for ETO companies developing software intensive manufacturing systems, and that SPLE and Mass Customization originally was developed with the same purpose in mind. The research gap from section 2.1 concludes, that if a framework – which links the two research areas – is developed, then contributions from both areas can be used to bring the Mass Customization research further, with regards to software intensive products. Especially the Mass Customization Performance Assessment research is relevant in order to continuously improve the process of a successful Mass Customization implementation process. This paper proposes a framework addressing how ETOs could develop software intensive products, hence the applicability of the framework will initially mainly address the software related artefacts of the product. Therefore, further research must be conducted to show if the framework has limitations with regards to more hardware intensive systems.

References

[1] Apel, S., Batory, D., Kästner, C., Saake, G.: Feature-Oriented SoftwareProduct Lines. Springer, Heidelberg (2013)
[2] Bossen, J., Hansson, M.N.: Realizing mass personalization (2013) (unpublished)
[3] Clements, P.C., Northrop, L.: Software Product Lines: Practices and Patterns. SEI Series in Software Engineering. Addison-Wesley (2001)

[4] Haug, A., Ladeby, K., Edwards, K.: From engineer-to-order to mass customization. Management Research News 32(7), 633–644 (2009)

[5] Heradio, R., Fernandez-Amoros, D., de la Torre, L., Abad, I.: Exemplardriven development of software product lines. Expert Systems with Applications 39(17), 12885–12896 (2012)

[6] Hu, S.J.: Evolving paradigms of manufacturing: From mass production tomass customization and personalization. In: Forty Sixth CIRP Conference on Manufacturing Systems, vol. 7, pp. 3–8 (2013)

[7] Kang, K., Lee, H.: Variability modeling. In: Capilla, R., Bosch, J., Kang, K.C. (eds.) Systems and Software Variability Management, pp. 25–42. Springer, Heidelberg (2013)

[8] Kristal, M., Huang, X., Schroeder, R.: The effect of quality managementon mass customization capability. International Journal of Operations and Production Management 30(9), 900–922 (2010)

[9] Krueger, C.W.: Easing the transition to software mass customization. In: van der Linden, F.J. (ed.) PFE 2002. LNCS, vol. 2290, pp. 282–293. Springer, Heidelberg (2002)

[10] Kumar, A.: From mass customization to mass personalization: a strategic transformation. International Journal of Flexible Manufacturing Systems 19(4), 533–547 (2007)

[11] Nielsen, K.: Mass Customization Assessment and Measurement Framework for Industrial Applications. Department of Mechanical and Manufacturing Engineering (2014)

[12] Nielsen, K., Brunø, T.D., Jørgensen, K.A., Taps, S.B.: Mass customizationmeasurements metrics. In: Proceedings of the 7th World Conference on Mass Customization, Personalization, and Co-Creation, pp. 359–375 (2014)

[13] Pine, J.B.: The mass customization manifesto (unpublished 2014)

[14] Pohl, K., Böckle, G., van der Linden, F.: Software Product Line Engineering. Springer, Heidelberg (2005)

[15] Salvador, F., de Holan, P.M., Piller, F.: Cracking the code of mass customization. MIT Sloan Management Review 50(3), 71–78 (2009)

[16] Storbjerg, S., Brunø, T., Nielsen, K.: Mass customization and performanceassessment: Overview and research directions. In: Proceedings ofthe 7th World Conference on Mass Customization, Personalization, andCo-Creation, pp. 333–347 (2014)

[17] Zhang, G., Shen, L., Peng, X., Xing, Z., Zhao, W.: Incremental and iterativereengineering towards software product line: An industrial case study. In: 2011 27th IEEE International Conferenceon on Software Maintenance (ICSM), pp. 418–427 (September 2011)

A Regulation Mechanism Based on Work Activity to Improve Lean Approach

Patrick Badets[1,2], Véronique Pilnière[1,3], and Christophe Merlo[1,2]

[1] ESTIA, Estia-Recherche, Technopole Izarbel, Bidart, France
[2] IMS, UMR 5218, University of Bordeaux, Talence, France
[3] CREG-UPPA, UPPA, Pau, France
{p.badets,v.pilniere,c.merlo}@estia.fr

Abstract. Companies adopting Lean increase their productivity, quality of product and delivery in the short term. But in the medium term, these performance criteria are mitigated by events such as absenteeism, sickness leaves, turnover, etc. To explain this, Occupational Health scientists identify contradictions between the components of Lean and human functioning. One of these contradictions relates to the regulation mechanism of human work activity, specific to human functioning, which would be inhibited in a Lean working environment. In this article, we focus on the integration of this mechanism in the Lean performance approach and, to illustrate our approach, we choose the example of semi-finished stock lying between each workstation: the 'work in progress' inventory. We propose to use a performance indicator that measures the need of 'work in progress' inventory taking into account the regulation mechanism of the work activity. We call this indicator "number of regulating 'work in progress' inventory".

Keywords: Work in Progress Inventory, Work Activity, Working Regulation, Lean, Performance, Margin of Maneuver, Occupational Risks.

1   Context

Lean[1] is a production and management approach that aims to eliminate production waste in a transformation process in way to only retain the value-added activities [1]. This approach focuses on the reduction of production costs, delivery times and production scrap (Quality). Lean has been theorized in the 80's by researchers from MIT (Massachusetts Institute of Technology), drawing on the Japanese methods, specifically the Toyota Production System (hereinafter abbreviated as "TPS" for Toyota Production System). Lean has been a major attraction in the auto companies and their subcontractors in the 1990's and 2000's [2]. Since the crisis of 2008, all sectors of activity were concerned by this appeal. In 2006, a study estimated that 28% of French employees work in companies that have adopted Lean [3].

---

[1] In this paper, we will use "Lean" as an abbreviation for the Lean approach.

B. Grabot et al. (Eds.): APMS 2014, Part III, IFIP AICT 440, pp. 124–130, 2014.
© IFIP International Federation for Information Processing 2014

2   Research Problem

Today, several studies show a correlation between the use of Lean by companies and a drop of the commonly used performance criteria (Quality, Cost, Delay) because of events such as absenteeism, sick leaves, accidents and turnover [3], [4], [5].

To explain it, several scientists from Occupational Health research area have identified strong contradictions between Lean and human functioning at work [6].

One of these contradictions is about the consideration of the level of autonomy of a worker in his working activity, i.e. of his 'margin of maneuver'. This level of autonomy is the opportunity given by an organization that allows a worker to choose its own way to work according to the production variability considering the constraints of the organization. On the one hand, Lean considers that this regulatory mechanism is not necessary to be taken into account since the production process can be stabilized. On the other hand, Occupational Health scientists believe that this mechanism is a fundamental contribution to the performance of the company due to the autonomy it infers to the worker in order to manage uncertainty and to regulate its process of work [7]. One of the operational consequences of this lack of integration is, for example, the level of 'work in progress inventory', and more precisely how workers regulate their work activity with the help of semi-finished stock of products. This example comes from a cooperative project with an automotive SME, dedicated to the improvement of the deployment of Lean.

On the basis of it, we ask the following question: how to promote the consideration of this regulatory mechanism in the Lean approach of performance adopted by companies?

To provide some answers, we will define the concept of performance and specifically criteria used in Lean. We will describe how the regulation mechanism of work activity plays an important role in performance. In this paper, we will propose to change the approach of performance, underpinned by Lean, by integrating this mechanism. Finally, we will propose an indicator that allows measuring this mechanism using the example of 'work in progress' inventory.

3   State of the Art

3.1   Performance

We propose, in this article, to change the approach of performance underpinned by Lean. But what do we mean by performance? Performance is defined as the quality reflecting the ability of a system to achieve its goals. It characterizes the relationship between the functions to be performed by the system and the compliance of the service actually provided by the resources. Performance is defined from the goals (criteria) chosen by a company (e.g.: economic, legal, social, ecological) and may have a multi-dimensional nature [8]. Thus, we will see in the next section that Lean selects Quality, Cost and Delay as criteria to evaluate the performance of a production system. To complete the definition of performance, we draw attention to the fact that criteria are measured by indicators.

3.2   Lean and Its Performance Approach

We choose to select two components of Lean: technical variability and waste elimination. Technical variability elimination aims to reduce variations observed in a production process, for example by ensuring the quality and consistency of suppliers raw materials or products before they enter the production process (via quality assurance programs for example) or doing preventive maintenance to minimize random breakdowns [9]. This kind of elimination is a prerequisite for implementing another major Lean component: waste elimination. Eliminating waste aims to reduce production process steps considered as non-added value.

Taichi Ohno [9], one of the main Lean theoreticians, identified 7 types of waste involved in a production process:

- Transport, e.g. unnecessary products displacements.
- Inventory.
- Motion, e.g. people or equipment moving more than is required to perform the processing.
- Waiting, e.g. interruptions of production during shift change or maintenance operations.
- Overproduction.
- Over Processing, e.g. under dimensioned tools for scheduled production.
- Defects, e.g. the effort involved in inspecting and fixing defects.

Ohno specifies that waste elimination aims to reduce delivery time, cost and quality defaults. Thus, Lean uses Quality, Cost and Delay criteria to evaluate the performance of a production process. In this paper, we will focus on a specific indicator aimed to measure one of the seven types of waste above mentioned. This indicator measures the number of 'work in progress' inventory. 'Work in progress' inventory is composed of semi-finished products located between two workstations. This indicator is used by Lean to assess Cost and Delay criteria of performance.

Indeed, getting too much 'work in progress' inventory in a production site generates several problems such as:

- Trapped capital (Cost criterion)
- Financial risk of being obliged to sell obsolescent products (Cost criterion)
- Decreased flexibility in changeovers (Cost and Delay criteria).

Lean focuses on the production process and believes it can be stabilized. As we explain below, this approach can be challenged by another one that focuses on human functioning at work and which believes that the process cannot be stabilized.

3.3   Work Activity Regulation

We now introduce this approach. This approach is centered on mankind at work and focuses on work activity.

Work activity refers to the activity actually performed by workers and differs from the area of assigned tasks (e.g.: procedures). Work activity depends on goals and means that are assigned to the worker, as well as its personal characteristics.

According to available means (e.g.: tools, support from another worker) and goals which are assigned (e.g.: cycle time, quality criterion), a worker will make compromises to achieve the stated objectives. The compromise is done between given means ("External Means") and the worker internal state ("Personal Resources"). This process is called "Work Regulation". As a result of this process, the worker will choose a way to do his work ("Modus Operandi"). Variously, this compromise would be made to the detriment of the worker internal state (e.g.: working faster in despite of fatigue) or of the results of the work (e.g.: not achieving the appropriate quality) [10].

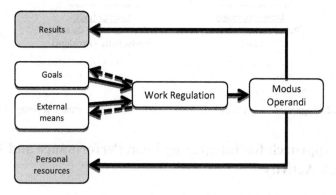

Fig. 1. The work regulation mechanism [10]

Thus, the worker is led to build up 'margin of maneuver' in its working environment that allows him to regulate his work activity against variability in a way to preserve his health (internal state) and to reach the objectives (see Fig.1). In a production environment, 'margin of maneuver' can take the form of time (e.g.: moving ahead on a chain transfer) or space (e.g.: building up a buffer stock). In this human-centered approach, performance is rather seen as the ability of an organization to let worker building up the pertinent 'margin of maneuver' to face variability, rather than the ability to stabilize a process.

On this topic, the Occupational Health scientists' community, particularly through French institutions such as ARACT[2] and INRS[3], agrees that technical stability, one of the Lean components, has never been observed in a production process. However, it has been observed that, in Lean, work activity 'margin of maneuver' have been removed assuming that technical process is stabilized. Applied to 'work in process' inventory, Lean considers them as wasteful whereas the Occupational Health scientists' community considers them as 'margin of maneuver'. In short, we refer to the illustration done by Bourgeois which sets work activity regulation as a leverage for performance in the production process [11].

---

[2] ANACT : Agence Nationale pour l'Amélioration des Conditions de Travail (National Agency for Working Conditions Improvement).

[3] INRS : Institut National de Recherche sur la Sécurité (National Institute Of Health and Safety Resarch).

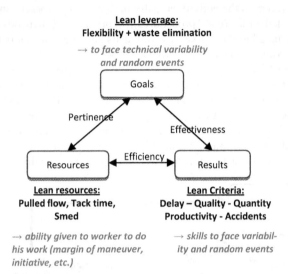

Fig. 2. Regulation mechanism of work activity as a performance leverage [11]

4   An Approach for Integrating Lean Performance and Human Work Activity

4.1   Introducing a Multi-level Regulation Mechanism

We consider the canonical model of Le Moigne [12] (Fig. 3) that breaks up an organizational system into three sub-systems: a decision system that regulates an operative system through an information system that supports information flows. This model is generally a recursive model that allows modelling the system at different levels of granularity [13]. This model helps us to highlight the information feedback between operating and decision systems.

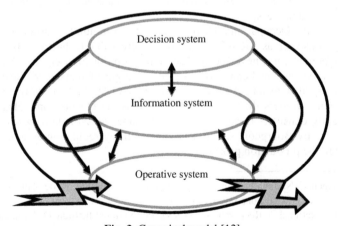

Fig. 3. Canonical model [12]

Thus, we have seen in Figure 1 that the regulatory mechanism of work activity is an adequate leverage for performance and that Lean does not integrate this mechanism into its components, considering it as a waste to eliminate. So, how to promote the integration of this mechanism as a performance leverage in Lean and, accurately, how to promote the integration of 'margin of maneuver'?

On the basis of the previous elements, we propose a new Lean approach of performance. In this approach, we believe that the regulation mechanism of work activity is a leverage.

Our aim is to define a global approach that allows the control of a whole system, i.e. on the operational, tactical and strategic levels, integrating this regulatory mechanism. This mechanism is located at a very detailed system level where human activity is performed.

We propose to characterize the information flows and the decision activities in order to take into account the regulatory mechanism for each worker. Especially, the decision-making system will receive bottom-up feedback information about indicators related to 'margin of maneuver'measured in the production environment (operating system). Our method consists here in defining new kind of indicators that represent 'margin of maneuver' reducing the impact of the process variability on the performance.

4.2   A 'Margin of Maneuver' Indicator: The Number of Regulating 'Work in Progress' Inventory

Referring to Figure 3, which indicator is able to inform the decision-making system about a 'margin of maneuver' state or a 'margin of maneuver' need status? We propose to use an indicator related to 'work in progress' inventory which integrates the pertinent number of 'margin of maneuver' to do the job. As located at an operational level and involved in the regulation of work, we propose to name it "number of regulating 'work in progress' inventory".

We oppose this definition with the one used in Lean: "number of 'work in progress' inventory". Indeed, Lean focuses on the number of products between workstations and tries to reduce it, regardless of whether these products could be necessary to the performance of work because of the existing variability.

How to measure the "number of regulating 'work in progress' inventory"? We could calculate the standard deviation from the upstream and downstream work in progress inventory consumption and use it as a reference value.

To do so, it is important to base the calculation on observations and interviews with several workers involved by the production environment, repeating measurements taking into account variations observed in production (e.g.: beginning of the day, unplannified orders, seasonality).

This indicator would be a "steering" type indicator. It would help to check how 'work in progress' inventory requirements vary during a production cycle, compare this value with the means given to workers in the production situation and adjust these means in way to come close to the reference value previously calculated.

5   Conclusion

Thus, we propose to change the Lean approach of performance to integrate the regulation mechanism of work activity. We use Le Moigne model to feed the decision-making system with bottom-up feedback information though indicators related to 'margin of maneuver'measured in the production environment. As an example, we propose to use an indicator that measures the needed 'work in progress' number in order to adapt the means of production necessary to help workers to do their work properly.

Aside from the question of changing the lean approach of performance, we are aware of the importance of defining a generic method to implement the proposed approach into companies, and especially SME's. This method should change the "waste elimination" mental picture. It will help stakeholders to sort out useful operations for the regulation of work activity from non-added value operations. By this way, decision stakeholders will be able to get the appropriate 'margin of maneuver' indicators and thus base their performance analysis on more global and long-term Quality, Cost and Delay criteria.

References

1. Womack, J.P., Jones, D.T.: Lean thinking: banishwaste and createwealth in your corporation. Simon and Schuster (2010)
2. Peter, K., Lanza, G.: Company-specific quantitative evaluation of lean production methods. Production Engineering 5(1), 81–87 (2011)
3. Valeyre, A., et al.: Working conditions in the European Union: Workorganization. Office for Official Publications of the European Communities, Luxembourg (2009)
4. Landsbergis, P., Cahill, J., et al.: The impact of lean production and related new systems of work organization on worker health. Journal of Occupationnal Health Psychology 4(2), 108–130 (1999)
5. Conti, R., Angelis, J., Cooper, C., Faragher, B., Gill, C.: The effects of lean production on worker job stress. International Journal of Operations & Production Management 26(9), 1013–1038 (2006)
6. Bourgeois, F., Gonon, O.: Le lean etl'activitéhumaine. Quelpositionnement de l'ergonomie, convoquée par cette nouvelle doctrine de l'efficacité?Activités 7(1), 136–142 (2010)
7. Bourgeois, F.: Que fait l'ergonomieque le lean ne sait / ne veut pas voir? Activités 9(2), 138–147 (2012)
8. Neely, A.D.: Measuring Business Performance: Why, What and How. The Economist Books, London (1998)
9. Ohno, T.: Toyota Production System: Beyond Large-Scale Production. Productivity Press (1988)
10. Guérin, F., Laville, A., Daniellou, F., Duraffourg, J., Kerguelen, A.: Understanding and transformingwork. The practice of Ergonomics. ANACT, Lyon (2007)
11. Bourgeois, F.: Fil rouge. Actes des Journées sur la pratique de l'ergonomie de Bordeaux, Mars 6-18 (2011)
12. Le Moigne, J.L., Landry, M.: Towardsatheory of organizational information system - A general system perspective. In: Gilchrist, B. (ed.) Information Processing. IFIP, vol. 77, pp. 801–805. North-Holland Publishing Company (1977)
13. Doumeingts, G.: Méthode GRAI (Doctoral dissertation) (1984)

Management of a Production Cell Lubrication System with Model Predictive Control

Andrea Cataldo[1], Andrea Perizzato[2], and Riccardo Scattolini[2]

[1] Institute of Industrial Technology and Automation - National Research Council,
Milan, Italy
andrea.cataldo@itia.cnr.it
[2] Politecnico di Milano, Dipartimento di Elettronica,
Informazione e Bioingegneria, Milan, Italy
{andrea.perizzato,riccardo.scattolini}@polimi.it

Abstract. The energy efficiency of manufacturing systems represents a topic of huge interest for the management of innovative production plants. In this paper, a production cell based on three operating machines has been taken into account. In particular, each machine has an independent lubrication system whose lubricant is cooled by a centralized cooling system, while the lubrication fluid temperatures must be maintained inside known upper and lower bounds, and the controller of the centralized cooling system has to minimize the cooling power. In order to control the lubrication and cooling processes, a Model Predictive Controller (MPC) has been designed, synthetized, implemented and simulated.

The main advantage of the proposed algorithm consists in the possibility to directly consider the temperature limits together with the maximum bound of the cooling power directly into the optimization problem. This means that the control action is computed using the a-priori knowledge of these bounds, resulting in better temperature profiles then those obtained with standard controllers, e.g. with saturated Proportional, Integral, Derivative (PID) ones.

Keywords: Model based control, Model predictive control, Hybrid optimal control, Production plant energy efficiency, Plant energy optimization.

1   Introduction

Improving the energy efficiency of manufacturing production systems is nowadays a topic of huge interest. In fact, limiting the CO2 emissions [1, 2], resizing factory energy supply infrastructures and minimizing plant energy consumptions are leading factors to save plant installation and production costs.

In particular, the reduction of energy consumption is possible through the optimization of the algorithms developed to manage their working function [3, 6].

This paper is focused on the definition of the control algorithms for the optimization of the machines' energy efficiency. Specifically, the control policy for a production cell lubrication system has been designed, synthetized and implemented by

B. Grabot et al. (Eds.): APMS 2014, Part III, IFIP AICT 440, pp. 131–138, 2014.

adopting optimal model-based control techniques. These development activities consist in the modeling of the physical process to be controlled, the definition of the constraints on the process variables', and the solution of a suitable optimization problem which has then been implemented into a C++ control platform. A simulation experiment is proposed in the paper to evaluate the resulting control performances.

The paper is organized as follows. Section 2 describes the production cell and the control functional requirements. Section 3 describes the dynamic model of the operating machine lubrication system and details the MPC design, synthesis and implementation. Section 4 shows the results coming from a simulation experiment. Section 5 concludes the paper by summarizing the obtained results and the advantages of the proposed approach, besides hinting to future developments.

2   Description of the Cell Lubrication System

The considered production cell is part of the engine assembly line described in [7] whose model is sketched in Fig. 1. The production line machining operation sequence consists of *Milling – Welding – Screwing – Drilling* activities. However, only the machines *M1, M3* and *M4* (for simplicity renumbered in the following as machines 1,2,3) belong to a single production cell because they share some centralized auxiliary systems, such as the fluid lubrication cooling system.

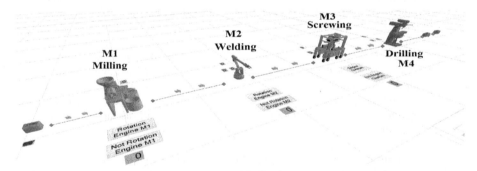

Fig. 1. Engine assembly line layout

During its machining process, each machine produces a specific quantity of heat exchanged with the lubricant fluid, which in turn is cooled from the cooling fluid flowing into the centralized cooling system circuit. As the lubrication fluid temperature grows, the machine control system is able to open an On-Off valve that allows the cooling fluid to flow and thus the lubricant fluid to be cooled.

More specifically, the overall cooling systems operates as follows. Denote by P_{cool} the thermal power of the centralized cooling system, which can be modulated by the control action, and by $\gamma_i \cdot P_{cold}$ the thermal power exchanged with the *i-th* $(i=1,2,3)$ machine lubrication fluid with temperature T_i. If all the temperatures T_i, $i=1,2,3$, are inside some prescribed limits, the On-Off valve is closed and the no thermal power is provided to the machines. On the contrary, if at least one of these temperatures exceeds an upper bound T_{hoti}, $(i=1,2,3)$, the valve opens and it is set $P_{cold}= P_{cool}$.

The logic behavior of the cooling system can then be defined by the following relations:

$$if \quad \vee_{i=1}^{3}(T_i \geq T_{hoti}) \quad \rightarrow \quad P_{cold} = P_{cool} \tag{1}$$

$$else \quad P_{cool} = 0$$

Note however that, due to the different machine characteristics and machining processes, the transferred heat to the lubricant fluids is different from machine to machine, and it is not constant during the machine working cycle.

Table 1 lists the maximum and minimum lubrication fluid temperatures for each machine, referred to a specific machining operation. In addition Table 2 presents the thermal power produced by the considered machining operations. The minimum power produced from a machine is equal to 0 that means that it is not working.

Finally, the room temperature T_a is assumed to lie in the range 10-45 [°C] while the available cooling power can be modulated between the values 0-3500 [W].

Table 1. Machine lubrication systems temperature ranges [°C]

Machines	T_{1min}	T_{1Max}	T_{2min}	T_{2Max}	T_{3min}	T_{3Max}
M1	10	140				
M2			10	250		
M3					10	125

Table 2. Machine lubrication systems thermal power ranges [W]

Machines	P_{1min}	P_{1Max}	P_{2min}	P_{2Max}	P_{3min}	P_{3Max}
M1	0	750				
M2			0	500		
M3					0	650

3   MPC Design, Synthesis and Implementation

The control problem related to the centralized lubrication fluid cooling system consists of maintaining the three lubrication fluid temperatures in each specific range by minimizing the energy consumption of the centralized cooling system.

Standard control systems based on industrial controllers are able to manage each lubrication fluid temperature, but they cannot minimize the overall cooling system energy consumption because, due to the resulting decentralized architecture, each local controller only knows the process under its control.

A more suitable technique to solve this class of control problems is Model Predictive Control, or MPC. Nowadays, MPC represents the most widely used advanced control method in the process industry. This is due to the possibility of reformulating the control problem as an optimization one, where different and possibly conflicting goals can be taken into account, as well as to explicitly include constraints on the input and output variables. Moreover, MPC allows for the design of multivariable regulators for large scale systems, with tens or hundreds of variables, see [8]. Thanks to these unique advantages, MPC-based solutions are widely popular in many industrial fields characterized by continuous processes, such as the chemical, petro-chemical, pulp and paper industries, power networks control and related energy mar-ket, see e.g. [9, 10, 11].

3.1   MPC Design

The first step for the application of MPC consists of the modelling of the process to be controlled. In view of the previous considerations, each lubrication fluid receives heat from the machining operation and transfers this energy to the cooling fluid. Therefore, the dynamics of the temperature of the *i-th* machine can be described by the energy balance equation (2), where τ denotes the continuous time index:

$$\frac{dT_i(\tau)}{d\tau} = \gamma_i \cdot \left(T_a - T_i(\tau)\right) + k_{hi} \cdot P_{hoti}(\tau) - k_{ci} \cdot P_{cold}(\tau) \tag{2}$$

where

γ_i is the convection coefficient that models the thermal coupling between lubri-cation fluid and the external environment at temperature T_a;

k_{hi} is the coefficient modelling the heat exchanging between the machine and the lubrication fluid;

k_{ci} is the coefficient modelling the heat exchanging between the cooling fluid and the lubrication one.

MPC techniques rely on discrete-time models. Therefore, by exploiting the simple Forward Euler discretization, and denoting by $\Delta\tau$ the adopted sampling time, the dis-cretized form of (2) is:

$$T_i(k\Delta\tau + \Delta\tau) = T_i(k\Delta\tau) + \Delta\tau\left[\gamma_i \cdot \left(T_a - T_i(k\tau)\right) + k_{hi} \cdot P_{hoti}(k\tau) - k_{ci} \cdot P_{cold}(k\tau)\right] , \quad k = 0,1,2,\dots \tag{3}$$

or, denoting by t the discrete-time index,

$$T_i(t + 1) = T_i(t) + \Delta\tau \cdot \left[\gamma_i \cdot \left(T_a - T_i(t)\right) + k_{hi} \cdot P_{hoti}(t) - k_{ci} \cdot P_{cold}(t)\right] \tag{4}$$

Equations (1), (4) represent the set of dynamic equations and logic statements ac-cording to which the MPC can be synthetized.

3.2   MPC Synthesis

The MPC synthesis is carried out by implementing the hybrid model defining the discre-tized physical process (4) and the control logic propositions (1), by means of the HYSDEL software tool [12] which translates the corresponding high level structured language into a Mixed Logic Dynamical (MLD) system formalism [13] of the form (5):

$$\begin{cases} x(t + 1) = Ax(t) + B_u u(t) + B_\delta \delta(t) + B_z z(t) \\ \quad y(t) = Cx(t) + D_u u(t) + D_\delta \delta(t) + D_z z(t) \\ E_\delta \delta(t) + E_z z(t) \le E_u u(t) + E_x x(t) + E_c \end{cases} \tag{5}$$

where x is the state variable representing the temperatures T_i, u is the control variable representing the cooling power P_{cool}, y is the output corresponding to the measured state x, while δ and z are vectors of logical and continuous auxiliary variables, respectively.

As previously discussed, the optimization problem is stated to minimize at any sampling time the peak of the overall cooling power P_{cool} along a future prediction horizon specified by the positive integer N. Therefore, the adopted performance index J is:

$$J = \min_{k=t,\dots,t+N-1} P_{cool}(k) \tag{6}$$

In order to fulfil the required bounds on the lubricant fluid temperatures, the optimization problem is subject to the following constraints:

$$T_{1,min} \leq T_1(t) \leq T_{1,max} \tag{7-a}$$

$$T_{2,min} \leq T_2(t) \leq T_{2,max} \tag{7-b}$$

$$T_{3,min} \leq T_3(t) \leq T_{3,max} \tag{7-c}$$

$$P_{c,min} \leq P_{cool}(t) \leq P_{c,max} \tag{7-d}$$

At any sampling time t, once the optimal sequence $P^o_{cool}(k)$, $k = t, \dots, t + N - 1$ of future control variables has been computed, only its first element, i.e. $P^o_{cool}(t)$, is effectively applied. Then, according to a moving horizon strategy, at the new sampling time $t+1$ the overall procedure is repeated.

It is important to note that the optimization problem above stated may be infeasible due to the nature of the problem under study. In fact, since the cooling system is shared among different machines, it may not be possible to fulfil all the constraints at the same time. For instance, if only one machine is operating and its lubricant has to be cooled, then the others will be cooled as well, by possibly violating their lower bounds. In order to prevent infeasibility of the control solution, it is common practice to transform the hard constraints into soft constraints, in order for them to be violated only if infeasibility occurs. This feature is achieved by heavily weighing these violations in the cost function to be minimized.

In order to complete the MPC synthesis, the heating powers $P_{hot\,i}$ have been considered as disturbances acting on the processes. Two solutions are commonly exploited in order to take these disturbances into account, depending on the availability of their future behavior:

a) Prediction available: whenever the future value of the disturbances is available, it should be included into the optimization problem in order to achieve the optimal solution;
b) Prediction not available: if it is not available, it is common practice to assume that the disturbances are constant over the whole prediction horizon, and in particular equal to the current value.

In this work the production cycles have been assumed to be known, then the solution a) has been considered.

3.3   MPC Implementation

The application of the MPC law to a real lubrication system or to an equivalent dynamic simulation model, requires to run the algorithm into a control platform. Then a customized control environment based on the C++ object oriented programming language has been used, by implementing the MPC according the steps showed in Fig. 2:

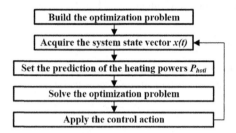

Fig. 2. MPC implementation into the C++ customized control environment

4   Simulation Results

Since it has not been possible to apply the developed control system to the real production cell, some simulation experiments have been carried out by running the MLD model of the lubrication system in the MATLAB platform [14] and the MPC in the C++ customized control platform, by interfacing them by means of synchronizing signals. The constraints on the lubricant fluid temperatures have been set accordingly to Table 1. In addition, soft constraints on upper bounds of the temperatures have been used to prevent infeasibility, as previously discussed. The must-be-cooled temperatures T_{hoti} have been set equal to 100, 110 and 85 [°C] respectively for $M1$, $M3$ and $M4$ while the ambient temperature to 25 [°C] constant. Finally, the cooling power range is 0-3500 [W]. The left plots in Fig. 3 depict the selected heating power profiles, corresponding to the working cycles of $M1$, $M3$ and $M4$, from top to bottom. The first three plots on the right in Fig. 3 show the lubricant temperatures (in solid blue) together with their bounds (in dashed red) and the must-be-cooled temperatures (in solid-dotted magenta). It can be noted that the lower bounds are never violated because they are set as hard constraints. On the other hand, the soft upper bounds are occasionally crossed. As expected, the violations only occur when at least one temperature is close to the lower bound, which cannot be crossed, leading to the upper one crossing (e.g. see the plots at time 7-10s). The bottom-most plot on the right presents the cooling power which always lies inside the given range.

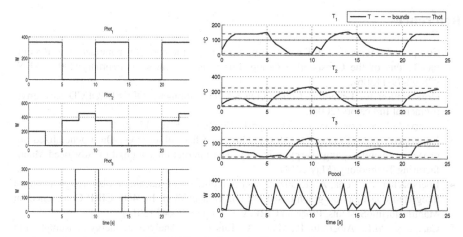

Fig. 3. Simulation experiment results

5   Concluding Remarks

In this paper, a production cell based on three operating machines has been considered. In particular, the centralized lubrication cooling system energy management has represented the case study for the design, synthesis and implementation of a model predictive controller. The simulation experiment that has been carried out shows the ability of the MPC to cope with the hybrid control problem in which continuous process variables and corresponding logic constraints have been taken into account. The control action is computed using the a-priori knowledge of the bounds, resulting in better temperature profiles then those obtained with standard controllers. Moreover the small system dimensions require a low computational demand, which leads to fast computing time.

Future works should firstly focus on the deployment of the controller in a real production cell in order to compare the simulation experiment results with the real data acquired from the field. Secondly, a more detailed cooling system modelling would allow for more accurate MPC law calculation and a more realistic control action definition. Finally, an explicit formulation of the MPC, which is currently under study, will allow to replace the on-line optimization with an equivalent, and much lighter, piecewise affine controller, see [15].

Acknowledgements. The research leading to these results has received funding from the European Union's Seventh Framework Programme (FP7/2007-2013) under grant agreement n° 285363 (EMC2-Factory Eco Manufactured transportation means from Clean and Competitive Factory).

References

1. European Commission: ICT and energy efficiency - the case for manufacturing, Recommendations of the Consultation Group, European Commission (February 2009) ISBN: 978-92-79-11306-2
2. Organization for Economic Cooperation and Development (OECED),OECD Key Environmental Indicators (2004),
   http://www.oecd.org/dataoecd/32/20/31558547.pdf
3. Fysikopoulos, A., Pastras, G., Alexopoulos, T., Chryssolouris, G.: On a generalized approach to manufacturing energy efficiency. The International Journal of Advanced Manufacturing Technology (May 2014)
4. Eberspächer, P., Verla, A.: Realizing energy reduction of machine tools through a control integrated consumption graph-based optimization method. In: 46th CIRP Conference on Manufacturing Systems. Procedia CIRP, vol. 7, pp. 640–645 (2013)
5. Calvanese, M.L., Albertelli, P., Matta, A., Taisch, M.: Analysis of energy consumption in CNC machining centers and determination of optimal cutting conditions. In: Proceedings of the 20th CIRP LCE (2013)
6. Frigerio, N., Matta, A.: Machine Control Policies for Energy Saving in Manufacturing. In: 2013 IEEE International Conference on Automation Science and Engineering (CASE), Madison, WI, August 17-20, pp. 651–656 (2013)
7. Cataldo, A., Taisch, M., Stahl, B.: Modeling, simulation and evaluation of Energy consumption for a manufacturing production line. In: 39th Annual Conference of IEEE on Industrial Electronics Society, IECON 2013, Vienna, Austria, November 10-13 (2013)
8. Camacho, E., Bordons, C.: Model Predictive Control. Springer (2007)
9. Bauer, M., Craig, I.K.: Economic assessment of advanced process control – a survey and framework. J. of Process Control 18, 2–18 (2008)
10. Bendtsen, J., Trangbaek, K., Stoustrup, J.: Hierarchical Model Predictive Control for Resource Distribution. In: 49th IEEE Conf. on Decision and Control, Hilton Atlanta Hotel, Atlanta, GA, USA (2010)
11. Negenborn, R.R., Beccuti, A.G., Demiray, T., Leirens, S., Damm, G., De Schutter, B., Morari, M.: Supervisory hybrid model predictive control for voltage stability of power networks. In: American Control Conference, ACC 2007, New York City, USA, July 9-13, pp. 5444–5449 (2007)
12. Torrisi, F.D., Bemporad, A.: HYSDEL—A Tool for Generating Computational Hybrid Models for Analysis and Synthesis Problems. IEEE Transactions on Control Systems Technology 12(2) (March 2004)
13. Bemporad, A., Morari, M.: Control of systems integrating logic, dynamics, and constraints. Automatica 35, 407–427 (1999)
14. MATLAB, MathWorks, http://www.mathworks.com
15. Bemporad, A., Borrelli, F., Morari, M.: Piecewise linear optimal controllers for hybrid systems. In: Proc. American Control Conference, pp. 1190–1194 (2000)

Selecting Theoretical Models for IT and Supply Chain through a Bibliometric Research

Marcelo T. Okano, Fernando A.S. Marins, and Oduvaldo Vendrametto

Abstract. The objective of this research is to identify the major works in IT and supply chain and selecting the main theoretical models for analysis. A literature search was performed on the major knowledge bases to determine and select the conceptual models being used. This resulted in the choice of Gunasekaran et al model. SCOR (https://supply-chain.org) and GSCF (http://www.gsb.stanford.edu/scforum). As a result, we analyze these three mentioned models. The research is important because it provided a bibliographical study on the use of information technology in managing supply chain by means of theoretical models.

Keywords: IT, SCM, SCOR, GSCF.

1 Introduction

Most companies are more and more applying IT (Information technology) systems, especially in Supply Chain Management (Supply Chain Management - SCM) to enhance their performance in competitive global markets [1].

According to Prajogo & Olhager [2], Information (and communication) technology plays a central role in supply chain management in the following aspects. First, IT allows firms to increase the volume and complexity of informations which needs to be communicated with their trading partners. Second, IT allows firms to provide real-time supply chain information, including inventory level, delivery status, and production planning and scheduling which enables firms to manage and control its supply chain activities. Third, IT also facilitates the alignment of forecasting and scheduling of operations between firms and suppliers, allowing better inter-firms coordination.

There are several conceptual models and many discussions on measures of supply chain performance in the literature, however, there is a lack of empirical analysis and case studies on performance metrics and measurements in an environment of supply chain [3], impacted by the use of information technology.

The objective of this research project is to identify the main works on IT and supply chain and selecting the main theoretical models for analysis. We performed a literature search in major knowledge bases to determine and select the conceptual models being used. This resulted in the choice of models Gunasekaran et al.[3], SCOR (https://supply-chain.org) and GSCF (http://www.gsb.stanford.edu/scforum). As a result we have the analysis of these three models mentioned. The research is important because it provided a detailed study on the use of information technology in managing supply chain by means of theoretical models.

B. Grabot et al. (Eds.): APMS 2014, Part III, IFIP AICT 440, pp. 139–147, 2014.

2   Material and Methods

A broad survey of a relevant theoretical framework was done to investigate the IT applied to SCM from a literature survey conducted in major databases in the area of Information Technology, Logistics and Supply Chain Management. A bibliometric survey, or bibliometrics was performed for a quantitative analysis of the written communication of journal articles. Citations and cocitations were analyzed. The citation analysis is based on the premise that authors cite articles that are important in the development of their research.

Tarapanoff et al [4] defines bibliometrics as the study of quantitative aspects of production, distribution and use of recorded information from mathematical models for the process of decision making.

Some researchers observed that the frequency distribution of the data in a text or a set of references follows certain standards. These observations led to the bibliometric laws: Lotka's law that determines the contribution of each author to the advancement of science; Bradford's Law which is a method to select the most representative journals for an area of science; and Zipf's Law which found that words that occur in a text are counted and sorted in descending order of number of occurrences, the multiplication of the number of occurrences by the ranking position for each word is a constant [13].

Among the various bibliometric indicators formed from citation data, stands out even though the identification of the number of references to a specific set of work you want to qualify is possibly as important evaluation process of research activity, and operationally difficult to be applied to the funding agencies. These difficulties are mainly due to the large amount of documents involved in these situations and the known inconsistencies in the rates of citations and bibliographies.

Given these limitations, the data categorized quote by periodical and published in the form of indicators in the Journal Citation Reports (JCR) of the Institute for Scientific Information (ISI) began to be used as an evaluation parameter of researchers and institutions. Are published annually in the JCR three indicators, by journal title: the immediate index citation (immediacy index), the half-life of citations (cited HalfLife) and finally the bibliometric index most known and used, the impact factor (impact Factor) [14].

For international journals the research was conducted through the site ISI Web of Science (http://apps.webofknowledge.com), using the advanced search terms for IT or Information Technology and SCM or Supply Chain Management in the titles of articles . For Brazilian publications, we used the site SciELO (http://www.scielo.org) through the advanced search with the terms of Information Technology and Management of the supply chain. 36 articles, 27 of which were international and national 9 were found.

The publications are from the period 1999-2013, distributed according to Figure 1, and the relation of this periodic consulted in Table 1.

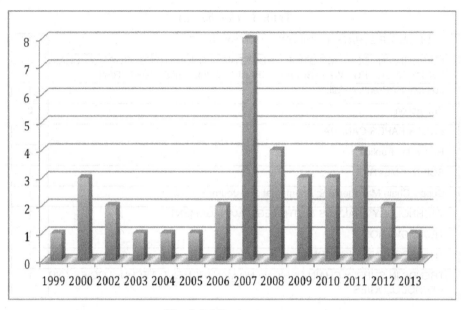

Fig. 1. Publications per year

Table 1. List of publications by periodicals

Periodic	Publications
AIRCRAFT ENGINEERING AND AEROSPACE TECHNOLOGY	1
COMPUTERS IN INDUSTRY	1
DYNA-COLOMBIA	1
Gest. Prod.	2
IEEE TRANSACTIONS ON ENGINEERING MANAGEMENT	1
INDUSTRIAL MANAGEMENT & DATA SYSTEMS	1
Industrial Management	1
Interações (Campo Grande)	2
INTERNATIONAL JOURNAL OF ADVANCED MANUFACTURING TECHNOLOGY	2
INTERNATIONAL JOURNAL OF OPERATIONS & PRODUCTION MANAGEMENT	1
International Journal of Production Economics.	2
INTERNATIONAL JOURNAL OF PRODUCTION RESEARCH	1
INTERNATIONAL JOURNAL OF TECHNOLOGY MANAGEMENT	2
JISTEM J.Inf.Syst. Technol. Manag. (Online)	1
JOURNAL OF BUSINESS-TO-BUSINESS MARKETING	1
JOURNAL OF OPERATIONS MANAGEMENT	1

Table 1. (*Continued.*)

JOURNAL OF STRATEGIC INFORMATION SYSTEMS	1
LOGISTIK IN DER AUTOMOBILINDUSTRIE: INNOVATIVES SUPPLY CHAIN MANAGEMENT FUR WETTBEWERBSFAHIGE ZULIEFERSTRUKTUREN	2
London: FT Prentice-Hall.	1
Production	2
PULP & PAPER-CANADA	1
Rev. Adm. Pública	2
SCIENTOMETRICS	1
Supply Chain Management: An International Journal	1
TECHNOLOGY ANALYSIS & STRATEGIC MANAGEMENT	1
TECHNOVATION	1
TRANSPORTATION JOURNAL	1
TRENDS IN SUPPLY CHAIN DESIGN AND MANAGEMENT: TECHNOLOGIES AND METHODOLOGIES	1

Table 2. Periodics used in research

Títle	Author	Contribution to research
Information technology, operational, and management competencies for supply chain agility: Findings from case studies	Ngai, Eric W. T.; Chau, Dorothy C. K.; Chan, T. L. A.	Definitions of terms Competence of IT, IT Flexibility and Integration of IT.
A framework for analysing supply chain performance evaluation models.	ESTAMPE, D., LAMOURI, S.	Indicators Model SCM GSCF - Global Supply Chain Forum
A framework for supply chain performance measurement,	GUNASEKARAN, A.; PATEL, C.; MCGAUGHEY, R.E.	Model proposed by Gunasekaran et al. (2004) - strategic, operational and tactical levels are hierarchies in the function, where policies and compensation can be distinguished and proper control exercised (Ballou, 1992).
Better supply chains through information technology.	LEVARY, R.R.,	Proposes the benefits of the use of IT in supply chain
The performance prism: The scorecard for measuring and managing business success.	NEELY, A.; ADAMS, C.; KENNERLEY, M.	define performance appraisal
Use of information technology in managing supply chain in São Luís, Maranhão, and opportunities for the development of local suppliers	Morais, Káty Maria Nogueira; Tavares, Elaine.	Proposes the benefits of the use of IT in supply chain

There are several conceptual models and many discussions on measures of supply chain performance in the literature, however, there is a lack of empirical analysis and case studies on performance metrics and measurements in an environment of supply chain [3], impacted by the use of information technology.

The criteria used to select the models were originally cited in the articles studied. Thereafter, which related to IT and supply chain and covering at least the areas of customers, suppliers, delivery and production.

After reading the articles, the articles selected from table 2 and their major contributions to the research.

3   Analysis of Results

A) Model proposed by Gunasekaran et al. [3], a framework for performance measures and metrics is presented (see Table 3), considering the four major supply chain activities/ processes (plan, source, make/assemble, and deliver). These metrics were classified at strategic, tactical and operational to clarify the appropriate level of management authority and responsibility for performance.

According to Rushton & Oxley [10], this hierarchy is based on the time horizon for activities and the relevance of the decisions and the influence of different levels of management.

Table 3. Supply Chain Performance Metrics Framework

Supply chain activity/ process	Strategic	Tactical	Operational
Plan	Level of customer perceived value of product, Variances against budget, Order lead time, Information processing cost, Net profit Vs productivity ratio, Total cycle time, Total cash flow time, Product development cycle time	Customer query time, Product development cycle time, Accuracy of forecasting techniques, Planning process cycle time, Order entry methods, Human resource productivity	Order entry methods, Human resource productivity
Source		Supplier delivery performance, supplier leadtime against industry norm, supplier pricing against market, Efficiency of purchase order cycle time, Efficiency of cash flow method, Supplier booking in procedures	Efficiency of purchase order cycle time, Supplier pricing against market
Make/ Assemble	Range of products and services	Percentage of defects, Cost per operation hour, Capacity utilization, Utilization of economic order quantity	Percentage of Defects, Cost per operation hour, Human resource productivity index
Deliver	Flexibility of service system to meet customer needs, Effectiveness of enterprise distribution planning schedule	Flexibility of service system to meet customer needs, Effectiveness of enterprise distribution planning schedule, Effectiveness of delivery invoice methods, Percentage of finished goods in transit, Delivery reliability performance	Quality of delivered goods, On time delivery of goods, Effectiveness of delivery invoice methods, Number of faultless delivery notes invoiced, Percentage of urgent deliveries, Information richness in carrying out delivery, Delivery reliability performance

Measures to influence the strategic decisions manages high level, often reflecting the broad based policy research, corporate financial planning , competitiveness and the level of adherence to organizational goals.

The tactical level deals with the allocation of resources and measure performance against targets to be met in order to achieve specified outcomes at the strategic level. The measure of performance at this level provides valuable feedback on decisions mid-level management.

Measurements and metrics for operational level require accurate data and evaluate the results of management decisions at the operational level. Supervisors and workers must adjust the operational objectives that, if achieved , result in the achievement of tactical objectives [3].

B)   *SCOR® - Supply Chain Operations Reference Model*
It is a reference model of supply chain operations, coordinated by the Supply Chain Council - SCC (http://supply-chain.org/), analyzing their structure, composition and its performance indicators [11].

It was designed to assist in learning companies in relation to internal and external processes to their field of expertise [11].

The SCOR Framework is the basis for all supply chain management. It helps companies describe how a supply chain is organized, how well it performs and capabilities it possesses. The metrics in SCOR provide a solid foundation for measuring performance and identifying priorities, the processes are the common language in your supply chain operations..

The model allows companies the following advantages:

- Evaluation of effective processes themselves;
- Compare your performance with other companies;
- Looking specify the competitive advantage;
- Uses benchmarking information and best practices to improve their activities;
- Quantify the benefits in implementing change;
- Identifies the best software tools to meet their specific needs.

The SCOR ® is version 10.0, and is based on five core management processes - planning, supply, produce, deliver and return, as illustrated in Figure 2.
The description of the five processes:

a) Plan - the scope of the planning process and management of supply and demand as a reference model has been the definition of resources and demand planning inventory, distribution, production and capacity planning;

b) Supply - acquisition of raw materials, qualification and certification of suppliers, quality monitoring, negotiating contracts with vendors and receiving materials;

c) Manufacturing - manufacturing of the final product, testing, packing, process changes, product launch and ownership;

d) Deliver - order management and credit, warehouse management, transportation, shipping and customer service. Create database of consumers, products and prices;

e) Return - the raw material, finished product, maintenance, repairs and inspection. These processes extend to the supporting post sale to the consumer.

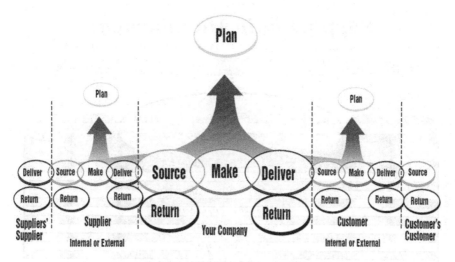

Fig. 2. – SCOR Model- version 10.0
Source: *Supply Chain Council*

C)   SCM Model - GSCF – *Global Supply Chain Forum*
This model GSCF was developed at Ohio State University in 1994 by Professor Douglas Lambert (http://fisher.osu.edu/research/faculty-expertise/marketing-logistics/lambert). He describes three levels (strategic, tactical and operational) and highlights the links between the process and structure of the supply chain. It focuses on eight processes: customer relationship management, customer service management, demand management, order fulfillment, manufacturing flow management, relationship management vendor, product development and marketing and management of return [6].

Figure 3 illustrates the eight business processes along the supply chain and presents the network structure of the supply chain, flow of products and materials, and key business processes interrelated, and borders intra-company involved in a chain supplies [12].

The GSCF suggests the classification of the processes of supply chain management for the four types of business, according to Santos [12]:

1. Managed processes: business processes conducted with a set of key companies along the supply chain will be treated and managed in an integrated manner.

2. Monitored processes: are not as critical to the company focus as managed processes, but it is important that they are integrated and constantly monitored.

3. Unmanaged processes: unmanaged processes are those that focus the company decides not to get involved in their management that considers not to be critical or monitored.

4. Processes of non-members: those involving members of the supply chain of the company focus and not members of the supply chain.

These metrics and models will be the basis for the development of performance indicators of the supply chain impacted by the use of IT.

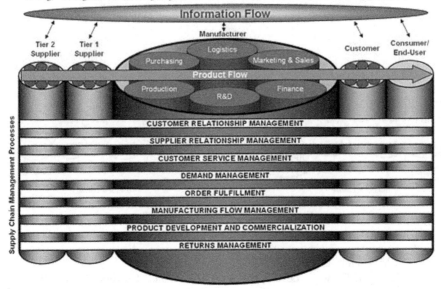

Fig. 3. Supply Chain Management: integration and management of business processes through the supply chain [12]

4   Final Considerations

The survey reached a view to identifying the main models for IT systems used in the supply chain.

The research objective was achieved because we can identify the major works in IT and Supply Chain using bibliometrics and selected the main theoretical models for analysis. As a result we get three Gunasekaran, Scor and GSCF models. Based on the conceptual framework in three related models verified that the six key areas are engineering, manufacturing, delivery, return, suppliers and customers.

Despite the lack of literature found in the survey, we perceive its importance for the occurrence of the continuity of the articles, which began early in this century and remain to the present day, presenting an increase in cocitações the last five years.

The literature is using bibliometrics is important to check what is being written on the subject in the major countries and academic centers tool.

One sees a lot of interest from various authors on the subject and the relevance of academic articles written on various research bases.

As a future project, is expected to use these this search to reassessment and development of indicators in order to measure the level of impact in different areas of the company, as well as contribute to improving the analysis of information technology systems in supply chain management supplies.

References

1. Ming-Lang, T., Kuo-Jui, W., Thi, T.N.: Information technology in supply chain management: a case study. Procedia - Social and Behavioral Sciences 25, 257–272 (2011)
2. Prajogo, D.L., Olhager, J.: Supply chain integration and performance: The effects of long-term relationships, information technology and sharing, and logistics integration. International Journal of Production Economics 135, 514–522 (2012)
3. Gunasekaran, A., Patel, C., McGaughey, R.E.: A framework for supply chain performance measurement. International Journal of Production Economics 87(3), 333–347 (2004)
4. Tarapanoff, K., Miranda, D.M., Aráujo Júnior, R.H.: Técnicas para tomada de decisão nos sistemas de informação, p. 86. Thesaurus, Brasília (1995)
5. Ngai, E.W.T., Chau, D.C.K., Chan, T.L.A.: Information technology, operational, and management competencies for supply chain agility: Findings from case studies. The Journal of Strategic Information Systems 20(3), 232–249 (2011)
6. Estampe, D., Lamouri, S.: A framework for analysing supply chain performance evaluation models. International Journal of Production Economics 142(2) (April 2010)
7. Levary, R.R.: Better supply chains through information technology. Industrial Managementv 42(3), 24–30 (2000)
8. Morais, K.M.N., Tavares, E.: Uso da tecnologia da informação na gestão da cadeia de suprimentos em São Luís do Maranhão e oportunidades para o desenvolvimento de fornecedores locais. Interações (Campo Grande), Campo Grande 12(2) (December 2011)
9. Neely, A., Adams, C., Kennerley, M.: The performance prism: The scorecard for measuring and managing business success. FT Prentice-Hall, London (2002)
10. Rushton, A., Oxley, J.: Handbook of Logistics and Distribution Management. Kogan Page Ltd., London (1989)
11. Rodrigues, C.M.T., Donadel, C.M., Lorandi, J.A., Kieckbusch, R.E.: O modelo de referência das operações na cadeia de suprimentos - (SCOR-model). Anais do XXVI ENEGEP - Fortaleza, IN (2006)
12. Santos, A.C.: Modelo de referência para o processo de desenvolvimento de produtos em um ambiente de scm. Tese (Doutorado Em Engenharia Mecânica). Programa De Pós-Graduação Em Engenharia Mecânica da Ufsc. Florianópolis (2008)
13. Amaral, R.M., et al.: Uma visão da produção científica nos Anais do Encontro Nacional de Engenharia de Produção através da Bibliometria. Anais do XXIV Encontro Nacional de Engenharia de Produção, Florianópolis - SC (2004)
14. Strehl, L.: O fator de impacto do ISI e a avaliação da produção científica: aspectos conceituais e metodológicos. Ci. Inf., Brasília 34(1) (January 2005)

Product Upgradability:
Towards a Medical Analogy

Yannick Chapuis*, Frédéric Demoly, Eric Coatanéa, and Samuel Gomes

IRTES-M3M,
Université de Technologie de Belfort-Montbéliard (UTBM),
90010 Belfort Cedex, France
{yannick.chapuis,frederic.demoly,samuel.gomes}@utbm.fr,
eric.coatanea@aalto.fi

Abstract. This paper explored the analogy between the medical area and product design. Many similarities, shared between the genetic mutation permitting human to ensure its survival and the product undergoing the introduction of new technologies to meet the market fluctuation, are found to propose this analogy. From creating genetic reference space to transplant technology into product, fundamental process of survival and evolution will be described and allows the parallel with a product, to understand how the evolution of product respond to future needs. It also ensures the durability of resources in an ecological perspective. We discuss the complexity of establishing the right diagnosis for directing the design to choose the right technology and to enable its future integration into a living product. This uncertainty in the technological maturity but also the integrability of this technology in the current product at first, then in the future will allow its product development. Conclusions for the use of this analogy and the justification to describe "living product" will be drawn.

Keywords: Upgradability, DFX, Living product, Changeable product, Technology introduction, Proactive engineering.

1 Introduction

Nowadays, products with a long life span such as airplanes, oil rigs, diggers or centrals power generation need to be progressive, scalable and/or upgradable. As well, this products type are increasingly complex mostly in the area of high value-added products. More generally, these products are more complex due to successive and concatenation of innovations introduction while product constraints need a capitalization of all developed technologies. This faculty belongs to the design phase but more and more in the post design phase, with different maintenance laps time, updates, and duration of utilization need to be explored. When the product is designed, mature technologies are introduced to ensure a best performance and attractive product, but, with this large time scale, it

---

* Corresponding author.

B. Grabot et al. (Eds.): APMS 2014, Part III, IFIP AICT 440, pp. 148–155, 2014.

is more and more important to take into account the future. Today, the consumer society encourages people to consume even more, and in a lapse of time shorter and shorter. Sometimes, minimal changes in consumer behavior lead to modifications in the product use. This is the paradigm of the 21st century as the company tries not to consume more resources to ensure the sustainability of resources for the next generations. Therefore, to mix the two issues that are totally different, it is necessary to make more "alive", scalable products, and to make products in time. They must be able to withstand genetic mutations, technological transplants, but also to integrate the technological future years to come based on what is known at the present time. That is why we propose in this paper a medical analogy to our live product to fit best with the needs of the market while minimizing the total redesign of product.

2   Background and Positioning

2.1   Global Positioning

Nowadays, researchers efforts are focused on three mains parts. Some of them are concerned by getting ownership on past and present design intents [6] (left loop), some others work on the best way to use capitalized knowledge to reuse into product [14](connection between the two loops). This paper evolve on future predictions to predict potential evolution of the product to ensure his upgradability with new technologies. As shown in the Fig. 1, mains steps included in the right loop are ①, ②, ③, and ④. This positioning deals with predictions of future evolution and/or introduction technologies [3] [4], evaluation of scenarios

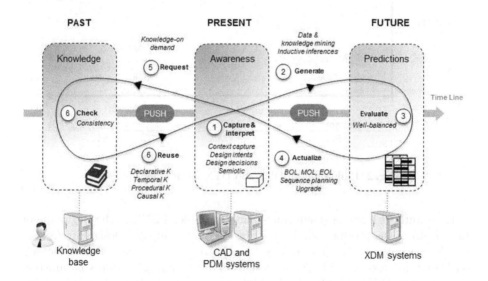

Fig. 1. Current research approaches

maturity level and integrability of news technologies and permit present product to enhance with potential mutation during its life. That's why we propose the notion of "living products" to present its capability to change his architecture throughout its life.

2.2 Developed and Ongoing Methods and Tools

The last decade has seen many DFX grow to meet different issues [7]. The DFX for Design For X, where X target a part of product lifecycle, is a methodology to take into account some constraints to be be proactive in the design phase. we can note two mains DFX and one specific DFX call DTX Design To X where X represent a specific parameter of the design in the middle of life of the product. So, we can resume this global philosophy on the Fig. 2.

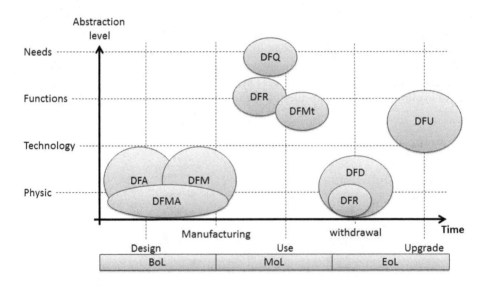

Fig. 2. Philosophy of DFX and DTX on product life cycle

Here, authors have represent some mains example of DFX in the Beginning of Life (BoL) of the product like Design For Manufacturing [2], Design for Assembly [5] and both [1] [16]. The End of Life (EoL) of the product is more focused on Design for dis-assembly [8] or Design for Recycling [11]. Mains parameters targeting for DTX in Middle of Life (MoL) are Quality [9], Reliability [12], Maintainability [15] or performance of the product. Only one virtue DFX impacted all the life cycle of the product, is the Design For Environmental friendly [10] [13], which impact form use of the natural resources, the less consumption, and for it impact less when it is withdrawing. Authors propose to take into account all aspects of the design of a product, from need to physic architecture. As shown in (Fig. 2), the Design for Upgradablity is posted at the end of product life cycle and consider needs, functional architecture, technologies and concept, physic architecture. The analogy of genetic mutation is used to prepare present to integrate a potential future, and allow to be proactive in the development of evolution scenarios of product technology and exhibit the need of product to be upgradable.

2.3 Industrial and Market Challenges

Nowadays, logical consumption involve on product design, but, today's industry need to impose their product with the faculty on to be proactive on predictive scenario of evolution of their product to drive customers to their solution.

3 Vocabulary and Mutation Analogy

3.1 Genetic Code

The genetic mutation is based on a common reference for each individual, i.e. the genetic code, the DNA (DeoxyriboNucleic Acid). DNA is considered as a chemical carrier of genetic information (possibility to enter the nucleotide sequence that characterizes each chromosome). It is necessary to build an information card to elaborate a map using the data present in a PDM (Product Data Management), a set of concatenation information. This informational card must contains information relating to RFLP model, namely, Requirement, Functional, Logical and Physic. The routing from data to knowledge via information is through the understanding context. Information is a data that have a meaning where an interpretation was given. Information allows an operational manager to make a decision (local or global scale) on action to be taken. Knowledge is the result of a reflection on the information analyzed, based on their experiences, ideas, values, opinions or on its own expertise and those of its peers. Each DNA strand includes a sequence of nucleotides, which are themselves composed of nitrogenous bases, monosaccharides (deoxyribose) and phosphate groups. There are four different nucleotides in the DNA, denoted A, G, C and T, the name of the corresponding bases. These nucleotides are grouped by special pairs:

- A with T
- T with A
- C with G
- G with C

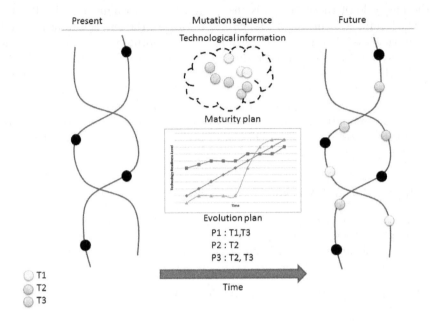

Fig. 3. Genetic code

These types of pairs correspond with the sequential logic design, namely, the need with requirements and functions with the organ. That is why, in a fixed context, we are in measure to validate the requirements with the needs and to propose functional and organic architecture to meet their needs. Here, in the context of product design, we will add a dependency between A and C (and conversely between C and A) because it is obvious that the function must fulfill the requirements. Any change in the nucleotide sequence is a mutation. As in the product,when the need and the solution proposed are not linked, we need a genetic mutation. So, if you link market with the A and T and the solution with C and G, when a change happens in one of this two area, a mutation is required.

3.2   mutagen Factor

The mutation in evolution is paramount, it is the only source of new genes. Adapting to a new situation requires a certain level of genetic variation to provide a mutation. The origins of a mutation called mutagenic or mutagen factor, can be physical or chemical. So the new situation mutagen may as well come from the inside and outside of the product. Indeed, a reversing caused by a distortion between the product and the customer creates a new situation to define the introduction of new technology in the product. That's why customer could not be prepared to this evolution. As already said, the market with impact on A and T sequence is an outside mutation. When there is changes in consumer habits, namely a new application for a product or service, manufacturers are often forced to respond with a new product which guarantees the sustainability of the company. However, in anticipation of these developments, it should be possible to change only part of the product because there is rarely a sudden change in the basic product. But it is possible that the change comes from industry itself through the introduction of new technology or by adding a new feature. At this time, it is a mutation affecting the sequences C and G and an internal transfer mastered by the company. This mutation can have a strong impact on consumption patterns and also on another product.

4   Process and Fitness

4.1   Diagnosis

The diagnosis is still based on a state that is generally accepted by all and represents the reference state. In the field of genetic mutation, this reference is called the karyotype. Karyotype is the standard arrangement of all chromosomes of a cell taken from a microscopic view. Chromosomes are photographed and arranged in a standard format by pair, classified by size and by the centromere position. The karyotype was performed in order to detect chromosomal aberrations (such as trisomy 21) or to identify several aspects of the human genome, such as sex (XX or XY). Note that a karyotype is in the form of photography. Etiology is the study of causes and factors of disease, etiology defines the origin of a disease based on semiotic events (Medical semiology is part of medicine that studies symptoms, signs and how to identify and present it in a diagnosis). Be careful sophistry, a cause does not necessarily correspond to the same effect, and vice versa, this is where the justification for the use of some Bayesian network for research and effect analysis. For medical diagnosis, two examinations could be done:

- Clinic, for physical examination, in this case, presence of two dichotomies:
  - The first information is about the general signs (temperature, fatigue ...) and focal signs (delimits a zone ...)
  - The second is about functional information signs (pain that is not verifiable) and physical signs (redness, noise ...).
- Para-clinical and then for additional radios, scanner, blood test...

4.2   Mutation

Product mutation is triggered after a gap between past and present or present and future. Currently, automobile manufacturers recall many vehicles which don't reach past needs comparing with vehicles currently produced. In the medical field, mutations are classified according to their consequences (phenotypic), that's why we can take again cases to organize them depending on mutation reason, curative or proactive. In this field, genetic mutation is seen as an alteration of the genetic information in a cell or virus genome. So as soon as there is a change of the solution or the need, we are in the presence of a mutation. A genetic mutation is called hereditary if the mutation forms a new organism, it may will an evolution of the species, this implies that it is possible to make a non-inherited mutation in a fleet of product already sold, but to be hereditary it must impacted all products already marketed but also his definition in the design of future product. Dynamic mutation is a mutation evolving from one generation to another, this is the typical case for updates software or with each new release, a number of functionality of the old version's recovery, while preparing the future features, at least, allow their development. In general, the mutation seeks to increase the "fitness" long-term (chance of survival), as humans, the basis must be durable in time, to find there the more evolution possible. When there is change of design data following a genetic mutation (realignment of the solution with respect to the need), only one said germ cell allows the propagation of the mutation (fertilization). Therefore, depending on healing mutations, it is necessary to have a Feedback on design data reflecting the need to create new, or how the product responds again. So we can build a summary table of all cases of mutation and to extract paths mutation based on problem identification.

4.3   Fitness or Fixing

The fitness is the consequence of the mutation, i.e. an improvement of the product relative to need. this is generally the case when a new technology is introduced. The fixing matches upgrading the product relative to need is the case of repairs, or the level of need has not changed, but the product became obsolete relative to its expected level.

5   Conclusions and Future Work

In this paper, authors proposed a method to take into account the earlier as possible the technological introduction in product design with a life-cycle point of view. This consideration is necessary in order to achieve innovative process to improve the product and to be able to be more competitive. Finally, different issues needs furthers research as criterion of technologies resources, tree learning occurs through the technological knowledge, generation algorithm scenarios taking into account the maturity and technological integrability. And in the more distant future, architecture is able to learn all technological links with associated system in the product and vision board quantitative change of entry criteria in relation to overall suitability.

Acknowledgments. The research activity is part of the INGéPROD (Productiveness for Product-Process Engineering in a Design Chain context), which has been funded by French Automotive Cluster Pôle de Compétitivité Véhicule du Futur. The authors would like to thank General Electric for this collaboration and all the financial supports of this research and technology program: DRIRE de Franche-Comté, Communauté dAgglomération du Pays de Montbéliard, Conseil Général du Doubs and Conseil Régional de Franche-Comté.

References

1. Barnes, C.J., Jared, G.E.M., Swift, K.G.: Decision support for sequence generation in an assembly-oriented design environment. Robotics and Computer-Integrated Manufacturing 20, 289–300 (2004)

2. Bralla, J.: The design for manufacturability handbook, 2nd edn. McGraw-Hill, New York (1999)

3. Chapuis, Y., Demoly, F., Gomes, S.: Towards an approach to integrate technological evolution into product design. In: International Conference on Engineering Design (2013)

4. Chapuis, Y., Demoly, F., Gomes, S.: A novel framework for technological evolution within product architecture. In: Prabhu, V., Taisch, M., Kiritsis, D. (eds.) APMS 2013, Part I. IFIP AICT, vol. 414, pp. 219–226. Springer, Heidelberg (2013)

5. Edwards, K.L.: Towards more strategic product design for manufacture and assembly: priorities for concurrent engineering. Materials and Design 23, 651–656 (2002)

6. Gruhier, E., Demoly, F., Abboudi, S., Gomes, S.: A spatiotemporal mereotopology based theory for qualitative description in assembly design and sequence planning., United Kingdom, J.S. Gero. (2014)

7. Holt, R., Barnes, C.: Towards an integrated approach to Design for X: an agenda for decision-based DFX research. Research in Engineering Design 21(2), 123–136 (2010)

8. Kroll, E., Hanft, T.A.: Quantitative evaluation of product disassembly for recycling. Research in Engineering Design 10, 1–14 (1998)

9. Kuo, T.-C., Huang, S.H., Zhang, H.C.: Design for manufacture and design for: concepts, applications and perspectives. Computers and Industrial Engineering 41, 241–260 (2001)

10. Luttrop, C., Lagerstadt, J.: EcoDesign and the ten golden rules: generic advice for merging environmental aspects into product development. Journal of Cleaner Production 14, 1396–1408 (2006)

11. Masanet, E., Auer, R., Tsuda, D.: An assessment and prioritization of design for recycling guidelines for plastic components. In: IEEE International Symposium on Electronics and the Environment, pp. 5–10 (2002)

12. Minehane, S., Duane, R., O'Sullivan, P.: Design for reliability. Microelectronics Reliability 40, 1285–1294 (2000)

13. O'Shea, E.K.: Design for environment in conceptual product design a decision model to reflect environmental issues of all life-cycle phases. The Journal of Sustainable Product Design 2, 11–28 (2004)

14. Petrazoller, N., Demoly, F., Deniaud, S., Gomes, S.: Towards a knowledge-intensive framework for top-down design context definition. In: Prabhu, V., Taisch, M., Kiritsis, D. (eds.) APMS 2013, Part I. IFIP AICT, vol. 414, pp. 210–218. Springer, Heidelberg (2013)

15. Slavila, C.-A., Decreuse, C., Ferney, M.: Maintainability evaluation during the design phase. In: Proceedings of the IDMME 2004 Conference, Bath, UK, pp. 5–7 (2004)

16. Swift, K.G., Booker, J.D.: Process selection: from design to manufacture, 2nd edn. Butterworth-Heinemann, Oxford (2003)

A Hybrid Method for Solving Buffer Sizing and Inspection Stations Allocation

Mohamed Ouzineb[1], Fatima-Zahra Mhada[2], Robert Pellerin[3], and Issmail El Hallaoui[3]

[1] Institut National de Statistique et d'Economie Appliquée and GERAD, B.P.:6217 Rabat-Instituts, Madinat AL Irfane, Rabat, Morocco
[2] University Mohammed V- Souissi/ENSIAS, B.P. 713, Rabat-Instituts, Madinat Al Irfane, Rabat, Morocco
[3] Polytechnique Montréal and GERAD, CP 6079 succ Centre-Ville, Montreal, Qc, Canada H3C 3A9
mohamed.ouzineb@gerad.ca, f.mhada@um5s.net.ma,
{robert.pellerin,issmail.el-hallaoui}@polymtl.ca

Abstract. The buffer sizing problem in unreliable production lines is an important, indeed, complex combinatorial optimization problem with many industrial applications. These applications include quality, logistics and manufacturing production systems. In the formulation of the problem, the system consists of n machines, n fixed-size buffers and m inspection station in series. The objective is to minimize a combined storage and shortage costs, and also specifying the optimal location of inspection stations in the system. The present paper aims at optimizing a generalization of the model previously proposed in (Mhada et al., 2014) using a novel approach. In this approach, we combine Tabu Search (TS) and Genetic Algorithm (GA) to identify search regions with promising locations of inspection stations and an exact method to optimize the assignment of buffer sizes for each location. This approach provides a balance between diversification and intensification. Numerical results on test problems from previous research are reported. Using this approach, we can reduce the solution time by more than 97% in some cases.

Keywords: Inspection, Production lines, Quality, Combinatorial Optimization, Meta-heuristics.

1 Introduction

Apart from rare exceptions ((Kim & Gershwin, 2005, 2008), ((Colledani & Tolio, 2005, 2006a,b, 2011)), the current and standard quality analysis models tend to consider separately the problem of developing strategies for the quality preservation in production lines (positioning stations inspection for example) and the development of strategies to optimize the production problem (kanban, CONWIP, or others). Yet as noted it so well ((Kim & Gershwin, 2005, 2008) and (Colledani & Tolio, 2005, 2006a,b, 2011)), both whole decision are interdependent. We illustrate this interdependence through the example of the analysis of

B. Grabot et al. (Eds.): APMS 2014, Part III, IFIP AICT 440, pp. 156–166, 2014.

kanban strategies introduced by Toyota in the sixties and have since become the paradigm of "lean manufacturing": they essentially advocate areas of limited storage between successive machines in a production line. The objective of these storage areas is to allow certain degree of decoupling between machines to increase productivity of the line (limitation of the effects of parts shortage for downstream machines or blocking machines upstream a broken down one). These stocks should be limited because they are associated with a frozen capital, a storage costs and a parts extended transit times in the workshop.

In a "just in time" ideal, there would be no intermediate stock and finished parts would be pulled from the system as they are produced. However, hazards, such machinery breakdowns and lack of raw material or operators, will come to question this idealized vision, unable to ensure a sufficient continuity of the workshop output. The sizes of the storage areas are directly related to the statistics of these hazards, as well as the estimated costs of the service losses that may result.

So if, we choose to size the kanban by ignoring totally the production quality dimension in the problem, we risk likely to overestimate the security service level with a storage areas which may contain important quantities of defective parts. These defective parts play a negative role for at least two reasons: on one hand they correspond to a misused production line time, since they decrease the efficiency of individual machines; they systematically undermine the "efficiency" of the intermediate storage for its ability to help increase the productivity of the line. On the other hand, as the investments associated with production line come from the same source, the costs associated with storage within the line are going to burden the budget associated with the improvement of the quality and vice versa. (Inman, Blumenfeld, Huang, & Li, 2013) present a survey of recent advances on the interface between quality and production systems design, they provide evidence that production design impact quality and quality impact production design. Also the location of the inspection station affects both the expected production cost per item and the production rate of the line.

They are many research (see (Mandroli, Shrivastava, & Ding, 2006)) that focus in determining the optimal inspection station position in n serial production lines with or without: i) scrapping, ii) rework, iii) off-line repair, without considering the concept of buffer sizing.

Like the work of (Kim & Gershwin, 2005, 2008), we propose to work with a continuous production models (fluid models). However, the analogy with (Kim & Gershwin, 2005, 2008) stops there. In (Kim & Gershwin, 2005, 2008), although the models are continuous, quality, remains attached to a discrete part and we see this as a potential source of contradictions in the modeling.

In our case, we consider a tandem machines where every machine has to satisfy a demand rate of good parts per time unit. We consider the problem of sizing the inventory level taking into account that the stock is mix of good and defective parts; we assume at first all outstanding in the production line continuously observed. Here, the modeling becomes more complex given that there is generally elimination of defective parts along the line by positioning a number of inspection stations. A steady effort was made to develop methods of decomposition, to reduce the analysis of the line to a series of equivalent machine that can be isolated and sequentially analyzed (Mhada et al., 2014).

The present paper efficiently solves a generalization of the model proposed in (Mhada et al., 2014) where the question of the optimal position in the production line of a number m of inspection stations will be treated (m also must be optimal). We combine Tabu Search (TS) and Genetic Algorithm (GA) to identify search regions with promising locations of inspection stations and an exact method to optimize the assignment of buffer sizes for each given location. Hybridizing TS and GA has been proven to be very effective for high-dimensional combinatorial optimization problems. Actually, when the number of solutions is huge, which is the case in this paper, this step aims at locating promising search regions. This approach provides a balance between diversification and intensification. First, the selection of solutions by GA allows the identification of promising regions in the search space. One intended role of using GA is to facilitate the exploration by guiding the search to unvisited regions with good potential. This leads to a certain diversification in terms of subspaces to explore. Second, TS intends to search intensively around good solutions found in the past search. This leads to intensification by exploiting the neighborhood of each solution selected by GA.

The exact method of (Ouzineb et al., 2013) has been shown to be efficient when dealing with the small instances of buffer sizing and inspection stations allocation. This approach is an Exhaustive Search Method (ESM) because the search is guaranteed to generate all possible locations of inspection stations. For each fixed location, the problem is reformulated as a network flow optimization problem that can be efficiently solved by a fast polynomial algorithm. Actually, the space that will be searched is finite by very large and the exhaustive search method may need hours for large instances. The approach proposed in this paper finds near optimal solutions in a fraction of time compared to the exhaustive method proposed in (Ouzineb et al., 2013).

The remainder of the paper is organized as follows. In Section 2, the problem statement is presented. A short description of the proposed approach is given in Section 3. Numerical results are reported in Section 4 and some conclusions are drawn in Section 5.

2   Problem Formulation

Figure 1 represents the production system studies, it consists of n machines separated by $n-1$ buffers and contain (m+1) inspection stations. Machines can be either up or down, starved or blocked. A machine M_i is starved if one of the upstream machines is down and all buffers between this machine and the machine M_i are empty. M_i is blocked if one of the downstream machines is down and all buffer between this machine and the machine M_i are full. When a machine is neither starved or blocked and operational, it transfer parts from the upstream buffer to the downstream in a continuous way. We assume that the first machine can never be starved and an inspection station is located after the last machine to ensure the conformity of parts received by the customer.

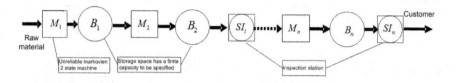

Fig. 1. The production line

All machines $M_i, i = 1...n$ could be modeled as a continuous time Markov chain that produce a single part type with two different quality levels: conforming and non conforming with the same predefined ratio of non-conforming parts to conforming parts β. We consider that all the machines have the same maximal production rate k, failure rate p and repair rate r.

We denote d the demand rate for good parts from the last buffer, x_i the inventory level on the buffer i, $\tilde{d}_i$ the long term average number of parts pulled per unit time from the stock x_i, c_p the storage cost per time unit and per part, c_I the inspection cost per pulled part, and a_{des}^n the required conforming finished parts availability rate.

A binary variable λ_i determine whether or not there is a station before the machine $M_{(i+1)}$ to ensure that all the parts be processed by $M_{(i+1)}$ are conform. We suppose that m inspection stations are dispersed along the line (m is not known) i.e. $\sum_{i=1}^{n-1} \lambda_i = m, m \in \{0, 1, ..., (n-1)\}$ and $\lambda_n = 1$.

The optimization problem is the minimizing of the long term per unit time average global cost of storage , production shortages, and inspection. Meaning, the cost to be minimized is:

$$J_{T(\tilde{d}_i,\lambda_i)} = \lim_{T \to \infty} \frac{1}{T} \sum_{i=1}^{n} E[\int_0^T (c_p\, x_i(t) + c_I\, \tilde{d}_i\, \lambda_i) dt] \tag{1}$$

under conditions:
$$\sum_{i=1}^{n-1} \lambda_i = m, m \in \{0, 1, ..., (n-1)\} \text{ and } \lambda_n = 1$$

The average long term combined storage, shortage costs and inspection costs in (1) expressions can be written after development and calculation (see article Mhada et al. (2014)) as:

$$J(a, \lambda) = \sum_{i=1}^{n-1} T^{(i)}(a, \lambda) + T_F(a, \lambda) + c_I \sum_{i=1}^{n-1} \lambda_i \tilde{d}_i \quad (2)$$

$$T^{(i)}(a, \lambda) = c_p \left(\frac{k \frac{(r(1-a_{i-1})+p)}{a_{i-1}}}{\sigma_i (k - \frac{\tilde{d}_i}{a_i}) \frac{(r+p)}{a_{i-1}}} - \frac{k (1-a_i)}{\sigma_i (k - \frac{\tilde{d}_i}{a_i})} - \left[\frac{1}{\sigma_i} - \frac{(1-a_i) \frac{(r+p)}{a_{i-1}}}{\sigma_i^2 (k - \frac{\tilde{d}_i}{a_i})} \right] \right.$$

$$\left. ln \left[\frac{\frac{(r(1-a_{i-1})+p)}{a_{i-1}} \frac{\tilde{d}_i}{a_i}}{r (k - \frac{\tilde{d}_i}{a_i})} - \frac{\sigma_i \frac{(r(1-a_{i-1})+p)}{a_{i-1}} \frac{\tilde{d}_i}{a_i}}{\frac{(r+p)}{a_{i-1}} r (1-a_i)} \right] \right), i = 1, ..., n-1 \quad (3)$$

$$T_F(a, \lambda) = \frac{\rho_n c_p \left(\frac{k_n (1-\exp(-\mu_n(1-\rho_n) z_n(a_n^{des})))}{1-\rho_n} - \frac{(r+p)}{a_{n-1}} z_n(a_n^{des}) \exp(-\mu_n(1-\rho_n) z_n(a_n^{des})) \right)}{\frac{(r+p)}{a_{n-1}} (1 - \rho_n \exp(-\mu_n(1-\rho_n) z_n(a_n^{des})))}$$

$$(4)$$

with: $\sigma_i = \frac{(\frac{(r+p)}{a_{i-1}}) \frac{\tilde{d}_i}{a_i} - k r}{(k - \frac{\tilde{d}_i}{a_i}) \frac{\tilde{d}_i}{a_i}}$, $\rho_n = \frac{r(k - \frac{\tilde{d}_n}{a_n^{des}})}{\frac{(r(1-a_{n-1})+p)}{a_{n-1}} \frac{\tilde{d}_n}{a_n^{des}}}$, $\mu_n = \frac{(r(1-a_{n-1})+p)}{a_{n-1}(k - \frac{\tilde{d}_n}{a_n^{des}})}$ and

$$z_n(a_n^{des}) = -\frac{ln \left[\frac{1}{\rho_n} \left(1 - \frac{(1-\rho_n)}{(1-a_n^{des})(\frac{(r+p)}{(r(1-a_{n-1})+p)})} \right) \right]}{\mu_n(1-\rho_n)}$$

- $a_i, i = 1...n-1$ is the total parts wip availability coefficient at buffer x_i ; this coefficient has a lower and an upper bounds (Sadr & Malhamé, 2004):
  The upper bound : the minimum of a_i is achieved when the levels of intermediate stocks are at zero, in this case a_i is therefore equal to $a_{i-1} \frac{r}{(r+p)}$. i.e. $a_i > a_{i-1} \frac{r}{(r+p)}$. Also a_i must be smaller than 1. So $a_{i-1} < min \left(\frac{a_i(r+p)}{r}, 1 \right)$
  The lower bound : a_{i-1} must guarantee the feasibility of demand $\tilde{d}_i$ by M_i, i.e $\tilde{d}_i < a_{i-1} k \frac{r}{(r+p)}$ then $\frac{(r+p) \tilde{d}_i}{r k} < a_{i-1}$. Also $a_i > a_{i-1} \frac{r}{(r+p)}$ and we suppose that $a_0 = 1$, then $a_{i-1} > \left(\frac{r}{(r+p)} \right)^{i-1}$. So : $a_{i-1} > max \left[\left(\frac{r}{(r+p)} \right)^{i-1}, \frac{(r+p) \tilde{d}_i}{r k} \right]$.

- $\tilde{d}_i, i = 1...n$ is the long term average number of parts pulled per unit time from stock x_i. The $\tilde{d}_i, i = 1...n$ expression depends on the selected position along the line of the m inspection stations. So if $e_j, j = 1...m$ the inspection station's position, i.e.

$$\lambda_i = \left\{ \begin{array}{l} 1 \text{ if } i = e_j, j = 1...m \\ 0 \text{ if not} \end{array} \right\} \quad (5)$$

then:

$$\tilde{d}_i = \left\{ \begin{array}{ll} d(1+\beta)^n & \text{if} \quad 1 \le i \le e_1 \\ d(1+\beta)^{n-e_1} & \text{if} \quad e_1 < i \le e_2 \\ \cdot & \quad \cdot \\ \cdot & \quad \cdot \\ \cdot & \quad \cdot \\ d(1+\beta)^{n-e_{m-1}} & \text{if} \quad e_{m-1} < i \le e_m \\ d(1+\beta)^{n-e_m} & \text{if} \quad e_m < i \le n \end{array} \right\} \tag{6}$$

The problem can be formulated as follows: find the minimal average global cost system structure (a, λ, m) that satisfies both constraints. That is,

minimize $J(a, \lambda, m)$ $\qquad$ (7)

subject to

$$\sum_{i=1}^{n-1} \lambda_i = m \qquad \forall m, \ 1 \le m \le n-1, \tag{8}$$

$$max \left[\left(\frac{r}{(r+p)} \right)^{i-1}, \frac{(r+p)\,\tilde{d}_i}{r\,k} \right] < a_{i-1} \le min \left[\frac{a_i(r+p)}{r}, 1 \right], \ \forall i, \ 1 \le i \le n, \tag{9}$$

$$\lambda_n = 1 \ \text{and} \ a_n = a_n^{des}, \tag{10}$$

$$\lambda_i \in \{0, 1\} \qquad \forall i, \ 1 \le i \le n-1. \tag{11}$$

$$a_i \ge 0 \qquad \forall i, \ 1 \le i \le n, \tag{12}$$

This problem is a Mixed Integer Nonlinear Programming (MINLP) problem which refers to a mathematical programming with continuous and discrete variables and nonlinearities in the objective function (7) and constraints ((8), (9), (10), (11), and (12)). This problem simultaneously optimizes the system structure: the location of the inspection stations (discrete) and parameters and the buffer sizing (continuous).

The variables a_i, $1 \le i \le n$, $\lambda_i \in \{0, 1\}$ $1 \le i \le n-1$ and m are the decision variables.

The constraint (10) represents the final conditions set by the customer.

The constraint (9) is a nonlinear constraint function which represents the line configuration, it is a cumulative constraint type that represents a guarantee the functioning of the production line.

The vector of binary variables ((8),(11)) is connected to the line structure.

3   Solution Methodology

As mentioned earlier, the objective function to minimize is the average long term combined storage and shortage costs, while also specifying the optimal location of inspection stations that meets a specified final condition set by the customer. The goal is to solve the optimization problem given by Eqs. (7-12) for a large test problem with 20 machines.

The exact method of (Ouzineb et al., 2013) has been shown to be efficient when dealing with the small instances of buffer sizing and inspection stations allocation. This approach is an Exhaustive Search Method (ESM) because the search is guaranteed to generate all possible locations of inspection stations.

This approach is an Exhaustive Search Method (ESM) because the search is guaranteed to.

It is clear that while the exhaustive exact method (ESM) of (Ouzineb et al., 2013) finds optimal solutions to small instances in reasonable times, the running time appears to be unreasonable for larger ones. In fact, ESM generate all possible locations of the inspection stations.

If we especially increase the number of machines, this method becomes drastically inefficient. The number of possible locations of the inspection stations, which is exponential, explodes. It is observed that the large amount of these locations are not profitable. For solving the combinatorial optimization problem formulated in 7-12, it is important to have an effective and fast procedure to smartly locate the extra m inspection stations. To do so, we propose a combination of Genetic Algorithm (GA) and Tabu Search (TS), which has been proven to be very effective for high-dimensional combinatorial optimization problems.

For each fixed location, we use a network flow problem, that can be efficiently solved as the standard shortest path problem to find the optimal assignment of buffer sizes. Because of such a combination, this method is said to be hybrid. Hereunder, we will refer to this hybrid method as EM/TG, EM and TG being acronyms of Exact Method and Tabu-Genetic, respectively. This approach finds optimal or near optimal solutions to the same instances in a fraction of time compared to the exhaustive method proposed in (Ouzineb et al., 2013) as will be shown by the experiments. The hybrid method is presented in details in the next section.

3.1 Hybrid Optimization Method

The genetic algorithm used in this paper is based on the method commonly known as the steady-state GA or GENITOR (Whitley & Kauth, 1988). Starting from a randomly-generated initial population (feasible solutions), the genetic algorithm applies iteratively four operators: selection, crossover, mutation and culling to produce a new population of solutions.

The search space S is composed of all possible λ_i values, for $i \in \{1, ..., n-1\}$. The production line can contain inspection stations located at the exit of buffer B_i and the provisioning point for machine M_{i+1}. The presence or absence of these stations is captured by a binary variable λ_i that takes 1 if there is an inspection station at the exit of the buffer B_i and 0 if not, respectively.

To avoid creating infeasible solutions after the crossover operator, we choose to generate solutions with same address. We divide the solution into two same parts and we create an address for each solution as follows:

The address of λ is defined by: $Address(\lambda) = (\sum_{l=1}^{n/2} \lambda_l, \sum_{l=n/2+1}^{n} \lambda_l)$.

Compared to standard genetic algorithm, the mutation step is replaced in EM/TG by Tabu Search. These operators can be summarized as follows:

1. **Selection operator:** it randomly selects, from the population, two solutions of same address named parent 1 and parent 2 that will "reproduce" to create a new solution.
2. **Crossover operator:** it produces a new solution (child or offspring) from a selected pair of parent solutions. We use the so-called one-point crossover operator, which, as illustrated in Table 1, creates the child string O for the given pair of parent strings λ_1 and λ_2 by:
   (a) Copying string elements belonging to the first fragment from λ_1;
   (b) Copying the rest of string elements from λ_2.

Table 1. An example illustrating the 1-point crossover procedure

Parent string λ_1	0	0	0	1	0	0	1	0	0	0	0	1	0	0	0	0	0	1	0	1
Parent string λ_2	0	0	0	0	1	0	1	0	0	0	0	1	1	0	0	0	0	0	0	1
Child string	0	0	0	1	0	0	1	0	0	0	0	1	1	0	0	0	0	0	0	1

3. **Tabu Search (TS)** (this replaces the Mutation operator): it looks for the best solution in the subspace associated with the new child using the TS algorithm described previously. The best solution found becomes the new child.
4. **Culling operator:** it generates the new population. Each new solution obtained by TS is decoded to obtain its fitness value. The fitness value, which is in fact a measure of quality, is used to compare different solutions. This fitness is evaluated according to the objective function $J(a, \lambda)$ optimized as a subproblem with an exact method (for more details see Section 3.2). If the new solution obtained by TS is better than the worst solution currently in the population, it replaces it, else it is discarded. After N_{rep} new solutions have been produced, new randomly constructed solutions are generated to replenish the population, and a new genetic cycle begins. The GA is terminated after N_c genetic cycles. The final GA population contains the best solution.

3.2   Flow Optimization Model

For a fixed location λ, the subproblem used to evaluate the fitness can be reformulated as a network flow problem. Consider the connected network $G(E, V)$ consisting of a set of nodes E and a set of links V as illustrated by Figure 2. Each column i corresponds to a set of possible buffer levels for a machine i, such that:

$$a_{i1} = 100 \times \max((\frac{r}{r+p})^{i-1}, \frac{d}{k}\frac{r+p}{r}) \quad \text{and} \quad a_{in_i} = 100 \times \min(\frac{a_i(r+p)}{r}, 1).$$

Each node is connected to all nodes in the next column. To each link is associated some real number $c_{i,i+1}$ that corresponds to the shortage costs and inspection costs, such that: $c_{0,1} = 1$, $c_{i,i+1} = T^i(a_i, a_{i+1}, \lambda) + C_I \times \lambda_i \times d_i$ and $c_{n-1,n} = T_F(a_{n-1}, a_n)$. The main objective is to find for each λ the shortest path between a_0 and a_n.

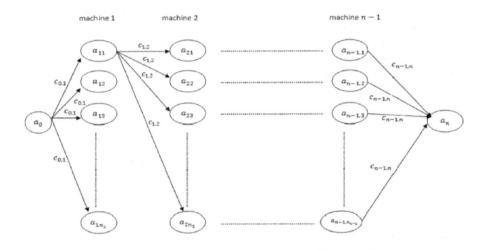

Fig. 2. The production line

4   Numerical Results

To analyze the solution method introduced in this paper, we tested it on a large problem with 20 machines, one of the problems benchmarked in previous research. This problem was first introduced and solved by the exact ESM method in (Ouzineb et al., 2013). The exact method applied to this problem takes hours while the new approach finds optimal or near optimal solutions in a fraction of time. Our algorithm was implemented in $C++$. The numerical tests were performed on an Intel Core i7 at 2.8 GHz with 8 Gbytes of RAM running under Linux.

Table 2 shows the parameters used for the experimentation. To compare the proposed hybrid approach EM/TG to ESM, we re-implemented ESM and re-tested it and EM/TG in the same conditions (computer, programming language, operating systems, etc.).

Table 2. System parameters

	n	p	r	k	β_i	d	c_p	c_I	a_n^{des}
20 machines	20	0.2	0.9	9	0.1	1	0.1	0.2	0.95

This allows us to determine the optimal solutions to compare to. We define two ratios in terms of the objective value and CPU time to determine which solution method performs better:

$$\text{MPCI} = 100\% \times \frac{(\text{Minimal ESM Cost - Minimal EM/TG Cost})}{\text{Minimal ESM Cost}}. \quad (13)$$

$$\text{MPTI} = 100\% \times \frac{(\text{Minimal ESM Time - Minimal EM/TG Time})}{\text{Minimal ESM Time}}. \quad (14)$$

Comparison results are given in Table 3 . The column m indicates the number of inspection stations to use. We varied this number between 1 and 10. We see that EM/TG obtains optimal solutions in 90% of the cases in less time. It reduces the solution time by huge factors up to 40 compared to ESM. Table 4 shows the

Table 3. Comparison results for 20 machines

m	Cost			Running time (s)		
	ESM	*EM/TG*	*MPCI*	*ESM*	*EM/TG*	*MPTI*
1	**8.3125**	**8.3125**	**0.00**	08.44	424.63	**-98.01**
2	**6.2645**	**6.2645**	**0.00**	75.82	709.54	**-89.31**
3	**5.9802**	**5.9802**	**0.00**	432.83	1610.94	**-73.13**
4	**6.0663**	**6.0663**	**0.00**	1792.58	1535.98	**14.32**
5	**6.2772**	**6.2772**	**0.00**	5402.57	2254.07	**58.28**
6	**6.5230**	**6.5230**	**0.00**	12509.7	1675.02	**86.61**
7	**6.7959**	**6.7959**	**0.00**	23037.5	1714.70	**92.56**
8	**7.0965**	**7.0965**	**0.00**	34423.4	1739.85	**94.95**
9	**7.4298**	7.5000	**-0.94**	41982.9	1322.47	**96.85**
10	**7.7947**	**7.7947**	**0.00**	42057.9	1222.84	**97.09**

results obtained for the test problems with 20 machines by using the proposed hybrid method and the exact approach limiting the running time to 3600 seconds. In all test cases, EM/TG performs as well as ESM in 40% of the test cases and better in the remaining 60% of the test cases when we limit the solution time to one hour.

Table 4. The results obtained by the proposed method and exact approach for 20 machines during 3600 seconds

m	1	2	3	4	5	6	7	8	9	10
EM/TG	**8.3125**	**6.2645**	**5.9802**	**6.0663**	**6.2772**	**6.5230**	**6.7959**	**7.0965**	**7.5000**	**7.7947**
ESM	8.3125	6.2645	5.9802	6.0663	6.2774	6.8639	7.3566	7.8709	8.4458	8.9299

N.B: For instance (m=9) the algorithm has converged locally after 1322 seconds and could not improve this solution even after more time.

5   Conclusions

This paper proposes an efficient hybrid approach based on an exact method and methaheuristics to solve the buffer sizing problem in unreliable heterogeneous production lines with several inspection stations. This is a very hard mixed integer nonlinear program. The proposed approach uses ideas from genetic algorithm and tabu search to identify profitable configurations (locations of the inspection stations). For these locations, we use an exact approach to decide the optimal sizes of the buffers to use. Our final goal is to find an optimal design.

This hybrid approach provides a balance between diversification and intensification that shows to work well on such heterogeneous production lines with up to 20 machines. When compared to the exhaustive exact method, the hybrid approach results are superior in terms of CPU time.

Future research will focus on applying our heuristic to solve larger instances (up to 30 machines and a variable number of inspection stations).

References

Colledani, M., Tolio, T.: Impactofstatisticalprocesscontrol (spc) onthe performance ofproductionsystems-part2 (largesystems). ZakynthosIsland, Greece (2005)

Colledani, M., Tolio, T.: Impact ofquality control on production system performance. Annals of the CIRP 55(1), 453–456 (2006a)

Colledani, M., Tolio, T.: Performance evaluation of production systems monitored by statistical process control and offline inspections. Information Control Problems in Manufacturing, 317–322 (2006b)

Colledani, M., Tolio, T.: Integrated analysis of quality and production logistics performance inmanufacturing lines. International Journal of Production Research 49(2), 485–518 (2011)

Inman, R., Blumenfeld, D., Huang, N., Li, J.: Survey of recent advances on the interface between production system design and quality. IIE Transactions 45(6), 557–574 (2013)

Kim, J., Gershwin, S.: Integrated quality and quantity modeling of a production line. OR Spectrum 27, 287–314 (2005)

Kim, J., Gershwin, S.: Analysis of long flow lines with quality and operational failures. IIE Transactions 40, 284–296 (2008)

Mandroli, S., Shrivastava, A., Ding, Y.: A survey of inspection strategy and sensor distribution studies in discrete-part manufacturing processes. IIE Transactions 38(4), 309–328 (2006)

Mhada, F., Malhamé, R., Pellerin, R.: Joint assignment of buffer sizes and inspection points in unreliable transfer lines with scrapping of defective parts. Production and Manufacturing Research 1, 79–101 (2014)

Ouzineb, M., Mhada, F., El Hallaoui, I., Pellerin, R.: An exact method for solving the buffer sizing and inspection stations allocations problem. In: Proceedings of the 2013 International Conference on Industrial Engineering and Systems Management (IESM), October 28-30, 2013, pp. 1–6 (2013), http://ieeexplore.ieee.org/stamp/stamp.jsp?tp=&arnumber=6761508&isnumber=6761346

Sadr, J., Malhamé, R.: Unreliable transfer lines: decomposition/ aggregation and optimisation. Annals of Operations Research 125, 167–190 (2004)

Whitley, D., Kauth, J.: Genitor: A different genetic algorithm (Tech. Rep.No.CS-88-101). Colorado State University (1988)

Negative Side Effects of Lean Management

Andreas Mueller and Stanisław Strzelczak

Warsaw University of Technology, Faculty of Production Engineering, Warsaw, Poland
a_mueller_84@yahoo.de, s.strzelczak@wip.pw.edu.pl

Abstract. This paper investigates the problem of unplanned negative effects, which may result from implementation of lean management. Using as the basis empirical evidence from European machine tools industry it is argued, that in majority of cases targeted effects (mostly cost savings, production and utilization increase) are followed, with a delay, by negative side effects (mostly unplanned increased costs, quality issues, customer dissatisfaction). It is suggested, that using the controlling framework as management tool may enable to avoid these unlikely effects. Its relevant adoption, to support multi-perspective assessment of lean management implementations is presented within the paper.

Keywords: Lean Management, Effects, Multi-perspective Assessment.

1 Introduction

In 2007 the Industry Week published an article about a widespread survey performed in USA, which has shown that only 2% of companies applying Lean Management initiatives meet their planed results [1]. In addition Liker [2] stated that a majority of organizations, which went through improvement programs argue, that after positive effects, a fall back turns in to reverse initial efforts. Recently, the Shingo Award Committee confirmed the last thesis, after investigating on sustainability of business excellence performance of past award winners [3]. The above mentioned fallbacks seem to appear frequently, despite application of modern Lean Management leadership approaches supported by organizational culture changes and intensive trainings. However, the scientific literature usually ignores the problem or walks along its surface, as it mainly lacks empirical background for its deeper analysis.

The purpose of this paper is to reflect on findings from literature and own research, with the intention to analyze roots and reasons, as well as possible ways to tame the above problem. This paper presents different research findings. Eight cases (including expert panels) from four different OEM machinery manufacturing companies are a basis for empirical data, illustrating negative side effects resulting from wrongly controlled or implemented Lean Management initiatives. Apart from that, the literature review regarding the effects of Lean Management and potential ways of their assessment, are presented in the paper, with the intention to avoid the unlikely effects. The conclusions from the research are used as inputs for development of a framework for holistic multi-perspective assessment of Lean Management implementations, by an adoption of the idea of universal controlling [19].

B. Grabot et al. (Eds.): APMS 2014, Part III, IFIP AICT 440, pp. 167–174, 2014.
© IFIP International Federation for Information Processing 2014

2   Existing Knowledge

One of the first difficulties met by anybody researching the Lean Management is its fuzzy definition, allowing various interpretations and implementations to be put under the same name. By researching on the term Lean Management a various range of definitions can be identified. Furthermore it seems difficult to identify a definition, which is not affected by lean consultancy. The shortest and easiest definition identified with a scientific background is as follows: Lean management implementation leads to generation of more value for customers with fewer resources as input [4]. Inputs could be described as materials, human resources and financial inputs.

Following the above definition, promising improvements are outlined in the literature, which seem to be dominated by authors directly involved in Lean Management Consultancy. It is often suggested, that with Lean Management it is possible to achieve significant effects, e.g.: lead time reduction of 60-90%, decrease of inventories by 10-50%, shop floor utilization increase by 5-40% or productivity improvement by 5-25%, just naming few benefits reported e.g. in [5]. This kind of promises makes decision-making and budget allocation for majority of Lean projects easy. However, it is not always sure, if at all, if the mentioned effects will bring only wealth in a long term perspective, as it is presumed in all cases. As was suggested by the quotations in the former section, there are also second momentum effects of Lean management implementation [1,2,3]. Other examples of firms suffering from distortions and turbulences after becoming lean corporations are described in some papers [6].

The question arises, when reading publications reporting Lean Management effects is how these were controlled (ex ante and ex post). Surprisingly all quoted publications bypass the methodological of how to control these effects. In general there are various accounting and controlling possibilities to support implementation and observation of Lean Management initiatives. Kaplan and Cooper outline that conservative controlling systems are insufficient for feedback and learning due to delays in reporting, straight attention on financial measures, top-down implementation, focus on localized improvements, individual control and adherence to traditional standards, which cannot support lean [7]. Maskell argues [8], that most of relevant accounting essentials, which modern managers work with, date back to 1930s. He suggests practical lean accounting as a relevant basis for improvements, however with no exact recommendations. Grasso reviewed accounting and controlling possibilities for Lean Management implementation assessment, including the following approaches [16]:

— Kaplan & Norton: Balanced scorecard [9]
— Staubus: Input/Output costing or Activity Based Costing (ABC) [10]
— Sharman: Flexible margin costing (ger.: Grenzplankostenrechnung - GPK) [11, 12]
— Merwe & Keys: Resource Consumption Accounting (RCA) [13]
— Dixon, Nanni & Vollmann: Stage II systems [14]
— Horvath: Process costing (PC) [15]
— Horvath: Integration of PC and GPK in RCA [16]
— Goldratt: Throughput accounting [17]
— Maskell: Lean accounting [18]

Some of the listed publications directly suggest, that companies should think of a lean controlling system with a practical and simple lean accounting approach [8,16]. Universal controlling, as a management tool, is being described by three dimensions: function (strategic or operational), scope (financial, operations and financial or complex) and category (production, logistics etc.). It may incorporate controlling of results and controlling of structures. Aside from controlling dimensions two approaches are used to control different outputs: quantitative outputs and qualitative outputs. The quantitative controlling focuses on mathematic models or applications and reflects to measurement theory and support to the decision-making process. Especially in the past, a pure financial controlling in terms of controlling results and structures had broad attention. Qualitative controlling focuses more on individual attitudes, behavior, group processes, considers industrial psychology, while motivation is a driving force. It is widely applied for qualitative differentiation (characterization) of an organization and enables monitoring or evaluation in a form of non-financial logic.

It is also visible from the reviewed literature, that a multi-perspective method of lean Management assessment is not available, despite several controlling approaches existing in the literature. Quantitative controlling seems improper to create value due to straight attention to monetary benefits, while qualitative controlling might be interesting due to its universalism. The field of multi-perspective assessment of Lean Management is not yet enforced by available literature. The research described below targets to eliminate theses shortcomings, by looking at case study findings and analyzing its results.

3   Research Methodology and Findings

Considering the main objective of the research, i.e. finding the means to avoid side negative effects of lean management implementation, potentially by a better way of assessment of the effects, two major directions seem to be crucial: to understand the reasons of why negative effects appear and to investigate the tools which may help to recognize the negative effects, if possible in advance, and to measure them.

Apart of the review of existing knowledge, which can be based on the literature sources, there is also evident need to directly recognize the phenomena through empirical research. Unfortunately, due to limited access to the company data (particularly to the quantitative data), the scope of possible approaches for such research is very limited. It has been decided, to avoid any bias, to develop case studies of different implementations of Lean Management, starting from data collection during semi-structured interviews, than eventually followed by successive expert panels. These could be also helpful to verify conclusions drawn from the empirical data, which refer to the eventual assessment framework or method. The synthesis of such conclusions was presumed as fundamental for formulation of the holistic multi-perspective method for Lean Management effects assessment, following the integrated global analysis approach. The framework is rooted in the ideas of universal controlling, according to the literature recommendations. The plan of research is presented in a structured way in the below table.

Table 1. Structure of Research

Phase	Scope	Methods / Tools
Initial	Problem conceptualization Evidence of possible effects Assessment approaches	Analysis of literature
Empirical	Planning interviews Interviewing	Semi-structured interviewing Expert panels (2nd iteration)
Analysis of results	Results assessment Summary of findings	Conceptual analysis Simple statistical analysis
Synthesis of results	Proposal of multi-perspective as- sessment method	Theoretical synthesis

Targeting the interviews, four globally operating OEM machinery manufacturers have been approached, to receive first-hand information on specific lean initiatives. All companies have an in house production and engineering. The interviews have been done in different departments in EU. After onsite face to face introduction eight interviews were arranged with middle and senior managers from different work areas (Table 2). Afterwards findings have been later discussed, during the expert panels, to receive detailed information and protect against any bias. Due to confidentiality companies are unnamed. As key performance indicators were not allowed to be published, synthetic quantification of effects or costs is used in the paper.

All eight interviews have been conducted, aiming to discover targeted effects, which managers committed on, prior to lean project starts. In addition, discovery of negative side effects was indirectly targeted. All identified types of targeted effects and side negative effects are listed in table 3.

Table 2. Performed Interviews

Company	Location	Workforce	Lean Topic	Interviewees
A	South Germany	1000+	Product Development	Chief technical officer Head of product development
B	North Germany	600+	Procurement LCC	Head of procurement Senior category manage
A	South Germany	1000+	Assembly Tact	Head of assembly Head of outgoing goods
C	Switzerland	500+	Assembly LCC	Head of assembly Diverse sales managers
C	Switzerland	500+	Engineering Relocation	Head of engineering Head of business excellence IT
A	South Germany	1000+	Production LCC	Head of assembly Head of human resources
D	West Germany	1000+	Machine Investment	Head of production Head of quality management
B	North Germany	600+	Sales KPIs	Head of sales Line manager assembly

Table 3. Overview of Targeted and Side Effects

Interview	Field and Topic	Targeted Effects	Negative Effects
1	Product Development	Low development cost Transparent spending	Additional costs Quality issues Customer dissatisfaction
2	Procurement LCC	Saving supply cost LCC quote	Additional costs Penalties, Fall outs Quality issues
3	Assembly Tact	Cost savings Double output Productivity increase	Additional costs Increased stock
4	Assembly LCC	Saving personnel costs Saving production costs Low cost suppliers	Additional costs Customer dissatisfaction Reduced sales volume Non-acceptance by own staff
5	Engineering Relocation	Saving production costs Utilization of plants Standardization	Additional costs Quality issues Missing responsibility
6	Production LCC	Saving production costs Low investment cost Growth in market	Additional costs Quality issues Non-acceptance by own staff
7	Machine Investment	Saving production cost Technological advantage Utilization	Additional costs
8	Sales KPIs	Revenue increase Better motivation	Additional costs Quality issues Customer dissatisfaction

It has appeared that for all cases, which were subject of interviewing, implementation plans existed. All of them were including a list of expected gains. Such list in all cases summarized mainly the expected financial benefits and the one-time cost reductions to be achieved. By categorizing findings it becomes clear, that nearly all lean initiatives primarily targeted cost savings, followed by some kind of growth targets (increased sales, etc.) and utilization targets.

When looking at negative side effects observed, it becomes evident that in all cases the implementations of Lean Management initiatives were later followed by some unexpected additional costs (losses), around or even inside the lean system, and additionally by unplanned quality issues (in every second project), and by some kind of customer dissatisfaction (in about every third project).

An effort to measure all effects was also undertaken during the performed research. As they were of different type and some could not be measured easily in a natural way, all interviewees were asked to allocate a weight ranging from 0 as minimum to 6 as maximum, to the targeted (i.e. positive) and negative (i.e. side) effects. The average assessments for all cases are illustrated at Fig.1.

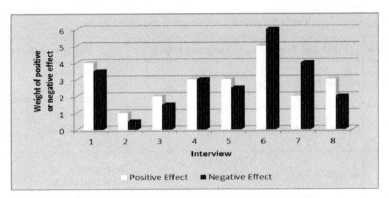

Fig. 1. Absolute Quantification of Lean Management target and side effects (sequence of interviews as in table 3)

By comparing the initially planned targeted effects with the observed negative side effects, it is clear that in some cases side negative effects are higher than the priory planned effects, reflecting that unplanned costs overtake planned benefits. Furthermore, in even no one case the planned effects exceeded significantly (i.e. by one order) the negative side effects.

The interviewed managers were also asked about their opinions concerning assessment of the effects. A fixed numerical baseline in a form of starting point, to track the progress, was always considered as a basis to follow up targeted savings. This means that a kind of primitive controlling of targeted effects was applied in all cases. A general opinion can be also formulated, that a strong focus on financial controlling seems to be an inappropriate for Lean projects implementation. Many interviewees stressed, that missed link between Lean initiative and overall strategy, together with changing environmental conditions, ignored risks due to profitability pressure, drive negative side effects, making counteracting after first appearance nearly impossible.

The scale of identified negative effects of Lean Management implementations together with the existing methodological shortcomings support the conclusion that the Lean Management implementations should be preceded, then monitored in a more systematic and rigid way. Particularly choosing the Lean Management initiatives and their targeted effects should be rooted in the strategic planning and done with reference to the strategic company goals, then rigidly monitored by the controlling means.

4   Multi-perspective Assessment of Lean Management

Following the conclusions from research, an initial framework for multi-perspective assessment of Lean Management implementations has been developed to overcome existing methodological shortcomings, using the idea of universal controlling (Fig.2). The intention behind the proposed model is to maintain a connection between strategic planning, which embeds strategy, objectives, time frame and risk assessment of an entire corporation, with a way of selection of particular processes to be improved by the Lean Management methodology. This way the targeted processes improvement initiatives receive information inputs for further detailed analysis directly from the overall company data, including key performance indicators and their trendlines.

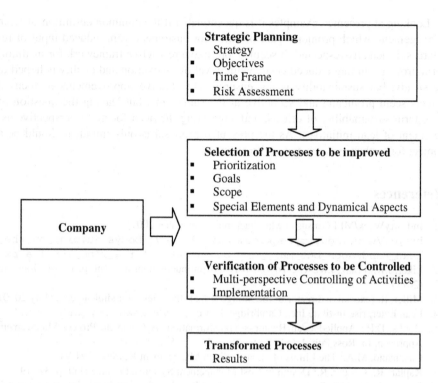

Fig. 2. Framework for a method for multi-perspective assessment of Lean Management

After prioritization and goals setting the scope of implementation may be defined in a justified way. Then some special elements or dynamical aspects may be considered. Within a verification stage a multi-perspective controlling of activities is being applied before an implementation starts. Finally when implementation has taken place, results are being evaluated, monitored and considered as new baseline for next improvements.

5   Conclusions

The evidence form performed research suggests, that all the interviewed managers agree about existing practices on Lean Management assessment, as having many shortcomings. Particularly strict financial controlling of arbitrary selected savings should not be used as a stand-alone instrument for Lean project implementation. An initial model for multi-perspective assessment been therefore developed, intending to connect Lean Management with strategic planning and qualitative controlling, to overcome the problem of negative side effects of Lean Management implementations.

Despite the fact that quantitative controlling, or in particular a focused financial controlling of reduced cost items is applied to plan and monitor benefits and costs of projects, it is confirmed that in most cases unplanned turbulences appear to reverse, or at least significantly reduce initially planned target effects.

Looking at presented examples it is questionable if the common definition of Lean Management, which promotes gain of value for customers from reduced input of resources, is actually respected. It seems more like a restrictive framework for medium-term projects, aiming reduced costs, while level of innovation and quality is hoped to be steady, but sustainability is not ensured. Quantitative improvements of focused effects seem promising and seductive at the same time, but leaving the question of long-term sustainability of effects, and suggesting the need for multi-perspective assessment of lean initiatives. As the presented proposal is only initial, it should be a subject for further research and verification.

References

1. IndustryWeek/MPI Census of Manufacturers (November 2007),
   http://www.industryweek.com/articles/everbodys_jumping_on_the_
   lean_bandwagon_but_many_are_being_taken_for_a_ride_15881.aspx
2. Liker, J.K., Franz, J.K.: The Toyota Way to Continuous Improvement, p. 12. McGraw-Hil (2011)
3. Miller, R. (executive director of the Shingo Prize): Interview on radiolean.com (July 2010)
4. Lean Enterprise Institute Inc., Cambridge, http://www.lean.org/whatslean/
5. Hobbs, D.P.: Applied Lean Business Transformation: A Complete Project Management Approach. In: Ross Pub, J. (ed.) J. Ross Pub. Inc., p. 5 (2011)
6. Cusumano, M.A.: The Limits of "Lean". Sloan Management Review 1994/VI
7. Kaplan, R., Cooper, R.: Design of Cost Management Systems, Prentice Hall, p. 37 (1998)
8. Stenzel, J., Maskell, B.: Lean Accounting: Best Practices for Sustainable Integration, p. 55. John Wiley & Sons (2007)
9. Kaplan, R.S., Norton, D.P.: The Balanced Scorecard: Translating Strategy Into Action. Harvard Business School Press (1996)
10. Staubus, G.J.: Activity Costing and Input-Output Accounting, Richard D.Irwin (1971)
11. Sharman, P.: The Case for Management Accounting, Strategic Finance, 2003/X
12. Sharman, P.: German Cost Accounting, StrategicFinance, 2003/X
13. Van der Merwe, A., Keys, D.E.: The Case for Resource Consumption Accounting, Strategic Finance, 2002/IV
14. Dixon, R., Nanni, A., Vollmann, T.: The New Performance Challenge: Measuring Operations for World-Class Competition, Dow Jones-Irwin (1990)
15. Prozeßkostenmanagement: Methodik und Anwendungsfelder, Vahlen, Horvath & Partner GmbH, 1998/VI
16. Grasso, L.P.: Are ABC and RCA Accounting Systems Compatible with Lean Management? Management Accounting Quarterly 7/1 (2005)
17. Goldratt, E.: What Is This Thing Called Theory of Constraints. North River Press (1990)
18. Maskell, B.: Practical Lean Accounting: A Proven System for Measuring and Managing the Lean Enterprise. Productivity Press (2011)
19. Marciniak, S.: Controlling – Theory and Applications, ch. 2&3. Diffin (2007) (in Polish)

Integrating Real-Time Analytics and Continuous Performance Management in Smart Manufacturing Systems*

Senthilkumaran Kumaraguru, Boonserm (Serm) Kulvatunyou, and K.C. Morris

Systems Integration Division, Engineering Laboratory, NIST
Gaithersburg, MD, USA.
`{fns1,boonserm.kulvatunyou,kcm}@nist.gov`

Abstract. This paper proposes an approach to integrate real-time analytics with continuous performance management. The proposed system exploits the increasing availability of industrial process and production performance data. This paper identifies components of such a system and the interface between components within the system. The components presented in this paper form the basis for further research on understanding potential interoperability issues and required standardization efforts to support development of a system.

Keywords: performance management, smart manufacturing, continuous improvement, real-time analytics.

1   Introduction

Smart manufacturing (SM) systems are envisioned to have the ability to adapt to new situations by using real-time data for intelligent decision-making, as well as predicting and preventing failures proactively in real time.   The nature of plant data today is characterized by large volume, large varieties, high velocity, low veracity (accuracy), uncertain validity, and volatility (timeliness). Data analytics can use this type of data to provide insights for the purpose of performance management. SM will need performance management systems that have the capability to generate and consume such data to continuously monitor, measure, and control performance in real time [1]. In this context, this paper presents an approach for integrating performance management of SM systems with real-time data analytics. Performance management systems employing such an approach enable continuous improvements to performance criteria such as costs, safety, and sustainability. Over time, the result of deploying such a performance management system will benefit manufacturers by providing a more dynamic response to performance concerns. This in turn will enable realizations of smart manufacturing systems that benefit end customers with low cost, sustainable, and customizable product choices [2]. The proposed integrated system for performance management is discussed in detail in the next section.

---

* The rights of this work are transferred to the extent transferable according to Title 17 U.S.C. §105.

B. Grabot et al. (Eds.): APMS 2014, Part III, IFIP AICT 440, pp. 175–182, 2014.
© IFIP International Federation for Information Processing 2014 (Outside the US)

2   Real-Time, Continuous Performance Management System

Effective performance management is both reactive and proactive. Reactively, performance measurements drive two actions when there is a performance deviation—diagnosis and resolution. Diagnosis involves pinpointing potential problem areas, while the resolution involves finding and applying corrective actions. Proactively, when there is no deviation from a target performance for a period of time, the system can identify an opportunity for more improvements to the performance. In other words, manufacturers can and should continuously monitor and adjust target performance. Also proactively, performance management can be used to predict performance issues in real time.

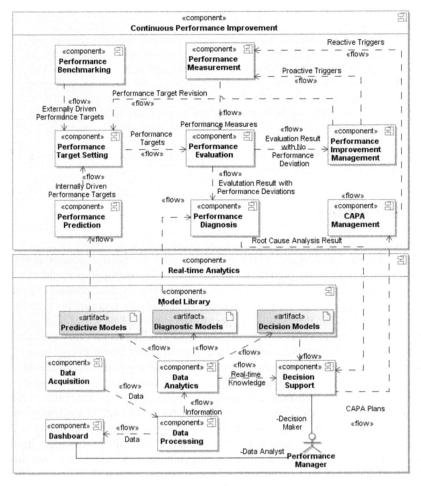

Fig. 1. Real-time analytics and continuous performance management system components

These desired functionalities necessitate the following major characteristics in the system: 1) data needs to be available for an intelligent and informed decision in real time; 2) performance and exceptions need to be predicted regularly and evaluated against performance targets; 3) performance deviation needs to be continuously monitored and improved; and 4) performance diagnosis and resolution capabilities need to be available online and evolved over time.

Figure 1 highlights the major components of the proposed system.   At the top level the system is divided into two components: *Real-time Analytics* and *Continuous Performance Improvement*.   The *Real-time Analytics* component discussed in section 2.1, is responsible for turning data from the system into information that can guide decision making.   It recommends corrective and preventive actions (CAPA) and produces analytical models that are used by the *Continuous Performance Improvement* component.   The *Continuous Performance Improvement* component discussed in section 2.2, focuses on measuring and evaluating data against targets. Deviation from targets will cause diagnosis and resolution.   The system components are identified by <<components>> and flow of information between the components are specified by <<flow>> and is marked by a dotted line in Figure 1 and the interactions of a performance manager with the components are specified by a solid line.

2.1   Real-Time Analytics

The main functions of the Real-time Analytics component are to: (1) gather data and convert it into useful knowledge and intelligence, and (2) develop predictive, diagnostic, and decision models. The models developed are maintained in a library as shown in Figure 1. This library is a growing knowledge base about the system based on past performance. The other components described below support both the construction and use of these models. The models are also used by the *Continuous Performance Improvement* component.

Data acquisition and Data Processing
The data used to calculate performance metrics is often available in multiple locations, in multiple formats, and from multiple systems. MTConnect [3] and Open Platform Communications (OPC) (previously Object Linking and Embedding for process control) Unified Architecture (UA) [4] are two extensible standards for exchanging shop floor data between systems. These standards enhance the utility and reduce computational complexity of mining unstructured information. Currently supported data types in these standards include measured physical quantities such as forces, acceleration, energy, flow rate, positional data, and clock time. The calculated data supported includes strain, torque, and wattage; and sensed events such as availability, error traces, emergency stops, part counts, and power state. This data needs further data cleaning and processing to deliver information to a system for modeling and decision making.

Figure 2 shows data flow between *Data Acquisition*, *Data Processing*, and *Data Analytics*. Unstructured data from a Human Machine Interface (HMI) may be processed by a Supervisory Control and Data Acquisition (SCADA) system, possibly followed by a Manufacturing Execution System (MES) system and by an Enterprise

Resource Planning (ERP) system. Data for the manufacturing decision maker is available in a structured way through each of these systems typically with increasing levels of abstraction by aggregating the data. Historical data from these systems are used to generate performance predictions.

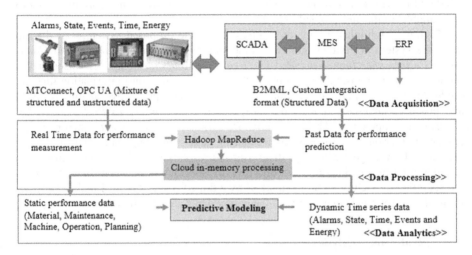

Fig. 2. Real-time data processing for performance management

Recent advances in processing capabilities dealing with large data sets through distributed data handling methods make it possible to extract useful, timely information from the unstructured data files. *Data Processing* shown in Figure 2 outlines the idea of using Hadoop for distributed processing to generate information from both structured and semi-structured data for real-time performance prediction. MapReduce [5] is a programming model for processing large data sets with a parallel, distributed algorithm on a cluster. Hadoop MapReduce is an open source implementation of this data processing programming model. Using this paradigm, a master node in a cluster takes log files as input and divides them into smaller sub-problems and distributes them into worker nodes. The worker nodes try to synthesize the information from the assigned sub problems by matching the codes. This is followed by a reduce step that collects the codes and combines the output in the form of a time-series of the actual events, alarms, and meta-data from the log files. The cloud in-memory processing provides the ability to connect to existing data sources and access to visually rich interactive dashboards. Easy navigation and ability to modify queries on the fly is an appealing factor to many users. Since these dashboards can be populated with fresh data, it allows users to have access to real time data and perform analytics quickly, which is a critical factor in real-time performance management.

Data Analytics Model Library and Dashboard

When dynamic time-series data is available, the *Data Analytics* component uses this information to generate prediction models for the chosen performance metrics. ARIMA (Autoregressive Integrated Moving Average) modeling methodology and GRACH

(Generalized Autoregressive Conditional Heteroskedasticity) are popular statistical methods for prediction using time series data [6]. The multi-layer perceptron (MLP) with back propagation learning is a machine learning technique often employed in recent time-series studies [6]. Employing these methodologies in a plant or equipment prediction model, aids in goal settings for key performance metrics [7]. The *Model Library* component stores these prediction models for use by the *Performance Prediction* component. Similarly, diagnostic and decision models are also developed and stored for use by the *Continuous Performance Improvement* components.

Processed information is used to compute performance measures through the *Performance Measurement* component and visually present them in a *Dashboard*. The *Dashboard* component provides a visual interface that displays common key performance indicators to the end-user in a single view. For real-time data fed into the dashboard, the connections to the database and visualization modules are updated on a chosen frequency.

Decision Support

The *Decision Support* component uses the *Model Library* to help the decision maker choose corrective and preventive actions. The corrective action could be to choose a new set of operating parameters to deal with a problem situation or to change or modify the component of a physical resource or to adjust the production levels to suit a new control recipe. These decisions are targeted towards different stakeholders and are made available to the *Continuous Performance Improvement* component for dissemination.

2.2   Continuous Performance Improvement

The main functions of the *Continuous Performance Improvement* component are to: (1) measure performance, (2) evaluate performance against targets, and (3) recommend areas for improvement either through diagnosis of problems or identification of opportunities. The primary interaction with the *Real-time Analytics* component is through the library of analytics models. *Performance Prediction* uses the predictive models to set performance targets, revise forecasts and change input conditions. *Performance Diagnosis* uses diagnostic models to categorize exceptions and trigger exception handling that produces root cause analysis results. It interacts with the *Decision Support* subcomponent of *Real-time Analytics* to produce CAPA plans with assistance from the human *Performance Manager*. The CAPA plans are fed into the *CAPA Management* subcomponent to manage performance corrections, e.g., scheduling a preventive maintenance. After a corrective action it triggers *Performance Measurement,* which is followed by *Performance Evaluation*. The *Performance Evaluation* subcomponent compares measured performance to predicted performance, and closes the continuous performance monitoring and diagnosis loop by triggering *Performance Diagnosis* when it finds a deviation. When there are no deviations during an evaluation, the *Performance Evaluation* subcomponent triggers the *Performance*

Improvement subcomponent to adjust performance targets if possible. The *Performance Improvement* subcomponent aims to maximize performance by revising performance predictions and targets and sending the recommended changes to different stakeholders. *Performance Benchmarking* develops and collects both internal and external benchmark data and helps set performance targets. The process will continue even when the system reaches a level where the system performance fails to improve over a certain period of time. The subcomponents shown in Figure 1 are described below.

Performance Measurement and Evaluation
The key performance indicators (KPIs) are identified among many performance measures and their definitions are modeled. The *Performance Measurement* subcomponent manages the KPI definitions and their data requirements and uses the *Data Processing* sub-component to compute the real-time KPIs for the predefined frequencies. The *Performance Evaluation* component compares the predicted KPI target values and current measured values to look for deviations.

Performance Prediction, Benchmarking, and Target Setting
The *Performance Prediction* subcomponent sets time periods and predicts thresholds for the performance targets using prediction models from the *Real-time Analytics* component. The prediction interval varies as the real-time data is added to update the prediction model. Performance data is systematically checked against the prediction model to look for performance problems.

   Performance Benchmarking is used in setting targets that are driven by external drivers. The benchmarking process may make use of data collection from best of breed organizations through surveys, interviews, focused group and industry meetings, publications and site visits. Performance targets should be revised when performance measurement and prediction indicates an opportunity for improvement by comparing current performance with the benchmarks.

Performance Diagnosis and CAPA Management
Figure 3 shows details of how the *Real-time Analytics* and *Continuous Performance Improvement* components interact to diagnose performance issues. The left side of the Figure 3 depicts the *Data Analytics* subcomponent as related to diagnostic modeling, while the right side depicts the *Performance Diagnosis* subcomponent. During performance evaluation when a deviation from a predicted performance target is found, a performance diagnosis procedure is triggered. The essential function of Performance *Diagnosis* in the case of asset performance management as shown in Figure 3 is the root cause analysis. In the root cause analysis process, a Pareto analysis is carried out to separate the vital few problems from the trivial many. A weak point analysis followed by a criticality analysis is carried out to understand the severity of the problems and their root causes [8]. Based on the maintenance policy, suitable corrective and preventive actions are suggested.

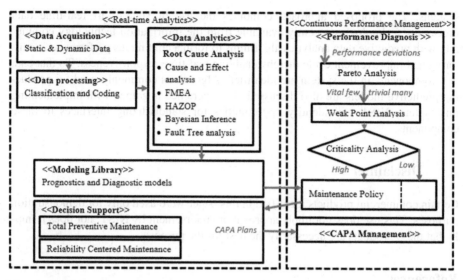

Fig. 3. Performance diagnosis and diagnostic modeling in case of asset performance management

The D*ata Analytics* component shows different root cause analysis methods that may be used alone or in combination to develop diagnostic and prognostic models relevant to a performance management of assets as shown in Figure 3. Cause & effect analysis, Failure mode effect analysis (FMEA), hazard and operability study (HAZOP) are the commonly used root-cause analysis methods used in the weak point analysis stage [9]. After the weak point analysis, a Bayesian inference and a fault tree analysis can be used in the criticality analysis stage. These analyses are part of the *Data Analytics* component identified in Figure 1.

Continuous Improvement Management
When the performance evaluations report no deviations in performance, the continuous improvement process is triggered. The continuous improvement process may follow a PDCA cycle (Plan, Do, Check, Act) or DMAIC (Define, Measure, Analyze, Improve, Control) approach to arrive at an incremental or breakthrough performance improvement [10]. The *Performance Improvement* sub-component also revises prediction algorithms and targets based on plans for introduction of new technologies, products, processes, and services.

3   Conclusions and Future Work

In this paper, an approach for utilizing data-driven models for a real-time, continuous performance management system has been proposed. The system is motivated by the smart manufacturing system vision in which adaptability and responsiveness are characterized as important metrics and capabilities for the next generation manufacturing systems. The proposed approach combines the use of state-of-art real-time data processing technologies recently available from the information technology community with predictive data analytics algorithms to form a continuous performance monitoring and improvement cycle thereby enabling real-time responsiveness. To that end, key components in the system are identified. Algorithms commonly used for producing predictive models are also discussed. As experience is gained with implementing this system, NIST will identify opportunities for standardizing interfaces to these components.

4   Disclaimer

Certain commercial products identified in this paper were used only for demonstration purposes. This use does not imply approval or endorsement by NIST, nor does it imply that these products are necessarily the best for the purpose.

References

1. Davis, J., Edgar, T., Porter, J., Bernaden, J., Sarli, M.S.: Smart manufacturing, manufacturing intelligence and demand-dynamic performance. Computers & Chemical Engineering 47, 145–156 (2012)
2. SMLC, Implementing 21st century smart manufacturing, Workshop summary report (2011)
3. Vijayaraghavan, A.: MTConnect for realtime monitoring and analysis of manufacturing enterprises. In Proceedings of the international conference on digital enterprise technology, Hong Kong (December 2009)
4. Mahnke, W., Leitner, S.H., Damm, M.: OPC unified architecture. Springer, Heidelberg (2009)
5. Dean, D., Ghemawat, S.: MapReduce: Simplified data processing on large clusters. In: Proceedings of OSDI (2004)
6. Box, E.P.G., Jenkins, M.J., Reinsel, G.C.: Time series analysis: forecasting and control, 4th edn. John Wiley & Sons, Inc. New Jersey (2014)
7. Shin, S.-J., Woo, J., Rachuri, S.: Predictive analytics model for power consumption in manufacturing. Procedia CIRP 15, 153–158 (2014)
8. Lei, et al.: Asset management. Springer, New York (2012)
9. Latino, R.C., Latino, K.C., Latino, M.A.: Root cause analysis: Improving performance for bottom-line results, 4th edn. CRC Press, USA (2013)
10. Sokovic, M., Pavletic, D., Pipan, K.K.: Quality improvement methodologies – PDCA cycle, RADAR Matric, DMAIC and DFSS. Journal of Achievements in Materials and Manufacturing Engineering 43(1), 476–483 (2010)

Supply Uncertainty in Food Processing Supply Chain: Sources and Coping Strategies

Atanu Chaudhuri[1], Iskra Dukovska-Popovska[2],
Cecilie Maria Damgaard[2], and Hans-Henrik Hvolby[2]

[1] Department of Business and Management, Aalborg University, Copenhagen, Denmark
atanu@business.aau.dk
[2] Centre for Logistics, Department of Mechanical and Manufacturing Engineering,
Aalborg University, Aalborg, Denmark
iskra@m-tech.aau.dk, cmd@mcelog.dk, HHH@m-tech.aau.dk

Abstract. Supply uncertainty aspects haven't been treated specifically in the food processing supply chain management literature, as the focus was mainly on the demand aspects. This paper provides an initial survey on the existing literature dealing with supply uncertainty of food processors. Specifically, the focus is on the types of supply uncertainty and sources that are causing them, as well as how the food processing companies are coping with it in the food supply chain.

Keywords. Supply Uncertainty, Food Industry, Coping Strategies.

1 Introduction

Most of the food industry is characterized by uncertainty in the supply of raw materials [1, 2]. In addition, some food producers, because of contracts with suppliers, are obliged to buy the supply of raw material, independently of quantity, quality, and in some cases even the type of specific product [2]. Adequate and timely supply is a pre-requisite for producers' and suppliers' value creation, making it possible for producers to reach their service level targets and allowing the supplier to stay in business.

In many industries supply is considered important, but unproblematic because of predictability and possibility of keeping inventory [1]. However, this is not always the case for food products, where the effects of the environment and long supply lead times affect the predictability of the volume and the quality of the supply. In the literature, uncertainties in supply and demand are recognized to have major impact on the manufacturing function [3]. However, focus of the existing literature has been mostly on balancing demand and supply through creating a demand driven system [4]. This can be challenging when a part of the supply chain (SC) is supply driven [2] and the market price is often influenced by fluctuations in supply [5].

On analyzing the frameworks dealing with supply-demand uncertainty, we realize that the types of uncertainties and uncertainty reduction strategies described may not be entirely relevant for food industry. Lee [6] expands Fisher's framework for linking

B. Grabot et al. (Eds.): APMS 2014, Part III, IFIP AICT 440, pp. 183–191, 2014.

demand uncertainty with SC strategy, to include supply uncertainty. The general strategy he proposes for situations of uncertain supply is risk-hedging through inventory pools or developing multiple supply bases. Van der Vorst and Beulens [3] identify sources of uncertainty and propose SC redesign strategies for food industry, however they do not look in detail for the supply aspects. The contribution in [2] is one of the few which draws attention to the supply driven chains. However, the focus is to explain the concept of supply driven chains and not necessarily to analyze specific supply uncertainties faced by food processing companies.

Thus, we can conclude that there is limited research on how food processing companies can develop appropriate strategies to address the supply uncertainty. Hence, the objectives of this paper are based on literature: *first*, to identify the supply related characteristics and their related uncertainties faced by food processing companies, and *second*, to identify the various coping strategies used by the food processing companies in order to deal with the supply uncertainties.

2   Supply Uncertainties in Food Processing Supply Chains

Uncertainty can be defined as a situation in which decision makers do not know for sure what will happen and therefore cannot accurately predict external changes [6–8]. This will become more critical if there is a high complexity in the environment (higher number and dissimilarity of the external elements) as well as high instability (the elements shift abruptly) [6, 7]. One of the latest characterizations of food supply chains [9] considers supply uncertainty to be mainly a result of seasonality, demand amplification and economy of scale thinking, and otherwise highly reliable. But, other sources of supply uncertainty do exist in food supply chains (FSCs). Based on FSC case studies, van der Vorst and Beulens [3] identify the following supply-related decision making uncertainties: *supply quantity, supply quality* and *supplier lead time*. From the SC risk management literature [8, 10] *supply cost (price)* appears as relevant uncertainty. In addition, *size (weight) of the product* is uncertainty in the fish and meat industry, while *type of the product* is a typical uncertainty for the fish industry.

In order to deal with uncertainty one needs to understand the sources leading to it. van der Vorst and Beulens [3] categorize the sources of SC uncertainty as: *inherent, chain related*, and *exogenous*. In addition, SC risk literature identifies number of *supplier related* sources of uncertainty. Below we elaborate on each of these characteristics and how they relate to supply uncertainty. Even though exogenous factors such as governmental regulations affect the supply aspects, these will not be considered in this paper.

Inherent characteristics are "built in" the nature of the supplied product and process, such as: perishability of the raw material, seasonal/variable harvest, being influenced by weather and environment conditions, product's nature of having variable size, and the inverted BOM structure (single raw material consisting of co-products with different demand). Product perishability creates uncertainty for the buyer with respect to product quality and quantity. When there are distinguishable variations in quality among products, food processors face uncertainty in finding sufficient quantity of the product [11]. Seasonal availability and weather conditions are leading to variability. For fishing industry, wild catch volume of different species of fish varies from year to year and also for the same months in different years [1], [12].

Chain related characteristics have been divided into: configuration, control structure, chain information system, and organization and governance.

- *Chain configuration* relates to the location and the number of the suppliers. Having international suppliers may on one hand decrease quantity uncertainty, but on the other increase supply lead time and quality uncertainty. The distance of supply sources to the producer, can enhance perishability while in transit for fresh produce and may induce stress to chicken or pig and thus influence quality of the meat. For fish procured from fish farms, disease and quality problems are common [12].
- *SC control structure* relates to information and decision process lead time, supply/ distribution lead time, and coordination of logistic decisions and processes. This may affect the supply lead time and pricing uncertainty as a centrally controlled SC or a cooperative with pricing responsibility may limit pricing uncertainty.—
- *SC information system* relates to data timeliness, accuracy and data definition, and can have positive impact on decreasing all the uncertainties. However, information secrecy is typical for supply driven chains [2] since if supplier has difficulty selling its products this information can create dampening of the price by the food processor. This can create price uncertainty.
- *SC organization and governance structure* is related to division of responsibilities, and in relation to the supply can be seen through the commitment, and contracts that exist between the supplier and the processor. Longer-term commitments and contracts can on one hand secure needed quantity and quality, but on the other create unnecessary supply.

Supplier related characteristics encompass internal supplier processes and organization: supplier capacity constraints [13] and uncertain supply capacity [14], supplier quality failure due to failing to maintain capital equipment, lack of supplier training in quality principles and techniques, and damage that occurs in transit [13, 15], business risk when the supplier faces financial problems and may not be in business for long [13, 15], risks due to inability of suppliers to stay abreast of technological changes which may have a negative impact on costs, competitiveness of products in the market, and lead-times [13]. In contrary to other industries where supplier high capacity utilization is considered as a source of risk [15], for a supply driven chains, which is a characteristic of the upstream part of the FSCs, high capacity utilization may be desirable as production below optimal or full capacity may not be economically viable and can result in possible reverse bullwhip effect [2].

Further on we identify, based on literature, how the uncertainties are characterized at four fresh food industries (Table 1).

Table 1. Characteristics of supply uncertainties in food processing supply chain

	Fish processor	Dairy	Meat processor	Fruits and vegetables processor
Supply quantity	High uncertainty [16], High catch variety from year to year and for the same month for different years [12],some parts of the fish have higher demand than others.	High uncertainty until delivery [17], weather induced variability [18], whey, generated with cheese, has low margin [2]	Variation in individual bird weights which can result in varying proportions of heavier and lighter birds [19], some parts of the chicken have higher demand then others [2]	Crop yield uncertainty due to weather conditions, contagious bacterial diseases [20], fresh produce heavily exposed to environment [21]
Supply quality, product size and type	Uncertainty depending on periods and biology[1, 16, 22], Temperature sensitive [16], quality degradation depends on microbial growth [22]	High contamination risk [23]	High and variable mortality, weight or fat variability, poor lairage control at abattoir affecting pig quality [24], variable quality of beasts and microbial growth [22, 25]	High uncertainty from environment (air, soil, water, insects, rodents, etc.) and manual manipulation and thus intrinsically potentially heavily contaminated [21, 26]
Supply lead time	High uncertainty, between 4 to 13 weeks [12]	Low uncertainty, daily delivery [27, 28]	24–30 months [24, 25]	Reach their peak value at the time of harvest; product value deteriorating exponentially post-harvest until the product is cooled to dampen the deterioration [27]
Supply Price	Total cost uncertainty from having to buy all from fishermen [2, 16]	High variation in price [5, 28], Total cost uncertainty [17, 18]	Mix of auction (rather variable price) and deadweight procurement (rather fixed price) for beef [29]	Total cost uncertainty from having to buy all output of fruits and vegetables [2]

3   Coping Strategies

We specifically analyze literature addressing supply uncertainties in processing fish, meat, dairy, and fruits and vegetables to identify coping strategies. We aim to identify and relate coping strategies with the sources of uncertainty.

Coping strategies at fish industry. Some of the coping strategies address the uncertainties related to the *inherent characteristics* of the supply. These include: farming and thus controlling the type and size of raw products at the supplier [5]; optimizing the product mix [1], flexible product mix planning [5], sorting and grading [5] at the processor to ensure quality and maximize margins while considering the variable demand of different co-products. Other strategies deal with the *SC related sources* of uncertainty. Backward integration by owning a stake in fishing vessels to signal commitment and ensure availability of supply [30] is a SC organization aspect. Maintaining a portfolio of suppliers and focusing on specific types of vessels to get the desired catch are SC configuration related coping strategies [30], which can be used to reduce uncertainties of volume and quality, reduce supplier related uncertainty of capacity constraints faced by individual suppliers due to quota restrictions or limited number of vessels or manpower and also to reduce supplier opportunism. Another strategy is catch-based aquaculture [1] where a fish is caught in periods when it is close to shore and easy to catch, then kept alive, and fed to better serve the market demand for fresh fish. This coping strategy addresses the inherent uncertainty by decreasing the influence of the seasonal variations. It also deals with SC control related uncertainty as it enables better coordination between processor needs and the supply. It may be considered similar to having a raw material or semi-finished inventory buffer to match supply with demand but can result in additional costs and is time consuming [1]. In addition, it addresses supplier capacity characteristics by reducing its uncertainty. Finally, we identified some coping strategies that deal with *supplier related sources* of uncertainty. Processors could offer various services to the fishing vessels to make themselves attractive, motivate the staff to stay extra time onboard by paying the crew a fixed portion of the sales revenue [1], offer good prices to attract and educate specific suppliers [30], while suppliers could exercise volume flexibility by varying the length of time at sea to catch the allotted quotas.

Coping strategies at meat industry. Many coping strategies focus on reducing the *inherent sources* that are causing quality uncertainties. Such strategies include: environmental control in broiler houses, reducing pre-slaughter stress, care in handling and transportation [31] at the supplier; quality assurance schemes [29], and automated carcass identification system to enable traceability [32] at the processor. Other strategies deal with the inherent sources leading to quantity uncertainties and involve: quick and efficient rerouting of low demand co-produce to different markets, and optimal planning and scheduling of various end products [19]. A number of strategies have been identified that deal with *SC related sources* of uncertainty: collaboration between farmer co-operatives, processor and retailer to strengthen links with farmers thereby ensuring consistency and improved quality [8], and selecting firms to minimize transport distances to the abattoir [24] thereby reducing transportation lead time. Another SC organization/governance aspect is related to a common price set by co-operative system based on objective measurement of carcass grade [32] which reduces pricing uncertainty.

Coping strategies at dairy industry. Some of the strategies that cope with *inherent characteristics* of the raw material include: keeping the milk at the right temperature [33], storing larger unused amounts of fat from the milk, or processing into milk powder when excess supply amounts appear [9], efficient vehicle routing. From a *SC organization and governance* perspective, long-term partnerships and contracts are typical for dairy industry[23, 34], as well as efficient management of the co-operatives. Incentivizing them to improve yield as well as on-time payments to ensure regular supply is used as a *supplier related* strategy [23]. *SC configuration strategies* include buying and collecting milk within certain kilometers of distance and from a larger amount of farmers, thus ensuring needed quantity.

Coping strategies at fruits and vegetables industry. Inherent sources of uncertainties related to perishability can be managed by efficient temperature controlled logistics to reduce supply quality variations [35], by substituting fresh products with frozen products wherever possible, and optimal product mix planning. Blackburn and Scudder [27] propose designing a hybrid of a responsive SC from post-harvest to cooling, followed by an efficient one in the remainder of the chain. The authors demonstrate that these two segments of the SC are only loosely linked, implying that little coordination is required across the chain to achieve value maximization. Thus, it also obviates some chain related uncertainties due to lack of co-ordination and information sharing. *Supply chain related* strategies include: having multiple suppliers, classifying suppliers to take care of variable quality [35], using spot-markets [36], profit sharing based on quality parameters to ensure quality and foster collaboration [37], using revenue sharing contract to coordinate a two stage agri-supply chain by selecting suitable wholesale price and revenue sharing percentage [38], using inventory policies with re-order point model under supply uncertainty [39]. Supplier related strategies include quality based pricing which can result in improvement in quality and on-time delivery of quality fruits [40]. Fig. 1 summarizes the different coping strategies.

Coping strategies for inherent characteristics of the supply	Coping strategies for supply chain related sources of uncertainty	Coping strategies for supplier related sources of uncertainty
• Control of type and size at the supplier • Optimizing product mix • Flexible product mix planning • Sorting and grading products • Environmental/temperature control • Reducing pre-slaughter stress • Care in handling and transportation • Quality assurance schemes • Automated carcass identification system • Rerouting of low demand co-produce • Planning of various end product • Storing unused part of co-product • Processing into less perishable products • Efficient vehicle routing • Substituting fresh with frozen products • Hybrid supply chain design	• Backward integration • Maintaining a portfolio of suppliers • Focusing on specific types of fishing vessels • Catch-based aquaculture • Collaboration in supply chain • Selecting firms to minimize transport • Set price by co-operative system • Long-term partnerships and contracts • Management of the co-operatives • Having multiple suppliers • Classifying suppliers • Using spot-markets • Using profit sharing based on quality • Using revenue sharing contract • Using inventory policies	• Offer more services • Motivate the staff and suppliers • Offer good prices • Educate specific suppliers • Varying capacity constrains • On-time payments • Quality based pricing

Fig. 1. Overview of the different coping strategies

The fish processing industry is practicing strategies dealing with all three types of sources of uncertainties. Some of the strategies are focusing on *reducing* the uncertainties (quantity and type/size) through various risk hedging mechanisms (farming, SC configuration), while other focus on *dealing with* the uncertainties (volume and product mix flexibility). The meat processing industry seems to focus more on the inherent and SC related sources. *Reducing* uncertainty is done through supplier quality improvement, lead time reduction, and common/transparent pricing, while *dealing with* uncertainty is through product mix planning. Dairy industry focuses primarily on reducing inherent related uncertainties of quality (environment and transport control) and of quantity (partnerships and contracts), as well as supplier related uncertainties (incentivizing suppliers). Fresh produce industry focuses on reducing inherent uncertainties because of perishability (temperature control) and dealing with it (hybrid SC design), as well as dealing with supply chain related uncertainty. Design of contracts to deal with pricing uncertainty has emerged as a separate field of literature.

Looking across industries, all involve strategies that reduce and deal with the inherent sources of uncertainty. From the strategies coping with SC related sources, SC configuration is considered in all the industries, followed by SC organization (in all except fresh produce). SC control appeared only in fish industry, while SC cooperation in the meat industry. Supplier related strategies were evident in all industries besides meat.

4   Conclusion

This paper characterizes the supply uncertainties of the food processors in terms of supply quantity, quality, lead time and price, and links them to the sources of such uncertainties which are broadly classified as inherent, chain related and supplier related. This characterization also helps in analyzing the different coping strategies adopted by fish, meat, dairy and fresh produce processors. Few gaps emerge from our analysis of the characterization and the coping strategies.

While all food processing industries do get impacted by the configuration of suppliers and their control structure, there is limited research on deciding the appropriate network structure for example the number and type of suppliers and the kind of engagement with them. In addition, we didn't observe any SC information sharing mechanisms passing on the information, for example about the type and quality of raw material. This is surprising, since information sharing is a main strategy for reducing uncertainty. There is a need to analyze supply patterns, quality and prices, and develop analytical solutions or decision support to determine the appropriate network structure and contracting mechanisms with the objective of maximizing profit for appropriate quality constraints. There are also possibilities to develop combined sourcing and product mix planning decisions and to empirically determine the impact of sourcing uncertainty reduction strategies on the performance of the firms.

Acknowledgement. This paper is possible because of the LogiNord project funded by NordForsk.

References

1. Dreyer, B., Grønhaug, K.: Coping with unpredictable supply: the role of flexibility and adaptation. European Journal of Marketing 46, 1268–1282 (2012)
2. Hull, B.Z.: Are supply (driven) chains forgotten? The International Journal of Logistics Management 16, 218–236 (2005)
3. Van der Vorst, J.G.A.J., Beulens, A.J.M.: Identifying sources of uncertainty to generate supply chain redesign strategies. International Journal of Physical Distribution & Logistics Management 32, 409–430 (2002)
4. Van der Vorst, J., van Dijk, S.J., Beulens, A.J.M.: Supply Chain Design in the Food Industry. TheInternational Journal of Logistics Management 12, 73–86 (2001)
5. Ottesen, G.G., Grønhaug, K.: Market orientation and uncertain supply in upstream markets: an exploratory study. European Journal of Purchasing & Supply Management 8, 209–219 (2002)
6. Lee, H.L.: Aligning Supply Chain Strategies with Product Uncertainties. California management review 44 (2002)
7. Daft, R.L., Murphy, J., Willmott, H.: Organization Theory and Design. CENGAGE Lrng Business Press, Mason (2010)
8. Leat, P., Revoredo-Giha, C.: Risk and resilience in agri-food supply chains: the case of the ASDA PorkLink supply chain in Scotland. Supply Chain Management: An International Journal 18, 219–231 (2013)
9. Romsdal, A.: Differentiated production planning and control in food supply chains. Doctoral theses (2014)
10. Tang, C.S.: A review of marketing–operations interface models: From co-existence to coordination and collaboration. International Journal of Production Economics 125, 22–40 (2010)

11. Hobbs, J.E., Young, L.M.: Closer vertical co-ordination in agri-food supply chains: a conceptual framework and some preliminary evidence. Supply Chain Management: An International Journal 5, 131–143 (2000)
12. Hameri, A.-P., Pálsson, J.: Supply chain management in the fishing industry: the case of Iceland. International Journal of Logistics Research and Applications 6, 137–149 (2003)
13. Zsidisin, G.A., Panelli, A., Upton, R.: Purchasing organization involvement in risk assessments, contingency plans, and risk management: an exploratory study. Supply Chain Management: An International Journal 5, 187–198 (2000)
14. Tang, C.S.: Perspectives in supply chain risk management. International Journal of Production Economics 103, 451–488 (2006)
15. Tummala, R., Schoenherr, T.: Assessing and managing risks using the Supply Chain Risk Management Process (SCRMP). Supply Chain Management: An International Journal 16, 474–483 (2011)
16. Ivert, L.K., Dukovska-Popovska, I., Kaipia, R., Fredriksson, A., Johansson, M., Dreyer, H., Chabada, L., Damgaard, C.M., Tuomikangas, N.: Sales and operations planning: responding to the needs of industrial food producers 2014 (2014)
17. Hovelaque, V., Duvaleix-Tréguer, S., Cordier, J.: Effects of constrained supply and price contracts on agricultural cooperatives. European Journal of Operational Research 199, 769–780 (2009)
18. Guan, Z., Philpott, A.B.: A multistage stochastic programming model for the New Zealand dairy industry. International Journal of Production Economics 134, 289–299 (2011)
19. Bisht, B., Pandey, S.: Planning Efficiency in perishable food operations (2012)
20. Kazaz, B., Webster, S.: The Impact of Yield-Dependent Trading Costs on Pricing and Production Planning Under Supply Uncertainty. M&SOM 13, 404–417 (2011)
21. Jacxsens, L., Luning, P.A., van der Vorst, J.G.A.J., Devlieghere, F., Leemans, R., Uyttendaele, M.: Simulation modelling and risk assessment as tools to identify the impact of climate change on microbiological food safety – The case study of fresh produce supply chain. Food Research International 43, 1925–1935 (2010)
22. Rong, A., Akkerman, R., Grunow, M.: An optimization approach for managing fresh food quality throughout the supply chain. International Journal of Production Economics 131, 421–429 (2011)
23. Gorton, M., Dumitrashko, M., White, J.: Overcoming supply chain failure in the agri-food sector: A case study from Moldova. Food Policy 31, 90–103 (2006)
24. Taylor, D.H.: Strategic considerations in the development of lean agri-food supply chains: a case study of the UK pork sector. Supply Chain Management: An International Journal 11, 271–280 (2006)
25. Cox, A., Chicksand, D.: The Limits of Lean Management Thinking: Multiple Retailers and Food and Farming Supply Chains. European Management Journal 23, 648–662 (2005)
26. Chai, L.C., Robin, T., Ragavan, U.M., Gunsalam, J.W., Bakar, F.A., Ghazali, F.M., Radu, S., Kumar, M.P.: Thermophilic Campylobacter spp. in salad vegetables in Malaysia. International Journal of Food Microbiology 117, 106–111 (2007)
27. Blackburn, J., Scudder, G.: Supply Chain Strategies for Perishable Products: The Case of Fresh Produce. Production and Operations Management 18, 129–137 (2009)
28. Romsdal, A., Strandhagen, J.O., Dryer, H.C.: Linking supply chain configuration with production strategy; the case of food production. In: 4th World P&OM Conference (2012)
29. Fearne, A.: The evolution of partnerships in the meat supply chain: insights from the British beef industry. Supply Chain Management: An International Journal 3, 214–231 (1998)

30. Ottesen, G.G., Grønhaug, K.: Primary Uncertainty in the Seafood Industry: An Exploratory Study of How Processing Firms Cope. Marine Resource Economics 18, 363–371 (2003)
31. Baracho, M.S., Camargo, G.A., Lima, A.M.C., Mentem, J.F., Moura, D.J., Moreira, J., Nääs, I.A.: Variables impacting poultry meat quality from production to pre-slaughter: a review. Revista Brasileira de Ciência Avícola 8, 201–212 (2006)
32. Hobbs, J.E., Kerr, W.A., Klein, K.K.: Creating international competitiveness through supply chain management: Danish pork. Supply Chain Management: An International Journal 3, 68–78 (1998)
33. Entrup, M.L.: Advanced planning in fresh food industries - integrating shelf life into production planning. Springer (2005)
34. Deimel, M., Frentrup, M., Theuvsen, L.: Transparency in food supply chains: empirical results from German pig and dairy production. Journal on Chain and Network Science 8, 21–32 (2008)
35. Wilson, N.: Supply chain management: a case study of a dedicated supply chain for bananas in the UK grocery market. Supply Chain Management: An International Journal 1, 28–35 (1996)
36. He, Y., Zhao, X.: Coordination in multi-echelon supply chain under supply and demand uncertainty. International Journal of Production Economics 139, 106–115 (2012)
37. Formentini, M., Boscari, S., Romano, P.: Quality Based Pricing and collaborative negotiation in agrifood supply chains. In: Presented at the 20th EUROMA Conference, Dublin (June 2013)
38. Zhao, X., Wu, F.: Coordination of agri-food chain with revenue-sharing contract under stochastic output and stochastic demand. Asia Pac. J. Oper. Res. 28, 487–510 (2011)
39. Yeo, W.M., Yuan, X.-M.: Optimal inventory policy with supply uncertainty and demand cancellation. European Journal of Operational Research 211, 26–34 (2011)
40. Hines, P., Francis, M., Bailey, K.: Quality-based pricing: a catalyst for collaboration and sustainable change in the agrifood industry? International Journal of Logistics Management 17, 240–259 (2006)

Outline of a Methodic Realization of Construction Kits for Changeable Production Systems

Michael Quade[1], David Jentsch[2], and Egon Mueller[2]

[1] Siemens AG Corporate Technology, Munich, Germany
michael.quade@siemens.com
[2] Chemnitz University of Technology,
Department of Factory Planning and Factory Management, Chemnitz, Germany
{david.jentsch,egon.mueller}@mb.tu-chemnitz.de

Abstract. This paper outlines a method to structure a construction kit system for assembly and manufacturing systems in a way, that a realised system from those building blocks fulfils the requirement of ease in reconfiguration considering specified change criteria (i.e. variants, capacity) at an adequate degree. An overview regarding the major engineering domains and applicable literature is given. The basic flow in this method is given and important steps described. This paper finishes with describing further steps for finalizing the method.

Keywords: Production equipment, reconfigurability, flexibility, change enablers, construction kit.

1   Introduction

Due to increased market competition, globalisation combined with changes in customers' requirements towards higher product variance and uncertain market prediction increase the pressure for changeability of production environments. This topic is discussed on different levels of factory and production system since years (e.g. [1], [2].

Nevertheless, on various levels sufficient changeability from industries perspective is yet not achieved. Uncertainties regarding the change criteria as well as the unspecific implementation of changing enabling measures often negate the positive impact of changeability. This results in increase in systems cost hindering dissemination of the changeability paradigms.

This paper outlines an approach for a methodical design process for construction kit systems. A construction kit establishes building blocks (or modules) suitable to set-up a large (sometimes infinite) number of final products by combining these elements. Assembly and manufacturing systems consisting of building blocks structured by the method fulfil requirements for flexibility and reconfiguration regarding defined change criteria. This is intended to provide systems with a fit of cost and changeability.

Realizing changeability on production system level is subject of a variety of publication (e.g. [3]–[5]). Its huge complexity combined with its impact on productivity makes this level highly attractive for investigation. Various system suppliers developed modular assembly systems, which are accepted by industry and provide limited

B. Grabot et al. (Eds.): APMS 2014, Part III, IFIP AICT 440, pp. 192–199, 2014.

changeability by rather fixed solutions. Nevertheless, applicable methods to guarantee deliberately designed changeability by considering the requirements for changeability in the design process of the construction kit system for realized machinery are yet not available to industry.

In this initial publication, the fundamental flow when using the methodic approach from the perspective of production equipment manufacturers is given. Future work will further elaborate on details.

2   Overall Goal

The approach for setting-up equipment with a construction kit designed by the presented methodology is depicted in Fig. 1:

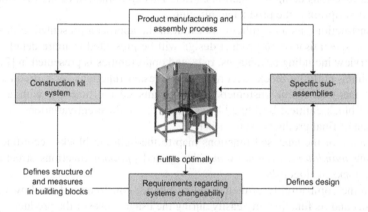

Fig. 1. Setting-up of changeable, kit-based production equipment

Optimally, for a new production process a system consists of building blocks from the construction kit, enriched by specific sub-assemblies. This allows setting up the system quickly and efficiently, while addressing special production processes accordingly. On the one hand, requirements for changeability (e.g. change criteria) define the design of specific sub-assemblies. On the other hand, they also lead to adequate structuring of the construction kit and defining measures in the blocks. Whereas in some blocks measures for e.g. high mobility are required, others may require a different set of enabling measures depending on their functionality.

Implementing a change enabler in a particular building block is beneficial only in case that it is relevant for the criteria in conjunction with the function realized in the building block. Which measures need to be implemented in a specific building block depends on two facts:

1. The dependencies of the functions realized by the building block on relevant change criteria
2. The dependencies of the change enabler on the relevant change criteria

3   Review of Relevant Engineering Domains

In this section, an overview shall be given regarding the relevant engineering domains being part of the presented approach.

3.1   Domain Design Methodologies

Different methodologies for product design had been established in the past years: besides traditional product development processes [6], [7], special processes for modular structures and construction kits emerged [8]–[10]. Generally, those processes include a functional analysis, being the basic step in defining the product. Components, modules or in the case of construction kits building blocks are allocated to one or several functions being its function carrier. This combination of the functional and physical description is the product architecture.

As construction kits are explicitly relevant in the approach presented in this publication, this specialisation of product design will be presented in more detail. A thorough overview including advantages, risks and opportunities is presented in [7], [11].

Combining building blocks according to requested functions for a product allows fulfilling many different customers' requirements cost efficiently with a limited amount of block entities. Building blocks may exist in different variations, increasing the amount of final products even further.

The nature of the analysed functions map to the building blocks accordingly: distinguishing *mandatory*, *eventually mandatory* and *optional* functions structures the building blocks analogously.

Due to the compatibility of their building blocks, construction kits allow adapting the product and its functionality easily during the usage phase of the product.

3.2   Domain Production Systems

Basically, the term *production* includes all aspects for transforming raw material into final products. Auxiliary material as well as energy could be required for this transformation, which will take place on *production equipment*. Relevant publications considering *production systems* (the actual utilization of the construction kit) include [12], [13].

Two major areas being part of a production system include *manufacturing* and *assembly systems*. Manufacturing as defined in [14] includes all processes changing the material composition or spatial relationships of products. Although joining processes are part of this definition, assembly as defined in [15] is often examined separately.

A functional analysis of systems in assembly and manufacturing may indicate large similarities; nevertheless, the detail requirements differ tremendously (e.g. in the case of mechanical requirements on manufacturing systems to prevent vibration). These differences clearly influence the design of adequate building blocks and their relationships. For the method presented below, both production areas are considered.

Another fundamental aspect for the method presented is the production level, which is object of matter. According to [16], those levels range from a distributed factory network level, via site, segment, system, cell to a single station, realizing one particular process. As the presented method reflects on the realization of production equipment from building blocks, the relevant level is on *cell* and *system level*.

3.3   Domain Changeability

In a variety of publications, the concepts of change processes are subject of matter [4], [17]–[20]. Although differences exist in the details, many aspects are identical:

- Change drivers, such as *demand volatility* and *company strategy*, trigger the need for a change process
- Change criteria, such as *product variant* or *volume* (which often are defined vaguely), are the objective of the change process
- Change enablers, such as *mobility* or *compatibility* (whose relevant measures according to a given change object are often vague), allow a system to be changed easily according to the change criteria

Some authors employ the hierarchical view on production systems (levels as presented above) in order to discern different kinds of change. A frequently cited source [21] draws attention to different modes of adaption: flexibility and reconfiguration. The difference of either of these modes is depicted in Fig. 2.

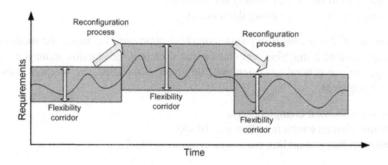

Fig. 2. Comparison of flexibility and reconfiguration (according to [21])

Following this logic, the definition is as follows:

- Flexibility: Ability of a system to economically adapt to changes of requirements in a given corridor
- Reconfigurability: Ability of a system to easily change the flexibility corridor

4   Outline of Basic Approach

The three major domains briefly reviewed above will be combined to describe a methodic approach for realizing a construction kit for assembly and manufacturing systems, which fulfills the requirements for changeability in an optimal fashion. The basic idea is depicted in Fig. 3:

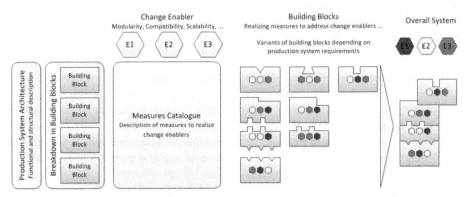

Fig. 3. Realization of changeable production equipment from building blocks

It needs to be highlighted, that detailing the methodic approach divides in two parts:

1. Required analysis for developing the method
2. Required analysis when using the method

The content of this publication focuses on the second part, i.e. using the method from the perspective of a machine supplier or end user (e.g. production management). At this stage, only a general overview will be given. Simplified, the method consists of the following steps:

1. Assessing relevant change criteria
2. Defining change enablers in building blocks
3. Realizing change enabling measures in building blocks

4.1   Assessing Relevant Change Criteria

As described above, relevant change criteria to consider in assembly or manufacturing systems realized by building blocks need to be captured. This is a tremendously important step, as only structuring a kit which addresses valid change criteria will lead to a system useful during its usage period.

If optimal reconfiguration of a system addresses an unnecessary change criteria, instead of increasing efficiency the opposite effect will occur (more expensive systems and change processes).[1]

---

[1] In further development of the method itself, weighting of change criteria against each other could be implemented, allowing emphasizing one relevant criterion over another one.

4.2   Defining Change Enablers in Building Block

Based on the previous step of the method, identification of change enablers to be realized in certain building blocks is required. It is inefficient to realize the whole set of change enablers in each building block. Instead, enablers to implement in a specific building block are defined by evaluating the functions, which are fulfilled by the building block.

As outlined above, two facts need to be taken into account:

- The dependencies of the functions realized by the building block on relevant change criteria
- The dependencies of the change enabler on the relevant change criteria[2]

Exemplarily, a function *Move and orientate product* (intra-system handling) is heavily impacted by the change criteria *product variant*. Additionally, regarding handling functions, the enabler *universality* strongly relates with the criteria. Thus, the building block realizing the function shall include measure to implement *universality*[3].

4.3   Realising Change Enabling Measures in Building Blocks

As in the previous step a set of change enablers were defined for each building block, finally measures to be implemented during the design of the construction kit system will be chosen. This can be done in conjunction with the set of functions realized by the building block, and a measures catalogue is envisaged to guide designers during developing the kit.

To fulfill the enablers in the designated kit modules appropriately, this catalogue includes

- Specific design elements for building block (e.g. wheels to address *mobility*)
- Non-functional requirements for the building block (e.g. minimal weight of building block to address *mobility*)
- Solution component for function (e.g. jointed-arm robot for pick and place process to address *universality*)
- Description of interfaces between building blocks and environment (to address *compatibility*)

Implementing change enablers in building blocks at different extend may be relevant, allowing realizing a manufacturing or assembly system optimally according to the specific requirements of the application case. Although some generic catalogue entries will be given, its content largely depends on the domain, in which the system suppliers or end users business takes place.

---

[2] Defining the relationship between change criteria and enablers depending on the system functions is amongst the major developments to be conducted in the future.

[3] In case that weighting the change criteria will take place, clearly different change enablers in building blocks are rated, too. In case of contradicting enabling measures in one building block, this allows guidance in the design process.

5   Conclusion and Outlook

In this paper an overview was given regarding the development of a method to support the developing of a construction kit system. A construction kit realized by this methodic approach, allows setting up manufacturing and assembly systems, which address crucial change criteria in an optimal, cost efficient way. This will strengthen the dissemination of changeable systems in industrial application.

Although the basic steps of the method had been defined, further work is required:

Decomposing the functions of manufacturing and assembly systems is the first crucial step in construction kit design. One major difference to other products is the high degree of uncertainty on the requirements of a realised system. Major reason for this lies in an unknown assembly and manufacturing process and the characteristics of the processed parts. Generally, when structuring the kit, these products are unknown and only general constrains could be assumed.

A catalogue for implementing specific measures according to defined change enablers need to be defined. This includes the structure of the catalogue as well as the initial content. It is envisaged to perform an analysis of available catalogues presented in a number of publications.

The relationship between crucial change criteria and relevant change enablers and measures for certain function carriers needs investigation. The linkage currently is rather vague and based on expert knowledge of industrial and equipment engineers. A more structured approach is required to formalize this aspect.

References

[1] Wiendahl, H.-P., Nyhuis, P., Zäh, M.F., Wiendahl, H.-H., Duffie, N., Brieke, M.: Changeable Manufacturing - Classification, Design and Operation. CIRP Ann. - Manuf. Technol (January 2007)
[2] ElMaraghy, H.A., Wiendahl, H.-P.: Changeability – An Introduction. In: Changeable and Reconfigurable Manufacturing Systems (2009)
[3] Koren, Y.: The rapid responsiveness of RMS. Int. J. Prod. Res. (November 2013)
[4] Pachow-Frauenhofer, J.: Planung veränderungsfähiger Montagesysteme (2012)
[5] Ackermann, J., Börner, F., Hopf, H., Horbach, S., Müller, E.: Approaches for planning and operation of adaptable factories. Int. J. Prod. Res. (2013)
[6] Grote, K.-H., Engelmann, F., Beitz, W., Syrbe, M., Beyerer, J.: Entwicklung und Konstruktion. In: Hütte das Ingenieurwissen, Berlin, Heidelberg (2012)
[7] Ehrlenspiel, K., Kiewert, A., Lindemann, U.: Kostengünstig Entwickeln und Konstruieren. Springer, Heidelberg (2007)
[8] Stone, R.B.: Towards a Theory of Modular Design (1997)
[9] Baumgart, I.M.: Modularisierung von Produkten im Anlagenbau (2005)
[10] Göpfert, J.: Modulare Produktentwicklung (1998)
[11] Pahl, G., Beitz, W., Feldhusen, J.: Konstruktionslehre (2006)
[12] Schenk, M., Wirth, S., Müller, E.: Fabrikplanung und Fabrikbetrieb (2014)
[13] Spur, G.: Produktion. In: Hütte das Ingenieurwissen (2008)
[14] DIN, DIN 8580: Einteilung der Fertigungsverfahren (2003)
[15] DIN, DIN 8593: Fertigungsverfahren Fügen, no. 0005 (2003)

[16] Wiendahl, H.-P.: Wandlungsfähigkeit, Schlüsselbegriff der zukunftsfähigen Fabrik. 92, 122–127 (2002)
[17] ElMaraghy, H.A.: Flexible and reconfigurable manufacturing systems paradigms. Int. J. Flex. Manuf. Syst. (October 2006)
[18] Landers, R.G., Ruan, J., Liou, F.: Reconfigurable Manufacturing Equipment. In: Reconfigurable Manufacturing Systems and Transformable Factories (2006)
[19] Pritschow, G., Kircher, C., Kremer, M., Seyfarth, M.: Control Systems for RMS and Methods of their Reconfiguration. In: Reconfigurable Manufacturing Systems and Transformable Factories (2006)
[20] Nyhuis, P.: Wandlungsfähige Produktionssysteme (2008)
[21] Zäh, M.F., Möller, N., Vogl, W.: Symbiosis of Changeable and Virtual Production. In: International Conference on Changeable, Agile, Reconfigurable and Virtual Production (2005)

Framework for Resilient Production Systems

Matthias Heinicke

Otto von Guericke University Magdeburg, Universitätsplatz 2, 39106 Magdeburg, Germany
Matthias.heinicke@ovgu.de

Abstract. To respond to turbulent changes in customer demand in a flexible and timely manner, an adequate configuration of production systems in terms of an increasing agility is crucial. In contrast, robust processes, which avoid or at least reduce any kind of dissipation, are increasingly in the focus of practitioners. This includes standardized material and information flows. Furthermore, the concept of resilience combines both agility and robustness and represents the ability of a system to cope with change effectively. This paper highlights the relevance of production control as regards the implementation of resilience in an organizational context. Against this backdrop, a functional map revealing the interactions of the individual tasks of production planning and control enables a systematic analysis of the causes of dissipation. Moreover, socio-technical aspects in terms of the identification of hierarchically structured roles within these activities are considered.

Keywords: resilience, functional map, production control, configuration.

1 Introduction

Various influencing factors work on an existing production system. Accordingly, their impact is currently represented mainly by the effort of increased agility in recent years. This concept includes increased responsiveness to changing environmental conditions (customer demand, pricing pressures, and supplier development). Consequently, an anticipation and adaptation to the turbulence of the environment is imperative. However, the ideal measures to meet these requirements in various fields are discussed in literature intensively as regards resilience (Bhamra et al., 2011). Resilience serves as means in order to cope with turbulence (Wieland and Wallenburg, 2013; Ivanov and Sokolov, 2013). However, its impact and effects require thorough empirical evidence.

In productions systems it is aimed at avoiding or at least reduction of dissipation. In this context, *dissipation* describes all actions or events in terms of perturbations, which affect efficiency and lower productivity. To overcome the consequent issues resulting from turbulence, various efforts are made within the scope of production planning and control. Particularly production control aims at reliable and robust production processes ensuring a rapidly response to changes and the achievement of production targets despite turbulent environmental influences. However, an accurate

B. Grabot et al. (Eds.): APMS 2014, Part III, IFIP AICT 440, pp. 200–207, 2014.

execution of control principles often fails due to a lack of understanding of the inter-dependencies and effects (Schuh et al., 2013).

Therefore, this paper introduces an approach providing a framework for analysing the interactions of the individual tasks of production planning and control. Thus, transparency is increased and operational users are enabled to track the information flow in this regard. The approach additionally intends to reveal interactions between environmental conditions and organizational aspects of production systems in the context of ensuring a reliable operation of organizational processes. For this purpose, a hierarchical pattern is deduced to specify the roles and the corresponding tasks of production planning and control. The focus of the following approach is the optimization of the transformation process as regards the avoidance of operational and organizational errors.

2   Definition of Resilient Production Processes

2.1   Agility and Robustness in an Organizational Context

Robustness is the property of a system to resist change or external influences without adapting its initial stable configuration and continuously provide a desired output (Ivanov and Sokolov, 2013; Wieland and Wallenburg, 2012). Accordingly, a robust system is insensitive to disturbances of the system during its operation (Zhang and Luttervelt, 2011). In general, robustness refers to a proactive strategy, which prevents supplier-related volatility from restricting the functionality of a supply chain (Wieland and Wallenburg, 2012) and thus production processes also. This concept implies resistance to anticipated changes (Wieland and Wallenburg, 2013).

The possibilities to design a robust system configuration are limited to ongoing internal and external changes. In this context, path dependency (Codes and Hülsmann, 2013) is a crucial factor in terms of an appropriate determination of a specific agility level. In addition to the robustness requirement, agility enables a reaction to severe disturbances that cannot be endured by the robustness of a production system (Ivanov and Sokolov, 2013). Identifying the correct manner and time of response to this kind of influence is crucial for the sustainability of production. The concept of speed is inherent to agility (Wieland and Wallenburg, 2012; Bhamra et al., 2011). Agility refers to a quickly and adequate response to unexpected changes and thus is similar to flexibility (Ivanov and Sokolov, 2013). Therefore, a perception of current changes is imperative for a fast reaction to perceived issues (Wieland and Wallenburg, 2013).

2.2   Resilience in an Organizational Context

The concept of resilience contains ecological, social, individual/psychological and organizational/socio-technical aspects (Bhamra et al., 2011). Resilience always is the ability of a system to cope with change (Wieland and Wallenburg, 2013). In the context of production systems, the resilience domain combines two dimensions: agility, which expresses reactive strategies, and robustness including proactive strategies (Wieland and Wallenburg, 2013); thus it is similar to changeability (Wiendahl, 2002). The first one meets environmental changes with corresponding organizational action by re-configuring operating states of a production system rapidly and flexibly. The latter is based on forecasting and prevention. Thus, robust systems endure rather than respond to changes due to the preservation of a stable system configuration. As a result, resilience implies self-regulation and resistance to disturbances of a system (Bhamra et al., 2011).

In summary, operational and organizational robustness expresses the ability of a system obtaining its functionality even under fluctuating environmental conditions. With respect to the resilience definition, both aspects, robustness and agility, have to be considered in terms of a closed-loop control system as regards production systems. Minor perturbations endured by the robustness of the system differ from grave disturbances that require a rapid re-configuration of the production system based on its agility property.

3   Resilience by the Means of Production Control

3.1   Influencing Production Systems by Production Control

In addition to production planning, the main factor to influence existing production systems represents production control. Production planning produces an image of the desired target state by the generation of default values for manufacturing and assembly. Empirically, the target state will not occur due to uncertainties as well as disturbances during production. In this context, production control ensures compliance with the desired management objectives (lead time, capacity utilization, inventory, on-time delivery) by intervening in current production processes. Based on the production program, results of the respective upstream planning level within the operational volume planning, scheduling and capacity levelling represent the input data for the next item. This is called cascaded loops (Nyhuis et al., 2009). Figure 1 illustrates a cascaded loop in production, which represents a hierarchical pattern of individual functions. For this purpose, the respective input and output variables of the individual viewing areas are represented and analyzed in their dependency and interaction (cf. Section 4.2).

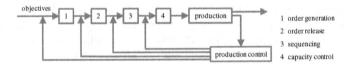

Fig. 1. Cascaded closed-loop production control

Unforeseen dissipation in a production system necessarily effect that its targets cannot be met. Consequently, in these cases an intervention at an operational level is required to ensure compliance with deadlines and other objectives. It is assumed that certain interactions between the various functional areas exist within production systems (Zülch, 1990). In this context, the kind of order release, the sequence of production orders and the batch size (order generation) are crucial parameters (Nyhuis et al., 2006). The combination of these parameters enables specific control methods (e.g. kanban, load-dependent order release, etc.). According to the presented task groups, following strategies in the production control can be distinguished:

- strategies for determining batch size,
- strategies for resource allocation (selection and scheduling),
- strategies for sequencing and
- strategies for order release.

A reasonable combination of these strategies is crucial. In this context, for employees both informal and formal degrees of freedom apply in exercising their functions.

3.2   Deficits in Production Control

In contrast to the deterministic effects assumed by existing approaches in terms of production control configuration, the influence of socio-technical aspects on the performance of control principles is nearly neglected (Schuh et al., 2013). In this context, various problems in the accurate implementation of control principles result from the diversity of choice, a lack of communication and a deficient comprehension of the effects of decisions. Therefore, degrees of freedom as a function of the applied control method, the specific task within the production control as well as in consideration of the respective groups of people (production planners, foremen, and workers) necessitate a clear definition in terms of the hierarchical structure of control processes. It is assumed that within production systems people adapt processes and its control. Regardless of the existing configuration of a production system in terms of robustness and agility, all the persons involved affect the level of its resilience.

Production planners primarily control the flow of information as regards production program. Task of foremen is the organization of the production processes. Workers will perform the actual manufacturing techniques and processes. In this context, it is assumed that the formal rules of the production control in terms of their effectiveness are limited in multistage production systems. This entails other organizational rules for trapping occurring negative effects that cannot be confined by common control principles. Therefore, identifying an appropriate operating point regarding the balancing between the degree of freedom of the employees and the deterministic execution of control principles is imperative depending on factors of influence and disturbances.

4   Approach for Resilient Production Systems

4.1   Closed Loop of the Tasks of Production Control

Production control serves to determine or rather anticipate derivations and to make the necessary adjustments accordingly. A proper balance between stability in terms of robust processes and dynamic adaption based on the agility of the system can be realized by appropriate principles of production control (Schuh et al., 2013). Thus, production control and adequate decisions of people implement the concept of resilience within production systems. For an expedient adaption by decision, it is essential to identify the cause-effect relationships for the individual operational targets in advance. Thus, this enables a positioning of the production in the tension of operational objectives.

A robust order processing in compliance with the logistic objectives therefore requires the mapping and analysis of all relevant processes and their interdependencies (Schuh and Stich 2, 2012). The efficiency of production is determined by a variety of factors. In this context, order generation and order release represent possibilities to influence the manufacturing system directly. In contrast, organization and availability of resources are two aspects that individual persons hardly can work on. Those can be characterized as random and thus are not directly affected by the decisions of the production control. The production resources include equipment, personnel and material. A lack of availability leads to a decline of the efficiency and the intrinsic flexibility of production. A reduction of availability even by disturbing environmental factors is possible. The organization provides a restrictive framework for the objectives, which exists before the implementation of production control. Predominantly, the workplace layout, the legal guidelines, the process principle of the production (operational organization) as well as the flow of information are determined as the most important factors that affect the attainable targets in advance.

4.2   Functional Map of Production Control Tasks

During a production process, variations and disturbances that complicate the control of production typically occur. Plan deviations appearing at different points of the production processes can be of various kinds and entail different consequences. In this context, robustness is measured in form of deviations as regards the four logistic objectives mentioned above. In order to protect against deviations, a high transparency in the planning and control processes is necessary. The functional map (Figure 2) represents such a tool depicting the individual tasks of production planning and control dependent on the hierarchy levels. The concatenating representation of the entire planning and controlling activities includes the appropriate dissemination of information. This tool depicts a self-contained and interactive structure. Thus, effects of a re-configuration of the flow of information and the scope for decision-making are assessable. Thereby, the functional map allows for the determination of the causes of problems as regards occurring deviations or faults. In addition, this facilitates coping with such disturbances by adopting effective measures quickly. The feedback of the results obtained in terms of data is very important to initiate improvements in a timely manner. Moreover, it is crucial that an adequate communication between the hierarchical levels proceeds (Schuh and Stich 1, 2012). As a result, the functional map systematically reveals both potentials and capabilities regarding the ideal interaction of the tasks of production planning and control. Thus, it supports the operational process of decision making.

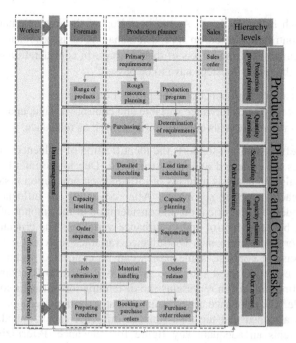

Fig. 2. Functional map of the basic tasks of production control

4.3   Implementation of Robust Processes

A robust configuration of manufacturing systems needs to meet several requirements. In this context, it is aimed at an accurate and controllable execution of tasks as regards fault prevention by anticipation (occurrence of errors) as well as reducing the effects of disturbances due to preparedness (coping with errors). Moreover, robustness implies various operational objectives. Hereby, the focus is on a comparably qualitative and quantitative yield of repetitive production processes. This requires a precise definition of all operations and a reliable understanding of one´s role within the hierarchical structure of the production system. In addition, operational key figures should be insensitive to disturbances of a production based on robust processes. In this context, robustness of production systems is assessable by the degree of change in the achievement of objectives in terms of production-related indicators as a function of environmental factors (Jodlbauer, 2008). This implies that the production program is fulfilled in spite of unforeseen variations reliably.

Furthermore, a clear understanding of the course of processes within in the production system is imperative. Apart from the production control activities, all input-output-relations of the execution of orders have to be considered. For that purpose, the functional map reduces the complexity of the entire production planning and control by a classification of individual tasks with respect to hierarchy levels. Thus, the effects of respective measures can be assessed easily. To realize insensitiveness to disturbances, potential fault causes has to be determined first. Subsequently, an identification of potential effects of disturbances allows a definition of the scope and manner of measures for each hierarchy level. At the backdrop of the implementation of robust processes, this contribution offers an approach managing all issues related to the identification and elimination of the effects of disturbances. In consideration of each operational objective, the following steps have to be passed:

- Identification of influences on the production system,
- Classification in disturbance variable and control variable, and
- Prioritization as regards controllability as well as relevance.

A cause and effect diagram supports the identification of influences. Hence, all potential influences are collected and well-structured. Due to the interdependencies of management goals, the analysis in terms of influence on production systems has to be conducted for each objective separately. After collecting all influences, identified issues should undergo a classification. In consideration of the amount of influences, it is differentiated between control and disturbance variables. The crucial difference is the potential exertion of influence. Disturbance variables represent external or environmental aspects. In contrast, some issues can be controlled within a production system. Lastly, every detected influence is assessed as regards controllability and relevance. The first dimension represents the differentiation between control and disturbance variable. The relevance aspect is an indicator for the effects of corresponding influences. It is assumed that the total time an influence factor impedes production processes represents an adequate key figure for relevance. Prioritizing influences enables operational users to take the ideal measures. With respect to different hierarchy levels, the individual scope of action is crucial in this regard.

4.4   Beyond Robust Production Systems

In consideration of organizationally robust processes, a limitation of the scope of action and decision of the individual process owners is required regarding the sequence and priority of individual orders. This consequently affects the departmental job control in terms of self-organization and self-optimization (Hartmann, 1998). Thus, if the robustness is no longer sufficient, the agility properties are claimed. Moreover, an establishment of a defined corridor of flexibility is necessary (Terkaj et al., 2009). In this context, various aspects of changeability come into consideration (Wiendahl, 2002). To meet the requirements of a turbulent environment, an examination of the effects of structural and organizational aspects of agility is imperative. Furthermore, the focus is on recognizing the need for changes of production systems in terms of structure (elements and resources) or organization (organizational structure and operational organization).

5   Conclusion and Future Work

In summary, this paper introduces an approach that combines socio-technical aspects and deterministic interactions of the tasks of production control. Due to the fact that several operators are unable to cope with complex control principles, their involvement is imperative in order to estimate the effects of the freedom of choice as regards the individual tasks of production control. The functional map enables an analysis of key levers influencing production systems. Based on the hierarchical pattern possibilities of intervention are drawn systematically, so that operational users will be in a position to act independently within coordinated control loops. Production control executed by operational users enables an adaptive balancing between robustness and agility and thus represents the implementation of the concept of resilience within production systems. However, the more intricate the production system and its organization are, the more difficult the application of this approach seems to be. In this regard, additional research is necessary.

References

Bhamra, R., Dani, S., Burnard, K.: Resilience: The concept, a literature review and future directions. International Journal of Production Research 49(18), 5375–5393 (2011)

Ivanov, D., Sokolov, B.: Control and system-theoretic identification of the supply chain dynamics domain for planning, analysis and adaption of performance under uncertainty. European Journal of Operational Research 224(2), 313–323 (2013)

Wieland, A., Wallenburg, C.: Dealing with supply chain risks. International Journal of Physical Distribution & Logistics Management 42(10), 887–905 (2012)

Wieland, A., Wallenburg, C.M.: The influence of relational competencies on supply chain resilience. International Journal of Physical Distribution & Logistics Management 43(4), 300–320 (2013)

Schuh, G., Potente, T., Thomas, C.: Design of Production Control's Behavior. In: Forty Sixth CIRP Conference on Manufacturing Systems 2013, pp. 145–150 (2013)

Zhang, W.J., van Luttervelt, C.A.: Toward a resilient manufacturing system. CIRP Annals - Manufacturing Technology 60(1), 469–472 (2011)

Cordes, P., Hülsmann, M.: Dynamic Capabilities in Manufacturing Processes: A Knowledge-based Approach for the Development of Manufacturing Flexibilities. In: Windt, K. (ed.) Robust Manufacturing Control, pp. 519–534. Springer, Berlin (2013)

Nyhuis, P., Hartmann, W., Kennemann, M., Münzberg, B.: Produktionsregelung mit logistischen Kennlinien. wt Werkstattstechnik 99(4), 239–243 (2009)

Nyhuis, P., Begemann, C., Berkholz, D., Hasenfuß, K.: Konfiguration der Fertigungssteuerung. wt Werkstattstechnik 96(4), 195–199 (2006)

Zülch, G.: Systematisierung von Strategien der Fertigungssteuerung. In: Zahn, E., Bullinger, H. (eds.) Organisationsstrategie und Produktion, pp. 151–178. Gfmt, München (1990)

Schuh, G., Stich, V.: Produktionsplanung und -steuerung 2: Evolution der PPS. Springer, Berlin (2012)

Schuh, G., Stich, V.: Produktionsplanung und -steuerung 1: Grundlagen der PPS. Springer, Berlin (2012)

Jodlbauer, H.: Produktionsoptimierung. Springer, Berlin (2008)

Hartmann, M.: Merkmale zur Wandlungsfähigkeit von Produktionssystemen bei turbulenten Aufgaben. GESIS, Barleben (1998)

Terkaj, W., Tolio, T., Valente, A.: Focused Flexibility in Production Systems. In: Elmaraghy, H.A. (ed.) Changeable and Reconfigurable Manufacturing Systems, pp. 47–66. Springer (2009)

Wiendahl, H.: Wandlungsfähigkeit: Schlüsselbegriff der zukunftsfähigen Fabrik. Werkstattstechnik 2002 92(4), 122–127 (2002)

Achieving Responsiveness in Small and Medium-Sized Enterprises through Assemble To Order Strategy

Shoaib ul Hasan[1,2], Marco Macchi[1], Alessandro Pozzetti[1],
and Ruth Carrasco-Gallego[2]

[1] Department of Management, Economics and Industrial Engineering,
Politecnico di Milano, Piazza Leonardo da Vinci 32, 20133 Milano, Italy
{sayyed.shoaibulhasan,marco.macchi,alessandro.pozzetti}@polimi.it
[2] Escuela Técnica Superior de Ingenieros Industriales,
Universidad Politécnica de Madrid, C/José Gutierrez Abascal 2, 28006 Madrid, Spain
ruth.carrasco@upm.es

Abstract. With an aggressive economic competition on a global scale, more educated and demanding customers, and a rapid pace of change in process technology, responsiveness in manufacturing is becoming a key competitive advantage. The present paper examines how responsiveness can be achieved in SMEs operating according to an Assemble to Order strategy. The framework – proposed starting from literature analysis and tested through a first case study – will be used in future works to drive a systematic analysis of responsiveness in SMEs.

Keywords: Responsiveness, Flexibility, Agility, Assemble To Order.

1 Introduction

Manufacturing companies, nowadays, are facing fierce pressure to cope with rapidly changing market demands for high variety, more customized products and quick delivery [1,2]. Manufacturing is in fact evolving from mass production to mass customization and personalization paradigms [3]. However, these new paradigms face many new challenges, such as high cost and increased lead times, due to the complexity induced by high variety [4,5]. This complexity increases on the shop floor because of additional product changeovers, more routing alternatives, larger volumes of work in process, assembly line balancing problems with mixed models, increasing process variability, etc. [5]. Nevertheless, to stay competitive, companies require delivering customized products rapidly and cost-effectively [6], and this responsiveness is considered as a key challenge for future manufacturing.

Interestingly, a recent survey ([7]) found that Small and Medium-sized Enterprises (SMEs) in Italy are more responsive than large enterprises, claiming that they are capable to deliver faster because they manufacture and assemble items very quickly. Notwithstanding the findings, there is still little empirical evidence to clarify how SMEs are actually adapting to provide quick response to a changing demand.

B. Grabot et al. (Eds.): APMS 2014, Part III, IFIP AICT 440, pp. 208–215, 2014.
© IFIP International Federation for Information Processing 2014

Then, the aim of our research is to explore different approaches that SMEs adopt to enhance their responsiveness. This study is part of the research and particularly focuses on the assembly process with the purpose to investigate different characteristics that lead to higher responsiveness in SMEs operating according to an Assemble To Order (ATO) strategy. Two research questions are driving the work: i) what are the different approaches that SMEs adopt to enhance responsiveness of their production systems? ii) how can manufacturing responsiveness be achieved in the context of SMEs operating an ATO strategy with manual assembly? As it is an initial work within the frame of our research plan, the paper will provide preliminary findings in this regard. Owning the exploratory nature of this phase of the research, the case study approach was considered to be an appropriate methodology [8] to identify and analyze key approaches adopted and how they help to achieve higher responsiveness. In this regard, the unit of analysis selected for the case study is one of the manufacturing plants of a selected SME in Italy because of its high responsiveness: the plant has been investigated using unstructured interviews and by on site visit to observe its actual functioning.

Section 2 provides the results of literature analysis, section 3 presents the conceptual framework; the case study is eventually discussed in section 4.

2   Literature Analysis

2.1   Manufacturing Responsiveness

The original debate about manufacturing responsiveness was focused on the concept of *"time-based competition"* [9,10]. Soon the debate enlarged the scope, considering competitiveness based on the capabilities to react to all kinds of changes rapidly and cost-effectively [6]. In particular, changing demand and market needs have been emerging as relevant issues, as remarked by [11] in his definition of responsiveness: *"the ability to react purposefully and within an appropriate time-scale to customer demand or changes in the marketplace, to bring about or maintain competitive advantage"*. Therefore, the changing demand regards also the modifications in the product portfolio, as pointed out in [12] where responsiveness refers to the speed at which a plant can meet changing business goals and produce new product models. Overall, the above mentioned (and other similar) definitions focus their attention on the competitive priorities and resulting benefits that the manufacturing system should address to achieve a winning position in the market through responsiveness. Conversely, the conditions that enable the system to be responsive are not particularly taken into account: a further insight from an operations management perspective is required.

In this regard, it is worth citing again [11] that identified three dimensions of responsiveness: product, volume and process. The dimensions concern respectively the ability to renew the product range through the rapid introduction of new models, to modify the production volumes, and to quickly manufacture and deliver items. Responsiveness of a production system is influenced by different variables such as position of customer order decoupling point [11], set-up times [7], production resources and system design (equipment and workers) etc. [6], [12].

2.2   Flexibility and Agility as Lever for Responsiveness

Flexibility has been at the focus of academic discussion for a long time. It is considered as "an operating characteristic" being defined as "the ability of a system to change status within an existing configuration (of established parameters)" [13]. As originally conceived, flexibility is characterized by three types of operational flexibility, relating to technology, labor and infrastructure [14] as the levers to support changes of an existing configuration. Different concepts implementing flexibility are then proposed: as a meaningful example, it is worth mentioning the concept of Flexible Manufacturing System (FMS) [15], one of the most popular in the history of flexibility in manufacturing. Although the FMS was claimed as a response to the increasing need to produce variety of parts, some limitations such as high complexity [16] and low system output [17] constrain its capability to cope with challenges of high fluctuation in the product demand and mix, as new market conditions demand a higher degree of flexibility than traditional FMS. Moreover, with high cost of general flexibility [18] and low output, a relatively high cost per part is expected with FMS. Also flexibility through FMS is obtained by assuming a constant amount of information and absence of learning process [19], while over time manufacturing plants should be able to make different decisions – for their structural and infrastructural resources –, learning from past experience and adapting to changing needs. Therefore, to be more responsive, manufacturing firms have been looking for approaches towards other forms of flexibility, capability to cope with dynamics, hence particularly looking at the effective use of changeable and reconfigurable structural and infrastructural resources within a plant. Agile manufacturing has emerged to this end. Agile manufacturing, or agility, is defined as *"an ability of the system to rapidly reconfigure (with a new parameter set)"* [13]. The concept of Reconfigurable Manufacturing System (RMS) has been proposed to achieve agility in manufacturing systems. RMS is intended as *"a system designed at the outset for rapid change in structure, as well as in hardware and software components, in order to quickly adjust production capacity and functionality within a part family in response to sudden changes in market or regulatory requirements"* [6]: this definition provides the major emphasis on the design of manufacturing systems with adjustable resources, in order to enhance the responsiveness to changes. More specifically, [17] asserts that six core characteristics of RMS: customization (leading to adjustments to guarantee the production of parts within given product families), convertibility (enabling to easily transform the functionality of existing systems and machines in order to suit new production requirements) and scalability (supporting to easily modify the production capacity by adding/subtracting manufacturing resources and/or changing components of the system) can be considered as the key characteristics to enable reconfiguration; modularity (leading to the manipulation and optimal arrangement of modular units between alternate production schemes), integrability (with the purpose to integrate modules rapidly by a set of mechanical, informational, and control interfaces) and diagnosability (representing the ability to diagnose the problems, and quickly correct operational defects) contribute to the rapid reconfiguration. A manufacturing system having these characteristics is considered as highly responsive.

2.3   Achieving Responsiveness through an Assemble To Order Strategy

ATO is a production strategy for customer order fulfillment, proposed as a form postponement [20] and implemented in assembly systems to produce unique variants within a product family [21]. As an order-driven production strategy, ATO production system faces swings in demand, thus high variability in the capacity utilization of the assembly systems; moreover long order lead times can be expected as only the component parts/sub-assemblies are hold in stock while finished products are not [22]. Therefore, to remain competitive, the production system must be properly designed with the objective to be responsive to the customer issues and, at the same time, achieve production quality and productivity.

To this end, different strategies have been proposed especially with the purpose to mitigate complexity. According to [23], to effectively manage the variety, in-house reengineering should be initiated when an ATO strategy is decided, with the purpose to flatten bills of material, simplify designs and standardize components and to obtain commonality in as many of the base components as possible within a product family. Component family and commonality enable then to reduce the number of setups on the shop floor, thereby decreasing manufacturing and assembly lead times [24]. Other ways to enhance performances and to minimize complexity in an ATO production environment are found in proper assembly sequence planning and assembly system configurations [25,26]. Furthermore, different types of assembly systems (manual, semi or fully-automated) would require specific concerns. In the case of ATO using manual assembly systems (with human assemblers operating usually with the aid of simple power tools [12]), of particular interest for this paper, the presence of human assemblers naturally leads to high potential for "convertibility", as humans qualified and trained may be easily adaptable to new tasks when the demand requires changes; but this potential could still suffer from complexity. In fact, as the product variety becomes high in manual, mixed-model assembly systems, the system performance could be negatively affected by the complexity that is induced, including also the risk that human errors occur [27]. Thus, in order to achieve higher responsiveness, in an ATO production environment, the main concern should be to induce as much flexibility and agility in the system; besides the reduction of complexity on the shop floor should be considered as a key priority.

3   Framework

Literature suggests that "*manufacturing companies adopt different approaches and practices to respond to changing needs from the environment. These approaches and practices induce flexibility and agility in the system and minimize complexity, which ultimately impact different dimensions of responsiveness such as product, process and volume*". Thus, based on literature, a conceptual framework is developed as shown in Figure 1. The framework is composed of different elements in four layers:

— the changing needs emergent from the business environment, for which the manu-
    facturing firms should be capable to be responsive in order to remain competitive;

— the responsiveness and its dimensions to address different needs, also providing a means to classify the determinants of responsiveness;

— the capabilities in a production system based on flexibility and agility that impact different dimensions of responsiveness;

— the manufacturing approaches and practices adopted at operations level, particularly for production planning and system design, that induce/enable flexibility and agility in the production system.

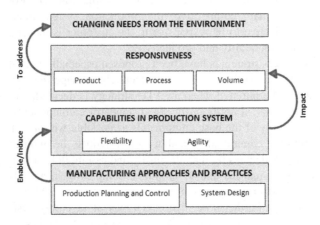

Fig. 1. Conceptual framework

4   Case Study

The case study is analyzed according to the framework developed in previous section. Considered as a leader in its industry, the company manufactures food processing machines for retailers or domestic use. Currently, besides the national market, it fulfills the needs of 125 countries worldwide, including Europe, North America and China. An interesting issue is that, regardless of the wide product variety, the company can deliver finished products within 5 days, achieving high responsiveness.

The key changing needs experienced by the company relate to the product variety and to the quick delivery, with the purpose to be competitive on the global market. Product variety depends mostly on the requests of customization, technical, to cope with local legislations for food equipment, and aesthetic, to maintain the image of the brand. Demand fluctuation is also high, as effect of the mix of customers distributed worldwide and locally. Due to these changing market needs the company decided to change its production strategy, transforming it from the past, Make to Stock (MTS), to the current, ATO. Different practices remarked as relevant for this transformation and for achieving responsiveness are identified in the remainder, reflecting 4 core characteristics of RMS, i.e. customization, convertibility, scalability and integrability.

Customization is based on component standardization and product familiarization, with subsequent effect on the organization of operators in assembly isles, combining high skilled workers – with expertise on a product family, then capable to manage the variety induced complexity by items within the family –, and low skilled workers – with expertise on the standard components, therefore a task specialization for the first phases of the assembly process.

Convertibility is based on a flexible tracking of information, implemented at the MES (Manufacturing Execution System) level by a decoupled coding system of pallets and components– which supports the ease introduction of new components in the inbound logistics management –, and on the qualification of operators in the shop floor – especially the high skilled operators of assembly isles.

Scalability of inbound logistics and assembly systems is achieved thanks to the adjustment of capacity during the shop calendar day of the picking area, where the assembly kits are prepared, and of the assembly isles: this is possible primarily because the workers, with task specialization on standard components, can rotate amongst different work places.

Integrability is based on the coordinated control of inbound logistics and assembly operations at MES level to achieve the required delivery performance. Firstly, this is achieved by scheduling the automated warehouse to send components in the picking area in close coordination with the assembly program. Secondly, the assembly program execution for batch is based on a work load control principle, being the capacities adjusted so that the assembly lead time of the batch stays within the limits

Overall, it is worth remarking that different types of operational flexibility emerge based on the skills of labor, technological support through a MES of inbound logistics and assembly, product familiarization, and component standardization.

Table 1 summarizes the practices observed for the case, and classified according to the conceptual framework, considering the induced capabilities and their impact on different dimensions of responsiveness; it is worth pointing out that, in some cases, more dimensions are closely connected, since one benefit from the other.

Table 1. Summary of practices, induced capabilities and impact on responsiveness dimensions

Practices	Induced capability	Dimensions of responsiveness		
		Product	Volume	Process
Customization based on component standardization and product familiarization + Organization in assembly isles using a mix of skilled operators (for tasks specialization on components and for the whole assemblies within a product family)	Flexibility	√		√
Scalability of inbound logistics and assembly systems, thanks to the adjustment of capacities during the shop calendar day	Agility		√	√
Convertibility based on a decoupled coding systems of pallets and components + qualification / training of assembly operators	Agility	√		√
Integrability based on coordinated scheduling of inbound logistics and assembly + work load control of assembly operations	Flexibility + Agility		√	√

5   Conclusions

The paper, based on literature analysis and a case study, envisions the variables to identify the key characteristics of manufacturing responsiveness. This is aligned with the long term purpose of our investigation, i.e. to understand how SMEs are adapting to provide quick response to changing demands. The proposed framework, and its future developments, will be used in order to drive a systematic analysis of the impact of different approaches and practices on responsiveness; indeed, different dimensions (product, process, volume) and capabilities in the production system (flexibility and agility) will be the leading concepts to this end. The case study presented in the paper is a first test for the framework. Overall, the findings from our investigation – after the extension to different cases – are expected to help SMEs to analyze and adopt different approaches and practices according to their needs, especially concerning the use of proper approaches in ATO strategy. Two particular interests, arising from the case study analyzed in the paper, and worth for future considerations in next cases, can be: i) the customization based on component standardization and product familiarization, to facilitate the introduction of process responsiveness in the shop floor; ii) the integrability of inbound logistics and assembly as a key determinant to guarantee process and volume responsiveness. Further on, considering the social aspect in the SME context, it will be worth concentrating on the role of labor, its support to manufacturing responsiveness, and the achievement of a good balance between economic needs for quick response and social needs of satisfactory working conditions.

Acknowledgments. This paper is produced as part of the EMJD Programme European Doctorate in Industrial Management (EDIM) funded by the European Commission, Erasmus Mundus Action 1.

References

1. Salvador, F., Forza, C.: Configuring products to address the customization-responsiveness squeeze: a survey of management issues and opportunities. International Journal of Production Economics 91(3), 273–291 (2004)
2. McCutcheon, D.M., Raturi, A.S., Meredith, J.R.: The customization-responsiveness squeeze. Sloan Management Review 35(2), 89–99 (1994)
3. Hu, S.J.: Evolving Paradigms of Manufacturing: From Mass Production to Mass Customization and Personalization. Procedia CIRP 7, 3–8 (2013)
4. Åhlström, P., Westbrook, R.: Implications of mass customization for operations management: An exploratory survey. International Journal of Operations & Production Management 19(3), 262–275 (1999)
5. Blecker, T., Abdelkafi, N.: Mass customization: state-of-the-art and challenges. In: Mass Customization: Challenges and Solutions, pp. 1–25. Springer, US (2006)
6. Koren, Y., Heisel, U., Jovane, F., Moriwaki, T., Pritschow, G., Ulsoy, G., Van Brussel, H.: Reconfigurable manufacturing systems. CIRP Annals-Manufacturing Technology 48(2), 527–540 (1999)

7. Belvedere, V., Grando, A., Papadimitriou, T.: The responsiveness of Italian small-to-medium sized plants: dimensions and determinants. International Journal of Production Research 48(21), 6481–6498 (2010)
8. Yin, R.K.: Case study research: Design and methods (Vol, vol. 5. Sage (2009)
9. Stalk, G.: Time – the next source of competitive advantage. Harvard Business Review 66(4), 41–51 (1988)
10. Stalk, G., Hout, T.: Competing Against Time: How Time-based Competition is Reshaping Global Markets. The Free Press, New York (1990)
11. Holweg, M.: The three dimensions of responsiveness. International Journal of Operations & Production Management 25(7), 603–622 (2005)
12. Koren, Y., Shpitalni, M.: Design of reconfigurable manufacturing systems. Journal of Manufacturing Systems 29(4), 130–141 (2010)
13. Ednilson, S.B., Mark, D.H.: A theoretical review of flexibility, agility and responsiveness in the operations management literature: Toward a conceptual definition of customer responsiveness. International Journal of Operations & Production Management 29(1), 30–53 (2009)
14. Slack, N.: The flexibility of manufacturing systems. International Journal of Operations & Production Management 7(4), 35–45 (1987)
15. Tetzlaff, U.A.: Flexible manufacturing systems, pp. 5–11. Physica-Verlag, HD (1990)
16. Setchi, R.M., Lagos, N.: Reconfigurability and reconfigurable manufacturing systems: state-of-the-art review. In: IEEE International Conference on Industrial Informatics, pp. 529–535 (2004)
17. Koren, Y.: General RMS Characteristics. Comparison with Dedicated and Flexible Systems. In: Reconfigurable Manufacturing Systems and Transformable Factories, pp. 27–45. Springer, Heidelberg (2006)
18. Mehrabi, M.G., Ulsoy, A.G., Koren, Y.: Reconfigurable manufacturing systems: key to future manufacturing. Journal of Intelligent Manufacturing 11(4), 403–419 (2000)
19. De Toni, A.F., Tonchia, S.: Manufacturing flexibility: A literature review. International Journal of Production Research 36(6), 1587–1617 (1998)
20. Van Hoek, R.I.: The rediscovery of postponement: a literature review and directions for research. Journal of Operations Management 19(2), 161–184 (2001)
21. AlGeddawy, T., ElMaraghy, H.: Design of single assembly line for the delayed differentiation of product variants. Flexible Services and Manufacturing Journal 22(3-4), 163–182 (2010)
22. Pil, F.K., Holweg, M.: Linking product variety to order-fulfillment strategies. Interfaces 34(5), 394–403 (2004)
23. Tesrine, R.J., Tesrine, M.G.: Cholesterol and inventory: healthy choice guidelines. International Journal of Services and Operations Management 1(2), 168–184 (2005)
24. Blecker, T., Abdelkafi, N.: Variety management in assemble-to-order supply chains, MPRA Paper, 5250, pp. 39–56 (2006)
25. Zhu, X., Hu, S.J., Koren, Y., Marin, S.P., Huang, N.: Sequence Planning to Minimize Complexity in Assembly Mixed-Model Lines. In: IEEE International Symposium on Assembly and Manufacturing (2007)
26. Wang, H., Hu, S.J.: Manufacturing complexity in assembly systems with hybrid configurations and its impact on throughput. CIRP Annals-Manufacturing Technology 59(1), 53–56 (2010)
27. Hu, S.J., Zhu, X.W., Wang, H., Koren, Y.: Product variety and manufacturing complexity in assembly systems and supply chains. CIRP Annals 57(1), 45–48 (2008)

TCO Evaluation in Physical Asset Management: Benefits and Limitations for Industrial Adoption

Irene Roda and Marco Garetti

Politecnico di Milano, Department of Management,
Economics and Industrial Engineering Milan, Italy
{irene.roda, marco.garetti}@polimi.it

Abstract. Nowadays, the evaluation of the total cost of ownership (TCO) of an asset for supporting informed decision-making both for investments and managerial issues within the asset management framework is gaining increasing attention in industry. Nevertheless its application in practice is still limited. The aim of this paper is to analyze the benefits and limitations of the adoption of TCO evaluation in asset management. Based on a literature review, the paper defines a framework that categorizes the benefits and potential applications that a TCO model can have for different stakeholders. Together with that, industry related issues that influence its implementation are also considered. Finally, empirical evidences are analyzed through a multiple case study to understand if those benefits are recognized in practice and which are the limitations for the practical adoption of a TCO model that should allow exploiting such benefits.

Keywords: Total Cost of Ownership, asset management.

1 Introduction

In the industrial sector, the operating time of the production asset after the green-field investment is typically long and during such time numerous rebuilds, replacements and expansion investments take place. All of these decisions, together with the chosen operations and maintenance strategies, affect the productivity of the physical capital (Komonen et al., 2006; Tam and Price, 2008). In order to meet the challenge of low returns on investment and realize value from asset, enterprises need to adopt an asset management strategy and system (ISO 55000:2014(E), 2014). Within it, one of the challenges for supporting decision-making along the asset lifecycle, is to improve the quantification process of costs so to be able to evaluate the total cost of a production system throughout its life cycle (i.e. the Total Cost of Ownership (TCO)) (IAM, 2012; Parra et al., 2009).

2 Methodology

This paper aims at defining a framework that categorizes the benefits and potential applications that a TCO model can have in asset management for different stakeholders. In order to do so, an extensive literature review has been developed as a keyword

B. Grabot et al. (Eds.): APMS 2014, Part III, IFIP AICT 440, pp. 216–223, 2014.

search, both through library services (Scopus, Google Scholar etc.) and a wider surfing in the web to consider journals and conferences publications, but also white papers and industrial reports. The analytic categories that allowed the classification of the reviewed literature and the definition of the framework have been derived both deductively considering the body of theory in the physical asset management and inductively from the material analyzed by means of generalization (Mayring, 2003). Once defined the framework, empirical evidences have been analyzed so to confirm it from a practical point of view. This also allowed identifying the main limitations for the adoption of TCO models, trough the development of a multiple case study. Details on the related methodology are given in Section 4.

3   TCO Applications and Benefits: Definition of a Framework

It is widely accepted in the academic literature (Schuman and Brent, 2005) that TCO should be an integral part of an asset management strategy and the same is assessed by the body of standards ISO 55000 on asset management (ISO 55000:2014(E), 2014). In the latter, it is indicated that: "[...] Life cycle cost, which may include capital expenditure, financing and operational costs, should be considered in the decision-making process". Moreover, companies are acknowledging how TCO can represent a reliable economic-sound support for taking decisions and to convey the information to people in different parts / functions of the same organization, or outside the company, such us costumers / suppliers. The ability to effectively identify cost drivers and manage cost reductions is a competitive advantage for companies (Heilala et al., 2006).

3.1   The Framework

Based on the literature review, a framework has been developed identifying the benefits for a company of having a TCO evaluation model supporting the decision-making process. The framework is organized on three main dimensions: i) type of stakeholder, ii) type of supported decision, iii) phase of the life cycle.

- **Type of stakeholder.** Different stakeholders with different perspectives can be interested in TCO analysis. Given the meaning itself of TCO, it is evident that asset users (industrial equipment or plant owners / managers) are the primary interested subjects. Nevertheless TCO is also a relevant issue for asset providers (industrial equipment or plant builders / manufacturers) (Barringer, 2003). Clearly it has to be considered that each of the two types of stakeholders has some common and some distinguishing reasons for interest on TCO. Besides, it must be considered that the ability of a provider to perform TCO evaluation is affected by the quality of information available in a higher way than the users' one (Korpi and Ala-Risku, 2008).
- **Type of supported decision.** A TCO model has potentiality to support different kinds of decisions. In particular, two main categories have been identified: (i) configuration decisions and (ii) management decisions. The first category includes all those decisions that have direct influence on the asset configuration, while the second one refers to those decisions that deal with the management, operation and maintenance of the asset.

- **Phase of life cycle.** TCO analysis is preferably carried out in any and all phases of an asset's life cycle to provide input to decision makers (Kawauchi and Rausand, 1999; Schuman and Brent, 2005). According to the conventional perspective, the lifecycle of an asset is composed by three main phases: beginning of life (BoL) including the activities for bringing an asset into operation (conceptualization, design, construction, installation and acquisition), middle of life (MoL) including the activities involved in asset operation and maintenance and finally the end of life (EoL) involving the final retirement of the asset (Amadi-Echendu, 2004).

The developed framework (Table 1) shows which benefits a TCO model can bring to each of the two types of stakeholder at each lifecycle phase by supporting different kinds of decisions (configuration or management decisions). In the following subsections the content of the framework is articulated considering each lifecycle phase.

BoL- According to several authors; cost must be an active rather than a resultant factor throughout the system design process (Fabrycky and Blanchard, 1991; Waghmode and Sahasrabudhe, 2012; Woodward, 1997). Though, generally speaking only 15% of the total TCO is consumed during the design phase, research has shown that as much as 85% of the remaining TCO is determined by decisions made during this stage (Lad and Kulkarni, 2008). TCO evaluation at this step allows providers and users to economically evaluate different scenarios at a pre-design step (Carpentieri and Papariello, 2006); determining the most cost efficient design amongst a set of alternatives; identifying cost drivers for design changes and optimization and, determining the cost of a design for budgetary purposes (Korpi and Ala-Risku, 2008). TCO can be seen also as a procurement (from the user perspective) and sales and marketing (from the provider perspective) tool. (Snelgrove, 2012) asserts that at the heart of pricing and selling in the twenty-first century is the ability to price based on created value. Moreover, TCO allows abandoning traditional feature-based marketing showing how the offered asset creates specific benefits considering its lifecycle and its effect on customer profitability. On the other side, through TCO, users are able to support their suppliers selection and evaluation steps (Ellram and Siferd, 1998). In the BoL phase the supplier can also be interested in TCO evaluation in case there is the possibility to enter into a service contract. TCO model is also able to support investment decisions supporting budget planning and costs control helping preventing decision makers from incurring investments which might be cheaper in acquisition, but significantly more expensive in O&M and consequently in total costs over their life cycle. Finally TCO plays a supporting role during the construction & installation phase for asset providers. In fact, although it is a late stage in the project for major changes, recommendations should still be considered in terms of TCO and the most favorable solution implemented. Spare parts requirement and provision can be evaluated at this phase (Schuman and Brent, 2005).

MoL- The evaluation of TCO and its usage for decision making support does represent a relevant aspect also during the MoL phase of an asset, both for configuration and management decisions, mostly for the asset users. At this stage, the asset is operative and, compared to the design stage, the level of uncertainty for the TCO evaluation is lower (Kawauchi and Rausand, 1999). Opportunities for reduced support costs and more effective support are based on the systematic capture and reuse of all information throughout the equipment life cycle; hence the best scenario is the case where data for technical performance evaluation are regularly collected. If this is not possible, the uncertainty in cost evaluation is anyways lower given that even if the analysis are based on estimations by people working on the field, these are related to an existing and operative asset. The use of TCO in this step can support asset users for configuration decisions such as the evaluation of the reconfiguration of the asset by applying some changes in the current layout for achieving a better availability level, involving also considerations on the WIP level (Tomasella and Parlikad, 2012). Moreover TCO evaluation can support management decisions such as the evaluation of changes in the actual maintenance strategy (Lad and Kulkarni, 2008; Woodward, 1997). Likewise, decisions on the operative conditions of the asset; its utilization and the production strategies can be supported by the TCO evaluation.

EoL- TCO has got relevance also at the End of Life of an asset. In fact, in this stage the asset is taken out of service for disposal or redeployment. In the latter case a potential new TCO may begin (Woodward, 1997), therefore the asset manager may use the TCO evaluation of the existing asset in order to support decisions for rehabilitation or reuse of the asset itself (Asiedu and Gu, 1998; Shahata and Zayed, 2008).

Table 1. Framework

	ASSET PROVIDER		ASSET USER	
	Configuration	Management	Configuration	Management
BOL	- Evaluation of project alternatives - Comparison and optimization of design alternatives - Components / equipment procurement and construction alternatives evaluation - spare parts requirements estimation. [4], [13], [2], [17]	- Communicating value to the customer and selling support - Propose to the clients specific design solutions - Pricing - Contracting maintenance services provision [4], [13], [17] , [19]	- Evaluation of design alternatives offered by a provider [6]	- Suppliers and tenders evaluation & selection - Maintenance service contract evaluation - Investment, budget planning, cost control [13], [5],[17], [22]
MOL	- Proposal of re-configuration solutions	- Maintenance service provision offering - Spare parts provision offering	- Reconfiguration decisions - WIP sizing [21]	- Maintenance scheduling and management - Repair level analysis - Asset utilization and production strategies [3],[14],[13]
EOL	- Proposal of reconfiguration for EoL optimization	- Evaluation and proposal of rehabilitation strategies	- Reuse strategies for components / machines	- Evaluation of rehabilitation strategies [2], [18], [22]

What emerged is that TCO is useful in asset provider – asset user communication, and helps in trade-off analyses of system concepts (Heilala et al., 2006). The core aim of a TCO evaluation is to avoid problem shifting decisions by keeping an integrating perspective.

3.2   The Industry-Influence

An additional aspect that emerged from the literature analysis is about the influence of the type of industry a company belongs to, on the value given to TCO analysis. The TCO concept was firstly introduced for procurement purposes by the US Department of Defense in 1960 and its importance in defense was stimulated by findings that operation and support costs for typical weapon systems accounted for as much as 75% of the total cost (Asiedu and Gu, 1998). Since then the need for more extensive application of engineering economy methodologies in the planning and control of production systems has been more and more recognized. The applications of LCC analysis have then spread to other industries such as oil and chemical industries (Kawauchi and Rausand, 1999). Not surprisingly, the concept originally spread among the process industry and more in general in capital-intensive industries where physical asset management represents a strategic resource given the high vulnerability to disturbances and the need for production / operation regularity that characterize them. Currently, the interest for TCO is rising in the discrete manufacturing industry too. In fact, the emergent global competition is forcing companies to estimate and optimize the overall system life cycle cost with reference to performance, safety, reliability and maintainability (Waghmode and Sahasrabudhe, 2012) to be able to compete not only on price, but also on cost effectiveness and technological leadership (Lad and Kulkarni, 2008). More and more contracts are based on TCO evaluation in several sectors such as the automotive, the packaging and the food sectors. Table 2 presents the concept emerged highlighting the critical factors connected to the TCO relevance for capital-intensive and discrete manufacturing industries.

Table 2. Relevance and critical factors of TCO in process and manufacturing industries

Type of industry	Critical factors	TCO relevance
Process industry (power, mining and oil, chemical sectors…)	• capital-intensive assets • high vulnerability to disturbances need for production regularity	• High strategic relevance of TCO for supporting decision making in physical asset management
Discrete manufacturing industry (packaging…)	• high competition and need to compete on cost effectiveness and technological leadership than just on price	• TCO is getting more and more relevance to demonstrate value for money of investments.

4   Practical Implications: Empirical Evidences

In order to corroborate the developed framework from an empirical point of view a case study was developed. The aim is to understand if the benefits that have been identified in literature are recognized in practice and which are the limitations for the adoption of TCO. Two companies belonging to different industries were selected. Company A is a small medium company in the discrete manufacturing industry while company B is a big company belonging to the process industry. They have different perspectives on asset management since company A is asset provider while company B is asset user. These differences have been selected referring to the different dimensions of the framework, and to the industry dependency highlighted in section 3. The case has been based on semi-structured interviews and on a defined questionnaire.

A first aspect that emerged from the case study is the different involvement and interest in using the TCO in different life cycle phases depending on the kind of stakeholder the two companies represent. Indeed, Company A (provider) declared to be directly involved and being able to take decisions mostly in the BoL phase. In fact, the company is responsible of the design and installation of the asset it produces and its role in the MoL phase is limited to providing the clients with manuals and guidelines for the maintenance activities. No service is provided in this case by A to its clients. On the other side, Company B is an asset user and it is directly interested in the management of its assets in the MoL phase and in the evaluation of investments for new installations. It has to be specified that Company A recently started to look at TCO as a potential tool and is now pushing its importance at strategic level; instead for Company B the TCO concept is consolidated even if it is still looking for a tool able to integrate technical evaluation into cost estimations. The following table refers to the proposed framework and shows which are the decisions that TCO evaluation can support according to the judgments of the two companies; based on the relevance for the business.

Table 3. The TCO benefits: results from the case study

		COMPANY A (ASSET PROVIDER)		COMPANY B (ASSET USER)	
		Configuration	Management	Configuration	Management
BoL		- Comparison and optimization of design alternatives	- Communicating value to the customer and selling support - Propose the clients specific design solutions	- Evaluation of design alternatives	- Suppliers and tenders evaluation & selection - Maintenance service contract evaluation - Investment, budget planning, cost control
MoL		- System reconfiguration proposals	- Possibility to develop service offering	- Reconfiguration decisions	- Maintenance scheduling and management - Repair level analysis

The results from the two cases endorse what was expected by the literature and confirm the benefits defined in the framework. The case study was also useful to identify the main limitations in the adoption of TCO in practice. In particular, the main findings that emerged are the following:

- both companies assessed the need for a TCO tool able not only to consider all the relevant cost items along the asset lifecycle, but also the technical aspects that have influence on it (the authors developed a literature review about this issue in (Roda and Garetti, 2014));.
- there is the need for a reliable database with both economic and technical parameters to be used for the TCO evaluation; in particular, the main problem for Company A is the necessity for a strict collaboration with its customers in order to get data for the evaluation of the OPEX of the asset under analysis; while Company B needs to focus on a system able to record relevant data regarding the behavior of its asset (failures events, set-up times etc.);
- the use of the TCO at the disposal phase is not considered as a relevant issue for both companies at the moment;

- general desires to minimize the initial expenditures in order to increase return on investment, and general lack inside the organizations of the adequate consideration of the asset life cycle that requires inter-functional cooperation and alignment;
- in general, TCO is seen as a powerful communication tool by both kind of stakeholders, being able to inform different kind of actors, the customers but also the top management by supplying the value of the asset through the language of money, eventually incorporating technical considerations.

5   Conclusions and Future Research

The paper presents a framework that describes the main applications and benefits that the evaluation of the TCO of industrial asset has got both for asset users and asset providers along the asset life cycle. Moreover, a case study analysis was implemented for an empirical assessment. The investigation confirmed that TCO represents a useful indication for guiding asset managers in the decision making process for harmonizing the never ending conflicts by focusing on facts, money, and time (Barringer, 2003) and, if properly estimated it does represent a competitive advantage for companies. It was possible to identify benefits of TCO for decision-making support at each life cycle phase of an asset and it emerged that its application can have positive effect on cost control, management of the asset, investments evaluation, sales and marketing strategy support, etc. Nevertheless, up to day, there are still a number of difficulties that limit a TCO model widespread adoption by industry. This problem emerged from the case study and it is a fact that there is no single calculation model that has been accepted in practice as a standard so far. The research plan of the authors of this paper is to develop a generalizable TCO evaluation methodology based on a critical analysis of some of the existing proposed solutions that go in this direction too. Future research should try to overcome the adoption limitations by identifying which are the existing barriers and defining a methodology for evaluating TCO that can be used as a real support in decision making. A step of the research may include widening to other companies the industrial assessment through the case study development to better identify the practical adoption's criticalities.

References

1. Amadi-Echendu, J.: Managing physical assets is a paradigm shift from maintenance. In: Proceedings of hte IEEE International Engineering Management Conference, pp. 1156–1160 (2004)
2. Asiedu, Y., Gu, P.: Product life cycle cost analysis: State of the art review. International Journal of Production Research 36, 883–908 (1998)
3. Barringer, H.: A life cycle cost summary. In: Conference of Maintenance Societies (ICOMS 2003), pp. 1–10 (2003)
4. Carpentieri, M., Papariello, M.: A life cycle cost framework for automotive production lines. In: 3th CIRP International Conference on LCE, pp. 711–716 (2006)

5. Ellram, L., Siferd, S.: Total cost of ownership: a key concept in strategic cost management decisions. Journal of Business Logistics 19, 55–84 (1998)
6. Fabrycky, W.J., Blanchard., B.S.: Life-cycle cost and economic analysis (1991)
7. Heilala, J., Helin, K., Montonen, J.: Total cost of ownership analysis for modular final assembly systems. International Journal of Production Research 44, 3967–3988 (2006)
8. IAM, Asset Management – an anatomy (2012)
9. ISO 55000:2014(E). Asset management — Overview, principles and terminology (2014)
10. Jönsson, M., Andersson, C., Ståhl, J.-E.: Conditions for and development of an information technology-support tool for manufacturing cost calculations and analyses. International Journal of Computer Integrated Manufacturing 26, 303–315 (2013)
11. Kawauchi, Y., Rausand, M.: Life Cycle Cost (LCC) analysis in oil and chemical process industries. Toyo Engineering Corp, Chiba (1999)
12. Komonen, K., Kortelainen, H., Räikkonen, M.: An asset management framework to improve longer term returns on investments in the capital intensive industries. In: London, S. (ed.) Engineering Asset Management, pp. 418–432 (2006)
13. Korpi, E., Ala-Risku, T.: Life cycle costing: a review of published case studies. Managerial Auditing Journal 23, 240–261 (2008)
14. Lad, B.K., Kulkarni, M.S.: Integrated reliability and optimal maintenance schedule design: a Life Cycle Cost based approach. Int. Journal of Product Lifecycle Mngmt 3, 78 (2008)
15. Parra, C., Crespo, A., Moreu, P.: Non-homogeneous Poisson Process (NHPP), stochastic model applied to evaluate the economic impact of the failure in the Life Cycle Cost Analysis (LCCA). Safety, Reliability and Risk Analysis: Theory, Methods and Applications, pp. 929–939 (2009)
16. Roda, I., Garetti, M.: The link between costs and performances for Total cost of Ownership evaluation of physical asset State of the art review. In: ICE 2014 Proceeding (to be published, 2014)
17. Schuman, C.A., Brent, A.C.: Asset life cycle management: towards improving physical asset performance in the process industry. International Journal of Operations & Production Management 25, 566–579 (2005)
18. Shahata, K., Zayed, T.: Simulation as a tool for life cycle cost analysis. In: Proceedings of the 40th Conference on Winter Simulation, pp. 2497–2503 (2008)
19. Snelgrove, T.: Value pricing when you understand your customers: Total cost of ownership–Past, present and future. Journal of Revenue & Pricing Management 11, 76–80 (2012)
20. Tam, A.S.B., Price, J.W.H.: A generic asset management framework for optimizing maintenance investment decision. Production Planning & Control 19, 287–300 (2008)
21. Tomasella, M., Parlikad, A.K.: Through-life management of engineering assets. In: Engineering Asset Management and Infrastructure Sustainability, pp. 931–944. Springer, London (2012)
22. Waghmode, L.Y., Sahasrabudhe, A.D.: Modelling maintenance and repair costs using stochastic point processes for life cycle costing of repairable systems. International Journal of Computer Integrated Manufacturing 25, 353–367 (2012)
23. Woodward, D.: Life cycle costing—theory, information acquisition and application. International Journal of Project Management 15, 335–344 (1997)

Flexibility in Lean Mixed Model Assembly Lines

Natalia Svensson Harari[1,2], Christer Osterman[1,3], Jessica Bruch[1], and Mats Jackson[1,2]

[1] Mälardalen University, Department of Product Realization, Eskilstuna, Sweden
{natalia.harari,jessica.bruch,mats.jackson}@mdh.se
[2] VolvoCE, Manufacturing Research, Eskilstuna, Sweden
{natalia.svensson.harari,mats.jackson}@volvo.com
[3] Scania CV AB, TD, Södertälje, Sweden
christer.osterman@scania.com

Abstract. The purpose of the research presented in this paper has been to characterize flexibility in lean mixed model assembly lines through exploring mechanisms used to achieve flexibility. The study combines a literature review and a multiple case study in two manufacturing companies. Scenarios of volume, mix and operation flexibility, as well as flexibility to introduce or remove products were studied. The results showed that to achieve flexibility related to these scenarios other kinds of flexibilities were used. Common mechanisms to achieve flexibility have been found in the two cases. A characterization of mixed model assembly lines regarding flexibility will be discussed.

Keywords: Mixed model assembly lines, lean, flexibility.

1 Introduction

Due to changing demands and shorten product life cycles, manufacturing companies deal with strategies to handle a variety of products and production volumes in their assembly systems. Assembly systems in the automotive industry in Sweden today are usually semi-automated mixed model lines where different product variants are assembled and operators are in charge of performing most of the assembly processes. Influenced by lean strategies, approaches to level production volumes and rationalization through elimination of the so called non-value-adding work are used. Different dimensions of flexibility have been described in the literature and difficulties of generalizing flexibility measures may be encountered [1]. Manufacturing settings are usually used when defining flexibility characteristics, and more information about them in assembly systems is needed beyond the efforts on describing Flexible Assembly Systems. These have been most of the times referred to as automated systems. The purpose of the research presented in this paper has been to characterize flexibility in lean mixed-model assembly lines (MMAL) through exploring mechanisms used to achieve flexibility taking into account the constituents of the assembly system described in the literature: human system, technical system, material handling system, information system and building and premises [2].

B. Grabot et al. (Eds.): APMS 2014, Part III, IFIP AICT 440, pp. 224–231, 2014.

2   Frame of References

2.1   Flexibility Dimensions and Measures

There are differences in meanings regarding flexibility as well as variation in perspectives specially when broken down into its dimensions, elements, and measures [3]. To characterize flexibility, Upton (1994), presented a framework of flexibility management regarding dimensions, time horizon and elements. Dimensions concern the required flexibility and need to change. Time horizon is related to the timeframe in which the change will occur. Elements of flexibility concern range, uniformity or mobility [4]. Dimensions of flexibility have been described by different authors such as Browne et al. (1984), Sethi and Sethi, (1990), and Gupta and Somers (1992) [5, 6, 7]. Koste and Malhotra, (1999), proposed a theoretical framework to analyze flexibility dimensions where 10 dimensions of flexibility were considered; Machine flexibility (number and variety of operations the machine can perform), Labor flexibility (number and variety of operations/task that workers can perform), Material handling (number of paths and variety of material), Routing flexibility (number of products with alternate routes and extend of variation between routes), Operation flexibility (number of products with alternate sequencing plans and variety of plans), Expansion flexibility (number and variety of expansions), Volume flexibility (extend of change and degree of fluctuations in output level), Mix flexibility (number and variety of products that can be produced), New product flexibility (number and variety of products that can be introduced), Modification flexibility (number and variety of product modifications), all of them without incurring in high transition penalties or large changes in performance outcomes [1]. The elements of flexibility have been then defined by them as; Range-Number (number of tasks, products, etc), Range-heterogeneity (differences in task, products, etc.), Mobility (transition penalties - time, cost, effort) and Uniformity (similarity of performance outcomes such as quality, cost, time) [1]. Based on Atkinson, (1984) and Allvin and Aronsson, (2013) some definitions of labor flexibility are further described; Functional flexibility (capacity of the job and the organization of work such as teamwork. It implies a reorganization and conversion of the operators to new work tasks. These methods are used for practical and immediate purposes), Numerical flexibility (adaption of the workforce to the changes in production not related to the performance of work. Some examples of this are: temporary employment, outsourced personnel and staffing agencies.), Temporal and financial flexibility (adjusting working time or labor cost. It could also include variable salaries.) [8,9].

2.2   Lean Mixed-Model Assembly Lines

The necessity of using the same equipment and line for different models was one of the driving forces behind the development of the Lean methods and principles [10]. In a Lean assembly line the Takt time is used to organize and balance the line. When producing a mix of models, some degree of leveling is necessary [11]. Even when the cycle-time of each particular model could be different, the overall takt time remains the same. This can be accomplished with internal buffers acting as de-couplers in the process but preferable with set up time reduction [12]. Just-In-Time (JIT) is a concept where the parts used in assembly are paced using a Kanban system to create pull in production and avoid waste [13] where the upstream process only produces as much as the downstream process consumes. The pull principle requires consistent leveling to reduce variation in demand. A Kanban system has several aspects and can be used to regulate the material flows as well as the assembly orders [14]. Standardized work connects resource efficiency with flow efficiency through the balancing of the process. Standardized work is connected to standard time [15] thus reducing variation in the assembly process. To handle different work content that products could have, solutions such as variation of workers in assembly, utilizing sub assembly lines, and concentrating imbalances to particular points of the assembly process are used [15]. Regarding setup times, different products require different fixtures. Changing can take time, reducing the flow efficiency of the process. Commonality of interfaces, generalized tools and fixtures and various SMED principles are used [12]. Planning and mixing rules are used to handle variation of customer demands. Problem solving and continuous improvement activities are carried out.

3   Methods and Techniques

The research method was based on a multiple-case study design as described by Yin (2014) [16]. It was a quali-quantitative and participative study. The literature review gave input to the design of the research study. The study focused on flexibility of volume, mix, operation and flexibility to introduce new products and remove existing ones. The assembly system was analyzed from all its constituents: human system, technical system, material handling system, information system and building and premises [2]. The study was conducted in two Swedish manufacturing companies, defined as Case A and Case B producing the same component in MMALs with production systems based on lean principles. The study was conducted by two researchers from June 2013 until April 2014. The design of the data collection protocol consisted of: Informed consent, background information of the participant, recorded semi-structured interviews, observations protocol. A pilot study was developed at the same companies but in different assembly areas. Active observations were made at the lines. In total 11 semi-structured interviews of around 1 hour were conducted to production managers, production technicians and logistics managers. The interviews were developed by function, conducted in Swedish, recorded and transcribed for reliability. The analysis of the data used the approach of Miles and Huberman, (1994) [17]. The collected data and transcriptions went through data reduction process and analysis supported by the frame of references. The results of each case were then used to draw cross-case conclusions.

4   Empirical Findings

The study concerned the assembly of a specific component referred as component X, Y and Z. Three assembly lines were studied in Case A which assembled X, Y and Z according to the final products. Case B had different assembly lines for X, Y and Z for different final products. Two assembly lines were studied in Case B. Both companies worked with modularization in their products, and mutual processes, tools, infrastructure, resources between models were used. Case B had a modular system established at the company. Both worked with semiautomatic hand-tools connected to andon systems and also customized fixtures and tools. Teams of 5 or 7 operators and 1 team leader worked along the lines. One or two operators worked in parallel by station depending on the product variant. Operators were employed by the company or outsourced in permanent and temporal terms. Stairs salary systems related to the competence were used. The takt time of the cases had differences. Case A used stop and go AGV´s systems. Operators rotated according to a schedule. Training and education of new operators was done in the line by the team leader. The company used a centralized material handling area. Some parts were delivered using poka-yoke solutions. Around 6 to 14 variants were assembled. The number of operators per line varied from 7 to 15, and the main lines had 3 or 4 stations. Case B used a continuous moving overhead conveyor as well as robots at some stages and elevators to transport the parts. Operators rotated every half an hour. Training and education of new operators was done in a separate area. Different material handling areas were dedicated for each line. Kits and moving racks beside the line were used. More than 100 variants were assembled. The number of operators per line varied from 70 to 105 and the main lines had 20 to 30 stations plus internal buffers and one area for special products.

4.1   Mechanisms to Achieve Flexibility

Volume Flexibility. Related to the capacity of the system, the cases analyzed scenarios of volume change followed by a decision making process. The balance of the line was a determining factor in the decisions. According to the magnitude of the volume change, they usually started with changes in shift-forms and working times, increasing or decreasing the number of employees avoiding possible changes in the current takt time and rebalancing the line, until the point when the capacity was exceeded and investments were needed. Logistics needed to adapt its capacity according to assembly. When assembly volumes decreased, they tried to maintain the same takt time using strategies such as takt holes. One consequence of decreasing personnel was that competence needed was lost also for scenarios when volume increases again. Case B had agreements with the Union concerning flexible working times and time banks for periods of increase or decrease of the based takt time. Mechanisms used to achieve volume flexibility are shown in Figure 1.

Mix and Operation Flexibility. Both companies delivered a variety of products. Assembly shared resources and processes for a variety of products. Alternate areas were used for products with high differences in work content in Case B. About operation flexibility, an assembly plan containing the variety of models was delivered in the first positions at the line specifying the sequence of models to be assembled. Some distinctions should be made in relation to the definition of sequence in assembly. Sequence could be referred as the sequence of processes in which the products are assembled, but sequence is also referred to as the order in which the different models will be assembled during the shift connected to customer orders and balance in the line. Mechanisms used to achieve product mix and operation flexibility are shown in Figure 2.

	Human System	Technical System	Material Handling System	Information System	Building and premises
Volume Increase	-Flexible Working Time -Adjust Shift Form -Recruit personnel -Decrease Takt time -Rebalance the line -Employee involvement	-Optimize equipment, increase speed -Analyze stations length connected to conveyor speed -Man-machine charts to reduce waiting times -Analyze technical capacity vs. Forecast -Optimize takt time without increasing staff -Time studies - Work close to the teams -Check flow capacity -Identify technical limitations -Investments, new skills -Number of stations	-Increase personnel according to assembly -Increase tugger trains/Forklifts -More battery for tugger trains/Forklifts -Check positions and competence -Traffic flow -Reduce waiting time -Control time points to deliver -Area	-Balancing software to measure times, divide the work and film every position and torque to eliminate idle time and check ergonomics. - Change instructions -Screens with times, number of units to be produced and current status, number of stops. -Systems to register the maintenance status of equipment, more use required more maintenance.	-Stop and go AGVs and continuous moving lines -Reduce or enlarge stations length, increase or reduce number of stations -Increase or move equipment -Material handling space beside the line
Volume Decrease	-Flexible Working Time -Adjust Shift Form -Reduce personnel -Reallocate permanent personnel - Maintain takt and takt with holes -Increase Takt time -Rebalance the line	-Not remove the installed capacity -No technical limitations	-Reduce personnel -Rebalance the groups -Reallocate in other tasks -Flexible working time		

Fig. 1. Mechanisms used to achieve volume flexibility and its relation with the assembly system constituents

	Human System	Technical System	Material Handling System	Information System	Building and premises
Product Mix	-In general, mutual/ standarized/repetitive assembly processes and task for a variety of models -Specific processes/tasks depending on the model/variant -Specific assembly areas for special variants with higher work content	-Mutual technology between product variants/models -Automatic setup of tools -Customized fixtures and tools	-Generic methods for a variety of models. -% of common parts between models	-Work instructions and standards -Assembly orders with part numbers -Colours/images to identify parts/variants -Scanners with barcodes to identify variants and automatic changeover/setup of tools and equipment. -Screens and control systems for specific product parameters connected to tools and Andon systems	-One assembly line for a variety of product models with similar station setups -Other areas or lines for different variants
Operation Flexibility	-Flexible working time -Re-planning, re-schedule of the product and inform first position -Routines and instructions for planned sequence changes -Teamleader receive the signal, change sequence list and distribute to the influenced -Andon system	-No sequence rules -Check the heaviest variants -Use adjustment areas -Use product reserves that could be adapted to different variants	-Check material availability and in place -Check with suppliers -No sequence material and have it available beside the line	-Andon system -Planning systems -Sequence lists -Communication with suppliers -Routines -Instructions	-Stop in the line -Adjustment areas

Fig. 2. Mechanisms used to achieve operation and product mix flexibility and its relation with the assembly system constituents

New Product and Removal of Existing Product Flexibility. The introduction of new products was considered a complex project in both companies. Challenges were related to cooperation between product design and assembly upon the technical implications from both perspectives and e.g. due to ergonomics. The companies analyzed the design of new products in relation to the existing ones to make possible the use of e.g. existing technology and resources. However, evaluations of possible modifications that did not destabilize the current assembly were also made as well as due to a potential need of building new assembly areas. Involvement of different levels of the organization was mentioned to be needed, due to possible new methods, instructions, times, technology, etc. Removal of existing products required the participation of preparation areas in coordination with assembly and logistics. Mechanisms used to achieve new product and removal of existing ones are shown in Figure 3.

	Human System	Technical System	Material Handling System	Information System	Building and premises
New Product Flexibility	-Project managers (Assembly) are involved from the beginning and work together with Product Development. -Train operators and try prototypes -New working methods -Time studies	-Adjust the new product according to the current assembly -Check if existing technology could be used, test assembly, technical tests -Modify equipment or invest in new one	-New part numbers -Allocate new material -Prepare stock -Place material -Evaluate space, if it is not enough, start picking material -Changes in packaging -Labelling	-Prepare systems -Labels -Update standards and instructions	-Adapt the line -New stations
Removal of product	-Preparation Unit stablish a deadline in assembly and work with logistics	-Remove equipment if its not used	-Change part numbers -Remove material	-Update or remove standards and instructions -Update systems	-Check stock -Clean shelves beside the line - In some cases reduce subassemblies

Fig. 3. Mechanisms used to achieve new product/removal of existing products flexibility and its relation with the assembly system constituents.

5   Analysis

The cases illustrate mechanism used to achieve flexibility and its relation with the assembly system constituents. To achieve volume, mix and operation flexibility and new product/removal of existing products flexibility, other flexibilities have been used. An overview of these results is shown in Figure 4.

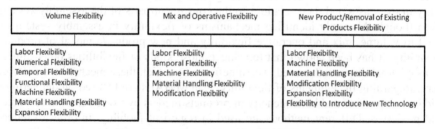

Volume Flexibility	Mix and Operative Flexibility	New Product/Removal of Existing Products Flexibility
Labor Flexibility Numerical Flexibility Temporal Flexibility Functional Flexibility Machine Flexibility Material Handling Flexibility Expansion Flexibility	Labor Flexibility Temporal Flexibility Machine Flexibility Material Handling Flexibility Modification Flexibility	Labor Flexibility Machine Flexibility Material Handling Flexibility Modification Flexibility Expansion Flexibility Flexibility to Introduce New Technology

Fig. 4. Overview of identified flexibilities

According to the results, the timeframe in which those mechanisms were used varied. Different kinds of labor flexibility such as functional, numerical and temporal took place in shorter periods of time compared to expansion flexibility or flexibility to introduce to new products due to e.g. investments. Already mentioned in the literature, introduction of new product flexibility could be related to flexibility to introduce new technology [18]. Routing flexibility is not really used in MMAL; instead the assembly sequence is taken into account. When differences are considerable between products, they are clustered or other assembly areas are used. The results suggest that the flexibility of a MMAL is related to its design and the options it has to be flexible are until some extent circumscribed by it.

Even though one of the cases had a modular system established at the company, common mechanisms to achieve flexibility were found between the cases. However, differences exist e.g. in the number of models assembled. This suggest that modularity could until some extend facilitate the introduction of new products, but other capabilities are still needed such as cooperation between assembly and product design, appropriate technical evaluations, involvement of different levels of the organization, and infrastructure to test the new designs.

Regarding flexibility elements described in the frame of reference by Koste and Malhotra (1999) [1] and its relation to MMAL, it was identified that concerning range-number and range-heterogeneity various product models were assembled which until some extend shared assembly processes, tasks, information, parts and equipment. The products can be customized, meaning that still differences between models could exist. Regarding mobility, methods are used to reduce setup times, and there could be short tool change over times between models, some of them adjusted automatically by scanning product barcodes. About uniformity, the models are expected to follow mutual and standardize assembly processes through all the stations. The models are delivered following the same takt time. To balance the line, work content measured in time is divided in similar proportions between stations for the variety of models. The products passed through quality control checks, sometimes one station at the end of the line was also dedicated to this purpose. Information systems are used to control and secure uniformity in quality and time.

6   Conclusion

Flexibility is a complex definition and different perspectives exist. A characterization of lean MMALs has been presented through analysing mechanisms to achieve flexibility in two cases and their relations to the constituent parts of the assembly system. Even though this study identified mechanisms of flexibility in assembly system related to volume, mix and operative flexibility and new product/removal of products flexibility, it has been shown that to achieve those kinds of flexibilities other dimensions of flexibility are also used. The timeframe by which these mechanisms are used vary. Regarding the elements of flexibility, lean MMALs are focused on delivering a wide range number and heterogeneity of products models by using common resources and processes. Different methods are used in regard of mobility, in order to reduce setup times and change overs. Uniformity is achieved by e.g. takt times, quality controls and standardization. By characterizing flexibility in MMALs taking into account the constituents of the assembly system, it could possible to better understand and evaluate its implications as well as its relation to the assembly system design from a holistic perspective.

Acknowledgment. The authors gratefully acknowledge the contributions from all the participants in the case study companies. This research work has been funded by the Knowledge Foundation within the framework of the INNOFACTURE Research School and the participating companies, and Mälardalen University. The research work is also a part of the initiative for Excellence in Production Research (XPRES) which is a joint project between Mälardalen University, the Royal Institute of Technology, and Swerea. XPRES is one of two governmentally funded Swedish strategic initiatives for research excellence in Production Engineering.

References

1. Koste, L.L., Malhotra, M.K.: A Theoretical Framework for Analyzing the Dimensions of Manufacturing Flexibility. Journal of Operations Management 18(1), 75–93 (1999)
2. Rösiö, C.: Supporting the Design of Reconfigurable Production Systems. PhD Thesis, Mälardalen University, Eskilstuna (2012)
3. D'Souza, D.E., Williams, F.P.: Toward a Taxonomy of Manufacturing Flexibility Dimensions. Journal of Operations Management 18(5), 577–593 (2000)
4. Upton, D.: The Management of Manufacturing Flexibility. California Management Review 36(2), 72–89 (1994)
5. Browne, J., Dubois, D., Rathmill, K., Sethi, S.P., Stecke, K.E.: Classification of Flexible Manufacturing Systems. The FMS Magazine 2(2), 114–117 (1984)
6. Sethi, A.K., Sethi, S.P.: Flexibility in Manufacturing: A Survey. International Journal of Flexible Manufacturing Systems 2(4), 289–328 (1990)
7. Gupta, Y.P., Somers, T.M.: The Measurement of Manufacturing Flexibility. European Journal of Operational Research 60(2), 166–182 (1992)
8. Atkinson, J.: Manpower Strategies for Flexible Organizations. Personnel Management, pp. 28–31 (1984)
9. Allvin, M., Aronsson, G.: Flexibility, Boundarylessness and the Strategies of Work. In: Sandberg, Å. (ed.) Nordic Lights: Work, Management and Welfare in Scandinavia, pp. 420–435. SNS Förlag, Falun (2013)
10. Ohno, T.: Toyota Production System, Beyond Large-Scale Production. CRC Press (1988)
11. Wilson, L.: How to Implement Lean Manufacturing. McGraw-Hill (2010)
12. Shingo, S.: A Revolution in Manufacturing: The SMED System. CRC Press (1985)
13. Ohno, T., Mito, S.: Just-In-Time, For Today and Tomorrow. Productivity Press (1988)
14. Dennis, P.: Lean Production Simplified. Productivity Press (2002)
15. Baudin, M.: Lean Assembly. CRC Press (2002)
16. Yin, K.R.: Case Study Research: Design and Methods. Sage, USA (2014)
17. Miles, M.B., Huberman, A.M.: Qualitative Data Analysis: An Expanded Sourcebook, UK. Sage, London (1994)
18. Ohlager, J.: Produktionsstrategier, TPPE50, Institutionen för Produktionsekonomi, Linköpings Tekniska Högskola, Linköping (1996)

A Method to Create a Process Reference Model Adapted to Heterogeneous Organizations

Geovanny Osorio[1,2], Lorraine Trilling[1], Thibaud Monteiro[1],
Frédéric Albert[3], and Pierre-Alain Millet[1]

[1] INSA de Lyon, DISP (laboratoire de Décision et d'Information des Systèmes de Production),
Bât. Jules Verne, 19 av. Jean Capelle, 69621 Villeurbanne, France
[2] OVE, Œuvre de village d'enfants, 19 Rue Marius Grosso, 69120 Vaulx-en-Velin
[3] CERCLH
{geovanny.osorio-montoya,lorraine.trilling,thibaud.monteiro,
pierre-alain.millet}@insa-lyon.fr, frederic.albert@cerclh.com

Abstract. In some cases there is a need to compare similarities between different process models. For example, given two organizations that offer products or services with similarities, we would like to know how much they differ from each other. This paper aims at defining a method to create a process reference model, which can be adapted to heterogeneous organizations. In order to construct this, we propose a method using BPMN language and based on the value chain approach. This process reference model issued from heterogeneous structures could enable managers to achieve a more comprehensive and unified vision of their organizations, and promote a coherent monitoring of activities. This work presents a unified method of communication between managers and organizations as well as throughout the structures comprising the organization. It provides a basis to establish an alignment of different structures in term of goals and business process following two axes.

Keywords: process reference model, value chain, BPMN, process approach.

1   Introduction

The constant evolution of business world lead organizations to change their perimeter (acquisition, separation, reorganization, etc.). Those changes require an aggregation of heterogeneous business process with a consistent management approach. So that, companies need to react by improving their knowledge about the process they performed as well as the new process to integrate. The fact of knowing the process and capitalize them by using a Process Reference Model (PRM) allows managers to cope with frequent and rapid changes in the business environment [1]. In this way companies need spontaneous solutions which can hardly be derived from wavering development [10]. Furthermore industrial and service sectors are pushed to the creation of process, which can respond to a customer demanding more and more customization of products and services [11].

Managers witnessed many attempts to improve the process-awareness in order to achieve a more comprehensive and unified vision of their sector, and to promote

B. Grabot et al. (Eds.): APMS 2014, Part III, IFIP AICT 440, pp. 232–239, 2014.
© IFIP International Federation for Information Processing 2014

performance management organizations internally. A PRM should come from a **button-up approach** around the different types of organizations, in order to identify the variables that can affect the elements of the system as well as the specific activities of each type of organization [7]. If operational process models are unknown, structured **top-down approaches**, as conceptual methods, such as CIMOSA [19] or GRAI [20] cannot be useful.

The construction of a PRM comes from a collaborative and multidisciplinary work that seeks to develop a common language for operational, tactical and decision-makers at all levels. The combination of a PRM with management tools like balanced scorecards can play a crucial role in the development and structuring of the common vision, as experience shows [5-6].

The aim of this paper is to propose a method to obtain a PRM. This method is illustrated by an application in the socio-medical sector, but could be used in other fields. This article is divided into 5 parts. Section 2 highlights the necessity for the construction of a PRM, supported by a literature review. Section 3 explains the proposed method for the construction of a PRM. Section 4 gives the application of the proposed approach in socio-medical sector, which requires such reference model before being able to monitor activities. Finally, section 5 provides a conclusion and gives some perspectives on this research.

2   Related Works

The emergence of computer technology and the increase in data flows in the last two decades leads the organizations to improve its knowledge about the processes they perform using information systems. Early examples of these, seek to organize a process as a defined sequence of tasks. Such systems were called Workflow management systems (WFM) [14, 15]. At the present, these systems have evolved with a greater range allowing the processes simulation and monitoring of the activities [4, 16, 17]. These ones are now called Business Process Management (BPM). Either the WFM or BPM, both systems aim to support operational processes.

Process modeling allows structuring and visually representing activities of an organization. It facilitates communication around the processes between different actors and enhance the understanding of the functioning of the company [7]. The creation of a PRM for an organization raises several issues. It involves (1) the gathering and analysis of currents models, (2) a field study in a sample of different structures to complete the analyzed information, (3) a modeling of performed activities in each structure using a common language, (4) a comparison of the modelled activities with good professional practices and the respect of legal standards, (5) an identification of the main similarities and differences to retain the models or model's fragments [8]. Thus, using these fragments, we must create a PRM in which all the fragments can fit while avoiding duplication [9].

Indeed, there are several invariants in the set of structures that led to the institutionalization of successful process to be re-used. In this context, experts have developed generic models allowing a logical progression for resolution of problems. Our aim is to create a model that subsumes a collection of process models from each structure (representing variants of the same underlying process) with the aim of replacing the variants with the merged model. The challenge here is not the modeling of processes from each structure, but the creation of a method to integrate different activities from a set of heterogeneous structures which is not specifically proposed in literature.

3 Method for Construction of the Process Reference Model

In order to achieve one PRM which can be transposable to different kind of organizations, we proposed a method divided in three main steps Fig 1. The first step aims to collect information in the field in order to identify activities carried out in different organizations and the manner in which these are performed. The second step seeks to establish the working perimeter conditioned by good professional practice and the respect of legal standards in the field of the application, which should be integrated in the PRM. Finally, the goal of the third step is to compare and combine different existing models using a set of aggregation and transformation operators, which would lead to construct an activities reference model matching with all types of organizations and taking into account existing references.

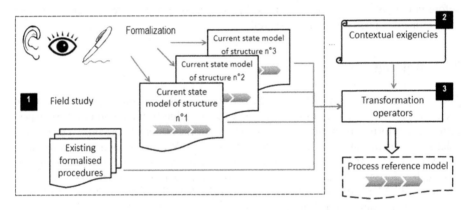

Fig. 1. Proposed method to create a process reference model

3.1 Current State Modelling

To gather the necessary information enhancing the knowledge of production flows and activities carried out by the organizations, it is necessary (i) to use reliable sources describing the process, as existing official procedures (flowcharts respecting the legal framework and referential quality) and (ii) to collect information from people in the field (information extracted from interviews with several professionals in different structures of the organization).

This set of information should be formalized for each structure using a simple and universal language allowing the modeling of business processes easily readable and understandable for all staff involved. We use a process map inspired by the Value Chain developed by Michael Porter [2] and a process approach [3] structuring activities around the three types of processes: **Value-added process**, **Control process**, and **Support process**.

To detail the processes as a flowchart of activities, we used the BPMN [15]. This language provides an easy notation that is intuitive for both technical users and business users. The Fig .2 illustrates the structure of the map and the principle of the processes decomposition (level 0) in an ordered organization of activities (level 1).

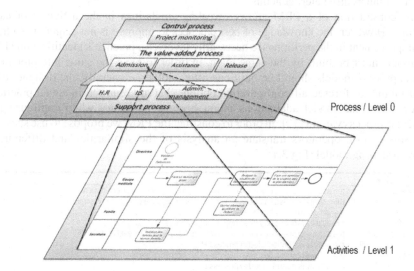

Fig. 2. Map of business processes and process detail with BPMN

3.2   Contextual Exigencies for a Process Reference Model

Even if professionals consider that modeled processes match to the processes performed in their structures, the modeling of these must drive to an assessment of activities. This is necessary to evaluate whether these activities actually correspond to good professional practice and assess if they are in accordance with the regulations of the sector. The formalization of existing practices helps to highlight deviations from best practices and conducts to the creation of a shared model.

To perform this step, we used a working group (composed by professionals of each modeled structure, and the deputy general director) with the aim to present the different practices carried out. This allows reaching a consensus on the practices to be used in the PRM as well as the way to name each of them.

3.3   Operators for the Construction of a Process Reference Model

The characteristic of a reference model is that it enables an entity or structure to recognize itself within a common framework which is not however specifically designed for this entity. The PRM is issued from current state models compared to the contextual exigencies. This construction has to minimize the gap between starting models and the final one. A particular attention is paid to integrate the constraints imposed by the consensus around contextual exigencies (best practices, legal standards…).

Furthermore, it is necessary to define the granularity level of the PRM; this one would be able to fit the different structures, while including specificities at a finer level of detail. It has to be able to report a board spectrum of activities. The PRM has to be precise enough to clearly describe the activities carried out in each structure which are inherently heterogeneous.

The construction of a PRM allows revealing similarities in the activities of each structure. However, the knowledge of best practices to improve is not acquired. So that, any improvement in the performance necessarily involves a practice's identification [12].

Models must be built by the same team, in order to have the same interpretation. Hence, process models should be built one after another. Generally, the designer of a PRM might not foresee all configuration options that are required in actual practice. Hence, additional model adaptations might become necessary when configuring a particular process variant [13]. In order to construct the PRM we propose to use specific operators. Those operators translate an analysis of the similarities and differences between starting model (Fig.3.)

Operator type		
I	for Identical	the activity/process has the same name as in the previous current state model established
R	for Rename	the activity/process has been renamed compared to the previous current state model established
X	for Suppression	the activity/process has been deleted
U	for Upgrade	the activity/process has been upgraded (from level N to level N-1)
D	for Downgrade	the activity/process has been downgraded (from level N to level N+1)
	D → process P	the activity is now included in process P
T	for transfer	the activity/process has been transfered to another process
	T → process P	the activity is now included in process P
S	for Spit	the activity/process has been split into 2 parts
A	for Alteration	the activity/process has been altered (content added, lost or modified)
		A can be associated to other operators (ex: D+A)

Fig. 3. Operators for the construction of the process reference model

4   Implementation and Results

4.1   Field of Application

In order to validate the proposed method, we conducted a work in an important medico-social foundation from Rhône-Alpes Region named OVE. Medico-social sector witnessed many attempts to achieve a more comprehensive and unified vision, and to promote performance management structures internally. Furthermore, on a work carried out by the National agency to support the performance (ANAP) express that "the medico-social structures produce little or no data about his performed activities" [18]. This sector is a whole wide range dedicated to the support of vulnerable people who are the users of the system (people in precarious situations, children or troubled teens, disabled persons and the elderly). Due to the heterogeneity of the sector and the large number of structures (around 8200 in France) this research must lead to a PRM, which takes into account several structures for centralized decisions.

4.2   Results

Using seven type of structures, we constructed seven different models taking into account the specific characteristics of activities carried out in each type of structure, afterwards, we classified these activities according to the three type processes: value-added, support and control processes. This model "all terrain" has allowed to adopt a common language, shared from top management to professionals, for naming all the activities performed by the structures.

Using the models process divided in two levels (Fig. 2) and the specific operators (Fig. 3), the construction of a PRM is a gradual process of comparison between the different starting models (Fig. 4).

The first reference model serves to identify the first activities as well as a first "sketch" of a process model. With the next models, we created a model that subsumes a collection of process models (typically representing variants of the same underlying process) with the aim of replacing the variants with the merged model. Then activities were reorganized into a common process that can be adaptable to the set of organizations using the operators proposed. Besides serving as a state of the art and show a first field- work of the functioning of the organizations, this process allows to identify the specific activities performed, as well as activities that do not correspond to good professional practice or that are not supported in the policies of the foundation. Making this comparison Fig. 4, we can observe that after the fifth modeled structure, specific processes found begin to decrease.

Code	Process name (First current state model)	Heterogeneous Structures							PRM	Process name (Final Process reference model)	
		1	2	3	4	5	6	7			
VA1	Admission to the user	I	I	I	I	I	I	I	I		VA1
VA2	Preparation of the assistance	I		R		R	I	R	R	Design and updating the PIA	VA2
VA3	User assistance	I	R	I	I	I	I	R	R	User assistance	VA3
VA4	Preparing the user release	I	I	I	I	I	I	I	I	Preparing the user release	VA4
VA5	Post-monitoring assistance	I						R	D-> VA4		
VA6	Collective meeting for new users		I			I			D-> VA1		
VA7	Hosting		I			I	I		I	Hosting	VA7
VA8	Speech therapist record								D-> VA2		
VA9	Assistance outside the structure							I	D-> VA3		
P1	GESTUSA 2	I	I	I	I	I	I	I	I	GESTUSA 2	P1
P2	Risk Management	I	I			I	I	I	I	Risk Management	P2
P3	Satisfaction survey	I	I			I	I	I	D-> P12		
P4	Steering of the assistance project	I	I	I	I	I	I	I	I	Steering of the assistance project	P4
P5	Tactical monitoring of project assistance	I	I	I	I	I	I	I	D-> 14		
P6	Operationnal monitoring of project assistance	I	I	I	I	I	I	I	I	Operationnal monitoring of project assistance	P6
P7	Professional Education	I			R				R	Education action	P7
P8	Advice and opinions with other structures	I	R	R		R	R		R	Animation of network partnerships	P8
P9	Achievement of firsts school days		I		R	R	R	R	X		
P10	Commission regulation with the MDPH	I				I	I	I	D-> VA1		
P11	Organization of extracurricular activities	I	I			I			D-> VA3		
P12	Meeting to evaluate the evolution of the structure	I	I			I	I		R	Quality approach	P12
P13	Management of post-admission period		I						D-> VA2		
P14	Monitoring of user professional assistance		I						D+A-> VA3		
P15	Monitoring of user social assistance		I						D+A-> VA3		
P16	Speech therapist record				i				D-> VA2		
P17	Commission studies of priority candidates					i			D+A-> VA1		

Fig. 4. Gradual process of comparison between the different starting models

This means that the model begins to converge and all the identified processes can describe almost entirely the process of the last two structures. This is however not sufficient for the construction of a PRM, which requires the continuous support of the general direction. This last is necessary to arbitrate the processes to be integrated into the reference model, as well as the flow charts of process information and samples of good practices. This PRM represents the starting point for activity monitoring and performance assessment while providing a unified method of communication throughout the structures of the foundation in order to establish an alignment in the set structures goals.

4.3   Validation of Process Reference Model Using a Software for Activities Monitoring: Gestactiv

In order to check whether the reference model is adapted to a set of heterogeneous structures we proposed a software to collect information related to the activities (formalized in the process reference model) that are performed in all structures. This survey information provided by this software enables us to confront the selected PRM with the activities performed by the set of structures.

The evaluation of the PRM was based in a real size experimentation. Nine "pilot" structures with almost 150 professionals and 350 users over a period of three months have entered their activities in the system according to the reference model. This has led to validate the ability of constructed PRM to reflect the day-to-day of professional activities. With the prospect of a generalization in 2015 to 65 structures from OVE Foundation, the PRM has proved robustness with respect to the reality of the implementation in the field activities. This is reflected by the significant integration of the tool in professional routines. The main indicators were the capture rate of foresight activities (43% of activities scheduled at least 3 days in advance), the degree of validation following the completion of them (95%) and the rate of implication of professionals to capture the positive returns.

5   Conclusions

The bottom up approach facing with contextual exigencies meets the need for a better knowledge about how an organization works. This approach provides a structured representation of the activities carried out within structures on which an activity monitoring tool is based. An experiment in the medico-social sector has validated the proposed approach.

For future works, the measures collected from the combination of process reference activities and monitoring tool will offer the possibility to answer questions at the operational level related to the user assistance and the consumption of resources. These measures establish a basis on which improvements can be developed: Balanced Scorecard (BSC), tools and methods to assist in the management organizations works. This approach combined with a tool allowing the lift up of the activities will translate strategy into operational action plans at all levels of the organization by providing information on the performance of each entity, useful to control them. These examples could open paths to numerous development opportunities in this sector.

References

1. van der Aalst, W.M.P.: Process-aware information systems: Lessons to be learned from process mining. In: Jensen, K., van der Aalst, W.M.P. (eds.) Transactions on Petri Nets and Other Models of Concurrency II. LNCS, vol. 5460, pp. 1–26. Springer, Heidelberg (2009)
2. Porter, M.E.: Competitive advantage: Creating and sustaining superior performance. Simon and Schuster Ed. (2011)
3. Brandenburg, H., Wojtyna, J.P.: L'approche processus. Eyrolles Ed. (2006)
4. Wohed, P., van der Aalst, W.M.P., Dumas, M., ter Hofstede, A.H.M., Russell, N.: On the Suitability of BPMN for Business Process Modelling. In: Dustdar, S., Fiadeiro, J.L., Sheth, A.P. (eds.) BPM 2006. LNCS, vol. 4102, pp. 161–176. Springer, Heidelberg (2006)
5. Kaplan, R., Norton, D.: Transforming the Balanced Scorecard from Performance Measurement to Strategic Management: Part I. Accounting Horizons 15(1), 87–104 (2001)
6. Martello, M., Watson, J.G., Fischer, M.J.: Implementing a Balanced Scorecard in a not for profit organization. Journal of Business & Economics Research 6, 9 (2011)
7. Ulrich, F.: Evaluation of reference models. Reference Modeling for Business Systems Analysis, 118–140 (2007)
8. La Rosa, M., Dumas, M., Uba, R., Dijkman, R.: Business process model merging: an approach to business process consolidation. ACM Transactions on Software Engineering and Methodology (TOSEM) 22(2) (2013)
9. Fiorèse, S., Meinadier, J.P.: Découvrir et comprendre l'ingénierie systéme. Cépadués Ed. (2012)
10. Mintzberg, H.: In a Dynamic Business World, Phrases Such as 'Strategic Planning', 'Marketing Planning' or 'Change Management' Are Oxymoronic! (2011) (retrieved 11)
11. Hau, L.L., Feitzinger, E., Billington, C.: Getting ahead of your competition through design for mass customization. Target 13(2), 8–17 (1997)
12. Jacques, J.: Amélioration de la performance industrielle à partir d'un processus Référent. PhD Thesis of Savoie university (2006)
13. Manfred, R., Weber, B.: Enabling flexibility in process-aware information systems: challenges, methods, technologies. Springer Ed. (2012)
14. Van der Aalst, W.M., Van Hee, K.M.: Workflow Management: Models, Methods, and Systems. MIT Press (2004)
15. Jablonski, S., Bussler, C.: Workflow Management: Modeling Concepts, Architecture, and Implementation. International Thomson Computer Press Ed. (1996)
16. Wynn, M.T., Dumas, M., Fidge, C.J., ter Hofstede, A.H.M., van der Aalst, W.M.P.: Business process simulation for operational decision support. In: ter Hofstede, A.H.M., Benatallah, B., Paik, H.-Y. (eds.) BPM Workshops 2007. LNCS, vol. 4928, pp. 66–77. Springer, Heidelberg (2008)
17. Rozinat, A., Wynn, M.T., van der Aalst, W.M.P., ter Hofstede, A.H.M., Fidge, C.J.: Workflow simulation for operational decision support using design, historic and state information. In: Dumas, M., Reichert, M., Shan, M.-C. (eds.) BPM 2008. LNCS, vol. 5240, pp. 196–211. Springer, Heidelberg (2008)
18. ANAP, Piloter la performance dans le secteur médico-social: Expérimentation d'un tableau de bord de pilotage (2011), http://www.anap.fr
19. Vernadat, F.B.: Enterprise modelling and integration: principles and applications. Chapman & Hall, London (1996)
20. Kromm, H., Ducq, Y.: Reference decision models in the medico-social service sector. In: Emmanouilidis, C., Taisch, M., Kiritsis, D. (eds.) Advances in Production Management Systems, Part II. IFIP AICT, vol. 398, pp. 422–429. Springer, Heidelberg (2013)

Activity-Based Discrete Event Simulation of Spatial Production Systems: Application to Fisheries

Eric Innocenti, Paul-Antoine Bisgambiglia, and Dominique Urbani

University of Corsica UCPP, UMR 6134 SPE CNRS, 20250 CORTE France
{eric.innocenti,bisgambiglia,durbani}@univ-corse.fr

Abstract. In this paper, we present a modular and generic object framework using the Discrete EVent system Simulation Specification (*DEVS*) and the activity concept. We plan to simulate coastal fishery policies in the aim of improving harvesting and the management of fisheries.

Keywords: Spatial Production Systems, Cellular Automata Model, DEVS.

1   Introduction

Application of long-term effective policies in natural production systems needs relevant decision-making indicators and quantitative assessments. This issue is critical in fisheries management facing the decline of world productivity due to pressures from overfishing, habitat change, pollution, and climate change [1]. It is possible to develop software tools dedicated to the election of strategies for sustainable fisheries management (fishing gear regulation, stock rebuilding projects, etc.) [2] – [4]. This work remains part of a computer tool designed to help fishery managers. The main goal is to assist in the definition of a responsible fishing policy in Corsica. We discuss the opportunity to develop a modular framework using the Discrete EVent system Specification formalism (*DEVS*) and the *activity* concept. We plan to develop software to simulate coastal fishery policies to improve the management of resources. We use a Cellular Automata Model (*CAM*) for spatial representation and taking into account the activity concept [5]-[8]. *CAM* are usually considered as an aggregation of discrete components with local interactions. The model of fish population growth is inspired by the literature [19], [20], and spatially explained with a *CAM*. The techniques developed are discussed, including challenges, perspectives and limitations. Section 2 reminds the theoretical concepts and section 3 details the software frame- work before presenting an illustrative application (section 4). The last section before the discussion and concluding remarks gives our   simulation results, we want to show that when *CAM* are jointly used with the *DEVS* formalism [9] and the *activity* concept, both the model and the simulator objects efficiently exploit the numerous spatial components.

B. Grabot et al. (Eds.): APMS 2014, Part III, IFIP AICT 440, pp. 240–247, 2014.

2   Backgrounds

2.1   Cellular Automata Modelling

Cellular Automata Model (*CAM*) are an evolved form of von Neumman's Cellular Automata (*CA*) [8], [9]. These computational models are well suited to capture essential features of spatial systems in which large-scale behaviour arises from the collective effect of a great number of locally interacting simple components. As *CAM* inherit their basic characteristics from *CA*, they get the benefit of emerging phenomena. From a simple and deterministic local rule, *CAM* can generate a surprisingly complex global behaviour. The spatial interactions between cells are key elements of such models. At each time step, a cell changes state according to the local rule linked to its neighbourhood. The successive states of the cells follow a state trajectory, in the discrete time base. The state of the *CAM* is the aggregation of the cell states. Over the last years, the study of IT implementation of *CAM* considerably increased [11-15]. The determination of active components in this kind of model is also an essential aspect to improve the computing model elegance and to guarantee acceptable simulation times. In the next subsection we give more information on the *activity* concept. .

2.2   Activity Concept

The activity concept is usually formulated as a measure of change in system behaviour [9], and is used to concentrate computations on the high rates of change [14], [15]. The activity in a *CAM* is determined by the measure of the active cells, i.e. by the set of cells that can change state between two global state transitions. The *activity* is measured at the highest level of the hierarchy, i.e., at the global level of the *CAM* in a set of active cells. The local level informs the global level on the model *activity*: (1) at time t, the simulator browses the *active cells* and executes their transition functions δ_{int} (*transition phase*); (2) at the same time, the neighbouring inactive cells are tested in order to determine if they can become active at $t+1$(*propagation phase*). This step is called and relies on the propagation rule. The inactive neighbouring cells of active cells are placed as active if they can become active at $t+1$. Whatever the size of the *CAM* considered, computations only depend on *activity*, thus the formulation of the *propagation rule* is a key element to enhance simulation times.

2.3   DEVS Formalism

DEVS formalism was introduced in [8] as a rigorous basis for the compositional modelling and simulation of discrete event systems. A *DEVS* model is either an *Atomic* (*AM*) or a *Coupled* (*CM*) model. An *AM* is a structure: $<X, Y, S, \delta ext, \delta int, \lambda, ta >$ with X the set of external events, Y the set of output events, S the set of sequential states, $\delta ext: Q \times X \rightarrow S$ the external state transition function, where $Q = \{(s,e) \mid s \text{ in } S, 0 \le e \le ta(s)\}$ and e is the elapsed time since the last state transition; $\delta int\ S \rightarrow S$ the internal state transition function; $\lambda : S \rightarrow Y$ the output function and $ta:S \rightarrow R+$ the time advance function. The *AM* describes the behaviour of the system.

A *CM* describes the composition of several DEVS sub-models, i.e *AM* or *CM*. We have developed our DEVS simulator inspired by pythonDEVS [16] and DEVS-Ruby [17], and in this work we use the *DEVS* simulator taking into account the activity concept previously described.

3   Framework

In this section, we give a brief description of our simulation software. Our approach is not based on Cell-DEVS [18], but on the multi-component concepts [8]. One atomic model aggregates the entire environment.

3.1   Activity-Based Discrete Event Simulation

The use of the *activity* concept implies the prediction of next active cells from a simulation procedure based on events. While applying these criteria to the *CAM* previously described, it is appropriate to use a discrete event system that cause transitions through the triggering of events based on message exchanges. For that, the model is established on the basis of *DEVS* formalism. The *CAM* used for the simulation is aggregated in an *AM*. It interacts with the simulator with ports and messages. The perimeter of the active area is updated when an internal event occurs (δ_{int}).

3.2   Object Implementation

Objects ensure modularity, genericity, and reusability and the DEVS formalismcomes with well established discrete event simulation algorithms. The main objects and the interconnections are presented in figure 1. The left part describes the simulation part, it is conventional in DEVS. The right part shows the encapsulation mechanism of CAM in an atomic model.

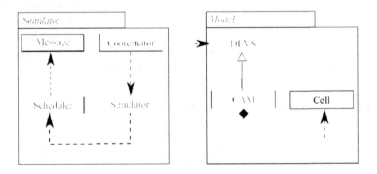

Fig. 1. The *CAM* and its *DEVS* objects

4   Illustrative Application: Fox Model Adaptation

To study the effect of the fishery on biomass and to estimate the Maximum Sustainable Yield (*MSY*) in each cell, we implement a Fox *Surplus-Production Model (SPM)* [19], [20]. The *MSY* corresponds to the maximum capture that does not exhaust the fish population. *SPM* models are advantageous as they allow to simply estimate both fish stock and fish rates. Moreover, they collect in the same production model the evolution rules of the biomass, the mortality and population growth. Thus, they only require temporal series of stock abundance indexes that eases their use. The Fox *SPM* [18] is a particular case of the Pella and Tomlison model [20]. It allows characterising the fish population x according to a set of coefficients, as:

$$f(x_t) = \frac{(p+1)}{p} \times r \times x \times \left(1 - \left(\frac{x}{K}\right)^p\right)$$ (1)

$$f(x_{t+1}) = x \times (1 - \varphi - r * log(x/K)) \times \varepsilon$$ (2)

Where is the fish rate, the environmental variability, r the population rate, K the maximum capacity of the environment, p an asymmetric coefficient.

In the Fox's model, p is near 0; this allows getting an asymmetric fish stock evolution. The model grows up to a K maximum constant, and it decreases keeping an asymptotic course. These models are relatively simple and well documented in literature. This model is implemented in each cell of the *CAM* with $K=90$.

4.1   SPM Model Settings

The environmental map is composed by *reef* and *fishing areas*: the *reef areas* model the life spaces of the fish. They have a strong attraction capacity as they feed the fish. The attraction coefficient *aCff* allows setting the attraction capacity of the cell. The value of *aCff* of each cell depends on the distance between the cell and the location of the *reef area*. The attraction capacity of the cells around the *reef areas* is randomly calculated at the initialization. The *fishing areas* are space with fishing production determined by the fishing rate . In the original Fox's model, the fish rate is applied to all the cells of the space. In order to clearly study the effect of fishing, we only apply it to the cells set as *fishing areas*. During simulation, we apply the transition rule in charge of the fish population evolution, and the propagation rule in charge of the movement of fishes in space (Fig. 2).

```
1: c: current cell, nCell: neighbouring cell, x: fish, K: max cell ca-
pacity, aCff: attraction coefficient
2: If c.nbFish > 0
3:   For each n in nCell {
4:     . If c.aCff < n.aCff Or c.nbFish > (K-20) Then
5:         #Different attraction da
6:         da <- n.aCff - c.aCff
7:         #Moving potential
8:         pd <- int(K - c.nbFish)
9:     . #Small attraction difference, little migration
```

Fig. 2. CAM Propagation phase algorithm

```
10:        migrCOEF = 6 #Migration coefficient
11:        If da <= 0.1 Then
12:          bmin <- 0              #Min value
13:          bmax <- pd/migrCOEF  #Max value
14:    .  #Medium attraction difference, medium migration
15:        maxMigrCOEF = 4 #Max migration coefficient
16:        minMigrCOEF = 8 #Min migration coefficient
17:        If da > 0.1 And da < 0.2 Then
18:          bmin <- pd / minMigrCOEF
19:          bmax <- pd / maxMigrCOEF
20:        Then
21:          bmin <- pd / maxMigrCOEF ,  bmax <- pd
22:    .  If c.nbFish >= K Then
23:          bmin <- 0 ,    bmax <- pd
24:    .  #Number of fish moving
25:        nFish <- random(bmin,bmax)
26:        moveFish(nFish)From(c)To(n)Location
27:        activateNCell(n)
28:        removeFish(nFish)At(c)Location }
```

Fig. 2. (*Continued.*)

4.2   Simulation Example

We compare the fish population evolution in fishing areas and in an area where fishing is prohibited. Thanks to the activity concept we can simulate a domain of 350x250 cells. We experiment a reef area with maximal attraction (1.0). The attraction around the reef area is randomly determined between 0.5 and 0.9. These coefficients have been empirically defined. The number of active cells evolves during the simulation process. The main values of the model's coefficients are detailed in table 1.

Table 1. Model's setting

	Ocean	Reef-	Fishing area	Fishing area t=40 (83 cells)
Population growth r	0	0.9-	0	0
Cell capacity K	9	9	9	9
Fish rate	0	0.4-	1	2
Attraction aCff	0	0.5-1	0.5-1	0.

The simulation results point out the fish quantities evolution in the simulated time.

4.3   Results

The curve presented in Fig. 3 shows the activity of cells. It decreases slightly with a stronger tendency to t = 40, corresponding to the beginning of overfishing. Trawlers have emptied cells and they have become inactive.

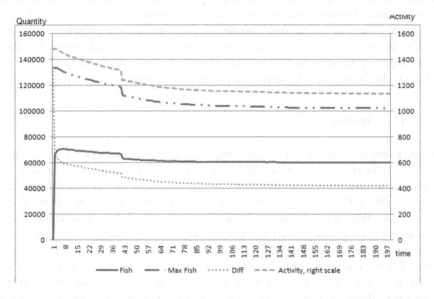

Fig. 3. Fish quantity and activity evolution. The blue curve represents the evolution of the fish population. The red curve describes the maximum capacity of the environment according of the K parameter and the number of active cells.

The fish population evolves as the *activity* level. The activity curve is a good indicator trend of the model.

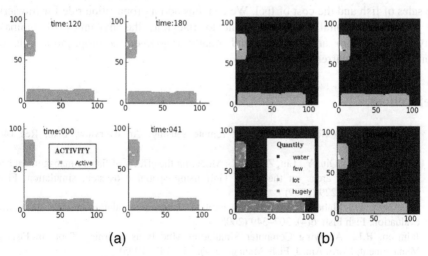

Fig. 4. Activity (a) and population (b) evolutions

Figure 4a represents the evolution of the activity, at t=0, 41, 120, 180. Active cells are greatly influenced by the reef areas and their attraction. Figure 4b shows the popula- tion fish at 0, 41, 120, and 180. After initialization, the homogenization of the fish population is due to the propagation rule. The fish population comes on the outskirts of the reefs. The results highlight the influence of attractions areas in the development of biomass, and the impact of fishing and overfishing. The activity does not directly increases with the increase of fish quantity, it is quite stable, and clearly shows to t=40 the increase in fishing. A targeted and intensive fishing activity quickly reduces the fish population per cell. To improve the model, we will substitute the fishing areas by agents following the fish population.

5   Conclusion

In this paper we described a research approach using the *activity* concept and the Discrete EVent system Simulation Specification formalism to model the management and harvesting of resources for fisheries. The *DEVS* formalism is coupled with a *Cellular Automata Model* to efficiently exploit numerous spatial components. With this approach we simulate a complex fishery production system with strong interactions between components evolving in huge spatial areas. Spatial data are generated in a modular and hierarchical way in reasonable computation times. We use our framework to explore the maximum sustainable yield (MSY) and to fix the max sustainable catch in a large fishing area. Using our software framework, decision makers can explore various policies and make choices to improve the management and harvesting of fisheries resources. Using a traditional population growth model from literature [19], we show how our theoretical approach can be used to integrate spatial dynamics, in spite of a huge number of components. Future works will require the integration of the findings and insights of experimental studies. As in [21], we plan also to add an economic model that takes into account the sales of fish and the cost of fuel. We can thus add a propagation rule for trawlers. At the environmental level, we want to integrate the dynamics of biomass (phyto/zooplankton) and currents and finally implement a propagation rule of biomass based on currents.

References

1. Klemas, V.: Fisheries applications of remote sensing: An overview. Fish. Res. 148, 124–136 (2013)
2. Chen, Z., Xu, S., Qiu, Y., Lin, Z., Jia, X.: Modeling the effects of fishery management and marine protected areas on the Beibu Gulf using spatial ecosystem simulation. Fish. Res. 100(3), 222–229 (2009)
3. Pelletieret, D., Mahévas, S.: Spatially explicit fisheries simulation models for policy evaluation. Fish Fish. 6(4), 307–349 (2005)
4. Johnson, B.L.: Applying Computer Simulation Models as Learning Tools in Fishery Management. North Am. J. Fish. Manag. 15(4), 736–747 (1995)

5. Innocenti, E.: Randomizing activity in fire spreading simulations. In: ITM Web Conf., vol. 1, p. 02003 (2013)
6. Innocenti, E., Muzy, A., Aiello, A., Santucci, J.-F., Hill, D.R.C.: Active-DEVS: a computational model for the simulation of forest fire propagation. In: 2004 IEEE International Conference on Systems, Man and Cybernetics, vol. 2, pp. 1857–1863 (2004)
7. von Neumann, J.: John von Neumann-Collected Works. VolumeV: Design of Computers. In: Taub, H. (ed.) Theory of Automata and Numerical Analysis, pp. 288–328. Pergamon Press (1961)
8. Zeigler, B.P., Praehofer, H., Kim, T.G.: Theory of Modeling and Simulation: Integrating Discrete Event and Continuous Complex Dynamic Systems. Academic Press (2000)
9. Muzyet, A., Hill, D.R.C.: What is new with the activity world view in modeling and simulation? using activity as a unifying guide for modeling and simulation. In: Proceedings of the 2011 Winter Simulation Conference (WSC), pp. 2882–2894 (2011), doi:10.1109/WSC.2011.6147991
10. Santé, A., García, M., Miranda, D., Crecente, R.: Cellular automata models for the simulation of real-world urban processes: A review and analysis. Landsc. Urban Plan. 96(2), 108–122 (2010)
11. Podrouzek, J.: Stochastic Cellular Automata in Dynamic Environmental Modeling: Practical Applications. Electron. Notes Theor. Comput. Sci. 252, 143–156 (2009)
12. Guinot, V.: Modelling using stochastic, finite state cellular automata: rule in ference from continuummodels. Appl. Math. Model 26(6), 701–714 (2002)
13. Krougly, Z.L., Creed, I.F., Stanford, D.A.: Astochastic model for generating disturbance patterns within landscapes. Comput. Geosci. 35(7), 1451–1459 (2009)
14. Zeigler, B.P., Jammalamadaka, R., Akerkar, S.R.: Continuity and Change (Activity) Are Fundamentally Related in DEVS Simulation of Continuous Systems. In: Kim, T.G. (ed.) AIS 2004. LNCS (LNAI), vol. 3397, pp. 1–13. Springer, Heidelberg (2005)
15. Qiuet, F., Hu, X.: Spatial activity-based modeling for pedestrian crow dsimulation. Simulation 89(4), 451–465 (2013)
16. Bolducet, J.-S., Vangheluwe, H.: A modeling and simulation package for classichierarchical DEVS. MSDL Sch. Comput. McGillUniv. Tech. Rep. (2002)
17. Franceschini, R., Bisgambiglia, P.-A., Hill, D.R.C.: DEVS-Ruby:a Domain Specific Language for DEVS Modelingand Simulation (WIP). In: CD Proceedings of the Symposium on Theory of Modeling & Simulation-DEVS Integrative M&S Symposium, DEVS 2014. SCS, Tampa (2014)
18. Wainer, G., Giambiasi, N.: Application of the Cell-DEVS Paradigm for Cell Spaces Modelling and Simulation. Simulation 76(1), 22–39 (2001), doi:10.1177/003754970107600102
19. Fox Jr., W.W.: An exponential surplusyield model for optimizing exploited fish populations. Transactions of the American Fisheries Society 99(1), 80–88 (1970)
20. Pella, J.J., Tomlinson, P.K.: A generalized stock production model. Inter-American Tropical Tuna Commission Bulletin 13(3), 416–497 (1969)
21. Duboz, R., Versmisse, D., Quesnel, G., Muzy, A., Ramat, E.: Specification of dynamic structure discrete event multiagent systems. In: Proceedings of SCS summer simulation 2006, Simulationseries, vol. 38(2), p. 103 (2006)

Implementation of Lean Project Planning:
A Knowledge Transfer Perspective

Lise Lillebrygfjeld Halse[1], Kristina Kjersem[1], and Jan Emblemsvåg[2]

[1] Molde University College, Specialized University in Logistics, Molde, Norway
{lise.l.halse,krisina.kjersem}@himolde.no
[2] Vard Group AS, Ålesund, Norway
jan.emblemsvag@vard.com

Abstract. During the last decades, the Norwegian shipbuilding industry has successfully delivered complex and customized offshore vessels for the global market. This industry has historically been characterized by highly skilled workmanship that makes flexible adaptations and improvements in the production process possible, which has been a competitive advantage of the industry. Nevertheless, more complex projects, competitive pressure and globally distributed value chains, call for more formalized planning and cross learning between shipbuilding projects. Consequently, shipyards in the industry have started to focus more on structured planning tools such as Lean Project Planning (LPP). In this paper, we consider the implementation of LPP from a knowledge transfer perspective, with emphasize on the role of the context in the implementation process.

Keywords: Project Planning, Knowledge transfer, Implementation, Lean shipbuilding.

1 Introduction

The Norwegian shipbuilding industry delivers complex and customized vessels for offshore purposes using an Engineer–To-Order (ETO) approach [1]. In this kind of production, customers' needs initiate the process of design, engineering and production [2]. Historically, this industry is renowned for highly skilled craftsmanship that makes independent adaptations and improvements in the production process, involving exchange of tacit knowledge [3]. In shipbuilding, project is the norm, and there is a problem with poorly planned and executed project [4]. The reason is claimed to be shortcomings of planning tools that were used earlier.

Consequently, Lean Project Planning (LPP) has been proposed as a new approach in this shipbuilding industry [4]. LPP represents a synthesis of Lean thinking ideas, Earned Value Management approach (EVM) and Last Planner System (LPP). In principle, however, Lean philosophy may not seem to be fully appropriate for ETO producers [5], and in particular manufacturing of low-volume products such as customized ships, which is the focus of this study. Moreover, in a production environment characterized by informal planning and tacit knowledge exchange, the implementation of a

B. Grabot et al. (Eds.): APMS 2014, Part III, IFIP AICT 440, pp. 248–255, 2014.

formalized planning system may be further complicated, as this necessitates the conversion from tacit to explicit knowledge through formalized procedures and statements. Previous research has rarely addressed this issue. We claim that in order to understand the barriers in the implementation of formalized planning systems, we need to view the process as knowledge transfer, where the context of the recipient organization will influence to what extent and in which way the knowledge is absorbed. In this study, the implementation of Lean Project Planning (LPP) in two shipyards is studied, representing two different organizational contexts.

The rest of the paper is organized as follows: First, we present theory related to implementation of management ideas from a knowledge perspective concluding with the need to do studies where the implementation context is addressed. Thereafter, the management idea in this study, LPP, is described. We briefly address the methodology used in this study, and present the research context and the findings, which is separated in two parts: status before implementation of LPP and the implementation into the two research contexts. Finally, we present the discussion, conclusions and contribution of this paper.

2   Literature Review

Implementation of Lean into the manufacturing industry has been considered as a spread of a management idea, which is translated into different organizational contexts [6]. However, such ideas also represent packages of knowledge that aim at improving organizations' performance and competitiveness. This suggests analyzing the implementation of management ideas as transfer and acquisition of knowledge, which is the approach in this paper.

2.1   Implementation as Knowledge Transfer

Generally, implementation of management practices, ideas and tools represents knowledge transfer between organizational units, where translators of the practices and ideas shape knowledge constructs in this process [7]. Several factors may affect how readily knowledge will transfer between organizational units. The nature or form of knowledge is an important aspect, and it has been claimed that explicit knowledge that is embedded in technology is more easily transferred than tacit knowledge not embedded in technology [8]. According to Gupta and Govindarajan [9], the *absorptive capacity* of the receiving unit is the most significant factor for successful transfer of knowledge in multinational companies. Here, knowledge inflow depends on the richness of transmission cannels, motivation to acquire knowledge, and capacity to absorb incoming knowledge. Hence, the absorptive capacity concerns the employees' ability *and* their motivation, and in particular the interaction between these [10]. Moreover, the absorptive capacity is claimed to develop cumulatively, building on the existing knowledge base [11].

Some claim that theoretical arguments and empirical research addressing the individual or interpersonal levels antecedents of absorptive capacity are still lacking in this field of research [12]. Furthermore, previous studies have shown that the implementation and outcome of management ideas such as Lean vary considerably across organizations [6, 13]. This implies that the knowledge these kinds of models represents, are 'translated' into a new context, where the recipient organization plays an active role in the adoption of practice and ideas. This will be addressed in the next section.

2.2   Knowledge Transfer and Context

In organizations, people have developed their own particular way of cooperating and sharing knowledge. In line with theory on absorptive capacity, the 'match' between new knowledge and the existing knowledge residing in the organization's social network will facilitate knowledge absorption. From this we would expect that social networks characterized by informal coordination and sharing of tacit knowledge would experience challenges when implementing formalized planning systems, since the existing knowledge base is not articulated, making it difficult to build on further by new and explicit knowledge. This dimension of knowledge acquisition can also be understood from a motivational point of view, as people will be motivated to acquire knowledge that fits their existing working practice and knowledge [10]. Hence, the motivation to acquire knowledge, and thus the absorptive capacity, is dependent on the social context.

This study addresses the gap in the literature regarding contextualization of absorptive capacity, and in particular, the translation of management practices and ideas, where previous studies have been at a higher level of abstraction. We contribute filling the gap by providing a case study of implementation of Lean Project Planning (LPP) in an ETO shipbuilding environment. The difference in context is addressed by studying the implementation of LPP in two shipyards. In the following, we will briefly describe LPP, which represents the knowledge that is sought introduced and implemented at these shipyards.

2.3   Lean Project Planning (LPP)

LPP is based on Lean thinking [14] adapted to construction industry (Lean Construction) including elements from Last Planner System (LPS) [15] and Earned Value Management (EVM) [16].

Lean Thinking is represented here by Plan Do Check Act (PDCA) cycle, a basic problem-solving approach, which in the LPP context involves making problems visible, finding proper solutions, checking the results and acting on deviations [17].

Lean Construction applies production-based ideas from lean thinking to project delivery within construction industry [18]. In such projects, lean changes the way project is managed during the building process. Lean Construction extends from the objectives of a lean production system - maximize value and minimize waste - to specific techniques, and applies them in a new project delivery process. Lean Construction is particularly useful on complex, uncertain and quick projects. It challenges the belief that there must always be trade-offs between time, cost, and quality. Since the 1990s, lean construction community recognized the need for a change in the way traditional project management plan and measure activities in a project.

LPS is a planning tool intended to increase planning reliability by decreasing workflow variability, through recognizing and removing activity constraints, identifying root causes for non-completion of plans and monitoring its improvement by means of Percent Plan Complete (PPC) [19]. LPS is a way to involve the 'last planner' – the last link in the decision chain – within the planning process by making 'promises' and then measure the percent of completed activities out of the promised ones (PPC) [20].

EVM is a technique used within the planning system for measuring the progress of a project by comparing the baseline of the project with reported physical results, the resources consumed and the remaining hours to the completion per activity [16]. A good performance metrics used by EVM is the Cost Performance Index (CPI) used to calculate and predict cost at completion of the project within a finite range of values after only 15-20 per cent completion of the project [21].

Each of the elements above has an important role in the LPP. PDCA involves identifying problems, find solutions and check the results. In LPP this is done in weekly meetings, starting with checking the status of previous week's planned activities. LPS is central for involving people within the planning process in order to achieve reliable promises and identifying problems in the near future. Important here is to involve the last link in the decision process, e.g. foremen as well as facilitating good communication and information flow between project participants. EVM contributes to making visible the progress and earned value at any stages during the building process.

3   Methodology

In this study, we aim at contributing to filling the gaps in the literature by studying the implementation of LPP in an ETO production environment, and where the differences in context are addressed. Despite having thorough knowledge of the LPP tool, the implementation of the tool is explorative in its nature, making a case study design appropriate [22]. Two shipyards are chosen as cases in this study: shipyard A and B. These shipyards were originally separate companies that were acquired by a larger group in the 1990s. They have, however, operated to a large extent as separate entities where most activities as design, engineering and production were carried out locally. Several years ago, the shipbuilding group started a centralization process by taking electro, design, piping, and accommodation departments outside shipyards and re-created them as distinct entities. This reorganization, together with the production of the hull outside Norway, created new challenges for the planning process. The present study involves a comparative research setting where the implementation process at the two shipyards is compared in order to find the relationship between barriers and the success of implementation.

Data is collected through participation in meetings and in-depth semi structured interviews employees in the head office and the two shipyards (three sites). Internal reports, minutes of meetings, and presentations constitutes additional data sources. Furthermore, one of the authors is the founder of LPP and has been involved in the implementation process at shipyard A. The interviews and the document study were aimed at revealing what parts of the LPP was sought implemented, how the implementation process was carried out and what kind of obstacles was experienced in the process. Furthermore, the planning systems and processes used before the implementation were mapped. Finally, the respondents were asked to reflect upon the reasons for the difficulties they experienced in the process.

4   Context – The Situation before Implementation

One of the most important characteristic of Norwegian shipbuilding industry is its flexibility, which gives customers the possibility to decide many features of the vessel quite late during the building process [23]. Maintaining this flexibility while dealing with increased complexity of vessels, competition on shorter delivery periods, and lower building prices, involves a constant focus on improving all processes in the building projects. The whole shipbuilding process is performed through a concurrent engineering approach, which implies that production of any part of the vessel can be started while the engineering phase is still being in progress. In concurrent shipbuilding, engineering, procurement and production activities are performed in near concurrency throughout the project execution – in contrast to the sequential approach where the vessel is engineered, equipment is ordered and then start the production process. The concurrent process, the participation of several different entities (internal and external), and the geographically distributed value chain (hull production outside Norway) represent demanding conditions for the implementation of a reliable planning system.

In this study the emphasis is on the planning process for the outfitting phase of the project. The outfitting phase is defined as the stage in which some of the last components are mounted on board, before the vessel testing phase. The number of participants during the outfitting phase in each project varies from 200-700 workers belonging to different specializations (steel workers, piping, accommodation, electro, etc.).

Before the LPP implementation, both shipyards were generally able to meet the requirements regarding cost and delivery times. This can be traced back to the long experience of the production workers, who were able to make prompt decisions based on their experience and tacit knowledge. Both shipyards were using formalized planning systems only to a moderate extent. In particular, the participation of people from production in the planning process was limited or absent, while a dedicated person, the Planner, created the plans based on data from previous projects. Furthermore, there were no recordkeeping of deviations in order to avoid recurrence of mistakes at both shipyards. In both shipyards, the communication flow took place mainly through informal channels.

However, there were some differences between the two shipyards regarding the structure and formalism of meetings. Shipyard B had before the implementation regular planning meetings on a weekly basis. From these meetings Minutes of meetings (MOM) were written by the Planner and sent to designated persons within the project. Such structure in meetings was not present at Shipyard A, where the meetings were more informally organized, and where MOM was seldom written. Furthermore, in shipyard B there existed a planning tool to follow the evolution of the projects in terms of resources. The diagrams were however based on the Planner's experience. In Shipyard A there was lack of formal control over the projects regarding resources and time, and decisions were made based on people's experience.

5   Implementation into Two Different Production Contexts

Demands of shorter building periods, organizational changes (centralization), and coordinating challenges due to the distributed production process (foreign hull producing shipyard and local shipyard for outfitting), motivated these shipyards to look into their planning processes. LPP was implemented and adapted with the purpose of enhancing communication within the planning process. This was done by standardizing the meeting structure, providing physical progress measurement, and proactively eliminating barriers that could affect completion of any activity. Another purpose for implementing this tool was to achieve commitment to the project plans by involving people executing the activities within the planning process. Shipyard A succeeded in implementing the most important aspects of LPP as described above. Participation was achieved by asking foremen to prepare week plans with activities that can be executed by own team during the next period, so that they were committed to the plan and felt responsibility to complete activities as planned. Furthermore, Discipline Coordinators (DC's) were formally invited to weekly meetings, and the meetings became more structured and formalized. Moreover, deviations became recorded systemically on the week plan and followed up by designated people. In general, communication flow in projects was improved, as more people were involved in the planning process, as well as increased commitment through written plans. The results of implementing this tool at Shipyard A were very good, which led the management of the shipbuilding group to encourage the other shipyards to implement LPP.

The second shipyard in this study, Shipyard B, approached the LPP differently than shipyard A. After being introduced to the planning tool, they tried it for a few months and then decided that it is not fitted for their way of working. Instead, they reinforced the usual meeting procedure with some small adjustments: The General Plan was updated based in the reporting from own Discipline (DCs) and presented during the weekly meeting. Furthermore, an adapted EVM version was introduced. However, this was adapted only at a general plan level, not at a lower level in the project organization. Moreover, deviation was only discussed and solved in connection with formal, however mostly in informal meetings, but there were no records made in order to prevent reoccurrence of the deviations.

6   Discussion and Conclusions

The purpose of this paper was to study the implementation of LPP in the shipbuilding industry from a knowledge perspective. In particular, we wanted to analyze the role of context in the implementation process, which has been done by studying the implementation of LPP at two separate shipyards in the same shipbuilding group.

We found that Shipyard B had somewhat more formalized planning routines than Shipyard A before implementation of LPP. Hence, we should expect that the knowledge base of Shipyard B should be more adapted to the new knowledge represented by LPP. However, this study finds that this has not been the case. On the contrary, the implementation of LPP has so far been more successful at Shipyard A. Literature on absorptive capacity emphasize the importance of interaction between the knowledge base and employees' motivation [11]. In our study, we found that there were differences regarding motivation at the management level. In shipyard A, the manager participated actively in developing LPP and implementing the planning tool at the shipyard. At Shipyard B, the managerial level found that the existing planning tool functioned satisfactory, and hence were not motivated to implement a new and more formalized tool. This finding illustrates the importance of the interaction between both knowledge and motivation for a successful implementation. Furthermore, the lack of formalized planning systems at Shipyard A could be considered as an advantage when implementing a new planning tool, as this organization may be more open to new ways for organizing working processes. Finally, our findings may indicate that these two shipyards despite of being a part of the same shipbuilding group residing in a cluster characterized by shared norms for knowledge sharing and extensive use of informal coordination [24], represent two different organization cultures. Based on preliminary findings, we can deduce that the organizational culture at Shipyard A emerges as more open to external impulses than at Shipyard B. The role of the organizational culture should be addressed in further studies. Furthermore, as this study is carried out in a relatively early stage of the implementation process, data should be collected at later stages in the implementation process, preferably including other shipyards in the group implementing LPP.

References

1. Haartveit, D.E.G., Semini, M., Alfnes, E.: Integration Alternatives for Ship Designers and Shipyards. In: Frick, J., Laugen, B.T. (eds.) Advances in Production Management Systems. IFIP AICT, vol. 384, pp. 309–316. Springer, Heidelberg (2012)
2. Hicks, C., McGovern, T., Earl, C.F.: A Typology of UK Engineer-to-Order Companies. International Journal of Logistics: Research and Applications 4(1), 43–56 (2001)
3. Asheim, B.T., Isaksen, A.: Regional Innovation Systems: The Integration of Local 'Sticky' and Global 'Ubiquitous' Knowledge. Journal of Technology Transfer 27(1), 77–86 (2002)
4. Emblemsvåg, J.: Lean Project Planning in Shipbuilding. Journal of Ship Production and Design 30(1), 1–10 (2014)
5. Cooney, R.: Is "lean" a universal production system? Batch production in the automotive industry. International Journal of Operations & Production Management 22(9/10), 1130–1147 (2002)
6. Morris, T., Lancaster, Z.: Translating Management Ideas. Organization Studies 27(2), 207–233 (2006)
7. Sahlin-Andersson, K., Engwall, L.: Introduction. In: Sahlin-Andersson, K., Engwall, L. (eds.) The Expansion of Management Knowledge. Carriers, Flows, and Sources. Standford University Press, Standford (2002)
8. Zander, U., Kogut, B.: Knowledge and the Speed of the Transfer and Imitation of Organizational Capabilities: An Empirical Test. Organization Science 6(1), 76–92 (1995)
9. Gupta, A.K., Govindarajan, V.: Knowledge flows within multinational corporations. Strategic Management Journal 21(4), 473–473 (2000)
10. Minbaeva, D., et al.: MNC knowledge transfer, subsidiary absorptive capacity, and HRM. Journal of International Business Studies 34(6), 586 (2003)

11. Cohen, W.M., Levinthal, D.A.: Absorptive Capacity: A New Perspective On Learning And Innovation. Administrative Science Quarterly 35(1), 128–152 (1990)
12. Minbaeva, D.B., et al.: A retrospective on: MNC knowledge transfer, subsidiary absorptive capacity, and HRM. Journal of International Business Studies 45(1), 52–62 (2014)
13. Giroux, H., Taylor, J.R.: The Justification of Knowledge: Tracking the Translations of Quality. Management Learning 33(4), 497–517 (2002)
14. Womack, J.P., Jones, D.T.: Lean thinking: banish waste and create wealth in your corporation. Free Press, New York (2003)
15. Ballard, H.G.: The last planner system of production control. In: Faculty of Engineering. University of Birmingham, Birmingham (2000)
16. Sumara, J., Goodpasture, J.: Earned value-the next generation-a practical application for commercial projects. In: Project Managment Institute 28th annual Seminars & Symposium, Chicago (1997)
17. Sobek, D.K., Smalley, A.: Understanding A3 thinking: a critical component of Toyota's PDCA management system. CRC Press, Boca Raton (2008)
18. Koskela, L.: Application of the New Production Philosophy to Contruction, In: Technical Report. CIFE, Standford University (1992)
19. Ballard, G., Howell, G.: An update onlast planner. In: IGLC, Virgina, USA (2003)
20. Olano, R.M., Alarcon, L., Razuri, C.: Understanding the relationship between planning reliability and and Schedule performance: A case study. In: IGLC-17, Taipei, Taiwan (2009)
21. Flemming, Q.W., Koppelman, J.M.: Using Earned Value Management. Cost Engineering 44(9), 32–36 (2002)
22. Yin, R.K.: Case study research: design and methods. Sage, Los Angeles (2009)
23. Halse, L.L.: Governance and transformation of clusters: theoretical models and the case of the maritime cluster in Mid-West Norway. In: 18th EurOMA Conference, Cambridge, UK (2011)

OntoSTEP-NC for Information Feedbacks
from CNC to CAD/CAM Systems

Christophe Danjou, Julien Le Duigou, and Benoît Eynard

Mechanical Engineering Systems Department, Université de Technologie de Compiègne,
Mechanical Laboratory Roberval UMR UTC/CNRS 7337, CS 60319,
60203 Compiègne cedex, France
{christophe.danjou,julien.le-duigou,benoit.eynard}@utc.fr

Abstract. This paper exposes a proposal to ensure manufacturing feedbacks from the CNC machine to CAD/CAM systems by using an ontology through information systems. Centered on the Manufacturing Process Management platform, the trades between Product Data Management and Enterprise Resource Planning platforms are based on the new semantic model OntoSTEP-NC – an ontology based on STEP-NC standard. This defines the Closed-Loop Manufacturing which provides and allows a data extraction from the CNC machine and reinjection of relevant information to the CAM systems. This would help CAM programmers making choices based on company good practices stored in the database.

Keywords: STEP-NC, OntoSTEP-NC, Closed-Loop Manufacturing, Manufacturing Process Management.

1 Introduction

To be more competitive and due to the globalization context, aeronautical manufacturers tend to improve the triptych: Cost, Time, and Quality.

This is why French FUI project called ANGEL (Atelier Numérique coGnitif intEropérable et agiLe) focuses on the capitalization of cuts know-how in order to improve the competitiveness of companies developing tools and methods to retrieve information from the CNC machine. To achieve the information flow bi-directionality from CNC machines to CAD, the systems must be able to exchange information and to use this information.

Defined as "The ability of two systems (or more) to communicate, cooperate and exchange services and data, thus despite the differences in languages, implementations, executive environments and abstraction models" [1], interoperability is described by 3 levels: Semantical, Technical and organizational [2]. The use of standard format which allows having a unified approach can be one of the various solutions for interoperability. To achieve the interoperability between the CAX software the STEP-NC standard seems to be one of the most promising [3].

B. Grabot et al. (Eds.): APMS 2014, Part III, IFIP AICT 440, pp. 256–263, 2014.

Beyond interoperability aspect this paper focuses on the feedback from the machining to the design and industrialization phases. The main question the paper would answer is: "How to integrate manufacturing expertise from manufacturing in the design / industrialization process for mechanical parts?". Indeed incrementing the cutting knowledge would help to manufacture the right part-the first time thus despite the files formats differences.

To answer this question, the next section presents a state of the art on STEP-NC standard as a basis for CAX software trades. The third section will explain the proposal to achieve the integration of manufacturing expertise and knowledge extracted from the CNC machining. Section 4 concludes this paper presenting future works.

2   State of the Art

2.1   STEP-NC a Solution for Data Exchange

Designing and manufacturing systems trades (CAD, CAM, Post-Processor, CNC machine, etc.) are led by specific file. Indeed, software has its own language and makes interoperability more difficult. For example, CATPart and CATProcess will be used respectively for Dassault Systems CAD and CAM systems, Top'CAM for Top-Solid CAM system, G-Code and M-Code will be used as specific inputs according the CNC controller, etc.

Therefore to ensure transaction between software, one solution consists in using standard format. Indeed this unifying approach allows having the same language for all the manufacturing technologies. To first achieve the data exchange between CAD and simulation, STEP standard has been developed (Lee, S.-H. et al., 2006). The STEP standard is an open and normalized standard that aims to promote the data exchange in a format which is understandable and shared by all. According to [5], the STEP standard provides a neutral, sustainable and scalable data exchange format.

In the last years, STEP-NC, a new standard format with enriched data has been developed in order to improve the systems interoperability [6] by integrating processing data. Indeed, the STEP-NC standard encompasses machining process, cutting tools description, and CAD features and requirements. This enriched standard format allows having in the same file all the information required for the whole development stage from the early design to the machining.

STEP-NC is led by two standards which are interested in two different levels – AIM (Application Interpreted Model) and ARM (Application Reference Model):

- ISO 10303 AP238 which concerns the AIM level. This level is based on the ISO 10303 standard which defines the STEP standard. The Application Protocol (AP) 238 untitled "Computer Numerical Controllers" mainly allows adding information for CNC machining. In this way, the STEP standard is enriched with the manufacturing feature.
- ISO 10649 deals with the ARM level. This level is higher than the previous one and it also defines the machining strategy.

The STEP-NC standard structures a large number of information. Therefore, the same file can be used for all the CAX systems and then all the modifications are propagated from one to another. The use of STEP-NC also helps to archive the modifications. Indeed there is no more coherence problem from CAM and CNC program. All the modifications and optimization made by the operators in the CNC machine are translated in the STEP-NC file. This program can be then archived and re-used if necessary. The use of STEP-NC can help to save time because the post-processor can be overpassed. Indeed, the machining intelligence is moved from CAM systems to CNC machines thus the translation from computer language to machine understandable language (Post-Processors and G-Code) is no more necessary. Therefore, the following works will be based on STEP-NC standard and not on G-code defining the information flow through the CAX systems from CAD to CNC [7].

2.2   STEP-NC Enabling Feedback, Cooperation and Optimization

As seen in the previous section, the use of STEP-NC standard file makes possible the propagation of modifications to all the other manufacturing systems. Therefore changes made directly in the CNC machine will be propagated back to CAM system.

In addition to the flow bi-directionality, STEP-NC standard will simplify the industrialization phase. As a result of optimization, according to the NIST, the STEP standard can potentially save up to a billion dollars a year by reducing the costs of interoperability in sectors such as automotive, aerospace and shipbuilding. The following list summarizes the major works using STEP-NC for feedback and optimization:

- [8] achieve vertical integration with STEP-NC in order to have a standard process monitoring and traceability programming. The traceability is ensured at three different levels: Business level, Manufacturing Level, and shop floor level. This allows monitoring the capitalization.
- [9] with DIMP system based on STEP-NC provides more flexibility for cooperative manufacturing environment.
- [10] use STEP-NC as a universal programming for CNC machines. Indeed the same CAM program can be spread to many CNC machines. Thus it has been made possible with the intelligence transfer from CAM system to CNC machines to use the same CAM program into many different CNC machines.
- Through the use of STEP-NC [11] define an automatic correction of cutting parameters based on the Machine Condition Monitoring. They have developed optiS-TEP-NC system which helps to perform cutting parameters optimization.
- In the same way, [12] has defined Closed-Loop Machining thanks to STEP-NC to achieve on-line inspection. To succeed this inspection they have developed a closed-loop between CAPP and CNC machine.
- Borgia [13] based on STEP-NC allows having automatic recognition of feature and generating toolpath based on machining working step. Then a mathematical optimization is conducted.

According to this short review on STEP-NC works, it appears that the standard is a promising solution for bi-directional trades and for optimization (Cutting parameters, toolpath optimization, feature recognition, etc.).

2.3   Lacks in STEP-NC

The previous study has highlighted that automatic correction/optimization and feature recognition are made reality thanks to STEP-NC use. But there is no feedback from the CNC machine to the CAD or CAM systems. This kind of feedback would help people in design or program choices. Indeed [14] formulated the following assertion: "Interoperability will enable manufacturing businesses to produce legacy components, based on the original process planning knowledge, on modern and future machine tools without the overhead of re-planning the fixturing, tooling and tool paths. This will enable future parts to be manufactured with confidence, as and when required without having to rely on the original equipment, past tooling and part programs which would be typically obsolete." Based on this assertion, it clearly appears STEP-NC is the basis for future data exchanges and to interoperability between CAX systems.

Although STEP-NC allows sharing and propagating data in both ways – CAD to CNC and CNC to CAD – STEP-NC is not yet a solution for archiving CNC machining information in order to be injected at the right time. This is why the next section will propose a solution to insure interoperability and a way to succeed in feedback from CNC machine to CAM systems. This feedback will create the Closed-Loop Manufacturing.

3   Solution for Data Feedback

3.1   Information Feedback Trades

As highlighted in the previous sections, STEP-NC standard file encompasses lot of information and permits the data propagation to the whole lifecycle. But STEP-NC does not allow incrementing manufacturing loops. In contrary to the Closed-Loop Machining which concerns a real time correction of machining parameters including the simulation, the Closed-Loop Manufacturing includes the CAM systems, simulation and CNC machines. Moreover this loop doesn't provide a real time feedback but allow incrementing the knowledge from the CNC machine. In fact, the n previous loops would impact and infer on the loop $n+1$.

As STEP-NC file in its own format cannot support the incrementing evolution of good practices. STEP-NC requires to be connected to information systems (PDM-MPM-ERP) to ensure traceability hence to improve the industrialization phase for the future manufactured products. This is why figure 1 exposes a proposition to achieve incrementing manufacturing loops. This implementation is being made possible thanks to the interaction between information systems and the CAX systems.

The proposal contains 3 stages in the Closed-Loop Manufacturing which can be clearly identified: The first one concerns the data extraction from the CNC machine, the second is about the validation process of good practices and third one deals with the geometrical and manufacturing recognition.

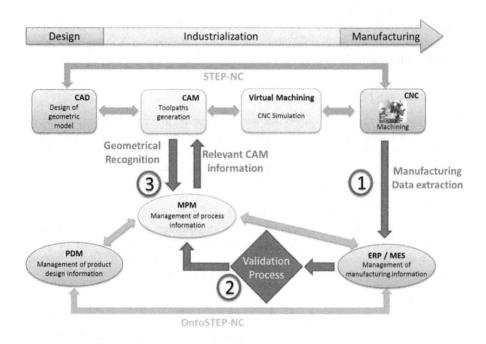

Fig. 1. Closed-Loop Manufacturing for data feedbacks

3.2   OntoSTEP-NC for PDM-MPM-ERP Trades

To achieve interoperability between information systems it has been chosen to use an ontology. In fact it has been chosen to use an ontology called OntoSTEP-NC based on the STEP-NC standard as support PDM-MPM-ERP trades [15]. The ISO 14649 standard has been chosen as a basis for OntoSTEP-NC model. The standard format is a meta-level model for CNC information so on OntoSTEP-NC describes a meta-level data. This model has been built using the Protégé software (edited by Stanford University) [16] defining entities as classes. Figure 2 and figure 3 describe the OntoSTEP-NC entities and its representation.

First based on ARM level the OntoSTEP-NC can be then modified to AIM model if necessary. Indeed the ontology lets a large range of possibilities to modify the model structure and to add new entities and features. Therefore the interoperability of the information systems is achieved thanks to the adaptability of the ontology model to perfectly fit with the data exchange between PDM, MPM and ERP. Moreover, the use of the recent developed OntoSTEP-NC will allow interoperability with CAX systems as explained by [14]: "Though STEP-NC has given the opportunity for machining process information to be standardized, the lack of a semantic and ontology representation makes it almost impossible to inter-relate the existing systems and languages."

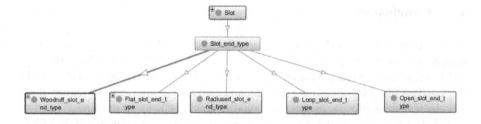

Fig. 2. OntoSTEP-NC graph

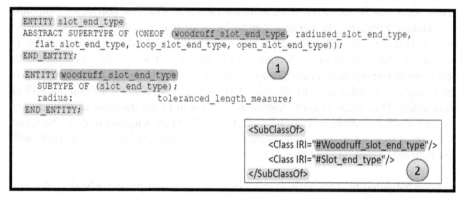

Fig. 3. STEP-NC comparison between EXPPRESS (1) and OWL language (2)

To improve the information feedback, OntoSTEP-NC is being developed as a database in which all the extracted data could be contained. As explained in Lee's work [17], the knowledge is not set in a relational database but organized according to the characteristics (class, properties, semantical links, attributes…) of the ontologies. This organization guaranties the unicity of the information in the database depending the process the feature belongs to.

To search information in the ontology, queries will be used and issue queries in query languages such as OWL-QL. This standard language for ontologies query offers the ability to export it to other ontologies if needed for future development by combining many ontologies to OntoSTEP-NC. For example, OntoSTEP-NC could be connected to ONTO-PDM [18] which is an ontology for ERP platforms and could also be connected to OntoSTEP [19] for the PDM and CAD platforms.

Moreover, according to [20] semantic queries enable to best capture a user's ontology requirement and rank the resulting ontologies based on their conceptual closeness to the given query. Hence, the information could be spread to all the manufacturing technologies which require this information. The ontology is the support of manufacturing loops and data feedback from the CNC to CAM systems.

4   Conclusion

As seen in section 2 STEP-NC can support through its rich data format, much information that can be integrated in the bi-directional flow CAD-CAM-CNC. Although STEP-NC allows feedback from the CNC machine to CAD and CAM systems, STEP-NC standard file does not allow archiving and capitalizing information. Indeed, there is no incrementing process in order to capitalize good practices yet existing.

This is why the proposition of this paper uses information systems (PDM-MPM-ERP) to ensure this capitalization setting the MPM as a pivot for trades between information systems and CAX technologies. Those trades are led using OntoSTEP-NC and allow having manufacturing loops.

This proposition will be tested in our future works on three industrial use cases. Those tests will be extracted from aeronautical parts. The first part is an aluminum one which presents a large number of manufacturing features (drilling, pocket, surfacing…). This first part will test the recognition of geometrical design and the ability to compare to the manufacturing features in the database. The second part which is an aeronautical turning-milling part also in aluminum will test the data extraction due to the numerous complex form of this part. The third part equal to the second one will be in titanium. This one will allow testing the increment of the database and also to test the answers from MPM concerning the relevant CAM information trades. The extrapolation of this proposition will concern complex forms for aeronautical parts with raw material as titanium and Inconel.

Acknowledgements. This work is done in the French FUI project ANGEL. We also thank all consortium partners for their contribution during the development of ideas and concepts proposed in this paper.

References

1. Wegner, P.: Interoperability. ACM Comput. Surv. 28, 285–287 (1996)
2. EIF European Interoperability Framework. White Pages, pp. 1–40 (2004)
3. Xu, X.W.: Realization of STEP-NC enabled machining. Robot Comput. Integr. Manuf. 22, 144–153 (2006)
4. Lee, S.-H., Jeong, Y.-S.: A system integration framework through development of ISO 10303-based product model for steel bridges. Autom. Constr. 15, 212–228 (2006)
5. Rachuri, S., Subrahmanian, E., Bouras, A., et al.: Information sharing and exchange in the context of product lifecycle management: Role of standards. Comput. Des. 40, 789–800 (2008)
6. Laguionie, R., Rauch, M., Hascoet, J.: Toolpaths programming in an intelligent STEP-NC manufacturing context. J. Mach. Eng. 8, 33–43 (2008)
7. Nassehi, A., Newman, S.T., Xu, X.W., Rosso, R.S.U.: Toward interoperable CNC manufacturing. Int. J. Comput. Integr. Manuf. 21, 222–230 (2008)
8. Campos, J.G., Miguez, L.R.: Standard process monitoring and traceability programming in collaborative CAD/CAM/CNC manufacturing scenarios. Comput. Ind. 62, 311–322 (2011)
9. Wang, X.V., Xu, X.W.: A collaborative product data exchange environment based on STEP. Int. J. Comput. Integr. Manuf., 37–41 (2013)

10. Xu, X.W., Wang, L., Rong, Y.: STEP-NC and function blocks for interoperable manufacturing. IEEE Trans. Autom. Sci. Eng. 3, 297–308 (2006)
11. Ridwan, F., Xu, X., Advanced, C.N.C.: Advanced CNC system with in-process feed-rate optimisation. Robot Comput. Integr. Manuf. 29, 12–20 (2013)
12. Zhao, F., Xu, X., Xie, S.: STEP-NC enabled on-line inspection in support of closed-loop machining. Robot Comput. Integr. Manuf. 24, 200–216 (2008)
13. Borgia, S., Matta, A., Tolio, T.: STEP-NC compliant approach for setup planning problem on multiple fixture pallets. J. Manuf. Syst. 32, 781–791 (2013)
14. Newman, S.T., Nassehi, A., Xu, X.W., et al.: Strategic advantages of interoperability for global manufacturing using CNC technology. Robot Comput. Integr. Manuf. 24, 699–708 (2008)
15. Danjou, C., Le Duigou, J., Eynard, B.: Integrated Platform from CAD to CNC: State of the Art. In: Proc. Int. Conf. Prod. Lifecycle Manag. Nantes, France (2013)
16. Noy, N., Klein, M.: Ontology Evolution: Not the Same as Schema Evolution. Knowl. Inf. Syst. 6, 428–440 (2004)
17. Lee, T., Lee, I.H., Lee, S., et al.: Building an operational product ontology system. Electron. Commer. Res. Appl. 5, 16–28 (2006)
18. Panetto, H., Dassisti, M., Tursi, A.: ONTO-PDM: Product-driven ONTOlogy for Product Data Management interoperability within manufacturing process environment. Adv. Eng. Informatics. 26, 334–348 (2012)
19. Barbau, R., Krima, S., Rachuri, S., et al.: OntoSTEP: Enriching product model data using ontologies. Comput. Des. 44, 575–590 (2012)
20. Ungrangsi, R., Anutariya, C., Wuwongse, V.: SQORE-based ontology retrieval system. In: Wagner, R., Revell, N., Pernul, G. (eds.) DEXA 2007. LNCS, vol. 4653, pp. 720–729. Springer, Heidelberg (2007)

Use of MCDM and AI Techniques for Mechanization of In-Service Inspection Planning Process

A.M.N.D.B. Seneviratne and R.M. Chandima Ratnayake

University of Stavanger, Stavanger, Norway
{chandima.ratnayake,dammika.seneviratne}@uis.no

Abstract. The in-service inspection planning process for topside piping equipment of aging oil and gas (O&G) production and process facilities (P&PFs) involves personnel with different kinds of expertise, experience, and knowledge as well as a vast amount of data and information. To simplify the inspection planning process and increase the quality of an inspection program, various industrial organizations as well as researchers have been developing numerous techniques in an isolated fashion to address the challenges pertaining to different activities involved in the inspection planning process. In order to mechanize the overall inspection process, suitable techniques need to be identified for the different activities carried out in a generic inspection planning process. This manuscript discusses the potential use of multi-criteria decision analysis (MCDM) and artificial intelligence (AI) techniques. It also provides evidence about the suitability of AI techniques in relation to fuzzy logic and artificial neural networks for the mechanization of the inspection planning process in a dynamic manner.

Keywords: In-service inspection planning, AI techniques, MCDM techniques, Inspection programs, Aging O&G P&PFs.

1 Introduction

In offshore P&PFs, the topside piping equipment plays a vital role in the production of hydrocarbons (O&G). In this process, performing equipment maintenance at a level anticipated to comply with the standards and guidelines imposed by regulatory authorities (i.e. Petroleum Safety Authority (PSA), Norway) is a mandatory task for the aging O&G P&PFs operating in the North Sea. Therefore, the owner/operator companies of the P&PFs conduct inspections to identify the equipment's fitness for service and the level of required maintenance and modifications (Ratnayake, 2012a). In this context, the in-service inspection planning process, which consists of a series of sub-processes, for instance, preparation of inspection programs, carrying out inspections at plant level, evaluating inspection results and updating the risk level of equipment, feedback for operation and maintenance and evaluation of resource allocation for the next inspection cycle, is of major significance.

Researchers have identified the importance of inspection planning in various industrial settings, and reliability-based and risk-based approaches were developed from 1963 onwards, gradually establishing risk-based inspection (RBI) concepts for the planning of inspections over the last 25-30 years (Ratnayake et al., 2011; Straub & Faber, 2006). The application of RBI planning has been limited in the past due to the significant numerical effort required by these methods. The MCDM methods, such as the analytic network

B. Grabot et al. (Eds.): APMS 2014, Part III, IFIP AICT 440, pp. 264–271, 2014.
© IFIP International Federation for Information Processing 2014

process (ANP), and the analytic hierarchy process (AHP) developed by Satty (1980), were applied by many researchers in different levels of the inspection planning process. Ratnayake (2012a, 2012b, 2013) and Ratnayake & Markeset (2010) used AHP in planning inspections for topside mechanical equipment. The views of the industry's professionals were considered in developing these AHP models to recommend critical thickness measurement locations (TMLs) (Ratnayake, 2012a, 2012b). The models were based on prioritizing the critical TMLs and optimising the cost for the inspections. Dey (2004) also used the AHP in hydrocarbon pipeline inspection planning, which was illustrated by case studies. The AI technique-based models were also developed to identify critical TMLs, considering the degradation mechanisms. The techniques, for instance fuzzy logic and artificial neural network (ANN), are used by Nesic et al. (2009), Singh and Markeset (2009), Zio (2012) in developing the models. Most of these models are based on empirical methods, in which planning personnel use these models together with their expertise for the planning purposes. The models which developed utilizing AI techniques are more able to incorporate expertise than the empirical models.

This manuscript discusses the advantages and disadvantages of the MCDM and AI approaches in the inspection planning process. The goal of this paper is to identify the sub-processes in the inspection planning process where it is possible to use the AI techniques for the mechanisation of the inspection planning process.

2   Background

The inspection planning work process is defined in several standards, for instance DNV RP G101 (2010) and API RP 581 (2008), and illustrates the sub-processes and flow of sub-processes. A generic inspection planning work process consisting of sub-processes that have been employed in the industry is illustrated in Fig. 1.

The main part of the inspection planning work process is the preparation of the inspection program. In planning inspection programs, the recommendation of critical TMLs for inspection is a primary task. A huge amount of data is gathered, and various techniques are used to identify TMLs by prioritization of criticality. In P&PFs, the topside piping equipment inspection planning personnel's primary concern is corrosion and erosion trends. However, there are other degradation trends, for instance, fatigue degradation, crack propagation due to fatigue, stress-induced cracking, slug effects, flow turbulence effects, stress generation, thermal effects, etc. In general, chemical and mechanical corrosion have been taken into consideration (i.e. CO_2 corrosion, H_2S corrosion, microbially-induced corrosion and sand erosion) during inspection planning. NORSOK M-506 (2005) and DNV RP O501 (2007) are examples of the models developed in standards to assist the inspection planning. The prioritization of identified critical TMLs is based on the thresholds provided by the governing documents, for instance plant strategy, RBI guidelines, piping standards (e.g. ASME B31.3), etc.

In executing inspections, resource allocation is another major part of the planning process. The TMLs' accessibility, methods for inspection, manpower and working hours needed to be calculated. The feedback process performs by comparing the current measurements and historical data to identify the current risk level of TMLs. Furthermore, the annual inspection budget, the annual activity plan and the feedback PM plan are assigned according to the feedback provided by the risk level of the TMLs. Therefore, the inspection planning sub-processes consist of data analysis, forecasting, optimizing and prioritizing. Currently this is performed by using basic calculations and primary software tools.

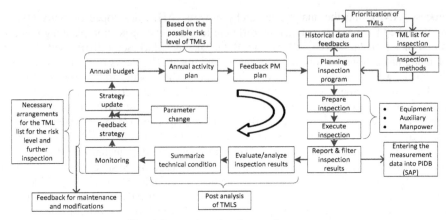

Fig. 1. Inspection planning work process

3   Static and Dynamic Modelling for Inspection Planning

The models developed in the condition based maintenance and monitoring paradigm, in particular to identify the inspection intervals and the prioritization of the inspections can be divided into static and dynamic models (Wang, 2003). Static models are driven by the fixed condition monitoring interval data, while dynamic models are driven by both fixed condition monitoring interval data and real-time condition monitoring data. Therefore, the dynamic model overrides the static model with real-time condition monitoring data, which keeps the equipment under close attention before an appropriate mitigation action takes place when it reaches a critical level (Wang, 2003). The currently developed static and dynamic models are less likely to connect to the real-time condition monitoring data (Jardine et al., 2006). However, the aging P&PFs are constantly affected by the changing production and process conditions where the deterioration and degradation trends are dramatically changing over time. Therefore, the dynamic behaviour of the models which can be connected to the condition monitoring data will be useful for the aging P&PFs to monitor the critical equipment regularly.

4   The Decision Support Modules in Inspection Planning

Different decision support modules (DSM) are developed based on the static and dynamic models to support the decision-making process of the sub-processes in inspection planning. DSMs are developed in an isolated fashion to address the different scenarios, such as the identification of different degradation trends for TMLs, the prioritization of TMLs, inspection methods, etc. However, a number of researchers have observed the difficulty in making proper decisions on the above analysing process and have suggested different approaches. The main model development is focused on degradation monitoring followed by the identification of critical TMLs. The techniques, for instance AHP, ANP, outranking, fuzzy logic, artificial neural networks and genetic algorithms, are used in developing the DSMs.

The main contribution of the DSM in inspection planning is through degradation models. Ratnayake & Markeset (2010) and Singh & Markeset (2009) have reviewed the degradations and degradation models for O&G topside piping and hydrocarbon transportation pipelines. The O&G piping equipment is frequently subject to different degradation mechanisms, internally and externally. A number of manuscripts address specific types of corrosion behaviour: Ramsamooj and Shugar (2001) offer a detailed description of corrosion and fatigue modelling in unfavourable conditions; NORSOK M-506 (2005), Singh & Markeset (2009) and Valor et al. (2010) address CO_2-driven corrosion and the problems of pitting corrosion; Walton et al. (1996) deal with the problems of modelling marine corrosion damage, and DNV RP O501 (2007) illustrates the erosion behaviour of the equipment subjected to produced sand. A large amount of degradation modelling causes the problem to converge into one variable situation, by treating individual items of equipment independently. For large systems, such as those found in the O&G industry, this is a practical assumption that allows the modeller to handle potentially intractable modelling problems. However, this is not usually a realistic assumption since the systems are undergoing different degradation mechanisms in different locations at different times. Therefore, the application of different degradation models (i.e. based on different degradation mechanisms) in one system will enable the identification of different degradation tends in the TMLs. The results from the different models can be used for cumulative prioritization to identify the most critical TMLs in a system.

5   Use of MCDM and AI Methods in Inspection Planning

The MCDM and AI techniques are used in static as well as dynamic modelling of the stages of the inspection planning process. The main functions of the exploited models are optimization, forecasting and prioritization. In MCDM, there are two different approaches for problem solving. The first is to evaluate problems which consist of a known number of alternatives in the solution domain. The second approach is where the number of alternatives for the problem is unknown. However, in this situation, the problem is solved by mathematical modelling to identify the solution (Triantaphyllou, 2000). Therefore, in the inspection planning process of O&G topside piping equipment, the alternatives are limited and the first approach in MCDM is used by many researchers.

Outranking methods, ANP and AHP are the three most frequently used MCDM techniques for prioritization (Bozbura and Beskese, 2007). The outranking methods determine which alternatives are being preferred to the others by systematically comparing each criterion instead of building complex utility functions (Brans et al., 2005). In AHP, pair-wise comparisons are made in between elements at each level of the hierarchy by means of a nominal scale to establish a comparison matrix. The eigenvector of the matrix is derived as the weights' vector of elements at the hierarchy. Finally, overall priority can be obtained by synthesizing local and global weights. The fuzzy version of AHP is preferred in the prioritization of problems for the following reasons: no measurement scale needs to be explicitly defined for each criterion/attribute in pair-wise comparison; representation of uncertainties such as vagueness; non-specificity and discord can be incorporated in the models (Klir and Yuan, 1995). However, there are limitations in using fuzzy-AHP, and these are some of the problems: a high number of computational requirements; only triangular membership functions can be used;, difficulties with criteria and attribute addition and deletion and the number of pair-wise comparisons are increased with the number of criteria (Buyukozkan et al., 2004).

Table 1. Comparison of usage of MCDM/AI techniques in inspection planning

Method	Usage in inspection planning process modelling	Advantages	Disadvantages
MCDM methods (Brans and Mareschal, 2005)	Extensively used in inspection planning. Static modelling behaviour due to the fixed designed methods by designer. Decision selection is from fixed alternative domain.	Easy interpretation of the criteria and alternatives. Easy for designing the models. Flexibility in defining the threshold limits.	Static behaviour of the models. Reflects the designer's perspectives. Fixed boundaries in generating decisions.
Fuzzy logic (Buyukozkan et al., 2004)	Relatively well used in the inspection planning. Represents the process uncertainty parameters. Modelling is static. However, by incorporating other AI techniques, dynamic behaviour can be obtained. Utilizes vagueness and impression of parameters to design noise-tolerant models. Rule base inferencing.	Interpretation of expert knowledge, intuition and experience. Interprets the vague, noise and imprecise data and information. Rule base is used to mimic human-like reasoning by using suitable inferencing methods.	More toward static behaviour in the modelling. Limitations in interpreting human-like reasoning behaviour. Inability of self-learning capabilities.
Artificial neural network (Zhang et al., 2004; Caputo & Pelagagge, 2002)	Relatively well used in inspection planning. Dynamic behaviour is observed in the neural network models. Equipped with the self-learning abilities to adapt the problem-solving capabilities.	Dynamic and good in modelling nonlinear and unstable processes. Trained for complex input output modelling. Self-learning abilities (adaptively). Different types of architecture for different levels and different types of complex problems.	Selection and designing of ANN for solving a problem situation is complex. Identification of proper network design needs extensive effort and research. Training and validation of the designed ANN requires large amount of data.
Genetic algorithms (Cavory et al., 2001)	Limited use in inspection planning. Shows more static behaviour in the modelling. Dynamic behaviour can be adapted using fitness function.	Easy representation of criteria and fast generation of outputs. Simple designing of a model.	Depends on the designers perspectives. No flexibility for imprecise data. Rigid in model construction.
Bayesian networks (Lee et al., 2014)	Extensively used in inspection planning. Static in behaviour since the model uses the statistical methods (probability).	Able to represent the historical behaviour. Easy for designing models and generating desired output. Reduction of number of parameters by conditional probability distribution.	Static in behaviour and relies on the designer's intuition and knowledge. Limited representation of the new data in the system. Less adaptability to the system behaviour.
Petri nets (Ratnayake, 2012a)	Limited use in inspection planning Static behaviour (less adaptability). Dynamically used, but cannot change the parameters.	Easy to model.	Limited alternatives in the modelling process. Needs extensive understanding of the process for modelling.
Hidden Markov model (Lee et al., 2014)	Limited use in inspection planning. In between static and dynamic (has some level of adaptability). Less dynamic in nature. Dynamic as a hybrid model with unknown state space parameters.	Can be used for fault and degradation diagnosis on non stationary signals and dynamic systems. Appropriate for multi failure mode.	Not appropriate when the failure state is observable. Large amount of data is needed for accurate modelling.

In recent years artificial intelligence techniques have also been used successfully in condition based maintenance planning. The earliest works made use of expert systems (Medsker, 1994); then came a number of studies using ANN (Caputo & Pelagagge, 2002). Jang (1993) proposed the adaptive network-based fuzzy inference system (ANFIS), a hybrid learning algorithm extensively used in forecasting problems. The ANN model is also used with a back propagation algorithm for predicting failure rates (Al-Garni et al., 2006). Ciarapica and Giacchetta (2006) experimentally used ANN and neuro-fuzzy systems to forecast activities in the rotating machinery preventive maintenance cycles. Genetic algorithms are used in optimizing the maintenance schedule tasks in production environments by Cavory et al. (2001). These are also used by Sortrakul et al. (2005) to solve an integrated optimization model for production scheduling and preventive maintenance planning. More recently, several works have employed fuzzy logic systems in the identification of critical TMLs (Ratnayake, 2014a, 2014b; Seneviratne & Ratnayake, 2013). However, the neuro-fuzzy approach integrates the neural networks and fuzzy logic to create powerful expert decision systems. Many authors have proposed various neuro-fuzzy models and complex training algorithms in inspection and maintenance planning (Zhang et al., 2004). Table 1 illustrates the usage of different methods for inspection planning process modelling in various industries with their advantages and disadvantages.

Although different models have been developed using different techniques, full mechanization of the inspection planning process has not yet been achieved. Researchers address the mechanization of some of the sub-processes illustrated in Fig. 1. To achieve total mechanization, as short-term goals, correct techniques for modelling the sub-processes needed to be identified. As middle-term goals, the knowledge bases for the models needed to be created. For long-term goals, full mechanization can be achieved by the integration of models, developed knowledge bases and the connection of condition monitoring sensors to the models.

6   Discussions and Conclusions

The planning process consists of several stages with different levels of data analysis. In this analysis the experience, knowledge and intuition of the field experts is extensively used. In the mechanization of the inspection planning process, prioritization techniques which can incorporate human-like abilities need to be used. The techniques, for instance fuzzy logic and ANN, demonstrate human-like reasoning abilities. However, referring to the advantages and disadvantages illustrated in Table 1, individual AI techniques show only a limited number of reasoning behaviours. Therefore, the use of multiple AI techniques in a model as hybrid AI techniques will enable human-like reasoning abilities to be embedded into the DSMs.

In the O&G P&PFs, the product and process condition variations cause the arbitrary degradation trends of aged equipment which are reaching critical levels. However, the financial productivity is less in aged P&PFs. Therefore, owner/operator companies face difficulties in performing inspections regularly to monitor the critical equipment. Hence, the dynamic modelling approach is necessary for the aged O&G P&PF inspection planning, where the condition monitoring data can be linked to the DSMs to identify the critical TMLs in a dynamic manner.

Acknowledgements. The authors would like to thank Roy Martin Zydeman and the in-service inspection planning team in Aker Solutions Offshore Partner, Norway, for their support in this research study.

References

API RP 581 Risk Based Inspection Technology, 2nd edn. American Petroleum Institute (2008)

Al-Garni, A.Z., Jamal, A., Ahmad, A.M., Al-Garni, A.M., Tozan, M.: Neural Network-Based Failure Rate Prediction for De Havilland Dash-8 Ttires. Eng. Appl. Artif. Intel. 19, 681–691 (2008)

Bozbura, F.T., Beskese, A.: Prioritization of Organizational Capital Measurement Indicators Using Fuzzy AHP. Int. J. Approx. Reason. 44, 124–147 (2007)

Brans, J.P., Mareschal, B.: PROMETHEE Methods. In: Multiple Criteria Decision Analysis: State of the Art Surveys, pp. 163–186. Springer, New York (2005)

Buyukozkan, G., Kahraman, C., Ruan, D.: A Fuzzy MulticriteriaDecision Approach for Software Development Strategy Selection. Int. J. Gen. Syst. 33, 259–280 (2004)

Caputo, A.C., Pelagagge, P.M.: An Inverse Approach for Piping Network Monitoring. J. Loss Prevent. Proc. 15, 497–505 (2002)

Cavory, G., Dupas, R., Goncalves, G.: A Genetic Approach to the Scheduling of Preventive Maintenance Tasks on a Single Product Manufacturing Production Line. Int. J. Prod. Econ. 74, 135–146 (2011)

Ciarapica, F.E., Giacchetta, G.: Managing the Condition-Based Maintenance of a Combined-Cycle Power Plant: An Approach Using Soft Computing Techniques. J. Loss Prevent. Proc. 19, 316–325 (2006)

DNV RP G101: Risk Based Inspection of Offshore Topside Static Mechanical Equipment. Det Norske Veritas (DNV), Norway (2010)

DNV RP O501 Recommended Practice DNV RP O501: Erosive Wear in Piping Systems. Det Norske Veritas (DNV), Norway (2007)

Dey, P.K.: Decision Support System for Inspection and Maintenance: A Case Study of Oil Pipelines. IEEE T. Eng. Manage. 51, 47–56 (2004)

Jardine, A.K.S., Lin, D., Banjevic, D.: A Review on Machinery Diagnostics and Prognostics Implementing Condition-Based Maintenance. Mech. Syst. Signal Pr. 20, 1483–1510 (2006)

Jang, J.S.: ANFIS: Adaptive-Network-Based Fuzzy Inference System. IEEET.Syst.Man Cyb. 23, 665–685 (1993)

Klir, G.J., Yuan, B.: Fuzzy Sets and Fuzzy Logic: Theory and Applications. Prentice Hall International, Upper Saddle River (1995)

Lee, J., Wu, F., Zhao, W., Ghaffari, M., Liao, L., Siegel, D.: Prognostics and Health Management Design for Rotary Machinery Systems – Reviews, Methodology and Applications. Mech. Syst. Signal Pr. 42, 314–334 (2014)

Medsker, L.: Design and Development of Hybrid Neural Network and Expert Systems. In: IEEE International Conference on Neural Networks-Conference Proceedings, vol. 3, pp. 1470–1474 (1994)

Nesic, S., Li, H., Huang, J., Sormaz, D.: An Open Source Mechanistic Model for CO2 / H2S Corrosion of Carbon Steel. NACE International, Corrosion 2009, Paper No. 09572 (2009)

NORSOK M-506 NORSOK Standard M-506: CO2 Corrosion Rate Calculation Model. Standards Norway, Lysaker, Norway (2005)

Ramsamooj, D.V., Shugar, T.A.: Modeling of Corrosion Fatigue in Metals in an Aggressive Environment. Int. J. Fatigue. 23(suppl. 1), 301–309 (2001)

Ratnayake, R.M.C.: Challenges in Inspection Planning For Maintenance of Static Mechanical Equipment on Ageing Oil and Gas Production Plants: The State of The Art. In: Proceedings of the ASME 31st International Conference on Ocean, Off-shore and Arctic Engineering,paper no. OMAE2011–49050 (2012a)

Ratnayake, R.M.C.: A Decision Model for Executing Plant Strategy: Maintaining the Technical Integrity of Petroleum Flowlines. Int. J. Decision Sciences, Risk and Management (IDJRSM) 4(1/2), 1–24 (2012b)

Ratnayake, R.M.C.: Utilization of Piping Inspection Data for Continuous Improvement: A Methodology to Visualize Coverage and Finding Rates. In: Proceedings of the ASME 32nd International Conference on Ocean, Offshore and Arctic Engineering, paper no. OMAE2013-10025 (2013), doi:10.1115/OMAE2013-10025

Ratnayake, R.M.C.: Application of a Fuzzy Inference System for Functional Failure Risk Rank Estimation: RBM of Rotating Equipment and Instrumentation. Int. J. Loss Prevent. Proc. 29, 216–224 (2014a)

Ratnayake, R.M.C.: KBE Development for Criticality Classification of Mechanical Equipment: A Fuzzy Expert System. Int. J. Disaster Risk Reduction 9, 84–98 (2014b)

Ratnayake, R.M.C., Markeset, T.: Maintaining Technical Integrity of Petroleum Flow Lines on Offshore Installations: A Decision Support System for Inspection Planning. In: Proceedings of the ASME 2010 29th International Conference on Ocean, Offshore and Arctic Engineering,paper no. OMAE2010-20035 (2010), doi:10.1115/OMAE2010-20035

Ratnayake, R.M.C., Samarakoon, S.M.S.M.K., Markeset, T.: Maintenance Integrity: Managing Flange Inspections on Aging Offshore Production Facilities. In: Proceedings of the ASME 30th International Conference on Ocean, Offshore and Arctic Engineering,paper no. OMAE2011-49050, pp. 19–32 (2011), doi:10.1115/OMAE2011-49050

Satty, T.L.: The Analytic Hierarchy Process: Planning, Priority Setting, Resource Allocation. McGraw-Hill, New York (1980)

Seneviratne, A.M.N.D.B., Ratnayake, R.M.C.: In-Service Inspection of Static Mechanical Equipment: Use of a Fuzzy Inference System for Maintaining the Quality of an Inspection Program. In: Proceedings of the IEEE International Conference Industrial Engineering and Engineering Management (IEEM), Thailand (2013)

Singh, M., Markeset, T.: A Methodology for Risk-Based Inspection Planning of Oil and Gas Pipes Based on Fuzzy Logic Framework. Eng. Fail. Anal. 16, 2098–2113 (2009)

Sortrakul, N., Nachtmann, H.L., Cassady, C.R.: Genetic Algorithms for Integrated Preventive Maintenance Planning and Production Scheduling for a Single Machine. Comput. Ind. 56, 161–168 (2005)

Straub, D., Faber, M.H.: Computational Aspects of Risk - Based Inspection Planning. Computer - Aided Civil and Infrastructure Eng. 21, 179–192 (2006)

Triantaphyllou, E.: Multi-Criteria Decision Making: A Comparative Study, p. 320. Kluwer Academic Publishers, Dordrecht (2000) ISBN 0-7923-6607-7

Valor, A., Caleyo, F., Rivas, D., Hallen, J.M.: Stochastic Approach to Pitting-Corrosion-Extreme Modeling in Low-Carbon Steel. Corros. Sci. 52, 52–910 (2010)

Wang, W.: Modelling Condition Monitoring Intervals: A Hybrid of Simulation and Analytical Approaches. J. Oper. Res. Soc. 54, 273–282 (2003)

Walton, J.C., Cragnolino, G., Kalandros, S.K.: A Numerical Model of Crevice Corrosion for Passive and Active Metals. Corros. Sci. 38, 1–18 (1996)

Zio, E.: Prognostics and Health Management of Industrial Equipment. Diagnostics and Prognostics of Engineering Systems: Methods and Techniques. IGI Global (2012)

Zhang, D., Bai, X., Cai, K.: Extended Neuro-Fuzzy Models ofMultilayer Perceptrons. Fuzzy Set. Syst. 142, 221–242 (2004)

Paths for Modularization

Modularization for Flexible Structural Platform for Boats

Bjørnar Henriksen and Carl Christian Røstad

SINTEF Technology and Society, 7465 Trondheim, Norway
{bjornar.henriksen,carl.c.rostad}@sintef.no

Abstract. Rapid product introduction and customization are keywords for competitiveness in many industries. This is often associated with modularization, where the objective is to create a flexible product design, not requiring changes in the overall product design every time a new variant is introduced. Modularization could be approached in many ways with focus on different enablers. This paper describes different approaches that are relevant to create a flexible, modularized structural platform for boats. The paper is based on the project "Marine Platform", where manufacturers for the professional and leisure market, are focusing on different, but complementary, paths towards modularization. This conceptual paper describes how high-speed innovation in the boating industry could be approached through modularization in material technology, moulds, and production processes, but where the most important enabler for a flexible structural platform for boats is knowledge – modularized knowledge.

Keywords: Product development, modularization, boating industry.

1 Introduction

Customization is one of the potentially most important competitive advantages for manufacturers in high cost countries such as Norway, especially when it is combined with innovations and frequent product introductions. However, this is challenging for example in the design and development of boats when also efficient production processes are required. "Mass customization" and modularized design/production would normally be key elements in a strategy to meet such challenges.

The overall objective for the R&D project "Marine Platform" is to reveal, create and combine the different presumptions and requirements into efficient development and production processes for boats. This is based on a new approach to design and the development of flexible standardized structural platforms as a basis for defined inter-phases for the different modules in boats. This then leads to new approaches to production and customization improving the companies' competitiveness. In our definitions of modules we have to go behind the traditional view of modules as physical parts and systems. Modularized processes, both in product development and production, and increasingly modularized knowledge (e.g documentation) are emphasized in modularization. Even though all of the above perspectives are interrelated and should be covered in a holistic modularization strategy, they are often not explicitly

B. Grabot et al. (Eds.): APMS 2014, Part III, IFIP AICT 440, pp. 272–279, 2014.
© IFIP International Federation for Information Processing 2014

described and approached. An important part of the project is to develop methodologies and solutions enabling these objectives.

The purpose of this conceptual paper is to illustrate different ways modularization could be approached using cases from the boatbuilding industry, where the overall aim is to enable rapid product development processes. The paper is based on a R&D project involving manufacturers of leisure boats and boats for the professional markets. The project is at an early stage and so far the activities have mainly been to develop hypothesis, challenges, and how to approach them in concrete contexts. The project is closely related to what is happening in the companies (case studies) and the researchers aim to participate in the product development processes in order to improve them through action research. Literature studies have also been important for the project (and this paper) at this early stage.

Section 2 presents theoretical perspectives on innovation and modularization. Section 3 presents the R&D-project while Section 4 focuses the different focus areas in the modularization of a structural platform for boats. Section 5 concludes.

2   Theoretical Perspectives

2.1   Product Development and Modularization

Module-based design funded on platform-thinking enables faster development processes e.g. through reuse of solutions. We can also assure robust design solutions from modules that have been tested and optimized over a long period of time. Modularity allows part of the product to be made in volume as standard modules while product distinctiveness is achieved through combinations or modifications of modules [1]. Modularization could bridge the advantages of: (1) standardization and rationalization, (2) customization and flexibility, and (3) reducing complexity [2].

The cost effects through reduced product development lead time and volume effects from standardization are important, but there are also revenue aspects of modularization: With a modular product platform structure, a set of building blocks (modules) are created where a great number of final products can be built, without increasing a company's internal complexity.

Parallel development activities are possible once the interfaces between the modules have been defined, and subsequent work conforms to the established interface specifications [3]. This reduces overall development time and resource requirements by eliminating the time-consuming redesigns when component interfaces are not fully defined and standardized during component development processes [4].

2.2   Components and Functions

We often find module-based design within incremental product development, where e.g. not all innovations or "novelties" are introduced at the same time. However, if modularity is identified and exploited in the initial conceptual or reverse engineering

Fig. 1. Component oriented modularization

effort, the immediate product design reaps benefits in several strategically important areas [5]. However, an early focus on products and components could freeze product architecture and solutions, making it less flexible for future requirements.

Products are normally supposed to fulfill functions or requirements defined by "someone". This could be from standards or regulations, but most often this is about meeting customer requirements. A function oriented approach implies focus on functions and organizing/prioritizing them before the physical function containers are defined. This could be perceived as a demanding and theoretical process, but today modularization based on functionality has become a common approach and methods have been introduced to cut out a module from function structures using module heuristics [3]. These methods, such as Modular Function Deployment (MFD™), identify modules from a functional model of a product, create rough geometric layouts and group products into families based on function [6]. Rather than a fixed product platform upon which derivative products are created through substitution of add-on modules, this approach permits the platform itself to be one of several possible options. After comparing function structures for common and unique functions, rules are applied to determine possible modules. This "inverse" process defines possible architectures. This approach increase the flexibility as it also represents a modularization of the basic platform [7].

Fig. 2. Function oriented modularization

2.3   Modules - Knowledge Containers

A systematic approach needs knowledge from people that know customer demands, service requirements, and from those producing the products. Concurrent engineering could be a key to mobilize and capture this knowledge [8]. An important part of the knowledge of the company is embedded in the products and reusing modules knowledge saves time and money. Also, the reuse of engineering specifications, testing, process engineering etc, may lead to the desired effects by blurring the boundary between knowledge management and traditional modularization [9].

The tendency towards a more abstract understanding of modularity is further strengthened by the fact that modularization in an industrial context can be seen as reuse of engineering and employee resources for companies that are increasingly aware of knowledge as a competitive advantage [10]. An important part of the knowledge of the company is embedded in the products and reusing modules. It is not necessarily the finished, physical modules that are reused in order to gain the benefits. Also, so-called *intellectual reuse* of earlier stages, like reuse of engineering specifications, testing, process engineering etc, may lead to the desired effects by blurring the boundary between knowledge management and traditional modularization [11].

2.4   Holistic Approach to Modularization

To get the desired effect of module-based design processes they have to be standardized in a way that matches the requirements from the physical products and modules. Processes could be production, but also product development or administrative processes such as documentation and system-support. Also the knowledge modules are premises e.g. for production or product development since they could give input on for example cost efficiency of the processes.

For the product development process modularization could give time and cost savings in addition to quality improvements since modules could be developed separately through testing, modules could be reused in subsequent development processes etc. One of the advantages of a holistic modularized product strategy is that modules could be "sub optimized" without risking reducing the performance of other modules or the product as a whole.

Fig. 3. Holistic approach to modularization

Modules and platforms are terms closely related and often mixed. One distinction is that while a module has a product- or function focus, platform are often more abstract, related to processes or basic principles. A platform could be basic geometry (e.g space between components), fixation, materials, common ways of dealing with interfaces and tolerance. In this way a platform have a longer life time than modules and could as is the case for the Marine Platform contain several modules.

3   The Marine Platform Project

Marine Platform is a 4-year R&D project co-financed by The Norwegian Research Council that started in 2012. The overall objective is to radically improve the product development process focusing on the critical and resource demanding phases related to the structural elements of the boat. The project aims to define the premises and solutions for a flexible structural platform.

The project has four Norwegian industrial partners, two SMEs producing for leisure boat markets, one large company producing for the professional market, and a SME supplier which is a key actor in the boatbuilding industry as it is the biggest and most important supplier of their products in the Scandinavian boatbuilding industry. The supplier is within the mechanical engineering industry, but still has many of the same characteristics of craft manufacturing as the other partners.

SINTEF is project coordinator and two other research partners are also contributing to the action research, namely The University of Agder and Inventas.

4   Different Paths towards a Flexible Structural Platform

4.1   Criteria for Structural Platforms

Flexibility and modularization enabling rapid product development can be achieved by using the different perspectives on modularization in different areas. In the Marine Platform project business cases have been defined for each industrial. This provides the objective for the research carried out and thus results in a higher technology readiness level [12]. The business cases are strongly revolving around how to make the development process for new models more efficient and more cost-effective in addition to catering for the ability to customize the products and thereby competitively fulfilling customer requirements. This requires a study of success factors, enablers, capabilities, the possible configurations and the possible critical issues [14].

As the knowledge aspect is crucial for modularization, an important criteria for modularity is that performance, data collection and knowledge could be linked to modules or be property-modules themselves in the product architecture.

Investigating and developing a structural platform that can act as a basis for several different models is well known in other industries like the automotive sector. However, with regard to boat manufacturing where there are very high demands for customization and where the number of boats sold of one model is significantly lower than in other industries, the need for a flexible structural platform arises. Such a structural platform can both consist of the hull/inner-liner/support structure themselves and modules on the boat acting as structural components providing stability and strength.

In the following, the project's focus-areas for establishing a flexible structural platform for boats are presented. Specifically, this paper addresses the following areas; standardization and outsourcing, material technology and adaptive process moulding.

4.2   Standardization and Outsourcing as Basis for a Structural Platform

Identifying structural properties for interiors, furniture, doors, windows, bulkheads are just some examples that to a large degree will have to be carried out in cooperation with suppliers and where one can achieve simplification through standardization and uniform quality requirements. By establishing concise structural properties and requirements for different modules and components in a boat, it will be easier to create requirement specifications to suppliers. The establishment will also make it easier and more efficient to identify suppliers and products that adhere to the sought-after product properties. Standardization also addresses strength requirements which in turn more clearly defines the single components and modules and thereby simplifies the work on the overall structure in boats. The main advantages with standardization are that a company achieve a holistic approach and have more available data with regards to a boat's structure. The greatest challenge is the amount of work needed in order to standardize, especially in craft manufacturing where there are many unique and one-of-a-kind solutions developed for single products.

Standardization also must capture customer needs of today and tomorrow in defined (and not defined) market segments. The Concurrent Innovation Process has been developed for involving customers and document needs and requirements. One of the boat producers used this methodology as basis for developing modularized concepts for a new range of boats for the professional markets and proved that common platform based on standardized solutions was a viable approach.

The project addresses standards and common solutions for interfaces, material solutions etc. This enables a higher degree of flexibility in supply chains and outsourcing, but will require extensive documentation and a general acceptance of standards.

4.3   Material Technology as Basis for a Structural Platform

By focusing on material properties, new material-solutions that provide strength and structural properties are within reach. Also, materials as enablers for modularization are equally important. Different materials with different kinds of properties can have different structural functions that may be utilized in order to ensure flexibility and structure. Examples are self-supported hulls, use of innerliners or grids.

New laminates and new or adapted materials provide greater possibilities to avoid the cost-driver of special reinforcement like ribs and/or innerliners. Also, a fact-based approach to the use of materials is needed in order to avoid over-dimensioning and excessive use of materials, resulting in higher material costs and e.g. heavier products (resulting in e.g. higher energy consumption). However, it should be noted that e.g. leisure boats are built based on strict international standards where the designers are restricted in choosing e.g. material thicknesses. One of the project's aims is to contribute towards new standard developments. The project has carried out several tests on new materials showing the possibilities that may be possible. One of the first business cases has been to develop, simulate and build a new modular boat using aluminum. The main objective of this endeavor was to take a new modular approach to the use of a fairly known material in the boating industry. Marine Platform also has a focus on laminate composites. Being able to describe and understand the relationship between the structure and composition of a material, its processing parameters and its properties is an important knowledge module for flexible and effective product developments of boats.

However, material testing and documentation is resource demanding and Marine Platform is now investigating methods for "multi-testing". Through a combination of lab-tests, reuse and simulation the aim is to be able to test and document a larger amount of different material properties from one panel.

4.4   Adaptive Moulds as Basis for a Structural Platform

Usually a new boat-model is developed on the drawing board and a prototype is made. The prototype is usually made as a mock-up and will later form the basis for cutting e.g. the hull on order to make a mould. However, the mould is very inflexible as you can only produce the specific hull. The ultimate objective of the project is to explore and develop adaptive moulds that fulfill the requirements for design, structure and strength. In theory this indicates that it should be possible to develop adaptive moulds that can facilitate an unlimited number of boat-designs by splitting the boat-design into modules. The project aims to develop and prove that adaptive moulds for smaller ranges of boats are possible and the work so far seems to confirm this. As the advances are still on a theoretical level there is still work to do in the business case connected to high-speed boats.

Several advances seem promising and fitting as starters for adaptive moulding. Using additive manufacturing is one such approach [13]. Here it is possible to create prototypes without cutting moulds. However, the sizes available for additive manufacturing will pose some challenges and one need to address interface-issues between modules made in order to create a structure that might be used as template for build 1 of the boat. In effect, the project has found that additive manufacturing is usable for prototyping and production of smaller hull-parts and modules.

A promising approach is flatbeds. Here one has a set of moulds that ensures that the basic requirements for a boat are addressed. The greatest advantages will be that it will no longer be necessary to cut moulds, thus removing a very costly and time-consuming process. It will also provide the possibility to merge modules that can create new models much more rapidly than before. "Flat bed methodologies" are showing great prospects, however there is still a long way to achieve what the project are aiming for; the flexible adaptive structural platform.

5   Conclusion

The flexibility and the cost effective aspects enabled by modularity could be an important driver for cost effective product development. In Marine Platform the focus is on the structural platform of the boats and the project has identified several paths for this. These paths' could be based on modularity in products/services, processes, and increasingly important, knowledge. In Marine Platform we have shown how standardization and outsourcing could represent a cost effective way to distribute development cost. Focus on material technology could give us a set of solutions representing modules in a structural platform for boats. Moulds from modules could also be a basis for modularity.

In Marine Platform all of these focus areas for modularity are combined and investigated. However, the basic element is modularized knowledge. Documentation and knowledge is fundamental for standards, for material solutions and how to design/assemble mould elements (modules). It is the knowledge modules that are the main enabler for fast creating the structural elements of the boats. The knowledge modules are also much more proprietary than the physical modules, hence more difficult to copy by competitors.

References

1. Duray, R.: Mass Customizers use of inventory, planning techniques and channel management. Production Planning & Control 15(4), 412–421 (2004)
2. Ericsson, A., Erixon, G.: Controlling Design Variants: Modular Product Platforms. ASME Press, NY (1999)
3. Stone, R.B.: A heuristic method for identifying modules for product architectures. A heuristic method for identifying modules for product architectures. Design Studies 21, 5–31 (2000)
4. Sanchez, R.: Using modularity to manage the interactions of technical and industrial design. Design Management Journal 2, 8 (2002)
5. Henriksen, B., Røstad, C.C.: Attacking the Critical Parts in Product Development. In: Prabhu, V., Taisch, M., Kiritsis, D. (eds.) APMS 2013, Part I. IFIP AICT, vol. 414, pp. 94–102. Springer, Heidelberg (2013)
6. Ericsson, A., Erixon, G.: Controlling Design Variants: Modular Product Platforms. ASME Press, NY (1999)
7. Dahmus, J.B., Gonzales-Zugasti, J.P., Otto, K.N.: Modular product architecture. Design Studies 22(5), 409–425 (2001)
8. Jo, H.H., Parsaei, H.R., Sullivan, W.G.: Principles of concurrent engineering. In: Chapman and Hall, Concurrent Engineering: Contemporary Issues and Modern Design Tools, New York, pp. 3–23 (1993)
9. Sanchez, R., Mahoney, J.T.: Modularity, Flexibility, and Knowledge Management in Product and Organization Design. In: IEEE Engineering Management Review. Reprint from Strategic Management, vol. 17, John Wiley & Sons Limited (1996) (special issue December)
10. Sanchez, R., Mahoney, J.T.: Modularity, Flexibility, and Knowledge Management in Product and Organization Design. In: IEEE Engineering Management Review. Reprint from Strategic Management, vol. 17. John Wiley & Sons Limited (1996) (special issue December)
11. Miller, T.D., Elgård, P.: Design for Integration in Manufacturing. In: Proceedings of the 13th IPS Research Seminar, Fuglsoe, Aalborg University (1998) ISBN 87-89867-60-2
12. Mankins, J.C.: Technology Readiness Levels. White paper, NASA Office of Space Access and Technology (1995),
    http://www.hq.nasa.gov/office/codeq/trl/trl.pdf
13. Dormal, T., Dam, J.L., Baraldi, U.: A new technology for the manufacturing of large prototype injection moulds: LLCC (Laminated Laser Cut Cavities). In: Proc. 7th Eur. Conf. on Rapid Prototyping and Manufacturing, pp. 327–336 (1998)
14. Corti, D., Taisch, M., Pourabdollahian, G., Bettoni, A., Pedrazzoli, P., Canetta, L.: Proposal of a Reference Framework to integrate Sustainability and Mass Customization in a Production Paradigm. In: 2011 World Conference on Mass Customization, Personalization and Co-Creation: Bridging Mass Customization & Open Innovation (MCPC2011), San Francisco, USA, pp. 1–10 (2011)

Flow Disturbance Analysis in Workshops with High Reworks Rate

Mélanie Noyel[1,2,3], Philippe Thomas[1,2], André Thomas[1,2], Patrick Charpentier[1,2], and Thomas Brault[3]

[1] Université de Lorraine, CRAN, UMR 7039, Campus Sciences,
BP 70239, 54506 Vandœuvre-lès-Nancy cedex, France
[2]CNRS, CRAN, UMR7039, France
[3]Acta-Mobilier, parc d'activité Macherin Auxerre Nord 89270 MONETEAU
{mnoyel,tbrault}@acta-mobilier.fr,
{philippe.thomas,andre.thomas,
patrick.charpentier}@univ-lorraine.fr

Abstract. Companies with high reworks rate have a real problem of flow management. Despite methods in place leading to minimize the number of reworks, they often must implement palliative solutions to manage disturbed flows. We propose in this paper a diagnostic approach based on reworks and flow disturbance indicators to enable them to view the disturbing status of their workshop. This work is a part of a more global work which aim is to develop a flow management control system based on product driven control concept and real-time indicators chosen from those presented in this paper.

Keywords: reworks, flow disturbance, indicator, simulation.

1 Introduction

Some companies present an unavoidable high reworks rate as shown with the lot of works pursued to include reworks in methods such as Economic Production Quantity (EPQ) optimization [2], production run time optimization [3] or replenishment policy [4]. Even if there are a lot of methods trying to decrease reworks rate, companies have to dealing with. Quality remains a priority number one, especially when there is an increased of customer demands in a context of difficult mastery of manufacturing process (unstable over time as example). The flow disturbances due to reworks have been analyzed since a long time by many authors [6]. But this problem was often studied only on simple or particular cases [8, 11]. Moreover, indicators for analyzing tested situations are often arbitrarily chosen without taking into account the different points of view. However in our meaning, simulation can help to understand each point of view of each indicator token into account. The master objective of this work is to bring to this type of companies a decision support based on several indicators to enable them to better understand the impact of their reworks rate on the complexity of their physical flows on the shop floor. That leads them to be able to anticipate the impact of quality drifts on flow control problems and to react quickly and well to decrease it thanks to cartography of the

B. Grabot et al. (Eds.): APMS 2014, Part III, IFIP AICT 440, pp. 280–287, 2014.

real-time state of their workshop. After presenting in more detail the purpose of this paper, possible indicators and their characteristics to handle reworks rate and flow disturbance are listed. Then, the simulation model and the selected test scenarios to compare their behavior rate are explained.

2   Background and Issues

The most relevant approaches to understand and control Quality [7] is based on manufacturing approach. It combines conformance to customer requirements and the "right the first time" concept to reduce costs and ensure quality. Non-quality products can be the result of a higher than usual customer requirement, which may occur during the conquest of new markets (export ...). In this case, processes are well mastered but a higher quality level is required to reach new customer requirements. Nevertheless, non-quality may also result from unstable manufacturing process or process drift. Many companies working for the luxury market face with this problem because quality requirements lead to be close to technological limitations of the manufacturing process. Because products are expensive, only two reactions are possible to fix the non-quality product detected at the xth workstation on the existing X workstations:

- Case 1 (Repair) : Sending it to a dedicated workstation W_{spe} leading to:
  - Two new flows created: $W_x \rightarrow W_{spe}$ et $W_{spe} \rightarrow W_{x+1}$
  - Maximum number of additional flows: $M_{apf} = 2 . N_{spe} . X$
    with N_{spe} the number of workstations dedicated to repairs
- Case 2 (Rework): Sending it to a previous workstation W_{x-y} leading to:
  - Only one new flow created: $W_x \rightarrow W_{x-y}$
  - Maximum number of additional flows: $M_{afp} = \sum_{i=2}^{X}(i-1) = \frac{X}{2}(X-1)$.

In practice, both cases have sometimes to be considered at the same time but this paper focus on case 2. We call reworks all products repaired by sending it to a previous workstation. If reworks rate is fluctuating, arising disturbances will also be fluctuant and unpredictable, which complicates production control. It is recognized that reworks affect the performance of system productivity [5]. COQ (Cost of Quality) method is appeared in the 50s thanks to the concept of the ghost factory which is a workshop parallel to the official workshop with the mission is to repair the defects of the official factory [6]. It represents 40% of the production capacity of the official factory. The first standard on the subject appears in France in 1986 (X 50-126) to evaluate the costs of non-quality [1]. A statistical analysis relative to one workstation problem points out the oscillatory phenomenon [11] that is also mentioned in other works where the aim is to evaluate performance on a workshop with multiproduct type [12]. The production flow disturbance by reworks is especially important if reworks emerged downstream in the production process [8]. So, for the production control, we have to follow and maintain a low reworks level to be sure to simplify the initial piloting problem [9]. However, even reducing and stabilizing the reworks rate, the resultant disturbance on the flow remains consistent and makes scheduling difficult.To evaluate the reworks rate in a company, an indicator that counts the number of defects is often used. Nevertheless, when reworks rate is growing, the probability to repair several times the same product is growing, too. So how to count these products becomes a critical issue and it is difficult to make a direct link between reworks rate and flow disturbance. As previously said, this paper is a part of a global work which aim is to analyze, compare and identify relevant indicators to measure the reworks impact on workflow disturbance. These indicators are presented in part 3.

3   Indicators Determination

3.1   Selection of Possible Indicators

Two kinds of indicators allow to measure reworks rate and product flow disturbance. For reworks, there are global (at the company scale) and local (related to the most stringent workstation, generally the bottleneck) indicators defined bellow:

- N_{config} is the number of reconfigured rooting sheets relative to normal ones. It is independent of the number of disturbed products if we don't work in unit lot size.
- N_{defect} is the number of products which have had at least one defect relative to expected products to make. It takes into account the exact number of disturbed products. There is no consideration of products repaired more than once time. There is a weakness due to the fact that some defects may not cause disturbance of the sequence of the manufacturing program but just a longer production time. In the case of a model with lot size unit, $N_{defect} = N_{config}$ because the number of lines reconfigured is directly equal to the number of products on which we have detected at least one defect. Effectively, detection of a defect involves repetition of one or more operations. Whatever the situation: $N_{defect} \leq P$.
- N_{work} is the number of products actually processed on the workstation relative to expected products to make. It is very simple to measure but we have to note that it cannot differentiate if added operations have been made on several products or on the same product. Moreover, N_{work} is always exceeding 100%.
- RO_{SD} and/or RO_{AV} is the Operation Ratio that corresponds to the number of real operations compared to what was expected in the routing sheet. As RO is relative to a specific product/lot, it is recommended to take into account the average/mean (AV) and/or standard deviation (SD). RO represents both the rooting sheet disturbance and the level of this disturbance. If any defect exists for one product, its RO is equal to one. It is more difficult to measure than previous indicators.

Similarly, there are possible indicators to measure the workflow disturbance:

- N_{WIP} is the work in process (average or max). It is important to note that a well distributed work in process is not necessarily penalizing, even if it is heavy. Note that it is not useful on one workstation because it will be equal to N_{stock}.
- N_{stock} is the stock level upstream an important workstation (average or max).
- C_{max} is the time to complete all the production. Commonly used in scheduling problems, it is equivalent to the end production date of the last product. Two schedules can give the same C_{max} but with a very different customer service rate.

- T_w is the waiting time.
- R_{max} is the maximum delay. Depending on the case, be an hour late is sometimes equivalent to be a week late, and sometimes, late penalties are too heavy.
- N_{late} is the number of late products.
- T_{break} is the out of supply time on the bottleneck workstation. It can be measured only on models with several workstations.

3.2   Model Presentation

The Petri net presented on Fig. 1 has been implemented in ARENA to analyze the impact of an increase of each reworks indicator on a manufacturing process. Despite the apparent simplicity of this model, model reduction often leads to summarize the problem with a one- or two-workstations model [10]. The two machines have the same production rates. There are others similar works in literature that performs a scheduling on a two-machine problem [7]. The lot size is unitary and each product is directly transferred to the next workstation, not involving additional time correspond- ing to the pending end of batch before transfer. It avoids the problem of splitting lots to remake only a part of product [11].

Fig. 1. Petri net representing our problem and implemented in ARENA

- P1: Wait in queue before workstation 1
- P2: Process on workstation 1
- P3: Wait in queue before workstation 2
- P4: Process on workstation 2
- P5: Finished state

- T1: Workstation 1 available
- T2: Operation end on workstation 1
- T3: Workstation 2 available
- T4: Operation end on workstation 2

Usually, different scenarios are established to test several types of workshops. In our simple case of one or two workstations, combinations are limited. Being able to apply several different piloting rules will allow to test different scenarios without having to complicate the workshop. Priority rules most commonly used are FIFO (First In First Out), EDD (Earliest Due Date) or the critical ratio. EDD is chosen in order to allow permutations between reworks and normal products in queues. The due date required for the implementation of the priority rule EDD was determined for each product to represent a "normal" situation with low reworks rate leading to no delay. Probability of reworks occurrence are explained on (Fig. 2) with the following particularity:

$$\begin{cases} T_{reworks}(M1 \rightarrow M1) = T_{reworks}(M2 \rightarrow M1) + T_{reworks}(M2 \rightarrow M2) \\ \quad T_{reworks}(M2 \rightarrow M1) = T_{reworks}(M2 \rightarrow M2) \end{cases}$$

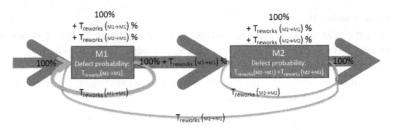

Fig. 2. Probability of reworks occurrence

To have different vision of reworks with unitary lots, only N_{defect}, N_{work}, RO_{AV} and RO_{SD} are tested. If there is no variability in the model, our indicators are dependents and it is possible to express them with a mathematical formula. But, in reality, variability involves disturbances (ex. Forester Effect). This variability is included in the model by using normal distribution for the product arriving in the first queue, the processing time on workstations and the probability of defect occurrences.

4   Analysis and Results

4.1   Analysis of Reworks Indicators

Two scenarios are tested: one and two workstations. All graphs are relatives to the reworks rate R_R applied on workstation(s). N_P products are send through the model.

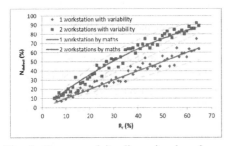

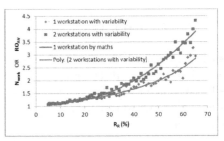

Fig. 3. N_{defect} and its dispersion based on reworks rate for 1 and 2 workstations

Fig. 4. N_{work} on both workstation based on reworks rate for 1 and 2 workstations

By mathematical definition, $N_{defect}(1W) = R_R$ and $N_{defect}(2W) = R_R \times (2 - R_R)$ (Fig. 3). The dispersion observed with model variability seems to be different between one (only increasing) and two workstations (increase then decrease). This indicator offer a view of the capacity to make product right the first time.

By definition, $N_{work}(1W) = \sum_{x=0}^{\infty} R_R{}^x = 1 + \frac{R_R}{1-R_R}$. Dispersion is also due to variability in the model. With two workstations, the formula is already difficult to determine but the same dispersion exist, too. With one workstation as with two workstations, RO_{AV} is directly equal to N_{work} (Fig. 5). These indicators offer a view of the volume of load on the workshop. As the number of operations increase in a non-linear mode with the reworks rate, it is important to work to decrease the reworks rate.

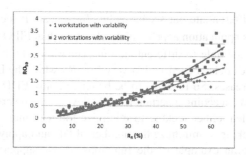

Fig. 5. RO_{SD} based on reworks rate for 1 and 2 workstations

RO_{SD} offers a view on the predictability on the respect of deadlines. Higher the reworks rate is, more difficult is to predict the number of necessary operations and so the product completion time.

There are many ways for representing the reworks on the workshop. The most appropriate choice to use the indicator may depend on the type of workshop but also the desired view. A combination of several of them can also give a more comprehensive understanding from different perspectives (capacity to make product right the first time, volume of charge on the workshop and predictability on the deadlines respect).

4.2   Analysis of Workflow Disturbance Indicators

The same model is used with two workstations but with two other scenarios: EDD and FIFO. The stock upstream the bottleneck machine 1 N_{stock} (Fig. 6) seems to be a good indicator of the disturbance flow as well as work in process N_{WIP} (Fig. 7). However, these two indicators are not able to differentiate EDD from FIFO. The similarity between these two indicators is also explained by the one machine model where N_{stock} is equivalent to N_{WIP}. Theoretically, R_R increasing tend to get some kind of

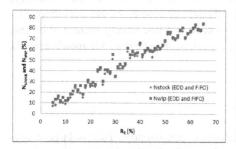

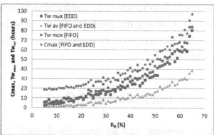

Fig. 6. N_{stock} and N_{WIP} based on reworks rate for 2 workstations

Fig. 7. C_{max} and T_W based on reworks rate for 2 workstations

system saturation. In practice, this still represents more pieces to handle, store, manage simultaneously, which negatively influence all production indicators. C_{max} indicator, commonly used in scheduling, has the same behavior that T_W. C_{max} and $T_{W_{av}}$

are also unable to differentiate our scenarios but $T_{W_{max}}$ can. It seems that, in relation to $T_{W_{max}}$, EDD rules application appears more effective than FIFO rules.

N_{late} and R_{max} are able to differentiate our scenarios (Fig. 8 and 9). The FIFO priority rule generates delays even with a very low R_R while the EDD rule generates delays when R_R increases. So it seems to be better to apply EDD at low reworks levels. However, when exceeding a certain reworks level to be determined according to the workshop modeled, either seeking to minimize the maximum delay and keeping the EDD rule, or seeking to minimize the number of late and applying the FIFO. This rule change may be an example of the functions of our support system workflow management. These two indicators seem particularly useful for controlling the system by the rules.

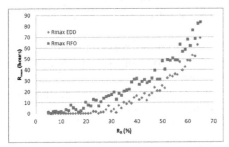
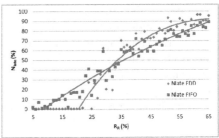

Fig. 8. R_{max} based on reworks rate for 2 workstations

Fig. 9. N_{late} based on reworks rate for 2 workstations

Flow disturbance is also a concept difficult to represent because it exists a lot of point of view. Depending on management objectives, some indicators alone are not appropriate. For example, it is impossible to differentiate the EDD and FIFO rules if we consider only N_{WIP}, N_{stock}, C_{max} or T_W. The best solution seems to be a combination of indicators. The latter figure shows that the same rule for controlling the workshop is not necessarily effective in all cases of running of the workshop. This therefore shows the usefulness of our support system. Flow management will be able to offer the user the best rule to use based on selected indicators for monitoring the workshop.

5   Conclusion and Outlook

Flows repairs due to reworks disturb production consistently. This is largely confirmed by the literature but rarely studied in depth. To develop a system for assisting the production piloting for companies with high reworks rates, we propose a thorough study on reworks and flow disturbance indicators. There are several ways to control reworks for companies. We must be aware of the different possible points of view and their advantages and drawbacks. In this paper we propose a new indicator, the Operation Ratio that has the advantage of combining the manufacturing program disturbance with the level of disturbance and appears correctly reflect the reworks rate in the workshop. Flow disturbance is also a difficult concept to measure. The usual indicators offer only a single view of the flow disturbance. If we want to have a global view, we need to work on a combination of these different indicators. As perspectives, we have to validate our analysis on a real scale industrial case, which will bring our work to a realistic level. We hope to develop a behavioral mapping of the workshop in order to locate it in real time and make the right decisions on the piloting rules.

References

1. Abouzahir, O., Gautier, R., Gidel, T.: Pilotage de l'amélioration des process par les coûts de non-qualité. In: $10^{\text{ième}}$ Séminaire CONFERE, Belfort, France, Juillet 3-4 (2003)
2. Chiu, S.W., Gong, D.C., Wee, H.M.: Effects of random defective rate and imperfect rework process on economic production quantity model. Japan Journal of Industrial and Applied Mathematics 21(3), 375–389 (2004)
3. Chiu, S.W.: Production run time problem with machine breakdowns under AR control policy and rework. Journal of Scientific and Industrial Research 66(12), 979 (2007)
4. Chiu, S.W., Chen, K.K., Yang, J.C.: Optimal replenishment policy for manufacturing systems with failure in rework, backlogging and random breakdown. Mathematical and Computer Modelling of Dynamical Systems 15(3), 255–274 (2009)
5. Colledani, M., Tolio, T.: Impact of quality control on production system performance. CIRP Annals-Manufacturing-Technology 55(1), 453–456 (2006)
6. Feigenbaum, A.V.: Quality control: Principles, practice and administration: An industrial management tool for improving product quality and design and for reducing operating costs and losses. McGraw-Hill, New York (1951)
7. Garvin, D.: What does product quality really mean. Sloan Management Review 26(1), 25–48 (1984)
8. Love, P.E.D., Li, H., Mandal, P.: Rework: a symptom of a dysfunctional supply chain. European Journal of Purchasing & Supply Management 5(1), 1–11 (1999)
9. Noyel, M., Thomas, P., Charpentier, P., Thomas, A., Brault, T.: Implantation of an on-line quality process monitoring. In: 5th International Conference on Industrial Engineering and Systems Management, IESM 2013, Rabat, Maroc, Octobre 28-30 (2013)
10. Rabiee, M., Zandies, M., Jafarian, A.: Scheduling a no-wait two-machine flow shop with sequence-dependent setup times and probable rework using robust meta-heuristics. International Journal of Production Research 50(24), 7428–7446 (2012)
11. Skidmann, A., Nof, S.Y.: Unitary manufacturing cell design with random product feedback flow. IIE Transactions 17(2), 188–193 (1985)
12. Skidmann, A., Schweitzer, P., Nof, S.Y.: Performance evaluation of a flexible manufacturing cell with random multiproduct feedback flow. International Journal of Production Research 23(6), 1171–1184 (1985)
13. Thomas, A., Charpentier, P.: Reducing simulation models for scheduling manufacturing facilities. European Journal of Operational Research 161(1), 111–125 (2005)
14. Zargar, A.M.: Effect of rework strategies on cycle time. Computers & Industrial Engineering 29(1), 239–243 (1995)

A Strategic Approach for Automation Technology Initiatives Selection

Maria Kollberg Thomassen[1], Børge Sjøbakk[1], and Erlend Alfnes[2]

[1] SINTEF Technology and Society, Industrial Management,
P.O. Box 4760 Sluppen, N-7465 Trondheim, Norway
{maria.thomassen,borge.sjobakk}@sintef.no
[2] Department of Production and Quality Engineering,
Norwegian University of Science and Technology, NTNU
erlend.alfnes@ntnu.no

Abstract. Despite the rapid development of new manufacturing technologies, a large portion of adoptions fail to achieve expected benefits. Existing models for technology selection are criticized for requiring large computations, and for being time consuming and difficult to use. This paper presents a strategic approach to support decision-makers in automation technology selection that is efficient and easy to apply in practice. It involves technology strategy decisions, process and technology analyses, technology/process ranking and considerations on investment and implementation. The approach has been developed through literature reviews and close collaboration with two case companies, utilizing the action research method. Its use is illustrated in an ongoing automation project at a world leading supplier of plastic pipes systems.

Keywords: Operations strategy, automation, process technology, strategic approach, technology selection, high variety production.

1   Introduction

Despite rapid developments of new manufacturing technologies, a large percentage of technology adoptions fail to achieve expected benefits [1, 2]. The risk of unsuccessful investments in advanced production equipment is high. Often, companies have insufficient foundation for investments decision-making [2]. Consequently, many companies tend to make large investments in equipment that give only limited payoff [3], often resulting in too much capacity, excess functionality and equipment that does not fulfill its potential [4]. A rapid increase in the number of available technologies and technology complexity has implied more challenging decision-making [5, 6]. Literature proposes numerous approaches to technology selection [7-9]. However, existing models are criticized for requiring large computations and for being time consuming and difficult to use due to their high level of sophistication [10, 11].

The purpose of this research is to develop an approach to support decision-makers in automation technology selection. The approach is self-explanatory, simple to apply and permits rapid prioritization of automation initiatives. The study expects to

B. Grabot et al. (Eds.): APMS 2014, Part III, IFIP AICT 440, pp. 288–295, 2014.

contribute to improved practices of how companies can arrive at better quality automation decisions by adopting a systematic approach.

The approach was developed using action research, including literature investigations and discussions with representatives of two case companies; a supplier of high-tech ship equipment and a plastic pipe system supplier. The companies provided detailed insights into their experiences from historical and ongoing automation processes, as well as their needs of how current practices should be improved.

The rest of the paper is structured as follows. A theoretical background is given, followed by a presentation of the suggested approach. An illustrative example of how the approach can be used is also included. After this, conclusions are presented.

2   Theoretical Background

Most of the traditional literature on automation, with focus on high-volume, low-variety production, claims that automation is highly suitable for standardized processes and products in high volumes [12]. Processes characterized by specific product features or high level of customization have traditionally been challenging to automate [14]. However, more flexible technologies have emerged in recent years that permit more efficient automation also of non-standard processes [15]. Decreased technology prices in combination with increased labor costs enable automation in areas that have not earlier been viable [13]. Consequently, the interest for automation is growing also among companies characterized by high variation and typically manual based labor. With this development, automation decisions become even more challenging.

A relatively large body of literature addresses technology selection and justification issues in manufacturing companies. There is especially a wide range of approaches for technology selection [7] and justification of new technology investments [8]. Basically, technology selection methodologies focus on how to select the best technology for a specific process whereas investment appraisal techniques provide support for analysing investment justification problems of specific equipment.

There is a large variation in process focus among existing approaches, meaning that they are developed for different purposes and settings. For example, Torkkeli and Tuominen [6] propose a process for integrating technology selection to a part of core competence management in large manufacturing companies, whereas the technology selection framework of Farooq and O'Brien [16] aims to ensure alignment of technology decisions to supply chain objectives. Moreover, most approaches are based upon specific methods that imply detailed and time-consuming analyses and calculations for a defined technology or process [e.g. 17, 18, 19]. Only a few approaches have been identified that address applicability or usability aspects and provide guidance on usage of approaches [20, 21]. Social and environmental aspects are rarely considered in current approaches.

A synthesis of the main phases of different technology decision-making approaches and typical areas of analysis in a selection of literature is presented in Table 1.

Table 1. Main phases and typical areas of analysis identified in literature

Main phase	Typical areas of analysis	Refs.
Strategic	Market characteristics, evolution and trends Manufacturing vision and strategy Core competencies definition Business objectives, opportunities and competitive priorities Strategic planning incl. technology strategy, mission and purpose	[1, 6, 9, 16, 18, 22]
Operations	Resources and competences Operational goals and requirements Product characteristics	[9, 18, 22, 23]
Technology	Technology alternatives identification Technology characteristics and performance Technology impact assessment incl. risk	[6, 9, 16, 18, 19, 22-24]
Investment	Technical, manufacturing and financial criteria definition Economic/financial, strategic and analytical justification	[9, 17, 18]
Implementation	Deployment and protection of core competencies Training and installation Technical knowledge	[6, 9, 18]

3   The Suggested Technology Selection Approach

The suggested technology selection approach is described in this section. It has been developed based on the literature and input from the two case companies. The companies seek increased efficiency in order to retain their production in Norway. Their high labor costs make automation the most efficient means of competitiveness. The companies are already highly automated; however, automation is applied in a rather "traditional" manner and includes mainly standard processes and simple products.

The approach aims to support prioritization of automation initiatives so that a few projects can be selected for more detailed analysis and evaluation for acquisition and implementation. Even though the process is structured in five steps, it is assumed that the process is highly iterative in practice and recurrence is a natural part of the process, and that findings in subsequent steps may lead to reassessment of previous ones.

The first step deals with *technology strategy* decisions. A key question is how manufacturing can support the business strategy in terms of various performance metrics. Corporate responsibility and environmental policies should be used to shape main principles for responsible manufacturing in terms of workplace health, safety practices and environmental stewardship. Industry trends and company technology capabilities are used to decide whether the company should be an 'innovator' or a 'follower' and whether technologies are to be developed in-house or purchased.

In step 2, *process analysis*, the overall manufacturing system should be understood in terms of: (1) its performance requirements in terms of volumes, batch sizes, capacity and utilization, for instance; (2) main products and their processing requirements, with regard to geometry and material specifications; (3) the processing activities performed by the manufacturing system. Thereafter, process candidates can be identified by calculating current and future processing times in machine hours and man hours for each process, selecting labor intensive candidates for automaton and adding candidates based on requirements for performance and responsible manufacturing.

Technology alternatives are analyzed in step 3. For each process candidate, potential technologies should be identified. For each technology, its maturity should be assessed together with the level of adaptation required to perform the process using the technology. Each technology should also be evaluated in terms of what performance it implies for the process. Selected technologies should be suitable for each process and be evaluated based upon short-term and long-term considerations.

Step 4 involves the *ranking of process/technology* combinations where process/technology candidates are assessed in terms of strategic importance and ease of implementation. Priority should be given to initiatives with a strong strategic impact that are also easy to implement.

Investment and implementation aspects are considered in step 5, where the economic viability is tested for the prioritized candidates, usually through development of business cases. Specific analyses to be carried out typically vary with the information requested by the company's board of directors. For viable projects, implementation plans with defined milestones and responsibilities should be developed. The main elements of the suggested approach are summarized in Table 2.

Table 2. The suggested approach

Step	*Input*	*Assessments and Decisions*	*Output*
Technology strategy	Business strategy CSR strategy Technology trends Competences	Define manuf. competitive priorities and responsibility objectives Define innovation position for main technologies	Technology strategy Areas of interest for automation
Process analysis	Manuf. performance and responsibility requirements Product processing requirements Bill of manuf. processes	Map processes Select labour intensive processes Add candidates based on additional requirements	Manufacturing process candidates
Technology analysis	Literature and patents Conferences, fairs Expert knowledge Internal documents and workshops	Identify alternative technologies Assess technology maturity and performance Select technologies for each candidate process	Technology/process combinations
Technology/ process ranking	Accumulated input from step 1-3	Assess strategic importance Assess ease of implementation Select project candidates based on strategic impact and ease of implementation	Ranked technology projects
Inv. and implementation	Sales forecasts Acquisition costs Operating cost Supplier quotations	Analyse investments Assess suppliers Assess competence requirements Select projects and plan implementation	Time phased technology implementation plan

4   Application of the Approach

This chapter describes how the suggested approach for structuring and selection of potential automation initiatives is applied in one of the case companies. The company produces pipes for water, sewage, gas, cable protection and electrical installations. Its standard products come in a large number of variants depending on aspects related to for instance color, material and geometry including shape, circumference and length. Non-standard variants are made in-house in a separate department. Here, standard products from the inventory are customized by means of manual labor and low-level, semi-automated process technology.

Step 1: Technology strategy decisions. In order to compete against low-cost competitors and retain production in Norway, cost efficiency is a key competitive priority for the company. As such, any technology investments should contribute to reduced operating costs. Further, the company continuously works on improving its workplace health and safety practices, and there is high priority on eliminating straining, manual and repetitive tasks. Being a Norwegian subsidiary of one of the world's leading suppliers of plastic pipe systems, the company seeks to be an innovator. Since the company has limited capabilities to develop new technology in-house, they primarily seek to acquire new equipment from external suppliers.

Step 2: Process analysis. The manufacturing performance requirements are mapped next, including an assessment of the production data over the last four years in terms of number of parts produced, cycle time, share of man hours, service level, other delivery terms, and so on. This is used to identify main products (plastic pipes and components in a range of variants) and map their processing requirements. The main processes carried out to produce these products are identified, including plastic extrusion or injection molding for standard product variants, with subsequent forming, joining (e.g. welding) and assembly for customized products. Products are grouped based on similarities in processing and product characteristics. For each of these groups, aggregate processing times in machine-hours and man-hours are calculated, see Fig. 1.

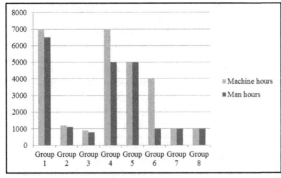

Fig. 1. Example of labor intensity mapping in the case company

This overview is used to select the most labor intensive candidates. Groups with high man-hours (1, 4 and 5) are selected as candidates. Group 6 is omitted because the process is already highly automated. Groups 2, 3, 7 and 8 are assessed based on additional requirements to evaluate whether they are potential candidates. However, these did not qualify for further enquiry.

Step 3: Technology analysis. For the selected groups, available technologies are identified based on internet searches and technical expertise, within the company and with external experts. These are characterized in terms of technological maturity, including working reliability, and level of adaptation required in order to implement the technology, and mapped in a framework. The left part of Fig. 2 shows an example where technologies for group 4 are mapped according to the two dimensions.

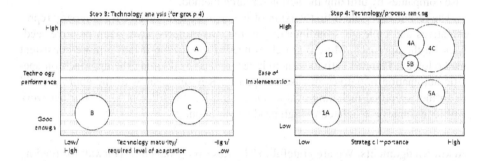

Fig. 2. Examples of technology analysis and technology/process ranking

Circles A, B and C represent three different pipe bending technologies. The size of each circle represents the total amount of products that the technology is able to process. Technology A is mature but can only handle 30 % of the total volume. Technology C is possible to use for 100 % of the volume; however, its cycle time is significantly lower. Technology B has low performance as well as low maturity, making it a less desirable candidate. Based on this mapping, technology A and C are selected for the next step. Similar mappings are carried out for groups 1 and 5.

Step 4: Technology/process ranking. Next, the selected candidates of alternative process/technology combinations are assessed in terms of ease of implementation and strategic importance. The right part of Fig. 2 above illustrates the positioning of different technologies for different product groups according to the two dimensions. The sizes of the circles indicate the share of products the technology is able to handle. By weighting the alternatives, final automation project priority came out as: 4C, 4A, 5B, 1D and 1A. Project 5A was discarded due to its lack of ease of implementation, although aspects of design for automation aspects were considered that might have helped to simplify implementation.

Step 5: Investment and implementation. The company is working on business cases showing the viability of the suggested automation projects. Being a part of an international group, it follows a corporate template for investment proposals. Several of the analyses proposed in the approach are carried out in order to fulfill the group management's requirements for investment proposals.

5   Conclusions

Automation technology constitutes a critical element for Norwegian manufacturing industry to increase productivity and stay competitive. Making sound automation decisions at the first attempt is crucial; however, existing models for selection of automation initiatives are not being used by industry due to their high complexity. In response, this paper presents a strategic approach for selecting automation technology projects that intends to be simple and efficient to use. The approach mainly addresses the early phases of the technology selection process, and contributes with improved understanding of how companies systematically can select appropriate automation initiatives. It has been developed based on literature and in collaboration with two case companies by utilizing the action research method.

The results represent a first version of the approach. Involved case company representatives and colleagues participating in the two projects have given positive feedback on the approach. More research is needed to develop it into a more consistent methodology. Planned activities include testing and developing the approach on specific automation initiatives in case companies. Key dimensions of the approach will be further specified including evaluation criteria for the different steps. Further work will focus on aspects related to high product variation.

Acknowledgements. We are grateful to The Research Council of Norway for funding this research. We would also like to express our appreciation to colleagues, especially Lars Erik Wetterwald, and case companies involved in the projects Effective Production of Advanced Maritime Equipment (EFFEKT) and Sustainable Multi-variant Manufacturing in Semi-process Industry (MIX), and the Center for Research-based Innovation Norwegian Manufacturing Future (SFI Norman), for their contribution.

References

1. Gouvea Da Costa, S.E., Platts, K.W., Fleury, A.: Strategic selection of advanced manufacturing technologies (AMT), based on the manufacturing vision. International Journal of Computer Applications in Technology 27, 12–23 (2006)
2. Small, M.H.: Planning, justifying and installing advanced manufacturing technology: a managerial framework. Journal of Manufacturing Technology Management 18, 513–537 (2007)
3. Chung, C.A.: Human issues influencing the successful implementation of advanced manufacturing technology. Journal of Eng. and Tech. Manag. 13, 283–299 (1996)
4. Mehrabi, M.G., Ulsoy, A.G., Koren, Y., Heytler, P.: Trends and perspectives in flexible and reconfigurable manufacturing systems. Journal of Intelligent Manufacturing 13, 135–146 (2002)
5. Morgan, L.O., Daniels, R.L.: Integrating product mix and technology adoption decisions: a portfolio approach for evaluating advanced technologies in the automobile industry. Journal of Operations Management 19, 219–238 (2001)
6. Torkkeli, M., Tuominen, M.: The contribution of technology selection to core competencies. International Journal of Production Economics 77, 271–284 (2002)

7. Farooq, S.: Manufacturing technology selection: a supply chain perspective. University of Nottingham (2007)
8. Raafat, F.: A comprehensive bibliography on justification of advanced manufacturing systems. Int. J. Prod. Econ. 79, 197–208 (2002)
9. Chan, F., Chan, M., Lau, H., Ip, R.: Investment appraisal techniques for advanced manufacturing technology (AMT): a literature review. Integrated Manufacturing Systems 12, 35–47 (2001)
10. Ordoobadi, S.M., Mulvaney, N.J.: Development of a justification tool for advanced manufacturing technologies: system-wide benefits value analysis. Journal of Engineering and Technology Management 18, 157–184 (2001)
11. Goyal, S., Grover, S.: Advanced manufacturing technology effectiveness: A review of literature and some issues. Front. Mech. Eng. 7, 256–267 (2012)
12. Sjøbakk, B., Thomassen, M.K., Alfnes, E.: Automation in the ETO Production Situation: The Case of a Norwegian Supplier of Ship Equipment. In: International Workshop of Advanced Manufacturing and Automation. Akademika Forlag (2013)
13. Wadhwa, R.S.: Flexibility in manufacturing automation: A living lab case study of Norwegian metalcasting SMEs. Journal of Manufacturing Systems (2012)
14. Frohm, J.: Levels of Automation in production systems. Chalmers University of Technology (2008)
15. Koren, Y., Shpitalni, M.: Design of reconfigurable manufacturing systems. Journal of Manufacturing Systems 29, 130–141 (2010)
16. Farooq, S., O'Brien, C.: An analytical approach to strategic technology selection. In: 19th International Conference on Production Research (2007)
17. Kengpol, A., O'Brien, C.: The development of a decision support tool for the selection of advanced technology to achieve rapid product development. International Journal of Production Economics 69, 177–191 (2001)
18. Efstathiades, A., Tassou, S., Antoniou, A.: Strategic planning, transfer and implementation of Advanced Manufacturing Technologies (AMT). Development of an integrated process plan. Technovation 22, 201–212 (2002)
19. Chan, F., Chan, M., Tang, N.: Evaluation methodologies for technology selection. Journal of Materials Processing Technology 107, 330–337 (2000)
20. Greitemann, J., Plehn, C., Koch, J., Reinhart, G.: Strategic Screening of Manufacturing Technologies. Enabling Manufacturing Competitiveness and Economic Sustainability, pp. 321–326. Springer (2014)
21. Phaal, R., Farrukh, C., Probert, D.: Technology management process assessment: a case study. International Journal of Operations & Production Management 21, 1116–1132 (2001)
22. Chuang, M., Yang, Y.S., Lin, C.T.: Production technology selection: Deploying market requirements, competitive and operational strategies, and manufacturing attributes. International Journal of Computer Integrated Manufacturing 22, 345–355 (2009)
23. Shehabuddeen, N., Probert, D., Phaal, R.: From theory to practice: challenges in operationalising a technology selection framework. Technovation 26, 324–335 (2006)
24. Punniyamoorthy, M., Ragavan, P.: A strategic decision model for the justification of technology selection. Int. J. of Adv. Manu. Techn. 21, 72–78 (2003)

Capability Maturity Model Integrated
for Ship Design and Construction

Serena Caracchi[1], Pavan Kumar Sriram[2], Marco Semini[2], and Jan Ola Strandhagen[2]

[1] Dept. of Engineering, University of Bergamo, Bergamo, Italy
serenac@stud.ntnu.no
[2] Dept. of Production and Quality Engineering,
Norwegian University of Science and Technology, Trondheim, Norway
{pavan.sriram,marco.semini}@ntnu.no,
JanOla.Strandhagen@sintef.no

Abstract. Project constraints are continuously growing in terms of time, cost, customer satisfaction, return on investment, quality. And also they are growing in terms of complexity, number of stakeholders, number of parameters to manage and number of interactions between these parameters. In this paper, we carry out literature study on capability maturity model integrated (CMMI) for Ship Design and Construction. The purpose is to understand, demonstrate and develop a structure for CMMI in Ship Design and Construction. Capability maturity models offer companies a simple but effective tool to organize, control and monitoring their processes. Emerged out of software engineering, the application fields have widened and maturity model research is becoming more important. So far, few limited studies exits on applicability of capability maturity models for Ship Design and Construction. The developed structure can be used as a structured matrix to assess the maturity levels of the company through measurable stages. In addition, the structured matrix can be used to assess and improve individual companies involved in the ship design and construction process, for example a yard and assess various value chain configurations, i.e., alternative configurations of actors to be performing a planned ship design and construction project.

Keywords: Ship Design and Construction, CMMI, maturity models, value chain configurations.

1 Introduction

Ship design and construction involves integrated activities, that includes tendering, contracting, concept and functional design, engineering, procurement, production, commissioning, delivery, and guarantee service (Andritsos and Perez-Prat 2000). In recent years, the ship design and construction community has become increasingly aware of the significance of the operational and managerial side of such activities, if they are to be effectively performed, coordinated and integrated (Semini et al., 2014). However, there is a lack of models and tools supporting the assessment, improvement and integration of these activities. Within project management in general, various

B. Grabot et al. (Eds.): APMS 2014, Part III, IFIP AICT 440, pp. 296–303, 2014.
© IFIP International Federation for Information Processing 2014

models for internal assessment and improvement of process quality/capability have been proposed. Among them, the capability maturity model (CMM) and its successor, capability maturity model integrated, (Chrissis et al., 2003) seem to be particularly suitable for more specific application in various sectors. Attempts have been made to adapt them to the industry characteristics within fashion (Battista and Schiraldi 2013), the automotive industry (Gonzalez et al., 2007), construction (Meng et al., 2011), and mechatronics and transportation (Pels and Simons 2008). To the authors' knowledge, no such studies have been performed for ship design and construction industry. This study seeks to fill the knowledge gap by developing a structure for a CMMI for ship design and construction. It aims to identify the activities the CMMI should evaluate (criteria), as well as the maturity levels in each of these activities. The main result of this paper is the CMMI matrix which could be used as a tool to assess and improve the capabilities of individual companies involved in the ship design and construction process, for example, a yard. It may also be in project-making in order to assess alternative configurations of actors to be performing a planned ship design and construction project. The concepts and results developed in the present research are mainly based on a literature review. International journals and conference proceedings, scientific textbooks, as well as white papers and relevant internet sources have been used in order to understand ship design and construction as well as to review existing research on maturity models.

2 Ship Design and Construction

Ships differ regarding the level of required customization, demand volumes and other characteristics (Semini et al., 2014). Ship design and construction is a complex process in which a lot of resources and areas of the company are involved, and requests a high level of coordination between parties. The project starts with the concept design, where customer requirements are translated into first set of documents with the principal characteristics of ships (area, volume, weight, speed). Then there's a deeper level, called basic and functional design, in which is created a specification book that collects technical details of the entire system and theirs economic feasibility. The contract design is built on a platform in which customer, yards, designers and engineers and constructions parties agree on specifications and costs about the entire project; the platform is continuously update.

Through engineering activities concept design is translated into drawings, sketches and concrete instructions to build the ship. In this step the ship project is integrated with the different systems and subsystems (electrical, control,..) and often the engineering is carried out concurrently with procurement and production. Planning and coordination is an essential activity to conclude the work on time. Essentially the building strategy is decided (how to build and with what), costs and time are estimated and the main schedule is anticipated. Finally the construction of the ship is carried out in the production and assembly stage, starting with the hull and finishing with the assembly of the various subsystems. After all the work in the dry dock is finished, the ship is launched on water. The procurement concerns the selection, the negotiation and the collaboration with suppliers. It's also a very important activity because it's necessary to complete it in little time, from the signed contract and the start of work. Then there's the commissioning, in which a long period test is carried and the ship is delivered to the buyer. The ship design and construction company agrees on maintenance and carries routine maintenance at an agreed time basis.

Above we introduced the main activities performed in ship design and construction. It did not distinguish between the ship designer and the ship builder (yard). In some cases, there are indeed fully integrated firms that carry out a large part of the project in-house and sometimes even own the finished product. Usually, however, the different activities are not performed by a single company, but a network of geographically dispersed parties with different roles and interactions. Even a single activity, such as engineering, can be split among several parties. The degree to which each party is involved in the various activities differs from project to project, and so does the level of integration and coordination between them. This is a characteristic of ship design and construction. Due to these differences, we find it useful to name the involved parties in terms of their predominant function. We concentrate on those with the most significant roles in actually carrying out the ship design and construction activities:

- The ship designer
- The shipyard
- Main equipment suppliers

3   CMMI: An Overview

3.1   Review of Existing Models

Maturity models generally arose at the beginning of the nineties when companies started to feel the need to assess the current state of their organizations in a structured way (Kohoutek 1996). Today, there are many different models, each oriented towards a specific domain (Table 1):

Table 1. Existing maturity models

Model	Domain	Developer and key reference
Capability Maturity Model Integration (CMMI)	Management	Carnegie Mellon University , Chrissis, Konrad et al. (2003)
Enterprise Architecture Maturity Model	IT Management	National Association of State CIO's (www.nascio.org/hotIs sues/EA/EAMM.pdf)
European Foundation for Quality Management (EFQM) Excellence Model	Business Management	EFQM , Wongrassamee, Simmons et al. (2003)
Process Maturity Model	Process Management	Rummler– Brache Group,(www.rummler-brache.com)
Project Management Maturity Model (PM3)	Project Management	Office of Government Commerce, UK (www.ogc.gov.uk/sdtoo lkit/reference/tools/PMMM_ release_v5.pdf)
Portfolio, Programme and Project Management Maturity Model (P3M3)	Project Management	AXELOS Limited (www.p3m3-officialsite.com/AboutP3M3/ AboutP3M3.aspx)
Organizational Project Management Maturity Model (OPM3)	Project Management	PMI , Farrokh and Mansur (2013)

Among the reviewed models CMMI appears to be particularly suitable for application to ship design and construction. First of all, CMMI reduces task uncertainty and helps manage complex interaction among actors, tasks and processes; this leads to a reduction in defects and rework. It supports process integration and the reuse of past knowledge, reducing time and costs. And another significant benefit is that it helps to integrate supply chains, contributing towards effective relationship management (Veldman and Klingenberg 2009). Quality schemes, such as ISO 9001:2000 and DNVs Manufacturer product quality assessment (MPQA) are outwards oriented, aiming to provide certifications towards customers and stakeholders (Bozarth and Edwards 1997). Maturity models, on the other hand, support internal assessment and improvement. They complement each other. ISO 9001:2000 has been associated with the third level in the CMMI structure (Yoo et al., 2006). Yoon et al. also proposed a method to implement both frameworks by initially implementing CMMI and adding further requirements for ISO 9001:2000. Further we define CMMI and discuss the maturity levels of CMMI in the following section.

3.2   Definitions of CMMI

Before defining a CMMI model is important to understand CMM model from which, CMMI is derived. The Capability Maturity Model is a framework representing a path of improvements recommended in order to reach a different stage of process capability (Paulk 1993). CMM integration (CMMI) is an extension of CMM model, composed by a collection of the best practices in the areas of product and service development, service establishment, management, delivery and product and service acquisition. There are two representation of CMMI: continuous and staged. The main difference between them is while the staged model rates the whole organization with one figure, a continuous model rates separately the performance of each of the processes that are assessed (Jokela et al. (2006), CMMI Product Team (2002)).

3.3   The Levels and Benefits of CMMI

In continuous representation CMMI has got six levels of maturity represented in figure 1 (CMMI Product Team (2002), Chrissis et al. (2003)):**Incomplete (Level 0):** In this level processes are not performed or partially not performed (every/some goals are not satisfied). **Performed (Level 1):** Process satisfies the specific goals of the process area but the procedures are not homogeneous. **Managed (Level 2):** Process is performed with a basic infrastructure in place to support itself. It is planned and executed in accordance with policy. People that work on it are skilled. Processes are also monitored, controlled and reviewed. **Defined (Level 3):** At this level processes are managed but also they follow precise guidelines about purposes, inputs, activities, roles, measures, criteria. **Quantitatively Managed (Level 4):** Defined processes are controlled using statistical and other quantitative techniques. With these is possible to handle quality and performances. **Optimizing (Level 5):** With a quantitatively managed process is possible to understand the different causes of variation in the process and improve it. For our matrix we ignore level 0.

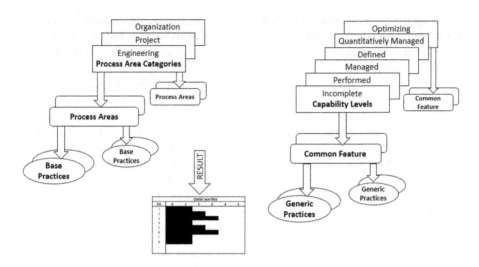

Fig. 1. CMMI model scheme

Benefits can vary during the different stages and for can be different for every company. But there are some general advantages that it is simple to lists. According to Goldenson and Gibson (2003) and Veldman and Klingenberg (2009), a CMMI maturity model can: increase customer satisfaction; reduce the costs of work products and the processes employed to produce; increase focus of quality with the reduction of defects over time; increase communication and coordination between actors; fit better the schedule of the project, improve the schedule predictability and reduce time required to do the work; improve productivity; reduce variability in lead times. Through the development of the structured matrix we aim to achieve similar benefits for ship design and construction.

4   Towards CMMI for Ship Design and Construction

The new model contains seven main criteria's. They are contract design, design and engineering, planning and coordination, production and assembly, procurement, logistics, and maintenance. However the main criteria's are not assess directly. Instead, each main criterion is broken down in three subcriteria. For example, the main criterion contract design is broken down into bidding, value chain configuration, negotiation and agreement. Both the main criteria's and subcriteria are developed on the basis of literature review (Meng et al. (2011), Veldman and Klingenberg (2009), Wendler (2012), James et al. (2012), Semini et al. (2014), Lamb (2004), Chrissis et al. (2003), Jokela et al. (2006), APM (2007), Netland et al. (2007), van Dokkum (2011)). The review of the literature on existing models also contributes to the identification of assessment criteria. In addition to the literature review, an expert group discussion confirms these indicators and gives a compliment.

As show in table 2, assessment criteria are described in a structured matrix. In the following matrix, the assessment descriptions of all criteria and subcriteria a different maturity levels are explained. This helps for in depth assessment.

Table 2. CMMI model for shipbuilding

Criteria	Sub Criteria	Performed	Managed	Defined	Quantitatively Managed	Optimizing
Contract Design	Bidding	Ad hoc	Repeatable but intuitive	Standard	Manage and measurable	Federated
	Value chain configuration	Random	Reactive	Structured	Proactive	Predictive
	Negotiation and agreement	Unaware	Tactical	Focused	Strategic	Pervasive
Design and Engineering	Concept, basic and functional design	Uncontrolled and isolated	Collaboration on major issues	Structured and collaboration on major issues	Structured and collaborating	Fully integrated
	Engineering and analysis	Individual	Incipient	Standardized	Consistent	Range of approaches
	Change Management	Implemented by instructions	Inconsistent assessment of change requests	Significant change consequences assessed	Time, cost and quality impacts assessed	Rapid and effective exploration of change options
Planning and Coordination	Project planning	Separated	Connected	Integrated	Controlled	Fully implemented
	Execution	Generally done	Organized procedures	Standardized procedures	Planned procedures	Improved procedures
	Monitor and control	Manual	Random	Scheduled	Planned	Improved
Production and Assembly	Hull production	Basic product implications identified	Production concepts identified	Capability to produce prototype components	Capability in place to begin full rate production	Full rate production demonstrated and lean production practices in place
	Outfitting	Uncertain and poorly controlled	Characterized for hull production and reactive	Characterized for hull production and proactive	Measured and controlled	Focused on continuous process and improvement
	Testing and commissioning	Authorized	Accordance with guidelines	Accepted and available	Implementation of all requirements	Incorporated and confirmed
Procurement	Working relationships	Confrontation or arms length	Limited cooperation	Collaboration	Close collaboration	Mutual help
	Innovation	No sharing learning and innovation	Little sharing learning and innovation	Sharing learning and innovation	Sharing learning and Innovation systematically	Continuous sharing learning and innovation
	Information exchange	Little information is exchanged openly	Some information is exchanged openly	Much information is exchanged openly	Most information is exchanged openly	Everything is exchange openly on a general platform
Logistics	Warehousing	Shared	Divided	Ordered	Measured	Reduced
	Transportation	Static information	Static information with limited real time alert	Multi channel information and account base alert	Location based, multimodal information	Location based, multimodal proactive re-routing
	Production logistics	Reacting	Transactional and anticipated	Operational and repeatable	Collaborated and Responsive	Integrated and agile
Outsourcing	Supplier identification and selection	The lowest price	Cost and quality	Cost, quality, ranking	Knowledge and tests	Development partnership
	Purchasing	Casual	Exploring	Emerging	Committed	Mastered
	Supplier evaluation	Formally established and communicated	Stakeholders are involved and controlled	Monitored and clearly defined performance measurement techniques	Have formal and quality assurance procedures	Metrics understood and continuously updated

5   Conclusions

This paper has proposed a structure for a CMMI for ship design and construction. Based on a literature study, relevant criteria and subcriteria have been identified and maturity levels proposed for each subcriterion. The most direct application is for internal assessment and improvement purposes at yards and other actors involved in ship design and construction. In addition, the CMMI can be used when configuring the network of actors to be performing a ship design and construction project. For example, it may be applied to a number of yards that are candidates for the construction of a specific ship. This can support both the selection of yards as well as deciding which engineering, procurement, and production tasks to assign to the yard. The ultimate goal of using the CMMI is to contribute to effective completion of ship design and construction projects. It should help to meet ever-increasing requirements to flexibility and responsiveness at highest quality and lowest cost.

The current study is literature-based, and a natural next step is to test, refine, and operationalize the CMMI by means of a number of case studies. Moreover, opportunities to apply the model in other engineer-to-order segments should be investigated, for example the manufacturing of maritime equipment such as thrusters, winches, and cranes.

Acknowledgement. This research was made possible by the SUSPRO project (Decision support for sustainable production of offshore ships in global fluctuating markets) as well as SFI Norman. The authors would like to thank the participants of the project for providing the inputs and fruitful discussions.

References

1. Capability Reviews (MPQA),
   http://www.dnv.com/industry/maritime/servicessolutions/
   cmc/approvalofmanufacturers/capabilityreviews
2. Andritsos, F., Perez-Prat, J.: The automation and integration of production processes in shipbuilding. State-of-the-Art report, Joint Research Centre. European Commission, Europe (2000)
3. APM, Models to Improve the Management of Projects (2007)
4. Battista, C., Schiraldi, M.M.: The Logistic Maturity Model: Application to a Fashion Company. International Journal of Engineering Business Management (2013)
5. Bozarth, C., Edwards, S.: The impact of market requirements focus and manu-facturing characteristics focus on plant performance. Journal of Operations Management 15(3), 161–180 (1997)
6. Chrissis, M.B., et al.: CMMI Guidlines for Process Integration and Product Im-provement. Addison-Wesley Longman Publishing Co., Inc. (2003)
7. CMMI Product Team, Capability maturity model® integration (CMMI SM), ver-sion 1.1. Software Engineering Institute, Carnegie Mellon University, Pittsburg, PA, Tech. Rep. SEI-2002-TR-012 (2002)

8. Farrokh, J., Mansur, A.K.: Project Management Maturity Models and Organizational Project Management Maturity Model (OPM3®): A Critical Morphological Evaluation. Project Management 2(7), 23–33 (2013)
9. Goldenson, D., Gibson, D.L.: Demonstrating the impact and benefits of CMMI: an update and preliminary results (2003)
10. Gonzalez, N., et al.: Measuring project maturity: example in a french automotive organization. International Conference on Engineering Design, ICED O (2007)
11. James, P., et al.: Key characteristics of SME procurement: An empirical study (2012)
12. Jokela, T., et al.: A survey of usability capability maturity models: implications for practice and research. Behaviour & Information Technology 25(03), 263–282 (2006)
13. Kohoutek, H.J.: Reflections on the capability and maturity models of engineering processes. Quality and Reliability Engineering International 12(3), 147–155 (1996)
14. Lamb, T.: Ship design and construction, Society of Naval Architects and Marine Engineers (2004)
15. Meng, X., et al.: Maturity Model for Supply Chain Relationships in Construction. Journal of Management in Engineering 27(2), 97–105 (2011)
16. Netland, T.H., et al.: How mature is your supply chain?-A supply chain maturity assessment test. In: Proceedings of the 14th International EurOMA Conference Managing Operations in an Expanding Europe (2007)
17. Paulk, M.: Capability maturity model for software, Wiley Online Library (1993)
18. Pels, H.J., Simons, K.: PLM maturity assessment. ICE, The 14th International Conference on Concurrent Enterprising: Concurrent Innovation: A New Wave of Innovation in Collabarative Networks, Lisbon, Portugal (June 2008)
19. Semini, M., et al.: Strategies for customized shipbuilding with different customer order decoupling points. Proceedings of the Institution of Mechanical Engineers, Part M: Journal of Engineering for the Maritime Environment (2014) 1475090213493770
20. van Dokkum, K.: Ship Knowledge: Ship Design, Construction and Operation, Dokmar (2011)
21. Veldman, J., Klingenberg, W.: Applicability of the capability maturity model for engineer-to-order firms. International Journal of Technology Management 48(2), 219–239 (2009)
22. Wendler, R.: The maturity of maturity model research: A systematic mapping study. Information and software technology 54(12), 1317–1339 (2012)
23. Wongrassamee, S., et al.: Performance measurement tools: the Balanced Scorecard and the EFQM Excellence Model. Measuring Business Excellence 7(1), 14–29 (2003)
24. Yoo, C., et al.: A unified model for the implementation of both ISO 9001: 2000 and CMMI by ISO-certified organizations. Journal of System and Software 79(7), 954–961 (2006)

Slack Resource as Evolutionary Determinant of International Manufacturing Joint Venture's Growth Performance

Stig B. Taps, Thomas Ditlev Brunø, Kjeld Nielsen, and Kaj A. Joergensen

Department of Mechanical and Manufacturing Engineering, Aalborg University, Denmark
taps@m-tech.aau.dk

Abstract. At present time in a world of change our understanding are constantly challenged with new knowledge that radically makes demand on prevailing theories and concept the scientific world for long have believed was unchangeable.

This article makes a back flash on innovation performance with some suggestion on how International Manufacturing Joint Ventures can enhance their learning capacity.

Manufacturing in a global world is a complicated management challenge because the supply chain is located in different national settings. Networkning and knowledge absorption is a key to get international competitiveness.

This paper claims a framework for building absorption capacity in international manufacturing firms.

Keywords: Growth performance, Innovation conceptualization, Slack resources, Absorptive capacity.

1 Introduction

International Manufacturing Joint Ventures (IMJV) is an organizational entity, constructed by two or more firms of different nationality [11], pooling a portion of their resources within a common legal organization [12]. These resources comprise firm-specific knowledge, and the knowledge base created in the entity is affected by each partner's sharing of knowledge with the other (Buckley, 1996). Productive resources of human technologies and mechanical technologies [5] are bundled from different sources, i.e., from partner transfer, by acquisition, and by engagement. Physical facilities are acquired, and technological equipment arrives, and is installed according to the focus. Managers, technical experts and labor are engaged, bundled together in a firm without a history by the simple fact that the IMJV is a new firm construct, a new 'child', to stand alone, and seeking to its own performance s through efficiency of combining those diverse bundling of resources. The IMJV is a synthetic organization [25], simultaneously establishing a structure and carry on operation. People have fragmented knowledge on parts of the focus, and the knowledge technology embedded in people is diffused and distinct, and acquired in working experiences from

B. Grabot et al. (Eds.): APMS 2014, Part III, IFIP AICT 440, pp. 304–312, 2014.

different organizational settings, maybe too, from other geographical locations outside the IMJV. Taking actions and making decisions within this newly structured 'child' are not supported by common understandings of actors or by common social and technological experiences.

How can such a synthetic construct growth?

Managers' must transform the IMJV from a synthetic organization through a process implying entrenched behaviors to stabilize organizational continuity whether as deliberate plans to establish patterns of behavior or as emergent patterns by which such patterns get established [16]. Accordingly the transformation process can be one of designing formal planning systems to imply entrenched organizational behavior through standardization of work, skills or outputs; and by focusing on collective so-cialization and individual cognition to establish an emergent pattern of coherence in behavior. Inter-correlation drive different parts in organization to coherence among their parts by means of manager's "tuning" of coordination mechanisms e.g., their choice among mechanisms to entrench behaviors in desired outcome and synergistic complementation between mechanisms.

Further, this dynamic capability approach acknowledge that resource endowments are "sticky", firms are to some degree stuck with what they have and may have to live with what they lack [24]. Features as bundling of resources, structural form of IMJV, appointment of managers to various departmental responsibility, and strategic direc-tion are commended contractual agreements among partners' founding conditions and therefore sticky for managerial actions within IMJV. Such imprinted stickiness makes demand on the ability of an IMJV to grow and innovate. Conditions could be barriers to transfer best practice inside the firm e.g., difficulty to transfer knowledge among subunits, and be hindering to integration and operational streamlining of practices, structures and systems.

The paper is organized in the following way. First, grow performance is elabo-rated from an innovative perspective and it is argued that building organizational slack resources to handle uncertainty influence firm's innovative performance. Second, a constructive approach for research in management capabilities to exploit resources for innovative purpose is argued.

2   Innovative Performance

Innovation has been conceptualized in many ways and studied from several perspec-tives. For instance, distinctions are made between studies of adoption and diffusion of innovations and at different levels of analysis: individual, organizations, industry and nations.

2.1   Economists

Economists conceptualize innovation at a high level of aggregation or abstraction, seeing it as one of the factors that cause increased productivity and economic growth at the industry or even national level [7].

According to Urabe [26]:

> *Innovation consists of the generation of a new idea and its implementation into new product, process or service, leading to the dynamic growth of the national economy and the increase of employment as well as to creation of pure profit for the innovative business enterprise.*

Firm is innovative only when 'newness' is transformed to economic benefit to society. Firm's innovativeness and rent generation are the outcome of the analytical fit between structure-conduct-performance of firms [2]. But when there are rapid changes in technology and market forces and defensible feedback effects from competitors such a monopoly rent generating strategy is difficult to defend. The growing uncertainty in today's turbulent competitive environment together with customers changing and unpredictable demand after products and services, accelerating pace of technological change affecting newness in manufacturing processes. For example, Pine claims [20] that our understanding of the market and the marketing concept is a misunderstanding because the market only exists as an individualist. Understanding customers idiosyncratic needs by development of a solution space makes increasing demand on robust process design [17].

2.2   Technologists

By technology researchers innovation is defined as a continuous process during which the innovation changes form as it is used and assimilated [21]. The processes of generating new technology and improving upon existing technology concern technologists and they study both product and process innovations from this perspective. Some technologists study the nature and dynamics of technological change within the context of the industry and attempt to understand the relationship between technological changes at the industry level and firm-level adaptations to these changes [1].

Other technologists researcher are concerned with factors that influence the generation of technological innovation at the level of organizational subunits such as the R&D or the manufacturing departments. They focus on factors that improve technical performances and criteria that influence the choice and use of technological innovations in various organizational subunits.

Thus, both generation factors and adoption phases of the innovation process within subunits is under study. For example, Salvador [22] proposes a process model approach based on three fundamental organizational capabilities: Solution Space development, Robust Process Design, and Choice Navigation that constitutes radical innovation to crack the code of mass customization. Wheelwright & Clark [28] argue that problem s in new product and new process development arises because of mismatch between anticipated benefits in resource utilization, organizational renewal and market position with strong defensible competitive barriers. They find causes for these mismatches from organization's analytical capability to alignment of external reality, and from lack of communication among functions within an organization and from locking into product and processes without innovative uniqueness and from managers fail to plan sufficiently.

2.3   Sociologists

Also sociologists research in innovation at the focus on the organizational features that are compatible with the adoption of innovation within the organizations. One definition of innovation within this school is that innovation is adoption of an internally generated or purchased device, system, policy, program, process, product, or service that is new to the adopting organization [6].

This school studies factors (as technologists) but factors as the importance of distinct contextual, structural and individual features that explain variance in innovation adoption at the level of organization. Hage [10]claim that complexity of the division of labor is critical for organizational innovation because the division would lead to much greater adaptiveness or flexibility of the intellectual or problem-salving capacities or learning capacities of the organization, what Cohen & Levintahl [4] refer to as absorptive capacity.

From the above discussion innovation is conceptualized in different ways. Innovation is seen as a product; a new idea; method or device and as a process of introducing something new, newness either as technology or as organization. Organization can either be generator or adopter on innovation. Organization as generator of innovation is linked to the organization's problem solving and decision making capability to remove ambiguities between successive stages of the innovation process: idea generation, project definition, problem-solving, design and development, and commercialization of new product s and processes.

3   The Level and Type of Analysis

The level of analysis is conceptualized differently across four levels: industry, organization, subunits and the innovation itself. At the industry level researcher are concerned with factors that distinguish innovation development patterns among industries such as technological appropriateness to the stages of the industry life-cycle. Research at the organizational level seeks to identify contextual, structural and behavioral characteristics that differentiate innovative from non-innovative organizations. They try to find group of organizational characteristics which relative more efficiently determine the outcome of organizational innovation such as its adaptability to the environment, capacity to allocate resources to innovative programs and overall performances. At the subunit level researcher try to identify and analyze factors that either facilitate or hinder innovations within a division or a department. The most widely studied organizational subunits are R&D departments.

The type of innovation under investigation also differs. Process innovations are defined as tools, devices, and knowledge in throughput technology that mediate between inputs and outputs and are new to an industry, organization or subunit. Product innovations, in contrast, are outputs or services that are developed to the benefit of customers.

Type of innovation is also conceptualized as either radical or incremental. Radical innovations changes fundamentally existing practices within an organization or an industry into new practices on how to make activities around in transforming

competences to new standards. Radical innovations give rise to new business possibilities, new strategies and new structures under increased environmental uncertainty. Incremental innovation improves the old product or process within the
existing structure and strategy and mainly reinforces the existing capabilities of
the organization's practices.

Type of innovation can be viewed as either technical or social. This distinction
reflects a more general distinction between technical innovation and administrative innovation. Technical innovation includes products, processes and technologies used to produce products or render services related to the technical core of an
organization. Administrative innovation is related to management processes in
designing organizational structure, administrative processes and human resources.

Differences in conceptualization of innovation among economists, technologists
and sociologists are summarized in table 1. Each group is only addressing a limited
aspect of innovation complexity whenever the position is focused and broad definition, and the product and process view s and the radical or incremental perspective.

At the introduction we argued that dynamic capabilities are the key role in adoption, integrating and configuring internal and external organizational skills, resources
and functional competences and are important determinants for IMJV's growth performance. Therefore in the next section the focus is on the organizational level of
analysis. The insights from other levels of analysis are gained to broaden the following argumentation about slack resource availability in organization as important
determinants for IMJV's innovation.

4   Slack Resources, Absorptive Capacity to Innovation

The slack serves as a buffer between organization and environmental discontinuities
and provides the organization with the internal capability to invest for innovation [8].
Evans[9] has labeled innovative capability as strategic flexibility keeping the organization both agile and versatile. Bugelman [1] argue that the rate which mutant ideas
were pursued seemed to depend on the amount of slack resources available at the

Table 1. Differences in conceptualization of innovation among economists, technologists and
sociologist (*Based [1]*)

	Stage of Process	Level of Study	Type of Innovation
Economists	Idea generation Adoption	Industry	Product, process Only technical Only radical
Technologists	Commercialization Diffusion Adoption	Industry context	Product, process Only technical Radical, incremental
Sociologists	Adoption Initiation Implementation	Organisation	Product and process Technical, administrative Radical, incremental

operational level. To keep it simple, we define slack as the pool of resources in an organization that is in excess of the minimum necessary to produce a level of organizational output [18]. The excess of absorptive capacity an organization on a given time has over the capacity to run the daily operation is the resource available to innovative performance.

A firm's absorptive capacity is defined as the ability prior related knowledge confers to recognize the value of new information, assimilate it, and apply it to commercial ends [4]. These abilities, collectively, constitute what they call a firm's absorptive capacity. They view absorptive capacity, at the firm level construct, as an ability the firm develops over time by accumulating a base of knowledge. The firm absorptive capacity is generated in a variety of ways: by product of a firm's R&D activities; by production experience, reorganize or automate particular manufacturing processes; and by investment in absorptive capacity directly, when sending personal for technical training.

How manager design the structural features of the institutional, managerial, and technical level [19]of a firm, and how they coordinate interrelated activities to a coherent whole, have great influence on a firm's absorptive capacity. This design process is complicated by the resource bundling, in so far as, an IMJV is a new "child", with people without experience in working together, and with prior knowledge acquired in variety of different organizational contexts. Knowledge may be nominally acquired, but not well utilized, because the individual do not possess the appropriate contextual knowledge necessary to make new knowledge fully intelligible [14]. Therefore, firm's absorptive capacity is not simply the sum of the absorptive capacities of its employees, but is dependent on the firm's capacity to transfer knowledge across and within subunits.

In the following section we shall shortly argue a complete theoretical framework we propose to be.

5   Theoretical Framework

Bundling of complex, heterogeneous resources, and capabilities of organizations that are usually dissimilar in culture, size, industry, an often country of origin present a managerial challenge. Because of partners' bundling of complementary resources, management within IMJVs typically lacks administrative tools. The organization is operated by people, who do not have a common tradition, and the organization does not form an entity. Lack of planning systems or blueprints force management to establish new structures and simultaneously carry on operations. Uncertainty is high on, how to manage an IMJV to a coherent whole entity. Because of the bundling of resources, complexity and differentiation increases, as well as in the risk of conflicts, opportunistic behavior, and competing goals between subunits. As a result management is confronted by the increasingly crucial need to monitor, coordinate, and integrate the activities of the IMJV [3], [15]. A structuration process [27] develops knowledge technologies e.g., the meaning and concepts to use mechanical technologies and human technologies in production [5], by which uncertainties are transformed to relatively certainties of how to act. Structuration suggest, then, that systems are built from rules and interactions; that resources, like actions, are tools people use to enact organizations; and that structures are the medium and outcome of the interaction [27].

Manager are bounded rational [23] in their acting, because the continuous, reciprocal interaction among variables, have a continuum of outcomes, that should all alternatives be examined no action would occur. Manager act accordingly to what they can see and take advantage of in their belief on what is satisfyingly. They are bounded by, what they know, and by what they value, and they are sensitive to norms of what is appropriate behavior [13]. IMJV, as a synthetic organization, is without organizational rationality, because of lack of rules, routines, and procedures, and "knowing that", and "knowing how" [13], is dispersed among organizational members, without common interpretation of the world. It is left to manager 's bounded rationality to implement a structuration process, satisfying their belief on the relation between the imprented targets from partner, knowledge technologies encoded in the context , and choice of coordination tuning, to facilitate an emerging learning process with in the IMJV. The theoretical framework for the research is outlined in Figure 1.

The first category of determinants in the framework comprises two exogenous determinants of IMJV forms: technology and organization structure. Technology is linked to organization structures through its requirements for procedures to control work and requirement for information, coordination and control intensity. How managers integrate mechanical technologies with the human technologies is dependent on their choices between mechanism: formalization, to make task simpler by routinization, and building information linkages; centralization, to distribute responsibility and decisions authority; socialization, the degree of motivation of workers and reduction of distractions. The organizational absorptive capacity is thus an outcome of management's cognitive skills to combine coordination mechanisms in a structuration process and building communication linkages supporting exploration of the new possibilities.

Fig. 1. Theoretical framework

6   Conclusion

This conceptual approach is descriptive. The intended empirical research is case study to explore, in natural settings, how this approach might contribute to deeper understanding of the phenomenon. But much more work must be done, especially in the scientific understanding and methodology proposal.

References

1. Burgelman, R.: Design for Corporate Entrepreneurship in Established Firms. Calif. Manage. Rev. 26, 154 (1984)
2. Chandler, A.D.: MIT Press, Cambridge
3. Child, J.: Organizations: A guide to problem and practise. Harper & Row, New York (1977)
4. Cohen, W.M., Levinthal, D.A.: Absorptive Capacity: A New Perspective on Learning and Innovation. Administrative Science Quaterly 35, 128 (1990)
5. Collin, P.D., Hage, J., Hull, F.: A framework for analyzing technical systems in complex organizations. In: Anonymous Research in the Sociology of Organizations. JAI Press, Greenwich (1986)
6. Damanpour, F.: Organizational Innovation: A Meta-Analysis of Effects of Determinants and Moderators. Academy of Management Journal 35, 555 (1991)
7. Damanpour, F., Gopalakrishnan, S.: Theories of Organizational Structure and Innovation Adoption: The Role of Environmental Change. J. Eng. Technol. Manage. 15, 1–24 (1998)
8. Eppkin, D.J.: Planning for Strategic Flexibility. Long Range Plann. 11, 9 (1978)
9. Evans, J.S.: Strategic Flexibility for High Technology Manoeuvres: A Conceptual Framework. Journal of Management Studies 28, 69–89 (1991)
10. Hage, J.T.: Organizational Innovation and Organizational Change. Annual Review of Sociology 25, 597 (1999)
11. Inkpen, P., Beamish, P.: Knowledge, Bargaining Powder, and the Instability of International Joint Ventures. Academy of Management Review 22, 177 (1997)
12. Kogut, B.: Joint Ventures: Theoretical and Empirical Perspectives. Strategic Manage. J., 319 (1988)
13. Kogut, B., Zander, U.: What Firms do? Coordination, Identity and Learning. Organization Science 7, 502 (1996)
14. Lindsay, P.H., Norman, D.A.: Human Information Processing (1977)
15. Mintzberg, H.: The structuring of organizations, a synthesis of the research. Prentice-Hall, New York (1979)
16. Mintzberg, H., Anestrand, B., Lampel, J.: The strategy safari. The Free Press, New York (2000)
17. Nielsen, K., Brunø, T.D., Jørgensen, K.A.: A Framework Study on Assessment of Mass Customization Capbilities. In: Proceedings of MCP-CE 2012, Novi Sad, Serbia (2012)
18. Nohria, N., Gulati, R.: What is the Optimum Amount of Organizational Slack?: A Study of the Relationship between Slack and Innovation in Multinational Firms. European Management Journal 15, 603 (1997)
19. Parson, T.: Structure and process in mordern societies. Free Press, Glencoe, III (1960)
20. Pine, B.J.: Mass customization: The new frontier in business competition. Harvard Business School Press, Boston (1993)

21. Sahal, D.: Original Research ArticleTechnological Forecasting and Social Change. Technology, Productivity, and Industry Structure 1, 1 (1983)
22. Salvador, F., De Holan, P.M., Piller, F.: Cracking the Code of Mass Customization. MIT Sloan Management Review 50, 71–78 (2009)
23. Simon, H.: Economic, Bounded Rationality and the Cognitive Revolution. In: Egidi, M., Marris, R., Viale, R. (eds.). Edward Publisher, Hants (1992)
24. Teece, D.J., Pisano, G., Shuen, A.: Dynamic Capabilities and Strategic Management. Strategic Manage. J. 18, 509–533 (1997)
25. Thomson, J.D.: Organization in aaction. McGraw-Hill, New York (1967)
26. Urabe, K.: Innovation and the Japanese Mangement System, 3 (1988)
27. Weick, K.E.: Technology as Equivoque: Sensemaking in New Technologies. In: Godmand, P.S., Sproull, L.S. (eds.) Technology and Organizations
28. Wheelwright, S., Clark, K.: Competing through Development Capability in a Manufacturing-Based Organization. Bus. Horiz. 35, 29 (1992)

Managing Uncertainty in Innovative Design: Balancing Control and Flexibility

Qiang Zhang[1], Ioana Deniaud[2], Claude Baron[3,4], and Emmanuel Caillaud[5]

[1] LPOID, Hefei University of Technology, Hefei, P.R China
zhangqiangonline@gmail.com
[2] BETA,Université de Strasbourg, Strasbourg, France
deniaud@unistra.fr
[3] CNRS, LAAS, Toulouse, France
claude.baron@insa-toulouse.fr
[4] Univ de Toulouse, INSA, LAAS, Toulouse, France
[5] ICUBE/ Université de Strasbourg, Strasbourg, France
emmanuel.caillaud@unistra.fr

Abstract. We investigate how control and flexibility can be balanced to manage uncertainty in innovative design. Emphasis is placed on two sources of uncertainty (technological and market) and two types of uncertainty (foreseen and unforeseen) that generate challenges in innovative design. After identifying project practices that cope with these uncertainties in terms of control and flexibility, a case-study sample based on five innovative design projects from an automotive company is analyzed and shows that control and flexibility can coexist. Moreover, it points out those projects that are suitable for achieving an optimal balance between control and flexibility.

Keywords: innovative design, control, flexibility, uncertainty, balance.

1   Introduction

Innovative design results in high technological and market uncertainty. Moreover, greater challenges arise from the unforeseen uncertainty due to the changing or emerging information about technology or market. To handle these uncertainties, traditional models have been control-oriented, emphasizing adequate on time delivery, cost-effectiveness and technological performance. However, its drawback lies in that it prevents identification and exploration of innovative opportunities in a rapidly changing environment [1]. Thus, many authors have identified project practices that enhance flexibility [2, 3]. With these practices a design team can respond to the dramatic shift in technology and market. Thus, striking an optimal balance between them becomes paramount for innovative design. Additionally, adopting control and flexibility are contingent upon the rapidly changing environment in which innovative design operates.

B. Grabot et al. (Eds.): APMS 2014, Part III, IFIP AICT 440, pp. 313–319, 2014.
© IFIP International Federation for Information Processing 2014

Thus, this paper aims to identify the relationships between different sources and types of uncertainty and specific project practices that support control or flexibility by means of a case-study of five completed innovative design projects from an automaker.

Consequently, the sources and types of uncertainty in innovative design are defined in Section 2.1, and the identification of project practices that could cope with these uncertainties in terms of control and flexibility are detailed in Sections 2.2 and 2.3. Research methodology and empirical findings, as well as managerial insights are discussed in Sections 4-5. In section 6 we present our concluding remarks.

2   Theoretical Background

2.1   Uncertainty

Innovative design often encounters two sources of uncertainty, namely, *technological uncertainty* and *market uncertainty*. The former is defined as the degree of uncertainty in respect of the design solution that will be needed in a project [4]. The latter refers to the level of uncertainty that exists in the external environment, with regard to determining the requirements that customers have of the resulting product.

Furthermore, in terms of type of uncertainty, innovative design faces not only foreseen uncertainties identified and understood at the beginning of this process, but also unforeseen ones that cannot be identified during project planning in a rapidly changing environment [5, 6]. As to foreseen uncertainty, the design team can anticipate possible risks. However, in the case of unforeseen uncertainty, the design team is unable to figure out and articulate relevant events that could impact innovative design and their functional relationships [7].

Therefore, innovative design suffers different sources and types of uncertainty. Figure 1 depicts a simple view of the issue. On the X-axis is market uncertainty evolving towards unforeseen uncertainty to the right. Here, the existing market breaks down and new ones emerge only slowly. The Y- axis depicts technological uncertainty.

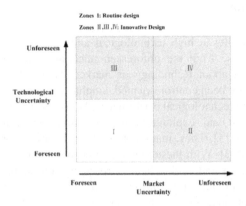

Fig. 1. Relationship between different uncertainties and designs

Similarly, we move from foreseen technological uncertainty to unforeseen uncertainty. If we map various designs depicted in Figure 1, it appears that Zone I corresponds to routine design. Zones II, III and IV stand for different environments of innovative design with unforeseen marker uncertainty, technological uncertainty, and both, respectively.

2.2   Control

As far as control is concerned, two types can be considered: *process control* and *output control* [1, 8]. Process control refers to a series of methods and activities adapted to design tasks; output control focuses on the result obtained relative to outputs goals and criteria. In this paper, six control practices based on these two aspects have been developed.

Process control can be represented by process structuration which refers to standardization. It consists of (i) *rigorous predefined design activities* that should be performed and (ii) *a rigorous operation sequence for these activities* [9]. Thus, a rigorous process structuration means that the design process should follow these predefined activities and their operation sequence.

Output control refers to gate evaluation whose criteria are applied to assess whether the project meets predefined goals or performance standards. Gate evaluation varies in terms of degree of rigor. Sethi and Iqbal (2008) identified the strictness, objectiveness and frequency of control as variables. Thus, we identified three control practices: (i) *strict evaluation criteria* (ii) *objective evaluation criteria* and (iii) *frequent evaluations*. Strictness is meant to ensure that all processes comply with the same criteria regardless of the nature of project. With respect to objectiveness, the evaluation criteria are not interpreted by different project managers and gate evaluators. Frequency emphasizes the number of evaluations within the whole process.

2.3   Flexibility

Flexibility is the ability to cope quickly with the environmental development by adapting to new technology and taking into account market information in order to satisfy the customer's needs with only limited penalty [2, 9]. A thorough review of the literature allows us to identify six flexible practices.

Parallel trials and iterative experiments. Parallel trials refer to several possible solutions tested simultaneously and selecting the best one *ex post*. This set of options is more likely to lead to the right solutions [10]. Additionally, iterative experimentations can generate information about how well the product functions from a technical perspective [11].

Early experiments involving customer. In addition to early experiments designed to solve a technological problem, experiments involving the customer provide the designer with information on those product features requested by customer [11].

Delaying concept freeze point. Delaying the concept freeze point probably permits the inclusion of new information fraught with technological opportunities and emerging customer requirements

Constructing a modular product architecture. Design modularity accommodates an early integration of the product design and changes in functionalities later in the process [11].

Exploitation of generation knowledge. Generation knowledge can facilitate these activities, allowing designers to find out an effective experiment strategy to match new pieces of information [2, 11]. In a highly uncertain environment, basic activities of innovative design consist in learning about new technological solutions applications.

Cross-functional and flat organization structure. When faced with the changes and requirements of possible creative product architectures, this structure can warrant openness and dynamic communication which in turn will lead to synchronized actions and greater collaboration between the different designers.

3   Research methodology

To deal with the research issues, a case-study approach is selected. A detailed and comprehensive view is needed and can be obtained by investigating ongoing projects.

(1)   Sampling

To be able to compare different project practices coping with different uncertainties in a similar context, we focus on projects managed by the same company. Moreover, in order to observe the innovative design process, it is important to follow the project from beginning to end. Based on these criteria, we selected five innovative design projects carried out by a Chinese automaker from 2000 to 2010.

(2)   Data collection

The method used for collecting data relies on interviews and document studies. Semi-structured and in-depth interviews were conducted with the main actors. In total, 18 interviews were made. The interviewees were asked to describe the way they coped with the uncertainties and the tools they used.

(3)   Data analysis

Data analysis was in two steps. Firstly initial uncertainties in each project were assessed from the point of view of sources and types of uncertainty. The end result is given: (i) Projects 2, 3 and 4 suffered unforeseen technological uncertainty. In terms of market, the three projects supported foreseen market uncertainty. (ii) Project 1 mainly dealt with unforeseen market uncertainty. (iii) Project 5 had to deal with unforeseen technological uncertainty and market uncertainty. Secondly, the adoption of control practices and flexible practices in each project was investigated. These practices were evaluated on the basis of interviews with the main actors in each project. Table 1 summarizes data collection per interviews and document studies. The rows stand for project practices that support management control and flexibility respectively, while the right columns list the five cases. The empty circle (O) means that this case adopts this specific project practice.

Table 1. Project practices in case studies with respect to control and flexibility

Project Practices		①	②	③	④	⑤
Control practices	• Rigorous predefined activities	o	o	o	o	o
	• Rigorous sequences of activities	o				
	• Strict evaluation criteria					
	• Objective evaluation criteria					
	• Frequent evaluation					
Flexible practices	• Parallel trial and iterative experiment		o	o	o	o
	• Early experiment involving customer	o				o
	• Delaying concept freeze point	o	o	o	o	o
	• Constructing a modular product architecture	o	o	o	o	o
	• Cross-functional and flat organization structure	o				o
	• Exploitation of generation knowledge		o	o	o	o

4   Empirical Findings

4.1   Adopting Control Practices

The first empirical finding relates to the adoption of control practices for different kinds of uncertainties. In terms of process structuration, all projects maintained predefined design activities, but did not strictly follow the sequences of these activities except for Project 1. With respect to gate evaluation, irrespective of the kind of uncertainty, all projects avoided the strict and objective evaluation criteria and frequent evaluation.

4.2   Adopting Flexible Practices

The second empirical finding is that these projects adopt adequate flexible practices commensurate with the uncertainties encountered. This empirical result is listed in Table 2 and discussed below.

Table 2. Flexible practices in case studies with respect flexibility

	Technological uncertainty	Market uncertainty
Different Practices	Parallel trial and iterative experiment Exploitation of generation knowledge	Early experiment involving customer Cross-functional and flat organization structure
Common Practices	Delaying the concept freeze point Constructing a modular product architecture	

(1)   Common Flexible Practices

According to Table 2, under any form of uncertainty, companies respond by delaying the concept freeze point and by constructing the modular product architecture. All projects prolonged the duration of the concept design stage to include information from different departments. However, constructing a modular product architecture may be the requisite for project practice with automakers. Given the high degree of sophistication of a new vehicle, even in low uncertainty projects, companies always perform design activities in accordance with the modular architecture.

(2)   Technological uncertainty

All projects characterized by unforeseen technological uncertainty adopted (i) parallel trials and iterative experiments and (ii) the exploitation of generation knowledge.

Parallel trial and iterative experiment. Indeed, when exploring unknown technological terrain, multiple trials and iterative experiments do provide the best hope of getting a satisfactory solution [10], whilst allowing designers to "probe and learn" rather than invest in accurate preliminary analyses.

Exploitation of generation knowledge. We captured the amount of generation knowledge in each design team of Projects 2-5 by asking project managers to assess the proportion of designers with several generations of experience. The result shows that the proportion of designers with greater than two generations of experience exceeds the other categories.

(3)   Market uncertainty

In that case, companies retained (i) early experiments with customer and (ii) cross-functional and flat organization structures.

Early experiment involving customer. When product specifications cannot be defined under unforeseen market uncertainty, innovative design should allow the evolution of customer needs to be tested continually as it rapidly evolves during the process [6].

Cross-functional and flat organization structure. Under unforeseen market uncertainty, the new information constantly provided by markets makes it impossible to define product concepts once and for all from the beginning.

5   Discussion and Managerial Implications

Firstly, according to these findings, all projects studied involving varying degrees of uncertainty followed the structured process, but avoided strict gate evaluation. Based on this, it is argued that by applying stricter, more objective, and frequent gate review criteria, the innovative design project will become less flexible. Thus, companies should refrain from frequently performing strict and objective gate review during this process. In addition, the result also shows that regardless of the kind of uncertainty suffered, each project still maintains similar control practices. Secondly, our empirical findings show that each project opted for not only similar control practices but also at least four flexible practices. In the event of unforeseen technological uncertainty, companies tend to rely heavily on parallel trials and iterative experiments and the exploitation of generation knowledge. In the case of unforeseen market uncertainty, the early experiment involving customers and a cross-functional and flat organization structure are much more effective.

Based on these results, it is the authors' opinion that process structuration and flexibility are compatible, and can therefore coexist within the process of innovative design. But the strict gate evaluation reinforces the inflexibility of innovative design. This has clear implications in practice. Companies should first diagnose the uncertainty profile of the innovative design project, and then simultaneously adopt adequate control practices and the corresponding flexible practices to cope with uncertainties inherent in innovative design.

6   Conclusion

This paper was to identify the relationships between different sources and types of uncertainty and particular project practices that support control or flexibility in innovative design. The first finding is that control and flexibility can coexist in this process. The second finding is about how to adjust practices to achieve an optimal balance between control and flexibility under different uncertainties.

References

1. Sethi, R., Iqbal, Z.: Stage-gate controls, learning failure, and adverse effect on novel new products. Journal of Marketing 72, 118–134 (2008)
2. Thomke, S.H.: The role of flexibility in the development of new products: An empirical study. Research Policy 26, 105–119 (1997)
3. Bhattacharya, S., Krishnan, V., Mahajan, V.: Managing new product definition in highly dy-namic environments. Management Science 44, 50–64 (1998)
4. MacCormack, A., Verganti, R.: Managing the sources of uncertainty: matching process and context in software development. Journal of Product Innovation Management 20, 217–232 (2003)
5. Calantone, R., Garcia, R., Dröge, C.: The effects of environmental turbulence on new product development strategy planning. Journal of Product Innovation Management 20, 90–103 (2003)
6. Buganza, T., Dell'Era, C., Verganti, R.: Exploring the relationships between product development and environmental turbulence: the case of mobile TLC services. Journal of Product Innovation Management 26, 308–321 (2009)
7. Sommer, S.C., Loch, C.H., Dong, J.: Managing Complexity and Unforeseeable Uncertainty in Startup Companies: An Empirical Study. Organization Science 20, 118–133 (2009)
8. Ramaswami, S.N.: Marketing controls and dysfunctional employee behaviors: A test of traditional and contingency theory postulates. Journal of Marketing 60, 105–120 (1996)
9. Biazzo, S.: Flexibility, structuration, and simultaneity in new product development. Journal of Product Innovation Management 26, 336–353 (2009)
10. Sommer, S.C., Loch, C.H.: Selectionism and learning in projects with complexity and unforeseeable uncertainty. Management Science 50, 1334–1347 (2004)
11. MacCormack, A., Verganti, R., Iansiti, M.: Developing products on "internet time": The anatomy of a flexible development process. Management Science 47, 133–150 (2001)

Motivations and Challenges for Engineer-to-Order Companies Moving toward Mass Customization

Aldo Duchi[1], Golboo Pourabdollahian[2], Davide Sili[2], Matteo Cioffi[2],
Marco Taisch[2], and Paul Schönsleben[1]

[1] ETH Zürich, BWI Centre for Industrial Management
[2] Politecnico di Milano, Department of Management Engineering, Milan, Italy
aduchi@ethz.ch, golboo.pourabdollahian@polimi.it

Abstract. ETO companies are mainly characterized by their ability to provide personalized products to customers. However, the current market trends and economic situation direct them to efficient manufacturing of customized goods. In this regard, moving toward Mass Customization and making a hybrid strategy of ETO-MC can be considered as a proper solution for ETOs. This study aims at investigating this topic using both theoretical and empirical data, and through analyzing the potential motivations for ETOs to move towards MC and the possible challenges they might face during such a transition.

Keywords: Engineer-to-order (ETO), Mass Customization (MC), Motivations and challenges, Product configuration.

1 Introduction

Engineer To Order (ETO) is considered as a manufacturing strategy in which all the necessary activities to deliver the product (design, engineering, manufacturing, assembly) are executed after receiving the customer's order [1]. Therefore each product is highly customized and the processes along the value chain differ for each product variant. Nowadays ETO companies are surrounded by several trends such as globalization, margin shrink, increased competition, delivery-time pressure, and turbulent technological advances. To achieve profitable business despite all these challenges, more and more ETO companies have started to pursue innovative strategies and a viable approach towards adapting Mass Customization (MC) in the ETO context. Mass Customization is referred as a *"production principle that emphasizes customized products that do not cost more than mass-produced products"* [2]. Despite of several similarities between ETO and MC, their interdependencies are rarely investigated in the literature. In fact, while traditional MC is focused on defining strategies for Mass Producers (MP) to increase the level of personalization without losing efficiency, ETO companies have dealt with the same trade-off (from a different perspective) trying to keep a high level of customization while increasing their productivity [3]. The few studies in the literature investigating both ETO and MC are mainly focused on the operational level. On the other hand, scarce contribution has been

B. Grabot et al. (Eds.): APMS 2014, Part III, IFIP AICT 440, pp. 320–327, 2014.

provided at the strategic level where there is a lack of support for ETO firms to evaluate the convenience of a shift towards MC [4].

To this end, this study aims at proposing a new term of ETO-MC, which suggests a
hybrid strategy to ETO firms combining the characteristics of MC and ETO. Moreover, the paper aims at identification and analysis of possible motivations and challenges that an ETO company might face during its transition toward MC in a value
chain perspective.

2   Methodology

With the intent to obtain a comprehensive overview of the topic, two main data
sources are used in this study namely literature and case studies. Accordingly, first a
set of opportunities and challenges resulting from an extensive literature has been
analyzed and collected in a framework for motivations/challenges identification. The
proposed classification is based on the distinguished elements of the ETO value chain.

In addition, leaving from the results of the literature review, a case study analysis
was carried out in order to deepen the findings and improve the results. In this regard,
four ETO companies were analyzed. The selection of case studies was mainly based
on the four defined independent variables within the study, namely the organization,
the characteristic of the product, the market, and the supporting IT Systems. A summary of case study companies is illustrated in Table 1.

Table 1. Case study companies: generalizability of the results

Company	A	B	C	D
Industry	Industrial Steam Turbines	Elevators	Concrete mixing and mineral processing plants	Asphalt plants
Product	Extremely diverse, offering ad hoc technologies for different customer	Slightly Diverse, high degree of commonality among product families	Very Diverse, core technologies are completely different	Moderately Diverse: will to standardize and uniform the technological characteristics
Market (Units/year)	Less than 50	More than 1000	300-500	Less than 300
Supporting IT Systems	Sales Configurator	Design Configurator (Generative)	Design Configurator (Adaptive)	Sales Configurator

3   Findings: Identification of Motivations and Challenges

Based on the data collected from the literature, the motivation and challenges in an ETO-MC environment have been traced back to common areas of concern that can be identified within the processes along the whole value chain [5]. The areas of concern are referred to the domains where the motivations and challenges of a shift toward MC are more likely to happen. They have been defined using a cluster analysis of the collected data. Eventually the final model is developed as a reference structure illustrating the positioning of each part of ETO value chain and their related areas of concern in a transition toward MC (Table2).

Table 2. ETO Value Chain and areas of concern

Phase	Description	Areas of concern
New Product Development	The process which is delegated to the introduction of new technological solutions matching emerging customers' need and requirements. NPD is critical to the success of ETO firms. A strategic shift towards MC can produce several changes to the performances delivered by this process.	- value creation within a stable solution space - knowledge management.
Sales	A potential customer order in the ETO segment is often initiated by an invitation to tender. The generation of a valid offer document, including mapping of customer requirements, definition of commercial characteristics as well as quotation of prices and lead times, is the general objective within the tender stage [6]. Since the success rate for winning a tender is quite low in the ETO sector, fast and cost-efficient processes are required during this stage [7].	- customer interaction and product configuration - cost estimation - supporting it systems
Order specific Engineering	With the use of configurable BOMs that efficiently implement both generative and adaptive configuration approaches [8], ETO-MC firms are able to adjust the product to fit the single customer's requirements without requiring deep modifications of the product structure. Increases in productivity in ETO-MC strongly relate on this capability and specifically the automation of engineering tasks.	- automation of engineering tasks
Procurement	Procurement obtains the specifications for components and sub-systems from the design function and deals with the relationship with the suppliers of components or sub-assemblies of the product. The effectiveness of procurement in the ETO environment depends upon whether the specifications are correct and appropriate (Caron & Fiore 1995).	- communication and sourcing strategy
Production & Logistics	To remain competitive, a company should synchronize the engineering, manufacturing and procurement processes [9]. That is mainly due to the fact that decisions made during the engineering and development phases affect every downstream process [10].	- operations - warehousing

3.1   Areas of Concern

New Product Development

Value Creation within a stable solution space: ETO firms addressing MC are able to determine a predefined set of solutions that can be represented within a configurator. This set of solutions is referred to as a solution space. The creation of a predefined product solution space involves the risk that the boundaries of that space are not properly defined [3]. Therefore, from a product design point of view, a transition to MC seems generally to be much more complex for an ETO company compared to a mass producer [3]. Moreover, the simplification of the product designs is an aspect that can have problematic consequences, since it may lead to problems such as *"loss of innovative capability and greater chance of imitation by competitors"* (Hvam et al. 2009). However, the area might contain some potential motivations for an ETO as well such as increased level of commonality and leading to higher number of product variants which can be designed and produced efficiently [8].

Knowledge Management: A crucial requirement that ETO manufacturers have to fulfil in order to shift towards MC is the creation of a *"new and more organized way of structuring the company's product line"* [11]. This can be made by adopting more rational ways of representing product variety (product families, platforms, modularity). Such effort makes *"the knowledge about the configuration system explicit"* [12], facilitating the task of product developers since they dispose of more standardized and clear knowledge of the product they are called to design [11]. It also enables the cross usage of component modules, thus reducing unnecessary redundancy [9], [13].

Sales

Customer Interaction & Product configuration: In an ETO environment, customers requests are constantly translated into technical specifications and production features [10]. In this regard, configurators are considered as a main resource and enabler for MC [14]. In fact, thanks to their systemized product offering, ETO-MC is able to direct customers to internally most easily producible, profitable component combinations [15]. However, the configurator design also implies some challenges. ETO products are often hard to standardize to a degree that allows configuration. This transforms the knowledge-based design to one of the main challenges of an ETO-MC company. [16,17].

Cost Estimation: ETO manufacturers often struggle with significant margin deviations[18]. Accordingly, a considerable high amount of their portfolio generates no or little profit. Such unexpected deviations typically results from poorly made cost estimation. The use of configuration systems is argued as a way to improve the quotation process of ETO products [19]. By calculating budget quotations, the configuration system manages to create sufficiently precise price estimations offered by one company providing a *"more consistent, fastest easier way to enter an order"* [3].

Supporting IT Systems: The rigidity of traditional systems makes it extremely difficult to configure customized products and manufacturing processes. Hence in an ET-MC environment specific BOM needs to be developed for the scope of technical configuration [20]. A knowledge-based system allows configurable BOMs by means of adaptive or generative techniques, they can be flexibly adapted to the single customer own requirements without needing deep modifications to the product structure [8].

Order Specific Engineering

Automation of Engineering tasks: There are several approaches to study the reuse of product and process knowledge with the aim to reduce the time and cost spent on product development thorough automation of repetitive design tasks [9], [21]. The CODP perspective proposed by Wikner and Rudberg [1], underlines the possibility of stocking engineering knowledge. Operationally, this means to find out repetitive design tasks, to standardize the knowledge related to them and to automatize these tasks. An impact of the reduction of repetitive engineering is that their expertise can be used for high-added-value tasks, since time is freed. On the other hand, the leaders of engineering teams are required to have high technical competences *"to follow the thinking of their colleagues when developing a customer specification"*. In addition, they should have excellent social skills *"to encourage colleagues to use existing parameters or to suggest sensible enhancements"* [8].

Procurement

Communication: People within an ETO-MC organization have to understand reciprocal needs and interdependence in a better way, coming to an agreement on the product characteristics that could be varied by the customer, taking into account the material planning [9]. In addition, thanks to the latest IT systems releases, third companies are sometimes allowed to interface directly with the product configuration system, thus improving the performances of the entire supply chain [21].

Sourcing Strategy: With regard to procurement and materials management, *"a firm applying a MC strategy should be able to source and ship small quantities of highly differentiated products efficiently"* [22]. Standard supply chains are generally geared toward handling large quantities of similar or identical products. Mass customizers thus must maintain relationships with more suppliers, spend more time on sourcing market research, and invest in the integration of supply chain management systems.

Production and Logistics

Operations: A successful transition toward MC is only possible if flexible manufacturing processes are supported by an increasing information richness of products and processes, that guarantees a cost efficient and individualized production [23]. Furthermore, when the level of standardization of the product increases, the level of correctness of product information improves as well [9]. Moreover, from a production point of view, the increased standardization of the customized products can lead to motivations, such as reductions of manufacturing costs and amount of error.

Warehousing: The MC strategy implies using some standard modules in the platform of a customized product which eventually leads to an increase in the amount of standardized orders for warehousing, while the dangers of imprecise forecasts will be reduced. In this sense, the risk of not being able to sell purchased items having the technical performances specified during the pre-award phase still exists, but in a smaller scale [3]. However, to avoid long response times, request should be emitted as soon as possible (at the Kick-off of a new project).

4 Empirical Findings

Empirical evidences collected from case study analysis provide a broader view toward motivations and challenges of ETO companies on their way to MC in practice. The following findings not only support a part of data collected from the literature but also highlight additional issues that these companies face in practice.

Although the analyzed companies show different characteristics, most of the motivations/challenges entailed by an MC strategy are concentrated in the design stages, new product development (NPD) and Order Specific Engineering (OSE). In particular, NPD, through the application of specific design approaches (modularity, product families, etc.), allows delivering part of the theoretically producible variety at low costs and reduced lead-time. MC approach to OSE can instead lead to savings in case the product needs additional manual working.

A crucial ETO-MC companies' feature is the increased standardization in the engineering phases. Many design activities, associated with the specification of a product, can be automated with the support of IT Systems, such as configurators, and standard documentation. In all the case studies, a reduction of routine/repetitive engineering activities was registered. Nevertheless, even if the companies have already reached a high level of standardization, from the analysis it emerges that additional value could be unlocked from the adoption of design configurator based on parametric design principles.

The interviewed managers pointed out the significant required amount of know-how as a main challenge. In particular, they put in evidence how strong skills are necessary in the design and use of product configurators as tools enabling the transition. However, the development of these capabilities is not immediate. The managers expressed the effort spent in the past to set up these tools and their concern for future developments and integration of this kind of systems. In fact, both the cost and complexity for adapting the configuration software are extremely high; furthermore, these tools express their potential only when they are properly used. Explanatory is the case of company D, which manages to get more standardized orders only when a technical engineer accompanies the sales agent during the customer configuration.

From the analysis, it emerges that a considerable level of integration between NPD, specific engineering and technical support to Sales is required for MC. In the case of companies A and C, engineering team and sales force are in contact on a daily base. In company B, there is full integration between NPD, Sales and OSE. The interaction between Sales and engineering can, indeed, lead to a better matching between customer needs and the product variety that the company is able to deliver without additional engineering.

Regarding production, logistics and procurement activities, the main motivations are conditioned to improvements in the upstream processes. Economies of scale in production and procurement arise, in fact, from a higher degree of standardization in the design phase.

5   Conclusions

This paper aimed at providing ETO firms with a model to clarify the strategic implication when addressing an MC strategy in an ETO-MC environment. Specifically, the model displays a collection of the most critical motivations and challenges entailed by MC, classified by the phase of the ETO process to which they are related.

Based on the results of data analysis, most of the motivations and challenges are concentrated in the design stages (NPD and OSE). In particular NPD, through the application of specific design techniques, contributes to deliver a pre-defined part of all the theoretically producible product variants at a lower cost and a reduced LT. On the other hand, the phase of Order Specific engineering (OSE) in ETO-MC firms is structured to be responsive to non-standard requests that are very differentiated solutions that the firm either is not able or prefer not to represent before the order was received.

The primacy of engineering comes from the evidence that MC is enabled by an increased level of standardization in the design activities. While the theoretical value of this statement is expressed in literature there are rare sources to support the firms which want to assess the practical consequences of the higher standardization implied by MC. This paper provided a deeper insight into the problem presenting a study of the strategic implications of MC thanks to a detailed case study analysis.

The adoption of case studies methodology helped in structuring the perception of managers about the effects of a shift towards MC. Nevertheless, the reduced number of companies limits the applicability outside the specified boundaries of this research. In particular, the generalizability of the results should be tested in the context of small-medium ETO enterprises.

Acknowledgement. This work is funded by the research project through the Swiss Commission for Technology and Innovation CTI (CTI no.: 15021.1 PFES-ES). The authors would like to thank all participating organizations for sharing their insights in the ETO industry.

References

1. Wikner, J., Rudberg, M.: Integrating production and engineering perspectives on the customer order decoupling point. Int. J. Oper. Prod. Manag. 25(7), 623–641 (2005)
2. Schönsleben, P.: Integral logistics management: Operations and supply chain management in comprehensive value-added. Auerbach Pub. (2007)
3. Haug, A., Ladeby, K., Edwards, K.: From engineer-to-order to mass customization. Manag. Res. News (2009)
4. Bonev, M., Hvam, L.: Performance measures for mass customization strategies in an ETO environment. In: 20th EurOMA Conf. (2011)

5. Gosling, J., Towill, D.R., Naim, M.M., Dainty, A.R.J.: Principles for the design and operation of engineer-to-order supply chains in the construction sector. Prod. Plan. Control, 1–16 (February 2014)
6. Willner, O., Rippel, M., Wandfluh, M., Schönsleben, P.: Development of a Business Process Matrix for Structuring the Implications of Using Configurators in an Engineer-To-Order Environment. In: Emmanouilidis, C., Taisch, M., Kiritsis, D. (eds.) Advances in Production Management Systems. IFIP AICT, vol. 397, pp. 278–285. Springer, Heidelberg (2013)
7. Hicks, C., McGovern, T., Earl, C.: Supply chain management: A strategic issue in engineer to order manufacturing. Int. J. Prod. Econ. 65(2), 179–190 (2000)
8. Schönsleben, P.: Methods and tools that support a fast and efficient design-to-order process for parameterized product families. CIRP Ann. Technol. (2012)
9. Forza, C., Salvador, F.: Managing for variety in the order acquisition and fulfilment process: The contribution of product configuration systems. Int. J. Prod. Econ. 76(1), 87–98 (2002)
10. Hvam, L., Bonev, M., Denkena, B., Schürmeyer, J., Dengler, B.: Optimizing the order processing of customized products using product configuration. Prod. Eng. 5(6), 595–604 (2011)
11. Reid, L.: Sharing ETO Knowledge, Managing the NPD process in ETO manufacturing Organisations. Manage. Sci. (2008)
12. Forza, C., Salvador, F.: Product Information Management for Mass Customization. Palgrave Macmillan, Basingstoke (2006)
13. Fleishanderl, G., Friedrich, G.E., Haselbock, A., Schreiner, H., Stumptner, M.: Configuring large systems using generative constraint satisfaction. IEEE Intell. Syst. their Appl. 13 (1998)
14. Zebardast, M., Pourabdollahian, G., Corti, D., Taisch, A.M.: Analysis of factors for successful implementation of Mass Customization: key resources and key activities. Annals of the Faculty of Engineering Hunedoara-International Journal of Engineering 11(2) (2013)
15. Heiskala, M., et al.: Mass customization with configurable products and configurators: a review of benefits and challenges. Mass Customization Information Systems in Business, pp. 1–32. IGI Global, London (2007)
16. Sabin, D., Weigel, R.: Product configuration frameworks-a survey. IEEE Intelligent Systems 13(4), 42–49 (1998)
17. Edwards, K., Blecker, T., Hvam, L., Salvador, F., Friedrich, G.: Mass Customization Services (2008)
18. Brunoe, T.D., Nielsen, P.: A case of cost estimation in an engineer-to-order company moving towards mass customisation. Int. J. Mass Cust. 4(3/4), 239 (2012)
19. Hvam, L., Pape, S., Nielsen, M.K.: Improving the quotation process with product configuration. Comput. Ind. 57(7), 607–621 (2006)
20. Piller, F.T.: Mass customization: reflections on the state of the concept. International Journal of Flexible Manufacturing Systems 16(4), 313–334 (2004)
21. Edwards, K.: Expected and Realized Costs and Benefits from Implementing Product Configuration Systems. Mass Customization for Personalized Communication Environments: Integrating Human Factors, pp. 216–231. Idea Group Publishing (2010)
22. Piller, F.T., Moeslein, K., Stotko, C.M.: Does mass customization pay? An economic approach to evaluate customer integration. Prod. Plan. Control 15(4), 435–444 (2004)
23. Dellaert, B.G.C., Stremersch, S.: Marketing Mass-Customized Products: Striking a Balance Between Utility and Complexity. Journal of Marketing Research 42, 219–227 (2005)

Metrics for Assessing Product Variety Utilization

Thomas Ditlev Brunø, Kjeld Nielsen, Kaj A. Joergensen, and Stig B. Taps

Department of Mechanical and Manufacturing Engineering, Aalborg University, Denmark
tdp@m-tech.aau.dk

Abstract. In mass customization, offering the right variety is critical and it is therefore proposed to develop an assessment system for the capabilities critical for mass customization success. This paper proposes different metrics and methods for assessing the utilization of a company's product variety. Two different methods are selected for further testing which is done on historical data for three different product families from three different companies. It is concluded that different metrics and methods may be relevant for different products, reflecting variety and complexity. However, in general, monitoring utilization of variety has potential to improve business for mass customization companies.

Keywords: Mass Customization, Assessment, Variety, KPI, Metrics.

1 Introduction

In any company, it is essential to offer products, which match the needs and desires of customers to achieve sales and profit. This is true for mass producers as well as mass customizers; however, in mass customization this issue is somewhat more complex than mass production due to a much higher variety and a more complex product structure. As pointed out by Salvador et al.[9], mass customizers need three fundamental capabilities to be successful: 1) Solution Space Development – Identifying the attributes along which customer needs diverge, 2) Robust Process Design – Reusing or recombining existing organizational and value chain resources to fulfill a stream of differentiated customer needs and 3) Choice Navigation – Supporting customers in identifying their own solutions while minimizing complexity and the burden of choice [4], [9].

In order for companies to be able to establish themselves as mass customizers or for existing mass customizers to improve performance, we proposed that an assessment system for Mass Customization performance is established [5], [6].

An essential element in mass customization is product variety. Variety is what differentiates mass customization from other business strategies, however the variety offered to the customer, the solution space, must be carefully designed, since a too high variety will imply higher costs and a too low variety will imply lost sales, since customers will not be able to buy the product matching their individual requirements [8]. Hence when developing an assessment system for MC, metrics addressing the size of the solution space and whether this size fits with the demand for variety is essential, since variety is a major driver for both cost and revenue. A number of

B. Grabot et al. (Eds.): APMS 2014, Part III, IFIP AICT 440, pp. 328–335, 2014.

metrics for this purpose have been proposed all related to solution space development [3]. These metrics however cover a broad area of capabilities related to solution space development, including the solution space at a certain point in time as well as dynamics of solution space development.

The metric "Used variety" (UV) introduced by Piller [7], referenced from [1] addresses how well the solution space is utilized by the customers, i.e. how much variety is offered vs. how much does actually make sense compared to the customers' requirements. The metric is calculated as indicated in the formula below:

$$UV = \frac{Number\ of\ perceived\ variants}{Number\ of\ all\ possible\ variants} \tag{1}$$

Using this metric may be difficult in practice, since the number of perceived variants is not readily available, as well as the number of all possible variants may be difficult to determine for various reasons, which will be addressed below.

The research question of this paper is: *How can the utilization of a mass customizer's solution space be measured?* The research question will be addressed with a basis on the "Used Variety" metric presented above, however due to certain practical issues in implementing this metric directly, further considerations need to go into defining the metric more specifically, which is done applying the method outlined below. The reasons for assessing the solution space include enabling mass customizers to optimize their solution space as well as their configuration systems, which both influence the performance in relation to solution space utilization.

2   Method

To answer the research question, a number of sub questions will need to be answered. In order to do this, the following methodical approach has been applied:

1. Clarify the purpose of the metric and based on this evaluate the feasibility of the originally proposed form of the metric.
2. Identify variables, which should be used to define and calculate the metric.
3. Evaluate the availability of data necessary for calculating a value for the metric.
4. Based on findings above, propose alternative methods to calculate the metric.
5. Verification of feasibility of calculating the metric by applying the proposed methods on different data sets containing actual historic product data.
6. Evaluate results from verification and identify the most suitable method in relation to the purpose identified in step 1.

3   Purpose and Evaluation of Existing Metric

The basic purpose of the metric UV is to evaluate the utilization of a company's solution space. The reason to do so is that variety comes at a cost, and variety, which is not being sold, does not generate income and may imply economic loss. The reasons for variety not being utilized can be very different but relating to the fundamental capabilities of MC, we expect low utilization to be due to either lack in capability for solution space development or choice navigation. Low utilization due to problems within solution space development will imply that a company has developed variety, which is simply not demanded by customers, i.e. development of the wrong products. On the other hand, utilization issues due to poor choice navigation imply that the company may have exactly the right variety, but is not able to guide the customer towards buying the product that matches the specific requirements. Either way, the result is that companies have made investments in introducing variety, which is not paying off.

Hence the metric should be able to assess to what extent the variety offered to customers is actually being utilized, i.e. sold, in order to enable companies to react to low utilization. The metric should be applicable as a KPI and should thus be able to track utilization over time. In order to track performance over time, the KPI should be calculated on a regular basis and therefore it should be possible to calculate based on readily available data from the company's IT systems and not require expensive market surveys or qualitative assessments from the company.

The way of assessing the utilization of variety proposed by Piller [7] using the metric Used Variety implies identifying the *number of perceived variants* and dividing this by the *number of all possible variants*. In general, assessing variety based on the measure "number of variants" is intuitively an obvious choice since this is based on a simple count. However, in many cases this will be impractical. One of the reasons for this is that in mass customization, the number of theoretical variants easily becomes astronomical. For example, when configuring a Mini Cooper online the configuration choices presented to the customer will result in a number of possible variants well above a 20-digit figure. Another issue that may arise when determining the number of possible variants is how to count continuous configuration variables, e.g. the height and width of a window, which can be any value within a predefined interval or custom printed T-shirts, which can have any image printed on them. In these cases, it makes little sense to determine the number of possible variants, since this figure is literally infinite. This is also the case for products composed by predefined modules or components, which can be combined in various ways to configure a product, where the number of modules included in the configuration is not bound. In this case, the number of possible variants will also literally be infinite. Hence, when determining the value of the UV metric the value will in many cases approach a zero value, as the denominator will be virtually or literally infinite. Furthermore considering an example where a given solution space is expanded with one extra binary option, this will effectively double the number of possible variants (given this option is offered for all products). This again implies that the value of the UV metric will be halved. Considering again the Mini Cooper example, adding an option to include floor mats will double the number of possible variants, thereby halving the value of the UV metric, even though the actual change in product variety would clearly not imply that the utilization of variety is reduced by 50%.

The numerator of the UV metric – number of perceived variants – may be determined in a number of different ways. The term "perceived" implies that the number should rely on the perception of the customer, which naturally is difficult to determine quantitatively. However, a reasonable way of measuring number of perceived variants is to assume this is equal to the number of different products (configurations) that have been sold over a period. If assuming this, it will be feasible in many cases to calculate an actual value for this metric, however as indicated above the value may not be a very good representation of the actual utilization of the solution space.

4   Variables and Calculation Methods

As described by Brunoe et al. [2], the utilization of a product family's solution space can be addressed using set theory. The solution space can be described using three sets; Configurable variety, configured variety and ordered variety. The set configurable variety contains all possible product variants, whereas configured variety contains all variants that have been configured and ordered variety contains all variants that have been configured and subsequently ordered. To assess the utilization of a solution space, it must be addressed what the relationship is between the set "configurable variety" and the set "ordered variety, i.e. a small difference between the two sets implies a good utilization of the solution space. However to assess the difference between the two sets, it must be determined what are the elements of the sets.

One possibility is to define the elements in the sets as product variants, which corresponds to the approach suggested by Piller [7] for calculating the "used variety" metric. This is in some cases a simple way of measuring the utilization of the solution space, however as pointed out above, there are certain issues in other cases. Calculation of the solution space utilization (SSU_1) can be done by applying the formula below:

$$SSU_1 = \frac{Number\ of\ distinct\ configurations}{Number\ of\ different\ product\ variants} \tag{2}$$

This form of the metric differs from the one defined by Piller [7], since the numerator simply counts the number of distinct configuration. The data needed to calculate the value of this metric is expected to be readily available, assuming the company has a product configurator, where the product family model defining the solution space provides the information needed for calculating the number of different product variants (simply by calculating the product of number of possible values for each configurable variable).

Another possibility for defining the elements of the sets is to let each outcome of each variable in a product configurator represent an element. E.g. if a configurator allows you to choose a product in three different sizes and three different colors, that would correspond to six elements. We define these elements as "configuration options". I.e. a configuration option corresponds to a specific value for a specific variable. Using the configuration options, the number of elements will not become astronomical when representing the solution space, but product configurators will typically contain configuration options in the order of hundreds or thousands. It is then possible, to calculate the solution space utilization based on the number of configuration options (SSU_2):

$$SSU_2 = \frac{Number\ of\ different\ configuration\ options\ chosen\ in\ configurations}{Number\ of\ different\ configuration\ options\ in\ solution\ space} \qquad (3)$$

This metric will also be able to assess the utilization of the solution space, however without the drawback of using the SSU_1 metric of e.g. reaching near zero values for larger solution spaces and being sensitive towards introduction of simple variety. On the other hand, if the sales of a product family reaches a certain level, it is expected that the value of the SSU_2 metric will approach one, as it is likely every configuration option will be chosen by a customer at least once. This leads to the issue regarding this way of measuring solution space utilization, which is that a configuration, which is chosen only one time by a customer, will count the same as a configuration option, which has been chosen thousands of times by customers. Clearly, a configuration option chosen thousands of times indicates a better utilization than a configuration option chosen only once, which this metric does not take into account.

Another way of assessing the utilization, using the configuration options, but taking the issues described above into account, would be to calculate the frequency by which each configuration variable is chosen by a customer. By doing this, it can be determined for each configuration variable, how well it is utilized. Furthermore, to assess the solution space as a whole, a distribution of the frequencies can be determined and illustrated in e.g. a histogram, which will indicate whether all configuration options are chosen similarly often, or some configuration options are chosen almost in every configuration whereas others are chosen very rarely. To represent this distribution, mean values and standard deviation can also be calculated for the frequencies for which configuration options are chosen. Although this way of assessing utilization of the solution space is not a metric in it's simplest form, i.e. a metric which can be calculated as a single figure, we include it in this paper as it gives a deeper insight than the other simpler metrics. The data used for calculating a value for this metric is identical to the SSU_1 metric

In this paper, the two methods – SSU_1 and determining the frequency and distribution of configuration options being chosen are tested on data from three different products from three different companies all producing mass customized products. The metric SSU_2 has not been included in the test because of the arguments presented above and since initial test showed that, the metric for all product families would reach the value 1.

5   Data

The data used for testing the different metrics and calculation approaches have been obtained from three different companies. The product families represent three entirely different product types in terms of application and complexity. Product family A is a family of mass customized capital goods equipment of high complexity. The product family is close to being Engineer to Order products and have thus a very large product variety, however they are standardized and can thus be considered mass customized products. Product Family B is a family of products, which are used as sub components of larger systems in the process industry. The products have medium variety and are customized to meet individual demands, by combining different components.

The complexity of these products is relatively low. Product Family C is a family of products for domestic utilities. The product family has medium variety but are slightly more complex than the products in family B but still much less complex compared to family A. Data obtained for the three product families consists of a product family model defining the variety, i.e. variables and there values, enabling determining the total number of variants and configuration options. Furthermore, historic data describing specific configurations which had been sold over a one to two year period was obtained for determining what variety had actually been configured.

6   Results

The results of testing the SSU_1 metric are shown in table 1. At first glance, it can be seen that all three product families have SSU_1 metric values very close to one, although product family A has a significantly lower value for the metric, for which the major reason is that the number of possible variants is significantly higher. Furthermore, it can be seen that the number of distinct configurations sold are not particularly high. This is due to the products being B2B products and thus not being sold in volumes comparable to consumer products. Furthermore, for families B and C it indicates that sales includes much repurchase of previously purchased configurations. I.e. one configuration is sold in larger volumes and in multiple orders.

Table 1. Results from applying metric SSU_1

Product Family	A	B	C
Distinct configuration sold	409	157	26
Number of possible variants	4,26E+61	1,91E08	9,17E09
Value of SSU_1 metric	9,59E-60	8,19E-07	2,83E-09

Table 2 and Figure 1 show the results of analyzing the frequencies of which configuration options are chosen by customers. In figure 1, the frequencies are divided into 20 even intervals. The bars in the histogram indicate the number of configuration options, which have been chosen the number of times, which corresponds to the frequency interval. E.g. the first bar for product family A indicates that 358 configuration options have been chosen by customers between 0 and 22 times. The number below each bar indicates the upper bound of the interval.

Table 2. Results from analysing frequency of which configuration options are chosen

Product family	A	B	C
Mean frequency	77,0	52,1	44,6
Mean frequency relative to no. of configurations	0,231	0,156	0,133
Std. Dev	109,6	79,28	62,48
Std. Dev relative to no. of configurations	0,267	0,183	0,345

Table 2 also reflects an analysis of the frequencies of configuration options being chosen, where the mean frequency and standard deviation are calculated. The mean frequency for e.g product family A indicates that configuration options are in average chosen 77 times by customers. The mean is also related to the number of configurations in row two in the table, where the value 0.231 indicates that the average configuration option is chosen in 23.1 % of the configurations. The table also shows the standard deviation for the frequencies, where it is notable that the standard deviation in all three product families is larger than the mean value indicating very spread frequencies, but also a long tail of configuration options where a few configuration options are chosen very frequently and a high number is chosen very rarely, which is also seen in figure 1.

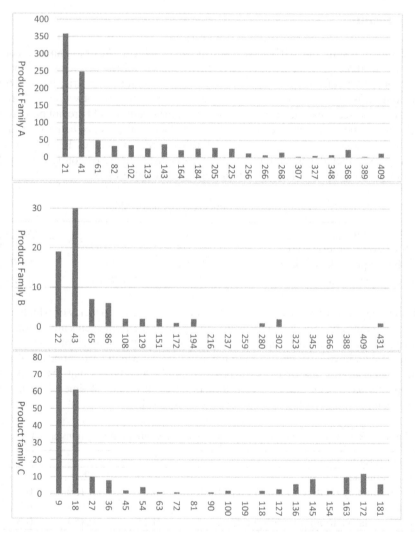

Fig. 1. Results from analysing frequency of which configuration options are chosen illustrated as distribution histograms. X axis labels indicate the upper bound of the interval.

7   Conclusion

The basic idea of the Used Variety metric [7] is intuitively good, however insufficiently described to operationalize it. Using the SSU_1 metric a very similar measure can be calculated, however testing on actual data showed that the method did not provide very useful information on utilization of product variety. The metric may however be useful in cases with low variety or in cases with a lower number of predefined product variants. Another method for assessing variety was tested, where the frequency of choosing a configuration option is counted, resulting in a distribution of frequencies, which indicates if there is a large spread in the utilization of configuration options and if there is a large part of the product variety which is rarely configured and thus potentially unprofitable.

The data used to test the methods is obtained from three different companies, however all operation in a B2B setting, limiting volume. The results may have been somewhat different if data were included for consumer products as well, however in terms of assessing the applicability of the method, we consider the testing done in this work as sufficient to draw the conclusions stated above.

Further consideration needs to go into the practical application of the methods, e.g. over how long time should data be sampled? Using data for 1 month will reveal a significantly different result than data for half a year. Furthermore, not all configuration variables may be relevant to include, since some may be redundant, if the configurator as an example contains variables for both user requirements and product characteristics.

In general, we expect the application of product variety assessment tools as a valuable tool for mass customizers in order to optimize their business in terms of determining the right level of product variety and diagnosing the configuration process.

References

1. Blecker, T., Abdelkafi, N., Kaluza, B., et al.: Key Metrics System for Variety Steering in Mass Customization. Munich Personal RePEc Archive (2003)
2. Brunoe, T.D., Nielsen, K., Joergensen, K.A., et al.: Describing Product Variety using Set Theory, pp. 105–114 (2014)
3. Brunoe, T.D., Nielsen, K., Joergensen, K.A.: Solution Space Assessment for Mass Customization. In: MCP-CE 2012, p. 56 (2012)
4. Lyons, A.C., Mondragon, A.E.C., Piller, F., et al.: Mass Customisation: A Strategy for Customer-Centric Enterprises. Customer-Driven Supply Chains, 71–94 (2012)
5. Nielsen, K., Brunoe, T.D., Joergensen, K.A., et al.: Mass Customization Measurements Metrics, pp. 359–375 (2014)
6. Nielsen, K., Brunoe, T.D.: Mass Customisation Assessment and Measurement Framework. In: Anonymous Enabling Manufacturing Competitiveness and Economic Sustainability, pp. 165–170. Springer (2014)
7. Piller, F.T.: Logistische Kennzahlen Und Einflussgroessen Zur Performance-Bewertung Der Mass-Customization-Systeme Von Selve Und Adidas (2002)
8. Pine, B.J.: Mass customization: The new frontier in business competition. Harvard Business School Press, Boston (1999)
9. Salvador, F., De Holan, P.M., Piller, F.: Cracking the Code of Mass Customization. MIT Sloan Management Review 50, 71–78 (2009)

Decentralized Approach for Efficient Simulation of Devs Models

Romain Franceschini and Paul-Antoine Bisgambiglia

University of Corsica, UMR SPE 6134 CNRS, UMS Stella Mare 3460, TIC team, Campus
Grimaldi, 20250 Corti
{r.franceschini,bisgambiglia}@univ-corse.fr

Abstract. This paper proposes to improve simulation efficiency of DEVS models based on the classical Discrete Event system Specification (DEVS) formalism by reducing the number of messages exchanged between simulators. We propose three changes: hierarchical modeling tree flattening based on closure under coupling, direct coupling and decentralized scheduling. The main idea is to relieve coordinators by giving to simulators more tasks to process.

1 Introduction

The study of production systems necessitates the development of specific tools. Discrete EVent system Specification formalism [Zeigler et al., 2000] is an expressive, open and flexible formalism that can be extended. Recent studies [Vangheluwe, 2000, Zei- gler, 2003], have shown that DEVS formalism may be called multi-formalism because, due to its open nature, it allows the encapsulation of other modeling formalisms to meet specific applications requirements. From a performance perspective, the formalism can be improved as it does not scale well with a large number of models to simulate. At hardware level, it is possible to scale vertically by increasing power of machines, and horizontally by parallelizing [Chow and Zeigler, 1994] simulations, with a cost [Bal- akrishnan et al., 1997, Chow et al., 1994, Glinsky and Wainer, 2006]. At software level, we can work on algorithms efficiency by reducing their complexity.

In the DEVS formalism, the model hierarchy suggests that each evolution of a model state can produce a message, which traverse all the hierarchy up to the root of the tree. The number of messages is therefore proportional to the output of the models, the number of models, and the level of the hierarchy. In certain cases, this can affect and raise simulation execution time. Previous works already proposed different approaches to improves simulation efficiency. We can cite: parallelization approach [Chow et al., 1994, Balakrishnan et al., 1997, Kim et al., 2000, Glinsky and Wainer, 2006, Zacharewicz and Hamri, 2007, Jafer and Wainer, 2009]; distribution [Kim et al., 2000, Liu, 2006, Zacharewicz and Hamri, 2007]; and software approaches. These last approaches improve simulation time by getting rid of the hierarchical structure [Jafer and Wainer, 2010, Jafer and Wainer, 2009, Lowry et al., 2000, Zacharewicz and Hamri, 2007], and suggests to use direct coupling between models [Chen and Vangheluwe,

B. Grabot et al. (Eds.): APMS 2014, Part III, IFIP AICT 440, pp. 336–343, 2014.

2010, Muzy and Nutaro, 2005]. The purpose of this article is to propose modifications to the simulation algorithms to reduce significantly the number of exchanged messages between components.

Currently, our approach is based on the classical DEVS formalism. The rest of the paper is organized as follows: first part, we present the DEVS formalism. In the second part, we detail the modifications we introduce to the classical DEVS formalism. In the last part, we present simulation results using our "decentralized" simulation approach.

2   Background

DEVS [Zeigler, 2003] allows representing any system whose input/output behavior can be described with a sequence of events. It allows defining hierarchical modular models with two distinct types: atomic (behavioral) and coupled (structural) models. The first describes the autonomous behavior of a discrete-event system; the last one is composed of sub-models, each of them being an atomic or a coupled model. Formally, an atomic model is described by: $\langle X, Y, S, \delta_{int}, \delta_{ext}, \lambda, ta \rangle$, and a DEVS coupled model is described by $\langle X, Y, D, \{M_d \mid d \in D\}, EIC, EOC, IC, Select \rangle$.

We use the DEVS formalism because of its openness and extensibility. It offers both a formal framework to define models and a flexible implementation in object-oriented programming. It allows modeling all types of systems. In some cases, depending on the system, the simulation can be very time consuming. To explain the excess messages must detail the simulation part [Jafer and Wainer, 2009]. There are many works that aim to accelerate the simulation. We can cite [Glinsky and Wainer, 2006, Hu and Zeigler, 2004, Jafer and Wainer, 2009, Jafer et al., 2013, Lee and Kim, 2003, Liu and Wainer, 2012, Muzy and Nutaro, 2005, Wainer and Giambiasi, 2001, Zacharewicz et al., 2010]. Some of these solutions propose to flatten the hierarchy of models in order to reduce communication overhead between models.

This is achieved by simplifying the underlying simulator structure, while keeping the same model definition and preserving the separation between model and simulator. There are two advantages to using a so-called flat structure: reduce exchanges of messages and simplify the simulation tree. This simplification is often used to allow parallelize or distributed simulations. These many works have shown that flat simulators outperform hierarchical ones significantly. They have also showed that although the hierarchical simulator presented in [Glinsky and Wainer, 2006, Zacharewicz et al., 2010] reduced the number of messages by introducing two specialized DEVS coordinators, the communication overhead was still high in some cases. Others propose modifications simulation algorithms to parallelize and/or distribute computations (outsource). We propose to improve the simulator structure to accelerate simulation time. Our approach to accelerate simulations is not based on outsourcing the computations, but on three items: flat structure, direct coupling and decentralized scheduling.

3   Our Approach

The objective of this work is not to provide a comparison with other approaches that are based on parallelization or distribution; we propose algorithms to improve the classical

DEVS formalism. The aim of our modifications is to simplify the DEVS formalism, in order to make it more effective and faster. To reduce the number of exchanged messages between DEVS components, we propose three changes while remaining in compliance with the universal properties of DEVS, such as closure under coupling.

3.1 Local Schedule

In order to avoid message overhead, we propose to avoid dispatching *-messages when possible, which we will call local or decentralized schedule. The purpose of this modifi- cation is to make the simulator more autonomous and to simplify the task of flat coordi- nator. Right after processing an *-message, a simulator checks if it is the next scheduled simulator by its parent and if there is no other simulator scheduled at the same time. If so, then the simulator will keep control and process the new *fictive* *-message at its *tn*.

3.2 Direct Coupling

Message generation in the DEVS formalism is caused by message routing, specifically routing induced by the hierarchical structure of the formalism. For example, a component C1 of level H2 cannot communicate directly with a component C2 of the same level (H2). This is the case for all components. Messages must always be propagated to the parent, in H1 or H0 level. This hierarchy is a source of communication too. The fact of not being able to communicate directly with a component of the same level is a problem. We propose to add a list of couplings in simulators as a state variable. The simulators know their coupling, that is to say, the components to which they are connected, and with whom they should communicate. This list of decentralized coupling has been added to simulators.

3.3 Flattening Architecture and Direct Connection

The hierarchy flattening, also called direct connection by [Chen and Vangheluwe, 2010], is not new and has become a key to improve simulation time. The property of closure under coupling demonstrated in [Zeigler et al., 2000] implies that any coupled DEVS model offers the same behavior as a resultant atomic model, which allows to delete all coupled models in the hierarchy. In the hierarchical structure proposed in the DEVS formalism, a root coordinator is placed on top with a coordinator just below (H0 level). To flatten the simulation architecture, all the coordinators below the H0 level are deleted. Other works already offer this mechanism [Jafer and Wainer, 2009, Zacharewicz and Hamri, 2007], usually in order to parallelize and distribute the simulation. Our goal is to make the simulator standalone by removing redundant communications. We still keep the top-most coordinator, positioned just below the root. It gives an execution order to simulators. It has a schedule with an event number equal to the number of simulators. Now that we flattened the hierarchy, the top-most coordinator still coordinates its components. A component that generates an y-message still pass by its parent, which could be avoided with direct coupling.

3.4   Algorithms

We are now going to present algorithms for the modifications we propose, based on the classical DEVS simulation algorithms defined in [Zeigler et al., 2000].

Decentralized simulator tend to reduce the number of messages generated during a simulation in two different ways: (1) by allowing a simulator to communicate directly another component of its parent whenever possible and (2) by keeping control of *-messages whenever possible.

Listing 1.1. Decentralized simulator algorithm

```
 1  variables:
 2    indirect-couplings = all parent ICs where oport host == self and parent
          EOC doesn't include oport
 3
 4  when receive (*, t) message do
 5    do
 6      raise synchronisation error if t != tn
 7
 8      y = model.lambda()
 9
10      for each (y, oport)
11        couplings = indirect-couplings(oport)
12        if couplings are empty and parent EOC doesn't include oport
13          send (y, t) to parent
14        else if couplings are not empty
15          for each (iport, v) in couplings
16            send (x, t, v) to iport host
17          end
18        end
19      end
20
21      model.internal_transition()
22
23      tl = t
24      tn = t + model.ta()
25
26      t = tn
27    end while tn == parent.min_tn and parent.imminent.count < 2 and tn !=
          end-of-simulation
28  end
```

We achieve direct coupling by introducing indirect couplings to the simulator variables. Indirect couplings represent the direct route to another component of the parent. They are all IC of the parent involving one of the output port of the simulator model, excluding output ports involved in a EOC of the parent coordinator. As Listing 1.1 shows, when an output is generated by the model, an y-message has to be dispatched to the parent coordinator only if no indirect coupling exists and that the port is not involved in a EOC. If that is not the case, an x-message is directly sent to each indirect coupling recipient.

To avoid to return control from *-message, a simulator checks at the end of *-message processing if it is the next scheduled message by its parent. Then, if it is the only scheduled model at that time, it is not necessary to the parent to call the Select method. In that case, the message time is set to the simulator tn and the *-message processing starts again unless we reached the end of the simulation.

4   Results

The suggested approach allows to reduce the complexity of the simulation algorithms. We still have to demonstrate through some examples that this is expressed by a ma- jor reduction of the number of messages exchanged. We propose to present the results obtained with a [Wainer et al., 2011] benchmark. DEVStone allows to evaluate the per- formance of DEVS-based simulators. It generates a suite of model with varied struc- ture and behavior automatically. The test environment is based on a Intel(R) Core(TM) i5-3210M CPU @ 2.50GHz, 8 GB (2 x DDR3 - 1600 MHz) of RAM, APPLE SSD SM128E hard drive, running on OSX 10.9.3. Software used for the benchmarking is DEVS-Ruby [Franceschini et al., 2014] (without C extensions enabled) running on the Ruby 2.1.2 VM. DEVS-Ruby is a DEVS-based simulation framework implemented with the Ruby language.

4.1   Simulation Results

Table 1 shows the total number of exchanged messages along with the CPU time of a simulation for each of the three approaches. The DEVstone model is parameterized with a depth between 3 and 9, a width from 5 to 15, with HO models type, a δ_{int} transition time of 1ms, and a δ_{ext} transition time of 0.1ms.

Results show a major drop of scheduled messages between flat simulations and classic simulations. This is predictable because of all messages no longer sent to sub coupled models since they have been deleted from the hierarchy. Those results are very interesting but were already obtained by previous works on hierarchy flattening. How- ever, decentralized simulation offers very encouraging results since we can observe an additional message drop. We obtain this by reducing the number of scheduled *- messages and by avoiding to each atomic model that produces an y-message to pass by its parent coordinator by dispatching directly an x-message to the recipient.

Table 1. Number of exchanged messages and CPU time for each approach using DEVStone

Depth	Width	Approach					
		Classic		Flat		Decentralized	
		Messages	CPU time(s)	Messages	CPU time(s)	Messages	CPU time(s)
3	5	132	0.027517	90	0.027047	**61**	0.027517
	10	359	0.07453	260	0.072432	**161**	0.071881
	15	722	0.172698	530	0.170959	**311**	0.148885
6	5	333	0.060773	195	0.058662	**133**	0.0571
	10	1043	0.177945	620	0.173918	**383**	0.198214
	15	2183	0.4381	1295	0.375843	**758**	0.370906
9	5	588	0.09689	300	0.093082	**205**	0.091734
	10	1952	0.285154	980	0.296403	**605**	0.276397
	15	4148	0.648915	2060	0.709434	**1205**	0.609233

Although we significantly reduce the number of messages and that CPU times shows slightly better results with our approach, the difference is not as impressive as the number of messages. In our case, this is due to the naiveness of the sorted list-based scheduler which is used for now in DEVS-Ruby. Indeed, the hierarchy flattening increase the number of atomic models to handle by the scheduler of the last present co-ordinator. Moreover, the HO type of coupling in DEVStone involves many collisions, which is a stress condition for the scheduler.

5   Conclusions

In this article, we presented an approach that aims to reduce the number of exchanged messages in the classic DEVS formalism. To reduce the number of messages exchanged, we propose to expand the role of simulators. Indeed, we propose three major changes compared to classical DEVS formalism: direct coupling, flat structure and local schedule. The goal is the decentralization of a number of tasks in order to make the simulators more autonomous, and relieve coordinators. Through these modifications the universal property of DEVS are preserved, and it is possible to couple a classical model with a decentralized model.

The results obtained with our framework are good; the number of exchanged messages is reduced by a factor of two. For complex systems with many components such as production systems, this method seems very interesting. As a future work, we plan to work on the PDEVS formalism.

Acknowledgements. The present work was supported in part by the French Ministry of Research, the Corsi- can Region and the CNRS.

References

1. Balakrishnan, V., Frey, P., Abu-Ghazaleh, N.B., Wilsey, P.A.: A framework for performance analysis of parallel discrete event simulators. In: Pro- ceedings of the 29th Conference on Winter Simulation, WSC 1997, pp. 429–436. IEEE Computer Society, Washington, DC (1997)

2. Chen, B., Vangheluwe, H.: Symbolic flattening of DEVS models. In: Proceedings of the 2010 Summer Computer Simulation Conference, SCSC 2010, pp. 209–218. Society for Computer Simulation International, San Diego (2010)
3. Chow, A., Zeigler, B., Kim, D.H.: Abstract simulator for the par- allel DEVS formalism. In: Proceedings of the Fifth Annual Conference on AI, Simulation, and Planning in High Autonomy Systems. Distributed Interactive Simulation Environments, pp. 157–163 (1994)
4. Chow, A.C.H., Zeigler, B.P.: Parallel DEVS: a parallel, hierarchical, modular, modeling formalism. In: Proceedings of the 26th Conference on Winter Simulation, WSC 1994, pp. 716–722. Society for Computer Simulation International, San Diego (1994)
5. Franceschini, R., Bisgambiglia, P.-A., Bisgambiglia, P.A., Hill, D.R.: DEVS-Ruby: a Domain Specific Language for DEVS Modeling and Simulation (WIP). In: DEVS 14: Proceedings of the Symposium on Theory of Modeling & Simulation - DEVS Integrative M&S Symposium, pp. 393–398. Society for Computer Simulation Interna- tional (2014)
6. Glinsky, E., Wainer, G.: New parallel simulation tech- niques of DEVS and cell-DEVS in CD++. In: Proceedings of the 39th Annual Symposium on Simulation, ANSS 2006, pp. 244–251. IEEE Computer Society, Washington, DC (2006)
7. Hu, X., Zeigler, B.P.: A high performance simulation engine for large-scale cellular DEVS models. In: High Performance Computing Symposium (HPC 2004), pp. 3–8 (2004)
8. Jafer, S., Liu, Q., Wainer, G.: Synchronization methods in parallel and distributed discrete-event simulation. Simulation Modelling Practice and Theory 30, 54–73 (2013)
9. Jafer, S., Wainer, G.: Flattened conservative parallel simula- tor for DEVS and CELL-DEVS. In: International Conference on Computational Science and Engineering, CSE 2009, vol. 1, pp. 443–448 (2009)
10. Jafer, S., Wainer, G.: Global lookahead management (GLM) protocol for conservative DEVS simulation. In: 2010 IEEE/ACM 14th International Symposium on Distributed Simulation and Real Time Applications (DS-RT), pp. 141–148 (2010)
11. Kim, K., Kang, W., Sagong, B., Seo, H.: Efficient distributed simu- lation of hierarchical DEVS models: transforming model structure into a non-hierarchical one. In: Proceedings of the 33rd Annual Simulation Symposium (SS 2000), pp. 227–233 (2000)
12. Lee, W.B., Kim, T.G.: Simulation speedup for DEVS models by composition-based compilation. In: SCS, editor, Summer Computer Simulation Conference, SCS, pp. 395–400 (2003)
13. Liu, Q.: Distributed Optimistic Simulation Of Devs And Cell-Devs Models With Pcd++. PhD thesis (2006)
14. Liu, Q., Wainer, G.: Multicore acceleration of discrete event system specification systems. Simulation 88(7), 801–831 (2012)
15. Lowry, M.C., Ashenden, P.J., Hawick, K.A.: Distributed highperformance simulation using time warp and java. Technical Report DHPC-084 (2000)
16. Muzy, A., Nutaro, J.J.: Algorithms for efficient implementations of the DEVS & DSDEVS abstract simulators, pp. 273–279 (2005)
17. Vangheluwe, H.: DEVS as a common denominator for multiformalism hybrid systems modelling. In: IEEE International Symposium on Computer-Aided Control System Design, CACSD 2000, pp. 129–134 (2000)
18. Wainer, G., Glinsky, E., Gutierrez-Alcaraz, M.: Studying performance of DEVS modeling and simulation environments using the DEVStone benchmark. Simulation 87(7), 555–580 (2011)
19. Wainer, G.A., Giambiasi, N.: Application of the cell- DEVS paradigm for cell spaces modelling and simulation. Simulation 76(1), 22–39 (2001)

20. Zacharewicz, G., Hamri, M.E.-A.: Flattening g- DEVS / HLA structure for distributed simulation of workflows. In: Proceedings of AIS-CMS International Modeling and Simulation Multi Conference, pp. 11–16. Buenos Aires, Argentine (2007)
21. Zacharewicz, G., Hamri, M.E.-A., Frydman, C., Giambiasi, N.: A generalized discrete event system (g-DEVS) flattened simulation structure: Application to high-level architecture (HLA) compliant simulation of workflow. Simulation 86(3), 181–197 (2010)
22. Zeigler, B.: DEVS today: recent advances in discrete event-based information technology. In: 11th IEEE/ACM International Symposium on Modeling, Analysis and Simulation of Computer Telecommunications Systems, MASCOTS 2003, pp. 148–161 (2003)
23. Zeigler, B.P., Kim, T.G., Praehofer, H.: Theory of Modeling and Simulation, 2nd edn. Academic Press, Inc., Orlando (2000)

A Production System Reconfiguration Model
Based on Repair Approach

Feno Mahenina Remiel, Aline Cauvin, and Alain Ferrarini

Aix-Marseille University – ENSAM – LSIS UMR CNRS 7296
Avenue Escadrille Normandie Niemen, 13 397 Marseille, France
{remiel.feno,aline.cauvin,alain.ferrarini}@lsis.org

Abstract. The frequency of new product introduction requires adaptable production system. In this context, this paper deals with the reconfiguration issue during factory layout design regarding the introduction of a new product in an existing production line. A repair approach from planning recovery is explored to address this issue. We show that long term performance can be reached if future products can be integrated easily in the existing production system with low disruptions on current operations during the reconfiguration phase.

Keywords: Factory design, reconfiguration, assembly systems, repair planning.

1   Introduction

Due to rapid changing market, product lifecycle is decreasing and model mix is high in most industrial organization. This generates highly individualized engineering tasks and repetitions of development and validation activities. In this paper we propose an approach which allows analyzing production line reconfiguration process taking into account the future product to be produced.

Even though a lot of research work has been done on flexible and reconfigurable production systems, the reconfiguration process itself is less supported by suitable methodology. The different cases of the reconfiguration problem and the activities involved in the reconfiguration process need first to be categorized. The operations to be performed are intended to minimize the disruption on the existing assembly line. Adequate selection criteria need to be identified to assess each alternative.

A critical review of various approaches in design and reconfiguration of assembly systems reported in the recently published literature is first presented with a special emphasis on new product introduction. A methodology based on repair is introduced to address the reconfiguration issue. Finally, a case study is presented to illustrate the introduction of new products on existing assembly line.

2   Context and Motivation

The context of this study is about capacity requirement analysis and product allocation to assembly unit during the preliminary factory design. Configuration is the

B. Grabot et al. (Eds.): APMS 2014, Part III, IFIP AICT 440, pp. 344–351, 2014.

arrangement of the production system layout and the associated assembly process to achieve production objectives. Reconfiguration is a more difficult process than initial configuration because we need to consider not only the desired outcome of a configuration process but also find the most suitable way to reach this state.

Reconfigurability is the ability to add, remove and/or rearrange in a timely and cost-effective manner the components and functions of a system which can result in a required set of alternate configurations [1]. Several cases may arise when introducing new product (1) develop new assembly line, (2) expand existing one or (3) reconfigure existing facility. We consider the reconfiguration process as any change between production phases. There is a need for a new approach to analyze these reconfiguration processes by taking into account future change and the complexity of the system.

2.1   The Reconfiguration Problem

The reconfiguration problem is similar to the initial design process, except that there are existing facility layout and resources constraints. Each new product introduction brings the following issues: *when* and *how* do we reconfigure? The first one depends on the performance required for the next period; if it is not satisfactory then the reconfiguration is considered. We will focus on the second one which is related to the choice of adequate reconfiguration operations to perform in order to satisfy the new product change and existing constraints.

Several alternatives can be identified and they usually differ by their flexibility level. The decision to develop flexible assembly line on the first product is one of the main issue in factory design. It should not be supported by profitability analysis only but by technical performance criteria as well. This is because economic advantages of flexible systems appear on long period and the decision does not refer to the same product. On the other hand the profitability rule for a facility investment in most companies is less than one year, which does not give advantage to flexible solutions.

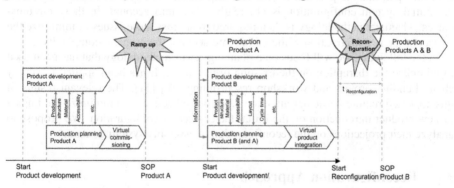

Fig. 1. Reconfiguration issue and the production system lifecycle [2]

Typical issue when introducing a new product B in a production system already producing A is represented in Fig.1. The decision we try to formalize is related to the operations to perform during the reconfiguration phase. Some research works related to this problem and their contributions are described below.

2.2   Literature Review

Several researches addressed the reconfiguration problem in different contexts. Most of them focus on operational planning and control of reconfigurable production system (RPS). Some deal with the balancing problem in reconfigurable manufacturing system (RMS) with genetic algorithm [3]. Economic justification of changeability in reconfigurable assembly systems (RAS) is proposed with a strategic point of view. Changeability classification and enablers for reconfiguration planning are presented but no specific methodology for the reconfiguration process has raised [4].

Others developed a methodology to choose between dedicated, reconfigurable and flexible production system   based on cost analysis and capacity investment [5]. Reconfigurability measurement has been also proposed based on axiomatic design and structure design matrix [6].

Some research works contributed to reconfiguration planning to minimize total lifecycle cost on several product generations. Assembly system reconfiguration planning problem (ASRP) has been resolved by dynamic programing and genetic algorithm [7].   Instead of generating new assembly plans from scratch, reconfigurable process planning (RPP) intends to generate portion of the master assembly planning referring to the new operations which are optimally positioned within the master plan [8] [9]. This approach enables local reconfiguration of assembly sequence plans.

A premise of reconfiguration methodology is proposed by [12], where several structures of RMS have been assessed according to their productivity. The study involves a simplified production line with only five stations to enable exact method analysis.

All the previous approaches deal with either operational planning and control of reconfigurable production system or the reconfiguration planning problem. Few deals with the operations to perform for the reconfiguration. The impact of the solution on the initial system configuration is not really taken into account. In these circumstances, adequate methodology is then required to address these issues to minimize the impact of the reconfiguration while taking into account the problem complexity.

In the following, we will focus on a planning repair methodology that has been used to minimize the disruption on the existing organization. It has been applied to supply chain, building project and workshop rescheduling [10] [11]. The relevant results of this approach require particular attention since our objective is to minimize the impact of new product introduction on the initial factory layout configuration. We propose to analyze their projections on the reconfiguration of assembly system domain.

3   Reconfiguration Approach

The reconfiguration problem can be seen as a planning repair as long as the objective is to minimize disruption on existing production system. The aim in project planning repair is to minimize the impact of the disruption on the initial master plan and associated organizational aspects, while in production system reconfiguration the aim consists in minimizing the impact of new product introduction on the initial system configuration. A plan repair can be seen as planning with re-use of fragments of the previous plan [13]. It can be defined as a local and limited modification of a previously calculated planning. The approach is particularly suited to solve scheduling problem or partially deficient resulting from any kind of disruption.

The principle of the studied method comes from the cooperative and distributed problem solving that has been already implemented in production and logistics, and extended to building site organization [14]. This principle is based on the development of solutions by the actors themselves for limiting the impact of disruptions throughout the organization while ensuring the achievement of objectives. Rather than implementing a new planning calculation, the purpose is to repair the existing plan.

In order to achieve this goal, strategies for responding to disruptions have been defined consisting in a sequence of repair operations applied to the disrupted planning. Initially these operations consisted in time shifts or tasks permutations within one or more resources. Solving strategies implement sequences of repair operations in order to limit the impact of disruptions on the organization. Each implemented strategy will be evaluated in term of cost and delay in order to decide of using a strategy.

The same idea is retrieved in a factory design and reconfiguration with an additional dimension to the timeline of a plan. Repair operations consist in limiting tasks that minimize the impact of the new product on the current production system configuration. Operations may involve layout change, additional resources, equipment replacement or logistic concept adaptation [2]. The reconfiguration approach is based on repair method to find reconfiguration solutions initiated by the decision to introduce a new product. Designers may therefore focus on minimizing the impacts of the new system configuration on production cost and logistics, layout requirement, operation and workforce need or equipment availability. To do so, an analogy between both domains is presented, followed by first steps of the decision process.

3.1   Analogy between System Reconfiguration and Planning Repair

Here we use the principle of analogy to transpose some concepts of the planning problem to the reconfiguration issue. This analogy enables us to consider assembly reconfiguration issue as a planning repair, which takes us from a temporal point of view to space occupation point of view. The idea is to show common concepts and methodology to use existing resolution based on repair approach.

In planning problem, a task is composed of several operations which need to be assigned to an actor with limited time capacity. Each operation may require one or several resources to perform the task. In the reconfiguration problem, an assembly unit is composed of several workstations to allocate on a limited layout. The same analogy between time and space has been successfully used for the arrangement of cable harness design [16] where scheduling method have been used to arrange cable allocation.

Table 1. Analogy between reconfiguration and planning

Task	Assembly unit
Temporal attributes	**Spatial attributes**
- Duration (required time)	- Surface (required space)
- Start date	- Loading station
- End date	- Unloading station
- Temporal margin	- Available space on the layout
Physical attribute	**Physical attribute**
Working unit produced by the task	- Production capacity in jop per hour
Resources	**Ressources**
- Equipment	- Workstation
- Tools	- Tooling and fixtures
Actors	**Worker**
- Quantity	- Workforce
Structural attributs	**Structural attributs**
- Interruptible	- Décomposable (Split into 2 blocs)

In our case, reconfiguration operations may involve layout change, additional resources, equipment replacement or logistic concept adaptation.

- **Minor reconfiguration:** develop new process with low disruption.
- **Significant reconfiguration**: reuse part of existing process (carry over)
- **Major reconfiguration**: redesign the whole factory layout.

3.2   The Decision Process in Production System Reconfiguration

The analogy enabled us to validate the principle of repair in a layout reconfiguration context, the next step consists in identifying and evaluates several categories of operations to perform and analyze their impact on the production system. The decision process follows the 4 steps, analysis, design, selection and implementation.

- **Analyze** the new product parameters and the actual assembly line capability
- **Design** : identify reconfiguration strategies
- **Decision or selection**: choose between alternatives based on several criterion
- **Implementation and evaluation**: implement reconfiguration operations.

4   Reconfiguration Case Study

We illustrate the design step with an automotive body shop example. For a new product introduction, an industrial company is dealing with flexibility investment decision to improve its production process. The cost of the new flexible equipment is known but the real operational cost is usually not. To support this decision we can compare the performance of the production system with and without the flexible equipment.

When a car body is made, the parts are first stamped from rolls of steel, the overall body is welded together to create a shell, and then the individual parts are welded together into the body on a moving assembly line. This part of the process is performed in the Body in White (BIW) workshop containing several layers:

- Mainlines or assembly units (ex: opening unit, main floor)
- Subassemblies (ex: front door) supplying the mainline.
- Cells (ex: robotic hemming cell)
- Workstation (ex: manual gun welding)

4.1   Description of the Case Study

We assume that a company produces a product A and plans to introduce a new product B in two years, as described in Table 2. Specific tooling for product (A) is installed on the line in Hypotheses 1 while flexible tooling is installed for products (A) and (B) in hypothesis 2. The idea is to illustrate the reconfiguration operations at T2.

Table 2. Investment cash flow for new product introduction

Year	0	1	2
Product	A	A	A + B
Hyp 1	C0 + a		C1 + b
Hyp 2	C + a		b

C: capacitary investment   a, b: specific investment for product A or B
C0: Tooling investment for A   C1: remove tooling for A and install for B

Figure 4 represents the investment cash flow for hypotheses 1 and 2. The vertical line defines the reconfiguration phase. For the same initial capacitary investment (left side of each hypothesis), the two year cash flow cost is higher for hypothesis 1. The study has been conducted in the context of profitability analysis between both solutions which enables us to identify investment related reconfiguration operations.

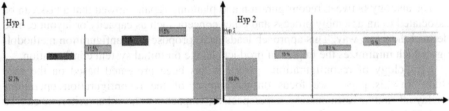

Fig. 2. Investment cash flow between product A and B

The difference between the two scenarios is due to the cost of operations to perform during the reconfiguration. The main characteristics of both cases are listed below.

Table 3. Difference between two reconfiguration strategies

Hyp 1	Hyp 2
Design and build additional fixtures	Build additional fixture with no extra design
Production stop during reconfiguration	No disruption to production (week end)
Find space for additional equipment	Space already available for added equipment
Recalibrate and re-plan robot trajectory	No need for recalibration
Need to restart production	No disruption to production

A solving strategy involves several reconfiguration operations starting from the least to the most disrupting one. Several criteria are used to assess their impact.

4.2   Performance Analysis and Selection Criteria

Even though cost related performance is important in the preliminary design, technical and human factor criteria need to be considered in reconfiguration. Evaluation of the reconfiguration process is based on the final state of the system, when the previous operations have been implemented. The main selection criteria are presented for the factory level or the subassembly level (manual or an automated system).

Factory	Manual assembly line	Automated assembly line
- Investment	- Value added time ratio	- Investment / capacity
- Required space	- Product flexibility	- Product flexibility
- Value added time ratio	- Volume flexibility	- Volume flexibility
- Operational costs	- Workforce	- Availability
- Availability	- Required surface	- Value added time ratio

Based on these criteria, an objective function mainly based on cost and time is defined to assess the relevance of the reconfiguration strategies. Those that satisfy the new requirement and respect constraint (available space, and resource capacity) are kept.

5   Conclusions et Future Research

The aim of this paper is to propose an approach for production system reconfiguration in new product introduction. One of the conditions to reach long term performance is to ease future reconfiguration. For that, a repair approach has been explored.

The analogy between reconfiguration and planning repair showed that a task can be associated to an assembly process and other concept such as capacity or layout can be defined the same way. This approach leads us to propose a reconfiguration methodology which minimizes the impact of product change on initial system configuration.

A typology of reconfiguration operations has been presented based on the case study. In this paper, we focus on the impact of the reconfiguration operations on layout and investment. As a perspective, impact on the other criterion can be analyzed. Further analysis also needs to be done regarding the reconfiguration methodology which consists in choosing the suitable combination of these operations. Objective function based on performance criteria can be used to support this decision.

References

1. Karl, F., Reinhart, G., Zaeh, M.F.: Strategic Planning of Reconfigurations on Manufacturing Resources. Procedia CIRP 3, 608–613 (2012)
2. Walla, W., Kiefer, J.: Life Cycle Engineering – Integration of New Products on Existing Production Systems in Automotive Industry, pp. 1–6 (2011)
3. Borisovsky, P.A., Delorme, X., Dolgui, A.: Genetic algorithm for balancing reconfigurable machining lines. Computers & Industrial Engineering 66(3), 541–547 (2013)
4. Wiendahl, H.-P., ElMaraghy, H.A., Nyhuis, P., Zäh, M.F., Wiendahl, H.-H., Duffie, N., Brieke, M.: Changeable Manufacturing - Classification, Design and Operation. CIRP Annals - Manufacturing Technology 56(2), 783–809 (2007)
5. Niroomand, I., Kuzgunkaya, O., Bulgak, A.A.: Int. J. Production Economics Impact of reconfiguration characteristics for capacity investment strategies in manufacturing systems. Intern. Journal of Production Economics 139(1), 288–301 (2012)
6. Farid, A.M.: Reconfigurability Measurement in Automated Manufacturing Systems (2007)
7. Bryan, A., Ko, J., Hu, S., Koren, Y.: Co-evolution of product families and assembly systems. CIRP Annals-Manufacturing Technology (2007)
8. Hu, S.J., Ko, J., Weyand, L., ElMaraghy, H.A., Lien, T.K., Koren, Y., Bley, H., Chryssolouris, G., Nasr, N., Shpitalni, M.: Assembly system design and operations for product variety. CIRP Annals - Manufacturing Technology 60(2), 715–733 (2011)
9. Azab, A., Elmaraghy, H., Samy, S.N.: Reconfiguring Process Plans: A New Approach to Minimize Change (2009)
10. Cauvin, A., Fournier, S., Ferrarini, A.: Disruption management in distributed organizations: a cooperative repair approach for reactive planning and scheduling. Progress in Economic Research 23 (2011)
11. Fournier, S., Ferrarini, A., Cauvin, A.: A Cooperative Agent – Based Scheduling Repair Method for Managing Disruptions in Complex Organisations. In: WETICE, 20th International Conference on Collaboration Technologies and Infrastructures (2011)
12. Koren, Y., Shpitalni, M.: Design of reconfigurable manufacturing systems. Journal of Manufacturing Systems 29(4), 130–141 (2010)
13. Komenda, A., Novák, P., Pěchouček, M.: Domain-independent multi-agent plan repair. Journal of Network and Computer Applications 37, 76–88 (2014)
14. Ferrarini, A., Fournier, S., Tranvouez, E., Cauvin, C., Cauvin, A.: Decision aid using multiagent models and simulation: Disruption Management in Building Site organization. In: 20th International Conference on Production Research (ICPR 2009), vol. (2004), pp. 61–68 (2009)
15. Zweben, M., Davis, E., Daun, B., Deale, M.J.: Scheduling and rescheduling with iterative repair. IEEE Transactions on Systems, Man and Cybernetics 23(6), 1588–1596 (1993)
16. Cerezuela, C.: Contribution à l' élaboration de méthodes et d' outils d' aide à la conception dans une perspective d'ingénierie concourante. Le cas du câblage électrique. T

Reconfigurable Manufacturing System Design

The Case of Mobile Manufacturing System

Thècle Alix[1,*], Youssef Benama[2], and Nicolas Perry[3]

[1] University of Bordeaux, IMS, UMR-CNRS 2518, F-33400, France
[2] University of Bordeaux, I2M, UMR5295, F-33400, France
[3] Arts et Métiers ParisTech, I2M, UMR5295, F-33400, France
`firstname.name@u-bordeaux.fr`

Abstract. Mobile manufacturing is an enabler to increase the possibility to change and to adapt to altering needs, where the geographical position is not fixed. The main idea with the mobile manufacturing concept is to easily and quickly reuse manufacturing capacities between different orders or projects. This paper examines the concept of mobile manufacturing system by addressing issues related to manufacturing system mobility management. Review of reconfigurable manufacturing system is conducted. Issues as reconfigurable manufacturing system design in the special context of multi-site environment are discussed.

Keywords: Mobility, RMS, manufacturing system design.

1 Introduction

It is becoming increasingly obvious that the era of mass production is being replaced by the era of high value added and specific market niches. The key to create products that can meet the demands of a diversified customer panel is a short development cycle yielding low cost and high quality goods in sufficient quantity. This makes flexibility an increasingly important attribute to manufacturing [1]. Manufacturing system must have the ability to be rapidly transformed due to new technologies and demand changes, and also the ability to change their facilities and even their locations. In addition, they are expected to produce instantly high quality while coping with these changes [2].

In the following sections we first discuss the concept of mobile manufacturing. Secondly, we address issues about reconfigurable manufacturing system and present a case study where this type of systems can be justified. Finally we present a design framework for mobile and reconfigurable manufacturing systems.

---

* Corresponding author.

B. Grabot et al. (Eds.): APMS 2014, Part III, IFIP AICT 440, pp. 352–359, 2014.

2   The Concept of Mobile Manufacturing System

2.1   A Specific Need for Mobility

Due to excessive production capability and economic globalization, the manufacturing environment becomes turbulent and uncertain. Manufacturing enterprises must reassess their production paradigms, so that a manufacturing system can be designed and operated efficiently in the ever-changing environment [3]. In some cases where customer's order books are deterministic, distributed in a unique place per customer and performed sequentially, a mobile manufacturing system can be a solution. That kind of system has to enable the changes i.e. the adaptation to altering needs, whatever the location. In each case, product specifications should be revised and adapted to cope with each country constraints (political, geographical, social, etc. constraints), supply chain can be modified and even the local workers knowledge can differ.

The purpose of the mobile manufacturing concept is to move manufacturing equipment from a stationary location (the site where the actor that controls and manages the capacity is) to a temporary location (the site where the capacity is used in operation) [4]. Reasons for introducing mobile manufacturing systems are fourfold:

- Mobility is needed to increase flexibility: Upton considered mobility as an operational form of flexibility: "the ability to change product being manufactured quickly, on an on-going basis is the capability which most frequently supports the ability to provide quick response" [5].
- Mobility is needed to improve efficiency: Mobile manufacturing capacity can be used to adjust the manufacturing system to an inconsistent workload. By implementing mobile manufacturing modules that quickly and easily can be used on different production sites, fewer investments are needed in manufacturing equipment. The effectiveness and the quality of the performed work are improved and the overall equipment efficiency is maximized.
- Mobility is needed to reach new markets: Mobility is used as a characteristic in strategic domain to describe manufacturing in a long-term perspective. "By using mobile manufacturing capacity, it is possible to enter geographically new markets while maintaining control of the business. The company could win a new order and produce part of the order in a local country, while a large part of the order could still be manufactured at the company's manufacturing site in [home country]" [4].
- Mobility is needed to reduce the manufacturing cost of the end product: In the case of products with important volume dimensions that are produced in important quantities and should be livered to different geographical locations, shipping costs can dramatically raise the final cost. In this case, Producing close to the client site could be an alternative to reduce the global manufacturing cost. Thereby economy of scale may be considered to split the investment on mobile manufacturing unit.

Several dimensions can affect mobility and consequently the way the manufacturing system can be designed.

2.2   Dimensions Affecting Mobility

Mobility refers to the movement of physical manufacturing resources [4]. It exists at the same time a geographical distance between the temporary and the stationary location in mobile manufacturing, and a technological, organizational, and social distances as well as cultural differences. Those distances and differences are not totally separated from each other, but rather connected. Ask and Stillström have highlighted two forms of distances through case studies [4]: the geographical distance defined as the distance that can be measured between the stationary and temporary location, in kilometers or yard for example, and the organizational distance corresponding to the distance between departments, functions, or levels. The organizational distance is not as easy to determine as the geographical distance, but it is of huge importance in information handling for example. Once the distances are determined it is possible to manage the mobility of the system.

2.3   Managing the Mobility of Manufacturing Systems

Stillström describes the main lifecycle of the system for one rotation, i.e operating cycle for one temporary location [4]: "*the life cycle starts with configuration of the manufacturing modules to a specific order. Thereafter, the modules are transported to the location where they will be used in production. When the order is finished, the manufacturing modules are transported to home site, or to another location, where they are reconfigured and reused*". In addition, we should consider other necessary stages detailed below (Figure 1):

- Factory set up: the plant is built on the end-user site. Before this stage, site preparation operations are already carried out. The manufacturing system is set up and commissioning operations are performed.
- Diagnosis control: at the end of the production campaign, all resources are controlled and reconfigured to prepare the next production campaign.

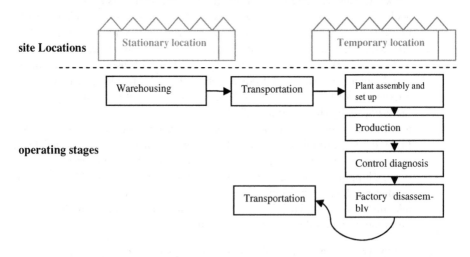

Fig. 1. Exploitation stages of a mobile production system, for one rotation

- Disassembly: the manufacturing system is disassembled, conditioned, and ready to be shipped to next end user location or to home location.

When considering operating cycle of mobile manufacturing unit between two rotations, we must consider the commercial order book of the firm. Indeed, in the case of several rotations, there are two possible scenarios:

- After the first rotation, the mobile manufacturing system is already reserved to produce on a determined location. In this case, maintenance operations and necessary modules replacement could be operated at: (1) the end of the first rotation, (2) before producing on the next location or (3) during the transportation stage. For each case, required components supplying, availability of the required operators qualification and delay constraints should be taken into account when deciding or choosing solution.
- The second scenario corresponds to the case when there is no immediate command after the first rotation. In this case, modules of the mobile manufacturing system should be stored for a period.

Furthermore, a specific stage corresponding to periodic inspection may be required. The need to consider this stage depends strongly on the technical solutions adopted to allow modules mobility. For example, to allow the mobility of machinery, it is possible to embed the machinery into a container. Due to regulation constraints on marine container shipment, resources must be inspected periodically.

3   Reconfigurable Manufacturing Systems as a Basis to Design Mobile Manufacturing Systems

Reconfigurable Manufacturing Systems (RMS) are able to cope with changes rapidly and cost effectively. In the context of a dynamic market demand with volume demand fluctuation and product mix variability, the manufacturing system adaptability is obviously valuable [6].

3.1   RMSs Features

RMSs allow changeable functionality and scalable capacity by physically changing the components of the system, by adding, removing or modifying machine modules, machines, manufacturing cells, material handling and/or complete lines". For Koren and Shpitalni, RMSs are designed "at the outset for rapid change in structure, as well as in hardware and software components, in order to quickly adjust production capacity and functionality within a part family in response to sudden changes in market or regulatory requirements" [7]. The authors conduct a comparison between Dedicated manufacturing lines (DML), Flexible Manufacturing System (FMS) and RMS based on several features (Table 1). Regarding the context described previously RMS are the most convenient system to consider reaching mobility.

Table 1. Comparison of RMS features with dedicated and flexible systems [7]

	DML	RMS	FMS
System structure	Fixed	Changeable	Changeable
Machine structure	Fixed	Changeable	Fixed
System FocusPart	Part	Part Family	Machine
Scalability	No	Yes	Yes
Flexibility	No	Customized	General
Simultaneously operating tools	Yes	Possible	No
Productivity	Very High	High	Low
Cost per part	Low	Medium	Reasonable

3.2   Design Framework for RMS

Manufacturing systems engineering frameworks can be classified into 3 families:

- frameworks that address the manufacturing system selection process [1],
- manufacturing system design [8],
- manufacturing system control [9].

Deif proposed a systematic design approach for reconfigurable manufacturing system [10]. The architecture is composed of two modules. The first one describes the design process of the reconfigurable manufacturing systems while. The second one describes the control of the design process at each level. The control module is based on performance measurements that reflect the strategic objectives of the RMS. The architecture of the design process is made of 3 layers: (1) market-capture layer, (2) system-level reconfiguration layer and (3) component-level reconfiguration layer. Determination of the decisions that drive the design of the manufacturing system is necessary. These decisions impact both the nature and the number of resources needed to satisfy the demand. We propose a design framework allowing to take into account and to structure the main decisions driving generation of manufacturing system configurations. This framework, adapted from Deif [10], is based on 3 layers :

Strategic Level: The objective of this level is to capture the market demand to generate the required capacity and functionality that will be used as inputs to the tactical level. Control module is based on performance measurements: cost, quality and responsiveness time.

Tactical Level: The objective of this level is to select the best configuration that will enable the satisfaction of the market demand. Figure 2 shows some examples of decisions that will impact the design of the manufacturing system. Generation of multiple configurations is enabled by the modular design of the manufacturing system components. Modeling and evaluation are based on a genetic algorithm. The selection of the best solution uses an evaluation module and a simulation tool.

The generation of reconfigurable manufacturing system configurations is controlled by constraints (cost, space, demand satisfaction...). Best feasible configuration among the generated ones is then selected using predetermined performance measurements: Time, Quality, Reconfiguration smoothness index.

Operational Level: Operational level deals with the physical implementation of a selected configuration. The implementation affects physical, logical and human components. Integrability and machine open control architecture are the major enabling technologies for the successful of the real physical implementation of the reconfigurable manufacturing system [10]. This level is controlled by performance measurements like cost, quality, time and reconfigurability.

3.3   RMS in the Solar Energy Field: Case Study

In the Solar Energy Field, shipping costs drive the global manufacturing cost of solar collectors. Currently, shipping costs are expensive due to the wide surface of solar collectors, light and uncompact structures. A solution to reduce the global manufacturing cost is to produce close to the end-user installation site. Moreover, in order to make the production system investment more profitable, it would be wise if the same production system can serve producing many solar fields i.e. if the manufacturing system can move between different production sites. Furthermore, as the market demand forecast fluctuates between two orders, the product volume and duration to satisfy this demand may vary. The manufacturing system may cope with this variability. Demand variation results in a necessary, cost effectively, up gradation or down gradation of the manufacturing system capacity. Solar fields are installed in desert environment, with high temperatures and rough climatic conditions the functionality of the manufacturing system must be adapted to the specifications of each site. Finally, the manufacturing system is operated by technical and human resources. The need to employ local labor requires adapting the mobile manufacturing system. Available qualification and socio-cultural background should be taken into account when reconfiguring the manufacturing system. For economic and feasibility reasons, the production system must be moveable to various end-user sites. The main idea is to easily reuse manufacturing capacity between different orders or projects. Manufacturing system must be prepared for reconfiguration according to market and order situation. System reconfigurability is driven by external change triggers such as:

- Variable volume demand: the demand profile is characterized by mass production, and high volume variability due to market uncertainties. Scalable capacity is needed to handle volume demand variability.
- Geographical location change: to be able to move to each final location, manufacturing system and all its components should be mobile.
- Location specifications: production system must be operational in various final locations with specific constraints (e.g. temperature, climate conditions).To cope with these changes, scalability, mobility and convertibility are considered as necessary characteristics and must be embedded into the manufacturing system. Figure 2 shows the RMS design framework we propose dedicated to the solar energy field.

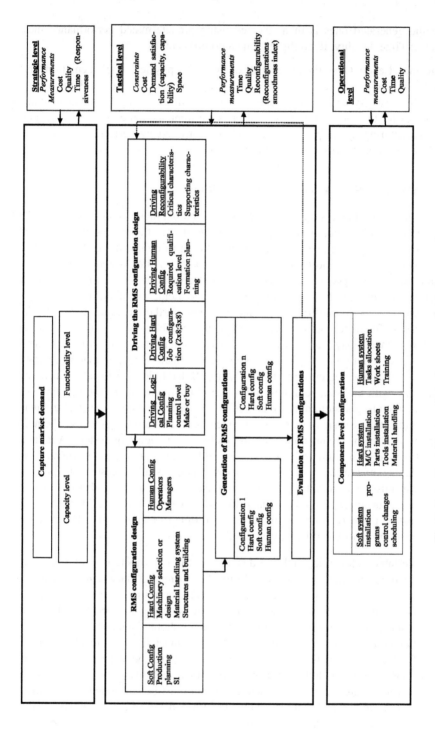

Fig. 2. Reconfigurable manufacturing system design framework

4   Conclusion

The concept of mobile manufacturing system has been presented, and the reasons why this solution could be needed were identified. Factors impacting mobility have been described. Special issues about the management of the mobility between the stationary and temporary location have been addressed. Furthermore, questions related to the interaction of the manufacturing system with its environment have been addressed as well as reflections induced by mobility constraints.

In addition to the need for mobility, the manufacturing system must cope with variability in demand volume and product mix. Reconfigurable manufacturing system paradigm has been analyzed. In this connection a design framework for RMS has been presented. Finally, the make or buy problem for RMS operation in multi-site context has been addressed, the reader is encouraged to consult [11] for in-depth analysis of this question.

References

1. Chryssolouris, G.: Manufacturing systems theory and practice. Springer, New York (2006)
2. ElMaraghy, H.A.: Flexible and reconfigurable manufacturing systems paradigms. Int. J. Flex. Manuf. Syst. 17(4), 261–276 (2006)
3. Bi, Z.M., Lang, S.Y.T., Shen, W., Wang, L.: Reconfigurable manufacturing systems: the state of the art. Int. J. Prod. Res. 46(4), 967–992 (2008)
4. Stillström, C., Jackson, M.: The concept of mobile manufacturing. J. Manuf. Syst. 26(3-4), 188–193 (2007)
5. Upton, D.M.: Flexibility as process mobility: The management of plant capabilities for quick response manufacturing. J. Oper. Manag. 12(3-4), 205–224 (1995)
6. Wiendahl, H.-P., ElMaraghy, H.A., Nyhuis, P., Zäh, M.F., Wiendahl, H.-H., Duffie, N., Brieke, M.: Changeable Manufacturing - Classification, Design and Operation. CIRP Ann. - Manuf. Technol. 56(2), 783–809 (2007)
7. Koren, Y., Shpitalni, M.: Design of reconfigurable manufacturing systems. J. Manuf. Syst. 29(4), 130–141 (2010)
8. Cochran, D.S., Arinez, J.F., Duda, J.W., Linck, J.: A decomposition approach for manufacturing system design. J. Manuf. Syst. 20(6), 371–389 (2002)
9. Chen, D., Vallespir, B., Doumeingts, G.: GRAI integrated methodology and its mapping onto generic enterprise reference architecture and methodology. Comput. Ind. 33(2-3), 387–394 (1997)
10. Deif, A.M., ElMaraghy, W.H.: A Systematic Design Approach for Reconfigurable Manufacturing Systems. In: Hoda, A.E., Waguih, H.E. (eds.) Advances in Design, pp. 219–228. Springer, Heidelberg (2006)
11. Benama, Y., Alix, T., Perry, N.: Supporting make or buy decision for reconfigurable manufacturing system. In: Multi-Site Context. presented at the APMS, Ajaccio (2014)

Assessing the Role of Plants in International Manufacturing Networks: A Tool to Monitor the Strategic Alignment

Donatella Corti, Luca Canetta, and Alessandro Fontana

University of Applied Sciences and Arts of Southern Switzerland, ISTePS, Manno, Switzerland
{donatella.corti,luca.canetta,alessandro.fontana}@supsi.ch

Abstract. The internationalization of operations has been quite a common trend for Western companies over the last 20 years. The development of manufacturing networks is a more and more common solution also for SMEs. In order to make sure that the whole network evolves according to the business requirements, each single plant needs to be assigned a precise role. Starting from the well-known framework proposed by Ferdows ([5]; [6]) on the strategic role of plants, a tool is developed to monitor the role of production plants by aligning the vision of the headquarters and the one of the plant itself. Four case studies are carried out to validate the model and some guidelines are then derived to interpret the output. This paper contributes to the field dealing with the strategic role of plants with a proposal that can be easily applied by practitioners.

Keywords: manufacturing networks, strategic role of plants, Ferdows' model, assessment model.

1 Introduction

Over the last decades, it has been a common trend for a large number of companies in industrialized countries to increase their international presence as a way to strengthen competitive position and increase their sustainability in the long term. Even though in the past this choice was mainly confined to multinational enterprises, nowadays production relocation is a more and more widespread option also for SMEs (see for example [3]). The recent evolution of the competitive context and, in particular, the huge economic crisis that hit the Western countries led to new trends for this phenomenon: as argued by Kinkel ([9]), production relocation has declined, whilst the number of backshoring activities has remained stable in the period 2007 to mid-2009. At the same time, a further relocation from East Europe to Far East has been noted ([9]). As shown by these recent findings, the research on international production networks is still an evolving topic that needs to keep pace with the dynamics of the macroeconomic environment. The academic interest for management of operations in offshored plants has increased and shifted from dyadic relationships to the networks framing and management ([11]; [8]; [7]; [6]). In this paper the focus is on a specific form of direct foreign investment that entails the set up of a fully owned plant by a

B. Grabot et al. (Eds.): APMS 2014, Part III, IFIP AICT 440, pp. 360–367, 2014.
© IFIP International Federation for Information Processing 2014

SME running a dispersed production network. In this context, attention is paid to the coordination of the network from a strategic point of view: companies need tools that could support them in continuously monitoring the configuration of the network and, in particular, if and how the single plant is contributing to the success of the network as a whole. The proposed model is a decisional supporting tool that aims at supporting SMEs in continuously monitoring the dynamics of the production network by making sure that each plant is acting according to the assigned role. The tool provides managers of both the parent company and the offshored plant with a common set of data to start sharing a strategic vision the running of the plant should be based on. This paper contributes to the literature debate by further testing the Ferdorws' model, whilst, at the same time, attempts to translate theoretical concepts currently mainly used only in the academic arena into a tool for practitioners.

2   The Strategic Role of Plants within an International Production Network

The literature on manufacturing networks mainly takes a macro and static perspective ([14]), neglecting the dynamics and lacking overall evidence on the interactions between the evolution of individual plants and the whole network ([2]). Although there are several models in defining strategic roles of the international network plants, the Ferdows's model ([5]; [6]) be considered as a milestone or a starting point for the development of a tool which enables the consideration of dynamic changes of a plant's role [10]. [6] addresses the roles of plants, introducing a model based on a matrix whose axis represent the strategic reason for choosing the location of a plant and the site's competence (measured on a low to high scale). Crossing the two dimensions, six strategic roles are identified. Unlike other classifications, the Ferdow's one introduces a clear analytical framework and allows the consideration of some dynamic aspects. He also pursued a more operations management-oriented approach focusing on the role and functioning of individual factories in international manufacturing networks rather than using the business unit as unit of analysis [10]. [16] state that the contribution of plants which have "low" level in the vertical axis of the Ferdows' model is to produce items, while "high" level in the vertical axis represents also important developments such as providing know-how for the other facilities of the network. However, the Ferdows' model lacks of a clear definition and operationalization of the site competence dimension [15]. Building on this reasoning, [10] have focused on the dynamic changes that occur in the strategic roles of factories and enhanced the site competences axis of Ferdows' conceptual model by identifying additional factors that contribute to the level of site competence. Different plants are source of different capabilities [4]: companies should work on the assessment of the plant's operations and performance management of single plants. Some possible indicators to be used are mentioned in [12] or [4]. Even though the importance of monitoring the network considering the different role of each plant within it, literature on the assessment of international production networks is still scarce and lacks of holistic frameworks.

3   An Assessment Model to Support the Strategic Role of Plants

This paper aims at contributing to the literature on strategic roles of plants by proposing a model that further extend Ferdows' proposal ([6]) by taking into account its recent extensions ([10]; [15]) and making it suitable for practitioners'use. Practical tools are needed to make sure, on the one hand, that strategic objectives are properly shared between the headquarters and each single manufacturing plant and, on the other hand, that performance of plants are aligned with the evolution of the network as a whole. The goal is to provide a dashboard (Figure 1) for both headquarters and foreign plants that can be used to determine the strategic role of the specific production unit of interest. This is done through mapping the current strategic role from the perspective of both headquarter and the plant itself and by analyzing possible gaps in order to build a shared set of believes. Furthermore, since the role of plants within the network is a dynamic one, the model is also able to timely highlight the need for a possible shift. The proposed model takes as a reference the two dimensions characterizing both Ferdows' and Meijboom and Vos's model, but the vertical axis (site competence) is redefined considering the current needs of the international production networks. The resulting framework becomes a tool that could be used to position different plants and monitor their role over time identifying possible misalignments. The tool includes kind of a dashboard that shows the results in a graphical way and a questionnaire that supports practitioners to define in a structured way the role of the plant. Since one of the aim of this tool is the measurement of how aligned are the perspectives of headquarter and foreign plants, the application procedure foresees the use of the same set of questions for both the parent company and the plant. By comparing the two resulting positioning it is possible to take into account possible misalignment characterizing the two visions. The present version of the model has been developed with Excel that provides the user with an immediate representation of the results that makes easier the comparison between the two visions. Like in the reference models, the key aspects to be investigated are: "Primary strategic reason for the location of the plant" and "Level of site competence & technical activities at the plant".

Primary strategic reason for the location of the plant
The main strategic reasons for opening a plant in a specific location are the three already proposed by [6], as also further confirmed by more recent researches, namely access to low cost production input factors, use of local technological resources and proximity to market. A first set of questions has been included in the tool to understand which factors have a stronger effect on the choice of the location for the plant. With a straightforward calculation considering all the factors and their relative importance, the main strategic reason is determined. For each strategic reason a set of related factors are identified and who fills in the questionnaire has to rank their relative importance on a 5-point scale (1= unimportant; 5 = very important). The total score for the single factor is then translated into a percentage that reflects the level of pursuing of that objective. More objectives are achieved at the same time, but one is the main trigger for setting up the plant. The strategic reason with the highest

probability is defined as the primary reason for the relocation. The complete list of elements is shown on the left side of Figure 1.

Level of site competence & technical activities at the plant

This dimension takes into consideration the site competence meaning the level of responsibility and autonomy assigned to the plant. Some changes compared to the list of activities proposed in [10] have been introduced and a total of 10 dimensions have been identified to characterize this axis. The choice of the dimensions has been driven by both literature analysis and expertise of authors in the fields of global operations management. In order to operationalize the framework each factor has been assigned equal importance (10%). The higher the percentage achieved by a plant, the more strategic its role is. In order to calculate the level of site competence expressed in percentage (100% means the highest strategic role), each one of the ten factors is analyzed by considering its constituting elements associated to the questions included in the questionnaire. Activities are presented in order of increasing importance so that the higher the number of elements included, the more strategic the role is.

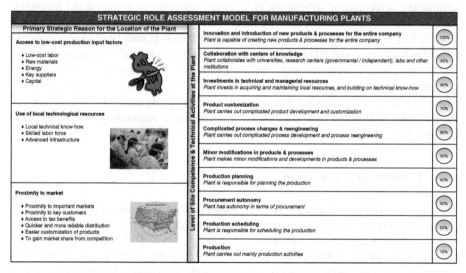

Fig. 1. Dashboard presenting the assessment scope and factors

Even though the list of proposed factors is partially overlapping with the one introduced by [10], some changes have been introduced in order to take into account recent literature on both operations management and global production networks. For instance, it has been considered important to make explicit the possible ability of a plant to customize products. On the one hand, the need to customize is aligned with recent trends of production paradigms (see for example [13], [1]) that are influencing also markets under development. At the same time, from the production point of view, the customization requires a higher level of autonomy for the management of processes. Also the factor "collaboration with center of knowledge" has been introduced in order to consider the closer and closer link between companies and research centers whenever the introduction of innovation requires important investments as well as cutting edge knowledge. The ten activities use to define the level of site competence are the following (for space constraints they are not detailed further):

- Production (1)
- Production scheduling (2)
- Procurement autonomy (3)
- Production planning (4)
- Minor modifications in products & processes (5)
- Complicated process changes & reengineering (6)
- Product customization (7)
- Investments in technical and managerial resources (8)
- Collaboration with centers of knowledge (9)
- Innovation and introduction of new products & processes for the company (10)

In Figure 1, the right side of the framework highlights the list of factors and the cumulative probability that determines the level of site competence. In order to determine the percentage of attainment of a certain competence is carried out following a similar reasoning than the one used for the strategic priority. For each competence a list of factors is assessed on a 5-point scale and then it is translated in to a percentage value between 0 and 10 in such a way that the ten factors can score a maximum of 100 % (the highest strategic role). The availability of a tool allowing a practical and systematic identification of the strategic role of plants and the observation of its evolution over time is recommendable for every manufacturing network, in particular for those run by SMEs that typically have a less structured monitoring system in place and have fewer resources to dedicate to this task.

4   Empirical Validation

The proposed assessment tool has been validated collecting empirical data from a sample of four Turkish companies running an international production network. The main selection criteria has been the location of the headquarter, Turkey, in order to avoid possible bias due to cultural differences in managing the network. Out of the nine companies that have been contacted, four have shown positive interest to take part in the case study research by answering the questionnaires and carrying out face-to-face interviews. One of the sampled companies is a big one even though the proposed assessment has as primary beneficiary SMEs. This case has been used to further check that the tool is coherent with already existing procedures in place in multinational and big companies. According to the aim of the assessment model, for each company both the headquarters and one plant of the network located in a foreign country have been involved in the research. Main features of the sampled companies are summarized in Table 1. The use of the tool allowed the assessment of the vision of the headquarters and the one of the production plant. To give an example of the output the tool can provide, the case of company C is discussed. The questionnaire has been filled in separately by the supply chain manager of the headquarters and the plant manager of the plant located in Russia. The analysis carried out by both the headquarters and the plant led to the identification of "proximity to market" as the primary reason for locating the plant: in both cases, this strategic reason was the highest ranked with respectively 26,7 % (plant, Figure 2) and 28,9 % (headquarters, Figure 2).

Table 1. Summary of information for the analyzed sample

	Sector	Turnover	No. plants	Analyzed plant	No. employees (total)	No. employees (plant)
A	Fabricated steel production	100-500 Mln	3	China	2400	270
B	Beer production	>1 billion	16	Russia	10000	4500
C	Building products	100-500 Mln	3	Russia	220	80
D	Construction	< 100 Mln	3	Russia	900	200

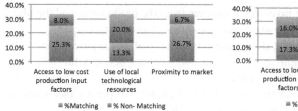 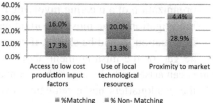

Fig. 2. Company C- Russian plant: assessment of % of matching with reasons according to the primary strategic reason (left: vision of the plant; right: vision of the headquarter)

This strategic reason has been also confirmed by the open interview that was carried out with the headquarter managers to interpret and validate the tool's results. Moving to the site competence, the overall score obtained from the headquarters is 59% out of a possible score of 100%, whereas the score assigned by the plant itself is noticeably higher and equal to 83%. This can be interpreted as the plant seeing itself as more strategically important than the headquarters views it. It is worth noticing that the plant is a new one, set up in 2010: it could take some time to fine-tune the management of a plant and, in the first of operation, misalignment are likely to happen. Being able to highlight such gaps timely is a way to achieve a better level of integration since the beginning with a positive impact not only on the single plant, but also on the network profitability. The fact that the plant identify a higher level of competence probably means that the headquarters are not fully aware yet of the full potentialities of the plant. The identification of the main gaps between the two visions provides the headquarters with some valuable inputs to improve the management of the plant. A more detailed analysis should be carried out to understand the sources of the biggest differences appeared in the activities "Complicated process changes & reengineering", "product customization" and "Innovation and introduction of new products & processes for the entire company".

5   Managerial Guidelines When Using the Tool

For the proposed tool to be easily accepted and put into use by executives, it has been designed as a self-evaluating tool, based on a set of simple and straightforward questions that graphically visualize the obtained results for facilitating their interpretation. As shown in the case study analysis, the tool allows highlighting possible gaps. At this point, it is important to be able to point out the difference, analyze it further to find the root cause and to take actions to increase the alignment. Some guidelines have been drawn to interpret the results of the tool. When the primary reason does not coincide between the two visions an important intervention is foreseen in order to realign the strategy, this entails a significant strategic change for at least one of the involved actors. On the contrary, a gap highlighted in the site competence could be confined to single activities that typically require interventions of a practical nature. In the case of a misalignment in terms of the current primary location driver, in order to quickly and objectively evaluate the scores the developed guidelines suggest the following actions:

- organization of a meeting involving managers from the headquarter and the plant;
- investigation of the most important causes or areas of misalignment;
- information should be shared, if necessary, in order to align the perceptions

The gap or the misalignment about the site competences between the two viewpoints can arise from three possible scenarios:

- the headquarters has a realistic view of the plant, but the plant either overestimates or underestimates its current competence level.
- the plant has a realistic view of itself, but the headquarter either overestimates or underestimates the current competence level of the plant.
- the headquarter and the plant have extreme views of the plant, one underestimating whereas the other overestimating.

The developed guidelines suggest different approaches to be adopted depending on the magnitude of the gap. For differences up to 5% no important intervention is foreseen. For gaps between 5% and 10% the situation is more serious and a careful analysis of factors for which the gap is higher is needed since there is a clear misalignment for some activities. For gaps higher than 10%, the intervention of the headquarters is urgent to limit the derivation of the two visions. Possible interventions depend on contingent factors thus making difficult the development of a general procedure.

6   Conclusions

The model proposed in this paper is a tool meant to support a company not only in identifying the role of a plant, but also to understand whether the same vision is shared by both the plant and the headquarter. The main benefit for the plant managers is that they will be able to better evaluate the strengths of the plant as well as major areas that may provide opportunities for future improvements. On the other hand, the headquarters will have a better picture of the whole network that should result in a more balanced set of actors. Additional empirical data collection is needed to further validate and fine-tune the tool. An extension of the model is already under development that introduces a more detailed assessment model including a set of indicators for the different factors defining the site competence.

References

1. Boër, C.R., Pedrazzoli, P., Bettoni, A., Sorlini, M.: Mass Customization and Sustainability. An assessment framework and industrial implementation. Springer (2013)
2. Cheng, Y.C., Farooq, S., Johansen, J.: Manufacturing network evolution: a manufacturing plant perspective. International Journal of Operations and Production Management 31(12), 1311–1331 (2011)
3. Corti, D., Egana, M.M., Errasti, A.: Challenges for off-shored operations: findings from a comparative multi-case study analysis of Italian and Spanish companies. In: Proceedings of 16th Annual EurOMA Conference, Gothenburg (2009)
4. Dossi, A., Patelli, L.: You Learn From What You Measure: Financial and Non-Financial Performance Measures in Multinational Companies. Long Range Planning 43, 498–526 (2010)
5. Ferdows, K.: Mapping international factory networks. In: Ferdows, K. (ed.) Managing International Manufacturing, Elsevier, Amsterdam (1989)
6. Ferdows, K.: Making the most of Foreign Factories. Harvard Business Review (March-April 1997)
7. Forsgren, M., Holm, U., Johanson, J.: Managing the embedded multinational: A business network view. Edward Elgar, Cheltenham (2005)
8. Ghoshal, S., Bartlett, C.A.: The multinational corporation as an inter-organizational network. In: Ghoshal, S., Westney, D.E. (eds.) Organization Theory and the Multinational Corporation, pp. 68–92. Palgrave MacMillan, Houndsmill (2005)
9. Kinkel, S.: Trends in production relocation and backshoring activities. Changing patterns in the course of the global economic crisis. International Journal of Operations & Production Management 32(6), 696–720 (2012)
10. Meijboom, B., Vos, B.: Site competence dynamics in international manufacturing networks: instrument development and a test in Eastern European factories. Journal of Purchasing & Supply Management 10, 127–136 (2004)
11. O'Donnel, S.: Managing Foreign Subsidiaries: Agents of Headquarters, or an Interdependent Network? Strategic Management Journal 21, 525–548 (2000)
12. Parthiban, P., Goh, M.: An integrated model for performance management of manufacturing units. Benchmarking: An International Journal 18(2), 261–281 (2011)
13. Piller, F.T.: Observations on the present and future of mass customization. International Journal of Felxible Manufacturing Systems 19(4), 630–636 (2007)
14. Rudberg, M., Olhager, J.: Manufacturing networks and supply chains: an operations strategy perspective. Omega: International Journal of Management Science 31, 29–39 (2003)
15. Vereecke, A., Van Dierdonck, R.: The Strategic Role of the Plant: Testing Ferdow's Model. International Journal of Operations & Production Management 22(5), 492–514 (2002)
16. Vereecke, A., De Meyer, A., Van Dierdonck, R.: The Strategic Role of the Plant in International Networks: A Longitudinal Study. Vlerick Leuven Gent Working Paper Series (July 2008)

Reducing the Research Space of Possible Order Release Dates for Multi-level Assembly Systems under Stochastic Lead Times

Oussama Ben Ammar[1], Hélène Marian[1], Alexandre Dolgui[1], and Dash Wu[2]

[1] École Nationale Supérieure des Mines, EMSE-FAYOL, CNRS UMR6158, LIMOS,
F-42023, Saint-Étienne, France
{obenammar,marian,dolgui}@emse.fr
[2] University of Toronto, Canada
dwu@fields.utoronto.ca

Abstract. This paper proposes tools which will be used to optimize multi-level assembly under lead time uncertainty. One type of finished products and several types of components are considered. We suppose that each component has a fixed unit inventory cost and the finished product has backlogging and inventory holding costs per unit of time. The lead times of components are discrete random variables, and the costumer's demand of the finished product is known. A reduced space of research is presented to strengthen optimization methods which have been applied for minimizing the sum of the average inventory holding cost for components and the average backlogging and inventory holding costs for the finished product.

Keywords: Stochastic lead times, multi-level assembly system, reduced space of research.

1 Introduction and Related Publications

For assembly systems, the lead times of components may be an uncertain parameter; it is rarely deterministic and mostly has a variable value. This unpredictability may be caused by technical problems such as machines breakdowns, limited capacity, delay of transport, etc.

Various techniques such as safety stocks and safety lead times are used by planners in order to lead the better anticipation of lead time uncertainties. For example Koh and Saad (2006) specified that the safety lead time can be used to handle uncertainties in supply chain, such as late delivery. Molinder (1997) showed that both the uncertainty of the lead time and demand variability involve the level of optimal safety lead times and optimal safety stocks.

Dolgui et al. (2008) studied the MRP parameterization problem for two-level assembly systems with random component procurement times. They explained that lead time uncertainties seem to be insufficiently studied for a long time, favouring the study of demand uncertainties.

B. Grabot et al. (Eds.): APMS 2014, Part III, IFIP AICT 440, pp. 368–374, 2014.

In the literature few researchers have studied lead time variability for assembly systems. Ould Louly and Dolgui (2002), Dolgui et al. (2009), and Ould Louly et al. (2008a) proposed a discrete Newsboy model for one-level assembly systems to minimize the average inventory holding cost for components while maintaining a high customer service level for the finished product. The same problem was solved by a Branch and Bound procedure in Ould Louly and al (2008b).

Hnaien et al. (2009) and Fallah-Jamshidi et al. (2011) modelled and optimized two-level assembly systems, in particular for a fixed demand, a known due date and an unlimited capacity. The same problem, but for multi-level assembly systems, is studied by Ben Ammar et al. (2012) and Ben Ammar et al. (2013a). Authors proposed analytical and simulation models to calculate the expected value of the cost which is the sum of the average component holding cost and the average finished product backlogging and holding costs. To minimize this expected cost, the proposed models are coupled with a GA which Hnaien et al. (2009) used in their studies. The same problem was solved by a Branch and Bound approach (Ben Ammar et al., 2013b). However, a reduction of the search space seems be necessary to improve these results.

A multi-level assembly system with stochastic lead times at each level is studied in this paper. It continues the work of Ben Ammar et al., (2013a). We propose a reduced space of research which depends on finished product costs.

The rest of paper is organized into five sections. Firstly, we describe the problem (section 2). The initial space of research is given in section 3. Some results are shown in section 4. Finally, we outline the work done in the conclusion and give some perspectives of future research.

2   Problem Description

To get closer to the industrial methods of planning, we consider a discrete temporal environment. The Figure 1 shows that the finished product is produced from

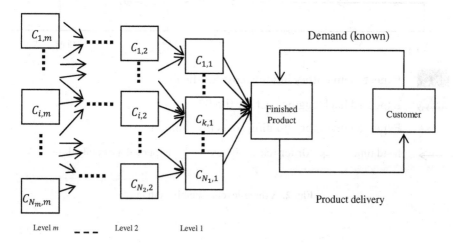

Fig. 1. A multi-level assembly system

components themselves obtained from other components. We limit our study into a single period. We assume that both the due date T and the demand for the finished product are deterministic and known. A unit backlogging cost and a unit inventory holding cost for the finished product, and a unit inventory cost for each component are considered. Actual lead times are modelled as independent random discrete variables with known probability distributions.

In this model, the MRP system is considered as a push-system. Thus, for each level, when all the necessary components are available, level m delivers the components to level $m-1$ with a random discrete lead time. When the semi-finished product arrives at the final level (level 0), it undergoes the necessary operations and afterwards the finished product is delivered to the customer in order to satisfy the demand. It is assumed that each component of level m is used to assemble only one type of component at level $m-1$.

The objective is to find the order release dates for components at level m which minimize the expected value of the total cost (it is given in Ben Ammar et al. (2013b)) which equals to the sum of the inventory holding cost for components and the backlogging and inventory holding costs for the finished product (see the example in Figure 2).

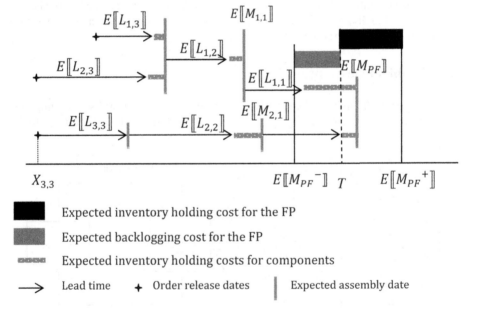

Fig. 2. A three-level assembly system

3   Reduced Space of Research

Let $u_{i,l}$ the maximum value of $L_{i,l}$ and $U_{i,m}$ the longest time between the release date for component $c_{i,m}$ and T. Each $L_{i,l}$ varies in $[1, u_{i,l}]$ and each order release date $X_{i,m}$ varies in $[T - U_{i,m}, T - m]$.

The idea is to reduce this search space of all feasible solutions. That is why we rely on the property related to the distribution of lead times. For this we decompose the multi-level assembly system (Figure 1) to N_m (the number of components at level m) multi-level linear supply chains (Figure 3). Each linear chain is composed of m components and delivers a finished product on a specified delivery date.

Let $c_{i_m,m}$ a component at level m whose lead time is equal to $L_{i_m,m}$. This component is necessary to make the component $c_{i_{m-1},m-1}$ (its lead time is equal to $L_{i_{m-1},m-1}$) ; itself compound the component $c_{i_{m-2},m-2}$ etc. The availability date of the product of this linear chain is equal to $\psi_{i_m} = L + X_{i_m,m}$ with $L = L_{i_1,1} + L_{i_2,2} + \cdots + L_{i_{m-1},m-1} + L_{i_m,m}$.

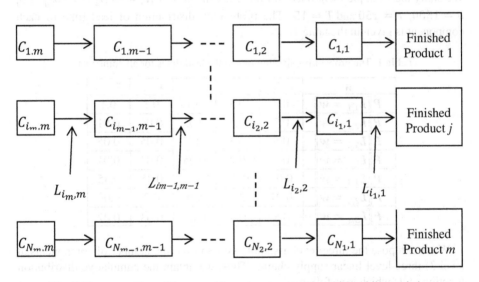

Fig. 3. Decomposition of the assembly system to several multi-level linear chains

Let b the unit backlogging cost for the finished product and r the inventory holding cost for the finished product. For each linear chain:

- The total expected cost $E[\![X_{j,m}]\!]$, which is equal to the sum of b and r, can be deduced from the proposition (2) in Hnaien et al. (2008) by changing the unit inventory holding cost at level 1 by the unit inventory holding cost for the finished product.

— The optimal solution $X_{j,m}^*$ which minimizes $E[\![X_{j,m}]\!]$ is also given in proposition (3) in Hnaien et al. (2008). It satisfies the optimality condition for the discrete Newsboy model, where the cumulative distribution function $F(.)$ of the total lead time L is used:

$$F\left(T - X_{j,m}^* - 1\right) \leq \frac{b}{b+r} \leq F\left(T - X_{j,m}^*\right) \tag{1}$$

For each order release date $X_{j,m}$ for component $c_{j,m}$ in the assembly system, $X_{j,m}^*$ can be the upper limit and the initial research space of possible solutions $[T - U_{j,m}, T - m]$ can be reduced to $[T - U_{j,m}, X_{j,m}^*]$. By contradiction, it can be easily proven. The complete proof will be published soon.

4   Experimental Results

We study the example mentioned in Figure 2 with $m = 3, N_3 = 3, N_2 = 2, u_{i,j} = 5,$ $b = 1500, r = 150$ and $T = 15$. The probability distribution of lead time of each component is given in the table 1.

Table 1. The probability distributions of the lead times for all components

w	1	2	3	4	5
$P[\![L_{1,1} = w]\!]$	0.4	0.3	0.1	0.1	0.1
$P[\![L_{2,1} = w]\!]$	0.7	0.2	0.05	0.04	0.01
$P[\![L_{1,2} = w]\!]$	0.5	0.3	0.1	0.05	0.05
$P[\![L_{2,2} = w]\!]$	0.7	0.2	0.05	0.04	0.01
$P[\![L_{1,3} = w]\!]$	0.09	0.01	0.1	0.35	0.45
$P[\![L_{2,3} = w]\!]$	0.01	0.1	0.6	0.2	0.09
$P[\![L_{3,3} = w]\!]$	0.8	0.1	0.05	0.03	0.02

We decompose the three-level assembly system to 3 (the number of components at level 3) three-level linear supply chains. Thus, we obtain the cumulative distribution function of L which is as follows:

- $c_{1,3} \rightarrow c_{1,2} \rightarrow c_{1,1} \rightarrow FP_1$

F(3)=0.018;   F(4)=0.0443;   F(5)=0.0832;   F(6)=0.1937;   F(7)=0.40875; F(8)=0.6129; F(9)=0.7543; **F(10)=0.86365; F(11)=0.94345**; F(12)=0.9785; F(13)=0.9915; F(14)=0.99775; F(15)=1.

- $c_{2,3} \rightarrow c_{1,2} \rightarrow c_{1,1} \rightarrow FP_2$

F(3)=0.002;   F(4)=0.0247;   F(5)=0.1735;   F(6)=0.3948;   F(7)=0.58905; F(8)=0.74045;   **F(9)=0.86385;**   **F(10)=0.93865;**   F(11)=0.97495; F(12)=0.99085; F(13)=0.99765; F(14)=0.99955; F(15)=1.

- $c_{3.3} \rightarrow c_{2.2} \rightarrow c_{2.1} \rightarrow FP_3$

F(3)=0.084; F(4)=0.2865; F(5)=0.48175; F(6)=0.65045; **F(7)=0.841525;**
F(8)=0.927;   F(9)=0.966055;   F(10)=0.987505;   F(11)=0.99658;
F(12)=0.998965; F(13)=0.99971; F(14)=0.99996; F(15)=1.

The optimal release date $X_{1,3}^*$ for the first linear supply chain $c_{1.3} \rightarrow c_{1.2} \rightarrow c_{1.1} \rightarrow FP_1$ is given by the expression (1):

$$F(10) \leq F\left(15 - X_{1,3}^* - 1\right) \leq 0{,}909091 \leq F\left(T - X_{1,3}^*\right) \leq F \qquad (11)$$

The optimal release date $X_{1,3}^*$ is equal to 4. It is the upper limit for the order release date $X_{1,3}$ for component $c_{1,3}$ in the assembly system. The initial research space of possible solutions $[0, 12]$ can be reduced to $[0, 4]$. $X_{2,3}^*$ and $X_{3,3}^*$ are determined in the same way and are equal to 5 and 7.

For each component, the upper limit $\sigma\left(X_{j,3}^*\right)$ of the initial research space i is equal to 12 $(T - m)$. Then, the cardinal of the initial space of research is thus equal to 13^3 $((T - m + 1)^{Nm})$ solutions. The cardinal of the reduced space of research is equal to 210 $(5 \times 6 \times 7)$ and is reduced the initial space by 90%.

To study the influence of costs, we fix r to 10 and vary b. Table 2 gives the upper limits of the reduced space of research.

Table 2. Upper bounds of the reduced space of research in function of inventory holding cost

b	1	10	10^2	10^3	10^4	10^5
$\sigma\left(X_{1,3}^*\right)$	9	7	4	2	1	0
$\sigma\left(X_{2,3}^*\right)$	10	8	5	3	1	0
$\sigma\left(X_{3,3}^*\right)$	11	9	7	4	2	0

Note that the backlogging cost for the finished product influences the cardinality of the space of research. For a fixed inventory holding cost, an increase of backlogging cost decreases significantly the cardinality of the space of research. In other words, we should order as soon as possible when the backlogging cost increases.

5   Conclusions

This paper deals with the reducing of the research space of order release dates of components which compound a multi-level assembly system under a fixed demand and uncertain lead times for components.

The reduced space of research will be used to choose the appropriate method to optimize multi-level assembly systems. For example, Local Search or a Branch and Bound method may be sufficient when the backlogging cost much greater than the inventory holding cost. For other cases, Genetic Algorithms coupled with others heuristics may optimize this problem.

Our future work will focus on the analysis of the correlation between different costs and the number of components in the level m of the nomenclature to choice the appropriate method to minimize the expected cost.

References

1. Ben Ammar, O., Marian, H., Dolgui, A.: Optimization for supply planning in multi-level assembly systems with stochastic lead-times. In: 5th International Conference on Industrial Engineering and System Management (IESM 2013), Morocco, October 28-30, p. 10 (2013a)
2. Ben Ammar, O., Marian, H., Wu, D., Dolgui, A.: Mathematical Model for Supply Planning of Multi-level Assembly Systems with Stochastic Lead Times. Invited keynote paper for a special session. In: Bakhtadze, N., Dolgui, A., Lototsky, V. (eds.) Proceedings of the IFAC Conference on Manufacturing Modelling, Management and Control (MIM 2013), St Petersburg, Russia, June 19-21, 6pages. Elsevier Science (2013b) IFAC-PapersOnline.net (ISSN 1474-6670)
3. Ben Ammar, O., Marian, H., Dolgui, A.: Configuration d'un système d'assemblage multi-niveau sous incertitudes des délais d'approvisionnement. In: 9th International Conference on Modeling, Optimization and SIMulation (MOSIM 2012), Bordeaux, France, June 6-8, 10 pages (2012)
4. Dolgui, A., Prodhon, C.: Supply planning under uncertainties in MRP environments: A state of the art. Annual Reviews in Control 31, 269–279 (2007)
5. Dolgui, A., Hnaien, F., Ould Louly, M., Marian, H.: Parameterization of MRP for supply planning under uncertainties of lead times. In: Kordic, V. (ed.) Supply Chain, pp. 247–262. I-Tech Education and Publishing (2008) ISBN 978–3–902613–22–6
6. Koh, S., Saad, S.: Managing uncertainty in ERP-controlled manufacturing environments in SMES. International Journal of Production Economics 101(1), 109–127 (2006)
7. Hnaien, F., Dolgui, A., Ould Louly, M.: Planned lead time optimization in material requirement planning environment for multilevel production systems. Journal of Systems Science and Systems Engineering 17(2), 132–155 (2008)
8. Hnaien, F., Delorme, X., Dolgui, A.: Genetic algorithm for supply planning in two-level assembly systems with random lead times. Engineering Applications of Artificial Intelligence 22, 906–915 (2009)
9. Fallah-Jamshidi, S., Karimi, N., Zandieh, M.: A hybrid multi-objective genetic algorithm for planning order release date in two-level assembly system with random lead times. Expert Systems with Applications (2011)
10. Molinder, A.: Joint optimisation of lot-sizes. Safety stocks and safety lead times in an MRP system. International Journal of Production Research 35, 983–994 (1997)
11. Ould Louly, M., Dolgui, A.: Generalized newsboy model to compute the optimal planned lead times in assembly systems. International Journal of Production Research 40(17), 4401–4414 (2002)
12. Ould Louly, M., Dolgui, A., Hnaien, F.: Supply planning for single-level assembly system with stochastic component delivery times and service level constraint. International Journal of Production Economics 115(1), 236–247 (2008a)
13. Ould Louly, M., Dolgui, A., Hnaien, F.: Optimal supply planning in MRP environments for assembly systems with random component procurement times. International Journal of Production Research 46(19), 5441–5467 (2008b)

Layout Design by Integration of Multi-agent Based Simulation and Optimization

Application to Underground Shopping Streets

Nobutada Fujii[1,*], Toshiya Kaihara[1], Tomomi Nonaka[2], and Shun Nogami[1]

[1] Graduate School of System Informatics, Kobe University
Rokkodai 1-1, Nada, Kobe 657-8501, Japan
[2] Dept. of Industrial and Systems Engineering, Aoyama Gakuin University, Kanagawa, Japan
nfujii@phoenix.kobe-u.ac.jp

Abstract. This paper proposes a layout design method by integration of multi-agent based simulation and optimization. The proposed method adopts 'optimization for simulation' approach to integrate simulation and optimization, in which optimization is executed first, then the result is evaluated through simulation by various scenarios. The optimization is repeated sequentially using an output data derived by the simulation executed in each previous turn. The proposed method is applied to a layout design problem for underground shopping streets, which is the problem determines store positions to be located. The objective of the layout design is to arrange store positions attractively for passers considering their preferences and target directions, which depend on the day of the week, time zones and seasons. Computer experiments are conducted to confirm the effectiveness of the proposed method.

Keywords: multi-agent based simulation, optimization, layout design, service engineering.

1 Introduction

Layout design for production systems and social systems is difficult to achieve both high levels of productivity and low cost simultaneously. Layout design methods have been proposed, however, most of them were implemented based on heuristic approaches to obtain better solutions without ensuring their optimality [1]. One of the most popular and practical methods is 'SLP (Systematic Layout Planning)' proposed by Muther [2]. A procedure of the SLP is as follows; (1) relationship between facilities based on their material flows by 'from-to charts' is revealed. (2) A chart named 'activity relationship chart' is developed based on the activities. (3) A required space is measured for each facility, and (4) a space relationship diagram is constructed by combining the activity relationship chart and the space requirement. (5) Alternative plans are developed to consider other remaining constraints. Finally, (6) a suitable layout plan is selected from the alternatives. The SLP method has been often implemented for the layout design of real plants and facilities, however, it is hard to

B. Grabot et al. (Eds.): APMS 2014, Part III, IFIP AICT 440, pp. 375–382, 2014.
© IFIP International Federation for Information Processing 2014

develop the 'activity relationship chart' using the 'from-to chart' to describe a material flow because of the huge combinations for the large scale problem.

Layout planning methods based on mathematical programming have been also proposed, in which the layout problem has been formulated as the quadratic assignment problems in the area of OR [3]. Recent developments of meta-heuristic approaches realize to solve a relatively large-scale optimization problem efficiently. In particular, many studies implement evolutionally computation-based optimization methods have been proposed [4][5]. The meta-heuristic based approaches enable to solve the real scale problems, however, it is usually required to set the static objective function such as fixed varieties of items or unchangeable available facilities in order to solve the facility layout planning within the framework of combinatorial optimization problem. Hence, the approaches should be extended to adapt current situations including dynamic and daily changes of production items and facility changes.

Simulation based approaches have been also proposed in order to consider probabilistic behaviors in systems or events which are difficult to be formulated. The approaches have no optimization logics, so that it is hard to change an experimental condition by using the simulation results. The simulation-based approaches can evaluate only predetermined layout plans. It should be demonstrated try and error processes to evaluate which plan is the best solution.

To overcome above mentioned limitations, integration methods of simulation based approach and optimization have been proposed [6][7]. The simulation and optimization are repeatedly executed; the obtained results derived from one method are incorporated into the other method as the input data. The simulation and optimization are implemented in a mutually complementary manner. In this paper, a layout design method by integrating multi-agent based simulation and optimization is proposed. To integrate the simulation and optimization, an approach of 'optimization for simulation' is implemented; the approach evaluates alternative plans by employing simulation, then optimization is executed by using the simulation results. The proposed method is applied to a social system layout design problem: underground shopping streets, in which the layout design problem is to determine the store positions to be located in the underground shopping streets. The layout design is implemented to arrange attractive stores for passers considering their preferences and target directions changing due to the situation such as the day of the week, time zones and seasons. The objective function of the optimization is to maximize total utilities for each store. The optimization and simulation are sequentially repeated using an output data derived by the simulation executed in each previous turn.

In the remainder of this paper will describe the framework of integration of multi-agent simulation and optimization in the section 2. Then, the application method of the framework to the layout design problem for underground shopping streets will be described in the section 3. In the section 4, computer experiments are conducted to confirm the feasibilities of the proposed method by comparing the current layout and the obtained layout by the proposed method. Finally, the conclusion and future works will be described in the section 5.

2   Framework of Integration of Simulation and Optimization

There are two purposes to integrate simulation and optimization [7]. The first one is to evaluate an alternative plan on simulation, then process optimization using the results by the simulation. In this approach, simulation is mainly demonstrated rather than optimization so that which is named 'Optimization for Simulation'. In the second one, optimization is demonstrated mainly and it is named 'Simulation for Optimization'. Optimization results are evaluated through simulations by scenario analysis. In this paper, the approach of 'Optimization for Simulation' is employed for a layout design method. Figure 1 shows the proposed framework of integration of multi-agent based simulation and optimization.

Multi-agent based simulation models components existing in the targeted system as agents and the system executes simulation as a distributed autonomous system. The agent can represent the model of either artifact or human in the simulation; it is relatively easy to introduce human objects into the simulation. Since human factor still plays important role in manufacturing systems as well as service production systems, human interventions have possibilities to enhance service quality or may influence on productivity. Furthermore, flows of products and humans in production and service systems are complex so that it is difficult to develop a complete model for mathematical programming. Therefore, it should be required to consider temporal influences derived by the product and human flows throughout spatial design of layout planning. Most of earlier studies in the area of OR, above mentioned temporal factors have been incorporated into the models by a simplified way with abstraction. Hence, the proposed approach by the integration of multi-agent simulation is expected to develop a layout planning method considering both products flows and human ones: spatial and temporal factors.

In addition, it is needed a large amount of computation time in order to implement high simulation accuracy when demonstrated by integration of optimization and simulation. To balance a tradeoff between accuracy and length of computation time, it is required to apply any solutions. In this paper, a solution to solve the tradeoff is incorporated into the proposed model, and it will be described in the following section.

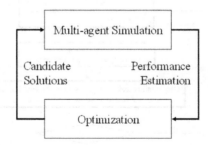

Fig. 1. Framework of Integration of Multi-agent based Simulation and Optimization

3   Layout Design for Underground Shopping Streets

3.1   Outline of the Proposed Method

An underground shopping street is something familiar with people's daily life in particular in urban areas. Recently passers who just want to go through the underground shopping streets as the passageway without any specific purpose for shopping or browsing are increasing. Competitions between stores located on the underground shopping streets and other stores located above ground have been growing. In general, customers can be categorized into two segments of planning purchases and non-planning purchases. This study targets the passers who just go through the underground shopping streets, so that increasing non-planning purchases of the passers is selected for the main evaluation criterion.

An earlier study showed the effectiveness of layout planning for retail stores targeted non-planning purchases as well as planning purchases [8]. In the layout design of the underground shopping streets, it is needed to consider specific characteristics of the underground shopping streets, which differ from general store layout problems; there are many entrances and exits and each passer has own target direction in the underground shopping streets. How passers select passing ways vary according to the passers' purposes and that are frequently changed depending on the situations such as day of the week, time zone and season's factor. Hence a store layout design should be implemented to arrange attractive stores effectively considering changing passers behaviors.

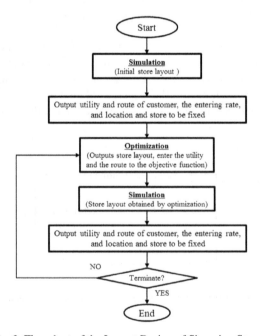

Fig. 2. Flowchart of the Layout Design of Shopping Street

Figure 2 shows the flowchart of the layout design of shopping street. The proposed method integrates multi-agent based simulation and optimization. Once a layout design is implemented, customers' migration paths will be changed according to the derived layout. The layout design is required to evaluate sequentially by repeating simulation and optimization. As a result, a large amount of computation time is needed. The proposed model implements sequential processing of simulation and optimization through fixing store's position partially to be incorporated into the repeating processes. Therefore, the optimizations are executed considering changing consumers' behaviors simultaneously and it enables to arrange attractive stores to improve total customer traffic rates for the underground overall shopping streets.

3.2   Algorithm of the Proposed Method

A flow chart of the layout design of shopping street is shown in Figure 2. Simulation and optimization are integrated and implemented to repeat in order to develop a layout gradually.

The purpose of the algorithm is to develop a layout design to let passers non-planning purchase. An objective function is to maximize total utilities of arranged stores. The objective function f is to determine where store j to be located in assignment place k, which is formulated as follows;

$$\text{maximize} \quad f = \sum_{i=1}^{I} g_i \tag{1}$$

$$g_i = \begin{cases} \dfrac{\sum_{j=1}^{J} \sum_{k=1}^{K} \max\{(U_{ij}-T_i),0\} \cdot x_{ik} \cdot y_{jk}}{m_i} \\ 0 \quad (if\ m_i = 0) \end{cases} \tag{2}$$

subject to

$$fix_{ljk} = \{0,1\} \ \left(for\ all\ l, j, k\right) \tag{3}$$

$$\sum_{j=1}^{J} \sum_{k=1}^{K} fix_{ljk} = 1 \ \left(for\ all\ l\right) \tag{4}$$

$$\sum_{k=1}^{K} y_{jk} = 1 \ (for\ all\ j) \tag{5}$$

$$\sum_{j=1}^{J} y_{jk} = 1 \ (for\ all\ k) \tag{6}$$

$$x_{ik} = \{0,1\} \ (for\ all\ i, k) \tag{7}$$

$$y_{jk} = \{0,1\} \left\{j, k \mid \sum_{l=1}^{L} fix_{ljk} = 0\right\} \tag{8}$$

Constraints are formulated as from Equation (3) to (8). In the decision variable (3), $fix_{ljk} = 1$ means that store j is arranged at place k in simulation turn l, otherwise $fix_{ljk} = 0$. The Equation (4) indicates that only one store is arranged at a place in each turn of the simulation. The constraint determines that a store is arranged at one place is shown in Equation (5). All places must be assigned any store shown in Equation (6). The decision variable Equation (7) represents $x_{ik} = 1$ means that customer i pass through along place k, otherwise $x_{ik} = 0$. Equation (8) indicates that $y_{jk} = 1$ means the store j is arranged at place k, which has not been assigned, otherwise $y_{jk} = 0$. The parameter m_i represents the total number of stores to be passed through by consumer i.

First of all, the simulation with the initial (current) layout is executed. The simulation derives the utility U_{ij} of customer i toward store j and the threshold values of $T_i, fix_{ljk}, x_{ik}, m_i$ to determine whether customer i enters store j or not. Then the optimization is executed using the above mentioned utilities and threshold values as input data by the decision variable y_{jk} to maximize the objective function value.

4   Computer Experiments

The target area represents the underground shopping street where 24 stores and 8 exits are located. The number of passenger is assumed 15,000. Figure 3 illustrates the current layout of the shopping street and that is modeled in 1/4 scale of the actual shopping street in this paper. The number of passers is calculated by using the decreasing ratio of the area space [9]. The exits along four dimensions are set neighboring four different facilities located on the ground. The left-hand side is located along

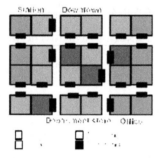

Fig. 3. Current layout of shopping street

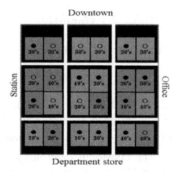

Downtown

Fig. 4. Obtained layout by the proposed model

station, the bottom side is located along department store, the right side is located along offices and the upper side is located along downtown, respectively. The assumption is set that business persons tend to prefer the station and office sides, housewives prefer the station and department store sides and students tend to move between the station and downtown sides. The located stores are categorized into three groups of restaurant, variety and clothing shop.

Table 1. Comparison results between current and the proposed layouts in terms of entering rate

	Current	Proposed
Entering rate	0.39	0.45

Figure 4 shows the experimental result when the simulation and optimization were executed with the policy fixing the store position, which has the largest number of customers to be entered in descending order. The proposed method was repeated 24 times and the simulations were executed 5 trials in the each time. The optimization problem is solved using the solver named 'CPLEX12.5' by IBM.

Table 1 shows the comparison results between current and the proposed layouts in terms of entering rate. The entering rate er is calculated by $er = v/p$, where v represents the total number of customers entered into shops and p means the total number of customers coming through the underground shopping street. The entering rate increases when the number of customer increases, who enters the shops as the result of achieving maximal utilities due to the layout change. The results show that the proposed method obtains the higher value of entering rate than that of current layout. The obtained layout by the proposed model is shown in Figure 4. Comparing the current layout shown in Figure 3 and the obtained layout shown in Figure 4, it can be observed that all the three categories of stores were arranged on the streets along passers' ways in a balanced manner in the obtained layout. The stores with same categories are not arranged on one or specific sides. In particular the category of restaurant stores which have higher entering rates are arranged with widely dispersed, so that it can lead the high total entering rate to be obtained.

5   Conclusion

This paper proposed a layout design method by integration of multi-agent based simulation and optimization. The method was incorporated into the layout design for underground shopping streets considering passengers' flow and applied to the computer experiments. Comparison results with the current layout of the store locations revealed the effectiveness of the proposed method. Applying on a larger scale and reducing the computation time can be pointed out as the further steps of the study.

References

1. Kochhar, J.S., Heragu, S.S.: Facility Layout Design in A Changing Environment. International Journal of Production Research 37(11), 2429–2446 (1999)
2. Muther, R.: Systematic Layout Planning, 2nd edn. Cahners Books (1973)
3. Hillier, F.S., Connors, M.M.: Quadratic Assignment Problem Algorithms and the Location of Indivisible Facilities. Management Science 13(1), 42–57 (1966)
4. Castell, C.M.L., Lakshmanan, R., Skilling, J.M.: Optimisation of Process Plant Layout Using Genetic Algorithms. Computers and Chemical Engineering 22(1), 993–996 (1998)
5. Kochhar, J.S., Foster, B.T., Heragu, S.S.: A Genetic Algorithm for the Unequal Area Facility Layout Problem. Computers and Operations Research 25(7), 583–594 (1998)
6. Andradottir, S.: A Review of Simulation Optimization Techniques. In: Proc. of the 1998 Winter Simulation Conference, vol. 1, pp. 151–158 (1998)
7. Fu, M.C.: Optimization for Simulation: Theory vs. Practice. INFORMS Journal on Computing 14(3), 192–215 (2002)
8. Kishimoto, A., Takahashi, T., Takahashi, M., Yamada, T., Tsuda, K., Terano, T.: An Agent Simulator for Analyzing Consumer Behaviors and Sales Promotion in a Retail Store. In: The 23rd Annual Conference of the Japanese Society for Artificial Intelligence, 2P2-2 (2009) (in Japanese)
9. Moriya, M., Kashihara, S., Yoshimura, H., Yokota, T., Sakata, K.: Investigation of Crowd Flow and the Number of People Staying in the Diamond Underground Street and its Influence on the Crowd Flow in the Adjacent Areas. Annual Report of the Division of Kinki Region of Architectural Institute of Japan 37, 121–124 (1999) (in Japanese)

Future of ERP: Challenges and Opportunities in the SaaS-era

Johan C. ("Hans") Wortmann and Kristian Peters

Faculty of Economics and Business, University of Groningen,
P.O. Box 800 9700 AV Groningen
http://www.rug.nl/staff/j.c.wortmann/

Abstract. This paper is concerned with ERP systems, which are defined as company-wide transaction processing systems based on packaged standard software. ERP systems provide the benefit of sharing data between functional areas in a firm. The paper argues that there is room for expansion of these benefits by sharing data with supply chain partners. The paper investigates the role of vendors and concludes that there are interesting new possibilities. These are related to the SaaS delivery model of enterprise software. This model calls for attention of the (enterprise) software supply chain in academic research.

Keywords: ERP, SaaS (Software-as-a-Service).

1 Introduction

ERP systems are standard software packages for transaction processing, which integrate various functional areas of organizations, such as finance, logistics and HRM. The term "integration" means in this context that data on objects are stored and maintained only once, and are made available to each functional area concerned. This creates a common communication language and a "single version of the truth". The value proposition of ERP systems is that organizational processes and transactions can be executed efficiently, even if these processes cross the functional boundaries in organizations. Accordingly, ERP systems have grown mature with the claim that the entire organization needs integrated transaction processing which can be covered by a single investment – in ERP. This paper investigates the value proposition of ERP in the nearby future.

The classical value proposition of ERP can be reviewed in the light of recent and ongoing developments in the ERP and business environment. Four relevant developments are observed. Firstly, the focus of organizational improvement has changed towards *supply chain* issues [1]. In the past, organizations were focused internally: streamlining all internal processes was a major goal. Nowadays, streamlined internal processes (enabled by e.g. ERP) are mostly in place, and room for improvement should be sought outside the boundaries of the own organization. Consequently it would be logical to explore if the benefits of ERP can be realized in the supply chain. Many of the supply chain opportunities that can be identified for ERP vendors are

B. Grabot et al. (Eds.): APMS 2014, Part III, IFIP AICT 440, pp. 383–390, 2014.

mentioned in academic literature on collaborative enterprise systems (see e.g., [2]). However, these opportunities still constitute considerable challenges in practice, because the technologies needed are perhaps described in research, but not available on the market (see [3] [p.817] for a list of business opportunities not yet fulfilled in collaborative commerce, which could be addressed by ERP vendors).

Secondly, much standard software for transaction processing is nowadays offered in the form of *Software as a Service* (SaaS). This offering creates cost reductions for most customers. However, SaaS creates also new opportunities for various standard software vendors. Vendors could move upstream or downstream in their own supply chain. This second development relates to the (standard) software supply chain.

Thirdly, modern information systems cover much more than merely transaction processing systems. There is ICT support for professionals executing their work (Decision Support and Work Flow Management), there are real-time systems governing the execution of processes, there are office applications and social media to support human communication and interaction, and so on. All these other forms of ICT usage in organizations do not exhibit the typical transaction processing nature and require different technologies than classical ERP.

Last but not least, implementing and maintaining ERP systems may (still) require considerable effort. This is not only due to the number of parameters, which have to be set in order to configure ERP systems, but it is also due to the organization-wide nature of ERP projects.

This paper explores the future of ERP against the background of the above four developments. The first development ("organizational improvement has changed towards *supply chain* issues") is explored in section 2. Section 2 analyzes the supply chain of a company using ERP and identifies opportunities for improvement in data sharing, using arguments that have been explained at length in academic papers. This leads to the conclusion that ERP customers would benefit from more sharing of data and processes with supply chain partners. Accordingly, section 3 analyses the vendor's position, again using well-known academic frameworks. In this section, we will also return to the second ("SaaS creates new opportunities for various standard software vendors") and third developments ("modern information systems cover much more than merely transaction processing systems"). This leads to the conclusion, that vendors can exploit opportunities to expand their offering into the (enterprise) software supply chain. Section 4 gives a view on ongoing and future academic research. Section 5 provides conclusions.

2   Towards a Supply Network of Content

As mentioned in the introduction, one of the main benefits of company-wide transaction processing systems, such as ERP systems, is that data on relevant objects are maintained at a single place and are made available to any authorized party in need of these data. This is sometimes called: the *single version of the truth*. Organizations that rigorously follow this principle have considerable benefits, as compared to organizations who still struggle with multiple versions of the truth. Additional advantages of focusing on the single version of the truth are the agreements that are obtained on the semantics and ontologies related to the objects involved, and the streamlining of business processes. The classical value proposition of ERP systems is largely related to these points [4].

However, *l'histoire se répète:* what used to be true for data content in single organizations is now true for the ecosystems in which these organizations operate. For example, a vendor catalogue's content is copied into the systems of all wholesalers who sell products of this particular vendor. This creates multiple update problems when the catalogue is maintained. It seems better to have these catalogues not copied, but retrieved as a service when necessary. This argument is not only true for so-called master data, but also for transactional content data on contracts, orders, shipments, receipts, invoices and payments, which can be stored in multiple systems. If we want to avoid multiple data storage efforts and the corresponding organizational burdens, the principle of a single version of the truth should be maintained. This principle leads to the idea of *objects servitization*: for each object there is a single data source and when data on this object ("content") is needed by authorized parties, these will be retrieved from the source via a service provided by the object.

Unfortunately, a caveat is needed with respect to this idea. While it allows organizations to retrieve data from business partners, it does not guarantee that data updates are consistent with the requirements of all these partners. For example, if a vendor eliminates an item from the vendor's catalogue, this data update may not be consistent with the requirements of a wholesaler who still has to deliver orders for this item. Such issues are covered by ERP but not by interfaces based on services.

Accordingly, ERP has been adopted as preferred solution by many organizations and even for business units across the globe, consisting of many local organizations residing under a joint owner. For such business units, the above considerations have resulted in so-called *multi-site ERP*: a multi-site ERP implementation covers several organizational units who share part of their data. For example, a company with both production facilities and distribution centers (DC) would *share* the orders from the DCs to the factories, rather than having all orders entered and maintained twice. In this way, a single version of the truth is created. However, remember the fourth issue given above: implementing and maintaining ERP systems is extremely cumbersome. For this reason, viz. to avoid complexity, multiple single-site implementations are sometimes preferred above a multi-site implementation in business units. If so, data are shared in the way mentioned above: there is one party responsible for a set of objects, e.g. a catalogue, and the other party retrieves the catalogue data when needed. The drawback, that data consistency is jeopardized, is taken for granted in order to avoid cumbersome implementation and upgrade issues.

Altogether, there is a need in supply networks to avoid multiple storage of the same data. In the energy branch, special metering companies manage delivery data. In freight transportation, the main carrier takes this role. Many projects are currently ongoing to enable electronic invoices, which may be regarded as a move to avoid duplicate data storage. In fact, e-commerce is often a way to ensure that duplicate data are avoided or that automatic synchronization of the same data objects is enforced.

Accordingly, the notion of a *content supply network* emerges: organizations create information on objects ("content"), and this content is delivered to business partners. Such delivery may be accompanied by payments, as in the case of energy metering services. Note, that the content supply network may consist of the same partners as encountered in the physical supply chain, but the direction of the value stream may be different (see figure 1). Also, independent players can take a position in this network, if they provide content related services to other network participants.

Finally, there may be also other players who add value in content networks. Examples are providers of consumer market sales (Nielsen), on stock exchange transactions (Bloomberg), on the organization's financial situation (accountants), etc.

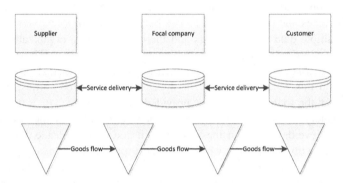

Fig. 1. Content supply network

3   Software-as-a-Service

3.1   Introduction

In recent years, ICT vendors have offered cloud-based solutions to their customers. The essence of this offering is that ICT infrastructures and platforms are not sold to customers and deployed by customers, but these are owned and run by vendors and offered "as-a-service". ICT can become much cheaper and more scalable when infrastructure and platform are shared between customers. Ultimately, the cost reduction of hardware infrastructure is based on Moore's law, which states that the costs of key hardware are reduced by 50% every 18 months, combined with the gains obtained from sharing risks. The cost reduction of platforms such as operating systems is based on virtualization techniques, allowing multiple software platforms to share hardware.

By itself, this cost reduction due to Infrastructure-as-a-Service (IaaS) and Platform-as-a-Service (PaaS) has nothing to do with applications such as ERP. However, there is also a good reason to have standard software such as ERP delivered as "as-a-Service": the costs of application management can be reduced considerably if the same standard software is shared between user organizations. Sharing of software reduces the number of different software variants which are maintained, and consequently bypasses many tasks, such as adopting platform changes, installing patches, testing upgrades, database backup and recovery, helpdesk work, contracting 2nd tier

ICT suppliers, and so on. Therefore an interesting value proposition for ERP vendors emerges, namely to offer their solution as SaaS to customers. Many major vendors have already begun exploiting this opportunity. However, the move towards SaaS brings vendors also into a different competitive arena. This issue will be analyzed in the next subsection.

3.2   Analysis of ERP Vendor Position When Adopting SaaS

SaaS can be regarded as a new technology emerging in the business context, and comes with new challenges and new opportunities for ERP vendors. However, ERP vendors who embrace the SaaS offering will normally not refrain from their classical "on premise" offering. In order to analyze this change, we will use the well-known organizational adaptation framework of Miles and Snow [5], who distinguish three types of adaptation problems in organizations: the entrepreneurial problem, the engineering problem, and the administrative problem.

In case of ERP vendors, the entrepreneurial problem is mainly concerned with selection (new) product-market strategies, the engineering problem is mainly concerned with the software design and infrastructure, and the administrative problem is mainly concerned with the vendor's internal organization structure and processes.

The adoption of SaaS concerns the transition from a product to a service offering, and may also include changing markets. SaaS also involves creating new ways of delivering value to customers. These are strategic decisions, and therefore concern the entrepreneurial problem. From there, the engineering problem is involved: an ERP product that really allows multiple customers to use the same software (and presumably the same database) requires additional software development in ERP. The software has to be made fit for SaaS and for multiple customers (also called "tenants"). Additionally, appropriate systems and infrastructure have to be implemented for providing the service(s) to tenants. There are many ways to design and implement multi-tenancy and SaaS architectures [6]. Finally, SaaS requires support from the organization and management processes. For instance, the monitoring and reward system should be adjusted in order to stimulate salesmen to sell the new value proposition based on SaaS.

When moving with an ERP product from the classical on premise delivery model to a SaaS model, ERP vendors should not only address the engineering problem, but also address the entrepreneurial and administrative problems. The value proposition of the ERP vendor shifts from a focus on product features to a focus on costs. In terms of the value disciplines of Tracey and Wiersema [7], ERP vendors are traditionally oriented towards product leadership and they start to compete on operational excellence. In terms of Porter [8], the vendors who used to have a differentiation strategy are seduced to compete on cost leadership. However, there is only one party in the market who can dominate based on cost leadership, according to Porter. For most ERP vendors, even for the vendors with a large market share, it is unlikely that they will survive in a market competing on costs. This brings the discussion to the following question: what options do ERP vendors have after adopting SaaS? The next section tries to answer this question.

3.3   Different Positions in the Software Supply Chain: Options for ERP SaaS

Like many other companies, software product companies are part of a supply chain. Actually, there are two supply chains involved, which should be properly distinguished, viz. the design-time supply chain and the run-time supply chain. The design-time supply chain describes partnerships during design and supply of (design) components for the product or service offered by the focal company. The run-time supply chain described partnerships during actual delivery of products and services to the final customer.

This distinction is well known and clear for physical goods, such as apparel, electronics or buildings. During new product development, the focal company searches for design partners who may either supply off-the-shelf knowledge products or perform design tasks for the focal company. However, this knowledge supply chain may be entirely different from the physical goods flow necessary to serve the market.

The same distinction is well known in the software industry. For designing a classical ERP product, the design team may use off-the-shelf components such as security components, user-management and authentication components, database management systems, a UI-framework, a java framework, 4GL tools, configuration management tools and so on. Also, an ERP package may be combined with other application software such as MS Project. After development, these components are delivered to customers jointly with the ERP offering. This is similar to physical products where e.g. an add-on is included in the delivery.

When designing a SaaS product, the situation changes. Five options are highlighted. First, in case of ERP SaaS, license contracts for additional ERP components, such as the DBMS, will be made with the SaaS supplier, i.e. with the ERP supplier, instead of with the DBMS supplier. This means that *the ERP vendor integrates upstream in the software supply chain.*

Secondly, the ERP vendor may also choose to refrain from added value upstream in the software supply chain. For example, the ERP SaaS provider could choose to leave all authentications to a third party authentication service in SaaS mode. If so, someone should pay for the authentication service, probably the ERP customer. Accordingly, the ERP SaaS vendor leaves the added value to suppliers and thus *refrains from integrating upstream.*

Thirdly, if the ERP package is designed to work with a third party applications e.g., CRM, warehousing or even finance, these third party applications could be delivered as part of SaaS ERP or it could run in SaaS mode. This option for service delivery may be called: *specialization in the software supply chain.*

Fourthly, ERP vendors have the option to *integrate downstream in the supply chain* by e.g. investments in mobile apps for specific sessions in ERP. (This option is not restricted to SaaS but fits well with a SaaS offering). Such investments would enhance the customer experience. Obviously, the vendors can also refrain from such investments and leave these e.g. to their resellers or implementation partners. An interesting example in moving downstream in the supply chain is the mobile app "MyOrder". MyOrder enables customers in any shop (or restaurant) to download a catalogue, place an order, pay, and receive the paid order from the shop's personnel.

Last but not least, ERP vendors or their competitors could *take a position in the content delivery network*. Section 2 describes there will be new players in the content delivery network, either to provide information services for several parties or to add value to information (such as in the case of financial analysis by accountants).

4   Discussion

This paper investigated the value proposition of ERP in the nearby future. In the above section we have argued, that there are many options for ERP vendors and others in implementing SaaS. In the current practice, it is unclear to what extent ERP vendors and other parties are implementing or have implemented the various options. Our pending research focuses on both the organizational context (organizational adaptation) as well as the institutional context of ERP vendors in adapting to software supply chain changes and SaaS developments.

First, SaaS adoption does not only require ERP vendors to address the engineering problem, such as new software and architecture design for SaaS, but also to address entrepreneurial and administrative problems, such as implementing new business models and update the financial and reward structures in the organization. Secondly, the three adaptation problems will be affected by how ERP vendors strategically employ SaaS. ERP vendors are originally product leadership and differentiation oriented with regard to their competitive strategies, yet SaaS may tempt ERP vendors to move towards cost leadership and operational excellence competition instead. Such a move makes it difficult to sustain a competitive advantage for most ERP vendors, because only one or a few players will survive in a cost competition arena.

It is therefore of interest to investigate 1) whether and how ERP vendors make the transition from their classical on premise solution to SaaS, and 2) whether and how they resist the temptation to move into cost leadership competition with SaaS.

Institutional theory, and institutional preconditions in particular, offer an explanation on whether and how ERP vendors make the transition from their classical on premise solution business to SaaS [9–11]. Institutional preconditions are related to three domains, i.e., the regulative, the normative and the cognitive domains, and concern e.g., perception of importance of SaaS adoption (cognitive), importance of relationships in the supply chain (normative) and the role of professional standards and rules (regulative). If the institutional preconditions are for example preventing a move towards a new value proposition, then it is unlikely that such a move will occur.

The five identified options for ERP vendors can be used to understand to what extent ERP vendors are shedding components and services to others in the software supply chain, and thus decrease their added-value and to what extent ERP vendors are integrating upstream and/or downstream, or specializing in their supply chains to increase their added-value. There may be also good opportunities to take a position in the content supply network, but this may contradict their institutional preconditions.

Accordingly, the case of ERP and SaaS is not only an opportunity to position these subjects in a theory of a supply chain of services as outlined above in sections 2 and 3. It is also an opportunity to add new insights to supply chain design choices from the perspectives of institutional theory and the framework of Miles and Snow as outlined in section 3.2. This line of research may lead to interesting cross-fertilizing towards physical supply chains.

5   Conclusion

In this paper, several challenges and opportunities for ERP in the SaaS era have been identified. Section 2 analyzed the role of ERP in supply networks. The conclusion was the following. ERP is not likely to be extended beyond the boundaries of organizations. However, the increasing awareness of content supply networks will give rise to new services around data, and may invoke new players to take roles in these networks. ERP vendors have many opportunities to move upstream and downstream in their own software supply chains. Although they could enter into the content supply networks, it remains subject of further investigation if they will do so, and how.

References

1. Miles, R.E., Snow, C.C.: Organization theory and supply chain management: An evolving research perspective. J. Oper. Manag. 25, 459–463 (2007)
2. Bititci, U.S., Martinez, V., Albores, P., Parung, J.: Creating and managing value in collaborative networks. Int. J. Phys. Distrib. Logist. Manag. 34, 251–268 (2004)
3. Alvarez-Rodríguez, J.M., Labra-Gayo, J.E., de Pablos, P.O.: New trends on e-Procurement applying semantic technologies: Current status and future challenges. Comput. Ind. 65, 800–820 (2014)
4. Wortmann, J.C('.), Don, H., Hasselman, J., Wilbrink, A.: Enterprise Information Systems as a Service: Re-engineering Enterprise Software as Product-Service System. In: Frick, J., Laugen, B.T. (eds.) Advances in Production Management Systems. IFIP AICT, vol. 384, pp. 496–505. Springer, Heidelberg (2012)
5. Miles, R.E., Snow, C.C., Meyer, A.D., Coleman, H.J.: Organizational strategy, structure, and process. Acad. Manag. Rev. 3, 546–562 (1978)
6. Kabbedijk, J., Salfischberger, T., Jansen, S.: Comparing Two Architectural Patterns for Dynamically Adapting Functionality in Online Software Products. In: PATTERNS 2013, The Fifth International Conferences on Pervasive Patterns and Applications, Valencia, Spain, pp. 20–25 (2013)
7. Treacy, M., Wiersema, F.: Customer intimacy and other value disciplines. Harv. Bus. Rev., 84–93 (1993)
8. Porter, M.: What is strategy? Harv. Bus. Rev. 19, 61–78 (November-December 1996)
9. Teracino, E.A., Seo, D.: Conceptualization of the Convergence Phenomenon to Develop an Applicable and Integrated Framework for the Emergence of Software-as-a-Service. J. Glob. Inf. Manag. 21, 1–16 (2013)
10. Greenwood, R., Suddaby, R.: Institutional entrepreneurship in mature fields: The big five accounting firms. Acad. Manag. J. 49, 27–48 (2006)
11. Scott, W.: Institutions and organizations. Sage, Thousand Oaks (2007)

Requirements for a Value Stream Mapping in Make-To-Order Environments

Christoph Koch and Hermann Lödding

Hamburg University of Technology, Hamburg, Germany
{christoph.koch,loedding}@tuhh.de

Abstract. Value stream mapping (VSM) is a widely proven method to optimize a production. The practical approach, the manageable effort and the target-oriented procedure are the factors of success of this method. However, the method is of limited use when applied to make-to-order (MTO) environments. This paper aims to describe the shortcomings of VSM with respect to an application in a MTO production. The paper concentrates on the different logistic targets VSM impacts, as well as the manufacturing control tasks VSM applies. To set the basis for an application of VSM in MTO companies, requirements are described both for the logistic targets of VSM and the related manufacturing control tasks.

Keywords: value stream mapping, make-to-order, production control.

1 Introduction

It´s not only the quality and the price of products but also the quality of logistic processes that satisfy customer demands. Especially for make-to-order companies, high delivery reliability is mandatory to satisfy the customer [1]. Value Stream Mapping (VSM) is a widely proven and powerful tool in the field of continuous improvement of logistic targets. It has been established as a de facto standard in the industrial environment. It is composed of common rules that help to support targets like low inventory levels, short throughput times and high productivity [2]. It was developed as a communication standard within the high-volume-low-mix (HVLM) industry [3]. Thus, the method is tailored to the needs of the corresponding production system. Its implicit assumptions (make-to-stock) and explicit recommendations (design guidelines) are of limited use for make-to-order (MTO) companies. Companies with a high number of variants particularly criticize structural problems of the method [4]. Therefore, we seek for an approach to apply this practical method even in a MTO environment.

This paper analyzes the shortcomings of VSM with respect to an application in the field of MTO. The analysis allows formulating requirements for a MTO specific VSM. The focus lays on the logistic targets and on the involved methods of manufacturing control.

B. Grabot et al. (Eds.): APMS 2014, Part III, IFIP AICT 440, pp. 391–398, 2014.

2   Make-To-Order Production

Production can be divided into different manufacturing strategies that come along
with different characteristics. The manufacturing strategy usually depends on the type
of product a company produces. In this context make-to-order (MTO) and make-to-
stock (MTS) are two ideal types of processing an order. These two concepts differ in
several criteria [5]:

The customer decoupling point describes the point in the value chain, where the
product is linked to a specific customer order. A MTS production usually produces
according to forecasts without concrete customer orders. The customer orders are
satisfied by stocks of finished goods. Contrary to that, manufacturing orders in MTO
companies are initialized directly by customers. A customer order triggers a manufacturing order, so that every manufacturing order can be connected to a customer [6].

MTS companies often produce standard products without any customer specific influence on the product design. Customers are then accustomed to a limited choice of
products. In a MTO environment the influence of the customer on the product is
usually higher, so that the number of different products is typically much higher than
in a MTS production and the volume per product is much lower [7].

According to the range of products, the structure of the products also differs. While
MTS companies often produce low priced products with a simple structure, MTO
companies typically have multi-part products with complex structures [6].

MTS companies typically organize their production as a flow production. The
workstations are arranged according to the flow of material. The number of variants
that can be produced is limited. MTO companies have complex and customer specific
products, so the flow of material is normally undirected and complex. Due to this fact
the manufacturing often is arranged as a workshop production to guarantee high flexibility. A job shop is a typical form of this arrangement [5].

Both types of firms also differ in their logistic targets. MTS companies serve their
customers from a stock. Therefore, it is necessary to have the relevant parts available
to immediately satisfy the customer demand. For MTO firms the logistic target is
different. Keeping the promised delivery date is one of the most important targets for
MTO companies [8].

3   Value Stream Mapping

Value Stream Mapping is the process of picturing both the material flow and the information flow to coordinate all activities [9]. VSM is divided into two stages: analysis and design. Rother and Shook deliver a standard procedure for drawing the current
state map [3]. This procedure can be separated into five steps that should be followed
in order to generate the current state map: 1) Select a product family; 2) Collect the
relevant data; 3) Incorporate the information flow; 4) Draw the timeline; 5) Interpret
the current state map.

After having established the current state map, the question arises how to get to a
future state map. The design stage provides structured guidelines that lead to future

state maps. Rother and Shook propose seven guidelines [3]: 1) Produce to takt time; 2) Implement continuous flow and FIFO lanes; 3) Use Kanban supermarkets; 4) Send the production planning information only to the pacemaker; 5) Level the product mix evenly; 6) Distribute the production volume evenly (batch sizes); 7) Manufacture every part every day.

By applying these guidelines, a future state map can be developed stepwise. The guidelines represent the standard configuration for a manufacturing control system for a MTS production.

4   Shortcomings of Conventional VSM for MTO Productions

The discrepancy between the conventional VSM and a MTO production can be illustrated by three points: Differences in logistic objectives, a mismatch of the applied tasks of manufacturing control and the manufacturing environment.

4.1   Logistic Objectives

Both types of companies, MTS and MTO, differ in logistic objectives amongst other criteria (see chapter 2). As the conventional VSM is tailored to a MTS environment, the method also inherits the logistic objectives of a MTS production. The conventional VSM thus omits the most important logistic objective in MTO environments: schedule reliability.

Schedule reliability is one of the most important internal logistic objectives for MTO companies [10]. The schedule reliability describes the stability of logistic processes within a production [11]. It directly affects the delivery reliability towards the customer. It is defined as the percentage of orders completed within a defined range of tolerance [12]. The schedule reliability is influenced by the lateness and by the sequence deviation. Kuyumcu developed a causal model that is able to separate the overall lateness into lateness resulting from backlog and lateness resulting from sequence deviation [13]. The current VSM ignores the schedule reliability as an important key figure for MTO companies.

In the analysis stage of the conventional VSM the focus lays on work-in-progress (WIP) and throughput time (TTP). The former key figure is directly recorded during the value stream analysis, the latter derived from the WIP level and the customer takt. Both figures are important also for MTO companies. However, the measurement method of both figures is not practicable for MTO companies. The WIP is measured in number of parts. This is sufficient and practicable for companies with standard products and standardized container contents. Recording the number of parts in a MTO environment with highly fluctuating processing times and batch sizes can be less helpful. Usually, the number of parts is not representative for the workload of the orders and the counting itself can be time-consuming if there are no standard container contents. The throughput time is calculated with Little´s Law by dividing the WIP level in front of the workstation by the customer takt. However, the customer takt is hardly to determine in a MTO production as the material flow is more complex and the order contents are varying strongly.

4.2   Applied Functions of Manufacturing Control

The design stage of VSM includes methods for controlling manufacturing in terms of guidelines. These guidelines act in accordance with the logistic objectives of a MTS production. In the section below the guidelines are evaluated with respect to their use in a MTO production:

1. *Produce to takt time:* The customer takt is highly fluctuating in a MTO environment, so that it is much more difficult to produce to takt time than in high volume MTS productions.
2. *Develop continuous flow with FIFO sequencing:* Due to highly fluctuating processing times and complex material flows the implementation of continuous flow is often not applicable in MTO productions. The FIFO lanes help to avoid a chaotic sequencing in MTO productions as well. However, they do not support schedule reliability because delayed orders won´t be accelerated when they are processed in their incoming sequence.
3. *Use Kanban supermarkets to control production:* The Kanban method is by definition a decentralized order generation mechanism for companies that produce to stock. In this case the Kanaban logic is responsible to refill the consumption of a stock / supermarket. Thus, it is not applicable for a MTO production.
4. *Send the production planning information only to the pacemaker:* The PPC information should only be sent to the pacemaker process, so that not all processes are controlled by a superior production planning department. The upstream processes should be decoupled by Kanban supermarkets, which is not possible for MTO companies.
5. *Level the product mix evenly:* To level the product mix evenly at the pacemaker process one need to have a good forecast of the individual demands and to know a constant pacemaker / bottleneck system. Both points can often not be achieved in MTO environments.
6. *Distribute the production volume evenly:* After leveling the product mix in the next step the production volume should be distributed evenly on the pacemaker process. This is often not possible to install immediately as it is necessary to know the exact demands and a stable pacemaker process.
7. *Build the capability to produce every part every day:* Building up the capability to produce every part every day means to decrease setup times and batch sizes to react flexible on changes in demand. Generally, this guideline is also useful for MTO companies. By reducing setup times the need for building setup families disappears.

Some of the guidelines, generally those who manage the informational flow, are based on a stable pacemaker process. As a MTO production often arranges their manufacturing in form of a job shop with complex and changing material flows, a stable pacemaker often is hardly to achieve. Quite the contrary: job shops have complex flows of material and changing bottlenecks. Other guidelines directly assume the functions of the manufacturing control tasks, e.g. installing supermarkets and FIFO-lanes. This is reasonable for a MTS, but not for a MTO production. The supermarkets connect the processes that are located upstream of the pacemaker process and stock semi-finished goods. Downstream of the pacemaker workstation, a continuous flow should be established with FIFO sequencing. As mentioned before, FIFO does not support the schedule reliability.

4.3 Missing Functions of Manufacturing Control

The guidelines aim to optimize the manufacturing area by introducing and accomplishing functions of manufacturing control in a structured manner. Both the information and the material flow are controlled to improve the logistic objectives WIP and throughput time. The following figure describes the relationship between the logistic objectives of a manufacturing system and the relevant tasks of manufacturing control to achieve the objectives.

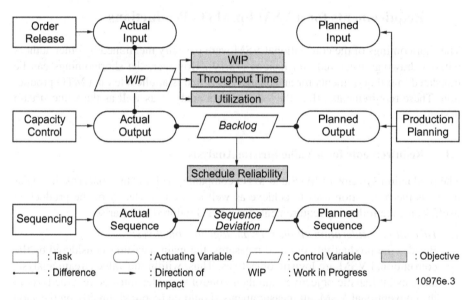

Fig. 1. A manufacturing control model [13]

The model contains tasks of manufacturing control that impact the logistic objectives of a production with the help of actuating and control variables. These tasks can be roughly divided in production planning (Fig. 1 right hand section) and production control (Fig. 1 left hand section) tasks. The model includes the following control tasks: order release, capacity control and sequencing.

While sequencing is handled by the conventional VSM approach (FIFO-lanes) both order release and capacity control are not taken into consideration. As mentioned before, FIFO sequencing does not support the schedule reliability actively. It merely avoids sequencing at the discretion of the operators, who sometimes may pursue different objectives than schedule reliability.

The capacity control is one of the two levers to control the schedule reliability. It decides about the adjustment of capacity which can mean overtime or shortened work hours [14]. The current VSM method completely neglects the capacity control. This is very problematic even for MTS environments, as backlogs can accumulate and affect the inventory level in the supermarket. It is even more problematic for MTO companies, as backlogs directly influence schedule reliability.

By releasing an order, the production is allowed to process the order. The order release can operate based on different criteria (e.g. WIP, due dates), which have to be defined. The order release provides a lever to control the work in progress and the throughput time in a MTO production. The need and effectiveness of a structured order release to control the mean throughput time have been quoted by several authors [15,16,17]. It is thus an elementary function of manufacturing control, which is missing in the conventional VSM.

5   Requirements for a VSM for MTO Productions

The shortcomings of the conventional VSM were partially mentioned by other authors without drawing structured conclusions [18,19]. However, the shortcomings can be translated into requirements for an adapted VSM that is applicable on a MTO production. These requirements affect the value stream analysis as well as the value stream design.

5.1   Requirements for a Value Stream Analysis

The production systems of MTS and MTO companies differ. This concerns the logistic goals the production tries to achieve as well as the complexity of the production itself. Thus, the following requirements for a MTO tailored VSM arise:

1. *Take into consideration all the relevant logistic objectives:*
    Besides the productivity oriented measures, the main measures considered by the conventional VSM are logistic objectives. Thus, within the value stream analysis all relevant logistic objectives and their control variables must be recorded. As in the conventional VSM, all measurements should be recorded directly on the shop floor. The WIP should be grasped in a unit more convenient for MTO environments. The throughput time depends on the WIP, so this relation must also be considered while choosing the appropriate units.
    The schedule reliability depends on the lateness of orders, which is influenced by backlog and sequence deviation [12]. Similar to the relation of WIP and throughput time, backlog and sequence deviation act as control variables for the schedule reliability. Both measures then have to be recorded in the analysis stage of the MTO tailored VSM.

2. *Cover the complexity of job shops:*
    The first step of the analysis contains the choice of an adequate product family using a product-process-matrix. Having a large amount of product families, this procedure becomes very extensive. A VSM for MTO should rather focus on the

entirety of work systems than on single product families. By doing this, the procedure will be to cover the complexity of production systems of MTO companies, such as backflows or shared resources.

5.2   Requirements for a Value Stream Design

For a VSM that is tailored for a MTO production new requirements regarding the guidelines occur.

1. *The guidelines should consider all tasks of manufacturing control:*
    It is not sufficient to concentrate on single tasks of manufacturing control. In order to configure the manufacturing control comprehensively, all the relevant tasks of manufacturing control must be considered. To have a lever on the control variable WIP, the order release mechanism must be controlled. The backlog results from the difference of actual and planned output. Thus, it is fundamental to configure the capacity control task, which directly affects the actual output. Additionally, the sequencing rule must be configured to minimize sequence deviations. Planned due dates of operations are often determined during the production planning. Thus, sequencing the orders according to their due dates could be possible.
2. *The guidelines should support the user with developing a future state map:*
    The configuration of a comprehensive manufacturing control system is a complex task. Thus, it is elementary to have a structured process for the configuration. The guidelines must support this by offering a consistent and logical sequence of introducing the manufacturing control tasks. Moreover, the guidelines should be independent of each others, so that the failure of one guideline does not automatically lead to the failure of another guideline.

6   Conclusion and Outlook

The paper evaluates the conventional VSM method with respect for a use in a MTO environment. Based on the field of application, the logistic targets aimed at by VSM do not correspond with the logistic targets of a MTO company. From this follows that the manufacturing control functions introduced by the value stream design, which should support the target achievement, also are either incomplete or impracticable for MTO productions. A VSM tailored for MTO should aim at all logistic objectives, especially at the schedule reliability. Therefore the appropriate manufacturing control tasks have to be considered, including order release, capacity control, and sequencing.

The ongoing studies at the IPMT include the development of a value stream analysis and a value stream design procedure. Therefore, a recording method for the logistic objectives as well as a standard configuration of manufacturing control for MTO companies must be developed and evaluated. Guidelines to develop a future state map must then be derived from the standard configuration of manufacturing control. Furthermore, the complete method has to be evaluated with different industrial partners to cover different types of MTO productions.

398   C. Koch and H. Lödding

References

1. Kingsman, B., Hendry, L., Mercer, A., de Souza, A.: Responding to customer enquiries in make-to-order companies – Problems and solutions. Int. J. Production Economics, 46-47, 219-231 (1996)
2. Irani, S.A., Zhou, J.: Value stream mapping of a complete product. Available at: Department of Industrial, Welding and Systems Engineering. The Ohio State University, Columbus (2011)
3. Rother, M., Shook, J.: Learning to see: Value stream mapping to create value and eliminate muda. The Lean Enterprise Institute, Brookline (1999)
4. Hämmerle, M., Rally, P.: Wertschöpfung steigern. In: Spath, D. (ed.). Fraunhofer Verlag, Stuttgart (2010)
5. Schuh, G.: Produktionsplanung und -steuerung – Grundlagen, Gestaltung, Konzepte. Springer, Berlin (2006)
6. Deep, A., Guttridge, P., Dani, S., Burns, N.: Investigating factors affecting ERP selection in made-to-order SME sector. Journal of Manufacturing Technology Management 19, 430–446 (2004)
7. Aslan, B., Stevenson, M., Hendry, L.C.: Enterprise Resource Planning systems: An assessment of applicability to Make-To-Order companies. Computers in Industry 63, 692–705 (2012)
8. Nyhuis, P., Wiendahl, H.-P.: Fundamentals of Production Logistics. Springer, Berlin (2009)
9. Jones, D.T., Womack, J.P.: Seeing the Whole: Mapping the Extended Value Stream. The Lean Enterprise Institute, Brookline (2002)
10. Lödding, H., Nyhuis, P., Schmidt, M., Kuyumcu, A.: Modelling lateness and schedule reliability: how companies can produce on time. Production Planning & Control 25, 59–72 (2014)
11. Wiendahl, H.-P.: Wie aus der Logistik eine Wissenschaft wurde. In: Wiendahl, H.-P. (ed.) Die wandlungsfähige Fabrik. Integrierte Sicht von Fabrikstruktur, Logistik und Produktionssystemen. Proceedings of the IFA-Fachtagung, pp. 107–142 (2003)
12. Yu, K.-W.: Terminkennlinie. Eine Beschreibungsmethodik für die Terminabweichung im Produktionsbereich. VDI Progress Reports, Düsseldorf (2001)
13. Kuyumcu, A.: Modellierung der Termintreue in der Produktion. PhD-Thesis, Hamburg Technical University, Hamburg (2013)
14. Lödding, H.: Handbook of Manufacturing Control. Spinger, Berlin (2013)
15. Land, M., Gaalman, G.: Workload Control concepts in job shops: a critical assessment, Igls, Austria. Preprints of the Eight International Working Seminar on Production Economics, pp. 201–226 (1994)
16. Hendry, L.C., Kingsman, B.G., Cheung, P.: The effect of workload control (WLC) on performance in make-to-order companies. Journal of Operations Management 16, 63–75 (1997)
17. Wiendahl, H.-P.: Load-oriented manufacturing control. Springer, Berlin (1995)
18. Chitturi, G., Paulls, F.: Value Stream Mapping in a Jobshop. In: Proceedings of International Conference on Agile Manufacturing, pp. 142–147 (2007)
19. Alves, T.D., Tommelein, I., Ballard, G.: Value Stream Mapping for Make-to-Order Products in a Job Shop. In: Proceedings of Construction Research Congress, pp. 1–10 (2005)

Enacting Innovation within Collaborative-Driven SOA Providers Networks

João Ferreira Santanna, Ricardo J. Rabelo, and Alexandra A. Pereira-Klen

Department of Automation and Systems Engineering,
Federal University of Santa Catarina, Florianopolis (SC), Brazil
joaosantanna@yahoo.com.br, ricardo.rabelo@ufsc.br,
xandaklen@gmail.com

Abstract. Software industry has become a very important sector nowadays. New ICT paradigms have emerged to cope with current global-local world challenges, such as Service-oriented architecture (SOA). SOA has the potential to raise SMEs to new levels of sustainability in terms of software innovation. However, SMEs are limited in their resources, and both innovation and SOA are complex, costly and risky. This paper presents preliminary results of an ongoing research towards developing an innovation model that relies on collaboration, enabling software/SOA providers to work as an open network to jointly develop an innovative SOA-base software product. The proposed model identifies not only the processes to be involved in but also identifies the most relevant supporting issues to be taken into account along the innovation and collaboration processes. Final considerations about the work are presented at the end.

Keywords: Collaborative Networks, Innovation, Software Services, SOA.

1 Introduction

Software industry has become a very important sector nowadays. In Europe, for instance, there are more than fifty thousand SMEs within the ICT sector [1]. Being by far composed of SMEs, they usually have tough difficulties for engaging assets to feasibly invest on innovation with acceptable risk [2]. So it is crucial to develop sustainable models to allow them taking advantage of more recent ICT and organizational trends and hence to innovate. Li et al. [3] point out that software innovation is a key aspect to increase SMEs competitiveness.

Some recent ICT paradigms have emerged with the potential to support that. This paper deals with SOA (Service Oriented Architecture) paradigm. SOA represents a new vision in terms of systems design, development, integration and servitization. In the SOA vision, all system's features are seen as independent and self-contained soft- ware modules – called *software services* – that jointly form virtually a single logical unit to create products and processes [2]. There are some technologies for implementing services-based systems, being *web services* the most used one.

B. Grabot et al. (Eds.): APMS 2014, Part III, IFIP AICT 440, pp. 399–408, 2014.
© IFIP International Federation for Information Processing 2014

Reports anticipate a SOA market of $15 billion dollars in 2019 [4]. However, SOA projects are complex, risky, costly and unique, impacting companies (both customers and providers) at many dimensions [2]. This paper exploits the premise that SOA providers SMEs can mitigate such barriers if they collaborate more intensively with each other towards jointly developing SOA-based innovative software *products*.

It is important to highlight that a SOA/software product has many differences when compared to manufacturing sector/product, in terms of e.g. development stages and methodologies, supporting constructs, physical deployment, SLA treatment, software / services quality, and product contracting, access and usage.

Working collaboratively is rather difficult. Companies are heterogeneous and autonomous, largely distributed, meaning that their different strategies must be accommodated and interoperate regarding their different priorities and trade-offs in terms of acceptable risks, trust and benefits [5].

A sort of collaborative/networked-based innovation models have been presented in the literature. However, none of them are devoted to SOA/software sector and do not consider a wider open scenario where services' providers can participate in all phases of the innovation process, collaboratively and as a network, sharing benefits, costs and risks. Besides that, most of models are very abstract, without providing more detailed processes and even less for a collaborative SOA scenario.

This paper shows preliminary results of an ongoing research which aims to contribute to face this gap, presenting an innovation model that deals with that general scenario. It has been conducted as an essentially research-action, qualitative, deductive and applied work, strongly grounded on literature revision.

The paper is organized as follows. Section has introduced the problem and research goals. Section 2 presents a basic foundations review. Section 3 introduces the proposed model. Section 4 provides a summary of the achieved results and next steps.

2   Basic Concepts and Revision of the State-of-the-Art

This section presents a resumed description of the main core theoretical foundations that have been used in the conception of the proposed innovation model.

2.1   Innovation Models

By innovation model it is meant the general conceptual construct that helps an organization and its actors to set up the innovation framework, to develop the innovation itself and to manage this progress and its results (adapted from [6]). The literature presents an extensive list of innovation models. In essence, they basically describe the main phases and general *processes* necessary to carry an innovation out via the so- called *funnel*, namely: *selection and/or generation of ideas, concept development, concept evaluation/selection, concept design/specification, implementation* and *exploita- tion* (adapted from [7]).

Innovation models have evolved from linear models to network and open models, which can go back and forth through each phase (*stage*). Evaluation actions (*gate*) use to be added between each stage so releasing or not the process continuation. Different actors can contribute along the innovation process' stages, being them intraorganizational members or external partners/ stakeholders, and even customers [8].

Regarding this paper's goal, two innovation models are of particular relevance: the *Network* and *Open* innovation models. Roughly, the Network model considers an open environment composed of companies prepared and willing to work on an innovative idea when it comes up. Processes and operating rules are then set up accordingly. Open innovation focuses on a new logic based in openness and collaboration. It has been often adopted by large corporations that have the innovative idea reasonably well clear and looks for some complementarities   and   added value in some processes or product's parts. This can come from established partners or from wider ecosystems.

2.2   Collaborative Networks

CN is a general concept that embraces the diverse manifestations of collaboration among organizations. Its essentials relies on allowing organizations to keep focused on their skills and aggregating competencies and diverse resources with other organizations – so creating networked organizations – in order to offer products with higher value to meet businesses in a better way [8].

Two manifestations are of particular importance in this work: VO (*Virtual Organization*) and VBE (*Virtual organization Breeding Environments*). Generally, a VO can be defined as a temporary alliance formed by autonomous and heterogeneous organizations that collaboratively join their complementary core-competences and resources to better attend to a given demand, dismantling itself after all its legal obligations have been accomplished. During its *lifecycle* (VO *creation, operation, evolution* and *dissolution*), new members can get in and existing members can get out from it. VOs are mostly originated from long-term alliances, namely a VBE. A VBE formally groups organizations aiming at creating VOs with the most adequate partners in a more agile and trustful way, thanks to enough pre-conditions and basic/common operating rules for collaboration which are set up when its members get into it [9].

A VBE is classically seen as a closed world, not supporting larger and open digital business ecosystem at all. Adaptations in the VBE concept towards handling such more ample scenarios have been proposed, as the *Federation* [5] and the *sectoral system innovation* [10] concepts.

2.3   Governance

Governance in Networked Enterprises can be defined as "the definition of rules, criteria for decision-making, responsibilities, and boundaries of actions and autonomy for the involved actors. It is created by the own set of organizations to regulate itself. The fundamental role of governance is not managing, but rather to delimitate the management. Actors can use their knowledge within the defined governance framework in way to help organizations to best reaching their common goals" [11].

During the collaboration life cycle companies share assets and sensible information. However, they are independent enterprises and have their own business strategies, creating a complex and intrinsically conflicting operating scenario. Therefore, it is extreme relevant to properly govern that in way to minimize conflicts among all the involved actors and hence the risks for achieving the innovation goals.

In the CN perspective, a VO embraces different partners, with different roles and hence rights and duties, according to the business' profile, VO life cycle and the VBE-like/network's principles, bylaws and rules. This should be regulated by the VBE-like and VO governance models. Costa et al. [12] have proposed an integrated VBE-VO governance model on top of some classical network governance models, e.g. [13] [14].

2.4   State-of-the-Art

The *Systematic Literature Review* methodology [15] was applied to support the state-of-the-art review. *IEEExplore, ACM,* and *ScienceDirect* databases were searched, collecting papers written in English and published in journals and conference proceedings in the period Jan 2000-Feb 2014. It also considered some *ad-hoc* searches over the Internet and a search at *CORDIS,* the EU research projects database.

Any work was found   out   which   dealt   with   the   envisaged   open   and networked based innovation models *and* devoted to SOA & software providers. On the other hand, 5 papers and 6 projects presented more useful insights for the proposed innova- tion model, its processes and constructs.

Du Preez et al. [7] have devised an innovation model for products and general services (i.e. not for *software* services) identifying the most important required macro processes. Berre et al. [16] have proposed supporting languages to express the value delivery and services chain for the general area of services. Hoyer et al. [17] have stressed the obstacles faced by SMEs when collaborating. Belussi et al. [18] have proposed a framework and services typology in the innovation context. Therefore, they are all innovation initiatives on services but anyone on *software* services/SOA. Li et al. [3] have proposed a model driven collaborative development platform for SOA-based e-business systems, but not devoted anyhow to support innovation.

In terms of EU projects, *BIVEE, ComVantage, IMAGINE, CoVES, Laboranova* and *PLENT* [19] have tackled innovation at different perspectives and levels, fundamentally devoted to manufacturing sector, some considering the open innovation model, some don´t. Anyone has applied the network innovation model and/or more directed to software or SOA sector.

3   Proposed Innovation Model

3.1   General Requirements and Rationale

Regarding the various aspects mentioned in the previous sections, the innovation model basically intends to endow groups of SOA-related and supporting software SMEs (belonging to a federation-like ecosystem) to carry an innovation out towards providing a (SOA) software (product) solution to attend to a given request.

In order to devise the model, this vision was decomposed into fifteen specific requirements. In a resumed way, the most relevant ones are: i) The 'product' is a SOA- based software, composed of existing web services; ii) Different companies own services or are in charge of developing such services; iii) This ownership should be protected and accounted; iv) Each web service and its supporting infrastructure can be developed / provided by one or by more companies or ad-hoc supporting partnerships; v) Companies that will participate in the innovation process should be properly selected; vi) Companies may participate along the entire innovation process and related software development cycle, depending on their agreed roles, rights and duties; vii) Companies may/can/should enter to, operate in, and exit from the collaborative innovation network in different moments and number of times, both in the normal operation of the network and when problems, changes or severe conflicts take place.

The model's structure took the "classical" processes proposed by Du Preez at al. [7] into account (section 2.1) as they can comprehensively embrace the general processes necessary for the envisaged model. Processes' names and sub-processes were adapted to better reflect their role regarding the intrinsic nature of SOA development.

Regarding that SOA & supporting software providers have web services assets and related expertizes, it is also important that the necessary expertizes can be joined, covering the diverse dimensions involved in an innovation, such as legal, financial, commercial, technological and software engineering.

3.2   The Proposed Innovation Model

The model is showed in Fig 1. It also uses the funnel notion to represent the multiple ideas that go through evaluation phases where only the approved ideas can go on.

However, differently from the classical models, the funnel is here split into two sequential but somehow decoupled macro phases. Whilst the first funnel aims to discuss and select the best ideas and then to define the respective members of the innovation network (i.e. t VO), the second one aims to develop the selected innovation(s) inside the formed VO(s). This separation is also important as there are different notions of budget, time and H resources allocations, the importance of the research, and the involvement of customers, experts and external supporting entities in each funnel.

Processes and nature of discussions, type of knowledge, information flow, type of responsibilities, etc., are intrinsically different in each funnel. Regarding that, the innovation behaves more like as the *network* type inside the first funnel and more like as the *open* innovation type in the second funnel. In terms of governance model, while the *all-ring no-core* and *buyer-driven* models [13, 14] tends to largely prevail in the first funnel, this tends to be more *corering with coordination firm* and *information-driven* in the second funnel. The innovation can move forward and backward in both funnels. However, this tends to happen much more frequently in the first funnel due to the natural not so structured way of exchanging more abstract/business ideas towards more concrete plans. In the second funnel this tends to be more controlled, based on evaluations performed in the intermediate gates (illustrated as "vertical lines" separating the processes within the funnels), deciding if the whole process can go on or not (and further actions). This decision involves interactions among partners, observing the governance model. It can be said that a more *human-driven* approach tends to predominate in the first funnel and a *process-driven* approach tends to do so in the second funnel, where the (software) development process is usually well defined and more structured.

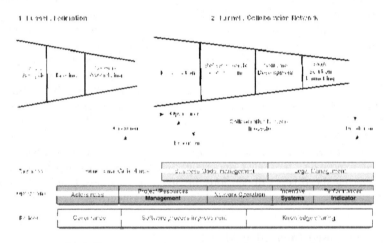

Fig. 1. The proposed Innovation Model. Source: authors.

Briefly, the processes are the following:

First funnel

1) *Idea Analysis*: one (or group of) company from the federation can propose a joint innovation to the federation's committee, which will firstly evaluate the idea's potential. At this moment the idea is presented shallowly.

2) *Briefing*: the idea is now detailed presented, describing the necessary technologies, potential partnerships, estimated ROI, foreseen market, etc.

3) *Network assembly*: formation of the VO that will execute the innovation. It involves partners' search and selection, negotiation, VO governance model and revenue mode setting up, and contract signature. Yet, performance indicators and eventual metrics upon partners and the innovation process itself.

Second funnel

4) *Presentation*: a complete project plan and ICT analysis are conceived and the business model is eventually refined. This is done by the involved companies helped by some external actor (from inside or outside the federation) depending on the VO governance model. It also includes issues of IPR and ownership, accounting, and knowledge gaps in the VO and in the federation.

5) *Software-service conceptualization*: it refers to the idealization of the SOA solution, the required services to be composed and expected end-to-end QoS.

6) *Software development*: this process basically deals with the same issues tacked in the previous step. However, at a much more detailed level, including the services coding themselves, their integration and final verifications. It covers the SOA/services life cycle development [20], but respecting the many particularities when the SOA project is developed by a group of companies [21].

7) *SOA solution launching*: this process ends the innovation development, making the idealized SOA solution available to who has requested it. Further actions are very much dependent on the business and contract / its term. Therefore, it may include processes that are out of a typical innovation framework, like the SOA product effective provision to clients/customers.

An underlying construct in the proposed innovation model is the *VO life cycle*. Its importance is twofold: i) knowing in which processes a VO can change its configurations, including partners' entrance/withdrawing and their respective roles; ii) helping partners in the VO management as this requires additional processes for each VO phase other than innovation or software engineering related. These processes have different complexities and demands different efforts, costs and supporting methods from the VO members [22].

3.3   Functional Guidelines

Functional guidelines (FG) correspond to supporting aspects that should be considered by network members along the collaborative innovation. It is a construct not presented in other innovation models. They represent methods, techniques, tools and foundations that are required at the different phases of the whole process and at different levels. Ten main FGs have been identified through an inductive method over a number of papers on innovation got from the literature review (e.g. [23] and [24]). FGs are grouped into categories, which act at three levels of the innovation process. Briefly:

- **Business Level:** it embraces the FGs related to the innovation commercialization, in more particular: *Business Model management* – guarantee that the innovation results are aligned with the defined business model; *Legal management* – guarantee that the innovation results have been developed and are aligned within the required legal framework, respecting contracts, IPR and services ownership.

- **Operational Level:** FGs to support the "daily" operation of the innovation development, in more particular: *Actors' management* – guarantee that all the involved actors will consider their rights and duties according to the governance model; *Project/Resources management* – it supports the usual issues related to manage the in- novation process as a project, e.g. financial, HR and material resources; *Network operation* – it is also related to the governance model, adapting the power and structural elements of decision-making; *Incentive systems* – issues to guarantee the correct application of collaboration incentives in the innovation also regarding productivity and adherence to the project's goals; *Performance indicators*: selection and application of adequate indicators to correctly measure and manage the performance of the project, individual services, partners and the innovation itself.

- **Policies Level:** FGs related to general relations among the VO, the VO with other actors (internal or external to the federation), and with customers, in more particular: *Governance* – rules and models to set up how the innovation will be executed and managed; *Software process improvement* – models, standards, specifications, practices and methodologies to guarantee the right way of developing software and services; *Knowledge sharing* – to guarantee that the necessary information and knowledge to support the innovation are properly shared and managed.

4   Final Considerations

This paper has presented preliminary results of a research which aims at conceiving an innovation model devoted to support collaborative innovation among SMEs of software/ services providers towards a SOA solution.

The proposed model has been developed in the light of Collaborative Networks, enabling SMEs to work as a network, so sharing costs, risks and benefits. A Virtual Organization (VO) represents the group of SMEs that jointly carry an innovation out. One of the underlying assumptions is that they should come from a VBE-like network of ICT companies which should have some preparedness to collaborate, which in- cludes sharing of common principles and operating rules.

It could be observed that quite few works have dealt with collaborative innovation targeting networked SMEs and anyone looking at the software services sector and related products. Besides that, most of the innovation models that have been proposed are directed to manufacturing, a sector very different than the SOA/software sector.

The proposed model also identifies the most relevant supporting issues that should be taken into account along the innovation process and the VO life cycle. To be highlighted the governance issue, fundamental to guarantee the correct evolution of a given innovation as long as it progresses, regulating partners' roles, rights and duties. This mitigates conflicts among companies and hence the innovation risks. Such issues, taken as functional guidelines in the proposed model, help companies to allocate proper resources and to be aware about different levels of complexities along the collaborative innovation life cycle. These FGs and their placement along the innovation process should however be seen here as a reference. Therefore, regarding the particularities of the given ecosystem in terms of e.g. existing culture, type of customers, adopted business models, and regional/national/international accounting and legal frameworks and associated requirements, they can support processes in a different way as and can have different degrees of importance. Yet, new FGs can also be added.

Regarding the particularities of software/SOA sector, the nature of the innovation process, and the fact companies should work in a network, the classical innovation funnel was adapted and split into two sequential but decoupled funnels.

Next steps of this research include the verification of the model and its elements (for further refinements) close to a real cluster of ICT/SOA providers already identified. This also comprises refinements on top of the work of [21] in terms of detailed processes and practices to develop SOA collaboratively with a focus on innovation.

References

1. http://www.ukita.co.uk/about-ukita/about-ukita.html
2. Westphal, I., Thobenand, K.D., Seifert, M.: Managing collaborationperformance togovern virtualorganizations. Journal of Intelligent Manufacturing 21(3), 311–320 (2010)
3. Li, Y., Shen, J., Shi, J., Shen, W., Huang, Y., Xu, Y.: Multi-model drivencollaborative development platform forservice-oriented e-Business systems. Advanced Engineering Informatics 22, 328–339 (2008)
4. PRWEB, http://www.prweb.com/releases/soa-services-oriented/architecturemarket/prweb10670370.htm
5. Rabelo, R.J.: Advanced collaborative business ICT infrastructures. In: Methods and Tools for Collaborative Networked Organizations, pp. 337–370. Springer (2008)
6. Tidd, J., Bessant, J., Pavitt, K.: Innovation Management. Willey (2001)
7. Du Preez, N.D., Louw, L.: A framework form an aging the innovation process. In: Proc. Portland Int. Conf. on Management of Engineering & Technology, pp. 546–558 (2008)
8. Rothwell, R.: Successful industrial innovation: critical factors for the 1990s. R&D Management 22, 221–240 (1992)
9. Baldo, F., Rabelo, R.J.: For a methodology to implement virtual breeding environments-a case study in the mold and diesectorin Brazil. In: Camarinha-Matos, L.M., Paraskakis, I., Afsarmanesh, H. (eds.) PRO-VE 2009. IFIP AICT, vol. 307, pp. 197–206. Springer, Heidelberg (2009)
10. Malerba, F.: Sectoral systems of innovation: concepts, issues and analyses of six major sectors in Europe. Cambridge University Press (2004)
11. Roth, A.L., Wegner, D., Padula, A.D.: Differences and Inter-Relations of Governance Concepts and Horizontal Networked Enterprises Managemen. Journal of Administration 1, 112–123 (2012) (in Portuguese)
12. Costa, S.N., Rabelo, R.J.: A Governance Model for Virtual Enterprises. In: Proc. XVI Symposiumon Manufacturing Management, Logistics and International Operations, pp. 1–12. SãoPaulo, Brazil (2013) (inPortuguese)
13. Storper, M., Harrison, B.: Flexibility, hierarchy andregional development: Thechanging structure of industrial production systems and their forms of governance in the 1990s. Research Policy 20, 407–422 (1991)
14. Gereffi, G., Humphrey, J., Sturgeon, T.: The governance of global value chains. Review of International Political Economy 12, 78–104 (2005)

15. Kitchenham, B., Pearl Brereton, O., Budgen, D., Turner, M., Bailey, J., Linkman, S.: Systematic literature reviews in software engineering- A systematic literatu rereview. Information and Software Technology 51, 7–15 (2009)
16. Berre, A.J., Lew, Y., Elvesaeter, B., de Man, H.: Service Innovation and Service Realisation with VDM Land Service ML. In: 7th IEEE International Enterprise Distributed Object Computing Conference Workshops (EDOCW), pp. 104–113 (2013)
17. Hoyer, V., Christ, O.: Collaborative e-business process modelling: a holisticanalysis framework focusedonsmallandmedium-sized enterprises. In: Proceedings 10th International Conference on Business Information Systems, pp. 41–53. Springer, Poznan (2007)
18. Belussi, F., Arcangeli, F.: A typology of networks: flexible and evolution ary firms. Research Policy 27, 415–428 (1998)
19. http://cordis.europa.eu/projects/home_en.html (accessed in September 2013)
20. O'Brien, L.: A framework for scope, cost and effort estimation for service oriented architecture (SOA) projects. In: Software Engineering Conference, ASWEC 2009, Australia, pp. 101–110 (2009)
21. Cancian, M.H., Rabelo, R.J., von Wangenheim, C.G.: Supporting Processes for Collaborative SaaS. In: Camarinha-Matos, L.M., Scherer, R.J. (eds.) PRO-VE 2013. IFIP AICT, vol. 408, pp. 183–190. Springer, Heidelberg (2013)
22. Camarinha-Matos, L., Afsarmanesh, H.: Collaborative Networks: Reference Modeling. Springer Publishing Company, Incorporated (2008)
23. Munkongsujarit, S., Srivannaboon, S.: Key success factors for open innovation intermediaries for SMEs: A case study of iTAP in Thailand. In: Proceedings of PICMET 2011 Technology Management in the Energy Smart World, pp. 1–8 (2011)
24. Van Zyl, J.: Process innovation imperative [software product development organisation]. In: Proceedings IEMC 2001 Change Management and the New Industrial Revolution, pp. 454–459 (2001)

Using DEVS and CELL-DEVS
for Modelling of Information Impact on Individuals
in Social Network

Youssef Bouanan, Merouane Bouhamidi El Alaoui, Gregory Zacharewicz,
and Bruno Vallespir

University of Bordeaux, Lab. IMS, UMR 5218, 33405 Talence, France
{youssef.bouanan,gregory.zacharewicz,
Bruno.vallespir}@ims-bordeaux.fr, alaoui.merouane@gmail.com

Abstract. We observe that major works about modelling and simulation within social science, especially for social, organizational and cultural influences on opinion information spreading over a population, do not use specification languages to describe their models. These models are specified in the shape of math formulas and then directly coded using classical programming languages. The specification language can be a missing link. For instance, the DEVS formalism (Discrete EVent system Specifications) being general enough to represent dynamical systems, can provide an operational semantics applicable to this domain. These models independent from implementation are easily reusable. In this article, we recall first the use of discrete modelling approaches in the social influence. Then we present models for human information treatment and propagation using DEVS and Cell-DEVS (Cellular DEVS). Finally, we present a simulation transposed from epidemic models to the impact of information on individuals using CD++, a simulation tool for DEVS and Cell-DEVS.

Keywords: DEVS Formalism, Information Impact, CELL-DEVS, Human Behaviour Modelling.

1   Introduction and Motivation

The reactions of populations to the dissemination and propagation of information are, up to now, not modeled appropriately. There is however an interest in the ability to simulate and accurately measure the impact of information on population. The SICOMORES project objective is to provide solutions to artificially generate structured social networks of realistic population and simulate the effects of information on population, with a propagation algorithm of the effects across networks. The intention is to go further than current models which generally reduce the individuals of a population as simple obstacles or information transmitters without enough nuances in their behaviour and the influence they can have on a message. This paper intends to present the premise of modelling and simulation of the impact of influence activities on individuals in social networks using Cell DEVS M&S formalism.

Cell-DEVS is a combination of CA (Cellular Automata) with the DEVS (Discrete EVent system Specifications) formalism that allows the definition of complex cell

B. Grabot et al. (Eds.): APMS 2014, Part III, IFIP AICT 440, pp. 409–416, 2014.
© IFIP International Federation for Information Processing 2014

based systems. It appears especially suited to this study that takes into account several layers of social graph related with geographical networks. CD++ is a modelling and simulation tool that implements DEVS and Cell-DEVS. We use CD++ to build a model of influence of information on individuals in social networks. In more detail, this paper will participate in the definition of a set of models that addresses the entities and the structure of a population. It will present a state of the art of modelling and simulation approaches to describe a social system at multiple levels including multi-agent systems (MAS) and discrete modelling approaches. In addition, it will provide models of individuals and groups of individuals characterized by a set of state variables (e.g. Using Maslow to construct the behaviour of an individual) and the mesh between the individuals within a social network.

2   Background

2.1   DEVS Formalism

The DEVS formalism for modelling and simulation (Zeigler et al., 2000) is based on discrete events, and provides a framework with mathematical concepts based on the sets theory and systems theory concepts to describe the structure and the behaviour of a system. With DEVS, there is an explicit separation between a model and its simulator: once a model is defined, it is used to build a simulator (i.e. a device able to execute the model's instructions). DEVS knows two kinds of models: the atomic models, which describe behaviour, and the coupled models which describe a hierarchy.

The tiniest element in DEVS formalism is the atomic model. It is specified as:

$$AM = < X, Y, S, ta, \delta int, \delta ext, \lambda >$$

The semantics for this definition is given as follows. At any time, a DEVS atomic model is in a state $s \in S$. In the absence of external events, the model will stay in this state for the duration specified by ta(s). When the elapsed time e= ta (s), the state duration expires and the atomic model will sent the output $\lambda(s)$ and performs an internal transition to a new state specified by δint (s). Transitions that occur due to the expiration of ta(s) are called internal transitions.

However, state transition can also happen due to arrival of an external event which will place the model into a new state specified by δext (s,e,x); where s is the current state, e is the elapsed time, and X is the input value. The time advance function ta(s) can take any real value from 0 to ∞. A state with ta(s) value of zero is called transient state, and on the other hand, if ta(s) is equal to ∞ the state is said to be passive, in which the system will remain in this state until receiving an external event.

Table 1 show the graphical notation to define the behaviour of atomic models.

Table 1. DEVS graphical notation

State	Internal Transition	External Transition
Name Ta	q0 Ta=e0 --q0!20--> q1 Ta=∞	q0 Ta=∞ --q0?10--> q1 Ta=e1

2.2   CELL-DEVS

Cell-DEVS (Wainer, 2009) has extended the DEVS formalism, allowing the implementation of cellular models with timing delays. It improves execution performance of cellular models by using a discrete-event approach. It also enhances the cell's timing definition by making it more expressive. Each cell is defined as an atomic model using timing delays, and it can be later integrated to a coupled model representing a cell space, as showed in Figure 1.

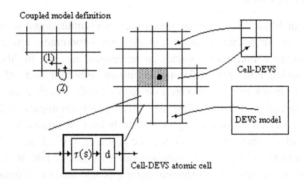

Fig. 1. Informal Description of Cell-DEVS

Once the cell behaviour is defined, a coupled Cell-DEVS can be created by putting together a number of cells interconnected with their neighbors. A cellular model is a lattice of cells holding state variables and a computing apparatus, which is in charge of updating the cell state according to a local rule. This is done using the present cell state and those of a finite set of nearby cells (called its neighborhood).

Each cell uses N inputs to compute its next state. These inputs, which are received through the model's interface, activate a local computing function (t). A delay (d) can be associated with each cell. The state (s) changes can be transmitted to other models, but only after the consumption of this delay. Two kinds of delays can be defined: transport delays model a variable commuting time (every state change is transmitted), and inertial delays, which have preemptive semantics (scheduled events can be discarded).

2.3   CD++ Toolkit

CD++ (Wainer, 2002) is a modelling and simulation toolkit that implements DEVS and Cell-DEVS theory. Atomic models can be defined using a state-based approach (coded in C++ or an interpreted graphical notation), while coupled and Cell-DEVS models are defined using a built-in specification language. We will show the basic features of the tool through an example of application. CD++ also includes an interpreter for Cell-DEVS models. The model specification includes the definition of the size and dimension of the cell space, the shape of the neighborhood and borders. The cell's local computing function is defined using a set of rules with the form:

{POSTCONDITION} {DELAY} {PRECONDITION}. These indicate that when the PRECONDITION is satisfied, the state of the cell will change to the designated POSTCONDITION, whose computed value will be transmitted to other components after consuming the DELAY.

3   Human Behaviour Modelling

3.1   General Approach

Human Behaviour Modelling is an important area of computational science with implications not only for social sciences, but also for economics, epidemiology and other fields. Scientific literature abounds in heterogeneous and highly specialized, theoretically founded concepts of human cognition, emotion and other behaviour aspects. There are many lines of research on such models, which span several disciplines, have different goals, and often use different terminologies and various approaches. Human behaviour modelling or human behaviour representation (HBR) is an important field of study in military service research (Fei et al., 2007), robotics [(Kubota and Nichida, 2006)], brain-computer interface (BCI), human machine interface (HMI) and some specially oriented anthropology studies. Human behaviour models are often represented by finite state machines, rules, fuzzy rules (Dorsey and Coovert, 2003), artificial neural networks, multi-agent based modelling (Sun, 2007). The need for a variety of modelling paradigms stems from the fact that the different domains of knowledge needed to represent human behaviour cannot be done by only one paradigm.

3.2   Using DEVS for Human Behaviour Modelling

Human behaviour can be difficult to understand and predict, thus it can be qualified as a complex system. DEVS is a well-defined formalism which has numerous advantages over other formalisms in the modelling of complex dynamic systems. A few related works have provided DEVS models of human behaviour that we will use with slight modifications; (Seck, 2004) present a DEVS based framework for the modelling and simulation of human behaviour with the influence of stress and fatigue, (Faucher, 2012) proposed a first approach using G-DEVS formalism for Civil-Military Cooperation actions (CIMIC) and Psychological actions (PSYOPS), which are actions of influence that take precedence over combat. The purpose of this work is to go beyond previous works by providing a simple model but more performant and accurate which will allow us not only to model the behaviour of an individual, but also the simulation of the propagation of an information among a group of individuals and its influence on their behaviour.

This model (Figure 2) is describing the influence of message on the behaviour of an individual and potentially its dissemination. The first state consists in being in contact with another agent in its social network neighbourhood and calculating the strength of connexion between them. When the message is received, it creates an impact on the individual which change its behaviour eventually depending on the strength of the message (Faucher, 2012). Then, if the message strength is still strong enough the receiver is preparing on its turn to transmit the message to its network neighbours considered as target info.

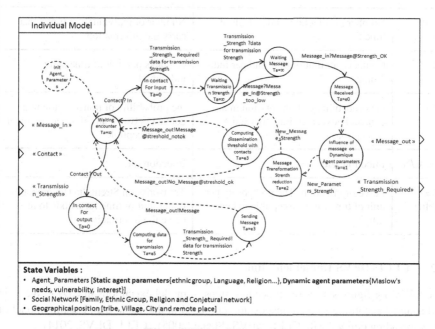

Fig. 2. DEVS individual model

4   Using CELL-DEVS to Simulate Information Propagation

4.1   From Epidemics Spreading to Information Diffusion

The phenomena of information propagation have known a great interest of researchers and still an active field of research as well (Bakshy et al., 2011). In the past, the propagation was mainly studied in the epidemiological field to better understand the process of propagation of infection in certain conditions. Therefore, the majority of recent works related to information diffusion are based on the epidemic researches. There is a basic analogy (Table 2) between the dissemination of information among a group of individuals and the transmission of infectious disease between the individuals themselves. In the two cases, something is communicated through a given contact.

Table 2. Analytical model parameters in epidemiology versus diffusion

	Epidemiology	Information diffusion
N	Number of individuals	Number of individuals
S(t)	Number of susceptible individuals at time t	Number of susceptible individuals at time t
I(t)	Number of infectious individuals at time t	Number of individuals at time t that carry the information
X	Contacts per unit of time and per individual	Contacts per unit of time and per individual
ß	the probability of transmission in a contact between an infective and a susceptible	the probability of transmission in a contact between an information holder and a susceptible
a= ßx/N	Infection rate	Infection rate
α = a*I(t)	Force of infection: The probability per unit of time for a susceptible to become infective	Transmission Strength: The probability per unit of time for a node to receive the information

4.2   CELL-DEVS Implementation

The following figure shows the procedure steps of model executions in CD++. We used and adapted according to the transposition proposed in the Table 2 an existing model of virus spreading defined with CELL-DEVS (Shang, 2005), (CELL-DEVS, 2014).

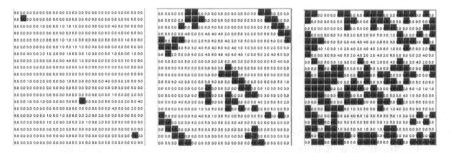

Fig. 3. Execution result at time 00:00:00:000; 00:00:00:500; 00:00:01:000

The model is intended to study the propagation of information within a group of individuals. Assume there is 20×20 mesh of cellular automata (CA). Each individual, residing in (i,j) node, is equipped with a number ranged from 0 to 9 indicating different Parameters of the individual. Each cell may represent one of two categories: one is person who did not receive the information represented by white color; the other is the person who received the message represented by red color. The individual can be opposed to the information and/or person that is transmitting the message and/or favourable to the emitter and message content. The simulation results show on the right picture of Figure 3 that depending on the opinion of individuals and the configuration of the social networks some individual can be reached by the information where some other not. This test is very simple; it is based on the abstract geographical situation of individuals and it takes into account only one dimension of a social network. We have not introduced yet the graph representation for defining the multilevel social network links between individuals or groups. Nevertheless the approach already validates the possibility to reuse epidemic algorithm for information spreading.

5   Conclusion

This paper introduced Formal Modelling and Simulation of the impact of Information on Individuals in Social Networks. We have presented how DEVS and Cell-DEVS can be very useful techniques for modelling and simulating of Social influence. At the individual level, the DEVS model proposed is very simple keeping raw Maslow parameters as state variables and being simply influenced by arriving messages. In its turn the individual model can transmit the message after having potentially transformed its strength according to several criteria. The Cell DEVS structure then use these models of human extremely simplified and start building on top of its connected modules to form Cell-DEVS network. In addition, the separation between the model and simulator followed by DEVS and CD++, has enabled the modeller to concentrate on building the behavioural model on one side and preparing the spreading logic on the other side using the CD++ toolkit. The model shows a correct, even very simple, human behaviour impact regarding information perception and treatment. Then the information spreading reusing the epidemic approaches seems accurate after some adaptations to propagate the information over the network.

6   Perspectives

The main perspective remains the definition of a multi-level social network. In detail the real social network is complex, it can refer for e.g. to the family environment, work, religion, geography to transport the information from one individual to another. The final result will be the combination of several networks graphs. The next step will also consider other experimental terrains, for instance enterprise and organization.

References

1. Bakshy, E., Hofman, J.M., Mason, W.A., Watts, D.J.: Everyone's an influencer: quantifying influence on twitter. In: Proceedings of the Fourth ACM International Conference on Web Search and Data Mining, pp. 65–74 (2011)
2. CELL-DEVS Models, `http://www.sce.carleton.ca/faculty/wainer/wbgraf/doku.php?id=model_samples:start` (accessed April 2014)
3. Diekmann, O., Heesterbeek, J.A.P.: Mathematical Epidemiology of Infectious Diseases. Wiley Ser. Mathematical and Computational Biology, England (2000)
4. Ding, W., Pei, L., Li, H., Xi, N., Wang, Y.: The Effects of Time Delay of Internet on Characteristics of Human Behaviors. In: Proceedings of the 2009 IEEE International Conference on Networking, Sensing and Control, Okayama, Japan (2009)
5. Dorsey, D.W., Coovert, M.D.: Mathematical Modeling of Decision making: A Soft and Fuzzy Approach to Capturing Hard Decisions. Human Factors 45(1), 117–135 (2003)
6. Faucher, C., Zacharewicz, G., Hamri, E.M., Frydman, C.: PSYOPS and CIMIC operations: from concepts to G-DEVS models. SpringSim (TMS) 42 (2012)
7. Fei, L., Ming, Y., Guobing, S.: Verification of Human Decision Models in Military Simulations. In: Proceedings of the IEEE 2007, The First Asia International Conference on Modeling & Simulation, pp. 363–368 (2007)
8. Kubota, N., Nishida, K.: Prediction of Human Behavior Patterns based on Spiking Neurons. In: The 15th IEEE International Symposium on Robot and Human Interactive Communication, ROMAN 2006 (2006)
9. Seck, M., Frydman, C., Giambiasi, N.: Using DEVS for Modeling and Simulation of Human Behaviour. In: Kim, T.G. (ed.) AIS 2004. LNCS (LNAI), vol. 3397, pp. 692–698. Springer, Heidelberg (2005)
10. Shang, H., Wainer, G.: A Model of Virus Spreading Using Cell-DEVS. In: Sunderam, V.S., van Albada, G.D., Sloot, P.M.A., Dongarra, J.J. (eds.) ICCS 2005. LNCS, vol. 3515, pp. 373–377. Springer, Heidelberg (2005)
11. Sun, Z.: Multi-Agent Based Modeling: Methods and Techniques for Investigating Human Behaviors. In: Proceedings of IEEE International Conference on Mechatronics and Automation (2007)
12. Wainer, G.: "CD++: A toolkit to develop DEVS models", Software - Practice and Experience, pp. 1261–1306 (2002)
13. Wainer, G.: Discrete-Event Modeling and Simulation: A Practitioner's approach. CRC Press (2009)
14. Zacharewicz, G., Frydman, C., Giambiasi, N.: G-DEVS/HLA Environment for Distributed Simulations of Workflows 84(5), 197–213 (2008)
15. Zeigler, B.P., Praehofer, H., Kim, T.G.: Theory of Modelling and Simulation. Editions Academic Press, San Diego (2000)

Toward Human-Centric Factories: Requirements and Design Aspects of a Worker-Centric Job Allocator

Gokan May[1], Omid Maghazei[1], Marco Taisch[1], Andrea Bettoni[2], Marco Cinus[2], and Annarita Matarazzo[1]

[1] Politecnico di Milano, Department of Management, Economics and Industrial Engineering, Piazza Leonardo da Vinci 32, Milano, 20133, Italy
{gokan.may,omid.maghazei,marco.taisch}@polimi.it
[2] University of Applied Sciences and Arts of Southern Switzerland, ISTePS, Galleria 2 Via Cantonale 2c, CH-6928 Manno, Switzerland
{andrea.bettoni,marco.cinus}@supsi.ch

Abstract. The new point of view in which factory and workers are seen is the person at the centre of the production system, so employees should be involved in job design and task balancing processes. The advantages coming by this paradigm shift, from the task-centric organization to the worker-centric factory is doubtless the high correlation among job and worker in terms of skill, experience, and worker's features. Human-centric system is useful to improve the knowledge and the capabilities of workers regardless of age and role, and in this kind of model the job suits the worker and his needs. In this context, it is of paramount importance to design and develop a worker-centric job allocator tool in which the human dimension is a key factor. This study therefore addresses the requirements and design aspects of a worker-centric job allocator as an enabler for human-centric workplaces of the future.

Keywords: worker-centric job allocator, human-centric factory, sustainable manufacturing, social sustainability, factories of the future.

1 Introduction

The manufacturing sector needs to react and adapt to the emerging sustainability trend, not only for environmental and economic reasons but also for social ones. In this sense, the new point of view in which factory and workers are seen is the person at the centre of the production system, so employees should be involved in job design and task balancing processes. The advantages coming by this paradigm shift, from the task-centric organization to the worker-centric factory is doubtless the high correlation among job and worker in terms of skill, experience, and worker's features. The new human-centric factory model in the Figure 1 below, as developed by the authors in May et al. (2014), highlights the needs and important aspects for designing the human-centric workplaces of the future whilst addressing the problem from different perspectives (i.e. worker, factory, and context).

B. Grabot et al. (Eds.): APMS 2014, Part III, IFIP AICT 440, pp. 417–424, 2014.
© IFIP International Federation for Information Processing 2014

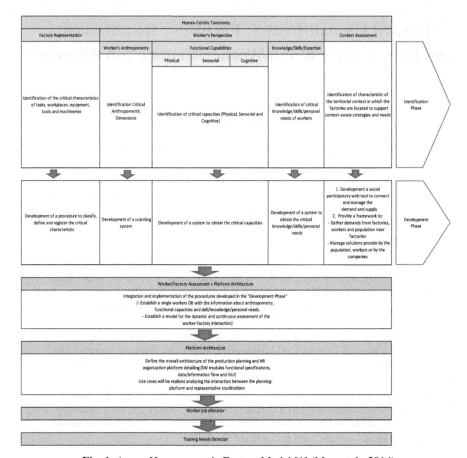

Fig. 1. A new Human-centric Factory Model [1] (May et al., 2014)

Human-centric system is useful to improve the knowledge and the capabilities of workers regardless of age and role, and in this kind of model the job suits the worker and his needs. In this context, it is of paramount importance to design and develop a worker-centric job allocator tool in which the human dimension is a key factor. Thus, in this research we address the research question *""How can the jobs in a workplace be allocated to workers to create human-centric workplaces?"*, on the way to design a worker-centric job allocator in which worker's skills, capacities and needs are considered. This study therefore aims at analyzing requirements and design aspects of a worker-centric job allocator to be used in human-centric workplaces of the future.

2   Theoretical Background

The review work in this section aims at describing the state of the art for traditional job allocation algorithms, and to find the bridges and the gaps between them and the relatively new research fields of worker-centric job allocator.

One of the main optimization problems in operations research is job allocation, and it aims at finding a maximum weight matching based on specific multi objective function or criteria. Thus, the problem of job allocation to tasks and workplaces is characterized by a large number of different possibilities for allocating employees to work functions [2]. There are many models for an optimal personnel assignment, but none of these incorporate the concept of human dimension in a holistic manner. The main aspect of a proper job allocator is the consideration of human factors like abilities, preferences, restrictions, and needs.

Dependent upon the type of personnel assignment problem, various instruments have been developed [3]. For instance, the ifab-Institute of Human and Industrial Engineering at the University of Karlsruhe develops a personnel-oriented simulation tool that considers the complex, dynamic interactions of personnel resources and machinery equipment and takes advantage of the vast array of opportunities for the planning and reassigning of personnel to work functions.

Zuelch, in his paper [3], highlights the key concepts in the way to design and conceive a worker-centric job allocator. However, the focus here is only on production planning, and themes like worker's abilities, preferences, skills, needs are only considered to the medium term production planning.

Corominas, in his research work [4] describes and models the allocation of a set of tasks to a set of workers, when the worker's performance on a task depends on the experience of the worker of this task and of the other tasks involved. The objective is to minimize the completion time. The model is very interesting because the performance is, at least in part, a consequence of experience. When a set of tasks is being performed, the experience acquired in the first stages can obviously influence the capacity of the worker to do this task and other tasks later. Despite this, the model takes into account only the experience factor and is not part of a worker-centric vision. There are essential elements missing in the model, such as needs, preferences, skills, features, and knowledge of workers.

Besides, Lin [5] constructs a general fuzzy assignment problem (GFAP) based on a real scenario and proposes a solution procedure. The model is based on a project team composed by n workers and a manager. The n workers are responsible for performing n jobs and the manager for restraining the total cost. Using the max–min criterion, a mixed nonlinear programming model of the GFAP is constructed, and an algorithm that combines simplex and trade-off approaches is proposed to solve the problem. In this model, the only objective is the increasing of team performance but main aspects of worker centric model are not considered. Thus, one weakness of the model could be the missing human dimension. However, the algorithm is very interesting and with some modifications could be used for future researches in designing worker-centric job allocators.

Koltai [6] suggests a balancing model for assembly workstations. The model assigns tasks to workstation taking into account skill requirement of tasks and skill level of workers (i.e. under skilled, average, and specialized). Nonetheless, this type of assignment is not dynamic because skills have been categorized a priori.

In traditional job allocation, algorithms are used in static way. However, it is important to have dynamic allocation of resources considering workers' evolution. The main gap found in the critical analysis of the literature is that models for job allocator and resource assignment are static. In the human-centric point of view, workers evolve during time, in which they could improve skills thanks to experience and training, change functional or anthropometric characteristics, improve knowledge, reconsider personal needs. So, the structure of job allocator should be dynamic, updating resource allocation based on workers' profile. Hence, this could enable us to redefine tasks, operations, jobs considering evolution of worker, factory, and contextual drivers. So, the worker-centric job allocator described in this work is built to address these emerging gaps.

3   The Worker-Centric Job Allocator

Job allocator module is a customer-centric production planning tool meant to dynamically assign the available workers to the different tasks and jobs considering workers' relevant characteristics, skills and availabilities; short-term production plans; time-schedules; job and task description. Different alternative jobs-workers matching are then ranked utilizing the assessment module. Job allocator runs when the   Production Manager needs to identify the better performing allocation of resources and to better manage human resources. This software module works on a short term basis and has a dedicated GUI for showing alternative for managing data entry, definition of allocation rules and for visualizing job allocations. Further considerations for this tool might be to have dedicated areas in which manager could find the best allocation by using filtering questions, and to have a customized and modular software tool in order to re-use the same software in different factory areas like technical department, production systems and other units.

3.1   Needs

The resource allocation in a company is a complex activity that employs many people in the organization. Big companies have a special department which deals this job. Despite all, for human resource management, it is difficult to take into account all worker's needs. The job allocator in a broad sense allows to assign tasks and jobs to the resources in a different way.

First of all, the analysis starts from a deep knowledge of the workers and their needs. This information becomes evaluation parameters to build the worker history and through these data, it is possible to better know the worker and to forecast the future needs, for example trainings. The tasks are then allocated according to the "best available resource" to perform that given asset. In this perspective, the role of training results are needed to improve knowledge and capabilities of each worker.

To derive the basic needs and requirements for a worker-centric job allocator, the process started with the interviews with two case companies from white goods and tooling industries. The companies listed the following functions as important for job allocator to be designed: communicate with work profiler; take into account a defined population; choose the best match between workstation skill requirements and worker profile to minimize the training gap up-front;   choose best match for each workstation on a set of workstations, in order to avoid looping; minimize the computational time; management of skill matrix – according to the critical workstation; identify the person who is the closest match to be trained in addition to that workstation, minimizing the training gap, matching interests and physical worker profile; have dedicated areas in which manager could find the best allocation by using filtering questions; a customized and modular software tool in order to re-use the same software in different factory areas like technical department, production systems and other units.

Besides, outputs required from job allocator tools are listed as for each workstation a list of operators with skills and qualifications, physical characteristics and limitations; and indication of match against workstation requirements and hints for designing workstations.

Despite the fact that defining an objective function is left as a further research stream, it is possible to define it in a generic way. According to the companies interview, it is better to shape a multi-objective function.

A multi-objective problem is defined as $\max\{f_1(x), f_2(x), ..., f_k(x)\}$ where Rk is the objective space. The multi-objective function for job allocator takes into account different objectives, some of them can be: maximize productivity P; maximize worker's satisfaction S; and minimize workers' related costs C.

Also, each single objective could be further specified into a set of decision variables along with a set of parameters. In this case decision variables can be workstations $W_i = 1, 2, .., N$ in a production system. Furthermore, constraints could be defined in a generic way accordingly, for example:

c_1: Assembly time for each workstation doesn't exceed the total working time T

c_2: Anthropometric factor AFi for each workstation is at least higher than the minimum required AF_{min}

The objective function might be defined as $\max\{P, S, -C\}$, where $c1 \leq T$, $c2 \geq AF_{min}$, and $W_i \geq 0$.

3.2   Requirements

Requirements analysis in systems engineering and software engineering, encompasses those tasks that go into determining the needs or conditions to meet for a new or altered product, taking account of the possibly conflicting requirements of the various stakeholders, analyzing, documenting, validating and managing software or system requirements [7].

It is possible to identify several types of requirements. In the following subsections will be listed three types of system requirements: functional, non-functional and technological. Requirements listed are MUST requirements, this means that the implementation of those requirements is essential to meet the initial specification to which the project is designed.

Functional Requirements. Functional requirements explain what has to be done by identifying the necessary task, action or activity that must be accomplished [8]. Functional requirements represent what user can do. Based on this, user can: create, delete, update worker data and its profile; share info with other company location/offices/premises; consult the system in every moment; find automatically the best job allocation; update the objective functions for the resource allocation; evaluate the different options on the basis of the objective functions; put in the system data of worker-factory-context; compare graphically different alternatives; and visualize statistics in different ways.

Non-functional Requirements. Non-functional requirements are requirements that specify criteria that can be used to judge the operation of a system, rather than specific behaviours. Non-functional requirements represent what system does. So, system: shows the workers list; shows measured data from each worker; shows the jobs' list; shows skills required from each job; compares worker skills with skills required for a specific job; communicates with existing production plan's data source (ERP); provides the optimum resource allocation considering worker-centricity; provides statistics; provides different alternatives for resource allocation; evaluates different options for resource allocation; keeps track of all job-worker alternatives; allows the communication among Job Allocator and job assessment modules; stores and retrieves data from knowledge database; allows the communication among Job Allocator and data coming from production plans; and provides a graphic interface in order to compare job-worker alternatives.

Technological Requirements. As technical requirement, system should have a GUI, a database, and different modules.

3.3   Use Case Diagram and Scenario

A use case diagram is a representation of a user's interaction with the system and depicting the specifications of a use case. As highlighted in the above use case diagram, the scenario is explained below:

- User can visualize suggested allocations, that is a list of jobs with assigned workers to each of it;
- User can evaluate job allocation alternatives;
- User can visualize job allocation statistics, that are statistics of jobs-workers matching;
- User can enter the required relevant data;
- To visualize statistics, it is necessary to have job allocation lists (include);

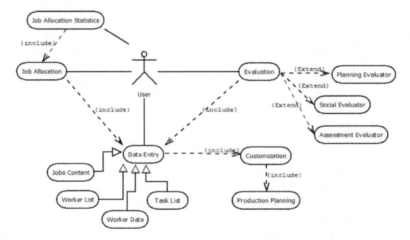

Fig. 2. Use Case Diagram

- Job Allocation and Evaluation have 'Data Entry' as a common feature (include);
- Evaluation is possible through different evaluator tools: planning evaluator, social evaluator, assessment evaluator (extend);
- Data Entry actions can be Job Content, Worker List, Worker Data and Task List;
- Customization is possible only through Data Entry (include): this function allows to customize the objective function.
- Production Planning is an external data source which stores production plans. The access to this tool is possible by Customization (include).

3.4   Class Diagram and Software Architecture

During the design phase of a software, it is very important to define the static view of the system, and a class diagram defines the basic elements in this context. The Figure 3 above hence illustrates the class diagram for the worker-centric job allocator.

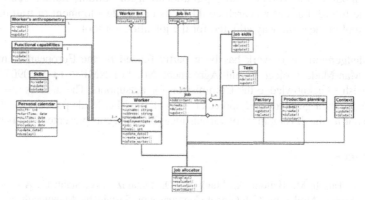

Fig. 3. Class Diagram for the worker-centric job allocator

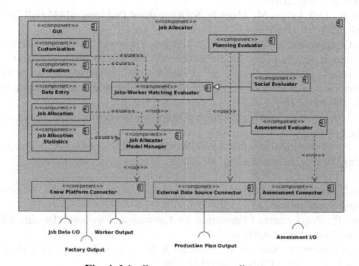

Fig. 4. Job allocator component diagram

The Figure 4 above represents the architecture of the job allocator software module which include the software elements and relationships in between them. Thus, building and documenting the software architecture fosters communication between stakeholders, and speeds up the decision process for the high-level design [9].

4   Conclusion

Designing human-centric workplaces of the future gains more and more importance in achieving socially sustainable factories and hence workers' satisfaction, which could lead to improvement of the overall performance in manufacturing plants. One of the main pillars in this direction is to design and assign jobs which better fit to workers' skills, characteristics, and needs. In this study, we analyzed the industrial needs and the requirements for designing such worker-centric job allocator. Hence, the results achieved and insights gained based on this study open the way toward development of software modules for worker-centric job allocation for building human-centric factories of the future. Further research could focus on the development of training needs detector tool in the same way adopted for the job allocator tool.

Acknowledgement. This work has been partly funded by the European Commission through Man-Made project (Grant Agreement No: FoF.NMP.2013-3 6090730). The authors wish to acknowledge the Commission for its support. The authors also wish to acknowledge their gratitude and appreciation to all the Man-Made partners for their contribution during the development of various ideas and concepts presented in this work.

References

1. May, G., Taisch, M., Bettoni, A., Maghazei, O., Matarazzo, A., Stahl, B.: A new Human-centric Factory Model. In: 12th Global Conference on Sustainable Manufacturing. Procedia CIRP (Forthcoming, 2014)
2. Burkard, R., Dell'Amico, M., Martello, S.: Assignment Problems. SIAM (2012) ISBN 978-1-61197-222-1
3. Zuelch, G., Rottinger, S., Vollstedt, T.: A simulation approach forplanning and re-assigning of personnel in manufacturing. Int. J. Production Economics 90, 265–277 (2004)
4. Corominas, A., Olivella, J., Pastor, R.: A model for the assignmentof a set of tasks when work performance depends on experience of all tasks involved. Int. J. Production Economics 126, 335–340 (2010)
5. Lin, C.-J.: Assignment problem for team performance promotion under fuzzy environment. Mathematical Problems in Engineering 6 (2013)
6. Koltai, T.: Formulation of Multi-Level Workforce Skill Constraints in Assembly Line Balancing Models, Manufacturing Modelling, Management, and Control 7(1), 772-777 (2013)
7. Hay, D.C.: Requirements Analysis: From Business Viewsto Architecture, 1st edn. Prentice Hall, Upper Saddle River (2003) ISBN 0-13-028228-6
8. Laplante, P.: Requirements Engineering for Software and Systems, 1st edn. CRC Press, Redmond (2009) ISBN 1-4200-6467-3
9. Bass, L., Clements, P., Kazman, R.: Software Architecture in Practice, 3rd edn., pp. 21–24. Addison-Wesley (2012) ISBN 978-0321815736

Exploring the Impact of National Culture on Performance Measurement

Ihssan M. Jwijati[*] and Umit S. Bititci

Heriot Watt University, Edinburgh, UK
{ij37,usb1}@hw.ac.uk

Abstract. The purpose of the research presented in this paper is to explore the impact of national culture on the design, implementation and use of performance measurement systems (PMS). Managing performance of organizations using management control system or performance management systems is essential for managers. As organizations are increasingly having to expand globally, they are forced to operate their original PMSs, but in different cultures. While, the impact of culture on PMS implementation have been revisited in the performance management literature from organizational perspectives, the impact of *national culture* on PMS was not clearly explored. Therefore the aim of the authors is to explore the impact of national culture on the lifecycle of PMS. Qualitative inductive research approach, and semi structured interviews of indigenous SMEs' were employed, and the findings suggest that national culture impact PMSs life-cycle and propositions are provided explaining the expected behaviour of different national cultures.

Keywords: performance measurement, cross-cultural management, change management, SME.

1 Introduction

Traditionally, measuring performance in organizations used to be achieved by monitoring financial performance only, until a time when the inadequacy of this approach was questioned by scholars such as (Johnson & Kaplan, 1987). The use of 'balanced' performance measures was advocated by many scholars such as Kaplan and Norton (1992), Neely (1996), and others. However, PMS implementation had high failure rate according to Neely and Bourne (2000), which lead the scholars to discover different forces behind successful implementation. Among the important factors that impact PMS design, implementation and use is culture. Culture according to Bourne, et al., (2000), is one of the important drivers of successful PMS implementation. However, most of these studies have been conducted from an organisational culture view point according to Henri (2006), and because of our vague understanding of the impact of national culture, Otley (2003) has called for more research to be performed to understand the impact of national culture. In addition, as we move deeper in to the 21st century we are seeing new forms of work emerging,

---

[*] Corresponding author.

B. Grabot et al. (Eds.): APMS 2014, Part III, IFIP AICT 440, pp. 425–432, 2014.

particularly with globalisation, advances in ICT technologies as can be experienced with global multinationals operating in different cultural settings as well as networks of smaller organisations collaborating in global networks (Bititci et.al., 2011). Furthermore, with the increasing impact of the emergent markets, organizations' need to conduct and manage businesses in other countries is more than ever, hence each organization should be able to cope with its internal and external environment in any country, as internal contextual factors are impacted with individuals' behaviour and culture.

Therefore, exploring the impact of national culture on PMS will help us contribute to the existing literature on performance measurement by (i) exploring the impact of national culture on the lifecycle of performance measurement systems, (ii) investigating moderating factors which is affecting the impact of national culture in organizations, and (iii) proposing methods of how to guide PMS implementation in different cultures.

2   Background Literature

2.1   National Culture

National culture (NC) has been defined by Hofstede as 'the collective programming of the mind which distinguishes the members of one human group from another' (Hofstede & Hofstede, 2005). The definition implies that culture is particular to one group and not others, and culture includes system of values. Schein (1985) has suggested that culture is the way in which a group of people solves problems and reconciles dilemmas. Kluckhohn and Strodtbeck, (1961) claimed that members of group exhibit constant 'orientations' towards the world and other people. Hall (1976) developed a model distinguishing between high-context and low-context cultures. In 1980 Hofstede first introduced his model, and he founded five dimensions: power distance (PD), uncertainty avoidance index (UAI), individualism vs. collectivism, masculinity vs. femininity, and long vs. short-term orientation. Although Hofstede's model had been criticised it has been widely used and confirmed. Later, other frameworks were introduced such as Laurent, Trompenaars, Schwartz, House etc. In this paper, two frameworks are going to be used, Hofstede and Trompenaars.

Trompenaars and Hampden-Turner (1993) created their framework on relationships of subordinates and rules (universalism vs. particularism), their relationship to the group (collectivism vs. individualism), their feelings and relationships (neutral and affective), the extent of their involvement with their tasks (specific vs diffuse), how status is awarded (ascription vs. achievement), how time is managed (synchronic vs. sequential) and how people relate to nature (Internalist vs. externalist).

2.2   Performance Management Systems

Traditionally, measuring performance in organizations used to be achieved by monitoring financial performance only, until a time when the inadequacy of this approach was questioned (Johnson & Kaplan, 1987). They advocated the use of non-financial measures in addition to financial measures in their seminal book *the relevance lost*. This lead many scholars to the introduction of different approaches such as Kaplan and Norton's (1992) Balanced Scorecard (BSC), Neely's performance prism, (Neely et al., 1996) among other performance frameworks. As the proliferation of PMS grew, as well as the failure rate of PMS implementation which amounts to 70% according to Neely & Bourne (2000). Attention then shifted from investigating implementation enablers and barriers to how to better use PMS results (Bourne et al, 2004).

Successful implementation of PMS depends on many factors such as: management commitment (de Waal, 200; Assiri, et al., 2006; Henri, 2006), aligning of strategy, (Kaplan & Norton, 1992; Bourne, et al., 2002; Assiri, et al., 2006), and culture (Bourne, et al., 2000; Bititci, et al., 2006), among other factors. Culture is one of the important drivers or factors impacting implementation of PMS (Henri, 2006; Bititci, et al., 2006; Bourne, 2005). Although national culture's impact has been researched in management control literature with mixed results, yet it's impact has not been properly investigated by performance management researchers. Otely (2003) has called for more research to understand the impact of national culture in performance management systems. It is therefore, vital to understand, the impact of national culture on PMS, as we are moving deeper in to the 21st century with new forms of work emerging, particularly with globalisation, advances in ICT technologies, network of smaller organisations collaborating in global networks (Bititci, et al., 2011).

Henri (2006) has found out that PMS can be used in four ways: monitoring, attention focusing, strategic decision-making, and legitimization. Monitoring when PMS provide feedback regarding performance to various stakeholders. If the results are used as a facilitator, then it is strategic use, while using the results to justify decisions or actions it legitimization. When the results are used to send signals throughout the firm, then the use is attention focusing or communications.

3   Methodology

In order to explore the impact of national culture on performance management systems, inductive qualitative research method was employed, as its more suitable for answering 'why', and 'how' questions in an iterative and flexible way, where the researcher's positions forms an integral part of the research process (Voss, et al., 2002) and Barratt et al., 2011). The research method used is multi-case study approach because it allows the researcher to explore the way companies in different cultures design, implement, and use their performance systems. The criteria for choosing different national cultures is based on Hofstede's *Power Distance v Uncertainty Avoidance* matrix as Hofstede suggested that there is an empirical evidence regarding the relationship between the country's position within the PD-UAI matrix and organizations' behaviour. Four cultures were chosen one from each quadrant in the PD-UAI matrix (Hofstede & Hofstede, 2005). The empirical study involved two Chinese, two Italian, two Syrian and two UK manufacturing SMEs.

For each company we collected information about PMS, PMS processes. Indigenous SMEs were chosen, as we expected large companies' policies, practices, and other factors to impact the influence the culture of the organisation. Additionally, in order to ensure that the chosen organizations representing their national cultures, only indigenous companies were chosen. All the case studies were having similar organization size, all were privately owned, all have industrial background, with minor differences in the firms' years of operation. Finally, ensuring -as much as possible- the clear impact of national, all case study organizations were chosen from non-regulated manufacturing sectors.

Wherever possible, interviews were held with the general managers and their top management teams. In one of the Chinese interviews, the decision maker was accompanied by members of his middle managers, where they participated in the discussion. In one of the Syrian organizations, the decision maker was interviewed alone in the beginning, and later the researcher was given time with two of the middle managers. It should be mentioned that the setting was left to the organizations involved, with the researcher expressing his wish to increase the scope, the length of the interview when the research needed more depth. In order to ensure objectivity, the interview result was triangulated with information company documents as well as researcher observations. In preparation for the company visits, a research protocol was designed. The research protocol was discussed between the authors and elaborated upon, and any question regarding the content was answered. Initially, the research protocol was piloted and tested on one UK organization, then the results of the interview was discussed, and minor changes were acted upon the research protocol, and then employed on the other case studies.

Semi structure interviews, observations, and archival sources were used to collect data, justified by the inductive nature of the research. The semi-structured nature of the interviews added exploratory richness to the research findings. Notes collected from interviews were prepared in a report that included observations from researcher, and relevant data from different sources such as internet sites or media reports. Visits to the company site helped in clarifying the nature of the organizations. Interviews were conducted by one researcher in three cultures, and conducted by another collaborating researcher for the fourth culture. Indigenous languages were the languages employed for each culture reducing translation errors. The number of researchers was ranging from one to two in the four cultures with interviewers discussing their notes on the interview. The length of the interviews depended on achieving the aim of the research ranging from two to three hours. Eight organizations were visited in the process of research. Each company is denoted by the name of culture, then C. No. denoting to the case number.

4   Findings

It seems that there is a pattern emerging across these eight cases with respect to the impact of national culture on PMS design and use. These patterns may be summarised as follows.

4.1   Chinese Culture

In Chinese companies with *family organization* culture, PMSs are designed by the top management board, with little input from the middle managers. The PMSs is formal, with formal meetings discussing the results. The use of PMS has been observed is mainly in managing strategy, in monitoring, communication, influencing behaviour, but not used in learning and development. The reason could be attributed to family culture, where this could be attributed to employees' obedience, stemming from the Chinese cultural value of vertical social order. Employee's willingness to cooperate and make the measurement process workable, and this could be to the Chinese cultural value of individual 'face' and reputation. The results resemble the results found by (Li & Tang, 2009).

4.2   Italian Culture

In the Italian culture, we can see two organizations with two different organization cultures. The first organization with an *incubator culture*, has deliberately designed its PMS by middle management, with balanced measures where we witnessed a highly used system in managing strategy, monitoring, communication, and learning and behaviour. In the second organisation with a *family culture* the PMS was designed by the top management with emphasis on financial measures. We observed evidence of resistance in its implementation where the PMS is mainly used for monitoring and legitimization.

4.3   Syrian Culture

In Syria, PMS used were mainly financial, but it was observed that the comprehensive use of PMS is reserved for the top manager. Middle managers used the measurement in their daily activities, but cross cooperation between managers was limited. The reports are kept with the top management, who in turn keep it under lock and key. Here PMS is used in legitimisation, which make some middle managers resistant to the measurement process, but it could said that the top managers are the main benefactor of the measurement who keep the result hidden from their managers, in a *knowledge is power* and *divide and conquer* approach.

4.4   UK Culture

In the UK, we have two organizations with two different decentralized cultures. The first UK organization is and *incubator* with an emphasis on people. It has a well-developed set of measures which is used for all purposes except legitimisation. Its use for learning and improvement is highly emphasised. The Second UK organisation is a *guided missile* with a greater task emphasis. It has less developed measures that are informally used for monitoring, communication, influencing behaviour purposes. Its use for learning and improvement is limited.

4.5   Impact of High Power Distance on PMS

It seems that high PD culture is associated with command and control use of PMS. Here the PMS systems are designed by top management only, where the role of middle management is diminished. As seen in Syria cases 1 & 2, China cases 1 &2, and Italy C.2. The high influence of top management is probably attributed to the high power distance, which leads to little or no middle management participation. The little involvement has probably lead to the reaction of middle management by mostly being either indifferent, or resentful or non-compliant to the measurement process. The difference between China and other high PD cultures could be due to *Guanxi*, which means in the Chinese culture "relationships" or "connections". Good guanxi will ensure minimization of conflicts and frustrations. It aims at building a supportive, genuine relationship founded on reciprocal respect (Yin, 2008). The only case that had some participation from the middle managers among the low PD was Syria C.1 case, and this may be attributed to the focus of the company's strategy on gaining market share, and educational level of these managers, or the high education level of the middle managers.

4.6   Impact of Engaging Strategy on PMS Use

It seems that organizations that shift decision making to middle management have better developed and used PMS. For example, in UK C.2, the performance measures are designed by middle manager, where the use of measures is through daily meeting, and where performance results are shared, elaborated in decisions making. Engagement has resulted in ownership of PMS design, implementation and use. However, is the high degree of use related to the flexible nature of the organizational culture? More research should address the impact of flexible organizational culture on the design, implementation and use of PMS.

5   Discussion and Conclusions

In high PD cultures one of the purposes of PMS is legitimisation, while in low PD cultures legitimisation is not a purpose for PMS. Low uncertainty avoidance cultures are associated with more democratic use of PMS

Although national culture seems to have some influence on the design and use of PMS in organisations, some strategic characteristics of the organisation also influence the design and use of the PMS...e.g.

- Strategy, it has been seen where innovation is a competitive requirement we are observing a more decentralised behaviour within the organisation that is accompanies with more empowered/delegated design and democratic use E.g. Italy C.1
- Governance structure of the organisation and possibly its history can affect the design and use of the PMS... e.g. China C.1

- Personality and outlook of the leadership has an impact on the use of PMS. For example in Italy. In C.1 the organization is lead by a relatively young management, with an innovation focus leadership, while in C. 2, where the leadership is conservative, the PMS aims go to monitoring only, not as far as Italy C.1 with innovation at the core of PMS. In Syria, such a difference exists between C.1 and C.2.

Concerning the design of PMS... uncertainty avoidance can impact the way performance information is communicated/shared in the organisation. For example, in high uncertainty avoidance cultures, information is circulated with caution in 'need to know basis' as seen in the Syrian organizations. Empowered approach is more helpful to gain the support and engagement from the employees. While in Chinese cases it was seen that PMS in high power distance cultures are of low maturity systems, command and control system. The more engagement will have more democratic systems. Although in the high PD and UCI cultures like Syria the closed secretive behaviours displayed by the top managers lead to themselves designing and using the PMS which in turn leads to significant resistance from other managers... A more empowered approach to the design and implementation of PMS although counter intuitive to top management behaviour may yield more sustainable results with more ownership and resistance from the organisation

Acknowledgements. The authors would like to thank Dr Patrizia Garengo from the University of Padova, Italy, and Dr Dan Wang from Harbin University for their invaluable assistance in collecting, translating and involvement in the data.

References

1. Assiri, A., Zairi, M., Edi, R.: How to profit from the balanced scorecard: An implementation roadmap. Industrial Manaement & Data 106, 937–952 (2006)
2. Bititci, U., Garengo, P., Dörfler, V., Nudurupati, S.: Performance Measurement: Challenges for Tomorrow. International Journal of Management Reviews (2011)
3. Bititci, U.S., et al.: Dynamics of performance measurement and organisational culture. International Journal of Operations & Production Management 12(1325-1350) (2006)
4. Bourne, M.: Researching performance measurement system implementation: The dynamics of success and failure. Production Planning & Control 2(101-113) (2005)
5. Bourne, M., et al.: Designing, implementing and updating perormance measurement systems. International Journal of Operations & Production Management 20(7), 754–771 (2000)
6. Bourne, M., Neely, A., Platts, K., Mills, J.: The success and failure of performance measurement initiatives: Perceptions of participating managers. International Journal of Operations & Production Management (2002)
7. Dastmalchian, Lee, Ng: The interplay between organizational and national cultures: A compariosn of organizational practices in Canada and Southe Korea using the Competing Values Framework. International Journal of Human Resources Management 11, 388–413 (2000)
8. Davis, S., Albright, T.: An investigation of the effect of Balanced Scorecard implementation on financial performance. Management Accounting Research 15, 135–153 (2004)

9. de Waal, A.: Behavioral factors important for the successful implementation and use of performance management systems. Management Decision 41, 688–697 (2003)
10. Deal, T., Kennedy, A.: Corporate Cultures: The Rites and Rituals of Corporate Life. Penguin Books, Harmondsworth (1982)
11. De Waal, A.A.: The Role of Behavioral Factors and National Cultures in Creating Effective Performance Management Systems. Systemic Practice and Action Research 19(1) (2006)
12. Garengo, P., Bititci, U.: Towards a contingency approach to performance measurement: An empirical study in Scottish SMEs. International Journal of Operations & Production Management 8(27), 802–825 (2007)
13. Greatbanks, R., Tapp, D.: The impact of balanced scorecards in a public sector environment. International Journal of Operations & Production Management 8(27), 846–873 (2007)
14. Henri, J.-F.: Organizational culture and performance measurement system. Accounting, Organizations and Society (77-103) (2006)
15. Hofstede, G.: Culture's Consequences. Sage, Beverly Hill(1980)
16. Hofstede, G., Hofstede, G.J.: Cultures and Organizatins Software of the Mind, 2nd edn. McGraw-Hill Books, New York (2005)
17. Hofstede, G., Hofstede, G.J.: Cultures and Organizations: Software of the Mind. McGraw-Hill Books, New York (2005)
18. Johnson, H.T., Kaplan, R.S.: Relevenece Lost: The Rise and Fall of Management Accounting. Harvard Business School Press, Boston (1987)
19. Kaplan, R., Norton, D.: The balanced scorecard - measures that drive performance. Harvard Buisness Review 70, 71–79 (1992)
20. Kluckhohn, F.R., Strodtbeck, F.L.: Variations in value orientations, xiv edn. Oxford, England (1961)
21. Li, P., Tang, G.: Performance measurement design within its organisational context— Evidence from China. Management Accounting Research (2009)
22. Neely, A.: The performance measurement revolution: why now and what next? International Journal of Operations & Production Management 2(19), 205–228 (1999)
23. Neely, A., Bourne, M.: Why measurement initiatives fail. Measuring Business Excellence 4(4), 3–7 (2000)
24. Otley, D.: Management control and performance management: Whence and whither? The British Accounting Review 35(4), 309–326 (2003)
25. Picard, R.R., Reis, P.: Management control systems design: A metaphorical integration of national cultural implications. Managerial Auditing Journal 5(17), 222 (2002)
26. Schein, E.: Organizational Culture and Leadership. Jossey-Bass, San Franciso (1985)
27. Taticchi, P., Balachandran, K., Tonelli, F.: Performance measurement and management systems: state of the art, guidelines for design and challenges. Measuring Business Excellence 2(41-54) (2012)
28. Tranfield, D., Denyer, D., Smart, P.: Towards a Methodology for Developing Evidence-Informed Management Knowledge by Means of Systematic Review. British Journal of Management 14, 207–222 (2003)
29. Trompenaars, F., Hampden-Turner, C.: Riding the Waves of Culture: Understanding Diversity in Global Business. Nicholas Brealey Publishing, London (1993)
30. Voss, C., TSikriktsis, N., Frohlich, M.: Case research in operations management. International Journal of Operations & Production Management 2(22), 195–219 (2002)
31. Yin, F.: An analysis of factors of success for Chinese/ European JVs in culture aspect. International Journal of Business Management 3(6) (2008)

Measurement and Management of Supply Chain Performance: A Benchmarking Study

Siham Lakri and Yves Dallery

Laboratoire Génie Industriel, Ecole Centrale Paris, Châtenay-Malabry, France
{siham.lakri,yves.dallery}@ecp.fr

Abstract. Over the past few decades, the role of Supply Chain (SC) has been evolving from cost centre to competitive advantage. That is why measurement and management of SC performance become particularly essential. However, such an undertaking is difficult due to the growing complexity of SC. As the literature review highlights it, there is a lack of survey dealing with measurement and management of SC performance, collecting data through interview process and especially addressed to large companies. This is the bias of the present paper. First, an overview of the benchmarking published on related topics is presented. Then, are detailed the selected sample, the methodology used to collect and analyse data and the preliminary results obtained. To finish, conclusions are presented followed by a discussion suggesting future research directions.

Keywords: Supply chain, Performance measurements, Performance management, Benchmarking study.

1 Introduction

Over the past few decades, the role of supply chain (SC) has been evolving from cost centre to competitive advantage. The International survey "Global supply chain survey 2013", led by PwC group, show that companies acknowledging SC as a strategic asset generate a 30% increase of profitability compared to the average (around 500 completed questionnaires from various industry sectors). Equally according to [1], supply chain management (SCM) is now recognised as one of the best means by which enterprises can make instant improvements to their business strategies and operations. Thus today's competition has shifted from inter-company level to inter-supply chain level [2,3,4,5].

Absolute growth lever of companies, SC formerly simple and linear, is nowadays considered as a complex system [6]. Although there are no generally accepted definitions of SC, in coherence with the perimeter of this paper the following definition is taken on: "A supply chain consists of all parties involved, directly or indirectly, in fulfilling a customer request. The supply chain includes not only the manufacturers and suppliers, but also transporters, warehouses, retailers, and even customers themselves. Within each organisation, such as a manufacturer, the supply chain includes all

B. Grabot et al. (Eds.): APMS 2014, Part III, IFIP AICT 440, pp. 433–440, 2014.

functions involved in receiving and filling the customer request. These functions include, but are not limited to, new product development, marketing, operations, distribution, finance and customer service" [7]. Besides, today's environment is more dynamic [1] and SC have to satisfy regulatory requirements (societal pressures for example) and profitability requirements (financial, flexibility, competitiveness...). That is why during the last few decades focusing on factory level management has been replaced by firm level management of SC [8]. SC being considered as a key factor of corporate success [9], measurement and management of SC performance become essential. Nevertheless, such an undertaking is complex due to the transversal characteristic of these processes, involving numerous actors having to cooperate in order to reach given strategic objectives.

Therefore, the purpose of this paper is to review at what stage big size companies are about SC performance measurement and management concepts, highlight their current practices and the related main issues they have to cope with. To do so, a benchmarking study has been carried out, based on data collected through interview process from eleven multinational companies. The rest of the paper is organised as follows. The next section presents a literature review focusing on benchmarking survey dealing with SC performance measurement and management or related topics. Section 3 describes our empirical analysis, detailing the sample, the methodology used to collect and analyse data and preliminary results obtained. To finish Section 4 presents a discussion and conclusions.

2   Overview of the Published Benchmarking Studies

In this section, a literature review is established on benchmarking survey dealing with SC performance measurement and management concepts, or related topics.

Benchmarking is a well-known process aiming to improve performance by learning from the best performers in the class [10]. In this paper, the idea is to carry out such a comparative analysis, in order to observe the practices of several companies in the area of measurement and management of SC performance. This part aims to position the present benchmarking and the published benchmarking studies on a common framework described hereinafter. [11] introduced a matrix composed of two types of components. The first one answers the question: "What is benchmarked?" Three options are possible: Performance – how good performance is compared to others, Process – methods and processes used to improve organisational effectiveness and Strategic – changes in strategic directions and decisions. The second one answers the question "What to benchmark against?" It could be Internal – within the organisation, Competitor – within industry/sector, Functional – technology and techniques used, Generic – best practices from any sector or industry.

Only external benchmarking studies are reviewed in this paper, giving it is the type of the present benchmarking study detailed in section 3. Indeed, by definition, internal benchmarking studies deal with comparison of processes or operations within an organisation only. In this type of benchmarking, the acquisition of information is facilitated. However, information obtained can be shortened and/or oriented, each one wanting to protect the interest of its department or its own.

In the literature review, two kind of benchmarking studies can be distinguished: 1-Benchmarking launched in order to validate a framework built, 2- Benchmarking studies without framework to validate.

2.1   Benchmarking Aiming to Validate a Framework Previously Developed

The literature review shows that usually benchmarking process is used in order to validate a framework previously developed. For instance, [12] conceptualized, developed, and validated six dimensions of SCM practices (strategic supplier partnership, customer relationship, information sharing, information quality, internal lean practices, and postponement) using data collected from 196 manufacturing firms. [13] has empirically tested a framework identifying the causal links among SCM and information systems (IS) practices, SCM–IS related inhibiting factors and operational performance based on a sample of 203 manufacturing Small and Medium Enterprises (SMEs) within the greater metropolitan area of Istanbul in Turkey. Equally in manufacturing industry, [14] examined which dimensions are used by the largest Danish companies to measure supply chain performance measurement (SCPM) at operational, tactical and strategic level, how can these dimensions be classified, and how do these empirical results have implications for practice and selected SCPM-theories. The SCPM model they proposed has been theoretically developed and empirically validated. In the airline and airport field, [15] applied a two-step Data Envelopment Analysis (DEA) procedure to evaluate the operational performance of a sample of the Association of European Airlines, whereas [16] developed a holistic performance measurement system (PMS) for airport ramp service providers with a process-based perspective, and conducted a benchmarking study in several European hub airports. The authors followed the action research approach for defining the PMS, which associates weights to the measures in an Analytical Hierarchical Process, and grouped measures into the perspectives of the Balanced Scorecard.

2.2   Benchmarking Studies without a Framework to Validate

In the transport logistics context of Hong Kong, [17] conducted a benchmarking study considering efficiency (economic use of resources) and effectiveness (fulfilment of customer requirements) measures. The 134 responses obtained allowed to evaluate their perceived SC performance in transport logistics from both cost and service perspectives. On the other hand, without specific context, in order to justify that leadership behaviour measurement can and should be part of any performance measurement system, [18] gathered exploratory empirical data from 11 Finnish SMEs located in Western Finland. Another kind of topic, investigate what relevant forecasting variables should be considered to improve companies' performance. [19] analysed equally whether some forecasting variables can interact and influence performance with a synergistic effect by means of data collected by the Global Manufacturing Research Group from a sample of 343 manufacturing companies in 6 different countries.

According to [20], while there is plenty of published literature that explains or espouses SCM, there is a relative lack of empirical studies examining SCM practices. [20] report the current status of SCM of manufacturing organisations in New Zealand. The outcomes suggest that although there is awareness of the SCM concept in New Zealand, the adoption of the newer concepts of SCM is not very advanced. [21] surveyed SCM practices in UK, collecting data from 288 industrial SMEs. The findings indicate a lack of effective adaptation from traditional adversarial relationships to the modern collaborative "e" – supply chain and also identifies issues businesses need to address to improve the performance of their supply chains. Similarly, [22] investigated practices and concerns of SCM in United States and concluded that all of significant SCM practices positively impact performance. Still about SCM practices but this time in Finland, [23] interviewed managers of six SC in order to analyse the change of SCM both in terms of operational practices and organisational capabilities. Some papers focus on metrics, as [24] which compared key performance indicators (KPIs) importance of 21 British companies or the collaborative survey [25] aiming at highlight KPI's use and consistency with companies' needs in France. While others are concentrated on process perspective, for instance [26] analysing the use of structured processes for the design of PMS in the UK (around 350 SMEs from a variety of industries) and [27] finding out about how SMEs in India apply Balanced Scorecard concept by the combination of three case studies and semi-structured interviews. The literature includes research works about strategy perspective as well. [28], using a representative sample of 156 organizations mostly from manufacturing, discuss SC strategies and structures in India whereas [29] conduct a survey that examines the success factors in developing and implementing SCM strategies for Hong Kong manufacturers. Finally, [30] compare performances of 68 European enterprises based on 5 KPIs from Supply Chain Operations Reference (SCOR) model, calculated using data from enterprise financial review.

To conclude, each of these studies are positioned in an adaptation of the matrix proposed by [11] in table1 presented below. Two main observations can be raised.

Table 1. Positioning of the studies reviewed on an adaptation of the [11] matrix

		What to benchmark against?		
		Competitor	*Functional*	*Generic*
What is bench- mark?	*Performance*	[15,16,17]	[19]	[30]
	Process	[13]	[14], [20]	[12], [18], [21], [23,24,25,26,27]
	Strategy		[28,29]	

First, obviously, there is an empty square at the intersection between strategy and competitor because for a start it is quite difficult to convince long term partners of an organisation to adopt this approach thus it seems even more unattainable to obtain competitors approval for such a partnership. Similarly, it is empty at the intersection between strategy and generic, as it seems to have little interest to compare strategy of companies from various industries. Moreover, by definition, strategy cannot be imitated. Secondly, by contrast, the majority of the studies are placed at the intersection between process and generic as the present benchmarking study. However, there is a difference among these eight research works in the way to collect data. Six [12], [18], [21], [24,25,26] use questionnaires whereas [27] use semi-structured interviews then case studies and [23] lead interviews. Another distinction between the "process-generic" benchmarking is the size of enterprises considered. Half of them concentrate only on SMEs ([18], [21], [26,27], two [12], [25] include SMEs as well as large companies and the two remaining [23,24] focus on large companies.

As the literature review highlights it, there is a lack of survey collecting data through interview process and especially addressed to large companies and their related research in the area of SC performance. This is the bias of the present paper.

3   Empirical Analysis

The sample constructed referred to 11 multinational corporations which employ by far more than 5000 people. Three of them are Native American companies and the 8 others are French companies. The sectors represented are Fast-Moving Consumer Goods (FMCG), Household appliance, Automotive, Luxury, Distribution and Steel industry. The selected companies represent also different geographical locations in France as well as have SC management differently organised. The aim of our undertaking is mainly to highlight current practices in today's large companies, understand the principal trends and identify correlations regarding concepts of measurement and management of SC performance.

3.1   Method to Collect Data and Data Analysis

We met each company twice and led interviews of about two hours based on a previously developed questionnaire in order to guide the discussions. All interviews were held at the respective companies' office, which allows insuring an environment conducive to obtain information easily even the sensitive ones. Two or three persons per company have been interviewed. Respondents met are SC directors, with a national or worldwide perimeter and/or internal SC experts.

The first step to analyse data was to choose adequate comparison criteria. Further to interviews, we selected 11 coherent criteria from five key aspects: from SC organisation aspect (chain perimeter, process perimeter, group organisation), from measurement aspect (number of KPIs, shared KPIs), from management aspect (who define KPIs, who set KPIs' targets, who manage in the sense of reaching objectives, management tools), from performance aspect (type of performance measured), and the last criterion but not the least, is about company performance culture. Indeed, the enterprise culture is rarely taken into account in benchmarking studies while it is an important factor which influenced decision-making in general. As interviews were rich in information, it was primordial to find a way to make the data comparable. To do so, we built synthetic profile of each company. We will not go into further detail in this article. The following section shows the preliminary results obtained.

3.2   Preliminary Results

First, there is a tendency to have many KPIs, more than 20 in 45% cases, which participate to the complexity of PMS. Clearly, the number and the choice of KPIs is still a problematic. The assessed performance remains predominantly economic, although we note ongoing project to evaluate environmental (36%) and social (28%) performance. Indeed, not only increasing societal pressures have an effect but also companies become more and more aware of the performance potential which could be resulting. Due to incomplete information about shared KPIs we feel inadequate to draw conclusions; however we can notice a difficulty to answer to that question which highlights a lack of visibility of what is shared with whom. The definition of KPIs for the most part occurred in centralized SC (45%), which has the advantage to insure homogeneity of KPIs set of SC sites. Decision about KPIs' targets is also handled by central SC (36%) in order to align overall objectives, i.e. strategic objectives, with SC sites objectives. On the other hand, local SC (64%) managers are in charge of performance management through KPIs. In that, we detect the general wish to manage SC performance as closely as possible to the field. Regarding SC culture, of course influenced by corporate culture, the following key messages are conveyed: get unquestionable KPIs, get less KPIs more standardized, get a wide vision of performance, simplify PMS, simplify reporting process, share more widely, measure collaborators performance, be committed. Today's companies direct their efforts toward simplification, collaboration based on a common language and commitment. Results about tools used will not be presented in this article.

Three correlations can be raised. First, B-to-B companies are organized by global business unit; have a process perimeter extended in comparison with B-to-C companies and make measurement system reviewed by central SC. On the contrary, B-to-C companies are organized by geographical zone and revise measurement system locally. Finally, in the majority of cases (80%), KPIs' targets setting process and performance management process, in the sense of manage through KPIs, are owned by the same level (local/local or central/central). However, we note two exceptions from this observation. KPIs' targets are set by local SC and the reaching of targets is managed by central SC. We understand that people from SC sites have a better knowledge of the field to choose ambitious targets but above all attainable ones. The second exception describes the opposite case, KPIs' targets set by central SC and management to reach targets owned by local SC. We explain it by the fact local SC as we said previously have a better knowledge of the field and thus are the most likely to make the objectives achieved.

4   Conclusions and Discussion

As the literature review highlights it, there is a lack of survey dealing with measurement and management of SC performance and especially which collect data through interview process and addressed to large companies. This is the bias of the present paper. We studied the current SC performance measurement and management practices of multinational corporations established in France. In this way, we cover a reasonable spectrum of firms from varied businesses. We highlighted, on one hand, measurement current tendencies as the density of measurement systems and type of performance measured in fact. On the other hand, we raised performance management current tendencies as KPIs definition, targets setting and performance management processes' decision levels in the SC. We also showed correlations illustrating B-to-B and B-to-C companies' profiles. We underlines that there is coherence between KPIs definition process and targets setting process being owned by the same decision level.

With this survey, we contribute with new findings that have implications for theory and offer to practitioners an up to date point of comparison. We proposed a cartography positioning published benchmarking studies, concerning several sectors, related to the SC performance issue according to the type of benchmarking. Moreover, through results, we delivered an overview of the state of progress of large companies regarding current key problematic.

Nevertheless, we present only a snap-shot view of the topic. First of all, a clear limitation to our study is the size of the sample. As we choose to proceed by interviews it would be difficult to drastically increase the number of companies to meet. Thus we can consider this study as an explorative one and not fully representative of the whole population. Besides, we collected data from SC directors and internal SC experts. It could be interesting to analyse the perceptions from other members of the SC or collaborators, such as suppliers or customers' points of view.

References

1. Kaihara, T.: Supply chain management with market economics. International Journal of Production Economics 73, 5–14 (2001)
2. Burgess, K., Singh, P.J., Koroglu, R.: Supply chain management: a structured literature review and implications for future research. International Journal of Operations & Production Management 26, 703–729 (2006)
3. Lambert, D.M.: Supply chain management: processes, partnerships, performance. Supply Chain Management Institute, Sarasota, Fla (2008)
4. Lummus, R.R., Vokurka, R.J.: Defining supply chain management: A historical perspective and practical guidelines. Industrial Management & Data Systems 99, 11–17 (1999)
5. Mentzer, J.T.: Fundamentals of Supply Chain Management: Twelve Drivers of Competitive Advantage. SAGE (2004)
6. Surana, A., Kumara, S., Greaves, M., Raghavan, U.N.: Supply-chain networks: A complex adaptive systems perspective. International Journal of Production Research 43, 4235–4265 (2005)
7. Chopra, S., Meindl, P.: Supply chain management: strategy, planning, and operation. Pearson, Boston (2012)
8. Gunasekaran, A., Williams, H.J., McGaughey, R.E.: Performance measurement and costing system in new enterprise. Technovation 25, 523–533 (2005)
9. Estampe, D., Lamouri, S., Paris, J.-L., Brahim-Djelloul, S.: A framework for analysing supply chain performance evaluation models. International Journal of Production Economics (2010)
10. Fong, S.W., Cheng, E.W.L., Ho, D.C.K.: Benchmarking: A general reading for management practitioners. Management Decision 36, 407–418 (1998)

11. Bhutta, K.S., Huq, F.: Benchmarking – best practices: An integrated approach. Benchmarking: An International Journal 6, 254–268 (1999)
12. Li, S., Rao, S.S., Ragu-Nathan, T.S., Ragu-Nathan, B.: Development and validation of a measurement instrument for studying supply chain management practices. Journal of Operations Management 23, 618–641 (2005)
13. Bayraktar, E., Demirbag, M., Koh, S.C.L., Tatoglu, E., Zaim, H.: A causal analysis of the impact of information systems and supply chain management practices on operational performance: Evidence from manufacturing SMEs in Turkey. International Journal of Production Economics 122, 133–149 (2009)
14. Algren, C., Kotzab, H.: State of the art of supply Chain performance measurement in Danish industrial companies. In: 23rd Annual NOFOMA Conference, Harstad, Norway (2011)
15. Barros, C.P., Peypoch, N.: An evaluation of European airlines' operational performance. International Journal of Production Economics 122, 525–533 (2009)
16. Schmidberger, S., Bals, L., Hartmann, E., Jahns, C.: Ground handling services at European hub airports: Development of a performance measurement system for benchmarking. International Journal of Production Economics 117, 104–116 (2009)
17. Lai, K.-H., Ngai, E.W.T., Cheng, T.C.E.: An empirical study of supply chain performance in transport logistics. International Journal of Production Economics 87, 321–331 (2004)
18. Kulmala, H.I., Ahoniemi, L., Nissinen, V.: Performance through measuring leader's profiles: An empirical study. International Journal of Production Economics 122, 385–394 (2009)
19. Danese, P., Kalchschmidt, M.: The impact of forecasting on companies' performance: Analysis in a multivariate setting. International Journal of Production Economics 133, 458–469 (2011)
20. Basnet, C., Corner, J., Wisner, J., Tan, K.-C.: Benchmarking supply chain management practice in New Zealand. Supply Chain Management: An International Journal 8, 57–64 (2003)
21. Quayle, M.: A study of supply chain management practice in UK industrial SMEs. Supply Chain Management: An International Journal 8, 79–86 (2003)
22. Tan, K.C.: Supply Chain Management: Practices, Concerns, and Performance Issues. Journal of Supply Chain Management 38, 42–53 (2002)
23. Kemppainen, K., Vepsäläinen, A.P.J.: Trends in industrial supply chains and networks. International Journal of Physical Distribution & Logistics Management 33, 701–719 (2003)
24. Gunasekaran, A., Patel, C., McGaughey, R.E.: A framework for supply chain performance measurement. International Journal of Production Economics 87, 333–347 (2004)
25. Salmon, K.: Generix Group, Aslog, Agora du Supply Chain Management: Supply chain - Quels KPIs pour les managers en 2014-2015? (2013)
26. Neely, A., Mills, J., Platts, K., Gregory, M., Richards, H.: Performance measurement system design: Should process based approaches be adopted? International Journal of Production Economics, 46–47, 423–431 (1996)
27. Bhagwat, R., Sharma, M.K.: Performance measurement of supply chain management: A balanced scorecard approach. Computers & Industrial Engineering 53, 43–62 (2007)
28. Sahay, B.S., Mohan, R.: Supply chain management practices in Indian industry. International Journal of Physical Distribution & Logistics Management 33, 582–606 (2003)
29. Chin, K.-S., Tummala, V.M.R., Leung, J.P.F., Tang, X.: A study on supply chain management practices: The Hong Kong manufacturing perspective. International Journal of Physical Distribution & Logistics Management 34, 505–524 (2004)
30. Estampe, D.: Benchmark de la supplychain. Techniques de l'Ingénieur (2011)

Simulation Analysis of Sweet Pepper Harvesting Operations

Zohar Elkoby[1], Bert van't Ooster[2,3], and Yael Edan[1]

[1] Dept. of Industrial Engineering & Management, Ben-Gurion University of the Negev, Israel
[2] Wageningen University, Farm Technology Group, Wageningen, The Netherlands
[3] Wageningen UR Greenhouse Horticulture, Wageningen, The Netherlands

Abstract. Greenhouse crop production requires extensive manual labor. The objective of this research is to analyze different work methods for harvesting in sweet pepper greenhouses. Operations research of harvesting work methods for a Dutch and Israeli sweet pepper greenhouse was performed. An existing discrete event simulation model on the crop handling processes inside a greenhouse, GWorkS, was used to simulate harvesting of sweet peppers in both countries. Results of simulation of one day showed that the model estimates harvesting time with an accuracy of 92% for NL data and 96% for IL data. The data analysis showed differences between the greenhouses in the existing harvesting procedures, logistic operations and data collection.

Keywords: Agriculture work methods, Simulation, Operations research, Pepper harvesting, Data Analysis.

1 Introduction

Greenhouse crop production requires extensive repetitive manual labor. A current problem in greenhouse horticulture is lack of human resources and high cost of human labor [4], [11]. Labor costs in greenhouse horticulture, constitute 29% and 25% of the production costs in the Netherlands [2] and in Israel (Israeli Central Bureau of Statistics) respectively. One solution is to improve labor efficiency. Work methods analysis is a commonly employed technique to improve production, operations management and increase efficiency [7]. In addition and as a complementary tool, simulation can be used to assess for cost-effectiveness, the effect of changing existing processes or the introduction of new processes in an actual system [9].

Advanced research has been applied to improve work methods in greenhouse horticulture for different crops such as sweet peppers [4], tomatoes [5], Gypsophila flowers [3], roses [11] using work methods analyses and simulation.

This paper focuses on operations research of harvesting work methods using a simulation model developed for sweet pepper harvesting processes in Israel and the Netherlands. The simulation model is based on a previous model developed for a different environment and crop: the GWorkS-rose model [11]. The focus of this paper is validating the GWorkS model for sweet pepper harvesting in two greenhouses from different countries.

B. Grabot et al. (Eds.): APMS 2014, Part III, IFIP AICT 440, pp. 441–448, 2014.
© IFIP International Federation for Information Processing 2014

2   Material and Methods

2.1   Company Characteristics and Data Acquisition

The Dutch Greenhouse

The greenhouse's production area is approximately 8.6 hectares of red peppers separated into two different greenhouses. Each greenhouse has a main aisle with crops on both sides, organized within paths. Each greenhouse has four sectors of 72-80 paths with path length 115 m. Not all workers of the greenhouse are qualified to perform all crop related tasks. The company uses electronic trolleys that has an adjustable height and is men-operated in the paths. Within a path, the trolley runs along a pipe rail system which is also used as a heating system.

The grower uses a SDF labour registration system (LRS) which records work hours, and enables work planning, tracking and tracing to analyse labour operations and worker performance. The LRS also registers the yield in each path. Automatic reports can be generated on every task done by the workers, on frequency of tasks and time required per task and day. The data was collected between the first week of 2012 (January 1st) and week 38 of 2013 (September 19th). Only the first greenhouse with 304 paths was simulated for testing and validation of the model.

The Israeli Net House

The net house's production area is approximately 2 hectares of red peppers separated into two different growing areas. One area is for growing peppers in the "Spanish" cultivation system and the other is in the "Dutch" cultivation system. The net house has a main aisle with crops on both sides, organized within paths. This research focus was on the "Dutch" cultivation area. This area has two sections with a total of 168 paths of 48 m length. The company uses hand-pushed trolleys to buffer the peppers harvested. During harvesting, the worker walks with the trolley in the path.

The grower does not use an automatic registration system, but he collects and fills Excel tables with the relevant data by himself. The data summarizes information about the yield and workers of the net house. The data was collected between the first week of 2010 and week 11 of 2014 (March 10th). For the model, only the second part of the greenhouse (the "Dutch" cultivation system) was simulated (168 paths) and compared to the whole season's data for this greenhouse area, from July 13th to March 10th.

2.2   Data Analysis

The procedure performed in order to process the data was described by a Process Flow diagram (**Fig. 1**). Data was processed in Excel, using pivot tables and in Access using queries.

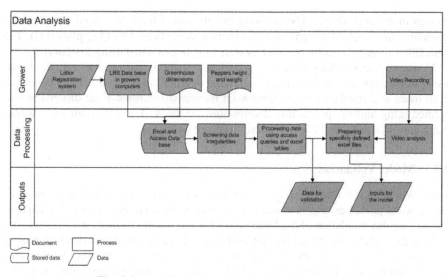

Fig. 1. Process flow diagram for stages of data analysis

The model inputs include: information regarding crop yield per day and per identifiable location, job frequencies, information about the resources of the greenhouse, and probability density function (pdf) parameters of the actions that constitute the harvesting process (**Table 1**). In order to prepare the pdf parameters video recordings were analyzed using Noldus Observer XT® ([1], [10]), which resulted in a series of

Table 1. Parameters of probability density functions (pdf) for sub actions of the harvest operation. The number of observations (n) is given and parameters p1 and p2.

For a normal distribution, p1 is mean and p2 is standard deviation, and for a lognormal distribution, p1 is μ and p2 is σ

Name	Description	Green-house	N	Pdf name	P_1	P_2
Grab and Cut Pepper	Service time (s) to cut a pepper when operator and Pepper are already in the place of action.	NL	7363	Lognormal	0.244	0.521
		IL	1195	Lognormal	0.843	0.597
Change path side	Service time (s) to switch sides on the trolley.	NL	7	Gaussian (Normal)	10	1
Log task	Service time (s) to log the start of a harvest task.	NL	4	Gaussian (Normal)	15	1
Store pepper in buffer	Service time (s) to put a Pepper stem in the buffer on the trolley (while the trolley is moving).	NL	7255	Lognormal	-0.576	0.531
		IL	1186	Lognormal	0.244	0.592
Boxes arrange	Service time (s) to arrange the boxes on the trolley to present an empty box.	IL	69	Lognormal	1.759	0.781

timings of defined actions. The resulting distribution of these measured service times resembled the shape of a lognormal distribution as confirmed by Q-Q plots ([1]). The probability density function parameters were best-fit estimated using Matlab ([6]).

Measured average daily yield (per greenhouse section) was used as a model input. Yield was assigned to paths using a lognormal distribution with parameters estimated from mean and standard deviation between measured locations. Fruit dispersion was defined using uniform probability distributions for the X, Y and Z coordinates within constraints that defined the space where fruits are harvested.

2.3   Model Validation

The GWorkS model was prepared to simulate each greenhouse according to its properties, work processes and resources and validated by analyzing a one day harvest. For the one day validation of the Dutch model, a run was performed on 25 paths (101-125) of the Dutch greenhouse for September 26th 2012 in order to calibrate the input parameters, and later the model was tested with other one day runs. In that date 14,244 peppers were harvested during 12.93 hours. The average labor time of a path, the total yield simulated and the cycle time per sweet pepper of the registered data and simulated process were compared. The Israeli model was validated for a one day run of November 8th 2013 which simulated the harvest of a complete section (section 3) with 84 paths. At that date harvesting was 15.75 hours and 6693 peppers were harvested. The total harvest time, yield and harvest time per pepper of the simulation were compared to the data. The accuracy rates for all validations are calculated according to:

$$accuracy = \left(1 - \frac{|model\ output - measured\ data|}{measured\ data}\right) * 100\% \qquad (1)$$

3   Results

3.1   Data Analysis of the Dutch Greenhouse

Using the data collected from the Dutch greenhouse it was possible to analyse behaviour and trends of different variables related to the harvesting process. Analyses

Table 2. Total working hours in the Dutch greenhouse in 2012-2013

Task	Time (h)	%
Harvesting	663	38.6
Trellising	439	25.6
Pruning and cutting plants	260	15.1
Sorting	244	14.2
Cleaning and maintenance	72	4.2
Other	39	2.3
Total time	1717	100

of total working hours in 2012-2013 for all main crop handling processes (**Table 2**) indicated that harvest (39%) and trellising (26%) represent the largest fraction of total labour time, followed by pruning (15%), sorting, and cleaning respectively.

The yield harvested during the season of 2013 (**Fig. 2**) teaches that the average harvested yield per path visit is 0.88 kg m^{-2} with a standard deviation of 0.29 kg m^{-2}. The variability of harvested yield per path is characterized by a lognormal distribution with parameters $\mu = -0.182$ ($SE = 0.0365$), and $\sigma = 0.350$ ($SE = 0.0260$). How-ever, as yield is a result of crop development, weather and operational planning, a measured time series was used as model input.

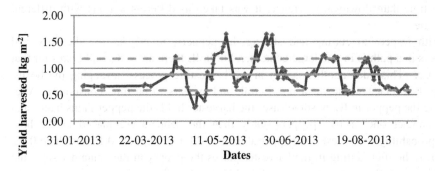

Fig. 2. The yield harvested in the Dutch greenhouse in 2013

To analyze the harvesting capabilities along the harvesting season, the relation be-tween the path yield and the harvesting time per pepper was determined. The yield is measured, in kg m^{-2} according to the peppers harvested on a specific day. The harvest time per pepper was calculated by:

$$Time\ per\ pepper = \frac{Total\ \text{harvesting}\ labor\ time\ in\ a\ path}{kg\ peppers\ harvested/\ average\ fruit\ weight} \quad (2)$$

A negative correlation between the two variables showed: as the yield in a path (x) is higher, the time to harvest each pepper (y) is lower: for 2012, y=3.3261x$^{-0.349}$ with R^2=0.6233 and 2013, y=-1.01ln(x) +3.7737 with R^2=0.3268.

3.2   Differences between the Harvesting Process of NL and IL Greenhouses

The harvesting process was compared by analyses of IDEF3 charts created for both greenhouses [6], [1]. Differences were studied to identify all the changes needed in order to simulate the harvesting process using the GWorkS-pepper model. The main differences are related to logistics and the order of actions, to work height adjustment, and to cutting and storing the peppers. With respect to logistics, in NL after harvest-ing one side of the path, the harvester turns around and harvests the other side. In IL both path sides are harvested at once. All the logistic operations on the container out-side the path, is automated in NL and manual in IL. This was excluded from the simu-lation model due to the high variance in the manual process and low importance when examining the harvesting process itself (approximately 15% of the total harvest labor time).

With respect to work height adjustment, in NL greenhouse, the harvester stays at the necessary height thanks to the electronic trolley. In IL the harvester is moving at the ground level of a path and only when necessary climbs to the appropriate height. The work height in NL is continuous within the height range of the trolley, but in IL the height of the harvester is discrete, either ground level or the height of the box. In NL, the trolley showed equal velocity for raising and lowering the platform. It was therefore defined as one action. In IL "adjusting the height" upwards takes more time than downwards. Hence, it was taken as different actions with different velocities.

With respect to cutting and storing the peppers, in NL storing the harvested peppers in a path is in one large container, but in IL there are 4-8 small boxes for that purpose. This adds another action in the harvesting process: arranging the boxes, which take place whenever a box is full, and appears to be time consuming. After cutting the pepper in IL, in some cases the harvester holds the pepper in his hands and cuts another one or two peppers. Only then the peppers are placed in the box. The probability to harvest one pepper alone is 0.79, two peppers 0.19 and three 0.02. In NL right after cutting it, the harvester places the pepper in the container since the container is in the ergonomic space of the harvester at all times.

Table 3. Summary of differences between the simulated Israeli and Dutch greenhouses

Criteria	Dutch greenhouse	Israeli greenhouse
Work methods and resources		
Total area examined	234 m · 182.4 m	96 m · 100 m
Paths amount	304	168
Amount of workers before harvest during harvest	 2-3 workers per hectare 3-5 workers per hectare	 5-8 workers per hectare 2-10 workers per hectare
Trolleys	36 electronic trolleys	20 manual trolleys
Containers	On each trolley one container with capacity of 290 kg.	On each trolley 6-8 boxes, each with the capacity of 10 kg.
Harvesting working process	Harvesting at one side to the end and return to main aisle via the other side.	Harvesting both sides of the path in one pass.
Numeric data base on season's databases		
Harvesting season examined	12-03-2012 to 29-10-2012 8 month	12-07-2013 to 15-02-2014 7 month
Average yield all season	30.0 kg m^{-2}	18.5 kg m^{-2}
Average yield harvesting day	0.8 kg m^{-2}	0.6 kg m^{-2}
Time per pepper	3.89 seconds	8.90 seconds**

**estimated and not definite (Taken from IL database from 2010-2011)

3.3   Validation Results

Model validation was performed as a one day run for a pre-defined part of the greenhouse. The NL validation results (**Table 4**) in 92.1% accuracy levels of the simulated yield (with 89% standard deviation). The average labor time per path accuracy is 91.9% and cycle time per unit is around 98%. The accuracy of standard deviation labor time (43.1%) and time per unit (84%) shows that the model has high variation between the different paths. Reality shows even stronger stochastic effects than the model. The data of IL (**Table 5**) does not include detailed information for each path, therefore only the following parameters were examined: sum of yield, total labor time and average cycle time per unit. The model simulates the reality of the net house at the accuracy levels of 85-95%.

For both **Table 4** and **Table 5**, model accuracy is indicated as the ratio between simulated mean for 10 runs and measured result (according to equation (1)). The 95% confidence level for the simulated mean is indicated in brackets (±ci).

Table 4. Results of a 1 day simulation of 25 paths in NL greenhouse on September 26th, 2012

#	Parameters	LRS data	Simulated mean (±ci)		Accuracy
1	Sum yield [u]	14244	16084	(±198)	92.1%
2	Standard deviation yield [u]	161.2	207.1	(±20.1)	89.0%
3	Average labor time per path [s]	1862	2076	(±27)	91.9%
4	Standard deviation labor time [s]	570.6	362.3	(±37.4)	43.1%
5	Average cycle time per unit [s]	3.27	3.34	(±0.03)	97.7%
6	Standard deviation time per unit [s]	0.43	0.41	(±0.03)	84.0%

Table 5. Results of a 1 day simulation of the IL net house on November 8th, 2013

#	Parameters	Grower's data	Simulated mean (±ci)		Accuracy
1	Sum yield [u]	6693	7272	(±41)	91.3%
2	Total labor time [s]	56700	54201	(±372)	95.6%
3	Average cycle time per unit [s]	8.47	7.46	(±0.05)	88.0%

4   Conclusions

The manual sweet pepper harvesting process is now modelled in a discrete event simulation model. The model was validated for two different greenhouses and can be used for other greenhouses and crops when needed, as the model was already successfully applied for cut roses [13]. The results of the one day simulation showed that the model estimates harvesting time with an accuracy of 92% for NL data and 96% for IL data. The simulation model can be used for sensitivity analysis of parameters, to examine changes in complex work processes and is planned as a basis for a model to optimize work-methods of a sweet pepper robotic harvester under development [8] that will work cooperatively with human harvesting.

Acknowledgements. This research was funded by the European Commission in the 7th Framework Program (CROPS GA no. 246252) and partially supported by the ABC Robotics Center funded by Helmsley Charitable Trust and by the Rabbi W. Gunther Plaut Chair in Manufacturing Engineering, both at Ben-Gurion University of the Negev.

References

1. Aantjes, G.W.J.: Data analysis and simulation trials of harvest in sweet pepper. Unpublished BSc thesis, Wageningen UR, Wageningen, The Netherlands (2014)
2. Bac, C.W., Edan, Y., Hemming, J., Van Henten, J.E.: Harvesting robots for high-value crops: state-of-the-art review and challenges ahead (in press, 2014)
3. Bechar, A., Lanir, T., Ruhrberg, Y., Edan, Y.: Improvement of work processes in gypsophila flowers. In: EFITA Conference 2009 (2009)
4. Bechar, A., Edan, Y., Krause, M.: Improvement of work methods in pepper greenhouses. In: XXXI CIOSTA-CIGR V Congress Proceedings, Hohenheim, Germany, September 19-21, pp. 249–255 (2005)
5. Bechar, A., Yosef, S., Netanyahu, S., Edan, Y.: Improvement of work methods in tomato greenhouses using simulation. Transactions of the ASABE 50(2), 331–338 (2007)
6. Elkoby, Z.: Analysis of Harvesting in Sweet Pepper Greenhouses for Human-Robot Collaboration. Unpublished BSc final project, Dept. of Industrial Eng. and Mngmt., Ben-Gurion University of the Negev, Beer-Sheva, Israel (2014)
7. Globerson, S.: Operations management and performance improvement. Dionon Publication (2002)
8. Hemming, J., Bac, C.W., van Tuijl, B.A.J., Barth, R., Bontsema, J., Pekkeriet, E., van Henten, E.: A robot for harvesting sweet-pepper in greenhouses. In: Proceedings of International Conference of Agricultural Engineering, Zurich, Switzerland (2014)
9. Law, A.M.: How to build valid and credible simulation models. Paper presented at the Proceedings of the 40th Conference on Winter Simulation, pp. 39–47 (2008)
10. Melman, N., Dotan, H.: Pepper harvesting as a case study for examinating the OLbserverxt software for work study. Unpublished BSc final project, Dept. of Industrial Eng. &Mngmt., Ben-Gurion University of the Negev, Beer-Sheva, Israel (2014)
11. van 't Ooster, A., Bontsema, J., van Henten, E.J., Hemming, S.: GWorkS – A discrete event simulation model on crop handling processes in a mobile rose cultivation system. Biosystems Engineering 112(2), 108–120 (2012)
12. van 't Ooster, A., Bontsema, J., van Henten, E. J., Hemming, S.: Simulation of harvest operations in a static rose cultivation system. Biosystems Engineering 120, 36–46 (2014)
13. van't Ooster, A., Bontsema, J., van Henten, E. J., Hemming, S.: Sensitivity analysis of a stochastic discrete event simulation model of harvest operations in a static rose cultivation system. Biosystems Engineering 116(4), 457–469 (2013)

The Effect of the Existence of Defective Items in Assembly Operations

Moshe Eben-Chaime

Department of Industrial Engineering & Management
Ben-gurion University of the Negev
P.O. Box 653, Be'er Sheva 84105, Israel
even@bgu.ac.il

Abstract. Quality is a principle issue in production management (PM). No process is perfect and the production of defective items is unavoidable. Very few studies regard the effect of the existence of defective items (EEDI) in production processes. Further, quality has been studied in isolation to high extent, of other PM domains. In this study, defect rates together with the assembly ratios of the bill of material are embedded in process charts. This facilitates the analysis of the EEDI in assembly operations and enables to quantify them. Apparently, defect rates grow dramatically in assembly operations due to the mutual effects of the assembly's components. Hence prior quality assurance effort is motivated

Keywords: Assembly, Bill of materials, Defect rate, Product structure, Quality.

1   Introduction

Feigenbaum (1991, page 47) minted the term "*hidden plant*": "the proportion of plant capacity that exists to rework unsatisfactory parts, to replace product recalled from the field, or to retest and re-inspect rejected units." He estimated that *hidden plant*s amount "to 15% to as much as 40% of productive capacity". Here, means to quantify these figures and more important to compare alternatives are provided.

2   Defect Rates and Input/Output Ratios

Let p_i denote the average defect rate (DR) of operation/activity i. Note that defects due to **common**, chance, or random causes are considered, not quality deterioration due to *assignable* causes as in Kim and Gershwin (2008). If activity i is performed on Q_i units, the mean number of acceptable units is only $(1-p_i)Q_i$. This easily extends to serial processes. If Q_0 units enter a serial process of n operations, the mean number of acceptable units at the end is (e.g., Freiesleben, 2005):

$$Q_n = Q_0 \prod_{i=1}^{n} (1 - p_i) \tag{1}$$

B. Grabot et al. (Eds.): APMS 2014, Part III, IFIP AICT 440, pp. 449–454, 2014.

Figure 1 portrays a serial process chart (e.g., Francis, McGinnis and White, 1992), where each node represents an activity. Each defective item divides its production process into three segments: prior to damage, between damage and detection and after detection. Detected defective items can be removed, thereby save the costs associated with, and the capacity required for future operations. A defective item can either be scrapped, used as it is for lower price, reworked or repaired. The last two cases involve costs and require capacity, additional to the regular capacity and costs, while in the first cases capacity is wasted and income is lost, which is equivalent to cost increase. In any event, larger quantities should be processed to compensate for the poor quality.

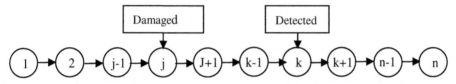

Fig. 1. A defect item divides the production process into three segments

Further, production mangers know how many end-items are needed. From these figures, order-quantities are calculated backward, as in material requirements planning (MRP; e.g., Nahmias, 2009). Whenever defective units are not used as intended, more units should be produce to replace these units. A reworked unit is just as an additional one with, perhaps, additional preparation activities, and repair requires additional repair capacity. Thus, (1) should be re-written as in (2), where p_i is the fraction of defective units that are not repaired:

$$Q_j^{in} = Q^{out} \Big/ \prod_{i=j}^{n} (1 - p_i) \qquad (2)$$

This calculation accounts for all items that will be damaged, and not repaired, in operation j and subsequent operations up to the last activity, n. Furthermore, this is the minimal quantity – larger quantity maybe processed in activity j if defective items from preceding operations have not been removed earlier. Suppose $j = n\text{-}19$; i.e. there are 20 operations to go, including j, and all share the same defect rate of 1%. Then, $Q_j^{in} = Q^{out} / 0.99^{20} = 1.2226 Q^{out}$. Namely, 1226 units will be processed, knowing that only 1,000 of them will be useful!

3   Assembly Operations

Products, however, are, usually, not structured serially, as in Figure 1, but in tree structures – a tree for each product. Figure 2 portrays a *product structure* and a bill of material (*BOM*) (e.g., Nahmias, 2009), which tell us which components are assembled and the assembly ratios: each assembly consists of 4, 2 and 1 units of component 1, 2 and 3, respectively. All these components should of course be conforming, but how can defective component be accounted for?

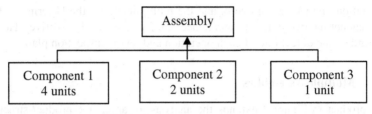

Fig. 2. A product structure

An assembly conforms only if all its components do or if it contains redundant components. Redundant components increase the load on the production system even more than defective items – they are added whether needed or not, and in order to simplify the analysis no redundancy is assumed herein.

3.1   Assembly's Actual Defect Rate

The requirement of more than one component to be conforming creates mutual effects between different components – not all the components should be defective – a single defective component may suffice to disqualify a whole assembly!

Accordingly, the defect rates of assembly operations depend not only on its self-defect-rate, pA, but on the defect rates of its components, too. Consequently, actual defect rate should be calculated for each assembly operation. Let K be the number of component types in an assembly, and mk, the assembly ratio of type k component in this assembly from the BOM. Then, the actual defect rate, P^a_A of the assembly is:

$$p_A^a = 1 - (1-p_A)\prod_{k=1}^{K}\left(1-p_k\right)^{m_k}$$ (3)

Consider for example the assembly of Figure 2. Suppose the components arrive with defect rates p1, p2, and p3, respectively. An assembly is conforming with probability: (1- p1)4(1- p2)2(1- p3)(1- pA). The complement of this probability is the actual defect rate, P^a_A of the assembly operation. This example demonstrates the dramatic increase of the actual defect rates of assembly operations. If the defect rate of each component is 1% and the defect rate of the assembly operation is 0.1%, then the actual defect rate of the assembly operation is about 7%!

Moreover, this increase is due to the mutual effect among components. If, say, 1,000 assembly units are required, then 1,074 units should be assembled, which contain 4,296 units of component 1, 2,148 units of component 2 and 1,074 units of component 3. As noted, a single defective component suffices to disqualify a whole assembly. Only 11 of the 1,074 units of component 3 are defective, the rest – 63 units are assembled with defective units of other components or a failure occurs during the assembly process. The same holds for the other components. Time and resources are required to diagnose the source of failure of each non-conforming assembly! Additional time and resources are required to fix a defective assembly.

As for the component defect rates; when no defect component arrives at an assembly station, the pk's are all zero, and the multiplication – the Π term in (3) equals 1. This cannot happen in reality and hence, the pk's are strictly positive. How positive? Depend on the defect rate of each operation and on the inspection plan.

3.2   Multiple Assemblies

The product in Figure 3 extends the analysis to larger tree-product-structures. It involves two assembly operations, the nodes numbered 10 and 14. The letter in each circle is the operation type and bellow is the defect rate, in percent's, of the corresponding operation. The numbers next to the edges entering assembly operations are the assembly ratios. In order to calculate the actual defect rate of the final assembly, which is numbered 14 in Fig. 3, the actual defect rate of the first assembly, #10, is required.

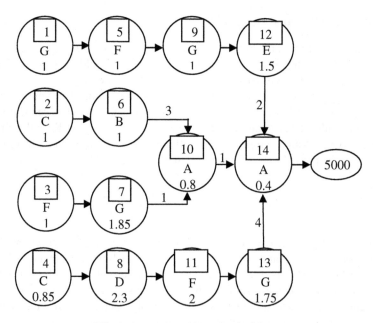

Fig. 3. A process with two assemblies

Assuming no intermediate inspection, the defect rates arriving at the first assembly from operations 2 and 6 are 100[1-(1-0.99)(1-.99)] = 1.99%, and 2.8315% from operations 3 and 7. Hence, the actual defect rate of assembly #10 is 100(1-.9801³*0.971685*0.992) ≈ 9.25%. Similarly, the arriving rate on the top branch is 4.425%, and 6.73% on the bottom. Finally, the actual defect rate of the final assembly is ≈37.5%!!

This example demonstrates a foremost implication of the mutual effects between assemblies' components – the calculations are separated. Defect rates must be calculated forward, first. Then, the quantities are calculated backward, using the assembly ratios of the BOM. If 5,000 end items are required, 8,000 = 5000/(1-0.375) units should be assembled. Backward MRP calculations form the three right columns of Table 1, which exposes a much more significant EEDI – the value of quality assurance. Poor quality adds 3 - 7.6% to the required quantities – the ratios between the numbers under perfect inspection to the numbers of a perfect process. 60% are added if no inspection is performed!! Perfect inspection does not exist, and any inspection adds cost and time to the process. A better solution is, of course, process improvements.

Table 1. The effect of poor quality – required numbers of units

Op. #	Op. type	Perfect process	Perfect inspection	No inspection
1	G	10000	10505	16000
2	C	15000	15490	24000
3	F	5000	5208	8000
4	C	20000	21529	32000
5	F	10000	10400	16000
6	B	15000	15335	24000
7	G	5000	5156	8000
8	D	20000	21346	32000
9	G	10000	10296	16000
10	A	5000	5061	8000
11	F	20000	20855	32000
12	E	10000	10193	16000
13	G	20000	20438	32000
14	FA	5000	5020	8000

4   Summary and Conclusions

The contribution of this study is two folds. First, the effect of the interaction between poor quality and assembly operations is explored. This has been achieved via the integration of defect rates with *process charts* and *product structure - BOM*.

The most significant conclusion emanates from Table 1. Even if all stations are in-control and performed as specified, still, many defective items are produced – the HIDDEN FACTORY. Consequently, quality should be considered right from the very beginning – the facility design stages. The numerical data of and BOMs can be easily stored in electronic spreadsheets, which can use it to compare alternatives; e.g., replacing a station with one of higher quality.

Another conclusion is the effect of the mutual effects among assembly's components – the rapid growth of the actual defect rates. This, too, should be considered during product and process design.

Finally, the stochastic nature of defects' occurrence should be considered. The calculations presented are of means and expected values but individual numbers are random variables. This strongly affects production management an effect which requires future research.

References

1. Feigenbaum, A.V.: Total quality control, 3rd edn., revised. McGraw-Hill, New York (1991)
2. Francis, R.L., McGinnis, L.F., White, J.A.: Facility Layout and Location: An Analytical Approach, 2nd edn. Prentice-Hall Inc., Englewood Cliffs (1992)
3. Freiesleben, J.: The economic effects of quality improvement. Total Quality Management 16(7), 915–922 (2005)
4. Kim, J., Gershwin, S.B.: Analysis of long flow lines with quality and operational failures. IIE Transactions 40, 284–296 (2008)
5. Nahmias, S.: Production and Operations Analysis, 6th edn. McGraw Hill, New York (2009)

Reliability Driven Standardization of Mechanical Seals for Petrochemical Applications

Lucio Compagno and Natalia Trapani

Dipartimento di Ingegneria Industriale (D.I.I.), University of Catania
Viale Andrea Doria 6, 95125 Catania (Italy)
{lcompagno,ntrapani}@dii.unict.it

Abstract. Mechanical seals are the most diffuse solution for rotating shaft sealing because of their high safety performances and low maintenance costs. The only requirement to meet high service level is a care in the choice of a sealing system suitable for fluids treated and operating conditions. Mechanical seal manufacturers usually have very large catalogues with a wide mix of products for each use and also offers to their clients customized solutions and maintenance service. This could result in high inventory cost for manufacturers which want to guarantee high maintenance service performances. This study shows a reliability driven methodology to reduce the mix and maintain high performances.

Keywords: Mechanical seal, reliability data, standardization, maintenance, life table.

1   Introduction

Today's challenge in Oil & Gas (O&G) industry is to become more "sustainable", that is to produce in a more efficient, economical and ecological way. To obtain this result, production systems require quality products and reliable equipments, able to guarantee high availability and service efficacy and efficiency.

As it is known, a significant proportion of industrial emissions occurs through spurious leaks in process system (fugitive emissions), and particularly from flanges, valves and rotating shafts. Fugitive emissions from European refineries were quantified up to 10,000 tons of dangerous substances per year [1, 2]. The primary purpose of a sealing system is to avoid a fluid loss to protect the environment from pollution due to hazardous substances and mechanical seals are the most diffuse solution for rotating shaft sealing because of their high safety performances and low maintenance costs.

A careful selection of mechanical seals, which requires an analysis of fitness for service (i.e. treated fluid, operating conditions), regular inspection and maintenance are the minimum requirements to obtain high performances [3], i.e. high reliability and low level of VOC (Volatile Organic Compound) emissions [1]. The concept of

B. Grabot et al. (Eds.): APMS 2014, Part III, IFIP AICT 440, pp. 455–462, 2014.
© IFIP International Federation for Information Processing 2014

Best Available Techniques (BAT) was introduced as a key principle in the European IPPC (integrated Pollution Prevention and Control) Directive [4]. In this Directive the word 'Techniques' includes both the technology used and the way in which the installation is designed, built, managed, maintained, operated and decommissioned according to a lifecycle management approach.

The selection criteria is often based on technical standards edited by API (American Petroleum Institute), such as API 682 [5] and ISO 21049 [6], EPA (Environmental Protection Agency), such as Method 21 [7], or ESA (European Sealing Association) [1].

In order to satisfy customer needs, manufacturers have developed very large catalogues with a wide mix of products for each use and also customized solutions, and they usually offers to their clients also the maintenance service.

For manufacturers which want or have (i.e. in a global service contract) to guarantee high maintenance service performances (as it is known [1], some solutions generically have a lower Total Emission Level/Lifecycle cost ratio), this could result in high inventory costs but also in higher production costs and maintenance time. In literature there are a lot of papers that define methods to estimate assets reliability and useful life left, in order to support condition based maintenance and prognostics. Most interesting is the GAMM method proposed by Barbera et al. [8], which uses a graphical approach based on a nonparametric estimation of reliability function using historical data; Abiri-Jaromi et al. [9] use an operational research approach to optimize maintenance expected costs; other methods to assess remaining useful life use knowledge-based approach (expert and fuzzy), life expectancy models (stochastic and statistical), Artificial Neural Networks and Physical, showing that the research on how estimate reliability of in service components is still popular [10, 11] and a unique solution method is not available.

In order to give a more efficient maintenance service and to reduce inventory and production costs for a mechanical seal manufacturer, a statistical data analysis approach was defined to obtain a standardization of installed base driven by operational conditions and reliability performances.

2   Case Study

The mechanical seal manufacturer has an installed base of 3,846 items in 8 plants of different clients. The seals can be classified into two macro categories (single or double) which generates 9 families and 21 different typologies (see Fig. 1).

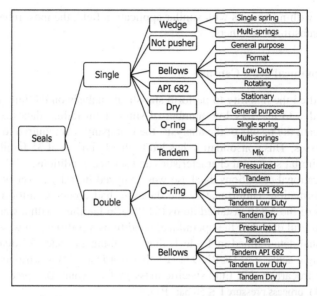

Fig. 1. Classification of seals into families and typologies

The installed base operate in different operational conditions that are caused by the potential combinations of the factors specified in Tab. 1.

Table 1. Operational conditions for the installed base

Variable	Values	ID
Process fluid	Hydrocarbon	I
	Not hydrocarbon	N
Specific mass	$\gamma \leq 0.5$ kg/dm³	D1
	$0.5 < \gamma \leq 0.8$ kg/dm³	D2
	$\gamma > 0.8$ kg/dm³	D3
Temperature	$T \leq 200$ °C	T1
	$T > 200$ °C	T2
Pressure	$P \leq 50$ bar	P1
	$P > 50$ bar	P2

3   Methodology

The methodology for the research is composed of three phases:

1. Installed mechanical seals census, to verify the correct classification according to Fig. 2 and the completeness of operational data according to Table 1;
2. Failure data analysis of seals typology, using Life Table technique [12] for assessing a "MTTF Family" (Mean Time To Failure) inside the present database;

3. Identify, within Families with similar application field, the most reliable and verify if it can substitute the others.

3.1   Mechanical Seals Census

Having verified the inability to perform statistical analysis on the failures suffered by each item, due to the very low number of single item failure data that would make non-significant the results of the analysis, the Company was required to group seals in uniform classes. This consolidation has led to the definition of 35 families containing seals with similar structural characteristics and service conditions.

The operational conditions database was analyzed in order to verify the completeness of information. Unfortunately the database had complete information only for 1,968 items of the 3,846 installed items (51.2%, 26 families) with a significant reduction of the useful data. For the operational conditions a codification was defined based on operational data defined in Table 1, thus obtaining 21 codes for dual seals and 23 ones for single seals, e.g. DCRND3T1P1 that is a Dual (D), Cartridge (CR), process fluid not hydrocarbon (N), fluid specific mass $\gamma > 0.8$ kg/dm³ (D3), process temperature T ≤ 200 °C (T1), process pressure P ≤ 50 bar (P1).

3.2   Failure Data Analysis

The Company provided the records of the dates of failure for each item, surveyed in 64 months, stating the causes of failure identified through a Root Cause Analysis (RCA).

The reliability analysis is based on the evaluation of failure times of items that are part of each family using Life Table theory to exploit as statistically significant also the reliability data of seals that have never failed in the observation period.

The data provided by the Company have the following characteristics:

1. the installation period is known for each component, but not the exact date of installation, then there are doubts on the "service start date";
4. seals are installed at different times and at each failure they were replaced with different seals (new or reconditioned); assuming that the reconditioning is able to return the seal "as new" it is as if, for any fault, a new component was installed;
5. dates of failure are note from 1 January 2006 to 30 April 2011 (64 months);
6. many components didn't fault in the period of observation.

Therefore, the data cannot be considered to be complete and adequate to run a "classical" statistical analysis. This led to the decision of executing an analysis using the Life Table methodology which allows to use data relating to seals that have never failed and data relating to the last period of service (from the last failure to April 30, 2011) by treating them as "censored data".

The Life Table is a table of extended frequency that, at discrete time intervals, counts the number of items still running at the beginning of the interval (Nr), of those failed in a period (Nf), and of those no longer controllable (e.g. lost to control or censored, Nc) to assess the elements at risk Ne, by the formula: Ne = Nr − Nc/2.

Using this technique it is possible to reach reliable estimates of the four main functions for the study of the life of a component (survival function, probability density function, failure rate, MTTF). The minimum size required for the analysis is 30 elements, including fault data and censored data.

In table 2 the life table of a dual seal family (DOTMS) is reported. The table shows all the variables that can be calculated (the calculated standard error often show very low values).

Table 2. Life table for DOTMS family

Int. Start [days]	Nr. Items running	Nr. censored	Nr. exposed	Nr. Dead
0	90	9	85.5	21
250	60	3	58.5	13
500	44	3	42.5	9
750	32	0	32.0	4
1000	28	4	26.0	6
1250	18	1	17.5	3
1500	14	1	13.5	2
1750	11	11	5.5	0
Int. Start [days]	Survived fraction	Cum. Survived fraction	PDF	Failure rate
0	0.75439	1.00000	0.00098	0.0011
250	0.77778	0.75439	0.00067	0.0010
500	0.78824	0.58674	0.00050	0.0009
750	0.87500	0.46249	0.00023	0.0005
1000	0.76923	0.40468	0.00037	0.0010
1250	0.82857	0.31129	0.00021	0.0008
1500	0.85185	0.25793	0.00015	0.0006
1750	0.90909	0.21972	-	-

The input data for the construction of the life table in this work are the times between repair and the service interval of items lost to control (censored data), according to the following assumptions:

1. installation date was considered to overlap the last failure date available in 2005, or the date of 01/01/2006 for all those items whose installation was before 2006;
2. if the item has no faults until 30 April 2011, it was assumed a service period overlapping the entire period of observation;
3. for items that have unknown installation period, the first failure date was considered as installation date.

A goodness-of-fit test for the PDF of each family was then executed by a statistical software application to determine whether it follows a known theoretical distribution (exponential, normal,...). Most of them are normally distributed, some of them are exponentially distributed, as shown in Fig. 2.

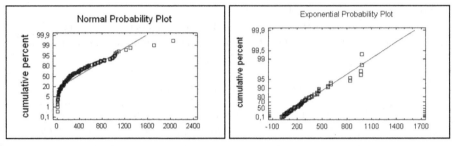

Fig. 2. Goodness of fit test of probability density function for two sets of data

In any case it is possible to calculate the MTTF using the formula (2):

$$MTTF = \sum_{k=1}^{n} t_k \cdot f_k(t) \cdot \Delta t_k \tag{2}$$

where t_k is the mean value of the Δt_k interval and $f_k(t)$ is the interval estimation of the PDF $f(t)$. The MTTF value will be the base for standardization.

3.3   Standardization

Crossing the MTTF data with the seals operational conditions it is possible to establish which families are more reliable for each service (operational conditions as specified in Table 1 and paragraph 3.1), as shown in Fig. 3.

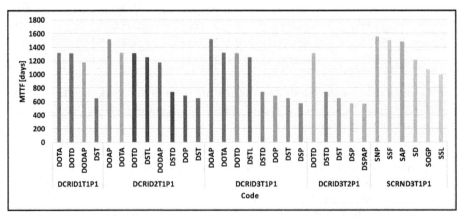

Fig. 3. Families MTTF vs construction and operational conditions

4   Discussion

Analysis of Figure 3 allows to establish that for the same range of operational conditions the manufacturer proposes from five to eight different seal families solutions but from the MTTF analysis it is clear that only a few of these can be considered reliable in the specific range, e.g. considering the code DCRID3T1P1 four of the installed families have a MTTF less than 800 days and four over 1200 days. The substitution of less reliable seals with the more reliable ones could generate benefits both for the manufacturer who could significantly reduce his catalogue and spare parts inventory with related costs, and for the customer who obtains reduced downtimes, reduced production costs, reduced potential environmental costs due to the better control of fugitive emissions, reduced seals maintenance and repair costs.

The cumulative results of standardization is synthesized in table 3.

Table 3. Seal families replacement as effect of standardization

Old Family	MTTF old [d]	ITEM Nr.	Total Item	New Family	MTTF new [d]
DOTA	1318	161			
DOTD	1310	97			
DSTL	1246	9			
DODAP	1173	61	450	DOAP	1512
DSTD	741	26			
DOP	689	48			
DST	645	48			
SD	1210	11			
SOGP	1068	8	115	SSF	1498
SSL	986	96			
DSP	575	56	81	DOTA	1318
DSPAP	560	25			
Total suggested replacement		646	646		

The overall results show that from 26 seal families it was suggested to reduce to only 16 families; the seal families replacement, that will be executed gradually (at the first maintenance intervention of each item), is referred to 646 item of 13 families which could be replaced by seal of only the three most reliable families specified in Table 3. In some cases, e.g. DOTA replacement of DSP or DSPAP generate a MTTF more than double, with obvious advantages for the reliability of the equipment.

5   Conclusions

Standardization effects are immediately visible both for the producer and customers. For the former in terms of stock costs reduction thanks to an increased interchangeability of spare parts which allows to reduce the size of the order quantity maintaining the same level of risk; for the customers in terms of increased reliability and availability of rotating shafts on which they are installed, with a direct effect on people and environment safety.

The manufacturer also experimented other less tangible benefits which consist of a greater maintenance specialization, a production mix reduced with benefits on maintenance lead time, customer service level, production lead time and ultimately lower costs of production.

Further studies on the long range effects of the suggested standardization on asset management costs will be probably available after a new census of the current installed base.

References

1. ESA Publication N° 014/09: Sealing Technology – BAT guidance note. European Sealing Association (2009)
2. Onat, A.: A review of fugitive emissions. Sealing Technology (October 2006)
3. Huebner, M.B., Buck, G.S., Azibert, H.B.: Advancements In Mechanical Sealing - API 682 Fourth Edition. In: Proceedings of the Twenty Eight Pump Users Symposium, Houston, Texas, September 24-27 (2012)
4. Directive 2008/1/EC of the European Parliament and of the Council of 15 January 2008 concerning integrated pollution prevention and control (Codified version). Official Journal L 24, 29.1.2008, 0008–0029 (2008)
5. API Standard 682, Fourth Edition: Pumps – Shaft Sealing Systems for Centrifugal and Rotary Pumps. American Petroleum Institute, Washington D.C. (2014)
6. ISO/FDIS 21049: 2011(E): Pumps – Shaft Sealing Centrifugal and Rotary Pumps. International Standard Organization, Geneva, Switzerland (2011)
7. EPA Method 21, Determination of volatile organic compound leak. Code of Federal Regulations. Title 40, Part 60, Appendix A. Washington, DC, USA
8. Barberá, L., Crespo, A., Viveros, P., Stegmaier, R.: A case study of GAMM (Graphical Analysis for Maintenance Management) applied to water pumps in a sewage treatment plant, Chile. In: Proceeding of 2nd IFAC A-MEST Workshop "Maintenance for Dependability, Asset Management and PHM", Seville, Spain, November 22-23 (2012)
9. Abiri-Jahromi, A., Parvania, M., Bouffard, F., Fotuhi-Firuzabad, M.: A Two-Stage Framework for Power Transformer Asset Maintenance Management - Part I: Models and Formulations. IEEE Transactions on Power Systems 28(2), 1395–1403 (2013)
10. Si, X.S., Wang, W., Hu, C.H., Zhou, D.H.: Remaining useful life estimation – A review on the statistical data driven approaches. European Journal of Operational Research 213, 1–14 (2011)
11. Sikorska, J.Z., Hodkiewicz, M., Ma, L.: Prognostic modelling options for remaining useful life estimation by industry. Mechanical Systems and Signal Processing 25, 1803–1836 (2011)
12. Cox, D.R.: Regression models and Life-Table. J. R. Stat. Soc. B 34(2), 187–220 (1972)

Building Blocks for Volume-Oriented Changeability in Personnel Cost Structure of Manufacturing Companies

Manuel Rippel[*], Jost-Wolfram Budde, Felix Friemann, and Paul Schönsleben

ETH Zurich, BWI Center for Industrial Management, Zurich, Switzerland
mrippel@ethz.ch

Abstract. Volatilities in global markets lead to rising importance of volume-oriented changeability (VoC) in the manufacturing industry. If the production demand is fluctuating, manufacturing companies often struggle to adapt their overhead costs, which are causing high variances in unit costs. Personnel is a main cost driver in overhead cost structure, in particular in high-wage countries. Therefore, this paper conceptualizes building blocks and analyzes impact relations for configuring VoC in personnel cost structure in production plants.

Keywords: Flexibility, Volatility, Volume-oriented Changeability, Personnel.

1 Introduction

Nowadays, companies are facing uncertainty in global markets as an omnipresent condition. For that reason, Wiendahl et al. introduced the concept of changeability as a system's potential to conduct technological, logistical, organizational and personnel changes beyond the available system-inherent flexibility corridors by means of an acceptable effort [1]. In particular manufacturing companies have to configure their capacities and capabilities in their production plant under the uncertainties of high volatility of order volumes [2]. Therefore, they are forced to find ways to economically adapt their cost structure to the fluctuating production volume, since manufacturing costs are highly sensitive due to fixed cost component [3]. Rippel et al. introduced the concept of "volume-oriented changeability" (VoC) focusing on the change dimension "volume", expand existing considerations of changeability to an socio-technical perspective and include *indirect* aspects in the plant environment [4]. This is particularly important, since around 50% of employees are working in support processes and their cost structure mainly consists of fixed costs [5]. Interdependencies of instruments, numerous influencing factors and general conditions, such as restrictive labor legislations, limitations due to social appropriateness and compliance with corporate cultural values, complicate the configuration of VoC of personnel cost structure [6]. Thus, the objective of this paper is to conceptualize building blocks for VoC and analyze their impact relations in order to support plant management to preventively set-up a holistic package with ready-to-use instruments for adapting personnel capacity and influence associated personnel costs.

B. Grabot et al. (Eds.): APMS 2014, Part III, IFIP AICT 440, pp. 463–470, 2014.

The findings have been developed through literature studies and interviews with three manufacturing companies from two industries (automobiles & parts, industrial goods & services). In addition, insights and findings were embedded, which were gained within the design and implementation of VoC at four production plants of a case study company (construction & materials, personal & household goods).

The multitude of existing obstacles reveal the need to systematize categories as building blocks for enhancing transparency and facilitating a basic configuration. The following questions will be answered: (1) Which decisive categories of enablers and levers do exist? (2) Which main influencing variables and impact relations have to be considered? (3) How does the combination of the building blocks look like?

2   Conceptualizing Building Blocks

This section presents the findings of the conducted case studies by conceptualizing building blocks as aggregated categories of instruments and design elements (see Fig. 1). It is intended to cover the most relevant topics but not to be exhaustive. The formalization differs from classical considerations, since the decisive factor of the category scheme is the mechanism contributing to VoC. Some instruments have a direct influence on the fields of impact, whereas some others indirectly affect them. The building blocks can be distinguished in "Enablers", which comprise the prerequisites for the set-up and execution of instruments, and in "Levers", which systematize instruments according to their impact mechanism.

2.1   Enablers

The enabler **"work organization"** provides the framework for the working-time-system, staffing levels, autonomous work groups as well as the organizational design of the system regarding structure and process organization. Depending on the design, the work organization itself provides flexibility potential or the requirements for the use of certain flexibility instruments. Thus the work organization can be seen as a condition or as an object of flexibility measures [7]. Work organization provides system-inherent capacity leeway by introducing employee-related instruments (e.g., job rotation, home office) and measures that increase the employability, which define the qualification for flexible workforce deployment with regard to shifting of capacities. Various measures of employability can be distinguished according to [8]. In addition to employee-related measures, such as improving workforce flexibility, career models and health promotion, there are also business-related measures, which focus on the change management style or changes in corporate culture and organizational structure. Besides, the work organization also facilitates instruments in the value chain (e.g., extended work bench) by reorganizing tasks for execution by third parties and establishing interfaces with external partners.

The enabler **"arrangement"** includes formalities related to the position, location and duration of working-time. Within the design of internal arrangements (e.g., labor contracts, agreements with work councils) the possible use of flexibility measures must be taken into account [9], e.g. scope of employment, periods of notice and contracts with for a limited period of time. Working-time flexibility can also be supported by clauses for additional or reduced working-time (e.g., employment leveling). The precise and transparent definition of rules and standards as well as trigger points and escalation levels for the activation of measures will enable mutual understanding and acceptance of both employees and employer. Employees benefit from minimized uncertainty with regards to the further approach. The employer benefits from a pre-aligned and prepared set of measures, which significantly increases the scope and speed of action in case of unforeseen demand fluctuations.

The enabler **"time accounts"** consists of working-time accounts, which are used to decouple contractual working hours and actual operated work. Working-time accounts are not independent models, but are often required as a basis for using working-time models. The combination of different types (e.g., work-time account, saving account, life-work-time account), their individual purpose and their interaction enable the implementation of various instruments by means of providing a reserve of work hours as "breathing volume". Thereby, position and duration of operated work can be adapted, when the demand differs from the contractual work time as regular baseline.

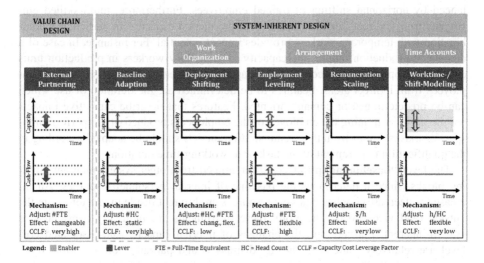

Fig. 1. Enablers and levers within value chain and system-inherent design

2.2   Levers

The lever **"worktime / shift-modeling"** consists of flexible working-time models (e.g., trust-based work time, flextime) and options to adapt the shift-model (e.g., shortening/extensions, additional shifts, holidays and weekends). Instruments of this block change the duration and the position of working-time.

The lever **"remuneration scaling"** defines ways of remuneration contributing to VoC. Roughly they can be divided into fixed salary, bonuses or flexible wage components. They must include a demand-oriented component instead or in addition to the common performance-oriented components.

The lever **"employment leveling"** comprises instruments to adapt the contractual working hours and thereby the capacity baseline, which couples the personnel expenditures (both direct and indirect labor costs), operated work and capacity demand. For example, a contractually regulated time-corridor defines which working-time must be fulfilled by the employee in case of deviations from the contractual working-hours. Thereby, the corridor can be used to extend or shorten working-time and time used within the corridor can be accounted on a working-time account. To provide a cash-effective capacity flexibility the accounting balance of the corridor can be determined with an effect on the remuneration. In that case a debt on the working-time account means a reduction of remuneration for the employee. The instrument "basis adjustment" can provide further system-inherent potential by means of an adaptation of working-time-related contractual components. It describes the possibility to adjust the time-corridor or the contractual working-hours after a certain contractual period.

The lever of **"deployment shifting"** consists of measures for flexible workforce deployment. The area of application of the flexible employee may be beyond department employee pools, plant-wide, company-wide or beyond the corporate boundaries [10]. Utilization deviations between working-groups or production units can be balanced by horizontal shifting of trained employees. Furthermore, multi-skilled employees from indirect functions can extend production capacity. In particular a combination with temporary workers provides impact potential. For instance, in case of a decline of production output, the capacity of temporary workers in production units can be disproportionately reduced. The gap can be filled by vertical shifting of employees from indirect areas. Features to be determined are the duration of use which can be predetermined or demand-oriented. Features that describe capacitive impacts are the need for training the employee or the employee's productivity to perform non-specialist tasks. Apart from that, remuneration models should be adapted according to the qualification requirement of the task or to working-time duration.

The lever **"baseline adaption"** is differentiated from other system-inherent building blocks, since it determines the baseline of internal personnel resources. An increase (or decrease) implies that new resources are brought inside the system from the outside (and vice versa). Therefore, these instruments are indirectly considered as system-inherent. Furthermore, the changes of internal capacity and associated cost level are relatively static (e.g., hiring, dismissal) and partially non-reversible (e.g., early retirement). The impact of the instruments is discrete and fairly long-term, whereby incremental and continuous adaptations prove to be difficult.

The lever **"external partnering"** contains options within the value chain to cover capacity demands. The design of the contract is crucial for utilizing external partnering as a VoC instrument, since the type of commitment allows adapting both capacity and associated payments: Firstly, the provision of service or capacities can be fixed by contract or aligned to the current demand. Thereby, the VoC potential depends, among others, on the period of notice, guaranteed purchase quantities, degree of risk participation by means of compensation payments in case of shortfall of minimum quantities [3] or the option of recurring basis adaptation of agreed services during the contract period in flexible intervals. Secondly, the cost model defines if the service should be considered as fixed or variable cost. In case of lump-sum contracts the fixed cost lead to a high operating leverage. This causes a deterioration of profitability in periods of demand decline [3]. If the payments depend on the amount of delivered services, the cost structure varies and is in line with the demand. Thirdly, it is important for a demand-oriented dimensioning of the service to compare the performance (e.g., productivity) of external capacity with internal resources.

3   Analyzing Impact Relations

The building blocks have impacts in technical, financial and social dimensions. In the following the individual, basic leverage effects on the most relevant fields of impact are displayed (see Fig. 2). Nevertheless, their existence, direction and extent depend on influencing variables, which are introduced initially.

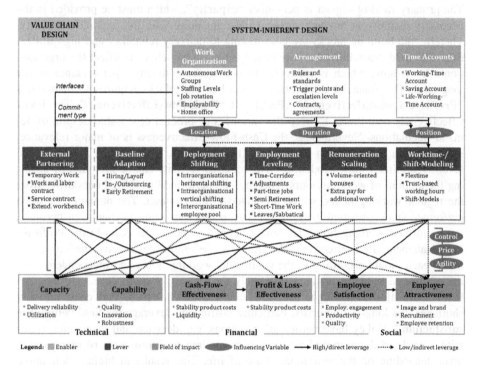

Fig. 2. Building blocks, influencing variables and fields of impact

3.1   Influencing Variables

The influential variable "**control**" has a crucial role in the process of configuring the building blocks, since the VoC potential of each measure strongly depends which stakeholder has which rights related to each measure. For example, the VoC potential of an employee-controlled working-time account significantly differs from an employer-controlled working-time account. The rights can be distinguished in decision and disposition right. The decision right determines a party's right to decide whether a measure is performed or not. The scope and timing of the measure are determined by the party with the disposition right [11, 12]. These rights can be hold by the employee, employer or both. **"Price"** involves the fact, that most instruments entail costs, since the risk of underutilized capacities is allocated to another party (e.g. employees or external partners). This party will demand a risk premium [4]. **"Agility"** underlines the importance of the temporal dimension, e.g. the required time to implement or to exploit the potential of a measure. The variable **"duration"** describes the duration of working-time in a given period and **"position"** comprises, when the work is conducted during a period. **"Location"** determines, where the task is performed, e.g. at another production unit or another plant.

3.2 Fields of Impact

The primary field of impact is personnel **"capacity"**, which must be provided in the necessary quantity at the right time at the right place with the required capability. Thereby, the building blocks are contributing to delivery reliability and high utilization. The field **"capability"** is considered, since instruments can affect the organization's know-how, which is indirectly related to the company's performance in the long-term. The financial implication of the building blocks requires to distinguish **"Profit & Loss-Effectiveness"** (P&L) and **"Cash-flow-Effectiveness"**. The P&L-Effectiveness contributes to keep the variances of product cost stable despite of demand fluctuations. Nevertheless, the Cash-Flow-Effectiveness is of major relevance, since it also affects the cash-flow. The difference can be illustrated by looking at the lever "Worktime / Shift-Modeling": The required capacity can be provided by adapting the amount of working hours. Thereby, the performed working hours differ from the regular working hours, which are stated in the contract. The deviation between performed and contractual working hours is recorded in a time account. Furthermore, the performed working hours are solely booked as personnel costs in the Profit-&-Loss statement (P&L-effective). Nevertheless, the employees receive the same payments each month according to the contractual working hours and independent from the performed working hours, respectively the capacity requirements. This implies that the cash-flow of the organization remains unaffected, which could cause liquidity shortages in a long-lasting crisis. Particular instruments leverage the field **"employee satisfaction"**, if they have participation options, e.g. decision and disposition rights with regards to duration and position of work-time or adjustments of employment level depending on the individual phase of life. This results in higher motivation, which can also increase the quality or productivity of their work [13]. The company can also enhance its **"employer attractiveness"** on the job market, if employee's needs are addressed in the design of the work-time system [14].

4   Combining Impact Potentials

Changeability in working-time-systems is usually determined by the possibility of a structural adaption to changing requirements [15]. The VoC potential in the scheme of the building blocks is exemplarily illustrated in Fig. 3 The combination of various building blocks results in increasing flexibility corridors and VoC potentials. It becomes apparent, that some instruments just enhance the potential with regards to capacity but do not affect the ability to adapt the corresponding cash-flow. This is crucial important for maximizing the ability to handle volume fluctuations economically. System-inherent instruments with an impact on cash-flow (e.g., employment leveling) are demanding a lot from employees, since their salaries are adapted. Instruments within external partnering enable to avoid the impact for internal employees. It is social reasonable to set up this potential in growth phases.

The concept provides guidance for practitioners within VoC in personnel capacities. A holistic package of ready-to-use instruments can be preventively implemented to increase the potential to act in volatile business environments. Thereby, responsiveness, speed and commensurability of actions as well as the transparency of associated impacts for both management and employees can be increased significantly. The benefits consist in the capability to adapt the personnel cost structure and associated multi-dimensional key performance indicators. The economic implications can be derived from the comparison of costs and benefits of the instruments.

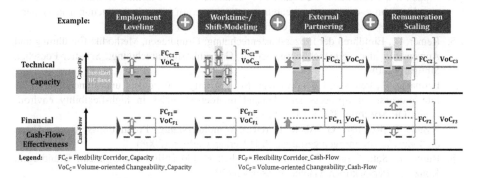

Fig. 3. Exemplary combination of impact potentials from a technical and financial perspective

5   Conclusion and Outlook

The building blocks provide companies a comprehensive overview of relevant design fields, which should be considered to use leverage effects. The concept gives direction to conduct a first basic configuration on strategic level. This creates the foundation for further dimensioning and detailing. The novelty lies in the provided transparency with regards to the scope, categories and impact relations of the various existing instruments. Decision-makers are enabled to consider multi-dimensional implications. Additionally, the distinction between P&L-effective and cash-flow-effective impact implies an aspiration level with regards to changeability, which is beyond the common focus in existing literature.

Limitations exist in the limited number of selected decisive influencing factors and fields of impact in order to make the scheme applicable for practical use on strategic level. In a next step, a simulation model is required for dimensioning the building blocks. The simulation of the working-time-system's behavior regarding the impact and interdependencies of the building blocks can be used to display fundamental effects on capacity and costs before starting implementation of VoC in the company. In addition, an appropriate and reasonable balance between technical, financial and in particular social aspects has to be considered.

References

1. Wiendahl, H.-P., ElMaraghy, H.A., Nyhuis, P., Zäh, M.F., Wiendahl, H.-H., Duffie, N., Brieke, M.: Changeable Manufacturing – Classification, Design and Operation. CIRP Annals – Manufacturing Technology 56(2), 783–809 (2007)
2. Raturi, A.S., Jack, E.P.: Creating a volume-flexible firm. Business Horizons 47(6), 69–78 (2004)
3. Wildemann, H.: Fixkostenmanagement – Leitfaden zur Anpassung von Kostenstrukturen an volatile Märkte. TCW Transfer-Centrum, München (2009)
4. Rippel, M., Lübkemann, J., Nyhuis, P., Schönsleben, P.: Profiling as a means of implementing volume-oriented changeability in the context of strategic production management. CIRP Annals – Manufacturing Technology, 8-11 (2014)
5. Remer, D.: Einführen der Prozesskostenrechnung: Grundlagen, Methodik, Einführung und Anwendung der verursachungsgerechten Gemeinkostenzurechnung. Schäffer-Poeschel, Stuttgart (2005)
6. Letmathe, P., Petersen, L., Schweitzer, M.: Capacity management under uncertainty with inter-process, intra-process and demand interdependencies in high-flexibility environments. OR Spectrum 35(1), 191–219 (2012)
7. Nyhuis, P., Reinhart, G., Abele, E. (eds.): Wandlungsfähige Produktionssysteme – Heute die Industrie von morgen gestalten. PZH Verlag, Garbsen (2008)
8. Rump, J., Sattelberger, T., Fischer, H. (eds.): Employability Management: Grundlagen, Konzepte, Perspektiven. Gabler, Wiesbaden (2006)
9. Armutat, S., Fassbender, P., Haberkern, K.-H., Kaiser, S., Steinbrücker, U., Szogas, C.: Flexibilitätsorientiertes Personalmanagement: Grundlagen, Handlungshilfen, Praxisbeispiele. W. Bertelsmann, Bielefeld (2006)
10. Bazenski, N., Stowasser, S.: Flexibilität in Unternehmen der Metall- und Elektroindustrie. In: Bornewasser, M., Zülch, G. (eds.): Arbeitszeit – Zeitarbeit: Flexibilisierung der Arbeit als Antwort auf die Globalisierung, pp. 61–76. Springer Gabler, Wiesbaden (2013)
11. Schmidt, D., Hasenau, K., Lehmann, C.: Betriebliche Strategien der Flexibilisierung: die Rolle der Arbeitszeit. In: Bornewasser, M., Zülch, G. (eds.) Arbeitszeit – Zeitarbeit: Flexibilisierung der Arbeit als Antwort auf die Globalisierung, pp. 100–114. Springer Gabler, Wiesbaden (2013)
12. Som, O.: Flexibilität und Stabilität in Betrieben des deutschen Verarbeitenden Gewerbes. In: FraunhoferInstitut für System- und Innovationsforschung (ISI): Flexibilität und Stabilität in Balance – Neue Erkenntnisse zu Einer Vertrauten Verbindung, pp. 15–46. MSK, Köln (2013)
13. Schulte, C.: Personal-Controlling mit Kennzahlen. Vahlen, München (2011)
14. Blum, A., Zaugg, R.J.: Praxishandbuch Arbeitszeitmanagement: Beschäftigung durch innovative Arbeitszeitmodelle. Rüegger, Chur (1999)
15. Kinkel, S., Kleine, O., Maloca, S.: Wandlungsfähigkeit messen und benchmarken. Fraunhofer Institut für System- und Innovationsforschung (ISI), Karlsruhe (2012)

Case Studies

Designing an Engineer-To-Order Performance Measurement System: A Case Study

Børge Sjøbakk and Ottar Bakås

SINTEF Technology and Society, Industrial Management
P.O. Box 4760 Sluppen, N-7465 Trondheim, Norway
{borge.sjobakk,ottar.bakas}@sintef.no

Abstract. The conventional maxim of "what gets measured gets done" has motivated many companies to systematically measure their performance over the years. From previously being focused solely on financial, backward-looking measures, it is now generally agreed that a performance measurement system (PMS) should align with a company's long-term, strategic objectives. These objectives are largely dictated by the company's production situation, and vice versa. When being approached by a Norwegian engineer-to-order (ETO) company requesting a PMS, the authors could not identify any literature explicitly referring to PMS for ETO. The authors therefore set out to design the PMS from scratch. The purpose of this paper is to illustrate how the PMS was designed in close collaboration with the case company, bearing the general characteristics and competitive priorities of ETO in mind.

Keywords: Performance measurement system, design methodology, engineer-to-order.

1 Introduction

There is a variety of production situations that can be used to meet demand. Most of the operations management and production literature would classify companies into a manufacturing continuum spanning across four types, depending on the position of the customer order decoupling point (CODP): make-to-stock (MTS), assemble-to-order (ATO), make-to-order (MTO) and engineer-to-order (ETO) [1]. In the ETO production situation products are manufactured to meet a specific customer's needs by unique engineering or significant customization [1]. The products are often complex, with deep structures consisting of both customized and standardized components [2]. Further, uncertainty in product- and process specifications, product mix and -volume [3, 4] often results in high lead times [5] and frequent change orders [6].

The competitive priorities of a company are largely dictated by its production situation, and vice versa. This should be reflected in the company's performance measurement system (PMS), i.e. the set of metrics used to quantify both the efficiency and effectiveness of actions [7]. Performance measures should focus on the order winners and market qualifiers for the different processes up- and downstream of the CODP [8]. This implies that the design of a company's PMS should vary with its

B. Grabot et al. (Eds.): APMS 2014, Part III, IFIP AICT 440, pp. 473–480, 2014.

production situation, and that a PMS for ETO in some way would differ from a PMS for MTS-, ATO- or MTO. For example, flexibility is regarded as an order winner in ETO, as opposed to price, which is more important in the MTS production situation [9]. As such, flexibility would necessarily have to be emphasized more in a PMS for ETO.

When being approached by a Norwegian ETO company requesting a PMS, the authors initially set out to identify what was already written about PMS for ETO. In this respect, quite a bit of literature on performance measurement in construction, which has the same discontinuity aspects of temporariness, uniqueness and multi-functionality as those found in ETO [10], was identified [e.g. 11, 12-15]. However, as noted by Beatham et al. [11] construction performance measures are often lagging measures used mainly as a marketing tool rather than as means for improvement. In ETO, a considerable portion of the manufacturing and assembly processes are carried out at the corporate premises using a production system managed according to established manufacturing policies, unlike the often 'ad hoc' construction projects [10]. As such, there would arguably be elements of repetition in ETO that could be measured using a more complete PMS consisting of both leading and lagging indicators. This PMS could be used as a means for improving the production system and its policies.

No literature explicitly referring to PMS for ETO was identified. The authors therefore set out to design the PMS from scratch, taking a PMS design methodology by Andersen and Fagerhaug [16] as a starting point due to their familiarity with this approach. The purpose of this paper is to illustrate how the PMS was designed in close collaboration with the case company, bearing the general characteristics and competitive priorities of ETO in mind. The focus lies at the process of designing the PMS rather than the details of the final PMS.

The remainder of the paper is structured as follows: First, the research method and case company are described. This is followed by some theoretical background, before the process of designing the PMS is described. Finally, the findings are concluded.

2   Research Method

The research was carried out by a qualitative approach, utilizing the action research method. Action research seeks to generate new knowledge both for the problem holder (in this case the ETO company) and the action researchers, through collaboratively solving problems in real life situations while having a research interest in mind [17, 18]. This research method is different from many other methods in that the researchers actively take part in the context of their research area, shaping a mutual reliance on the problem holder's and the researchers' skills and competences [17, 18]. Due to its nature, action research and its practitioners have met various types of critique over the years: It has been claimed to be nothing more than consultancy in not emphasizing the research in a sufficient (scientific) manner [18]; it is claimed to be inadequate in safely making causal inferences [19]; and, the researchers are said to be especially exposed for bias [18]. Further, it is prone to general critique of qualitative research; that it is hard to generalize from this type of research design, and it that it therefore lacks some key criteria for research quality [18]. The authors acknowledge that the idiosyncratic context of working closely with the problem holder restricts the possibility to fully generalize and replicate the research and its results. However; close collaboration was a critical success factor as the PMS needed to be tailored to the company. By investigating the requirements for a PMS for ETO, the research interest was also maintained, as this is a topic that has received little attention in the literature.

About the Problem Holder. The problem holder is a relatively small, high-tech company that specializes in design, manufacturing, technological development, installation and support of solutions for environmental monitoring. While being part of a larger international group, this particular subsidiary has its main office in the middle of Norway. For the PMS design activity, the production of ocean monitoring platforms was chosen as a case. These contain sensors for measuring various parameters, e.g. meteorological data and water quality. The platforms are categorized in four types based on different sizes and shapes of the floaters. There are some components that are common for all platforms, e.g. data loggers, floater (though different for each platform type) and electronics. Besides this, the platforms can be customized to a large extent. For each single platform that is delivered, the company has to engineer an anchorage system based on the seabed conditions in its area of operations. The production of a platform is triggered by a customer order, often resulting from tendering as the company has a high share of public customers. As is evident, the characteristics of the company coincide with typical characteristics of ETO, making it an interesting case for the design of a PMS for ETO.

3   Theoretical Background

The conventional maxim of "what gets measured gets done"[1] has motivated many companies to systematically measure their performance over the years. Earlier, performance was typically measured in terms of one or several financial ratios collectively suggesting how well a company was doing [20]. However, since the 1980s and 1990s other non-financial factors contributing to the performance of organizations have gained ground [16]. For example, in their balanced scorecard approach Kaplan and Norton [21] augment traditional financial measures with performance measures in the three areas of a company's relationship with its customers; its key internal processes; and, its learning and growth – arguing that financial measures and targets are not sufficient in measuring performance against a company's long-term strategic objectives. Today, it is generally agreed that performance measures should be derived from a company's strategic priorities [22].

There exist a lot of general methods for designing a PMS [e.g. 7, 16, 22]. Andersen and Fagerhaug [16] present an eight-step methodology: (1) Understanding and mapping business structures and processes; (2) developing business performance

---

[1]   Peters and Waterman attribute it to the organization theorist Mason Haire. In: Peters, T., Waterman, R.H.: In search of excellence: lessons from America's best-run companies. Harper & Row, New York (1982)

476   B. Sjøbakk and O. Bakås

priorities; (3) understanding the current PMS; (4) developing performance indicators; (5) deciding how to collect the data; (6) designing reporting and performance data presentation formats; (7) testing and adjusting the PMS; (8) implementing the PMS.

To assess organizational goal attainment, performance indicators play an important role in a PMS. A performance indicator is a variable that expresses quantitatively the effectiveness or efficiency (or both) of (part of) a process or system against a given norm or target [23]. Over the years, the list of available performance indicators has grown extensively, and for many companies step 4 in the methodology by Andersen and Fagerhaug [16] may be more a task of 'deciding' rather than 'developing' performance indicators. Further companies should decide on a few key performance indicators (KPIs), i.e. a set of performance indicators focusing on the aspects of an organization's performance that are most critical for the organizations present and future success [24], in order to make reporting and follow-up manageable.

Finally, the purpose of having a PMS generally exceeds that of "getting things done". Other stated purposes include motivation, promotion, celebration, learning and improvement, and performance measures should be chosen accordingly [20].

4 Designing the Performance Measurement System

In designing a PMS for the problem holder, the methodology by Andersen and Fager-haug [16] was taken as a starting point; however, it was not followed to the letter. First, the company's current PMS was mapped, referring to Step 3 in the methodology. Thereafter, five workshops with different departments in the company generated suggestions for necessary performance indicators, which were further refined by the researchers (Step 4). In this process, a brief evaluation of the measurability of the different indicators was carried out (Step 5). A preliminary set of performance indicators was then sent out to the management and other parts of the company for feedback. In this way a *top-down cascading method* was combined with a *bottom-up design process*, which is in line with what Andersen and Fagerhaug [16] recommend.

Aligning the PMS with the Problem Holder's Strategic Priorities. As noted in theory, a PMS should be derived from a company's strategic priorities. When the researchers were approached by the problem holder, the company had formulated a vision in its management system; however, it was agreed that it needed to be made easier to communicate both internally and externally. This realization served as an opportunity to rethink and reformulate the company's strategic priorities into something shorter and easier to remember for all stakeholders. Based on their experience with the company, the researchers were able to propose a vision and five strategic business goals with which the PMS could be aligned (Step 2). The strategic business goals were: (1) Safe and stimulating workplace; (2) efficient delivery; (3) high quality products and services; (4) preferred partner; and (5) sustainable production. In order to ensure balance of the PMS and measurements of relevance, these strategic business goals were further itemized into the following measurement dimensions: Customer focus; flexibility; safety; people; delivery time; delivery precision; quality; innovation and R&D; financial performance; and environment. Most of these dimensions would prove valuable for all production situations; however, flexibility, innovation and R&D are especially important for ETO due to the production situation's high product complexity and uncertainty in specifications and demand.

Workshops were carried out to secure the company's ownership to the new vision, strategic goals and measurement dimensions. As such, a byproduct of the PMS design process was that the researchers and the problem holder together developed a new vision for the company – concretizing its strategic priorities.

Understanding the Business Environment. The aforementioned workshops were further used to ensure that the main activities of the company were understood correctly (Step 1). These were structured in five business processes: (1) Sales; (2) planning; (3) engineering; (4) source and make; (5) delivery. Interestingly, the problem holder illustrated this as a 'customer journey', which in a neat way links the order-driven ETO business processes, the business functions responsible for each process and inherent handover activities (Fig. 1). This is important for the use and follow-up of the PMS, as this should be distributed over the many business functions involved in ETO production, with especially planning and engineering arguably being more important in ETO than in other production situations due to all operations being order-driven and the share of engineering done to every product.

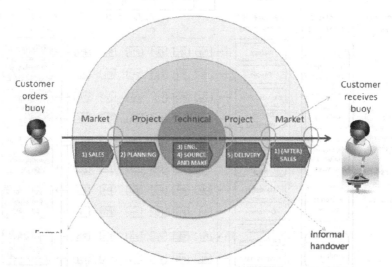

Fig. 1. The 'customer journey' showcasing responsibilities and handovers

From PIs to KPIs. During the workshops with the problem holder, 57 potential performance indicators were identified. For each indicator, the following was described: (1) Name and link to associated measurement dimension; (2) definition, i.e. a formula for calculating the performance; and (3) motivation, i.e. a description of its relevance. In collaboration with the case company, the performance indicators (PIs) were structured in accordance with the business processes of the company, as outlined in the customer journey: Sales (10 PIs); planning (6 PIs); engineering (10 PIs); source and make (13 PIs); delivery (9 PIs). Several indicators were found to occur in every process. These were gathered in a separate group coined 'common for all' (9 PIs). Both project- and production oriented indicators were considered in this process.

Based on the large number of relevant performance indicators, a limited set of KPIs was created to make the PMS more manageable. Such KPIs should in a simple and intuitive way display the current status in locations readily available for all employees, for example through a traffic light system. The KPIs should be easily linked with their underlying information in a drill-down manner. The previously developed strategic business objectives and measurement dimensions guided the task of creating KPIs, which were compound indexes calculated based on the status of underlying PIs. For example, the preferred partner index is aggregated based on the status of three underlying PIs: customer satisfaction measurement, percentage of re-sales to existing customers and tendering hit-rate.

Fig. 2 below illustrates the connection between the vision, the strategic business goals, the measurement dimensions, the business processes and the key performance indicators.

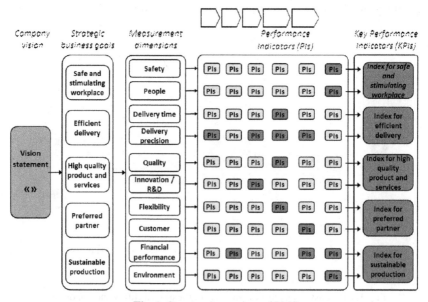

Fig. 2. Structural overview of PMS

Last, principles for implementation were described. The following five factors were described as vital: (1) Setting targets; (2) identifying measurement methods; (3) setting the frequency of registration and reporting; (4) principles for visualization; and (5) responsibility for measurement and follow-up.

5   Conclusion

The complex process of designing a PMS requires structure and methodology. Even though a step-wise waterfall model by Andersen and Fagerhaug [16] was applied, the researchers experienced going back-and-forth in the design process. To ensure that the PMS was derived from the company's strategic priorities in a consistent and integrated manner, four principles were applied: (1) Define strategic business goals supporting the company's vision; (2) construct measurement dimensions covering the strategic business goals; (3) relate performance indicators to business processes and measurement dimensions; (4) ensure that KPIs cover all measurement dimensions. Involving employees and managers from main business functions is critical.

The design process itself provided several unforeseen side effects. First, the 'customer journey' was found to be a helpful tool to structure the business processes and -functions within the company. Second, the PMS design process can serve as a catalyst for clarifying the vision and strategic objectives of the company. Third, the process can spur a number of improvement suggestions to existing processes and procedures.

Feedback from the problem holder supports the usefulness of the proposed PMS. However, as it has not yet been fully implemented at the company any numerical data to quantitatively assess its effects has not yet been made available. The researchers acknowledge that the findings are based on a single case, and that working closely with the problem holder limits the generalizability of the research and its results. Nonetheless, the case should be useful for others struggling to design their own PMS.

The topic of designing a performance management system for ETO companies is an area with much potential for further research, having received little attention in academic literature. The researchers therefore call for more studies describing the design process itself, and the actual resulting performance indicators that should be tailored to customer-specific and engineering-oriented production situations. Finally, as these may vary significantly, a minimum stability or degree of repetition required for an ETO company to fully exploit a PMS should be identified.

Acknowledgements. This work has been conducted within the MARGIN project (Integrated and responsive maritime supply chains) funded by the Regional Research Fund Mid-Norway and the SFI Norman (Norwegian Manufacturing Future) programme supported by the Research Council of Norway. The authors would like to thank the participants of the projects for providing valuable empirical data.

References

1. Amaro, G., Hendry, L., Kingsman, B.: Competitive advantage, customisation and a new taxonomy for non make-to-stock companies. Int. J. Oper. Prod. Man. 19, 349–371 (1999)
2. Hicks, C., McGovern, T., Earl, C.: Supply chain management: A strategic issue in engineer to order manufacturing. Int. J. Prod. Econ. 65, 179–190 (2000)

3. Bertrand, J., Muntslag, D.: Production control in engineer-to-order firms. Int. J. Prod. Econ. 30, 3–22 (1993)
4. Muntslag, D.R.: Profit and risk evaluation in customer driven engineering and manufacturing. Int. J. Prod. Econ. 36, 97–107 (1994)
5. Pandit, A., Zhu, Y.: An ontology-based approach to support decision-making for the design of ETO (Engineer-To-Order) products. Automat. Constr. 16, 759–770 (2007)
6. Riley, D.R., Diller, B.E., Kerr, D.: Effects of delivery systems on change order size and frequency in mechanical construction. Journal of Construction Engineering and Management 131, 953–962 (2005)
7. Neely, A., Gregory, M., Platts, K.: Performance measurement system design: A literature review and research agenda. Int. J. Oper. Prod. Man. 15, 80–116 (1995)
8. Olhager, J.: Strategic positioning of the order penetration point. Int. J. Prod. Econ. 85, 319–329 (2003)
9. Olhager, J., Rudberg, M., Wikner, J.: Long-term capacity management: Linking the perspectives from manufacturing strategy and sales and operations planning. Int. J. Prod. Econ. 69, 215–225 (2001)
10. Caron, F., Fiore, A.: 'Engineer to order' companies: How to integrate manufacturing and innovative processes. International Journal of Project Management 13, 313–319 (1995)
11. Beatham, S., Anumba, C., Thorpe, T., Hedges, I.: KPIs: A critical appraisal of their use in construction. Benchmarking: An International Journal 11, 93–117 (2004)
12. Chan, A.P., Chan, A.P.: Key performance indicators for measuring construction success. Benchmarking: An International Journal 11, 203–221 (2004)
13. Takim, R., Akintoye, A.: Performance indicators for successful construction project performance. In: 18th Annual ARCOM Conference, pp. 545–555 (Year)
14. Robinson, H.S., Carrillo, P.M., Anumba, C.J., A-Ghassani, A.: Review and implementation of performance management models in construction engineering organizations. Construction Innovation: Information, Process, Management 5, 203–217 (2005)
15. Navon, R.: Research in automated measurement of project performance indicators. Automat. Constr. 16, 176–188 (2007)
16. Andersen, B., Fagerhaug, T.: Performance Measurement Explained: Designing and Implementing Your State-of-The-art-System. ASQ Quality Press, Wisconsin (2002)
17. Greenwood, D.J., Levin, M.: Introduction to action research: social research for social change, Thousand Oaks, California, Sage (2007)
18. McKay, J., Marshall, P.: The dual imperatives of action research. Information Technology & People 14, 46–59 (2001)
19. Baskerville, R.L., Wood-Harper, A.T.: A critical perspective on action research as a method for information systems research. J. Inform. Technol. 11, 235–246 (1996)
20. Behn, R.D.: Why measure performance? Different purposes require different measures. Public Admin. Rev. 63, 586–606 (2003)
21. Kaplan, R.S., Norton, D.P.: Using the balanced scorecard as a strategic management system. Harvard Bus. Rev. 74, 75–85 (1996)
22. Bourne, M., Mills, J., Wilcox, M., Neely, A., Platts, K.: Designing, implementing and updating performance measurement systems. Int. J. Oper. Prod. Man. 20, 754–771 (2000)
23. Fortuin, L.: Performance indicators—why, where and how? Eur. J. Oper. Res. 34, 1–9 (1988)
24. Parmenter, D.: Key performance indicators (KPI): Developing, implementing, and using winning KPIs. John Wiley & Sons (2010)

The Importance of Emerging Markets for Petroleum Technology Companies in Norway: Management and Entry Operation Strategies

Jan Frick and Murshid Mikael Ali

University of Stavanger, Stavanger, Norway
{jan.frick,murshid.ali}@uis.no

Abstract. The petroleum industry today are characterised by local companies emerging to other markets. This paper evaluates from cases the importance of these markets, and how many actually export to them. The offshore technology petroleum industry is one of Norway's largest industry sectors. The main competitive advantage of this sector is its knowledge base. An important part of the industry supplies platforms and other highly specialised equipment to the petroleum industry. Constraints to achieving success in these markets are many; official data may be unreliable, corruption might flourish, there will be large cultural differences and the political and legal risks might be high. Prejudice against different societies can also be an obstacle in creating and developing organizations that promote trade.

Keywords: petroleum industry, competitive advantage, globalization.

1 Introduction

Multinational companies from developed countries are enhancing their presence in emerging markets because they see the impact on growth and related bottom-line effects of their decisions and actions. They have increased their competitiveness by engaging in emerging markets performance enhancing activities. Growth in any market opens up the necessity for exchange of knowledge and technology. Especially in the post-financial crisis era, companies from developed countries can spot opportunities in emerging markets.

According to the United Nations there are over sixty thousand firms operating internationally controlling at least half a million foreign affiliates. Together they produce goods worth more than eleven trillion USD. The trade between these companies have increased faster than the world trade overall (World Economic Forum, 2008). Private companies, through efficient organizations and capitalistic principles implement faster routines to enter new markets than others. These companies are now the global economy and drive the growth of different countries (UNCTAD, 2004). At the same time the largest economic growth of today is based in emerging countries. There is a shift in the world's economic power, from the West to the East (Enderwick, 2009). Usually globalization has been mentioned to describe

B. Grabot et al. (Eds.): APMS 2014, Part III, IFIP AICT 440, pp. 481–488, 2014.

free trade in goods and services, but the fast expansion of today's technological development has created a global arena of transfers of jobs and skills across borders, outsourcing and off shoring in order to cut costs. Part of the fast-paced globalization has occurred because companies find it hard to achieve growth in the already developed world. So they tend to turn against emerging markets, realizing that they yield better sales growth than can be found in the developed world (Pacek et al. 2007).

Business operations in emerging markets are a concept that is gaining popularity among many multinationals today. For many organizations it is not only a way of expanding their business, but also a part of the globalization that takes place around us today. Emerging markets accounted for about half of the world's GDP in 2006 and these markets continue to demonstrate a tremendous growth that outpaces those of the already developed markets (Pacek et al. 2007). As a result, many companies see the ability to sell effectively to these markets as integral to their long-term survival in an ever-increasing competitive environment. Business conducted in emerging markets enables companies to achieve lower production costs, gain access to new customers, obtain access to information or resources and spread business risk. This will also help companies react more quickly to changes in the market, and respond more promptly to customer requests.

2   Characteristics of Emerging Markets

- Countries generally considered to be emerging markets, possess some, but not necessarily all of the following
- Per capita income of less than US $10,725 (the current World Bank definition of low and middle income economies)
- Recent or relatively recent economic liberalisation
- Debt ratings below investment grade by major international ratings agencies
- Recent liberalisation of the political system and a move towards greater public participation in the political process

Studies of the different emerging markets have become more and more important, and several leading organizations have conducted studies on the subject and gives out yearly rankings. The most well-recognized and popular ranking of competitiveness of countries is the Global Competitiveness Rankings and World Competitiveness rankings.

The World Economic Forum conducts the Global Competitiveness Rankings study. Competitiveness is defined as the collection of factors, policies and institutions that determine the level of productivity of a country and thus determine the level of prosperity that can be attained by an economy.

The annual World Competitive Index is given by IMD. Competitiveness of nations could be described as an integrative process of all policies in a country in order to have a blueprint to increase prosperity (IMD, 2006). The World Competitiveness Index has four components, namely, economic performance, government efficiency, business efficiency and infrastructure. Knowledge has emerged and is accepted as the most critical resource (Bartlett and Ghosal, 1993; Moffet et al, 2010; Pillania, 2006). The main producers of wealth are information and knowledge generators (Moffet, 2010). Knowledge has an important role in advancing economic and social wellbeing and poor countries differ from rich ones not only because they have less capital, but also because they have less knowledge (World Economic Forum, 2008). Management scholars today consider knowledge and the ability to create and utilize knowledge to be the most important source of a firm's sustainable competitive advantage (Pillania, 2005).

3   How Important Is Emerging Markets in the Oil Industry Today?

To understand the importance of emerging markets for Norwegian companies within the petroleum industry, we should assess the upstream sites of one of the largest oil producers in the world. ExxonMobil is the largest oil company in the world, having a turnover of 1515 billion USD in 2013, and over 70 000 employees. An overview of the upstream activities shows that most of activities in production stem from emerging markets, and most of the major sites and new additions are also in connection to emerging markets. This indicates future activity that is expected to rise in these areas. These activities are also centred and mainly focused on emerging markets. For petroleum technology companies that offer new and more efficient technology, this is valuable information in order to understand where the future market for their products and services will be. The end-client for all of the case companies in this paper is eventually the petroleum operators such as BP, ExxonMobil, ConocoPhillips, Statoil and so forth.

4   Strategies to Enter Emerging Markets

When companies go global they will have to establish a global distribution system and an integrated manufacturing capability, and these factors gives the company a competitive advantage. However, going global poses also a lot of challenges, such as variety of commercial invoices, different bills of lading, and inspection certificates and in addition the company needs to comply with new domestic and international regulations. This will be discussed in the following chapters. According to Hisrich and al., there are different modes of entering or engaging in international business, these modes can be divided into three categories: Exporting, non equity arrangements as in turn-key contracts and licensing, and direct foreign investment as in joint ventures and wholly owned subsidiaries (see table under).

Entry Mode	Advantage	Disadvantage
Exporting	• Ability to realize location and experience curve economies	• High transport costs • Trade barriers • Problems with local marketing agents
Turn-key contracts	• Ability to enter returns from process technology skills in countries where FDI is restricted	• Creation of efficient competitors • Lack of long-term market presence
Licensing	• Low development costs and risks	• Lack of control over technology • Inability to engage in global strategic coordination
Franchising	• Low development costs and risks	• Lack of control over quality • Inability to engage in global strategic coordination
Joint Ventures	• Access to local partner's knowledge-based • Shared development costs and risks • Politically acceptable	• Lack of control over technology • Inability to engage in global strategic coordination • Inability to realize location and experience curve economies
Wholly owned subsidiaries	• Protection of technology • Ability to engage in global strategic coordination	• High costs and risks

(From Hisrich et al. 2011, page 531)

The most common way of starting an international venture is through exporting. Exporting is when a company or an organization sells and ships products or services manufactured in one country to another country. Towards the emerging market, Norwegian companies needs to have an emerging market agent that purchases the products or the services, and then sells them to the end costumer. Non-equity arrangements consist of licensing and turnkey projects. Joint ventures and wholly owned subsidiaries makes the Norwegian companies obliged to invest in Emerging markets, and be a part of the economical sphere there, thus an direct foreign investment.

5   Methodology

This paper is based on data collected through interviews of 40 different companies in the oil industry in near proximity to Stavanger. In addition all of the companies are characterised as Petroleum technology, this was also a prerequisite in order to be able to participate in the analysis. The primary source for this study was a semi-structured interview with 10 questions, in addition to an open and informal interview style in order to understand and get to know the organization and management on a deeper level. A typical interview lasted for about 60 minutes, with additional open-ended questions in order to understand the importance of sales and marketing in emerging markets for these companies.

6   Case Companies

1	Petroleum Tech Company AS	21	Module Solutions and Systems AS
2	Roxel elektro automasjon	22	MT Technology
3	Roxel Aanestad	23	Norwegian Hose Supply
4	Roxel AS	24	Norwegian Oilfield supply
5	Roxel Building Technologies	25	NOT AS
6	Roxel Energy	26	Align AS
7	Roxel Hvac	27	Completion Tech Resources AS
8	Roxel Klima	28	Vision Io AS
9	Roxel Products	29	IK Stavanger AS
10	Roxel Solutions	30	Oneco Technology AS
11	Stream AS	31	Oneco Solutions AS
12	Wiretech AS	32	Fjell Industrier AS
13	Xnor AS	33	Flowtec AS
14	Albatross Elektro AS	34	Hitec Products AS
15	Albatross Services AS	35	Light Weight Drilling AS
16	Aseon AS	36	Metallteknikk AS
17	IKM Testing AS	37	Norwegian Coating Technology AS
18	Bri Cleanup AS	38	Eureka Pumps AS
19	Bri Wellservice AS	39	Oil Treatment Technologies AS
20	Cyviz AS	40	Bolt Norge AS

Case Study Objectives

1) To understand if Norwegian petroleum technology companies are expanding to emerging markets.
2) Which emerging markets they operate in.
3) What kind of entry-strategy they use when entering into emerging markets.
4) Who in the organization are responsible for the export and establishment effort in emerging markets?

7   Study Results

All of the interviews were done with the top management of all of the companies. Top management is characterized by being one of the owners, CEO, CTO or others with key supervisory responsibilities. This has given this paper a unique insight into the management patterns of highly entrepreneurial companies during export to foreign countries, effectively mapping the most relevant countries.

- Top management gave 100% of the interviews.
- 75% of the companies operate within upstream, 25% within downstream.
- 100% of the companies export to foreign countries.
- 82% of the companies export to emerging markets.
- The most important emerging market was listed to be Middle East, with Brazil following closely afterwards.
- Only 25,5% has an office in an emerging market. Of these average age in the markets were 3,5 years.
- When exporting to emerging markets, these where the statistics on the different entry-modes:

Entry Mode	Total companies
Exporting	100%
Turn-key contracts	12,5%
Licensing	57,6%
Agent	55%
Joint Ventures	63,5%
Wholly owned subsidiaries	25,5%

- 72,5% cited that emerging markets were very important for their business, 17,5% said it was important, while approx. 10% claimed it to be less important.
- In 95% of all case companies, the top management were in charge of the operations towards emerging markets.

It is quite evident that emerging markets are important for most of the companies surveyed. A surprising fact is also that all companies have, at least once, exported products or services to foreign countries. One of the groups interviewed, Roxel Group, consists of several daughter companies who all fall under the SME and technology definition. In addition BR Industries were surveyed. This industrial group is one of the largest in Rogaland. Several of the companies surveyed belong to BR Industries. The case studies and interviews suggests that the oil technology companies have been clever in following the footsteps of the larger oil operators. We can refer back to our assessment and analysis of ExxonMobil and their focus of expanding operations. Interestingly but not surprisingly the Middle East were the most common emerging market to expand into.

Norwegian companies are eager to investigate possibilities and expand into new international markets as their own market space is becoming more and more competitive. Emerging markets has a good impression of Norwegian companies and is interested in cooperating with them in order to do business and create new opportunities. However, another interesting fact from the research shows that many of the companies just recently have established a link or a connection to emerging markets. The average age of being established were only 3,5 years for those companies who had an office in these markets. This suggests that our case companies just recently have acknowledged the importance of the emerging markets. Our discussions with those companies that have established themselves in emerging markets thus suggest that the Norwegian companies needs to invest in emerging markets for the long run and cannot expect to "take over" the market space in matter of months. The competition in emerging markets is fierce, but the benefits are great for the companies that think tactically and plan accordingly. Large cultural, religious and language differences are also often a barrier, however with time they are overcome.

8   Conclusions

Our research shows that the Norwegian companies surveyed are expanding and exporting to emerging markets, thus shown that they have acknowledged the importance of these markets to their companies. The emerging markets that they choose to expand to, and do business in – are mainly markets where large and known petroleum operators already do business. This is quite common in the petroleum industry, as our research also supports. Smaller companies, such as technology intensive SME, follows the larger corporations out into the rest of the world. For many of the companies that were investigated, much of their revenues, to an increasing extent came from emerging markets. The most popular mode of entry for most companies is exporting directly to the different markets. The importance of emerging markets are also evident for these companies, due to that almost all companies have assigned the task of expansion in these markets to someone in the top management of each company. The emerging markets are quite important for Norwegian SME technology companies within the petroleum industry, and that they are quite good in expanding to these market and that they have highly prioritized their operation strategies towards emerging markets.

9   Further Research

The authors of this paper recommends further research on the topic, especially in order to understand if there are differences in strategies when operating in different emerging markets.

References

1. Enderwick, P.: Responding to global crisis: The contribution of emerging markets to strategic adaptation. International Journal of Emerging Markets 4, 358–374 (2009)
2. Bartlett, C.A., Ghosal, S.: Beyond the M-form: Toward a managerial theory of the firm. Strategic Management Journal 14, 23–44 (1993)
3. Pillania, R.K.: Competitiveness and emerging markets. Business Strategy Series 10, 90–95 (2009)
4. Pillania, R.K.: Leveraging knowledge for sustainable competitiveness in SMEs. International Journal Globalization and Small Business 1, 27–39 (2006)
5. Moffet, M., Ronkainen, I., Czinkota, M.: International Business, 8th edn. John Wiley & Sons (2010)
6. Hisrich, R.D., Peters, M.P., Shepherd, D.A.: Entrepreneurship, 7th edn. McGraw-Hill International Edition (2008)
7. Hisrich, R.D.: International Entrepreneurship: Starting, Developing, and Managing a Global Venture, 2nd edn. Sage Publications (2012)
8. Pacek, N., Thorniley, D.: Emerging Markets: Lessons for Business Success and the Outlook for Different Markets. John Wiley & Sons (2007)
9. IMD, World Competitiveness Yearbook 2006, IMD, Geneva (2006), http://www.imd.org/wcc
10. World Economic Forum, Global Competitiveness Report 2008. Oxford University Press, New York (2008)
11. UNCTAD, World Investment report, New York and Geneva: United Nations Conference on Trade and Development (2004)

Supply Network Complexity: An Approach in a Global Aeronautic Industry in Brazil

Edison Sotolani Claudino[1] and João Gilberto Mendes dos Reis[1,2]

[1] Federal University of Grande Dourados, Postgraduate Studies Program in
Agribusiness
Dourados - Itaum Road km 12, 079804-970 Dourados, Brazil
[2] Paulista University, Postgraduate Studies Program in Production Engineering
Dr. Bacelar 1212, 04026-002 São Paulo, Brazil
edisonclaudino@ufgd.edu.br
betomendesreis@msn.com

Abstract. Operation management strategies have evolved from individual firms to clients and suppliers along the supply chain management.
Concomitantly, the use of information technology, outsourcing and globalization has increased the complexity of these chains which have been
recognized as supply networks. The aim of this study is presenting the
supply network complexity, which are networks in which are involved
products of high complexity encompassing global suppliers and clients
as well. For this purpose, we performed a study about the theme and
also presented a successful case related to the management of such network complexity in a Brazilian aeronautic industry.

Keywords: Globalization, Transnational companies, Aeronautic industry competition.

1 Introduction

In the last decades, world has evolved ever faster due to the constant improvement of the so-called Information and Communication Technology (ICT) which
together with the outsourcing of the production activities and feedstock supply
- and globalization as well - have significantly changed the scenery of the strategies in management operations [1], making them exceed the boundaries of the
individual firm. In this sense, the concepts of Supply Chain Management (SCM)
and Supply Networks [2] spring, using these new technologies for creating opportunities of business and efficiency income through the management of their
two networks: upstream and downstream.

To follow these changes, Production and Operations Management (POM)
has developed several systems and methodologies which allow a more strategic
management, from which we highlight: Just-in-Time (JIT), Total Quality Management (TQM), Flexible Manufacturing Systems (FMS), Computer Integrated
Manufacturing (CIM), Agile Manufacturing (AM), Lean Production (LP), Business Process Reengineering (BPR), Quick Response Manufacturing (QRM) and

B. Grabot et al. (Eds.): APMS 2014, Part III, IFIP AICT 440, pp. 489–496, 2014.
© IFIP International Federation for Information Processing 2014

Clean Production (CP) [1]. However, SCM springs as a major branch encompassing all these systems and methodologies aiming to increase the profitability of companies and to respond the requests from final clients.

In this context, it is worth mentioning that supply chains have been named as supply networks, due to the innumerous relationships among them. Furthermore, supply networks have become even more complex because of (i) the high unit cost, (ii) the high intensity of engineering, (iii) the characteristics of the products, which are developed to meet specific demands from customers and (iv) for the high capacity to integrate knowledge and skills [3].

In this work we named such networks as Supply Networks Complexity and they are characterized by the complexity of the final product and the relationship between global customers and suppliers. The main aim of this study was to analyze the dynamics of these complex supply chains by studying the strategies used by a Brazilian aeronautic industry in order to manage its network complexity as well as the accomplishments of this enterprise related to the management of products.

In order to develop this work a literature review on supply chain management and supply networks was performed. Based on this study, the concept of Supply Network Complexity was established, so that it was possible to examine a case study in a Brazilian aeronautic industry that succeeded in reducing design time and costs in the production of aircrafts through the management of its suppliers and global customers.

2   Supply Network Complexity

The most significant change in the paradigm of the modern business management consists in the concept that individual organizations do not compete among themselves as unique entities, but as supply chains [4]. The study of these supply chains allowed us to follow the strategies of relationships among companies, suppliers and clients. The following Figure (1) illustrates this evolution, suggesting it was developed to reflect the real business practices in a growing evolution..

As its possible to observe, in Figure 2 theres a deepening of the management activities and material flows (i.e. supply chains seen as centered processes). Moreover, recent approaches focus on supply chain management as a system (i.e. management members and their mutually beneficial relations) with clear strategic intention [5].

Supply chains have been conceptualized as a simple linear system represented by an event which depends on a series of companies interacting through dyadic relation [6]. However, the linear concept of sequential dyadic relationships simplifies and distorts the realities of modern supply chains.

Modern supply chains can be considered complex and the adaptation to changes are required. Thus, there is a need to re-conceptualize the lines of a simple linear system to a complex adaptive system of supply networks [7], [8].

The complexity of a supply chain can not be consider a simple linear structure where a small change often results in a chain reaction. When supply chain

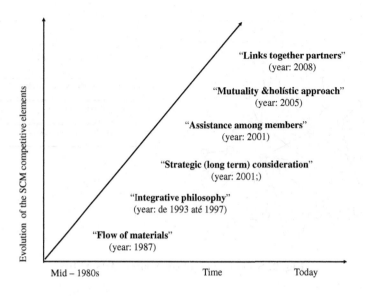

Fig. 1. Chronologic Evolution of the SCM competitive Elements. Source: Adapt [5]

complexity increases, monitoring and managing the interaction between different elements of the chain becomes more difficult [9].

Hearnshan and Wilson cited a complex approach of networks in which they propose that a supply chain is like a scale-free network (Figure 2) [10]. Thus, to reduce the vulnerability of the supply chain, the authors emphasize the need for managing constructions in redundancy, to undertake a strategy of multi-sourcing or intermediation among hubs companies, in other words, organizations that assume the responsibility of network management, either for the knowledge of the whole process, or for its economic power in the network relationships. More information about the model and BA scale-free network can be found in the work of [5].

Empirical models of the central-peripheral structure is observed in social systems of the real-world, including the flow of information in collaborative systems of researches in which pharmaceutical and biotech hubs companies collaborate closely sharing information for their mutual benefit. [10]. While all types of connections among hubs companies are possible to be found, the existence of a central-peripheral structure is further connected to the information flow since they have a closer triad structure [10].

In addition to the possible configurations and governance mechanisms for the supply networks, a company must currently not only manage its supply chain via active nodes, but also must have an adequate supervision on the supply network [9]. Thus, the identification of active and inactive members can be a strategic consideration for all the organization and part of its contingency plan related to supplier. One way to illustrate the differences between supply chains and networks can be seen in Figure 3.

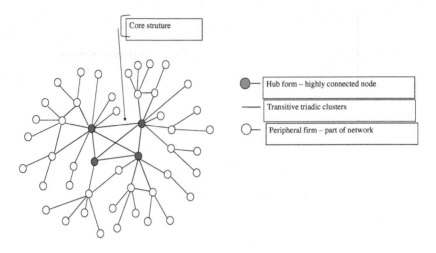

Fig. 2. Scale-free topology. Source: Adapt [10]

The supply chain is characterized by a perceivable linear structure (from raw material to final product), thus it is not totally complex, and its management is concerned to coordinate relevant flows as information, physical product and finance.

Supply networks, in turn, are an improved view of one or more supply chains, so the focus is on the net of relationships. As an example, an organization may have a connection with another company through a previous supplier who is not currently working. The integration in the supply network is more ad hoc, making it a complex, dynamic, nonlinear, based on trust and not-planned.

Moreover, supply network globalization of supply networks combined with the complexity of certain products makes the process of managing suppliers and customers a difficult task, which can only be accomplished through the use of ICTs.. Thus, such global networks of complex products that make a maximum use of these ICTs are named in this work as Supply Network Complexity.

Finally, the existing approaches towards complexity management in supply chains that can be found in literature can be structured into three essential process steps: identifying complexity drivers, measuring and evaluating the existing complexity, and developing strategies for managing complexity [11]. So, this study aim presents a case study that can show better these steps.

3   Case Study: Aeronautic Industry

The analysis of the Supply Networks Complexity leads us to a case of successful management of these networks, which is connected to a large Brazilian aircraft manufacturer. The Company is today one of the largest aviation industries in the world, acting onto the steps of project, development, manufacture, sale and

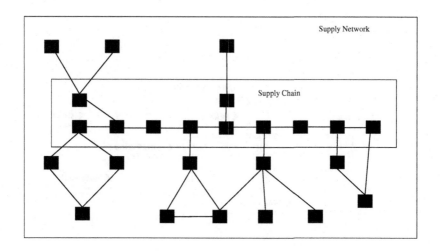

Fig. 3. Supply chain versus supply network. Source: Adapt [5]

after-sale support of aircrafts for both commercial and executive aviation, besides offering integrated solutions for defense/security and systems.

With offices and factories in many parts of the world the company is a leader in the commercial jet market with up to 120 seats, and the fifth largest manufacturer of business jets worldwide and the largest company of defense and security solutions in Brazil [12]. Figure 4 demonstrates the international factories and offices of the company.

The evolution of the company related to product development engineering, held jointly with suppliers resulted in the management of supply network in a strategic way, which was crucial to its competitive success [2]. The industry was vertically integrated, but since the '90s, has substantially altered its strategy to supply network to broaden its partnerships with key suppliers.

To illustrate this, in the '80s, the company worked with more than 500 component suppliers without substantial sharing of engineering effort and development. The aircraft development was done internally, making the resource constraints take a long period - around 8 years - for the product to be placed on the market.

However, trying to strategically manage their supply network, the organization sought for technologically strong partners around the world who were committed to a more cooperative relationship among suppliers and company from product design sharing risks and costs of development. Several companies have already been selected to develop and supply structure equipments and inside parts of the aircraft, allowing suppliers reduction from 500 to 350. This new model of supply management has generated a more technologically advanced product whose development period was reduced to five years.

In the '90s, the supply network managers of this company continued to evolve in their strategic effort to increase the speed of product launches, technological upgrading and flexibility in responding the market [2]. The development of the

Fig. 4. The global operation of aeronautic industry, with assembly lines in Brazil, China, Portugal and the USA and service operations in other locations. Source: Adapt [12]

aircraft project called ERJ 170, was innovative in several ways, either by engineering and institutional management of risk partnerships; or by the products integrated development tools (IDT) and the new management philosophy of co-design; as well for the built-edge technologies in the product, such as navigation systems fly-by-wire; and new production technologies, whose references are the techniques of lean production [3].

In project ERJ 170 one adopted the concept of group technology whose advantage is the commonality among the aircrafts and the co-design system for the development of the new aircraft project with risk partners. These two strategies are global trends, stimulated by technological nature of the product, market structure, high development cost and risk and rate of return on long-term investments, requiring from the risk partners a solid financial capacity for the investments supply. Table 1 highlights the risk partners of the project 170.

The set of risk partners to integrate the 170 - program were selected from the analysis of 85 potential partners. From these, 58 were qualified, but only 12 were chosen. Aiming to manage the project, a directory exclusively dedicated was established to organize two central working groups: (i) first group, named Integrated Program Teams (IPT), charged to ensure functional vision and quality of the design of the aircraft subsystems; (ii) the second group, named Design Build Teams (DBT), was responsible for each physical segment of the aircraft [3]. As a result of this new management model of this complex supply network, the company reduced the development period of the product to less than four years [2].

Other initiatives undertaken by the company to strengthen its relationships with the suppliers were: (i) the creation of the SAC (Suppliers Advisory Council) to improve communication, share strategic and tactical decisions and improvement of the trust level in the relationship; and (ii) the annual world congress with its suppliers, SC (Supplier Conference). The company currently has a collaborative and effective relationship with suppliers, sharing risks and benefits from the development of the product, which makes the organization a success in managing the Supply Network Complexity.

Table 1. 170 Projects risk partners (country and component)

Country	Component
Spain	Stabilizers and aft fuselage
Belgium	Slat / Central Fuselage II (Manufacturing)
USA	Interior
USA	Power generation system / APU, Tail Cut / air management system
USA	Flight control, fuel system and hydraulic system
USA	Avionics
Germany	Landing gear
Japan	Wings (board fixed attack, board fixed trail, stub, pylon, control surfaces
France	Central fuselage I/III / doors
USA	Engine / Nacelle
France	Providing the coating instrument panels and rib wings
USA	Production of transparencies / Windows

Source: Adapt [3]

4 Conclusion and Outlook

Globalization has allowed companies to have customers and suppliers around the world which makes the supply network management a complex task. Manufacturers of products that require a large number of parts and raw materials, skilled labor and high levels of security have increased this complexity and the management would not be possible without the use of modern Information and Communication Technologies. This study aimed to present that which was named Supply Network Complexity in order to represent networks that encompass this scenario.

The case study conducted in a Brazilian aeronautic industry has highlighted the results arising from the efficient management of these networks. Thus Brazil - a country where companies are generally multinational and whose main products are commodities - managed to develop a company capable of producing high-tech aircraft, security and international competitiveness.

Clearly, further studies on these Supply Network Complexity need to be performed and analyzed other segments of industrial production so that we can effectively consider this term in Production and Operations Management.

References

1. Gunasekaran, A., Ngai, E.W.T.: The future of operations management: An outlook and analysis. International Journal of Production Economics 135(2), 687–701 (2012)
2. Corra, H.L.: Gesto de Redes de Suprimento: Integrando Cadeias de Suprimento no Mundo Globalizado. 1 edn. (2010)
3. de Oliveira, L.G.: The development of complex systems projects in the aeronautical industry: The case of integrated management applied to the program embraer 170. Cadernos EBAPE. BR 7(1), 19–33 (2009)
4. Lambert, D., Cooper, M.: Issues in supply chain management - don't automate, obliterate. Industrial Marketing Management 29(1), 65–83 (2000)
5. Braziotis, C., Bourlakis, M., Rogers, H., Tannock, J.: Supply chains and supply networks: distinctions and overlaps. Supply Chain Management: An International Journal 18(6), 644–652 (2013)
6. Cox, A., Sanderson, J., Watson, G.: Supply chains and power regimes: Toward an analytic framework for managing extended networks of buyer and supplier relationships. Journal of Supply Chain Management 37(1), 28–35 (2001)
7. Pathak, S.D., Day, J.M., Nair, A., Sawaya, W.J., Kristal, M.M.: Complexity and adaptivity in supply networks: Building supply network theory using a complex adaptive systems perspective*. Decision Sciences 38(4), 547–580 (2007)
8. Li, G., Yang, H., Sun, L., Ji, P., Feng, L.: The evolutionary complexity of complex adaptive supply networks: A simulation and case study. International Journal of Production Economics 124(2), 310–330 (2010)
9. Cheng, C.Y., Chen, T.L., Chen, Y.Y.: An analysis of the structural complexity of supply chain networks. Applied Mathematical Modelling 38(9-10), 2328–2344 (2014)
10. Hearnshaw, E.J.S., Wilson, M.M.J.: A complex network approach to supply chain network theory. International Journal of Operations & Production Management 33(4), 442–469 (2013)
11. Aelker, J., Bauernhansl, T., Ehm, H.: Managing complexity in supply chains: A discussion of current approaches on the example of the semiconductor industry. Procedia CIRP 7, 79–84 (2013)
12. EMBRAER: Global presence (2014),
    http://www.embraer.com.br/en-us/conhecaembraer/presencaglobal/pages/home.aspx

Supply Chain Quality Management in Agribusiness: An Approach of Quality Management Systems in Food Supply Chains

João Gilberto Mendes dos Reis[1,2], Sivanilza Teixeira Machado[1],
Pedro Luiz de Oliveira Costa Neto[1], Rogério Monteiro[3],
and José Benedito Sacomano[1]

[1] Paulista University, Postgraduate Studies Program in Production Engineering
Dr. Bacelar 1212, 04026-002 São Paulo, Brazil
[2] Federal University of Grande Dourados, Postgraduate Studies Program in
Agribusiness
Dourados - Itaum Road km 12, 079804-970 Dourados, Brazil
[3] CEETEPS - College of Technology Zona Leste
Águia de Haia 2983, 03694-000 São Paulo, Brazil
betomendesreis@msn.com.br,
sivateixeira@yahoo.com.br,
politeleia@uol.com.br,
monteiro.rogerio@globo.com,
jbsacomano@gmail.com

Abstract. It is widely accepted that Quality Management Systems approach is indicated to ensure quality of products and services. Furthermore, Total Quality Management, Six Sigma, ISO Standards and Hoshin Kanri have established as important management systems for quality guarantee in many production processes. Unfortunately, these systems are not familiar to agribusiness companies. The aim of this study is to analyze the benefits of application of traditional QMS in food supply chains. For the purpose of analysis, this paper investigates a case study in a Poultry Slaughterhouse company. The results showed that whether the company adopted the traditional QMS, it was able to solve the problem of temperature variation in the freezing tunnel in a short period an effective way. This article is part of a work to identify Supply Chain Quality Management applications in agribusiness companies.

Keywords: TQM, Six Sigma, ISO Standards, Hoshin Kanri, Agribusiness companies.

1 Introduction

A major current focus on agriculture and livestock supply chains is how to ensure quality and food safety. The importance of quality and food safety increases due to consumers' information about products and services. Supply Chain Quality Management (SCQM) has been considered an adequate approach to manage

B. Grabot et al. (Eds.): APMS 2014, Part III, IFIP AICT 440, pp. 497–504, 2014.
© IFIP International Federation for Information Processing 2014

quality among organizations. Moreover, SCQM is a system for performance improvement that leverages opportunities created by suppliers and customers [1]. SCQM consists in the adoption of Quality Management Systems (QMS) along the whole supply chain. However, little attention has been provided to quality issues in supply chains [2]. In agribusiness, for example, researchers and firms are interested in achieving quality through the product characteristics and food safety [3], [4], [5], [6] and [7]. Therefore, it is difficult to find traditional quality management systems applied in food supply chains. This research identified that only a few authors reported applications of Total Quality Management (TQM), Six Sigma and ISO standards in food companies [8], [9] and [10].

TQM, Six Sigma, ISO standards and Hoshin Kanri (Police Deployment) have been studied for many years and they are used by different industrial companies. However, agriculture and livestock systems prefer to incorporate best practices, traceability, animal and crop control, government regulations and certifications to quality guarantee. Dora et al. argue that they did not find studies which integrate all concepts of quality like assurance, improvement, control, design and police in the food sector [4] and they established a Food Quality Management System (FQMS) to small and medium-size enterprises. Trienekens and Wognum studied the requirements of supply chain management in pork supply chains, which show the importance of quality for integrating supply chains and improve consumer confidence [11].

Although these approaches improve quality of food products, they avoid the adoption of traditional quality management systems. As a result, the chains can not be provided with knowledge and practice of these QMS.

This work examines a poultry productive chain and seeks to analyze the application of traditional QMS in problems resolution. With this aim the paper explores the production process in a Poultry Slaughterhouse. The hypothesis is that the adoption of QMS may solve the problem in an accurate way and allow company to ensure high levels of quality of products and food safety. In addition, this paper contributes to understanding of the small applicability of SCQM across food supply chains and agribusiness companies.

2   Quality Management Systems

2.1   Total Quality Management

There is a large volume of published studies describing the role of total quality management. These studies discuss and analyze the applications of TQM in industries and service operations with the purpose to show the advantages of this concept to ensure quality of products and services. TQM is applied in many organizations with the objective to improve product quality and increased customer satisfaction [12] and is divided into six elements: top management commitment; customer focus; supplier quality management; people management; continuous improvement; and process management [13].

TQM has its origin in Total Quality Control (TQC), and an administrative system improved in Japan from American ideas. Initially developed by Armand

Feigenbaum, TQC practiced in Japan is different from that originally proposed by Feigenbaum, because it is based on the participation of all sectors of the company and all the employees in studying and performing quality control.

2.2 Six Sigma

Six Sigma program is credited to Dr. Mike Harry, a statistician who was the principal founder of the Six Sigma Academy in Scottsdale, Arizona, United States. Motorola was the first U.S. company to adopt the system, followed by other organizations such as General Electric (GE) and Texas Instruments [14]. The idea behind the application consists of using statistical tools to reduce process variability.

The objective of the Six Sigma approach consists of search zero defect condition of services and products. However the goal is to reach 3.4 defects per million of opportunities and it uses a structure method named DMAIC (Define, Measure, Analyze, Improve and Control) [15].

2.3 ISO 9001 Standards

The ISO 9001 series is a designation given to quality management systems standards emerged in 1987 and became a worldwide phenomenon showing tremendous growth and dissemination across different countries [16]. In 2010, ISO 9001 was implemented in 1.109.905 companies in 178 countries [17]. ISO standards represent an international consensus on good management practices with the purpose of ensuring the supply of products that meet customer requirements and with a focus in continuous improvement [18]. Moreover, the ISO 9001 standard allows certification by assessed companies, which meets its requeriments.

2.4 Hoshin Kanri (Policy Deployment)

Policy deployment, known in Japan as Hoshin Kanri, is an administrative system for strategic management [19]. It was originally developed in Japanese industries as alternative to the concept of management by objectives [20]. To implement Hoshin Kanri, companies need (1) to provide a focus on corporate direction by setting, annually, a few strategic priorities; (2) to align the strategic priorities with local plans and programs; (3) to integrate the strategic priorities with daily management; (4) provide a structured review of the progress of the strategic priorities [19] and [20].

3 Methodology

This research was conducted in a company of food processing code PS (Poultry Slaughterhouse). The company was selected in Mato Grosso do Sul State, which is located in the center-western of Brazil. This region concentrates 10.6% of poultry production in the country [21].

The company was well characterized in the poultry respective supply chain and informations were collected from company, downstream and upstream partners. The company was evaluated with the purpose of identifying traditional QMS practices. Using traditional quality management approaches, a production process was chosen to check the advantages of implementing a QMS. After, TQM, Six Sigma, ISO standards and Hoshin Kanri were correlated with this process, emphasizing possible results of its application.

This method allows food companies to understand the importance of traditional QMS in operations management. Similarly, it enables firms to simulate the adoption of QMS providing a way of evaluating the system efficiency. A case study approach is used to permit an analysis in a real situation.

It is recognized that sample is quite small to characterize the application of the QMS in the food supply chains and unavoidable future work will be necessary. However, as the research is a case of study, this small sample does not invalidate the work results.

4   Case Study

The company operates in the frozen meat market (poultry and pork) and processing meat foods, dairy margarine, pasta, pizza and frozen vegetables. It is present in all regions of Brazil with 49 plants and its products reach consumers in 98% of Brazilian territory. Its international market involves more than 110 countries on the five continents. The company net sales in 2013 was 9,957 million Euros, where 56% in domestic market and 44% in international market. It is responsible for 20% of world trade in poultry [22].

In this study, a plant located in Brazil center-western was analyzed. It process 170 thousand poultry per day and animals are supplied by different farm producers in the region, that follow procedures established by PS. A simplified supply chain can be seen in Figure 1.

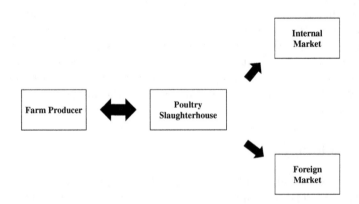

Fig. 1. Poultry Slaughterhouse supply chain

Figure 1 illustrates the main steps in this chain. Farm producers receive feed and pullets from PS and other sources. Then, the farm producers, after finishing process, send Poultry to PS where the company transforms these animals in fresh meat and industrialized products. Afterwards, these products are shipped to internal and international markets.

The company is responsible for ensuring product quality from the source to the consumer market. In the production process the quality of products is guaranteed by practices applied by company and by the Federal Inspection Service (SIF, in Portuguese language). SIF is a control system within the Ministry of Agriculture and Livestock that aims to assure quality and food security through meat origin and physical characteristics.

However, in this study, the purpose is to establish an example of the importance of application of the traditional QMS in this organization. Thus, the problem of the variability of temperature in freezing process was analyzed. To understand more clearly the problem, it is important known steps of the production process that can be seen in Figure 2.

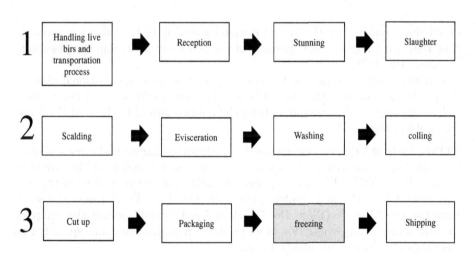

Fig. 2. Poultry slaughterhouse production process

The frozen meat is produced in a freezing tunnel (ACT. Automatic Control Tunnel), which works at temperatures between $-40\,°C$ and $35\,°C$ (Celsius degree). Products for the domestic market are shipped when the temperature reach $-12\,°C$, and the foreign market, only after $-18\,°C$. As operation of the freezing tunnel is automatic, company shell respect a standard time so that the products reaches the ideal temperature. Figure 3 shows na illustrative picture of a freezing tunnel.

The company's tunnel begun to change the temperature and time for freezing products, increasing the variability of the process. For some years, the company

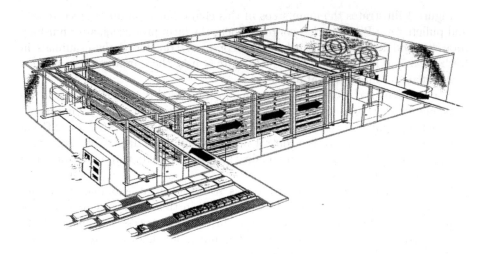

Fig. 3. ACT. Source: [23]

bored the problem, but the rise of demand forced it to try solve the problem. Now they are studying, an expansion of the plant and analyzing the possibility of change the ACT.

Our hypotheses are that, if the company had adopted a traditional QMS in the production process, they would be able to solve this issue many time before. Bellow are presented some ideas about the relationship of traditional QMS and the problem discussed.

TQM: Tools of TQM as control charts, Ishikawa's diagram and circles of quality, allowing to identify problems in a specific matter and possible corrective actions. Using TQM, PS could be able of finding out the variations in the process caused by ACT and applying solutions based on TQM tools. Moreover, tools like PDCA cycle (Plan, Do, Check and Act) should permit the company to make a continuing evaluation of its production process and consequently find answers and solutions to quality issues.

Six Sigma: Is a quality management system that aims to solve quality problems through the elimination of variation. In this specific case, the ACT presented variations in freezing temperature in comparison to the correct pattern. This variation between pattern time and real time might have been identified by quality control members of Six Sigma Belts and the corrective actions would be taken to resolve the issue.

ISO 9001 Standard: Represents a quality management system that aims to standardize process, ensuring quality of products and production processes. In this case, the variation of the ACT modifies the parameters of tunnel operation and generate ISO non-conformance, that needs to be solved by the company. Consequently the obligation of company in solving the non-conformance would permit the resolution of this problem.

Hoshing Kanri: Is a business management that can guarantee quality, because influences in the guidelines and goals set by management. Thus, these guidelines established for the production are directly related to process efficiency. So, failures in the ACT would need to be solved to ensure service guidelines and hence the quality of process and products.

5 Conclusion

The agribusiness enterprises have assured the quality of its products through sensory analysis made by consumers. Thus, the processes and activities are designed and crafted to ensure characteristics of the products to attend consumers' requirements. However, the control of the quality and food safety through physical characteristics of products does not indicate that the processes and products are controlled by quality management practices. QMS can increase the process efficiency and guarantee quality and food safety.

The case study showed that Poultry Slaughterhouse does not adopt traditional QMS. It seeks to assure quality of its products by having a SIF certificate. This certification is an obligation for the animal products in Brazil. However, this certificate was not enough to correct na ACT problem, as a consequence of the temperature variation, effect on the meat quality. If the company had implemented a traditional QMS, it would be able to solve the variation in ACT, thus ensuring quality of products and efficiency of process.

The analysis performed in this article shows that the hypotheses of adoption of QMS should solve the problems in PS in an proper way and ensure high levels of quality products and food safety is true.

One of the limitations of this paper is that only one case was be presented, which avoid the feasibility of establish a generalization of this study. So, the next steps of this research is to analyze other companies to validate the hypotheses presented.

The research about the quality in agribusiness is still in progress and is expected to interact with producers, researchers and industries in order to better understand this gap and find out solutions to guarantee improved quality of products in agribusiness companies.

References

1. Foster Jr., S.T.: Towards an understanding of supply chain quality management. Special Issue: Research in Supply Chain Quality 26(4), 461–467 (2008)
2. Mellat-Parast, M.: Supply chain quality management: An inter-organizational learning perspective. International Journal of Quality & Reliability Management 30(5), 511–529 (2013)
3. Troy, D.J., Kerry, J.P.: Consumer perception and the role of science in the meat industry. Meat Science 86(1), 214–226 (2010); special Issue: 56th International Congress of Meat Science and Technology (56th ICoMST). Jeju, Korea, August 15-20 (2010)

4. Dora, M., Kumar, M., Van Goubergen, D., Molnar, A., Gellynck, X.: Food quality management system: Reviewing assessment strategies and a feasibility study for european food small and medium-sized enterprises. Food Control 31(2), 607–616 (2013)

5. Aung, M.M., Chang, Y.S.: Temperature management for the quality assurance of a perishable food supply chain. Food Control 40(0), 198–207 (2014)

6. Aung, M.M., Chang, Y.S.: Traceability in a food supply chain: Safety and quality perspectives. Food Control 39, 172–184 (2014)

7. Chen, C., Zhang, J., Delaurentis, T.: Quality control in food supply chain management: An analytical model and case study of the adulterated milk incident in china. International Journal of Production Economics

8. Holt, G., Henson, S.: Quality assurance management in small meat manufacturers. Food Control 11(4), 319–326 (2000)

9. Kumar, M., Antony, J.: Comparing the quality management practices in UK SMEs. Industrial Management & Data Systems 108(9), 1153–1166 (2008)

10. Mensah, L.D., Julien, D.: Implementation of food safety management systems in the UK. Food Control 22(8), 1216–1225 (2011)

11. Trienekens, J., Wognum, N.: Requirements of supply chain management in differentiating european pork chains. Meat Science 95(3), 719–726 (2013)

12. Koilakuntla, M., Patyal, V.S., Modgil, S., Ekkuluri, P.: A research study on estimation of TQM 'Factors ratings' through analytical hierarchy process. Procedia Economics and Finance 3, 55–61 (2012)

13. Abusa, F.M., Gibson, P.: Experiences of TQM elements on organisational performance and future opportunities for a developing country. International Journal of Quality & Reliability Management 30(9), 920–941 (2013)

14. Mehrjerdi, Y.Z.: Six-sigma: methodology, tools and its future. Assembly Automation 31(1), 79–88 (2011)

15. Lin, C., Frank Chen, F., Wan, H-d., Min Chen, Y., Kuriger, G.: Continuous improvement of knowledge management systems using six sigma methodology. Robotics and Computer-Integrated Manufacturing 29(3), 95–103 (2013)

16. Sampaio, P., Saraiva, P., Rodrigues, A.G.: ISO 9001 certification research: questions, answers and approaches. International Journal of Quality & Reliability Management 26(1), 38–58 (2009)

17. Priede, J.: Implementation of quality management system ISO 9001 in the world and its strategic necessity. Procedia - Social and Behavioral Sciences 58, 1466–1475 (2012)

18. Quirós, J.T., do Justino, M.R.F.: A comparative analysis between certified and non-certified companies through the quality management system. International Journal of Quality & Reliability Management 30(9), 958–969 (2013)

19. Witcher, B., Butterworth, R.: Hoshin kanri: how xerox manages. Long Range Planning 32(3), 323–332 (1999)

20. Tennant, C., Roberts, P.: Hoshin kanri: Implementing the catchball process. Long Range Planning 34(3), 287–308 (2001)

21. Banco Central do Brasil: Evolução regional da atividade pecuária (July 2013), https://www.bcb.gov.br/pec/boletimregional/port/2013/07/br201307b1p.pdf

22. BRF: Annual and sustainability report 2013 (2013), http://www.brasilfoods.com/ri/siteri/web/arquivos/BRF_RA_EN_140228c.pdf

23. Scheidt, J.E.C.: O problema do tunel de congelamento. Tese de doutorado, Unicamp, Campinas (April 1996)

Development of the Auto Parts Industry in Brazil

Nivaldo Luiz Palmeri, Oduvaldo Vendrametto,
and João Gilberto Mendes dos Reis

Paulista University, Postgraduate Studies Program in Production Engineering
Dr. Bacelar 1212, 04026-002 São Paulo, Brazil
{nivaldoluiz,oduvaldov}@uol.com.br, betomendesreis@msn.com

Abstract. The purpose of this article is to demonstrate the evolution of the auto part industry regarding the Brazilian Automobile Industry. In 2013, even as Brazil ranked as the fifth largest producer of vehicles in the world, the commercial balance reached a new level of deficit. The studied hypothesis is that the national auto part industry is producing items of lesser technological value and importing items of greater value. This research highlights the importance of the technological development and the strengthening of competitiveness in the autopart industry for the success of the Inovar-Auto program.

Keywords: Auto part, Automobile industry, Inovar-Auto program.

1   Introduction

The Inovar-Auto program, developed by the Brazilian government [1] aims to reduce the number of imported auto parts in a growing domestic vehicle production. For that, the law offers tax incentives for companies that replace imported for auto parts produced in Brazil. The goal is to launch technology development in the country.

However, it can be noted in recent years that the complex auto parts tend to be imported from developed markets such as Europe, USA and Japan, while the domestic industry is responsible for complementary parts, such as the peripheral supplier. The Inovar-Auto program, implemented in 2012, still does not allow its effects to be fully observed.

Throughout its history, Brazil has been a country that tends to buy technology and not develop them; the automobile industry is an example of this behavior. Corporations throughout the whole country are all transnational. All the developed technology, even by Brazilian engineers, are linked to and patented abroad. The lack of long-term well-defined policies, development, and control stimulates import. In addition, there are difficulties in the development of technology, poor qualification of the workforce and low level of education in the country. Of the 100 largest Brazilian companies of this sector, only five develop technology and one is of national origin [2].

B. Grabot et al. (Eds.): APMS 2014, Part III, IFIP AICT 440, pp. 505–512, 2014.

This research studies the automobile and auto parts industry in Brazil from 2001 to 2012, featuring a pre-Inovar-Auto panorama. For this, the billing of the automotive and auto parts industry located in the country are evaluate, along with the volume of the import of parts.

2 Methodology

For this study, data was collected from the directories of ANFAVEA (National Association of Automobile Manufacturers) [3], DIEESE (Department of Statistics and Socioeconomic Studies) [4], and SINDIPEÇAS / ABIPEÇAS (National Association of Automotive Components Industry / Brazilian Association of Automotive Parts Industry) [5].

Once the data was identified, the next stages of the research were as following: (1) evaluation of the progress of vehicles manufacturers net sales in Brazil, including cars, light commercial vehicles, trucks and buses; (2) evaluation of the income and import of auto parts evolution, including the automobile industry, the aftermarket, exports, and intersectorial (other manufacturers) to determine the behavior of the Brazilian auto parts industry.

Objective evaluation findings have led to the billing growth of automobiles in the reference period, 2001/12 (Eq.1)

$$P = \frac{va}{vb} * 100 \tag{1}$$

Where, vb corresponds to the billing in 2001 and va in 2012.

Thus the development of the billing of vehicles in 2012 was given by:

$$P = \frac{83.676}{45.818} * 100 = 182.6 \tag{2}$$

The choice of the period between 2001 and 2012 for conducting the research is justified due to the global emphasis Brazil has been receiving, becoming the fifth largest producer of vehicles in the world. Furthermore, the crescent income of the Brazilian population favored the sales of vehicles, growing year by year, while the other sale areas find themselves stagnated. Finally, in 2012, the Inovar-Auto program was announced by the Brazilian government as a way to boost the domestic industry and stimulate the thickening of the Brazilian automotive chain.

It is important to emphasize that in the period between 2002 and 2012, the total production of automobiles (excluding CKD - Complete Knock Down) went from 1.63 million to 3.41 million units, a growth of 108.5%; with highlight to the light commercial vehicles segment that grew 251.4% during the cited period, followed by the truck sector, that presented a 216.4% growth during the same period [4].

Based on the data obtained from survey and the comparative calculations performed with the indicators of the automobile and auto parts industry, an analysis will be made of the Brazilian auto parts industry technological development.

3   Inovar-Auto

The Brazilian government's attempt to create the Inovar-Auto program is to promote technological research and enable the country's production to make more modern parts and components for the automobile industry, reducing the dependence on exportations and its consequences.

The automotive sector, due to its high competitiveness, continually invests in research and innovation. It is the third among the sectors that most invests; from 3% to 5%. Modestly, in 2013, the Inovar-Auto program proposed an initial investment of only 0.15% over the gross profit, reaching 0.5% in 2017 and furthered the application in engineering and basic technology to 0.5%, also in 2013, with a limit of 1% in 2017. Unlike to this logic, system suppliers, who are responsible globally for 60% of innovations in the segment, do not participate in the incentive to boost technological research. Therefore, the expectation of effective technological evolution is reduced [6].

The collected data leads to the hypothesis that the Brazilian industry (automakers and auto parts) are directing their production to items of smaller technological value, while they search for item of greater value available in centers such as Japan, European Union and the United States.

The main targets of the Inovar-Auto program are: (1) create favorable conditions of competitiveness for companies that produce cleaner and safer vehicles; (2) invest in the local supply chain and industrial engineering; (3) increase actions of the local R&D [3] and [4].

The consolidation of the country's competence is a necessary to maintain and improve their competitiveness. To follow this evolution, the existence of qualified suppliers in great quantities and development of global technologies is necessary, without, which the system would become fragile and dependent. Therefore, the national auto parts industry should be a priority in a proposition such as the Inovar-Auto [7].

4   Automobile and Auto Parts Industry in Brazil

The Brazilian automobile industry represents, in 2014, almost 25% of the industrial GDP and 5% of the total GDP, with billings above 100 billion dollars. Brazil has 61 industrial units among 46 cities in 10 states; with these numbers tending to increase [3].

The industry moves a chain that includes manufacturers, suppliers of raw materials, auto parts distributors, gas stations, insurance companies, repair shops, tire repair shops, media companies, and advertising agencies, among others, all interconnected and employing millions of workers [3].

The auto parts industry is directly related to the automobile industry. Their activities were initiated in the 1930s, and vigorously expanded in the 1950s. It was driven by the pioneer plan established by President Juscelino Kubitschek, who sought the introduction of a national automotive industry [8].

In 1990, the Brazilian auto parts industry began to face the scenario called globalization. The release of imported goods and economic stability encouraged the entrance of foreign products of better quality [8].

In the beginning of the XXI century, the process of global automobile industry restructuring repositioned brands and manufactures, expanding its global characteristics and enabling businesses to compete profitably in different regional markets. Taking the automakers as an example, the auto parts, machinery and equipment industry intensified its strategy of global competition, aiming to take the place of local suppliers [4].

In 2011, the trade balance of the Brazilian automobile industry has reached new level of trade deficit, reaching the 5.88 billion dollars mark: exports totaled 12.78 billion dollars, while imports totaled 18.66 billion [4].

In 2013, Brazil appeared as the fourth largest market in sales of light vehicles in the world, behind China, USA and Japan. The country has been consolidating its importance in the global market, with forecasts to double the sales by 2025; significantly increasing its share of the major brands in its market, especially Korean, Japanese and Chinese [4].

Among the foreign auto parts companies installed in Brazil, many plan to increase their investments in the country, such as the Continental company, which intends to double its production by 2015, and Magna and Dana who bought companies to strengthen their capacity. New companies are also planning to enter the country, such as the Korean companies DYMOS, Mobis, THN, and several Chinese suppliers [9].

The new industrial policy of the automotive sector (Inovar-Auto) is part of a long-term plan (2013-2017) with three main goals: (1) to stimulate investment and innovation; (2) to protect the domestic industry and (3) to growth Brazilian market against imports. Over the past five years, a sharp increase in the trade deficit and in the automotive and auto parts industry put in doubt the future of the national supply chain. This is not a small problem and it interferes in the local capacity to design parts, systems, and products. The analysis shows that Brazil's chances of becoming a center for the production and marketing of vehicle lacks technological expertise, as well as local projects with lower prices due to increased competition [10].

5   Results and Discussion

5.1   Brazilian Production and Sales of Vehicles

The growth in production of vehicles in Brazil grew alongside with the billing, from 2001 to 2012. While the production increased 188.8%, going from 1.8 million units built in 2001 to 3.4 million in 2012, the income increased from 45,818 million dollars to 83,676 million dollars during the same period of time, maintaining the balance shown in Table 1. Likewise, the profits per automobile remained stable, with a minimum cost of 22,184.77 million dollars in 2005, a maximum of 25,214.68 million dollars in 2001, and an average of 23,732.90 million dollars.

Table 1. Comparison between production and sales of vehicles

Year	Production		Billing		Billing/Production	
	Units	Growth(%)	US$ (*)	Growth(%)	US$ (*)	Growth(%)
2001	1,817,116	100.0	45,818	100.0	25,214	100.0
2002	1,791,530	98.6	43,402	94.7	24,226	96.1
2003	1,827,791	100.6	42,039	91.8	22,999	91.2
2004	2,317,227	127.5	52,009	113.5	22,444	89.0
2005	2,530,249	139.2	56,133	122.5	22,184	88.0
2006	2,612,329	143.8	60,110	131.2	23,010	91.3
2007	2,980,163	164.0	71,715	156.5	24,064	95.4
2008	3,216,381	177.0	76,245	166.4	23,705	94.0
2009	3,183,482	175.2	77,259	168.6	24,268	96.2
2010	3,646,548	200.7	86,066	187.8	23,602	93.6
2011	3,442,787	189.5	84,980	185.5	24,683	97.9
2012	3,430,604	188.8	83,676	182.6	24,391	96.7

* Million dollars
Source: Adapted [3]

5.2 Revenues of the Automobile Industry versus Auto Parts versus the Import of Auto Parts

When comparing the evolution of the automotive and auto parts industry's income between 2001 and 2012, the motor vehicles obtained a growth of 182.6%, while the auto parts grew 351.3%; sales of auto parts was 1.9 times greater than that of vehicles. During the same period, the imported auto parts presented a growth rate of 410.5%, an increase of 16.9% compared to auto parts and 2.2 times greater than that of the motor vehicles (Table 2)

The main variables used to explain the growth in auto parts import are related to the acknowledgement of the national currency towards the major currencies; increased costs of labor; elevated Brazilian tax revenue, and the relocation of new projects to more competitive countries. The combination of these variables has limited the investments of a large portion of the companies located in Brazil. These persistent factors can lead to de-industrialization of the segment [3].

5.3 Inovar-Auto Program

In an attempt to change this scenario, the federal government issued the 7819/12 - October 3, 2012, creating Program to Encourage Technological Innovation and Intensification of the Production Chain of Motor Vehicles or Inovar-Auto, aiming to support the technological development, the innovation, safety, environmental protection, energy efficiency, and quality of vehicles and auto parts [11].

A review of the government's proposition is premature, but is is possible to observe the repercussion of the program in the following recent publications:

Table 2. Billing and imports in US dollar millions

Year	Production		Billing		Billing/Production	
	Units	Growth(%)	US$ (*)	Growth(%)	US$ (*)	Growth(%)
2001	45,818	100.0	11,903	100.0	4,416	100.0
2002	43,402	94.7	11,309	95.0	4,147	93.9
2003	42,039	91.8	13,330	112.0	4,504	102.0
2004	52,009	113.5	18,548	155.8	5,825	131.9
2005	56,133	122.5	25,263	212.2	7,070	160.1
2006	60,110	131.2	28,548	239.8	7,237	163.9
2007	71,715	156.5	35,064	294.6	9,772	221.3
2008	76,245	166.4	40,992	344.4	13,558	307.0
2009	77,259	168.6	37,895	318.4	9,508	215.3
2010	86,066	187.8	49,767	418.1	14,855	336.4
2011	84,980	185.5	54,512	458.0	17,999	407.5
2012	83,676	182.6	41,818	351.3	18,129	410.5

* Million dollars
Source: Adapted [3]

Investments in the Nationalization of Motor Production in Industries Already Installed in Brazil. Toyota seeks to nationalize 65% of Brazilian motor, to be produced in the city of Porto Feliz, with an expectation of attracting 19 new suppliers and producing nationally parts such as block, cylinder head and crankshaft. The new project comes as a direct response to the Brazilian industrial policy, which until the initiation of the new regime, did not demonstrate any interest in fabricating motors in Brazil, even it being the fourth biggest importer of the country, importing 2.5 billion dollars and with a trade deficit of 1.7 billion dollars [12].

Nationalization of Engines and Components Made by Independent Developers. With the Inovar-Auto program, Cummins rises nationalization. Most of the car motors sold in Brazil are imported from China and receives only minor national contributions. The focal point before the new automotive regime was always the lowest cost and, often, the nationalization ceased to be a good option. Now the company seeks to offer products and components (turbochargers and after-treatment systems) with higher domestic content. [13].

Critics on the Success of Auto Innovate Program. Inovar-Auto protects the profit of inefficient car makers. So far Inovar-Auto program brought no solution to the lack of competitiveness of the domestic automotive industry. After its first year of operation, the Brazilian government's program, which aimed to increase technological inclusion and competitiveness in the domestic automotive industry, did not solve the efficiency problem. Production costs remain as high as ever, above the main competing countries, and the productivity continues to worsen [6].

Research and Development Projects (R&D). are blocked by the Ministry of Science, Technology and Innovation (MCTI), due to the lack of definition of what could be considered by the Lei do Bem (Law of Good). The 'Good Law' consolidates tax incentives that corporations can automatically benefit from, as long as they carry out technological research and development of technological innovation. MCTI blocks car makers in the 'Good Law', in the most recent list, 787 companies had their project approved by the 'Good Law' and 218 were cut off for presenting information inaccurate or inconsistent with the law. No vehicle manufacturer installed in Brazil when through the MCTI analysis, due to doubts on the actual application of resources in processes of R&D. All the initiatives of vehicle manufacturers have been omitted until the release of a better definition of what can be considered research and development for the sector [14].

6   Conclusion and Outlook

The practice of the Inovar-Auto program already increased foreign investment. However, as more parts are produced on Brazilian soil, more automakers buy parts and components abroad. Without technological inclusion and with the increase in competitiveness among the automotive parts industry, along with the decrease in other factors that undermine the efficiency of the national automotive industry, the chances of the Inovar-Auto program's success is small.

In this scenario, the ability of the Brazilian government in aligning the technological evolution of the domestic industry with the interests of foreign industries, backed by a consistent long-term policy, is fundamental for the reverse the current situation and the promotion of the long-awaited sustainable development.

References

1. Brasil: Lei 12.715/2012 (September 2012),
   http://www.planalto.gov.br/ccivil_03/_ato2011-2014/2012/lei/l12715.htm
2. dos Reis, J.G.M., de Oliveira Costa Neto, P.L.: Method for quality appraisal in supply networks. In: Emmanouilidis, C., Taisch, M., Kiritsis, D. (eds.) APMS 2012, Part II. IFIP AICT, vol. 398, pp. 519–526. Springer, Heidelberg (2013), http://dx.doi.org/10.1007/978-3-642-40361-3_66
3. Brazilian Automotive Industry Association: Brazilian Automotive Industry Yearbook. Centro de Documentação da Indústria Automobilistica - CEDOC, São Paulo (2014), http://www.anfavea.com.br/anuario.html
4. DIEESE: A indústria automobilistica no Brasil: diagnóstico do setor e análise do novo regime automotivo (2012),
   http://www.smabc.org.br/Interag/temp_img/%7B57336FD0-AA1A-4ED1-92AA-DE866CE178DA%7D_diagnostico%20do%20setor%20automotivo.uv.pdf
5. da Indústria de Componentes para Veículos Automotores Sindipeças, S.N.: Brazilian autoparts industry performance (2012),
   http://www.sindipecas.org.br/arquivos/Desempenho_Autopecas_2012.pdf
6. Kutney, P.: Inovar-auto protege o lucro de montadoras ineficientes (2014),
   http://www.automotivebusiness.com.br/artigo/827

7. Agência Brasileira de Desenvolvimento Industrial: Estudo prospectivo setorial automotivo (2009), http://www.abdi.com.br/Estudo/Automotivo.pdf

8. Rocha, A., Perrota, R., Vendrametto, R., Monteiro Junior, J.: Industrial warehouse under computerized customs control regime: some evidences from brazil. In: Managing Complexity: Challenges for Industrial and Operations Management, Abepro, Valladolid, pp. 1–12 (2013)

9. Karasawa, T.: The strategy of japanese autoparts companies in Brazil (2013), http://www.automotiva-poliusp.org/wp-content/uploads/2013/03/Karasawa-vfinal.pdf

10. Ibusuki, U., Kobayashi, H., Jin, Y.: Asian automobile manufacturers strategies in Brazil: impact of the new automotive policy (INOVAR-AUTO), Paris (2013), http://gerpisa.org/en/node/2108

11. Brasil: Decreto 7.819/2012 (2012), http://www.planalto.gov.br/ccivil_03/_ato2011-2014/2012/Decreto/D7819.htm

12. Kutney, P.: Toyota busca 65% de nacionalizao para motor brasileiro a ser feito em porto feliz (2014), http://www.automotivebusiness.com.br/noticia/19009

13. Riatto, G.: Com inovar-auto, cummins eleva nacionalizao (2014), http://www.automotivebusiness.com.br/noticia/19229

14. Kutney, P.: MCTI barra montadoras na lei do bem (2014), http://www.automotivebusiness.com.br/noticia/19326

A Macro Sectorial Study of Semiconductor Production

Antônio Sérgio Brejão, Marcos de Oliveira Morais, and Oduvaldo Vendrametto

Paulista University-UNIP, Postgraduate Studies Program in Production Engineering,
Dr. Bacelar St. 1212, São Paulo, Brazil
prof.sergiobrejao@uol.com.br

Abstract. The increasing demand of electronic components has expanded business and investment in research. Noteworthy is the development of materials, specifically semiconductors. This study analyzes the macro sector of semiconductor production and the cyclical growth prospects of international trade and investment in this sector. Through a quantitative exploratory study it was possible to identify in the cyclical context the recent insertion of Brazil in the semiconductor production scenario with a growing view in the industry.

Keywords: Production of Semiconductors, Electronic Components, International Trade.

1 Introduction

The conjunctural issues in the semiconductor manufacturing industry can give the companies opportunities of being more competitive. To be competitive, the company requires planning, research, development of new manufacturing processes, primarily in technology, skilled labor, efficiency, profitability, and investment. In Brazil, new production models, macroeconomic policies and the growth of technologies are making the electronic industries more specialized, thus increasing the value added to the product and/or process. The increase in these processes and projects that are improved, well-defined and strategically productive can provide a higher competitive advantage to the country.

Global economies are leading the productive semiconductor industry with significant production, sales and employment generation. These economies have previously defined strategies for all production processes, making them more competitive.

2 Methodology

The approach will be the quantitative exploratory research with cyclical and macro sectorial analysis of import, export, production and national and international investments in the semiconductor industry.

B. Grabot et al. (Eds.): APMS 2014, Part III, IFIP AICT 440, pp. 513–520, 2014.

3   Theoretical Framework

3.1   Processes of Semiconductor Production

The semiconductor fabrication begins with the production of wafers, namely a thin, round slice of a semiconductor material ranging in size from 152.4 mm to 304.8 mm in diameter. The finished wafer is approximately 15mm thick. After the production of wafers, integrated circuits that generate microprocessors and chips are assembled [1; 14].

3.2   Semiconductor Production in Brazil

Brazilian Company of Semiconductors - CBS was supported by the government through the Program of Technological Development Support for the Semiconductor Industry - PADIS. The unit installed in Minas Gerais was formed with capital from German companies and Brazilian Bank for Economic and Social Development - BNDES. The company will manufacture electronic integrated circuits assembled, unassembled or in the form of discs (wafers) that have not been cut into chips yet. Incentives for semiconductor plants are a priority of the new industrial policy of the country. Upon qualification, CBS will produce circuits with tax exemptions, and incentives will expire in 2022 [2].

Brazilian government's strategic option for a sustainable development model focused on industry competitiveness was consolidated through the Greater Brazil Plan - PBM. Such plan encourages the productive sector in its efforts to technological development and innovation, including mechanisms to support business expenditure on research and development. The support includes financial, tax and regulatory instruments to encourage investments [3].

In 2005 the activity in the chip design center was started at the National Center for Advanced Electronic Technology - CEITEC, with the announcement of CI-Brazil program to support the design of commercial chips in the country. In 2008, federal authorization for the institutionalization of a public company in semiconductors, named CEITEC, was conferred by Federal Law N° 11759/2008, and such company was operated judicially in the year 2009 in order to encompass the previous operations of the Center Design of CEITEC [4].

CEITEC is a public company linked to the Ministry of Science, Technology and Innovation - MCTI that operates in the semiconductor industry by developing solutions for automatic identification (Radio Frequency Identification and smartcards) and specific applications [5]. As an extension of the PBM, law N° 11484 was approved in 2007, granting incentives to industries of digital TV equipment and semiconductor electronic components and rules on the intellectual property protection of topographies of integrated circuits, thus instituting PADIS, whose purpose is to support technology development for the semiconductor industry in Brazil [6].

Also in this context, the Federal Revenue of Brazil – RFB, by Normative Instruction N° 852, dated June 13, 2008, established procedures to authorize the Program of Technological Development Support for the Semiconductor Industry in the country (PADIS) [7].

3.3   Brazilian Foreign Trade

According to Foundation for Research Support of the State of Sao Paulo - FAPESP magazine, the country exports metallurgical silicon at US$ 2/kg. After purified abroad, the silicon is transformed into sheets used in the manufacture of semiconductors or photovoltaic cells, and the cost in that stage ranges between US$ 50 and US$ 1,000, depending on the purity and crystallinity [8].

According to   Brazilian Association of Electrical and Electronics Industry - ABINEE, the trade balance of the appliances and electronics sector in the period from January to November 2013 showed the following results: exports of US$ 6.69 billion and imports of US$ 40.48 billion, thus generating a deficit of US$ 33.79 billion in the trade balance of electronics products. This result was 11% higher than the occurred in the same period in 2012 (US$ 30.35 billion) [9].

3.3.1   Imports and Exports

For CBS the rate of import duty levied on imported goods was reduced to zero for products such as machinery, apparatus, tools, equipment, computer tools - software for incorporation into their fixed assets, intended for tunneling activities and testing of electronic semiconductor devices [2].

Imports of electrical and electronic components totaled US$ 2.0 billion, being 14.7% higher than those occurring in November 2012, highlighting the components for telecommunications and semiconductors, which together totaled almost US$ 1 billion [10]. The three most imported items in such industry were: components for telecommunications (US$ 6.2 billion); semiconductors (US$ 4.9 billion) and computer components (US$ 3.0 billion) [10].

The Trade Balance of the components segment for the period 2002-2008 (Figures 1 and 2) had a small participation in the import and export of semiconductors and, in accordance with the BNDES, imports of discrete semiconductors (diodes, transistors, photodetectors and photoemitters) reached US$ 423.1 million and exports totaled US$ 29.6 million data is from September 2008 [4].

3.3.2   International Trade

The Semiconductor Industry Association - SIA, representing U.S. leadership in semiconductor manufacture and design, announced that worldwide semiconductor sales in 2013 reached $ 305.6 billion, the highest annual total ever in the industry, and an increase of 4.8% in relation to the 2012 total of $ 291.6 billion. Global sales in December 2013 totaled $ 26.6 billion, marking the strongest amount recorded in December, while December sales in the Americas increased 17.3% compared to the same period of the previous year [11; 12].

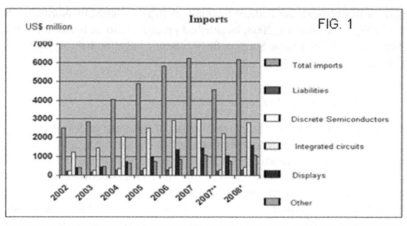

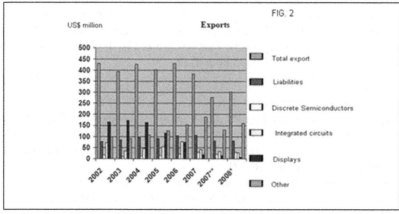

* until September 2008 ** until September 2007

Fig. 1. and **Fig. 2.** Adapted from Trade Balance of Components Segment Secex Aggregation
BNDES [4]

A research conducted by KPMG U.S. indicated that, worldwide, the semiconductor
market is extremely relevant, reaching a turnover of US$ 295 billion in 2010, against
US$ 220 billion in 2009, and that the segment generates 200,000 jobs, according to
the SIA [13]. Worldwide, some companies lead the semiconductor production as presented in (Table 1) in the biennium 2007/2008.

Table 1. Ranking of the top three semiconductor companies

Ranking 2007/08	Companies	Sales 2007 (US$ Bi)	Sales 2008 (US$ Bi)
1	INTEL	33.9	34.1
2	SAMSUNG	19.7	17.9
3	TEXAS INSTRUMENTS	12.3	11.5

Source: Adapted from BNDES - iSuppli, 2008 [4].

In Figure 3, BNDES presents a more updated scenario that shows a reduction of global semiconductor production between 2008 and 2011. With respect to investments in the semiconductor industry in the period of 2008-2011 (Figure 4), it is presented a sharp decline with signs of recovery in 2011.

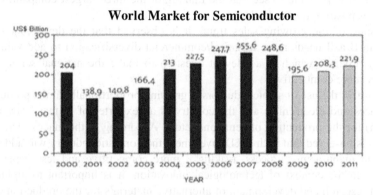

Fig. 3. World Market for Semiconductors (Adapted from BNDES *apud* SAI) [15]

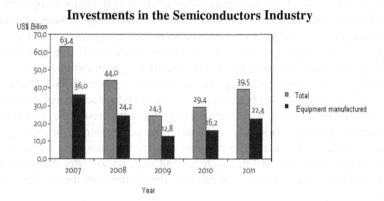

Fig. 4. Investments in the sector (Adapted from BNDES *apud* Gamerd; Fabtech) [15]

4   Results and Discussion

In Brazil, implementation processes for semiconductor production occurred in 2005, with the creation of CEITEC and, subsequently, various legal and tax incentives were adopted for the development of semiconductor and hence the creation of new businesses. On the national scenario of companies in the electronics industry subsystem, imports of semiconductors in 2013 grew 10% compared to 2012 with increasing trend.

There was a significant deficit in the trade balance of Brazil in the field of appliances and electronics, which includes semiconductors. Even so, discreetly, Brazil entered the international scenario of semiconductors export. The research shows the importance of the development of semiconductors with an increasing demand in many countries of the world and that, in 2013, the highest sales of semiconductors was recorded, in the order of 4.8%, according to ABINEE [10]. Semiconductors are among the most imported products in Brazil, with a variation of 10% in the period of 2012/2013. In 2007/2008, the sector had an important sales scenario, where in (Table 1) it is possible to see that the ranking of the three largest companies in US$ billions is positive for the leader.

Despite of the growing sales trend, it is observed that the development of the sector in Brazil needs more technical/commercial diversification to add value to the primary product, which is a relevant question to make the national semiconductor industry more competitive.

In Brazil, the use of semiconductors is growing proportionally to the production of appliances and electronics, and the country is an exporter of primary raw material (silicon) for the production of semiconductors. According to the macro sectorial scenario, it is observed that with R&D investment the domestic industry will add value to the input manufacture process, making it more competitive and less dependent on imports. In the context of technological innovation, it is important to highlight the need of research and development of alternative materials for the production of semiconductor, such as niobium, since Brazil is the largest global producer, with a share of 96% of the market [16]. Brazil exports silicon, which is the main component for the production of semiconductors, which after purification and processing abroad return to the country as finished product, with a much higher aggregate cost, making obvious the need for investments in the sector. However, such export does not bring great benefits to the country because the added value is low, with the trading of product at US$ 2.0/Kg, while after processing abroad it can cost around US$ 1000, depending on the degree of purity, thus obtaining an expressive and attractive market value.

Although speculatively, it is necessary to mention that researches on the quantum computer are growing worldwide. If feasible, the conversion of physical principles into technological equipment with properties where the transistors are not used will have a strong impact on the semiconductor industry, reason why the participants of the semiconductor chain must pay attention to the evolution of the quantum computer research.

5   Conclusion

As noted in the article, it is a sector in full development. Additionally to investments in technology, the issue of qualification of the workforce should be considered in a broader and strategic project for the country.

Upon the growing demand, companies in the electronics sector have been seeking for new technologies and new processes in order to meet their productive and economic needs. Strategies should be defined for optimized production processes and public/private investments, thus generating greater competitiveness. National companies will be more competitive if they start using well-defined strategies developed by the R&D sector of the government and organizations that facilitate investment to meet the demand.

It is observed that there is a structured and measured design over the years for such process, allowing for a guaranteed repeatability, thus favoring the industry. In the macro sectorial environment, the semiconductor industry is booming with a strong tendency to adjust alternative materials.

References

1. Companhia Brasileira de Semicondutores: Caracterização do Empreendimento (February 2011),
   http://www.semad.mg.gov.br/images/stories/Robson/Velhas2011/
   9.1-cia-semicondutores-pu.pdf (accessed on: February 20, 2014)
2. Sociedade Brasileira de Microeletrônica: Companhia Brasileira de Semicondutores terá incentivos até 2022 (February 2014),
   http://www.sbmicro.org.br/index.php?option=content&task=view
   &id=218&Itemid=2 (accessed on: February 28, 2014)
3. Brasil Maior: Agendas Estratégicas Setoriais (2013),
   http://www.brasilmaior.mdic.gov.br/images/data/201304/d874d3
   cdbd3a7e5d9cf32a28a3b083b0.pdf (accessed on: March 12, 2014)
4. BAMPI, S (Coord.) Perspectivas do investimento em eletrônica. Rio de Janeiro: UFRJ, Instituto de Economia, 2008/2009. 272 p. Relatório integrante da pesquisa. "Perspectivas do Investimento no Brasil", em parceria com o Instituto de Economia da UNICAMP, financiada pelo BNDES http://www.projetopib.org/?p=documentos (2009), projeto PIB e Perspectivas do Investimento no Brasil,
   http://www.bndes.gov.br/SiteBNDES/export/sites/default/bndes
   _pt/Galerias/Arquivos/empresa/pesquisa/pib/pib_eletronica.pd
   f (accessed on: March 7, 2014)
5. Diário Oficial da União (November 2008),
   http://www.ceitec-sa.com/assets/documentos/acesso_
   informacao/Decreto_6638_de_07112008_e_Estatuto_Social.pdf
   (accessed on: February 28, 2014)
6. Brasil: Lei nº 11.484, de 31 de maio de 2007, Do Apoio ao Desenvolvimento Tecnológico da Indústria de Semicondutores (2007),
   http://www.planalto.gov.br/ccivil_03/_ato2007-2010/2007/lei/
   111484.htm (accessed on: February 28, 2014)
7. Brasil: Instrução Normativa RFB nº 852, de 13 de junho de 2008, Programa de Apoio ao Desenvolvimento Tecnológico da Indústria de Semicondutores (Padis) (2008),
   http://www.receita.fazenda.gov.br/Legislacao/Ins/2008/in8522
   008.htm (accessed on: February 28, 2014)
8. FAPESP: Silício brasileiro para células solares Edição 197 (July 2012),
   http://revistapesquisa.fapesp.br/2012/07/16/silicio-
   brasileiro-para-celulas-solares/ (accessed on: Februay 13, 2014)
9. ABINEE – Associação Brasileira da Indústria Elétrica e Eletrônica: Balança Comercial (January/February 2014),
   http://www.abinee.org.br/abinee/decon/decon14.htm (accessed on: March 6, 2014)

10. ABINEE – Associação Brasileira da Indústria Elétrica e Eletrônica: Balança Comercial: do comércio exterior brasileiro (January/February 2014), http://www.abinee.org.br/abinee/decon/decon10.htm (accessed on: February 20, 2014)
11. Diário Comércio Indústria & Serviços: Setor de semicondutores apresenta vendas recordes em 2013 (February 2014), http://www.dci.com.br/pr-newswire/setor-de-semicondutores-apresenta-vendas-recordes-em-2013-id382545.html (accessed on: February 20, 2014)
12. PRNewswire: Semiconductor Industry Posts Record Sales in 2013 (February 2014), http://www.prnewswire.com/news-releases/semiconductor-industry-posts-record-sales-in-2013-243300871.html (accessed on: February 20, 2014)
13. KPMG: Enquanto Brasil tenta inserção, mercado de semicondutores (October 2011), http://www.kpmg.com/br/pt/estudos_analises/artigosepublicacoes/paginas/release-mercado-de-semicondutores.aspx (accessed on: February 20, 2014)
14. Pereira, A.L.: O que são wafers (May 2012), http://www.tecmundo.com.br/o-que-e/23660-o-que-sao-wafers-.htm#ixzz2tgGsIZ5g (accessed on: February 18, 2014)
15. Gutierrez, R.M.V., Mendes, L.R.: Complexo eletrônico: o projeto em microeletrônica no Brasil (July 2010), http://www.bndes.gov.br/SiteBNDES/export/sites/default/bndes_pt/Galerias/Arquivos/conhecimento/bnset/set3004.pdf (accessed on: March 31, 2014)
16. Instituto Brasileiro de Mineração: Nióbio (April 2014), http://www.ibram.org.br/sites/1300/1382/00000042.pdf (accessed on: April 15, 2014)

Integration of Decision Support Modules to Identify the Priority of Risk of Failure in Topside Piping Equipment: An Industrial Case Study from the NCS

A.M.N.D.B. Seneviratne and R.M. Chandima Ratnayake

University of Stavanger, Stavanger, Norway
{chandima.ratnayake,dammika.seneviratne}@uis.no

Abstract. The identification and prioritization of locations that have potential for failure (also referred to as thickness measurement locations (TMLs)) in the in-service inspection planning of offshore topside piping equipment requires a significant amount of data analysis together with relevant information. In this context, planning personnel analyze data and information retrieved from piping inspection databases through enterprise resource planning (ERP) software to investigate possible degradation trends in order to recognize the TMLs that have reached a critical level. It is observed that suboptimal prioritization occurs due to time restriction vs. amount of data and/or information that has to be evaluated. The suboptimal prioritization omits some of the critical TMLs, increasing the risk of failures whilst also increasing cost due to taking non-critical TMLs into inspection. Therefore, this manuscript illustrates an approach to integrate the decision support modules (DSMs) via an artificial neural network model for the optimum prioritization.

Keywords: In-service inspection planning, topside piping equipment, decision support modules, thickness measurement locations, artificial neural networks, ERP software.

1 Introduction

DSMs are used in the identification of possible failure locations in offshore topside piping equipment. The base of most DSMs is empirical engineering analysis of systems/equipment. The identification of possible failure location (TMLs) is a major part of inspection planning in offshore oil and gas production and process facilities (OO&G P&PFs) (Ratnayake and Markeset, 2010). Inspection planning is one of the key elements in maintaining the technical integrity of aging offshore production and process facilities (OP&PFs) (Ratnayake, 2012a). Standards, for instance Norsok Z-008, DNV RP-G101 and API 581, guide the operators and authorities in carrying out and maintaining inspection activities according to the rules and regulations defined by the governing authorities (Norsok Z-008, 2011; DNV RP G101, 2010; API 581, 2008).

B. Grabot et al. (Eds.): APMS 2014, Part III, IFIP AICT 440, pp. 521–529, 2014.

Inspection planning is an essential task in maintaining asset integrity at a prede-fined level in OP&PFs (Ratnayake, 2012c). In particular, of the process equipment in the OP&PFs, topside piping equipment, for instance, piping, valves, tanks, etc., un-dergoes in-service inspections to maintain the required health, safety, environment and quality (HSE&Q) limits imposed by the regulatory authorities on the Norwegian continental shelf (NCS) (Ratnayake, 2012b). The large amount of historical data and information is analyzed during the in-service inspection planning process, mainly to identify the critical TMLs for inspections (Ratnayake, 2013). The data is analyzed by field experts who have gathered experience in the inspection planning field for nu-merous years. The data is analyzed considering different scenarios (perspectives). For instance, the corrosion trends, erosion trends, fluid flow variations (turbulences) are considered in identifying the critical TMLs (Ratnayake et al., 2011). Therefore, DSMs developed to identify corrosion trends, flow patterns, etc., are helpful for the inspec-tion planning personnel in identifying the critical TMLs.

Researchers have developed different degradation prediction models for hydrocar-bon piping, which use corrosion and erosion empirical formulae. For instance, Nesic (2007), Nesic et al. (2009) and Norsok M-506 (2005) have developed a number of corrosion models for the use of hydrocarbon piping equipment for production and process facilities. Furthermore, erosion models developed in DNV RP O501 (2007) are used in the industry to identify erosive locations. The stress identification models are important in the identification of the wall thinning and crack propagation of equipment (Alvarado et al., 2007). Flow pattern identification models are also impor-tant in recognizing the critical vortexes developed inside the equipment under the multiphase flow, which generate erosion corrosion (Valle, 1998; Ferre et al., 1996). Moreover, Srinivasan et al. have developed a risk analysis model based on possible corrosion in petrochemical piping equipment (Srinivasan and Sueth, 2011). A DSM, which evaluates the risk level of TMLs based on the technical condition, has been developed by Seneviratne and Ratnayake (2013). However, there is limited use of the above models in the inspection planning field in identification of critical TMLs.

Within the industry, owner/operator specific software modules are used for re-cording and storing the piping and degradation data and information (Ratnayake, 2012a). Moreover, some of these modules are used for the basic analysis of the deg-radation rates of TMLs based on the measurements carried out in the field. The link-ing of the DSMs for the identification of the critical TMLs to the basic ERP software modules, for instance SAP, RIS etc., will improve the quality of recommendation regarding critical equipment for the inspections.

The ERP based software offers flexibility in integrating other software modules (Kahkonen and Smolander, 2013). The use of DSMs is specific to the particular in-dustrial case in which it is used and special attention is needed in integrating into a common ERP system. Kahkonen and Smolander (2013) have surveyed the develop-ment of the integration of DSMs into ERP systems and have stated that the integration must be work specific. Therefore, the manuscript suggests a methodology for integrat-ing the DSMs used in the inspection planning process into the existing ERP systems in the in-service inspection planning of offshore topside piping equipment using arti-ficial neural networks (ANNs).

The ANN is greatly used in data prioritization applications. ANN applications are used by Knapp and Wang (1992) and Becraft and Lee (1993) in manufacturing industries for prioritizing failures. Knapp and Wang (1992) used the ANNs for the recognition and prioritization of failure propagation by employing fluctuated data. Becraft and Lee (1993) developed a system using ANNs for fault diagnosis in chemical process plants under high risks. However, ANNs have relatively less use in the O&G industry for prioritizing purposes. The use of an ANN in this study is for the replacement of human judgment. The ANN model prioritizes the critical TMLs according to the criticality given by the DSMs. The ANN models try to imitate the inspection planner and analyze the prioritization like humans. The suggested neural network approach will be a very suitable method for replacing the humans involved in the prioritization system for TMLs. The background of the problem is illustrated in Section 2 of the manuscript, while the methodology is explained in Section 3. System development is explained in Sections 4 and Section 5 presents the concluding remarks.

2   Background

The current in-service inspection planning processes for OP&PFs involve several techniques, used worldwide, which are standardized by different standardization organizations. One of the widely used methods is risk based inspection (RBI), which is explained in the standards, for instance, API (2002, 2008) and DNV (2010).

After the risk assessment (based on RBI) for the equipment in the plant, inspection, test, maintenance and modification activities are planned based on the plants' historical and condition monitoring data. The inspection or maintenance plans reflects the risk (probability and consequence) of the equipment which tends to fail and the philosophy to maintain the fitness of equipment for service by detecting, preventing, controlling and mitigating. The condition of equipment is identified after inspections and necessary actions are taken for maintenance/modifications or re-inspections, if the equipment is not fit for the service.

The inspection planning process consists of several steps. The overall outcome of the inspection planning process is to identify the TMLs for inspections, allocate resources for inspections, and record the measurements and analysis of measurements for further evaluations. Furthermore, a quality inspection program aims to reduce plant downtime, minimize the cost and increase the effectiveness of the inspections.

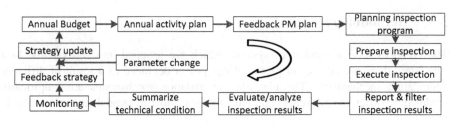

Fig. 1. Inspection planning process

The inspection planning process discussed above consists of the analysis of a vast amount of data with field experience in the identification of possible TMLs for inspections. The data and information are retrieved from condition monitoring systems, field measurements and standards. The TML analysis is performed by considering the historical thickness measurement data, degradation rates, potential degradation locations and potential failure locations. Therefore, the identification and prioritization of critical TMLs in a subsystem is a major part of the inspection planning process, as illustrated in figure 1 (Ratnayake, 2012b).

In handling and recording data, most of the piping inspection data bases (PIDBs) use the tag number or functional location, which is a number given to the specific equipment in a plant subsystem (Ratnayake, 2014). The system, subsystem and equipment (tag/functional location) numbering is illustrated in the industrial standards, for instance, DNV-RP-G101 (2010). The tag/functional location hierarchy is illustrated in figure 2. The data, for instance measurements from NDE equipment, trend analysis, equipment drawings, pictures, documents, data files and videos, are stored in PIDBs under the tag/functional location number.

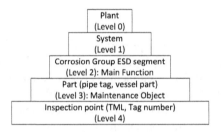

Fig. 2. Equipment level hierarchy

In aging OP&PFs, due to the effects of years of operational process cycles, the risk level of the plant equipment varies and the initial RBI assessments change over time. Therefore, inspection planning personnel use their experience and knowledge of the flow conditions and equipment condition to identify and prioritize the critical TMLs for inspection planning. This approach is on an ad hoc basis, and the quality of TML prioritization depends on the expertise of the planning personnel. Therefore, this manuscript discusses the utilization and integration of DSMs, for instance degradation prediction models, flow condition models, technical condition models, etc., using ANN to prioritize the critical TMLs for inspection planning purposes.

3   Methodology

The OP&PFs have a number of systems which are grouped into subsystems. In a subsystem there are number of pieces of equipment degraded as a result of different degradation mechanisms. The identified degradation mechanisms are empirically modeled by different researchers and industrialists. Most of these degradation models are formed as DSMs to identify the critical TMLs in the subsystem. Each DSM prioritizes the TMLs based on its empirical formula. By applying different DSMs, a different prioritization rank of TMLs is obtained. In current industrial practice, field experts make the final cumulative prioritization using their expertise and knowledge. Therefore, for a proper cumulative prioritization, a deployment of prioritization mechanisms is needed. The artificial intelligence techniques are appropriate in representing human knowledge in the prioritization process. Therefore, in this study an ANN (trained multilayer perceptron) model is proposed to obtain the cumulative prioritization to discover the critical TMLs in a subsystem. The method is shown in figure 3.

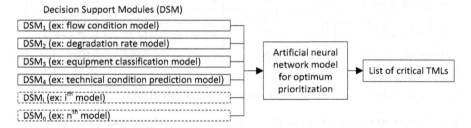

Fig. 3. ANN model for cumulative TML prioritization

3.1 Decision Support Modules

DSMs are used in the O&G industry for various purposes, especially the analysis and identification of critical TMLs. By using the DSMs in the inspection planning process, the TMLs are prioritized according to criticality. The prioritization of TMLs in a system by a selected number of DSMs is shown in figure 3. The individual prioritizations of the DSMs are analyzed by the experts to identify the critical TMLs. In this process the experts prioritize the DSMs' outcome, according to the significance of the importance of the decision support module. Then the most significant decision support module outcome is analyzed for TML prioritization. Moreover, by evaluating all the outcomes of the DSMs, a cumulative prioritization of the TMLs is made for the recommendation of the optimum prioritization of possible failure of TMLs. An example of TMLs of a subsystem prioritized according to the individual decision support module and the decision support module prioritization is shown in Table 01.

The DSM prioritization numbers are: P_{DMS1}, P_{DMS2}, P_{DMS3}, .., P_{DMSi}, .., P_{DMSn}. In an application, the DSM prioritization numbers are to be assigned with real numbers according to the reflection of the field experts. n is the maximum number of DSMs used for the prioritization of TMLs in the subsystem.

The TML prioritization numbers are: P_{1j}, P_{2j}, P_{3j}, ..., P_{ij}, ..., P_{nj},

$DSM_i = i^{th}$ DSM number; Inspection point $j = j^{th}$ inspection point (TML) number.

The prioritization from the DSM for each inspection point (TML) has been assigned according to the total number of inspection points in the system or on a ranking weight basis (based on the risk levels of TMLs).

Table 1. TML prioritization by DSM and DSM prioritization

	TML criticality prioritization DSM $_1$	TML criticality prioritization DSM $_2$	TML criticality prioritization DSM $_3$	TML criticality prioritization DSM $_i$	TML criticality prioritization DSM $_n$
DSM prioritization	P$_{DMS1}$	P$_{DMS2}$	P$_{DMS3}$	P$_{DMSi}$	P$_{DMSn}$
TML number					
Inspection point 1	P_{11}	P_{21}	P_{31}	P_{i1}	P_{n1}
Inspection point 2	P_{12}	P_{22}	P_{32}	P_{i2}	P_{n2}
Inspection point 3	P_{13}	P_{23}	P_{33}	P_{i3}	P_{n3}
...	...	...	...	...	...
Inspection point j	P_{1j}	P_{2j}	P_{3j}	P_{ij}	P_{nj}
...	...	...	...	...	...
Inspection point n	P_{1n}	P_{2n}	P_{3n}	P_{in}	P_{nn}

3.2   Use of Artificial Neural Networks in TML Prioritizing

In this proposed methodology, a prediction model is developed using the ANN technique and applied to the prioritized TML ranking from the DSMs to obtain a cumulative prioritization. The literature provides a number of different ANN architectures in the prioritization applications. Different types of neural networks are synthesized and, according to the research objectives, a multilayer feed forward ANN is used in this research study. The input value for each node of the ANN model will be (P_{ij}, P_{DMSi}). The output of the ANN model will be PC$_{ANNj}$ where PC$_{ANNj}$ is the cumulative prioritization number for the inspection point (TML) j.

4   Development of the Proposed Model

A subsystem in one of the matured OP&PFs is selected and the possible degradation mechanisms are identified to select the needed DSMs. The steps for the development, theoretical testing and validation of the proposed model are as follows: 1). Identify the subsystem degradation trends and failure mechanisms to select DSMs for identifying critical TMLs; 2). Obtain the experts' view on prioritization of TMLs and DSMs; 3). Build a priority list of TMLs and the DSMs with the view of the experts; 4.) Define the multilayer feed forward perceptron ANN model with the appropriate number of nodes (similar to DSMs used) and one hidden layer to replace the field experts' decisions; 5.) Define training data for the neural network from the experts' prioritization on TMLs and DSMs; 6.) Generate the test data for the neural network by running each DSM individually on the subsystem to prioritize the TMLs; 7.) Train and test the neural network and validate the results.

The total structure of the proposed model is illustrated in figure 4.

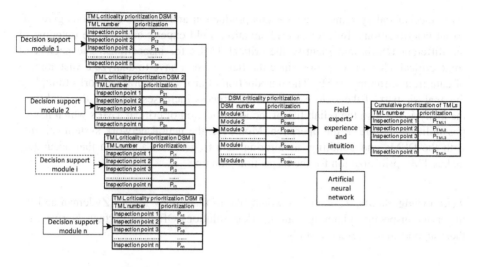

Fig. 4. Functional structure of the proposed model

The outputs from the DSMs for each inspection point (TML) have been ranked in a local manner (The ranking is based on the risk level of the TML. For instance, Seneviratne and Ratnayake (2013) ranked the TMLs according to the risk level based on the technical condition) and fed in to the trained ANN model with the criticality prioritization of the DSMs. A layout of tentative comparison is shown in Table 02.

PC_{FEj}: Cumulative prioritization of jth inspection point (TML) by field expert
PC_{ANNj}: Cumulative prioritization of jth inspection point (TML) by ANN model

Table 2. Tentative layout of the comparison of ANN model output and field experts' outcome

TML number	TML criticality prioritization DSM 1	TML criticality prioritization DSM 2	TML criticality prioritization DSM 3	TML criticality prioritization DSM i	TML criticality prioritization DSM n	Cumulative prioritization (by field expert)	Cumulative prioritization (by ANN)
Inspection point 1	P_{11}	P_{21}	P_{31}	P_{i1}	P_{n1}	PC_{FE1}	PC_{ANN1}
Inspection point 2	P_{12}	P_{22}	P_{32}	P_{i2}	P_{n2}	PC_{FE2}	PC_{ANN2}
Inspection point 3	P_{13}	P_{23}	P_{33}	P_{i3}	P_{n3}	PC_{FE3}	PC_{ANN3}
...	...	...	...	...	...	...	...
Inspection point j	P_{1j}	P_{2j}	P_{3j}	P_{ij}	P_{nj}	PC_{FEj}	PC_{ANNj}
...	...	...	...	...	...	...	...
Inspection point n	P_{1n}	P_{2n}	P_{3n}	P_{in}	P_{nn}	PC_{FEn}	PC_{ANNn}

5   Concluding Remarks

The proposed ANN model is suitable for identifying the critical TMLs in a subsystem which is undergoing different degradation trends and flow condition scenarios. The DSMs developed for degradation, flow condition and failure identification of the static mechanical systems under various production and process conditions give different prioritizations. In a real-world situation, field experts analyze the outcome of the different DSMs and identify the critical TMLs for inspections. The neglect of some critical TMLs is common since the field experts have to analyze a vast amount of data from different DSMs. The introduction of artificial neural networks to replace the analysis part of the field experts' work process increases not only the quality of the analysis but also the reliability of the identification of critical TMLs which have a possibility of failure in the operation. Moreover, the neural network system can link with the DSMs and condition monitoring data to generate a system that accurately makes TML prioritization for the inspection planning.

Acknowledgements. The authors would like to thank Roy Martin Zydeman and the in-service inspection planning team in Aker Solutions Offshore Partner, Norway, for their support in this research study.

References

1. Alvarado, M., Rodriguez-Toral, M., Rosas, A., Ayala, S.: Decision-making on pipe stress analysis enabled by knowledge-based systems. Knowledge and Information Systems 12, 255–278 (2007)
2. API RP 580. Risk Based Inspection, 1st edn. American Petroleum Institute (2002)
3. API RP 58. Risk Based Inspection Technology, 2nd edn. American Petroleum Institute (2008)
4. Becraft, W.R., Lee, P.L.: An integrated neural network/expert system approach for fault diagnosis. Computers & Chemical Engineering 17, 1001–1014 (1993)
5. DNV RP G101. G101: Risk based inspection of offshore topside static mechanical equipment, Det Norske Veritas (DNV), Norway (2010)
6. DNV RP O501. Recommended practice DNV RP O501: Erosive Wear in Piping Systems. Det Norske Veritas (DNV), Norway (2007)
7. Ferre, D., Ferschneider, G., Pauchon, C.: Method for modelling multiphase flows in pipelines. U.S. Patent No. 5,550,761. U.S. Patent and Trademark Office, Washington, DC (1996)
8. Kahkonen, T., Smolander, K.E.: Integration. ICEIS, 23 (2013)
9. Knapp, G.M., Wang, H.P.: Machine fault classification: a neural network approach. International Journal of Production Research 30, 811–823 (1992)
10. Nesic, S.: Key issues related to modelling of internal corrosion of oil and gas pipelines - A review. Corrosion Science 49, 4308–4338 (2007)
11. Nesic, S., Li, H., Huang, J., Sormaz, D.: An open source mechanistic model for CO_2 / H_2S corrosion of carbon steel. NACE International, Corrosion 2009, Paper No. 09572 (2009)
12. NORSOK M-506, NORSOK Standard M-506: CO_2 corrosion rate calculation model. Standards Norway, Lysaker, Norway (2005)
13. NORSOK Z-008. Risk based maintenance and consequence classification. Rev. 3, Standards Norway, Lysaker, Norway (2011)

14. Ratnayake, R.M.C.: Challenges in inspection planning for maintenance of static mechanical equipment on ageing oil and gas production plants: The state of the art. In: Proceedings of the ASME 31st International Conference on Ocean, Offshore and Arctic Engineering. Paper no. OMAE2011–49050 (2012a)
15. Ratnayake, R.M.C.: A decision model for executing plant strategy: maintaining the technical integrity of petroleum flowlines. International Journal of Decision Sciences, Risk and Management (IDJRSM) 4(1/2), 1–24 (2012b)
16. Ratnayake, R.M.C.: Modeling of asset integrity management process: A case study for computing operational integrity preference weights. International Journal of Computational Systems Engineering (IJCSysE) 1(1), 3–12 (2012c)
17. Ratnayake, R.M.C.: Utilization of piping inspection data for continuous improvement: a methodology to visualize coverage and finding rates. In: Proceedings of the ASME 32nd International Conference on Ocean, Offshore and Arctic Engineering, paper no. OMAE2013-10025 (2013)
18. Ratnayake, R.M.C.: Application of a fuzzy inference system for functional failure risk rank estimation: RBM of rotating equipment and instrumentation. International Journal of Loss Prevention in the Process Industries 29, 216–224 (2014)
19. Ratnayake, R.M.C., Markeset, T.: Maintaining technical integrity of petroleum flow lines on offshore installations: A decision support system for inspection planning. In: Proceedings of the ASME 2010 29th International Conference on Ocean, Offshore and Arctic Engineering. Paper no. OMAE2010-20035 (2010), doi:10.1115/OMAE2010-20035
20. Ratnayake, R.M.C., Samarakoon, S.M.S.M.K., Markeset, T.: Maintenance integrity: Managing flange inspections on aging offshore production facilities. In: Proceedings of the ASME 30th International Conference on Ocean, Offshore and Arctic Engineering. Paper no. OMAE2011-49050, pp. 19–32 (2011), doi:10.1115/OMAE2011-49050
21. Seneviratne, A.M.N.D.B., Ratnayake, R.M.C.: In-service inspection of static mechanical equipment: Use of a fuzzy inference system for maintaining the quality of an inspection program. In: Proceedings of the IEEE International Conference Industrial Engineering and Engineering Management (IEEM), Thailand (2013)
22. Srinivasan, S., Sueth, M.: Real time risk-based asset management - A framework for sustainable asset integrity solutions. In: Reliability and Maintenance Conference and Exhibition, Denver, pp. 416–431 (2011)
23. Valle, A.: Multiphase pipeline flows in hydrocarbon recovery. Multiphase Science and Technology 10 (1998)

CART for Supply Chain Simulation Models Reduction:

Application to a Sawmill Internal Supply Chain

Philippe Thomas[1,2], Marie-Christine Suhner[1,2], and André Thomas[1,2]

[1] Université de Lorraine, CRAN, UMR 7039, Campus Sciences, BP 70239,
54506 Vandœuvre-lès-Nancy cedex, France
[2] CNRS, CRAN, UMR7039, France
{philippe.thomas,marie-christine.suhner,
andre.thomas}@univ-lorraine.fr

Abstract. Evaluation of supply chain or workshop management is often based on simulation. This simulation task needs models which are difficult to design. The aim of this work is to reduce the complexity of simulation model design and to partially automate this task by combining discrete and continuous approaches in order to construct more efficient and reduced model. Model design focuses on bottlenecks with a discrete approach according to the theory of constraints. The remaining of the workshop is modeled in a less precise way by using continuous model in order to describe only how the bottlenecks are fed. This used continuous model is a regression tree algorithm. For validation, this approach is applied to the modeling of a sawmill workshop and the results are compared with results obtained previously by using a neural network model.

Keywords: Decision tree, CART, reduced model, simulation, supply chain.

1   Introduction

Planning or scheduling scenario evaluation is an important issue for internal/external Supply Chains (SC) control. Simulation is useful to perform this evaluation and allows to highlight evolution of the resources states, work in process and queues. This information allows to perform a "Predictive scheduling" [10] which concerns MPS which is initially established with the Manufacturing Planning and Control System. This first approach must not be confused with "Reactive scheduling" which gives new MPS solution, established after significant events occur on the shop-floor. The real time systems performing production reporting lead to obtain information into the management system very quickly [6]. However, it is difficult to use this huge of information to take a decision [13, 14]. At this level of planning, load/capacity balancing is obtained via the "management of critical resource capacity" function or Rough-Cut Capacity Planning which essentially concerns bottlenecks [19]. Goldratt and Cox [4] propose to manage all the supply chain by bottlenecks control and call it Theory of Constraints (TOC). For this purpose, the use of dynamic discrete event simulation of material flow is helpful [16]. Simulation models of real industrial cases are very com-

B. Grabot et al. (Eds.): APMS 2014, Part III, IFIP AICT 440, pp. 530–537, 2014.
© IFIP International Federation for Information Processing 2014

plex and can lead to problems of scale [12] that is why it is interesting to use simplest (reduced/aggregated) models of simulation [2, 3, 20]. To design these reduced model, different approaches may be used as using continuous flow model to approximate discrete manufacturing environments [5, 15], or using metamodels (linear regression, splines, Kriging) in order to perform simulation model [7]. Neural networks are also been used to perform this task [17, 18]. Another tool, regression tree, is able to find a suitable model useful for the model reduction. Classification and regression trees are machine learning methods able to fit a model to data. Models are obtained by partitioning data space and thanks to the association of a simple prediction model to each subspace [1]. The main goal of this paper is to evaluate the ability of regression trees to be used in order to reduce simulation model. In the second part, the proposed approach of reduction model and the regression trees are presented. The third part will be devoted to the presentation of an industrial application which is a sawmill flow shop case. In order to evaluate the pertinence of the proposition, the reduced simulation model of sawmill internal SC case is presented and, before to conclude, is compared to the same work performed by using neural network in the last part.

2   The Reduced Model

2.1   The Algorithm

Model complexity is relative to the number of elements, connections and model calculations [21]. Different approaches have been proposed to reduce model. To see a brief overview, see [18]. The proposed reduction algorithm is a modification of those presented by Thomas and Thomas [17]. The proposed approach is based on the association of discrete event models and continuous models (regression tree) in order to design a simulation model. Our objective is to maximize the bottleneck utilization rate and, at the same time, simplify simulation model design for modelers. Its main steps are recalled and explained below:

1. Identify the structural bottleneck (work center (WC) which for several years has been mainly constrained in capacity).
2. Identify the conjunctural bottleneck for the bundle of Manufacturing Orders (MO) of the MPS under consideration.
3. Among the WC not listed in 1 and 2, identify the one (synchronisation WC) satisfying these two conditions:
   (a) present at least in one of the MO using a bottleneck,
   (b) widely used considering the whole MO.
4. If all MO have been considered go to 5 if not go to 3.
5. Use regression tree for modelling the intervals between WC that have been found during preceding steps (figure 1).

Work Centers (WC) remaining in the model are either conjunctural or structural bottlenecks or WC which are vital to the synchronization of the MO. Other WC are incorporated in "aggregated blocks" upstream or downstream of the bottlenecks [18].

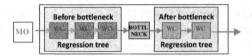

Fig. 1. Reduction model algorithm

2.2 Regression Tree

Decision trees are sequential models, which logically combine a sequence of simple tests. A regression tree looks like a classification tree, except that the output variable is a continuous one and a regression model is fitted to each node to give the predicted value of the output [9]. The first regression tree (AID) has been proposed by Morgan and Sonquist [11]. The principle of this regression tree is to begin to the root node, and then, for each node, find the test on the input patterns which minimizes the sum of the node impurities in its two child nodes. Classification and Regression Tree (CART) algorithm works on the same principle [1]. The main difference between AID and CART relies with the pruning and estimation process. CART is based on the generalization of the binomial variance called Gini index. The growing procedure of the tree is recursive and the process is stopped when [8]:

— there is only one observation in each of the child nodes,
— all observations within each child node have the identical distribution of predictor variables, making splitting impossible,
— an external limit on the number of levels in the tree or on impurity decrease level threshold is reached.

The resulting tree presents generally overfiting problem and needs a pruning phase, based on the impurity term used during the growing phase (Gini) associated to a penalty term corresponding to the number of terminal nodes. The final tree selection is performed by using a cross-validation procedure [1].

3   Overview of the Sawmill

The proposed approach is applied to build a simulation model of a sawmill workshop. In this actual case, managers need a tool to help them in their weekly decision-making Master Production schedule (MPS) process. They want:

— to evaluate the effectiveness of its MPS,
— to maximize its load rate, and so, its global productivity,
— to explain some unexplained congestion phenomena of the trimmer WC.

A first work [16] with a complete model has allowed to represent the congestion phenomena and to use this representation in order to improve the load rate. This model, has showed that a bottleneck load rate too high (higher than 60%) degrades productivity of bottleneck, and so, sawmill productivity. The difficulty is that bottleneck is the last sawmill WC but all influent factors on bottleneck productivity depend of the first WC. However, this complete model is unusable on a real case for the MPS dynamic evaluation because of time needed to modify it.

Sawmill can be described from a process point of view. It can be represented by two linear parallel flows for main and secondary products. This fact, associated to variation of log dimensions lead process to be non-linear. Therefore, the physical industrial production system can be divided into three main parts. To explain the process, the trip of a log from its admission into the process to its exit in planks form will be described. The first process part is the Canter line presented figure 2. Dashed arrows indicate the products flow. The considered log is taken into the process by using conveyors RQM1, RQM2, and RQM3. According to its characteristics (determined by scanner MS), the log is driven to conveyors RQM4 or RQM5, which are used as input inventory for the Canter line. After that, logs go on the first canter's machine and later on the CSMK saw, which transforms logs into square-shaped parallelepipeds.

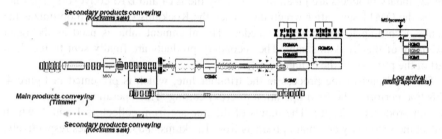

Fig. 2. The Canter line

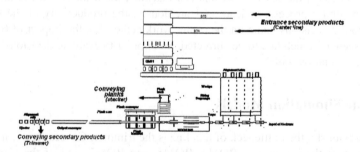

Fig. 3. The Kockums line

This step gives the two first sides of the parallelepipeds (the added value on the log) and produces two planks (secondary products), which are taken out of the Canter line by the BT4 and BT5 conveyors. The log is then driven on the RQM6 conveyors, rotated 90°, and stored in RQM7 awaiting its second passage on the CSMK saw. After the second passage, the squared is completed, and two other secondary products are taken out of the Canter line by BT4 and BT5 toward the second part of the process, the Kockums line. The squared log is cut on the MKV saw into three planks (called main products). These main products are driven to the third part of the process, the trimmer line.

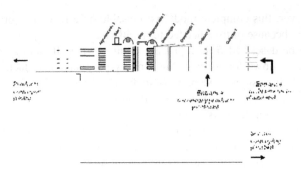

Fig. 4. The trimmer line

Figure 3 shows the second part of the process, where the main machine is the Kockums saw. Only secondary products are driven on this part. As previously said, the secondary products are taken in the line by the BT4 and BT5 conveyors. They are cut by the QM11 saw, after which they reach the Kockums saw, which optimizes the planks according to the products needed. The alignment table is used as the input inventory of the Kockums saw. The secondary products are finally sent to the third part of the process by the exit conveyor.

The third part of the process is the trimmer line, which is presented in figure 4. This line performs the final operation of cross cutting. This operation consists in cutting up products to length. The inputs of the line are from collectors 1 and 2, which collect the secondary and main products from Kockums and Canter lines respectively. Saw 1 is used to perform default bleeding and Saw 2 cuts up products to length. A previous work [16] has shown that this last machine, the trimmer saw, is the bottleneck of the entire process, and, as said previously, the productivity of the trimmer depends to the decisions taken on the canter work center. So, the impact of bad decisions are seen too much late to be corrected. So in order to evaluate decisions, managers need a simulation tool.

4   The Simulation Models

As said previously, the bottleneck of this line is the trimmer. Consequently, modeling the function of the inventories RQM4, RQM5, and RQM7, and of the Canter and Kockums lines is unnecessary and gave no direct and useful information for the evaluation of the MPS. In fact, only the arrival times of the products in the trimmer queue are useful for simulating the load of this bottleneck. So, in the complete model presented figure 5, all the parts surrounded with dashed line is unnecessary and may be replaced by a continuous model, here a regression tree.

According to the modeling process recalled in part 2, the specific sawmill model could be designed. To build this model, we need to identify the input variables. Thomas *et al.* [18] collected the available input data which can be classified into three categories: Data related to the products (here the logs), data related to the process and data related to the bill of material or routing (here the cutting plan). The data related to the products are mainly dimensional ones as length (lg) and three values for timber diameters (diaPB, diaGB, and diaMOY). The data related to the process are the process variables collected at the time of log arrival. In particular, we require the input stock and the utilization rate of the bottleneck, here the trimmer (Q_trim, and U_trim, respectively). The number of logs present in the process between the inputs and the exit of the Canter line (Q_RQM) and in the input inventories (Q_RQM4, Q_RQM5 and Q_RQM7) are needed.

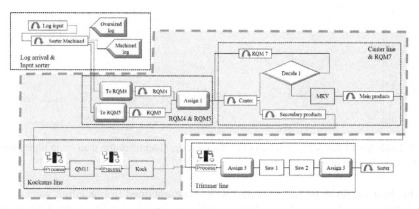

Fig. 5. Complete model

The data related to the routing correspond here to the information related to the cutting plan of the logs which must be cut into main and secondary products. This information is given by the type of part (T_piece).

Consequently, the model input variables are: Lg, diaGB, diaMOY, diaPB, T_piece, Q_trim, U_trim, Q_RQM, Q_RQM4, Q_RQM5 and Q_RQM7. In our application, 12775 products are simulated with the complete model. These data are used to fit the behavior of the reduced model to the complete one which serve as reference model.

The next step is to identify the output variable. Our objective is to estimate the delay (ΔT) corresponding to the duration of the throughput time for the 12775 products. ΔT is measured between the process input time and the trimmer queue input time. For regression problems, the goal is to reduce the distance between the model and the data. Hence, the RMSE criterion is suitable, and is used in this work:

$$RMSE = \sqrt{\frac{1}{N}\sum_{n=1}^{N}(y_n - \hat{y}_n)^2} \qquad (1)$$

where N denotes the number of data, y_n is the nth actual data point, and $\hat{y}_n$ is the predicted value.

Figure 6 presents the evolution of the RMSE in function of the number of nodes in the tree. This figure shows that classically, even if RMSE always decreases on the learning data set, it is not the same on the validation data set. It begins by decreasing before to increase. This fact illustrates the overfitting problem and the selection of the best model must be performed by using a cross validation strategy. In our case, the selected model comprises 296 nodes.

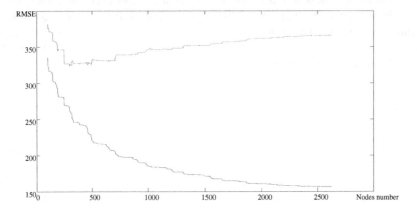

Fig. 6. Evolution of RMSE in function of nodes number – identification data set in blue dashed – validation data set in red

This best model must be compared with those obtained in preceding work which use neural network model [18]. These results are presented table 1. They show that regression tree outperforms neural model and allows to improve results of 20%.

Table 1. Comparison of RMSE for Neural network and regression tree models

RMSE	Identification	Validation
Neural model	408.45	413.93
Tree model	263.47	324.10

5   Conclusion

The use of regression tree in order to build a reduced simulation model is investigated here. The regression tree model is used to model the functioning of a part of the process that is not constrained in capacity. This approach has been applied to the modeling of a sawmill workshop. The results show that the complete and reduced models gave similar results even if the log arrival rule is changed. Moreover, the results are compared with results obtained with a neural network model and the comparison shows that regression tree outperforms neural network on this application. This means that it seems efficient to use a regression tree to model a part of a process instead of constructing the complete model. Assuming that the construction of a regression tree is a quasi-automated task, in which the modeler only collects and selects the input data set. It is faster and easier to design this kind of reduced model. This approach allows the modeler to focus on the management of bottlenecks. Our intentions for future works are the validation of this approach on different applications, particularly on several external supply chains, such that at least one particular enterprise belongs to different supply chains.

References

1. Breiman, L., Friedman, J.H., Olshen, R.A., Stone, C.J.: Classification and regression trees. Chapmann & Hall, Boca Raton (1984)
2. Brooks, R.J., Tobias, A.M.: Simplification in the simulation of manufacturing systems. International Journal of Production Research 38(5), 1009–1027 (2000)
3. Chwif, L., Paul, R.J., Pereira Barretto, M.R.: Discret event simulation model reduction: A causal approach. Simulation Modelling Practice and Theory 14, 930–944 (2006)
4. Goldratt, E., Cox, J.: The Goal: A process of ongoing improvement, 2nd revised edn., Great Barrington, USA. North River Press (1992)
5. Ho, Y.C.: Performance evaluation and perturbation analysis of discrete event dynamics systems. IEEE Transaction on Automatic Control 32(7), 563–572 (1987)
6. Khouja, M.: An aggregate production planning framework for the evaluation of volume flexibility. Production Planning and Control 9(2), 127–137 (1998)
7. Kleijnen, J.P.C., Sargent, R.G.: A methodology for fitting and validating metamodels in simulation. European Journal of Operational Research 120, 14–29 (2000)
8. Lewis, R.J.: An introduction to classification and regression tree (CART) analysis. In: Annual Meeting of the Society for Academic Emergency Medicine, San Francisco, California, May 22–25 (2000)
9. Loh, W.Y.: Classification and regression trees. Wiley Interdisciplinary Reviews: Data Mining and Knowledge Discovery 1, 14–23 (2011)
10. Lopez, P., Roubellat, F.: Ordonnancement de la production. Hermès, Paris (2001)
11. Morgan, J.N., Sonquist, J.A.: Problems in the analysis of survey data, and a proposal. J. Am. Stat. Assoc. 58, 415–434 (1963)
12. Page, E.H., Nicol, D.M., Balci, O., Fujimoto, R.M., Fishwick, P.A., L'Ecuyer, P., Smith, R.: An aggregate production planning framework for the evaluation of volume flexibility. In: Winter Simulation Conference, pp. 1509–1520 (1999)
13. Pritsker, A., Snyder, K.: Simulation for planning and scheduling. In: APICS (August 1994)
14. Roder, P.: Visibility is the key to scheduling success. In: APICS Planning and Scheduling (August 1994)
15. Suri, R., Fu, B.R.: On using continuous flow lines to model discrete production lines. Discrete Event Dynamic Systems 4, 129–169 (1994)
16. Thomas, A., Charpentier, P.: Reducing simulation models for scheduling manufacturing facilities. European Journal of Operational Research 161(1), 111–125 (2005)
17. Thomas, P., Thomas, A.: Multilayer Perceptron for Simulation Models Reduction: Application to a Sawmill Workshop. Engineering Applications of Artificial Intelligence 24, 646–657 (2011)
18. Thomas, P., Thomas, A., Suhner, M.C.: A neural network for the reduction of a Product Driven System emulation model. Production Planning and Control 22, 767–781 (2011)
19. Vollmann, T.E., Berry, W.L., Whybark, D.C.: Manufacturing, Planning and Systems Control. The Business One Irwin (1992)
20. Ward, S.C.: Argument for constructively simple models. Journal of the Operational Research Society 40(2), 141–153 (1989)
21. Zeigler, B.P.: Theory of modelling and simulation. Wiley, New York (1976)

Model-Driven Enterprise Resource Planning Specifications in SMEs

Clément Lacombe[1,2], Ramuntxo Pochelu[2], Said Tazi[3], and Yves Ducq[1]

[1] Univ. Bordeaux – IMS – UMR 5218 CNRS
351 cours de la Libération – 33405 Talence cedex, France
{clement.lacombe,yves.ducq}@ims-bordeaux.fr
[2] Sarl Atelier du Piment Elizaldeko Bidea, 64250 Espelette, France
{si,ramuntxo}@atelierdupiment.com
[3] UFR Anglet Université de Pau et des Pays de l'Adour
Allée du Parc Montaury 64600 Anglet, France
said.tazi@univ-pau.fr

Abstract. Small companies, like their larger counterparts, need information systems to drive and measure their performance. Until now, only large firms had access to ERP[1] technology, but the market is increasingly tapping into to the needs of small businesses. For many SMEs[2], however, the difficulty lies in navigating the choices available and defining their specifications for this type of information system, especially since few tools and methods exist to help them. This is why we have developed an enterprise modeling-driven method for needs specification: the information in a company's business model is used to prepare its ERP Functional Specification.

Keywords: Enterprise Resource Planning, specifications, Enterprise Modeling, SMEs.

1   Introduction

The research presented in this article was conducted in collaboration with the IMS Laboratory at University of Bordeaux 1, and with "Atelier du Piment" – a fast-growing company with a staff of ten, which grows, processes and markets the Espelette variety of chili pepper sold under the trade name "Piment d'Espelette AOP[3]". The company wanted to improve its organizational structure, and undertaking a project to overhaul its information system with the integration of ERP software was completely in line with this aim. The research presented herein was carried out simultaneously with the company's ERP project.

---

[1] Enterprise Resource Planning.
[2] Small and Medium Enterprises (SMEs).
[3] Protected Designations of Origin.

B. Grabot et al. (Eds.): APMS 2014, Part III, IFIP AICT 440, pp. 538–545, 2014.
© IFIP International Federation for Information Processing 2014

Regardless of its size, sector or line of business, a company has to implement various functions in order to exist:

- Procuring materials or goods, collecting information
- Processing, however simple or complex
- Selling products or services
- Keeping records for tracking, measuring and monitoring purposes
- Setting up a dashboard to understand and analyze

These functions need to be implemented in a coordinated, well-thought-out and efficient manner. Thus, a company can be seen as an organized system that is constantly changing.

To represent the organization of the complex "company" system [Le Moigne, 1977] breaks the company down into three sub-systems: a decision-making system, an information system, and an operating system.

The information system plays a central role in the company. Every company has an information system, which may be more or less formally structured, and which may be used by a single person or by a limited number of decision-makers, but the purpose of this system is the always the same: to enable understanding and analysis in order to improve performance. However, the larger the organization, the more complex the information system will be.

Information systems, especially ERP solutions, are key components of companies. The difficulty of integrating ERP software will depend not just on the size of the company, but above all on the scope of the project and the functional needs that the ERP will have to cover. Not only is deploying these solutions challenging, but these projects come with risks and the stakes are high. [Holland and Light, 1999] state that information system projects are first and foremost company projects.

Considering the difficulties that can arise in these projects, specialists look for the key success factors. [Mamoghli, 2013] has created a classification of studies on the risk factors and success factors for ERP projects. Of all the factors listed, in this article we will focus on the ERP software selection phase. Choosing an ERP solution is a complex task, particularly for SMEs. At this stage in the project, the company needs to be able to define and formalize its needs in order to choose one of the ERP solutions on the market.

The challenge for SMEs is that few resources are available to help them define their requirements. This is why we propose in this article a needs specification method based on the use of enterprise modeling.

In the first part, above, we have seen that a company can be considered a complex system, in which the information system plays a central role. We have also pointed out the difficulties that SMEs face in specifying their needs for ERP projects. In the second part, we will present a state of the art review of the main research on ERP software that has served as our reference base. We will then address the problem of the definition of needs in small companies, setting out our proposed method of using the company's enterprise modeling information for this purpose. Finally, we will illustrate the application of this method through a case study on "Atelier de Piment".

2   State of the Art Review

To establish the broader scientific context for our research, we will first examine the ERP life cycle. We will then discuss ERP alignment and enterprise modeling. Lastly, we will define the role and purposes of the Functional Specification in ERP projects.

2.1   ERP Life Cycle

There is a considerable body of research that has focused on ERP project phasing. [Mamoghli, 2013] presents a literature review. [Botta and al., 2001], [Deixonne, 2001], [Darras, 2004] proposes different ways of breaking down projects, which can be more or less detailed. There are five main phases: the pre-project phase, the pre-installation phase, the installation phase, the post-installation phase and finally the post-project phase. Our work focuses on the pre-installation phase. A poorly-realized definition of needs can negatively impact the ERP installation phase, since if the selected ERP software does not match the company's real needs, there is a greater risk of misalignment between the ERP and company processes.

2.2   ERP Alignment

[Mamoghli, 2013] defines the Misalignment Risk as the probability of misalignment associated with the ensuing loss if the misalignment occurs. It is the probability that the processes placed under ERP control will not be aligned with the company's real needs and processes.

For [Botta and Millet, 2005], managing ERP alignment is a necessary key success factor for ERP projects. [Mamoghli, 2013] proposes a model-driven engineering method called "Model Driven - ERP Alignment" which reduces the effect of Misalignment Risk. This method involves a model-based alignment process enabling the following:

- precisely identifying situations of alignment and misalignment between the models of the processes the company wants (AS-WISHED) and the models of standard ERP processes (MIGHT-BE);
- constructing the model of the processes to be installed (TO-BE), step by step, in a guided manner, through the combined use of evaluation criteria and decision-making.

For this method to be applied, the AS-IS, AS-WISHED and MIGHT-BE models need to be based on the same formalisms. While creating AS-IS and MIGHT-BE models is fairly straightforward, constructing the AS-WISHED model can be much more complex, as in order to do so, the company must first have a precise vision of its needs.

We find that this method works well in the context of a company that is already well-structured, and which has a fairly homogenous information system. However, we are not convinced that this type of method is appropriate in the case of small companies, which often rely on less sophisticated and somewhat informal information systems, and where there is too wide a gap between the existing system (AS-IS) and the target system (TO-BE).

In the following paragraph, we will lay out the modeling method and the interaction model that we presented in a previous paper [Lacombe and al., 2013].

2.3 GIM[4] and the Interaction Model

The GIM developed in the 1990s, based on the GRAI (Graph of Results and Interconnected Activities) method, was designed to provide tools for analyzing and designing complex production management-type systems in industrial engineering contexts [Chen et al., 1997].

This method uses three graphic models to represent the three modeling views:

- The decision-making view: GRAI grid,
- The information view: UML class diagram,
- The physical view: IDEF0 diagram.

The interaction model that we have developed incorporates these three modeling views. It does not model a specific system, but rather the interaction between these three modeling views. The purpose of the interaction model is to provide a graphical representation of a management step or process that can be defined as "special" – meaning a "non-standard" ERP function or process, one not supported by off-the-shelf ERP software.

We will now discuss how the information contained in the models produced is used to formalize the company's requirements in a Functional Specification.

2.4 Functional Specification

A Specification serves to formally express a need and to explain it so that it can be understood and validated by all stakeholders in a project. [Equey and Rey, 2004] explains that writing a high-quality Functional Specification helps limit cost overruns, increase companies' satisfaction and improve relations between the different stakeholders in the project. Another advantage is that this helps the project team appropriate the issues at stake in the project.

Writing the Specification is a key component of the ERP selection phase for companies of all sizes. However, the level of detail used to describe the needs is different for different-sized companies. Specifications for large-scale enterprises will include a highly-detailed and in-depth study of the functional requirements, whereas SMEs will not go into as much detail in defining the needs in their specifications.

---

[4] GRAI Integrated Methodology.

3   Model-Driven Needs Specification

In this scientific context, and drawing on our previous work [Lacombe and al., 2013], we propose a method for formalizing needs in a Functional Specification using the information contained in the GIM models and our interaction model.

Before explaining the method, however, let us first identify and define the main components of an ERP Specification.

- Presentation of the company

The purpose of this part of the Specification is to describe the company in terms of its legal structure, environment, line of business, market and offer. Going beyond these simple descriptors, this part should also convey the company's values and business dynamics.

- Description of current systems

There are two parts to this description of the current systems. The first serves to describe the company's physical processes, e.g., manufacturing, acceptance or goods shipping processes. The second part describes the existing information system, specifying the hardware and software in place within the company. This component of the Specification needs to define the precise status of the existing resources within the company.

- Presentation of the project

The purpose of this part is to identify the context and objectives of the ERP project. This is also where the scope and functions to be covered by the ERP solution will be defined, along with any interfaces with third-party applications that need to be taken into account.

- Description of needs

Two types of needs need to be defined: functional needs and decision-making needs. The first type, functional needs, can include aspects that are considered standard ERP functions or more specific "special" functions. The needs are classified according to company functions and defined in the models. The second type, decision-making needs, refers to management-related or performance measurement aspects. This is where needs in terms of statistical reports and dashboard performance indicators will be defined.

As shown in Table 1, the GIM models and our interaction model will provide the information needed to complete certain parts of the Functional Specification.

Table 1. ERP software requirement specifications and models used

	GRAI Grid	IDEF0 Diagrams	Interaction Model
Presentation of the company - 20%			
Legal structure	-	-	-
Environment	-	-	-
Factors specific to line of business	-	-	-
Customers	-	-	-
Products and services	-	-	-
Description of current systems - 10%			
Physical processes	-	X	-
Information system	-	-	-
Presentation of the project - 10%			
Objectives	-	-	-
Functional coverage	-	-	-
Description of functional needs classified by functions - 50%			
Standard needs	X	-	-
Special needs	-	-	X
Description of decision-making needs / Subject of subsequent research - 10%			

First, we will be able to use the IDEF0 diagrams to describe the company's current systems and physical processes. This modeling language is used to represent the series of activities in a process, the incoming and outgoing flows, the resources used and the monitoring data for the various activities.

Second, using the information in the GRAI grid, we will be able to create a detailed list of the desired functions to be supported by the ERP software. For this to be effective, it is important to use a GRAI grid that provides fairly detailed descriptions.

Finally, the interaction model will allow us to provide more detailed specifications for certain steps or management processes that require more in-depth analysis.

In the following section, we will illustrate the use of these three models through a case study.

4   Case Study: "Atelier du Piment"

The specific aspects to be taken into account for this activity are: traceability data entry and the weighing equipment used. In this case, the function is included in the GRAI grid, but requires special attention.

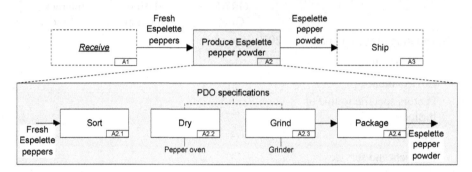

Fig. 1. IDEF0 – Chili powder manufacturing process, to be included as-is in the Specification

Manage procurement	Manage product processing	Manage shipments
Scheduling deliveries Receipt/acceptance of goods Receipt of delivery slip Printing shipment unit labels (EAN128)	Preparing manufacturing orders Ranking priorities	Scheduling shipments Shipping cost simulation Selecting carriers
Recording inputs and outpus inventory Managing multiple warehouses Reserving a quantity in stock	Launching manufacturing orders Monitoring raw material traceability	Preparing shipment units / pallets Preparing delivery slips Shipping shipment units / pallets

Fig. 2. GRAI grid – Tasks classified by function and organized into decision-making centers

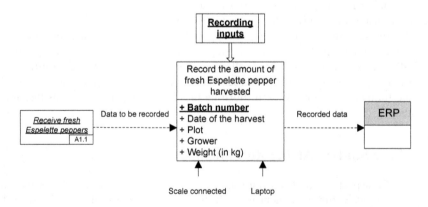

Fig. 3. Interaction model – Record of incoming fresh Espelette peppers in stock

5   Conclusion

In the first part of this article, we discussed how a company can be seen as a complex system, in which the information system plays a central role. We also pointed out the difficulties that SMEs face when it comes to specifying their needs for ERP projects.

In the second part, we examined the broader scientific context for our research, first discussing the ERP life cycle and the issue of ERP alignment, then presenting the GIM and the interaction model, and finally defining the role and purposes of Functional Specifications in ERP projects.

In the third part, we proposed a method for using modeling to write a Functional Specification. We first identified the main components of an ERP Specification, and then associated them with the most appropriate models, respectively.

In our ongoing work, we would like to develop a method to help SMEs specify their decision-making needs. While we have not yet addressed management aspects and the measurement of company performance through performance indicators and dashboards, these areas are of course highly relevant to our work on SME needs specification.

References

1. Botta-Genoulaz, V., Millet, P.-A., Neubert, G.: The role of enterprise modeling in ERP implementation. Industrial Engineering and Production Management 1, 220–231 (2001)
2. Botta-Genoulaz, V., Millet, P.-A.: A classification for better use of ERP systems. Computers in Industry 56(6), 572–586 (2005)
3. Chen, D., Vallespir, B., Doumeingts, G.: GRAI integrated methodology and its mapping onto generic enterprise reference architecture and methodology. Computers in Industry 33(2-3), 387–394 (1997)
4. Darras, F.: Proposition d'un cadre de référence pour la conception et l'exploitation d'un progiciel de gestion intégré. PhD, Institut National Polytechnique de Toulouse. Systèmes industriels, 230 pages (2004)
5. Deixonne, J.L.: Piloter un projet ERP: transformer et dynamiser l'entreprise par un système d'information intégré et orienté métier. Dunod. 2e édn, Paris (2006)
6. Equey, C., Rey, A.: La mise en place d'une solution de gestion moderne (ERP/PGI), quels enjeux pour une PME/PMI? 1ère partie: étude de cas détaillés, Working paper N°HES-SO/HEG-GE/C–06/1/4–CH (2004)
7. Holland, C.R., Light, B.: A critical success factors model for ERP implementation. IEEE Software 16(3-), 30–36 (1999)
8. Lacombe, C., Tazi, S., Ducq, Y.: Méthode et modèle d'interaction pour la spécification des systèmes d'information dans les Très Petites Entreprises. Congrès International de Génie Industriel. La Rochelle (2013)
9. Le Moigne, J.-L.: La théorie du système général, Paris: presse universitaire de France, 258 pages (1977)
10. Mamoghli, S.: Alignement des Systèmes d'Information à base de progiciel, vers une ingénierie dirigée par les modèles centrée identification des risques. National Institute of Applied Sciences of Strasbourg. Sciences et Technologies Industrielles, 254 pages (2013)

Life Cycle Evaluation of Factories: The Case of a Car Body Welding Line with Pneumatic Actuators

Tim Heinemann[1], Alexander Kaluza[1], Sebastian Thiede[1], Daniel Ditterich[2],
Johannes Linzbach[2], and Christoph Herrmann[1]

[1] Technische Universität Braunschweig, Institute for Machine Tools and Production
Technology, Chair of Sustainable Manufacturing- and Life-Cycle-Engineering,
Braunschweig, Germany
[2] Festo AG & Co. KG, Esslingen, Germany
t.heinemann@tu-braunschweig.de

Abstract. During the planning phase of the build up or overhaul of factories a
large share of the life cycle spanning impact of such production facilities is
determined. Furthermore it is very hard to evaluate the impact of possible
measures for improvement, resulting Total Cost of Ownership (TCO) and environmental impacts of factory systems. Against this background this paper presents an integrated life cycle analysis approach for a streamlined economical
and environmental life cycle assessment of factory systems. The approach gets
applied while using two interacting tools for a) energy efficiency evaluation of
pneumatic systems and b) life cycle evaluation of factory systems.

Keywords: life cycle evaluation, total cost of ownership, streamlined LCA, factory evaluation, sustainable manufacturing.

1 Introduction

When planning projects for new or overhauled factories are started, there is a high
degree of freedom about the configuration of the machines, the technical building
services (TBS) and the building shell. Also most of the later costs as well as environmental impacts (esp. for the use and disposal phase of the factory) get determined at
this stage. However, most of the information for a severe quantification of the financial and environmental impacts of planning alternatives are not available so that
wrong decisions can be taken easily. Especially when it comes to add-on measures to
reduce the environmental impact, often the budget restrictions impede the implementation as the TCO and financial benefits as well as the environmental improvements
cannot be estimated sufficiently. This problem will be solved by applying a Life Cycle Evaluation (LCE) Approach, which becomes manifest in the LCE Tool [1]. This
tool gets applied in combination with a specific tool for the evaluation of pneumatic
and electrical actuator systems to calculate the economical and environmental impact
of alternative system designs and improvement measures.

B. Grabot et al. (Eds.): APMS 2014, Part III, IFIP AICT 440, pp. 546–554, 2014.

2   Theoretical Background

Holistic System Comprehension and Factory Elements
In contrast to many approaches, which divide the factory planning process into sequences and induce a sequential planning of factory elements (e.g. [2]), this paper introduces a holistic system comprehension of factories, in which all factory elements are of equal importance. This is because in industrial environments all factory elements influence each other regarding the overall resource consumption. The introduced evaluation approach focuses on the factory system and its subsystems [3] [4]:

- production equipment: processes/machines/value adding process chains
- technical building services: responsible for providing production conditions and energy as well as media (e.g. compressed air)
- building shell: physical boundary of the factory system and to the outside

However, their individual design and control involves diverse disciplines which impedes a synergetic planning of the factory system. Thus, methods to overcome those interdisciplinary challenges are a proper way towards more sustainable solutions.

Life Cycle Evaluation
Life cycle evaluation (LCE) in the context of this paper addresses the evaluation of financial (Total Cost of Ownership, TCO) and environmental impacts (CO_2eq.) which result from physical flows during all life cycle phases of the factory system.

TCO is a selected perspective on life cycle costing (LCC), which considers all economically relevant monetary flows over the life cycle of products. Therewith, LCC allows analysing trade-offs between life cycle phases and supports to derive solutions from a comprehensive perspective [5]. Diverse frameworks for LCC in form of standards, norms or guidelines have been developed (e.g. VDMA 34160, VDI 2884, DIN EN 60300). TCO focuses solely on the operator/user perspective of the considered object and all the costs that occur during the course of ownership. To ease application, software based tools which also differ in terms of scope, field of application and general functionalities have been developed (e.g. [6]). However, those solutions tend to be quite specific for selected applications and less considering systems as a whole [1].

The calculation of environmental impacts can be done via Life Cycle Assessments (LCA). LCA focuses mainly on environmental impacts throughout a product's life cycle from raw material acquisition through production, use and end-of life treatment. It builds upon Life Cycle Inventories (LCI), which sum up the physical flows along the life cycle of a product [7]. From a product perspective the incorporated materials are usually well known and easy to assess in LCAs. However, the additional physical (energy/media) flows which occur during the manufacturing phase especially within a factory system are often hard to assess and demand for supporting tools (see also [1]).

3   Factory Life Cycle Evaluation Approach

Architecture of the Approach and Tool
All calculations and evaluations within the LCE approach are based on life cycle inventories (cumulated physical input and output flows) of the focused system, which can be a system element like an assembly line (see Fig. 1).

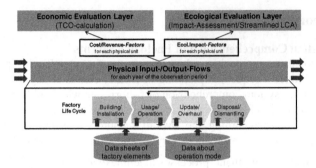

Fig. 1. Architecture of the life cycle evaluation approach

These flows are based on resource consumption profiles which are taken from data sheets and (simulated) forecasts of the factory's operation modes. During the use phase of the factory also the utilization, shift models, downtimes, etc. are used to calculate the overall physical flows. Every factory element gets described as a set of parameters with physical units. All evaluation is done by transforming the physical flow data into financial or environmental impacts by multiplying it with cost factors as well as environmental impact factors (e.g. CO_2eq.). This calculation gets supported through an Excel based tool, which supports the main parameterization of the individual factory system model through default templates of factory elements. Therefore the modelling and evaluation of alternative strategic factory settings gets facilitated for quick assessments in an early stage of the planning process. Fig. 2 shows an overview over the elements of the LCE Tool. Through these elements (user interface, reporting sheets, etc.) the usability gets enhanced. (For a deeper inside in the LCE tool and its data bases e.g. for environmental impacts of the building shell please see [1].)

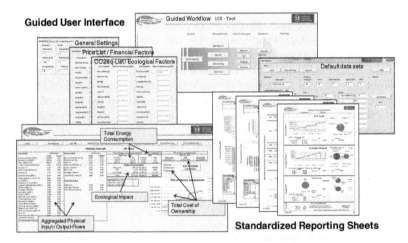

Fig. 2. Overview over the elements of the Life Cycle Evaluation Tool

Tool Interaction for Enhanced Evaluation Options

As the LCE approach demands reliable input data (e.g. technical behaviour of machines), it has to incorporate data from other tools. Especially in planning stages, when real consumption profiles of factory elements are not accessible, tools which simulate element or system behaviour become relevant. Furthermore the LCE Tool only considers factory elements down to the level of detail of machines, TBS or building shells. It cannot consider the behaviour of components (at acceptable effort). E.g. the behaviour of pneumatic components and resulting loads for compressors illustrate the resulting interplay of detailed machine component behaviour and the resource consumption of factory elements. Fig 3 visualizes an exemplary interplay of tools as it will be applied in the case study, which will be described afterwards.

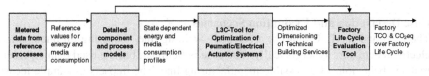

Fig. 3. Tool interplay and information flow

Supporting Tool for the Evaluation and Optimization of Pneumatic Actuation Systems

The LCE Tool benefits from an application of tools like the Life Cycle Cost Calculator (L3C-Tool, Festo AG & Co. KG), which can model actuation systems at a very high level of detail regarding single (pneumatic as well as electrical) actuation operations, resulting compressed air and electricity consumption (see Fig. 3). The L3C-Tool enables the right dimensioning of air compressors and the evaluation of improvement measures to the system of actuators, valves and tubes (see Fig. 4) [8].

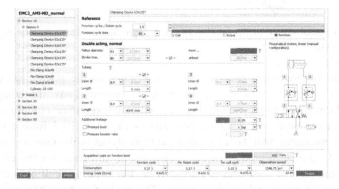

Fig. 4. Dimensioning of pneumatic system and calculation of compressed air demand in L3C-Tool (screenshot) [8]

A major advantage of the L3C-Tool is its ability to conduct transparent and comprehensible energy consumption calculations. This allows a direct cost comparison of different factory design options. Hence, this tool addresses the following main functionalities:

- Modelling of systems on component level and aggregation to machine level
- Calculation of energy costs and investment costs
- Performance of break-even analyses between different system configurations

The L3C tool also aims at identifying energy efficiency improvements, while quantifying energy saving potential, payback time for investments and maintenance costs. Thus, decision makers can carry out an energy diagnosis of configuration alternatives with little effort. Further information about the L3C-Tool can be found in [8] and [9].

4   Case Study: Optimized Planning of Car Body Welding Line through Improved Compressed Air Systems

Case Description and Evaluation Scenarios

The LCE and the L3C analyze a car body welding line, focussing on pneumatic and electrical actuators synergistically. The case is fictional, but the used data represents a realistic behaviour of a possible manufacturing line. The impacts of sample measures are analyzed, which get translated into financial and environmental KPIs through the LCE Tool. The car body welding line consists of different actuators within the manufacturing application, a compressor station and a building shell (exemplarily: Fig. 5).

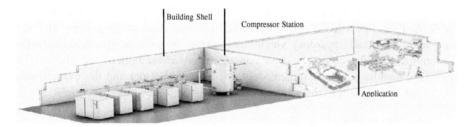

Fig. 5. Conceptual sketch of the analysed system, regarding the three factory elements (Festo AG & Co. KG)

As main improvement measure an optimization of the pneumatic components reduces the compressed air consumption of the system. Thus, the compressor can be resized compared to the standard setting with a conventional compressor. In order to highlight the broader evaluation potential of the LCE Tool further possible improvement measures will be evaluated exemplarily as well. Due to simplification reasons only the consumption of electricity has an influence on the environmental impact of the factory's use phase. Furthermore, the building shell only creates emissions during its setup and disposal phase. The evaluation time horizon is 30 years of use phase plus a setup and disposal of the factory. Tab. 1 introduces a selection of parameters, which describes the base scenario, and the parameter changes of improvement measures.

Table 1. Scenario description

Base scenario: Automotive car body welding line A car body welding line is used as reference. The model consists of a selection of the machines of the manufacturing line, the TBS (compressor station) and a sample building shell. The compressor capacity meets the demand of a car body factory as figured out with the L3C-tool. For the building shell a prede-fined reference factory has been used [1]. The following model parameters have been used besides others: • General: Annual operating hours: 4800 h; European electricity mix, price increase 1%/a • Manufacturing line: Process power: 69.1 kW; lifetime: 72000 h; maintenance interval/expenses: 4800h/~30k€; Investment: ~830 k€ • Compressor: Process power: 171 kW; lifetime: 24000 h; maintenance interval/expenses: 4800h/~19 k€; investment: ~94 k€ • Building shell: Aerated concrete walls, no windows; lifetime: 165000 h; maintenance inter-val/expenses: 4800h/~33 k€; investment: ~650 k€

Orga. measures	**Scenario 1: Alternative shift model** Application of an alternative shift model that might occur due to changing demands or the intro-duction of measures for improved working conditions. • Applied parameter changes: 2 shifts (3200 working hours) instead of three shifts • Sensitivity analysis: +/- 10% working hours
	Scenario 2: Alternative energy mix Substitution of the European Electricity mix with certified renewable electricity supplies. • Applied changes: Usage of the Swiss renewable energy mix (0.0098715 kg CO_2eq/kWh in-stead of 0.559 kg CO_2eq/kWh; price increase about 0.0015 €/kWh [10] [11] • Sensitivity analysis: +/- 10% energy price
Technical measures	**Scenario 3: Improved pneumatic components and system design, based on the recommendations from the L3C-Tool** Improving the compressed air system is a lever for decreasing energy cost in production [12] [8]. Overall system design (up to 9%), leakage detection (up to 20%) or more efficient compressors (up to 15%) can reduce the energy consumption significantly [12] [13]. For Sc. 3 a smaller com-pressor is installed due to improved pneumatic components, a more advanced system design and leakage detection. The total investment is assumed to remain constant as the measure's implemen-tation costs equalize the reduced compressor investment. The impact on the whole factory gets assessed. • Applied changes: Air compressor: 33% less electrical power input (115 kW instead of 171 kW) • Sensitivity analysis: +/- 10% electrical power input of air compressor
	Scenario 4: Energy efficient drives By increasing the energy efficiency of drives (e.g. according to the IEC 60034-30 standard) from class IE1 to IE3 efficiency increases of about 10% can be achieved [14]. • Applied changes: Drives: 10 % less electrical power input (62.2 kW instead of 69.1 kW for the considered section of the body welding line); Machine investment costs: +10% • Sensitivity analysis: +/- 10% electrical power input of production machines

Results

The car body manufacturing scenario could be modeled successfully within the Festo L3C-tool and the LCE-tool. Even though the LCE tool allows a separate simulation of the factory, the cumulated input data out of the L3C-tool enhanced a flawless applica-tion. Four scenarios have been applied in order to test the flexibility of the LCE-tool and the sensitivity of its results. For that matter the TCO and the greenhouse gas emissions (kg CO_2eq) have been evaluated (see Fig. 6 and Fig. 7.). An additional sensitivity analysis for Sc. 3 has been carried out (see Fig. 8).

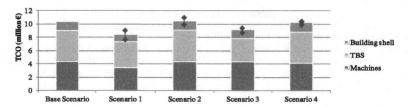

Fig. 6. Scenario evaluation results from LCE Tool, Total Cost of Ownership

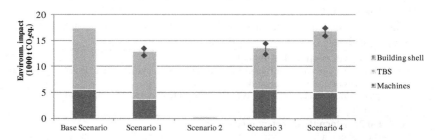

Fig. 7. Scenario evaluation results from LCE Tool, environmental impact (1000 t CO_2eq.)

The evaluated organizational measures include the change of the shift model (Sc1) and the use of a certified renewable energy mix (Sc2). Whereas the reduced working hours result in lower TCO (-19%) and greenhouse gas emissions (-26%), it has to be considered that the factory output would decrease simultaneously, not regarding additional efforts (e.g. ramp up and shutdown times). The change of the used electricity mix shows slightly higher TCO. The calculated carbon emissions decrease by 99%.

Variations in the installed compressor capacity (Sc3) and the use of more efficient electric drives (Sc4) have been discussed as technical measures. Based on the L3C-tool application and its optimization on component level, the use of a compressor with 33% less power demand becomes possible. This decreases the TCO by 11% and the carbon emissions by 22% (Sc3). Only marginal savings (2% TCO and 3% carbon emissions) could be achieved in Sc4. Based on these results, Sc. 3 has been selected to evaluate the influences of relevant input parameters on the TCO in more detail. A sensitivity analysis varies the compressor's electrical process power, changes energy prices as well as compressor lifetimes (Fig. 8). Increased compressor lifetimes are assumed due to the improved pneumatic system design.

Varying process power and energy prices show linear sensitivity effects. A larger influence can be observed for energy prices due to their influence on the factory system. The compressor lifetime shows a staircase-shaped course. This effect is induced by investments that become necessary for replacing compressors after their use phase.

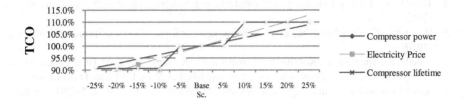

Fig. 8. Sensitivity analysis for TCO regarding variations of electricity price, compressor lifetime and compressor power

5   Summary

This paper presented an approach for a rapid life cycle evaluation regarding the economic (TCO) and environmental (CO_2eq.) impact of factory systems. This approach has been applied to a sample case of a car body welding line. In order also to assess the effect of changes in the configuration of its pneumatic actuation system, the specialized L3C-Tool was used and an optimized dimensioning of the air compressor set could be derived. The life cycle spanning effect of a variation of this factory system element has been evaluated as one improvement scenario via the LCE Tool. The effect of this measure has been compared to other technical as well as organizational improvement measures. By doing so the potential of an interaction of these tools was illustrated. As a result and according to the previously introduced holistic system comprehension of factories factory planning representatives should jointly assess the economical and environmental impacts of factory configuration options already at an early planning stage and under equal consideration of all factory elements.

Acknowledgements. The research leading to these results has received funding from the European Community's Seventh Framework Programme (FP7/2007-2013) under grant agreement n° 285363. The funded project's title is "Eco Manufactured Transportation Means from Clean and Competitive Factory" [EMC2-Factory]. For further information about the project please visit the website www.emc2-factory.eu.

References

1. Heinemann, T., Thiede, S., Müller, K., Berning, B., Linzbach, J., Herrmann, C.: Life Cycle Evaluation of Factories: Approach, Tool and Case Study. In: Proceedings of the 11th Global Conference on Sustainable Manufacturing (GCSM 2013), pp. 529–534 (2013)
2. VDI-guideline: VDI 5200 factory planning – planning process/VDI-Richtlinie: VDI 5200 Blatt 1 Fabrikplanung – Planungsvorgehen
3. Herrmann, C., Kara, S., Thiede, S., Luger, T.: Energy Efficiency in Manufacturing – Perspectives from Australia and Europe. In: Proceedings of the 17th CIRP International Conference on Life Cycle Engineering, pp. 23–28 (2010)

4. Thiede, S.: Energy Efficiency in Manufacturing Systems, pp. 38–39. Springer, Berlin (2012)
5. Herrmann, C.: Ganzheitliches Life Cycle Management, pp. 131–150. Springer, Heidelberg (2010)
6. Thiede, S., Spiering, T., Kohlitz, S., Herrmann, C., Kara, S.: Dynamic Total Cost of Ownership (TCO) Calculation of Injection Moulding Machines. In: Dornfeld, D.A., Linke, B.S. (eds.) Leveraging Technology for a Sustainable World, vol. 111, pp. 275–280. Springer, Heidelberg (2012)
7. Life cycle assessment – requirements and guidelines DIN EN ISO 14044:2006, DIN (October 2006)
8. Tools zur Planungsunterstützung. In: Green Carbody Project Consortium. Planung des effizienten Einsatzes von Druckluft im Karosseriebau, pp. 59–64 (2013), http://www.festo.com/net/SupportPortal/Files/327813/Greencar_Leitfaden_PDF_MD.pdf (accessed April 24, 2014)
9. Ditterich, D., Engler, W., Bredau, J.: Effizienter Drucklufteinsatz im Automobilbau. In: ATZproduktion 2011(4), pp. 2–7 (2011)
10. Ecoinvent 2.2, http://db.ecoinvent.org/
11. St.Gallisch-Appenzellische Kraftwerke AG. Broschüre Strompreise (2014), http://www.sak.ch/PortalData/1/Resources/01_sak_internet/de/24_e/05_strompreise_regelungen/Broschuere_Strompreise2014_SAK_Expert.pdf (accessed April 25, 2014)
12. Saidur, R., et al.: A review on compressed-air energy use and energy savings. In: Renewable and Sustainable Energy Reviews 2010(14), pp. 1135–1153 (2010)
13. Radgen, P., Blaustein, E.: Compressed air systems in the European Union. Germany: Energy, Emissions, Savings Potential and Policy Actions (2001), http://www.isi.fraunhofer.de/isi-media/docs/isi-publ/2001/isi01b04/compressed-air-long.pdf (accessed April 25, 2014)
14. ABB. IEC 60034-30 Norm zu den Wirkungsgradklassen für Niederspannungsmotoren (2009), http://www05.abb.com/global/scot/scot234.nsf/veritydisplay/36ef15c7594589a9c12578ab00264f67/$file/tm025%20de%20revb%202009_lowres.pdf (accessed April 25, 2014)

Integrating Aspects of Supply Chain Design into the Global Sourcing Process – Insights from the Automotive Industry

Gregor von Cieminski[1] and Alessandro Rossi[2]

[1] ZF Friedrichshafen AG, Friedrichshafen, Germany
[2] ETH Zurich, BWI Center for Industrial Management, Zurich, Switzerland
gregor.cieminski@zf.com, alrossi@student.ethz.ch

Abstract. This paper reports on enhancements of the global sourcing process proposed with the purpose of increasing the weight of criteria related to supply chain design in sourcing decisions. In a conceptual study carried out for a German automotive supplier, the global sourcing process proposed by Alard et al. was found to be most suitable for industrial application. From the technical perspective of the supply chain management function, even this comprehensive approach does not address important decision criteria, such as likely structure of global supply chains or the capacity flexibility required of suppliers in global supply chains. The enhancements proposed include new process steps making use of network optimization and simulation techniques to eliminate these shortcomings.

Keywords: Global sourcing, supply chain design, network optimization, simulation.

1   Introduction

In the same way as many other industries, the automotive sector is going through a phase of global expansion. Industry surveys provide evidence that market growth in the industry is shifting from its traditional strongholds in the western industrialized world to the emerging markets, especially in the Asia-Pacific region. The CEOs of automotive companies expect China to remain the specific national market that offers the biggest growth potentials [1]. This country alone is predicted to provide around 30 % of the global production of light passenger vehicles in 2020 [2].

Among other trends, these market developments are driving two changes in the global structure of the automotive industry. On the one hand, western OEMs (Original Equipment Manufacturers) and suppliers are forced to increase production in emerging markets in order to fulfil their growth objectives. On the other hand, automotive companies entering the market from the emerging nations have increased the cost pressure on their western competitors.

As a consequence, western automotive companies have increased the share of purchasing volume sourced from emerging markets. This is mainly for two reasons:

B. Grabot et al. (Eds.): APMS 2014, Part III, IFIP AICT 440, pp. 555–562, 2014.

1. Suppliers in emerging markets (or NSMs, short for "new souring markets") offer purchasing price advantages over the local or regional suppliers in Europe or the United States.
2. In their drive for global growth, western automotive companies aim to avoid the high transaction costs from their traditional production and supply base into the emerging markets. Therefore, new production facilities and a new supply base have to be built up in the emerging markets, i. e. on a global scale.

ZF Friedrichshafen AG (from here on referred to as "ZF"), a German automotive supplier, is also subject to the industry trends described above. In the specific market environment of the organisation, the importance of China as an NSM is growing. Given the growth of supply volumes sourced in China, the Supply Chain Management (SCM) function in the Asia-Pacific region is facing increasing difficulties in operating ZF's regional supply chains. For example, little attention may be paid to the impact of the location of a newly selected supplier on the structure of ZF's transportation network in China. The experience of the company confirms the findings of the analysis of Ruamsook et al.: SCM objectives are often assigned secondary importance in global sourcing decisions [3].

The SCM function of ZF in the Asia-Pacific region therefore initiated a study into possible improvements of the sourcing process [4]. This paper reports on the results of this study. First, it presents the case company and the methodology applied in, and the main findings of, the study. Second, it proposes enhancements of the global sourcing process from an SCM perspective in order to eliminate the shortcomings of the current sourcing practice. A set of general conclusions from the study completes the paper.

2   Initial Analysis of Global Sourcing Practices

This section first introduces the case company ZF Friedrichshafen AG. Second, the methodology applied in the analysis of the global sourcing practices of this company is presented and the main findings of the initial analysis are summarized.

2.1   Case Company

ZF Friedrichshafen AG is the third biggest German automotive supplier and a leading manufacturer of driveline and chassis technology. In 2013, ZF's total sales amounted to € 16.8 billion and the company employed around 72,500 staff worldwide in its 122 production locations and 33 service centres [5]. ZF Group is organized in four divisions defined with an orientation towards customers as well as technologies provided by the company. Additionally, the group encompasses two cross-divisional business units. ZF produces a range of driveline and chassis components – such as transmissions, powertrain modules, axle systems, suspension systems – for the automotive, marine, railway, aviation and wind-power industries.

ZF has been operating international production facilities for a number of decades, opening its first plant outside of Europe in Brazil as early as 1958. In recent years, the company has accomplished accelerating growth on a global scale. The biggest growth rates are in the Chinese operations. Here, as in the other global regions, the company has established regional headquarters that support the regional plants by providing corporate services across the main business functions. The regional SCM office initiated the analysis of global sourcing processes illustrated in this paper.

2.2 Methodology and Findings

The methodology applied in the analysis of global sourcing processes at ZF and in the enhancement of these processes was the "Systems Engineering" approach developed by Haberfellner et al. [6]. The Systems Engineering approach is structured into four phases (corresponding to the system life cycle). This section summarises the different phases with reference to the analysis presented:

1. *Trigger:* The problem trigger of the analysis of global sourcing processes were the increasing difficulties the Chinese corporate SCM team in the Asia-Pacific region faced in operating ZF's regional supply chains. The purpose of the analysis was to identify possibilities to involve the SCM team earlier in the decision process in order to more systematically and effectively consider the concerns of the function in sourcing decisions.
2. *System development:* The system development phase is sub-divided into a preliminary study, a main study and further detailed studies. Each study uses a defined problem solving cycle. This is described with regards to the global sourcing process in more detail below.
3. *System implementation:* The subject of this phase is the technical system implementation, i. e. converting the system concept into a tangible object or executable process. This phase was not within the scope of the global sourcing study and is therefore not presented in this paper.
4. *System use:* The system use phase represents the continuous use and improvement of the system under real operating conditions. This phase is also not covered by this paper.

The remainder of the paper focuses on the process steps of the second phase of the Systems Engineering approach, system development. As stated above, the problem solving cycle defined by Haberfellner et al. [6] provided the procedural framework:

1. *Situation analysis:* The situation analysis mainly examined the global sourcing practices at ZF in the Asia-Pacific region. The analysis included the documentation of the sourcing processes and practices currently in use in the region, challenges and problems associated with regional sourcing decisions and a SWOT analysis of the processes. It was shown that ZF has implemented an advanced global sourcing process in terms of the tasks typically associated with the purchasing function (determining the supply demand, supply market research, supplier identification, supplier evaluation, supplier selection). The analysis also revealed that the process neglects SCM-oriented decision criteria. Thus, sourcing decisions are taken that have a detrimental effect on supply chain performance and supply chain costs.

2. *Objective formulation:* For engineering the global sourcing process, the ZF SCM team Asia-Pacific defined the clear objective that aspects of supply chain design have to be integrated in the global sourcing process. The results of these analyses have to be considered as additional SCM-oriented criteria in the global sourcing decisions of the company.

3. *Solution search:* ZF's Asia-Pacific team engaged on a search for a blueprint on which to base improvements of the sourcing process of the company. The search considered reference processes for both, supply chain design and global sourcing, documented in industrial as well as scientific literature. A set of 10 relevant reference processes was thus identified and evaluated. Interestingly, a considerable number of process models from the field of purchasing were excluded because of their solely operational focus.

4. *Evaluation:* ZF based its evaluation of the 10 relevant reference processes on a set of defined criteria that covered both technical aspects (e.g. "Reference process includes procedure for rough supply chain design.") as well as application-oriented aspects (e.g. "Reference process includes clear documentation of process steps and their building blocks.") [4]. The criteria were weighted according to their importance and the corresponding scores determined for each of the reference processes under consideration.

5. *Decision:* As a result of the evaluation, the global sourcing process (GSP) developed Alard et al. [7, 8] was selected as the most suitable process reference for ZF. Figure 1 shows the sequence of fifteen steps Alard et al. have defined for GSP. Its advantages are explained with reference to the figure.

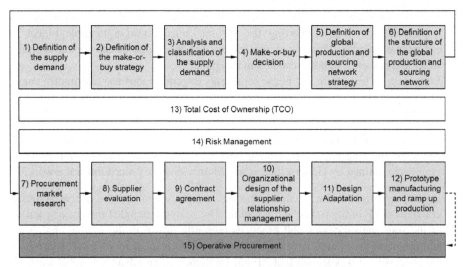

Fig. 1. Global sourcing process and its steps [7, 8]

The main advantage of GSP is the inclusion of two explicit steps concerned with the design of the production and sourcing network (steps 5 and 6). This ensures that strategic SCM-oriented aspects are considered in the subsequent sourcing decisions.

Also, if relevant, the GSP process steps integrate the total costs of ownership (TCO) as well as aspects of risk management in their analysis (steps 13 and 14, applicable along the chain of process steps). These elements guarantee a balanced consideration of relevant criteria for the sourcing decisions, including supply chain costs and risks.

3   Enhancing the Global Sourcing Process

Having selected GSP as the relevant process template, the purpose of the main study by ZF was two-fold. On the one hand, ZF matched the GSP process definitions with practices already applied by the company. On the other hand, the company analysed whether GSP matches all its requirements in detail. As this was not completely found to be the case, the process steps "static and dynamic analysis of the sourcing network" were newly defined. These are presented in section 3.1. Subsequent detailed studies were concerned with developing the process steps in more detail. As an example the process step "dynamic analysis of sourcing network" is described in section 3.2.

3.1   Supply Chain Design Steps in the Overall Process

Figure 2 depicts the GSP including the enhancements added by ZF.

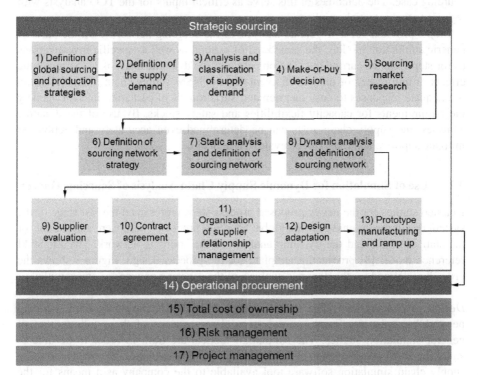

Fig. 2. Integration of supply chain design and global sourcing

Evidently, ZF did not change the overall structure of GSP. Indeed, steps 9 to 16 remain the same as before. Step 17 "Project management" was included as an additional cross-process activity to reflect the nature of GSP decisions. Also, in steps 1 to 4 less emphasis was placed on the make-or-buy strategy and other production-related aspects.

The main enhancements are related to steps 5 to 8 (cf. figure 2). First, the process "Sourcing market research" is drawn forward (step 5). This is to reflect the fact that before any specific analyses can meaningfully be carried out, general information about the NSM under investigation ought to be collected. On the basis of this, a first "Sourcing network strategy" (step 6) may be defined that specifies common guidelines for supply chain design in the NSM.

Steps 7 and 8 represent the essential new steps integrated into GSP. Step 7 entails a "Static analysis of the sourcing network". By means of network optimisation models, the overall structure of the NSM supply chain is analysed. Two types of investigation are conceivable: First, a generic study of the NSM based on probable scenarios of the supply chain structures. This serves the purpose of a general examination of the characteristics and challenges for supply chain designs in the NSM. Overall guidelines for designing the structure of the supply chain network should become apparent. Second, specific studies of the supply chain structures related to a concrete sourcing case. The outcomes of this serve as critical inputs for the TCO analysis with regards to the potential suppliers.

Step 8 provides for a "Dynamic analysis of the sourcing network". On the basis of generic simulation models, the same kind of general as well as specific investigations as for step 7 can be carried out. The objective of the dynamic analysis is to predict the effects of unforeseen or unplanned events on the NSM supply chains. The definition of adequate responses to customer demand variations is of particular interest, namely the requirements for capacity flexibilities and safety stocks. By use of the dynamic analyses, the supply chain costs can be determined even accurately and actions to mitigate supply chain risks can be evaluated in detail.

3.2   Use of Simulation for Dynamic Supply Chain Analysis of Sourcing Market

Detailed studies for the newly proposed process steps represented the last stage of the system development phase for the global sourcing process. These were carried out for the static analysis and the dynamic analysis of the sourcing network. The ZF SCM reference model [9] provided a template for the process design. Figure 3 shows the procedure defined for the dynamic analysis of the sourcing network as an example.

Design of process step. The overall process step "Dynamic analysis of sourcing network" is split into 7 sub-process steps. The sequence of these follows that of general simulation studies. The simulation models are built in order to be able to study the NSM supply chains under different operating scenarios. ZF intends to use a supply chain simulation software tool available to the company as a means for the dynamic analysis. As can be deduced from the inputs defined for the sub-process steps (cf. figure 3), the simulation models will be implemented as a comparatively high-level representation of the real supply chains. This allows the simulation studies to focus on a limited set of critical dynamic characteristics.

Designated use of process step. There are two critical advantages of analysing feasible supply chains in new sourcing markets by means of dynamic events-based simulation. On the one hand, the critical supply chain characteristics – e.g. customer demand, capacity flexibility – may be considered from the perspective of medium- to long-term capacity planning. The Asia-Pacific SCM team can thus clearly state the basic SCM-oriented requirements and make sure that potential suppliers meet these. On the other hand, similar requirements can be formulated for worst-case scenarios, which also have to be fulfilled across the sourcing network. The impact of a basic set of supply chain risks – e.g. supplier failure, failure of the transport infrastructure – can be accounted for. By means of this, ZF is able to support efforts for supply chain risk management in the sourcing network.

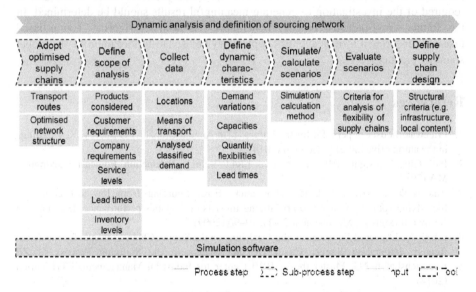

Fig. 3. Procedure for dynamic analysis of supply chains

Further development of process step. By putting the dynamic analysis of the sourcing network – as well as the other new process steps defined - into practice, ZF expects to obtain valuable information about the applicability of the design of the process steps. Most crucially, it should become apparent which characteristics of the NSM supply chains or sourcing networks need to be investigated in detail due to their criticality. Repeated applications of the enhanced GSP will thus lead to a continuously refined process design.

4   Conclusions

An analysis of the global sourcing processes at ZF Friedrichshafen AG illustrated that the sourcing decision process of the company does not adequately consider SCM-oriented aspects. The evaluation of relevant process models available in literature revealed these also to be lacking in this respect. For this reason, ZF enhanced the global sourcing process developed by Alard et al. by two specific steps: a static sourcing network analysis employing network optimisation approaches and a dynamic sourcing analysis on the basis of simulation experiments.

As a next step, ZF is planning a pilot application of the enhanced approach for global sourcing led by the corporate SCM team of the Asia-Pacific region. Clear recommendations on the practical design of the supply chains in China as an NSM are sought. At the same time, the practical applicability of the process enhancements presented in this paper will be evaluated. Specifically, the level of detail that is required of the investigation to generate meaningful results should be determined. In the future, cross-industry process benchmarks as well as rigorous action-based research (ensuring a formal scientific input) may be used to further improve the global sourcing practices.

References

1. PricewaterhouseCoopers: Fit for the Future: 17th Annual Global CEO Survey. Key findings in the automotive industry, London (2014)
2. IHS Global Insight: IHS Automotive Light Vehicle Production Forecast, Lexington, MA (2014)
3. Ruamsook, K., Russell, D.M., Thomchick, E.A.: Sourcing from low-cost countries: Identifying sourcing issues and prioritizing impacts on logistics performance. International Journal of Logistics Management 20(1), 79–96 (2009)
4. Rossi, A.: Impact of Future Sourcing Decisions on the Supply Chain Concepts for the Asian Region: Integrating Supply Chain Design Aspects in the Sourcing Process of ZF Friedrichshafen AG. Master thesis, BWI Center for Industrial Management, ETH Zurich (2014)
5. ZF Friedrichshafen AG: Annual Report 2013. Friedrichshafen (2014)
6. Haberfellner, R., de Weck, O.L., Fricke, E., Vössner, S.: Systems Engineering: Methodik und Praxis, 12th edn., OrellFüssli, Zürich (2012) (English edition forthcoming)
7. Alard, R., Bremen, P., Oehmen, J., Schneider, C.: Total Cost of Ownership Considerations in Global Sourcing Processes. In: Vallespir, B., Alix, T. (eds.) Advances in Production Management Systems. IFIP AICT, vol. 338, pp. 491–498. Springer, Heidelberg (2010)
8. Alard, R., Oehmen, J., Bremen, P.: Reference Process for Global Sourcing. In: Proceedings of 13th IEEE International Conference on Industrial Engineering and Engineering Management, pp. 367–371. IEEE, Singapore (2007)
9. von Cieminski, G.: Adapting and applying the Supply Chain Operations Reference model – a case study from the automotive industry. In: Frick, J. (ed.) Advances in Production Management Systems (2011)

The Supply Chain Design of Biomass Energy Plants: A Simulation Approach

Lorenzo Tiacci[1], Chiara Paltriccia[1], Stefano Saetta[1], and Eduardo Martín García[2]

[1] Università degli Studi di Perugia - Dipartimento di Ingegneria, Perugia, Italia
[2] Universidad de Valladolid, Valladolid, España

Abstract. Alternative energies nowadays have to be more competitive than energy derived from fossil fuels. In this study, the supply chain design problem for a biomass plant is considered. In order to reduce the cost per kWh of energy produced, the whole supply chain involving the biomass plant is modeled. A two-steps methodology, consisting in two sequential simulation experiments, is illustrated. The procedure allows to calculate the minimum total surface necessary for wheat production, and to find the size and the number of farms, which minimize the cost per kWh produced, varying different power rating of the plant. Given the general assumptions made, results can be utilized as a decision support tool for the supply chain design of biomass energy plants.

1 Introduction

The need to be more independent from fossil fuels is leading Europe to an increasing use of alternative energy sources. Among them, biomass is still little considered. In particular, in the Mediterranean area, despite it is a mainly agricultural area due to the mild climate, the numerous waste resulting from cereal production could be utilized for energy production from biomass.

In this paper, a support decision tool for the design of the supply chain of a biomass plant is proposed. This study is conducted through a simulation approach, which allows finding the best configuration for a network of farms that supply a biomass energy production plant placed in a central position. In fact, due to the high number of variables that have to be considered, the stochastic nature failures rate of machines and the limited capacity of storages, blockings and starvations phenomena arise along the nodes of the supply chain. For this reason it is very difficult to study the supply chain through analytical models.

The procedure proposed in this paper consists into two sequential steps. In the first one, the aim is to determine the necessary field extension related to different power rating of the plant. In the second step, the goal is to evaluate the optimal number and size of farms required to handle efficiently the resources in order to minimize the cost per kWh produced.

The paper is organized as follows: the next section provides a brief review of the literature on the design of the supply chain in the production of energy from biomass. In Section 3 and 4 the conceptual and the simulation model are respectively

B. Grabot et al. (Eds.): APMS 2014, Part III, IFIP AICT 440, pp. 563–570, 2014.

described. In Section 5 the design of experiment is illustrated. Results are discussed in Section 7 and in Section 8 a brief summary is drawn.

2   Literature Review

Alternative energy and Supply Chain (SC) have a central role in social and economic development at different stages [1]. As outlined in [2], the supply chain capacity is among the main issues for alternative energy development, together with project economics, technical constraints, social effects and environmental impacts .

The management of a biomass plants requires timely supply of feedstock with minimum logistics costs and an optimized biomass logistics system [3]. Several methods have been used to model and analyze different aspects of agricultural biomass supply chains. In [4] a location model for a biomass plant, based on an AHP approach, is proposed. Different type and issues on biomass supply chains were studied through static spreadsheet models in order to calculate the costs related to storage and transportations [5-7]. Indeed, as a further study, mathematical optimization-modelling tools were proposed as another methodology to optimize logistical decisions [8-10].

These static models are not able to describe the dynamic behavior and the complexity related to a biomass supply chain, that can be achieved only adopting simulation approaches [11]. Simulation approaches have been also utilized to validate analytical models developed for multi-echelon supply chains of bulk materials such as grain [12]. Among the simulation frameworks, the Integrated Biomass Supply Analysis and Logistics (IBSAL) model [11] considers various stages of the agricultural biomass logistics system. This model has been further enhanced considering the demand fulfilment and in-farm and at-plant storage management, considered in the IBSAL Multi Crop (IBSALMC) model [13].

In our work we developed a conceptual model inspired by IBSALMC, and a corresponding simulation model implemented in Arena. These models have been utilized to propose a design methodology and a decision support tool for the supply chain design of biomass plants.

3   Conceptual Model

A biomass plant, which produces energy from wheat biomass, is considered in this work. To provide this plant whit a sufficient quantity of wheat biomass it is necessary a specific area around the plant in which a certain number of farms is distributed. Each farm manages a different field surface cultivated with one cereal farming. Farms are allocated on an approximately circular area (Fig. 1).

Wheat is harvested during the summer. After harvesting, wheat is left on the field for a certain period, in order to dry. When the yield is ready, it is baled by a square baler, a machine used to compact yield into square bales of 1.2 m x 1.2 m x 2.4 m and 500 kg of weight each.

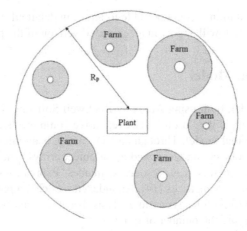

Fig. 1. Schematic representation of the plant and the network of farms

Bales are then left onto the field until a stinger stacker, a machine that picks up 8 bales per trip, collects and stores them into a farm Roadside Storage (RS). The operating turn of a stinger stacker begins at 6:00 a.m. and ends at 20:30 p.m., considering a break time for lunch at 12:30 p.m. Each farm owns a RS of a fixed capacity of 800 bales. The bailing collecting process is interrupted if the RS is full.

During the processes involved in the supply chain, while the bales stay in the field waiting to be stored, they lose weight due to the natural drying process. This mass loss causes a reduction of the total energy that can be produced by the plant.

The biomass plant owns a truck that collects bales from each farm to feed its grinder. When in the farm storage there are enough bales to fulfil a truck (at least 8 bales), the truck is called from the biomass plant, bales are loaded onto the truck by a tele-handler and then the truck drives bales to the plant, where they are stocked and then used to feed the grinder and to produce biomass energy. Farms that claim for the truck simultaneously are served following a FIFO policy. It is important to highlight that in this RS a sufficient number of bales should always be present in order to ensure a continuous feeding of the plant grinder.

The annual costs considered are divided into two main categories: logistics and storage costs. In detail, costs considered are: cost per hour of each machine, cost of failures, cost of transportations, and holding costs.

The processes that forerun the storing of bales at the plant are very important, because they are responsible of the continuous production of the plant. Blocking and starvation phenomena along the nodes of the described SC arise due to the following reasons:

1. Limited capacity of resources (balers, stingers stacker, tele-handlers, truck, RS, plant storage, grinder)
2. Stochastic failures of machines (balers, stingers stacker, tele-handlers, truck, grinder).

Due to space limitation it is not possible to report in detail all the features characterizing the model, which will appear in an extended version of the paper.

4   Simulation Model

The simulation model, built using Arena by Rockwell Software, is an indexed model. This feature of Arena is very useful when repetitive components are modelled, as the farms in our conceptual model. Through an 'ID', which is an integer number within a specific class, each object can be viewed as an object arrays. The index identifies the object in the array. In this way, resources, queues, expressions, processes can be represented by vectors or matrices [14]. An indexed model is a parametric model, and this is fundamental to perform scenario analysis, because it allows avoiding to reprogram the model varying the number of farms.

The hypotheses considered in the model are: times related to each process are deterministic; times related to failures of machines are stochastic and exponentially distributed. We validated our model through two widely adopted techniques [15]. The first one consists in computing exactly, when it is possible and for some measures of the input parameters, some measures of outputs, and using it for comparison. The second one, an extension of the first one, is to run the model under simplifying assumptions for which is the true characteristics are known and, again, can easily be computed.

The processes involved in the SC are modelled as seven blocks (Fig. 2).

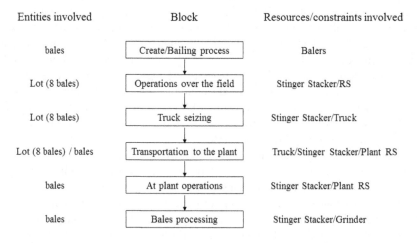

Fig. 2. Diagram representation of the main blocks of the simulation model

The simulation starts with the harvest. The first block is the creation of bales, which corresponds to the bailing process. Bales are created in according to the bailer capacity. The second block is related to the operations over the field, where the stinger stacker collects bales and forms lots, each containing 8 bales, that become the basic entities. When the number of lot waiting in the RS is reached, the truck is claimed. Truck availability depends on the state of the processes of the other farms. The third block represents the process related to the truck seizing and the bales loading. This process involves the stinger stacker and the plant truck and it is followed by the transportation to the plant and the bales unloading process, which involves the plant truck and the stinger stacker. The last two blocks are related to the at-plant operations, in particular to the storage and to the bales processing. Details related to resources involved and entities considered are described in Fig. 2.

The model is completed with three independent sub-models, which make use of dummy entities. The first one is realized for indexing motivations, and is related to the assignment of specific attributes to each farm (f.e. size of the farm, distance from the plant, etc.) varying the number of farms generated. The second and the third sub-models are essentially built to record statistics in specific moments of the simulation.

5   Design of Experiment and Results

In order to explain a methodology to design the optimal configuration of the supply chain that provides wheat to a biomass plant for energy production, two different experiments were built. The first experiment is aimed at evaluating which is the optimal extension of the total surface involved in the wheat production for a biomass plant of a given power rating. The second experiment is performed to evaluate the optimal number of farms, and therefore their optimal size, in order to reduce the unitary cost of energy produced. Each experiment is conducted for four different power rating of the plant: 200kW, 400 kW, 600 kW and 800kW, and has been replicated ten times. All the results refer to the average values obtained from the simulations.

5.1   Experiment 1

As before mentioned, the aim is to determine the extension of the total surface needed in the wheat production for a biomass plant, given the power rating of the plant. A specific area shall be managed by a high number of little farm or by a low number of big farms. To calculate the total surface for each power rating of the plant, a scenarios analysis have been performed. In each scenario the number of farms N_F varies in an interval of [10, 70], with N_F multiple of 5. The size of each farm has been generated randomly from a uniform distribution with a range [10, 30] ha.

The minimum number of farms which guarantees at least the 90% of utilization rate of the plant is considered for calculating the total surface required. By multiplying the number of farms N_F and their average extension, it has been possible to calculate the total surface required by the plant. This procedure has been replicated for different power rating of the plant.

In Table 1 the results are reported for each scenario. The total surface found are: 300 ha for a 200kW power plant, 600 ha for a 400kW power plant, 900 ha for a 600kW power plant and 1200 ha for a 800kW power plant.

Table 1. Results of Experiment 1

Farms	Total surface [ha]	200kW	% Demand fulfillment 400kW	600kW	800kW
10	200	68.11	-	-	-
15	300	**95.17**	-	-	-
20	400	99.72	-	-	-
25	500	99.83	81.04	-	-
30	600	99.86	**93.58**	-	-
35	700	-	99.63	-	-
40	800	-	99.33	84.49	-
45	900	-	99.89	**92.97**	-
50	1000	-	-	98.73	79.47
55	1100	-	-	99.90	86.21
60	1200	-	-	99.93	**92.46**
65	1300	-	-	-	97.64
70	1400	-	-	-	99.85

5.2   Experiment 2

Experiment 2 represents the second stage of the design methodology. Aim of this second stage is to evaluate the optimal number of farms, and therefore their size, in order to reduce the unitary cost of energy produced. Indeed the same surface can be managed or by a great number of small farms or by a small number of large farms (Fig. 3). The total surface necessary to guarantee a sufficient supply of wheat to the plant represents the fundamental input data.

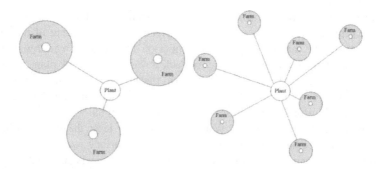

Fig. 3. Schematic representation about two possible opposite configuration of the network

The scenario analysis performed for each power rating is developed in the following way. A certain number of scenario are generated varying the number of farms N_F from 10 to 70. For each scenario, the average surface m_k of each farm is calculated as the ratio between the total surface required by the plant and the number of farms considered. Then the surface of each farm is randomly generated from a uniform distribution with range $[m_k-5, m_k+5]$ ha.

The optimal combination of number/size of the farms, which allows to minimize the cost per kWh of energy produced, is the one in which the appropriate number of machines and resources operates with reduced queues and idle times. In fact, it is not only necessary to own a sufficient area ensuring a sufficient total quantity of wheat, but is also important to ensure a continuous flow of material from the farms to the plant. Results related to Experiment 2 are reported in Fig. 4. It is possible to highlight that the functions that describe the costs per kWh, varying the number of farms, are always convex. The optimal number of farms, as expected, increases as the power of the system increase.

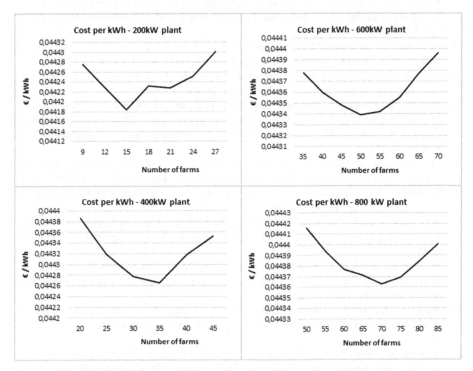

Fig. 4. Cost per kWh as a function of the number of farms

6   Summary

This research study analyzed the SC of a biomass plant evaluating costs for different power rating of the plant. This study was conducted adopting a simulation approach. The results achieved are valid under the assumptions made in the conceptual model. These assumptions are applicable to a large set of wet biomass supply chains. Thus, the relations found among the power rating of the plant and the optimal number and size of farms can be utilized as a supporting decision tool for the preliminary design of this type of supply chains. This model can be further developed considering other realistic aspects, such as weather conditions, the rotting process of the bales, and different variety of crops. Even other resource management policies could be considered, such as the sharing of resources like balers and stinger stackers among farmers.

References

1. Shi, V.G., Koh, S.C.L., Baldwin, J., Cucchiella, F.: Natural resource based green supply chain management. Supply Chain Manag. 17, 54–67 (2012)
2. Cucchiella, F., D'Adamo, I.: Issue on supply chain of renewable energy. Energ. Convers. Manage. 76, 774–780 (2013)
3. Sokhansanj, S., Kumar, A., Turhollow, A.F.: Development and implementation of integrated biomass supply analysis and logistics model (IBSAL). Biomass Bioenerg. 30, 838–847 (2006)
4. De Carlo, F., Schiraldi, M.: Sustainable choice of the location of a biomass plant: an application in Tuscany. International Journal of Engineering and Technology 5 (2013)
5. Allen, J., Browne, M., Hunter, A., Boyd, J., Palmer, H.: Logistics management and costs of biomass fuel supply. Int. J. Phys. Distr. Log. 28, 463–477 (1998)
6. Brundin, S.: Fuels from agriculture. Cost calculations of systems based on straw and energy grass. Department of Economics, Swedish University of Agricultural Sciences (1988)
7. Clegg, J.M., Noble, D.H.: A cost model of straw conservation systems. Agricultural Engineering (1987)
8. Eksioglu, S.D., Acharya, A., Leightley, L.E., Arora, S.: Analyzing the design and management of biomass-to-biorefinery supply chain. Comput. Ind. Eng. 57, 1342–1352 (2009)
9. Rentizelas, A.A., Tatsiopoulos, I.P., Tolis, A.: An optimization model for multi-biomass tri-generation energy supply. Biomass Bioenerg. 33, 223–233 (2009)
10. Rentizelas, A.A., Tolis, A.J., Tatsiopoulos, I.P.: Logistics issues of biomass: The storage problem and the multi-biomass supply chain. Renew. Sust. Energ. Rev. 13, 887–894 (2009)
11. Ebadian, M., Sowlati, T., Sokhansanj, S., Stumborg, M., Townley-Smith, L.: A new simulation model for multi-agricultural biomass logistics system in bioenergy production. Biosyst. Eng. 110, 280–290 (2011)
12. Saetta, S., Paolini, L., Tiacci, L., Altiok, T.: A decomposition approach for the performance analysis of a serial multi-echelon supply chain. Int. J. Prod. Res. 50, 2380–2395 (2012)
13. Ebadian, M., Sowlati, T., Sokhansanj, S., Townley-Smith, L., Stumborg, M.: Modeling and analysing storage systems in agricultural biomass supply chain for cellulosic ethanol production. Appl. Energ. 102, 840–849 (2013)
14. Altiok, T., Melamed, B.: Simulation modelin and analysis with Arena. Elsevier, USA (2007)
15. Law, A.M., Kelton, W.D.: Simulation Modeling and Analisys (2000)

Mini Factory: A Successful Model for European Furniture Industry?

Marco Seregni[1], David Opresnik[1], Christian Zanetti[1],
Marco Taisch[1], and Fred Voorhorst[2]

[1] Politecnico di Milano, Piazza Leonardo Da Vinci 32, 20133, Milan, Italy
[2] Scuola universitaria professionale della Svizzera italiana – SUPSI
Galleria 2 CH - 6928 , Manno, Switzerland
{marco.seregni,david.opresnik,cristiano.zanetti,
marco.taisch}@polimi.it, fred.voorhorst@supsi.ch

Abstract. Manufacturing system based on mini factory is one of the modern pervasive production models spreading as a response to demand for customized products with low cost and fast delivery time. However, as the term is far from being uniform and unique, its application in research and industry by managers is still challenging and represents somehow a riddle. Consequently, the various meanings associated with the term mini factory in literature are critically assayed. The results depicted three main areas of the model of mini factory: "Work organisation model", "Agile Assembly Architecture" and "Distributed mini factories network". Steming out from the third model, the possibility of using the mini factory model presented by Reichwald, Stotko & Piller was explored. Indeed, due to its characteristics, this model seems to be able to respond more effectively to the challenges in the European furniture sector, in particular for SMEs.

Keywords: Mini factory, Distributed mini factories network, transnational strategy, Furniture.

1 Introduction

The turnover of the European furniture industry in 2011 has been estimated at 90 billions of euro, with a total of 130.000 companies, consisted almost entirely of local small enterprise [1]. These data demonstrate the great importance of this sector both for the EU economy and its relevance among global furniture industry, where EU has a major role, among others, due to its ability to influence international fashion and design trends [2]. However, domestic demand, particularly in Western Europe, suffered a shock in 2009, due to the global crisis. Meanwhile, the growth of the global competition, particularly in the segments with lower unit value, caused a massive shift of production from EU countries to the Far East to reduce the overall production costs and, especially, labour ones [3].

In order to respond to the abovementioned challenges, European manufacturers have to radically change the production system paradigm. Especially to be able to satisfy the customers' dynamic needs and thus to increase the added value of their

B. Grabot et al. (Eds.): APMS 2014, Part III, IFIP AICT 440, pp. 571–578, 2014.

products. In this sense, the development of production system based on mini factories could be an effective solution, able to ensure higher performance than centralized mass production. However, due to the variety of models named mini factory, it is completely clear what exactly represents such model. Hence, the aim of this paper is twofold. First, it aims to clarify the term mini factory, while secondly it aims to identify the benefits of such models and to evaluate the possibility of implementation of this innovative production organization that can help European furniture SMEs to face the competition of the big international competitors. In order to fulfil those aims, the mini factory models are first categorized. Thus, as a result of the literature review three classes have been identified: Work organization model, Agile Assembly Architecture and Distributed mini factories network. In a second step, this paper explores potential benefits of the mini factory model proposed by Reichwald, Stotko & Piller [4], belonging to the third of the above mentioned categories. Finally, this model is evaluated for its potential applicability onto the field of European furniture, where customization is growing on importance.

Consequently, this article consists of two sections: the analysis of the literature and the verification of the adaptability and the potential benefits of the model of distributed mini factory networks in the field of furniture in Europe.

2   Mini Factory Models

An analysis of the manufacturing models identified as mini factory has been conducted using as keywords "mini factory" and "minifactory" on scientific databases Scopus, Web Science and Google Scholar. The most evident result emerging from this activity was the presence of this term in many areas that do not belong to manufacturing area; this issues was solved by narrowing the spectrum of research fields related to the industrial world. Taking as example Scopus database, only documents belonging to the subject areas "Engineering", "Computer Science", "Business , Management and Accounting", "Economics, Econometrics and Finance" have been selected and analyzed. Furthermore, this literature review showed a substantial lack of a unique and universally recognized definition of mini factory; on the contrary, it highlighted a strong variability in terms of characteristics and peculiarities of the models matched to that term. Due to this result, before proceeding with the study of mini factory characteristics compared with the challenges of European furniture industry, it was necessary to sort and classify the different models and case studies identified in the research. For this reason models presented under the name of mini factory are categorized in three classes: work organization model, Agile Assembly Architecture and Distributed Manufacturing Network.

2.1   Mini Factory as "Work Organisation Model"

Since the 80's the term mini factory has often been associated with innovative model for the innovation of work organisation. Ickis, Edelberg & Morales in 2000 in the description of the organizational changes implemented by the company TANIC during the second half of the 90s , the Nicaragua subsidiary of British American Tobacco, identified mini factory as "[...] a manufacturing cells with sequential and distribution of compact equipment and personnel" [5]. Gilbert, Raulet Teglborg & Crozet in 2013, describing the change in the organization of FAVI value chain activities, a French company specialized in the production of copper alloys, defined the mini factory as "[...] an island of production located in a particular area of the factory containing all the equipment and processes dedicated to a particular client" [6]. These two cases show a commonality in the goals, but a diversity in the organizational dimension. In fact, both cases' primary objective is the increase in the quality of the product, in TANIC as a response to decreasing trend in output quality while in FAVI as response to the high competition of Asian manufacturer, advantage on the cost side and resulting in aggressive pricing policies. Whereas for the organizational prospective the two cases show a substantial difference in the logic with which the mini-factories were created: in the first case mini factories are process-based while in the second they are customer-based.

In conclusion mini factory models included in this class can be defined as production organization with few hierarchical levels organized in teams, based on high job enrichment and enlargement; these units manage all production activities, including support ones needed for the completion of the customer's order.

2.2   Mini Factory as "Agile Assembly Architecture"

The models of mini factory that fall in this category do not refer to an entire production system, but concentrate on a specific phase of manufacturing production: the assembly. In particular in this area have been included models with both technological and functional features that get them in contact with FAS (Flexible Assembly System), defined as "an integrated, computer-controlled, robotic assembly of machines and automatic and programmable and automatic devices transport and handling, able to mount simultaneously medium volumes of a variety of different assemblies" [7].

Muir, Rizzi & Gowdy defined a system mini factory that are developing as "Potentially large collection of mechanically, computationally and algorithmically robotic modules [...]" [8]; furthermore they defined "high precision, self calibrating, agent based, distributed assembly system" [9].

Gaugel , Bengel & Malthan associated Mini Factory with "[...] a marketable, miniaturized highly flexible micro-assembly system capable of reproducing the correct size proportions between a product and its production environment and also able to intelligently integrated which had earlier run separate processes" [10].

The abovementioned models can be seen as FAS with extremely small (a room of an apartment or even a desk) through the use of miniaturized machinery, equipment and components, thus equalizing to concept of Microfactory [11]. These solutions could represent a technical instrument for facing assembly challenges related to high demand for customized products; however, as automated systems managed by an artificial control, they have a degree of flexibility that does not allow to work any type of piece. Consequently, they require a prior standardization of components in order to operate effectively in a customized production.

In terms of output these systems are widely used for the realization of products of very small dimensions, which need for high accuracy, in some cases in the vicinity of microns; for instance Printed Circuit Boards (PCB) is a product for which these assembly models are widespread.

2.3   Mini Factory as "Distributed Mini Factories Network"

In 2005 Reichwald, Stotko, & Piller defined mini factory as "[...] a designed scalable, modular, geographically distributed unit that is networked with other units of this type" [4]. In their model mini factory should performs all operations needed for the effective completion of the customer's order:

- design with an high involvement of customer and supported by user friendly tools;
- customized manufacturing on the basis of the customer's requests recorded in the previous phase;
- delivery, with the aim to guarantee a short delivery time;
- afters sales activities, such as repair, maintenance and other supplementary services.

The authors focus on the importance of networking all mini-factories installed with the aim of sharing various types of information (i.e. customer requirements, solutions to problems in mini factory management), thus giving the opportunity to personnel to access to a huge and global knowledge; moreover, localization near customers supports the growth of repeating purchase, hence increasing the customer retention rate. According to Zaeh and Wagner [12] this distributed instantiation of mini factories can also have economic positive impact by reducing logistic costs and delivery time.

The above described model also includes a central command unit which carries out support to the network of mini factories, such as the sourcing of standard components of the product, operators' training and definition of the basic characteristics of the product. Within mini factory, modularity means that each local unit is composed of modules that can be combined together thanks to their standard interfaces; thus local specificity of each mini-factory is easily ensured by a combination of these standard modules.

3   Model Application Onto the European Furniture Sector

The strong global competition and in particular the Asian player has pushed European manufacturers looking for ways to differentiate their offering in order to justify an higher price; this goal has markedly increased the relevance of the following abilities:

- quick and on demand supply;
- rapid response to changing tastes;
- customer support services.

Another very marked feature in the European furniture country in is the strong diversity in national markets, both in terms of design style, product mix and materials; thus selling into these countries requires a high knowledge of local customers and a large network of contacts. From a structural point of view, this sector is mostly composed, with the exception of a few international players, by SMEs, who are then more difficult to respond to these challenges. The model of distributed mini factories network presented, due to its characteristics, could be helpful for SMEs for meeting the growing need for customization of European furniture sector and eventually interfacing with different national markets.

3.1   Customization and Transnational Strategy in Furniture Industry

Reichwald, Stotko & Piller suggested their model of mini factory was particularly suitable "for creating customized products and services if a company's situation is characterized by a high degree of variability and specificity". For "specificity" the authors mean that products would withstand an high depreciation if rejected by the specific customer. Clearly this concept is strongly linked to customization, as the customized product means that specific product has a low value for other customers, even at the limit zero. Research conducted by Lihra, Buehlmann & Beauregard in 2008 showed that customized portfolio could be implemented as a successful strategy for US producers in order to face competing with low-cost offshore manufacturers, although with different impacts in different segments" [13].

Focusing on European furniture market, it presents a deep fragmentation in many segments with different features, linked with different customer's profile, as SERİN & ANDAÇ analysis within Turkish furniture showed [14]. According to a classification based on the intended use of furniture, at a very general level the sector can b partitioned into two segments: office furniture and domestic ones. Surely, customization is a competitive lever of primary importance much more in the second segment as a result of a variety and heterogeneity of characteristics required, ranging from functionality to aesthetics. More specifically, for its characteristics, distributed mini factories network can adapt better to specific groups of domestic furniture consumers [15] requiring customization in terms of size (i.e. "middle age singles") or in terms of style (i.e. "young couples").

In addition to customization needs, furniture industry in Europe has a strong heterogeneity among national markets [16], as confirmed by Tammela, Cane & Helo, a study on Time-Based Competition strategies of Brazilian and Scandinavian furniture companies that highlighted cultural diversity of customers and business partners was a key issue for strategic decision [17]. Thus a transnational strategy in which a company "[...] strives for global efficiency without losing on the advantages of offering a customized product tailored to local or regional habits" [18], could be a potentially successful solution. Consequently, distributed mini factories network, according to Reichwald, Stotko and Seifert conclusion [18], could be an effective way for the implementation of transnational strategy within European sector.

3.2   Potential Advantages for Furniture SMEs

Due to its characteristics, distributed mini factories network represents an intermediate solution with some aspects in common to large international companies and others with local SMEs; in particular SMEs, those represents more than 95% of the European furniture companies, could achieve competitive advantages [19] by joining a distributed mini factories network:

- centralized management of the support activities could enable SMEs to take cost advantage due to economies of scale;
- thanks to the integration between the design and production activities, and the logic of local lean supply chain, several inconsistencies between company's operations can be avoided, thus reducing significantly of the overall delivery time and its variance; this potential advantage has an enormous importance for producers in mature furniture markets in response to competitive pressure from manufacturers in the Far East, such as Mitchell & Watt stressed with reference to the American market [20];
- SMEs can obtain significant benefits in the knowledge management, due to the greater amount of information that can be accessed within the network of mini factories. Indeed, thanks to the network in which it is inserted, SMEs are able to access a variety of resources comparable to that of large firms. At the same time in this solution, single manufacturer is able to interact with the customer while obtaining from him complete information and a valuable feedback [21];
- providing to the customer a set of information about the product marked higher than any kind of catalogue, thus responding to increasing furniture customer's need for information due to technological knowledge, social values and socio-economic changing [22];
- reducing the downstream supply chain levels, thus increasing manufacturers' strength against furniture retailers, which has arisen their role over the past years due to their ability to interact directly with the customer [23].

4   Limitations and Further Research

The main limitation of this article is that it is on a conceptual level. This means that the model has not yet been applied and its success evaluated. However, the validity of the conceptualization has been reinforced by: a) working with widely recognized models, b) by working with reliable characteristics from the furniture industry, c) taking into account the trends in manufacturing as also on the furniture market and d) clearly defining boundaries of the mini factory model. The second limitation is that it does not take into account any more specific part of the furniture sector. However, due to the novelty in this field, the possibility from a general perspective had to be assayed first. Consequently, one of the next steps in terms of further research will be to focus on a specific sub-segment of the furniture industry. Furthermore, further research will be carried out in order to define more in detail the operational characteristics for the instantiation of a furniture mini-factories network, such as the supply chain, production planning logics, basic designs concepts. In particular, as demonstrated by some studies ([24],[25]), there is a growing attention of the customer with regard to environmental sustainability, which translates into a reward in terms of willingness to pay; thus, future research will explore the implications on mini factory model for ensuring high green performance.

5 Conclusions

In this article, the main models of the mini factory were identified and scrutinized, from which three main types were more closely depicted. The model of Reichwald, Stotko & Piller [4] has been identified to be the most proper one for further application. Based on the comparison between competitive conditions that were deemed optimal for the mini factory and the characteristics of the sector shows, that the model is applicable to the furniture industry, in particular for SMEs. The results of the analysis showed among others that that the furniture has the market condition suitable for the effective implementation of the distributed mini factory network. This means that the production model in question can increase the competitive advantage of the manufacturing enterprises in the furniture industry, thus indicating that this model is a viable answer for those manufacturers in time of economic crisis, supply surplus and lack of demand.

Acknowledgements. The work presented here is part of the project "CTC- Close To Customer"; this project has received funding from the European Union's Seventh Framework Programme for research, technological development and demonstration under grant agreement no FoF.NMP.2013-6 608736 – CTC.

References

1. Eurostat (2011),
   http://epp.eurostat.ec.europa.eu/portal/page/portal/statisti
   cs/themes From www.Eurostat
2. Oliver, R. (s.d.),
   http://www.itto.int/..download/topics_id=3466&no=1 from da
   www.itto.int
3. European Sector Monitor of the wood/furniture industry
4. Reichwald, R., Stotko, C.M., Piller, F.T.: Distributed mini-factory networks as a form of real-time enterprise: concept, flexibility potential and case studies. In: The Practical Real-Time Enterprise, pp. 403–434. Springer, Heidelberg (2005)
5. Ickis, J.C., Edelberg, G., Morales, M.: Tanic. Journal of Business Research 50(1), 123–137 (2000), doi:10.1016/S0148-2963(98)00109-X
6. Gilbert, P., Raulet Crozet, N., Teglborg, A.C.: Work Organisation and Innovation-Case Study: FAVI. European Foundation for the Improvement of Living and Working Conditions, France (2013)
7. Garetti, M., Taisch, M.: Automatic production systems, in italian, original title: Sistemi di produzione automatizzati, 2nd edn. CUSL, Milan (1997)

8. Muir, P.F., Rizzi, A.A., Gowdy, J.W.: Minifactory: A precision assembly system adaptable to the product life cycle. In: Intelligent Systems & Advanced Manufacturing, pp. 74–80. International Society for Optics and Photonics (December 1997)
9. Kume, S., Rizzi, A.A.: A high-performance network infrastructure and protocols for distributed automation. In: Proceedings of the 2001 ICRA IEEE International Conference on Robotics and Automation, vol. 3, pp. 3121–3126. IEEE (2001)
10. Gaugel, T., Bengel, M., Malthan, D.: Building a mini-assembly system from a technology construction kit. Assembly automation 24(1), 43–48 (2004)
11. Okazaki, Y., Mishima, N., Ashida, K.: Microfactory—concept, history, and developments. Journal of Manufacturing Science and Engineering 126(4), 837–844 (2004)
12. Zäh, M.F., Wagner, W.: Planning Mini-Factory Structures for the Close-to-Market Manufacture of Individualized Products. In: Proceedings of the MCPC, vol. 3 (2003)
13. Lihra, T., Buehlmann, U., Beauregard, R.: Mass customisation of wood furniture as a competitive strategy. International Journal of Mass Customisation 2(3), 200–215 (2008)
14. Serin, H., Andaç, T.: An investigation of the preferences of furniture consumers depending on education and age factors in Turkey. . African Journal of Business Management 6(22), 6658–6666 (2012)
15. CBI. The domestic furniture market in the EU (2007)
16. Arbeit und Leben Bielefeld e.V. (DGB/VHS). European Sector Monitor of the wood/furniture industry (2009)
17. Tammela, I., Canen, A.G., Helo, P.: Time-based competition: Relation to multiculturalism and logistics in international furniture companies. Benchmarking: An International Journal 20 (2013)
18. Reichwald, R., Stotko, C.M., Seifert, S.: Internationalizing Mass Customization–Minifactories as a transnational solution. In: Proceedings of the 2nd Interdisciplinary World Congress on Mass Customization and Personalization (2003)
19. Frohlich, M.T., Dixon, J.R.: A taxonomy of manufacturing strategies revisited. . Journal of Operations Management 19(5), 541–558 (2001)
20. Mitchell, P., Watt, H.: Strategies for the New American Furniture Industry. Cooperative Extension, North Carolina (2010)
21. Buehlmann, U., Bumgardner, M., Sperber, M.: How Small Firms Contrast with Large Firms Regarding Perceptions, Practices, and Needs in the U.S. Secondary Woodworking Industry. BioResources 8(2), 2669–2680 (2013), doi:10.15376/biores.8.2.2669-2680
22. Öztop, H., Erkal, S., Gunay, G.: Factors Influential in Consumers' Furniture Selection and their Preferences regarding Product Features. The International Journal of Interdisciplinary Social Sciences, 23–34 (2008)
23. Lihra, T., Graf, R.: Multi-channel communication and consumer choice in the household furniture buying process. Direct Marketing: An International Journal 1(3), 146–160 (2007)
24. Jensen, K.: Willingness to pay for environmentally certified hardwood products by Tennessee consumers (Doctoral dissertation, University of Tennessee) (2002)
25. Aguilar, F.X., Vlosky, R.P.: Consumer willingness to pay price premiums for environmentally certified wood products in the US. Forest Policy and Economics 9(8), 1100–1112 (2007)

Taxonomy of Engineer-To-Order Companies

Pavan Kumar Sriram and Erlend Alfnes

Dept. of Production and Quality Engineering,
Norwegian University of Science and Technology, Trondheim, Norway
{pavan.sriram,erlend.alfnes}@ntnu.no

Abstract. In this paper taxonomy has been developed to classify the different forms of ETO firms to enable a like-with-like comparison, arguing that existing taxonomies within the literature are inadequate for production planning and control research purposes. Successful production planning and control concepts from high volume, low variety producers cannot be directly applied, because of the unique nature of ETO products. Secondly through synthesis of the literature and the analysis of the three case studies we describe and examine the production planning and control activities characteristics of the ETO environment to distinguish the different environment within ETO production.

Keywords: Production planning and control, engineer-to-order, empirical study and review.

1 Introduction

Aspects of globalization have stirred an increase in demand for customized products. While having a customized product the customers also expect the products to be manufactured and delivered in short time, at a nearly same cost as mass production with relatively high quality [1]. This market trend requires manufacturing companies to be able to rapidly and cheaply produce customized products with a required quality level. This requirement is somehow controversial with conventional understanding, i.e. a trade-off between customization and low cost through highly efficient production mode, such as mass production. On the other hand, this market trend also provides the manufacturing companies with new opportunities, particularly for these small or medium sized enterprises (SMEs) in developed countries like Norway. The typical examples are customized thruster manufacturers, heavy-duty lifting and material handling equipment companies, special industrial equipment manufacturers, etc. In these manufacturing businesses, the customers normally require the orders to be specified with their specific requirements and to be filled within a short lead-time [2]. The high customization and short lead-time drive the customers to place their orders with a local company instead of an overseas competitor. However, the high cost of producing a customized product through a traditional production mode, e.g. job shop, may turn the customers away from these local companies [3]. Therefore, to keep the high customization, short lead-time and at meanwhile to effectively reduce the production cost become the high priority strategy for manufacturing companies to effectively compete with overseas large and cheap producers [4]. This is particularly true for SMEs in the developed countries Norway.

B. Grabot et al. (Eds.): APMS 2014, Part III, IFIP AICT 440, pp. 579–587, 2014.
© IFIP International Federation for Information Processing 2014

In this paper we focus upon different types of engineer-to-order companies and identify taxonomy that demonstrates the importance of the relationship between the degree of design activity, volume of manufacture, and of the distinction between products that are custom built from options, and those that involve custom design elements. This paper examines how these companies can effectively make use of the taxonomy to support management decision making in order to manage their manufacturing operations more effectively.

2   Methodology

The primary research methodology is multiple case study research, and by placing emphasis on the production planning and control (PPC) system framework of [5], we present empirical examples based on three companies operating within the heavy lift, crane & barge, and aluminum casting industry in Norway. This is carried out in accordance with a case-based approach [6]. The cases are conducted using data collected through semi-structured interviews of several informants in the companies, including the managing director and production manager(s). Production planners were also involved in the discussions. Direct observations and the analysis of secondary sources, such as company documentation and corporate website are used for triangulation, to check the internal consistency of data [7]. The central idea is to constantly compare theory and data, iterating toward a theory which closely fits the data [8].

3   Theoretical Background

3.1   Production Planning and Control

In ETO firms the time needed for engineering may represent a significant part of the total lead time. [9] developed a novel planning and scheduling model for ETO sectors where the MRPII was not a good fit.[10], presented a new framework for MRP system to be effective in ETO. The system was developed to allow aggregate production planning coordination between engineering, material acquisition and production activities, as well as the information structures but did not focus on coordination with supply chain. [1], presented that production planning and control are the most critical tools to meet customer demands and most of the existing systems are based on the superficial software's and there is a need for industry specific design. Stevenson's work mainly focused on the applicability of classical approaches to PPC, and highlighted the importance of workload control (WLC) concept to make-to-order (MTO) companies. But the scope is limited to assessing the applicability of various existing approaches to PPC.

More authors looked on development of methods/models on integration of Enterprise resource planning (ERP), Supply chain management (SCM), and innovative process as they considered them to be key elements for a successful planning and control system [11, 12]. But the frameworks don't address the effective planning of design, product configuration, and scheduling at different levels. And also it was focusing only on SCM in ETO and lacked applicability to various other planning and control issues in an ETO environment. [13], presented a concept for integrated manufacturing and innovative process in ETO environment. The work described a project management tool integration production planning. It highlighted the dependencies between logistics management and project management, but do not capture how to tackle planning and control in ETO in various stages of manufacturing. Also there have been both lean and agile strategies proposed in the ETO sector, wherein both paradigms attempt to rationalize tools, techniques, philosophies and approaches to manufacturing planning and control. But there are disagreements as to the boundaries, definitions and applicability of leanness and agility [4]. Also there are studies carried out by [14] shows a synergistic impact in combining the lean and ERP, but it is still not clear from the extant literature as to how either of these approaches can be successfully applied in ETO companies. [15], proposed a concept for an integrated planning and control conceptual framework based on 'seiban (meaning a manufacturing number in Japanese, is a technique for managing orders in the supply chain which is alternative to traditional MRP logic).' approach for project specific manufacturing, the main focus of the work was limited to development of a new ERP system. This work represents a fundamental difference in the information system requirements for MTS, ATO and ETO companies. A detailed literature on production planning and control approaches for ETO can be found in the article [15], in this paper we limit our discussions to the taxonomy. This paper aims to; briefly review the literature on the types of ETO companies based upon an analysis of literature review; distinguish ETO firms that provide a framework for identify similarities and differences between companies. This will be tested through a series of case studies as additional work.

3.2   Definitions of ETO

The increased number of academic articles on the topic of ETO is one example of the growing importance of the ETO concept. An overview of the number of the published articles shows that the research interest in the subject has been continually high over the past 5 years (source: EBSCO Business Source Premier Database). Although much has been published about ETO in the academic literature, commonly accepted definitions and frameworks have not yet been established. Many academic definitions exist, all of which differ in one or more aspects [4]. For this work we aim to develop a common comprehensive definition of the ETO concept, which will be deemed too broad to facilitate a common understanding in the work of the academics and of the industry research group on ETO: "Engineer-to-order (ETO) refers to a customer integrated process of unique products and services, which meet the needs of each individual customer with regard to certain product feature. All the operations are performed within a flexible solution space and high engineering responsive process".

3.3   ETO Existing Typology/Taxonomy

There are numerous articles presenting classification work in the field of ETO. To establish a more detailed understanding, a literature review of the existing classifications of ETO was conducted. Articles were first identified by using EBSCO and applying pre-defined search terms, through which we identified six articles presenting a classification of ETO. The details of the same are furnished in table 1.

Authors	Overview	Research Type	Industry Type	Evaluation Dimension
Gosling and Naim, (2009)	ETO is defined as a standard product range offered with the added availability of modifications and customizations. DTO, instead, is defined as where new product introductions with design, engineering and manufacturing based on new customer orders. The two manufacturing systems are therefore clearly distinguished one from the other. In addition ETO is divided, in turn, in ETO and ETS (engineer-to-stock).	Conceptual	Large and complex project in sectors such as construction and capital goods, film making, shipbuilding, law cases and software development	Degree of customer involvement, degree of product customization, and the operations environment
JG Wacker and Miller, (2000)	ETO environment is divided in two different categories: configure to order and invent to order. CTO consists in making product very similar to the previous ones and first engineering task is tailoring or configuring the product to meet the customer requirements. ITO needs more engineering time instead in inventing and designing the product; in ITO companies' previous products are rather different from the current ones.	Conceptual	Buildings construction	Degree of engineering time product customization, and degree of customer involvement

| Segers-tedt and Olofsson, (2010). | Construction concepts and projects also show different preparations before the customer order arrives and before realization of the project. The first and lowest degree of a defined building system is the well-known engineer-to-order where companies design products in ordinary construction projects. The design specification process is mainly based on client requirements, norms and standards. Winch (2003) divided the engineer-to-order further in concept-to-order (CTO) and design-to-order (DTO) reflecting the two main contractual forms between the client and the construction company; design-build and design-bid-build respectively. | Conceptual (though empirically validated) | Buildings construction | Degree of product customization, and degree of customer involvement |
| Hicks et al., (2001) | Four ideal types of company were developed to explain how production processes are organized within ETO firms.

The variables used to classify companies are the depth of product structure, which indicates product complexity, and the volume of production, which determines whether jobbing, batch or flow processes are employed. So type I is a vertically integrated company. Type II outsources component manufacture, but maintains assembly and construction activities in-house. Type III outsources all physical processes. | Conceptual (though empirically validated) | Capital goods: design, manufacture and construction plant (Power generation, offshore, power electronics and instrumentation, material handling, power generation, distribution and utilization) | Types of process, and depth of product structure |

Wikner and Rudberg, (2005)	ETO can be seen as a special case of MTO. In both cases the production flow is driven by actual customer orders. However, in the ETO case both the design and engineering activities are driven by customer orders, but these activities are not parts of the production flow. By doing this, a production dimension covering the typical CODPPD, is established. On the other hand we get an engineering dimension where the product can be designed and engineered based on customer orders.	Conceptual	Generic industry	Degree of customer involvement, and degree of product customization
Amaro et al., (1999)	Arrives at four basic degree of product customization which also holds classification aspects of different degrees of customer involvement. The result of the typology comprises of three attributes and eleven possible categories. The empirical validation is carried out through 22 company case.	Conceptual (though empirically validated)	Medical and military equipment, polymer and polymer products, magnets, conveyors and industrial automation, mechanical assemblies and switchgears	Degree of customer involvement, degree of product customization, and scope of internal responsibility/activities

4   Towards Taxonomy for ETO Companies

Case Study

Company A is an engineering company: that does project management (100%), contracts, engineering (90%, some is outsourced), doesn't have manufacturing at all (10%, just follow-up). Installation on site is limited to supervision and control (ca 25%). Mainly outsources low-cost production. Company A differentiates itself in the technology used in casting. Company B is an engineering and service company, and supplier of heavy-duty lifting and material handling equipment in a capacity range of 25 to 1000 tones and more. They develop designs, delivers, tests, commissions and carries out service on heavy lifting and material handling equipment for use in harsh and corrosive marine environments. Company C is a global supplier of marine structures with an innovative engineering- and expertise environment. The products are developed and marketed in collaboration with partner firms. They have established a long term co-operation with partners who are of the world's leading providers of ship design, marine equipment and complete system solutions. From the case studies, the significant differences between the three types of ETO are highlighted and elaborated. The differences found in the study are divided as distinguished features of ETO production environment.

Table 1. Distinguishing features of the ETO production environment in case companies

Characteristics	Company A	Company B	Company C
Product Design	Custom built using standard modules	Usually exclusive to one customer	Custom built
Product Size	Small and medium size	Generally big	Small and medium size
Product Change	Low	High	Medium
Production Volume	Medium to high volume	One to very low volume	Low to medium volume
Production planning	Stable and sometimes dynamic	Dynamic and sometimes chaotic	Dynamic and sometimes stable
Labour Skills	Little or no specialised skills required	Specialised skills	Some specialised skills required
Major production activity	Assembly and manufacturing	Assembly	Assembly and manufacturing
Customer input during design	Customer rarely involved during design	Customer gives input during design	Customer usually give input during design
Inventory	Medium	Low	Medium
Supplier involvement	Low	High	Medium
Product Design	Custom built using standard modules	Usually exclusive to one customer	Custom built

5   Conclusions

One of the main impediments in the study of ETO has been the absence of constructs and the little distinction that has been made between the ETO product delivery strategy and the managerial and organizational style of the companies. Although many of types of ETO firms may have common characteristics, there are many important differences. Through case study we have tried to highlight the significant differences between three firms. The effectiveness of ETO planning and control unfortunately lags far behind the level of manufacturing planning and control practices in, for example, make-to-stock (MTS) or assemble-to-order (ATO) producers. Successful manufacturing planning and control concepts from high volume, low variety producers cannot be directly applied, because of the unique nature of ETO products. This paper presents a taxonomy of ETO firms that provides a framework for identify similarities and differences between firms. It also provides a framework that will help with the transfer of best manufacturing planning and control practices. Secondly there are numerous areas for research in production planning and control for ETO firms. One of the major weakness of previous research is that little has been done to document present industry practice in case studies or surveys. This lack of practical criteria makes a realistic evaluation of the relative merits of the previous research difficult. Research on the various aspects of production planning and control in ETO firms needs more attention. A framework for integrated models considering all facets of production planning and control is needed. Future research must be grounded with industrial data to ensure that it is relevant to actual concerns.

Acknowledgement. This research was made possible by the EFFEKT, LIFT and SUSPRO project as well as SFI Norman. The authors would like to thank the participants of the project for providing the inputs and fruitful discussions.

References

[1] Stevenson, M., Hendry, L.C., Kingsman, B.G.: A review of production planning and control: the applicability of key concepts to the make-to-order industry. International Journal of Production Research 43, 869–898 (2005)

[2] Amaro, G., Hendry, L., Kingsman, B.: Competitive advantage, customisation and a new taxonomy for non make-to-stock companies. International Journal of Operations & Production Management 19, 349–371 (1999)

[3] Hicks, C., McGovern, T., Earl, C.F.: A typology of UK engineer-toorder companies. Int. J. Logis. Res. and Appl. 4, 43–56 (2001)

[4] Gosling, J., Naim, M.M.: Engineer-to-order supply chain management: A literature review and research agenda. International Journal of Production Economics 122, 741–754 (2009)

[5] Vollmann, T.E., Berry, W.L., Whybark, D.C., Jacobs, R.F.: Manufacturing Planning and Control for Supply Chain Management. McGraw-Hill, Boston (2005)

[6] Voss, C.A., Tsikriktsis, N., Frohlich, M.: Case Research in Operations Management. International Journal of Operations & Production Management 22, 195–210 (2002)

[7] Scandura, T.A., Williams, E.A.: Research methodology in management: Current practices, trends, and implications for future research. Academy of Management Journal, 1248–1264 (2000)

[8] Eisenhardt, K.M.: Building Theories from Case Study Research. Academy of Management: The Academy of Management Review 14, 532–549 (1989)

 [9] Little, D., Rollins, R., Peck, M., Porter, J.K.: Integrated planning and scheduling in the engineer-to-order sector. International Journal of Computer Integrated Manufacturing 13, 545–554 (2000)

[10] Jin, G., Thomson, V.: A new framework for MRP systems to be effective in engineered-to-order environments. Robotics and Computer-Integrated Manufacturing 19, 533–541 (2003)

[11] McGovern, T.O.M., Hicks, C., Earl, C.F.: Modelling Supply Chain Management Processes in Engineer-to-Order Companies. International Journal of Logistics Research and Applications 2, 147–159 (1999)

[12] Samaranayake, P., Toncich, D.: Integration of production planning, project management and logistics systems for supply chain management. International Journal of Production Research 45, 5417–5447 (2007)

[13] Caron, F., Fiore, A.: Engineer to order' companies: how to integrate manufacturing and innovative processes. International Journal of Project Management 13, 313–319 (1995)

[14] Powell, D., Olesen, P.: ERP Systems for Lean Production Control. presented at the 13th International Conference on Modern Information Technology in the Innovation Processes of Industrial Enterprises (MITIP), Norwegian University of Science and Technology, Trondheim, Norway (2011)

[15] Sriram, P.K., Alfnes, E., Arica, E.: A Concept for Project Manufacturing Planning and Control for Engineer-to-Order Companies. In: Emmanouilidis, C., Taisch, M., Kiritsis, D. (eds.) Advances in Production Management Systems. Competitive Manufacturing for Innovative Products and Services, pp. 699–706. Springer, Heidelberg (2013)

Author Index

Printed in the United States
By Bookmasters

Printed in the United States
By Bookmasters